Quick Reference Editing Shortcut Keystrokes

To:	Press:
Cut	Ctrl+X
Copy	Ctrl+C
Paste	Ctrl+V
Create a new document	Ctrl+N
Save	Ctrl+S
Print	Ctrl+P
Undo	Ctrl+Z
Select All	Ctrl+A
Edit the active cell	F2
Paste a cell name into a formula	F3
Change the reference type of a selected cell reference in a formula	F4
Complete an entry in the cell or Formula bar	Enter
Cancel an entry in the cell or Formula bar	Esc
Insert blank cells	Ctrl+Shift++ (plus)
Delete cells	Ctrl+- (minus)
Copy the value from the cell above the active cell	Ctrl+Shift+" (quotation mark)
Alternate between displaying cell values and formulas	Ctrl+ ` (grave accent)
Display the AutoComplete list	Alt+↓
Copy an entry down	Ctrl+D
Copy an entry to the right	Ctrl+R
Start a new line in a text-wrapped cell	Alt+Enter
Repeat the last action	F4 or Ctrl+Y
Insert an AutoSum formula	Alt+= (equals sign)
Enter the current date	Ctrl+; (semicolon)
Enter the current time	Ctrl+Shift+: (colon)
Insert a hyperlink	Ctrl+K

Quick Reference Navigation

To Move:	Press:
Down one screen	Page Down
Up one screen	Page Up
One screen to the right	Alt+Page Down
One screen to the left	Alt+Page Up
Top to bottom within a selection	Enter
Bottom to top within a selection	Shift+Enter
Left to right within a selection	Tab
Right to left within a selection	Shift+Tab

continues...

To Move:	Press:
To the end of a row or column of data	Ctrl+Arrow key
To the beginning of the row	Home
To the beginning of the worksheet	Ctrl+Home
To the lower-right corner of the worksheet	Ctrl+End
To the next sheet in the workbook	Ctrl+Page Down
To the previous sheet in the workbook	Ctrl+Page Up
To display the active cell	Ctrl+Backspace

Quick Reference Range Selection

To Select:	Press:
Entire table or list where the active cell is located	Ctrl+Shift+* (asterisk)
More cells for a selection	Shift+Arrow key
More cells to the beginning of the row	Shift+Home
Entire column	Ctrl+Spacebar
Entire row	Shift+Spacebar
Entire worksheet	Ctrl+A

Quick Reference Customization

To:	Do This:
Show all worksheet comments	On the **Tools** menu, choose **Options**, and click the **View** tab; click **Comment & indicator**.
Turn off worksheet gridlines	On the **Tools** menu, choose **Options**, and click the **View** tab; clear the **Gridlines** check box.
Change the default folder	On the **Tools** menu, choose **Options**, and click the **General** tab; type a new path in the **Default file location** text box.
Add or remove an AutoCorrect item	On the **Tools** menu, choose **AutoCorrect**; select an entry and click **Delete**, or type a new entry and click **Add**.
Change the direction in which the active cell moves when you press Enter	On the **Tools** menu, choose **Options**, and click the **Edit** tab; select a different direction in the **Direction** drop-down list box.
Turn fixed-decimal entry on and off	On the **Tools** menu, choose **Options**, and click the **Edit** tab; mark or clear the **Fixed** decimal check box.
Change the default font	On the **Tools** menu, choose **Options**, and click the **General** tab; select a different font in the **Standard font** drop-down list box.
Change your Excel username	On the **Tools** menu, choose **Options**, and click the **General** tab; type a new name in the **User name** text box.
Show or hide Chart ScreenTips	On the **Tools** menu, choose **Options**, and click the **Chart** tab; mark or clear the **Show Names** and **Show** values check boxes under **Chart tips**.
Change the default chart colors	On the **Tools** menu, choose **Options**, and click the **Color** tab; click a **Chart fills** or **Chart lines** color you want to change, then click **Modify**; in the Colors dialog box, click a new color, then click **OK**.

Using Microsoft® Excel 2000

Julia Kelly

A Division of Macmillan Computer Publishing, USA
201 W. 103rd Street
Indianapolis, Indiana 46290

Contents at a Glance

I Workbook Basics
1 Starting, Quitting, and Getting Help
2 Opening, Searching For, and Closing Files
3 Saving Files and Using Templates
4 Saving Excel Data as a Web Page
5 Selecting and Navigating Worksheets
6 Changing Your View of the Worksheet

II Building Worksheets
7 Entering Data
8 Copying and Importing Data from Other Files
9 Editing Data
10 Simple Calculations
11 Complex Calculations

III Formatting
12 Formatting Cells
13 Formatting Numbers
14 Formatting with Styles for Less Effort

IV Sorting, Filtering, and Summarizing Data
15 Sorting Lists
16 Filtering Lists
17 Finding Answers and Making Decisions
18 Summarizing Details with Consolidation or Subtotals
19 Summarizing Details with PivotTables and PivotCharts

V Charts
20 Creating a Chart
21 Formatting a Chart
22 Putting Data on a Map

VI Printing
23 Deciding What to Print
24 Formatting the Printed Page

VII Sharing Data with Other Users and Other Applications
25 Sharing a Workbook with Other Users
26 Sharing Data Between Applications

VIII Customizing and Automating
27 Customizing Your Excel Screen
28 Automating Repetitive Work with Macros
29 Using Excel's Built-In Templates

IX Creative Excel
30 Drawing Objects
31 Creative Worksheets
32 Creative Charts

Glossary
Index

Using Microsoft® Excel 2000

FIRST EDITION

International Standard Book Number: 0-7897-1862-6

Library of Congress Catalog Card Number: 98-86997

2002 2001 2000 99 4 3 2 1

Interpretation of the printing code: The rightmost double-digit number is the year of the book's printing; the rightmost single-digit, the number of the book's printing. For example, a printing code of 99-1 shows that the first printing of the book occurred in 1999.

Composed in Janson Text by Macmillan Computer Publishing

Printed in the United States of America

Executive Editor
Angie Wethington

Managing Editor
Thomas Hayes

Acquisitions Editor
Stephanie McComb

Development Editor
Brian Proffitt

Project Editor
Leah Kirkpatrick

Copy Editor
Kris Simmons

Indexer
Lisa Stumpf

Technical Editors
Jim Cooper
Bill Bruns

Team Coordinator
Karen Opal

Proofreader
Mary Ellen Stephenson

Layout Technicians
Steve Geiselman
Jo Anna LaBarge

Contents

Introduction 1

Why This Book? 2

Who Should Use This Book? 4

How This Book Is Organized 5

Conventions Used in This Book 7

I Workbook Basics

1 Starting, Quitting, and Getting Help 11

Starting and Quitting Excel 12
- Quitting Excel 15

The Excel Environment 15

Getting Help 18
- Using the Office Assistant 19
- Using the Contents, Index, and Answer Wizard 20
- Changing the Office Assistant's Behavior (a Bit) 24
- Asking What's This? 26

2 Opening, Searching For, and Closing Files 29

Opening Files 30
- Opening Non-Excel Files in Excel 34
- Opening More Than One File at a Time 35

Searching for a File 36
- Finding a File by Searching for File Properties 36
- Locating the File You Want with Quick View 39

Using Hyperlinks 40
- Connecting Files with a Hyperlink 40
- Opening Files Using Hyperlinks 42

Closing Workbook Files 42

3 Saving Files and Using Templates 45

Saving Files as Workbooks 46
- Saving a File 46
- Saving File Properties 47
- Saving a File in a Different Format 48
- Saving an Identical Copy of a Workbook 49

Creating and Using Templates 50
- Opening a Copy of a Custom Template 51
- Editing a Template 52
- Using Excel's Built-In Templates 53

4 Saving Excel Data as a Web Page 59

Saving a Worksheet as a Web Page 60

Saving a Static Web Page 60

Saving an Interactive Web Page 67

Using an Interactive Web Page 72

5 Selecting and Navigating Worksheets 79

Naming Worksheets 80

Selecting Worksheets 81
- Selecting a Single Worksheet 81
- Selecting Several Sheets at Once 82
- Deselecting a Group of Worksheets 82

Moving Around in a Worksheet 84

Selecting Cells in a Worksheet 85

Adding and Deleting Worksheets 87
- Deleting Worksheets 87
- Adding More Worksheets 88

Changing the Default Number of Sheets in a New Workbook 89

Rearranging Worksheets 89
- Moving Worksheets to Rearrange a

Workbook 89
Copying Worksheets Within a Workbook 90
Moving and Copying Worksheets Between Workbooks 92

6 **Changing Your View of the Worksheet 95**

Freezing Worksheet Panes to Keep Rows or Columns in View 96
Freezing Panes 96
Unfreezing Panes 98

Splitting Worksheet Panes to View Multiple Areas in a Worksheet 98

Using Multiple Windows 101
Arranging Multiple Windows to See Several Worksheets at Once 101
Arranging Multiple Windows to See Several Workbooks at the Same Time 104
Arranging Multiple Windows Manually 106

II Building Worksheets

7 **Entering Data 109**

Entering Data Directly in a Worksheet 110
Entering Data in a Single Cell 111
AutoFilling a Text Entry 111
Creating Your Own Custom List 112
AutoFilling a Number Series 113
AutoFilling a Growth Series 114
Repeating the Entry in the Cell Above 114
Entering the Same Data in Several Cells 114
Repeating an Entry in a Text List with AutoComplete 116

Entering Data with a Data Entry Form 117

Validating Data During Entry 118

8 **Copying and Importing Data from Other Files 121**

Trading Data with Other Programs 122

Copying Data from Word 122

Sending Data Over from Access 124

Sending Excel Data to Access 128

Importing a Text File 129

9 **Editing Data 133**

Editing Cell Entries 134

Finding and Replacing Data 136

Deleting Data 139

Undoing Mistakes 139

Moving and Copying Cells on the Same Worksheet 141

Moving and Copying Cells to a Different Worksheet 144

Inserting and Deleting Rows and Columns 146

Inserting and Deleting Cells 148

Separating a Single Column into Multiple Columns 150

Adding Worksheet Comments 152

Using AutoCorrect 154

Letting Excel Check Your Spelling 155

10 **Simple Calculations 159**

Simple Calculations, Quick Answers 160
Quickly Calculating Numbers Without a Formula 160
Using AutoSum to Enter a Formula 161

About Cell References 162
About Cell Reference Types 162
Changing References to Relative, Absolute, or Mixed 164

Writing Your Own Formulas 165
Writing a Simple Formula 165
Using AutoFill to Copy a Formula 166
Writing a Formula That Links Workbooks 169
Editing a Formula 171
Auditing a Formula 172

11 Complex Calculations 175

Understanding Functions 176

Using Functions 176
Writing a Formula Using Functions 177
Some Common and Useful Functions 179

Using Cell Names and Labels 201
Naming Cells 202
Writing Formulas with Named Cells 206
Writing Formulas with Labels 207

Converting Formula Results to Values 208

Locating Worksheet Errors 209
Locating Errors in Formulas 211
Finding Invalid Data in a Worksheet 211

III Formatting

12 Formatting Cells 215

The Formatting Toolbar 216

Formatting the Font 217

Making the Cell Fit the Text (and Vice Versa) 221
Aligning Entries 221
Changing Column Width and Row Height 224
Best-Fitting 224
Matching Precise Width or Height 226
Hiding and Unhiding Rows and Columns 226
Shrinking Entries to Fit in a Cell 228
Wrapping Text to Multiple Lines in a Cell 229
Transposing a Range from Vertical to Horizontal (or Vice Versa) 229
Merging Several Cells into a Single Cell (and Unmerging) 231

Formatting Borders 232

Formatting Colors 235

Copying Formatting with Format Painter 237

Using AutoFormat to Create a Table with Built-In Formats 239

Adding a Graphic Image to a Worksheet 241

13 Formatting Numbers 243

Applying Number Formats to Cells 244

Formatting Dates and Times 246

Formatting Text Entries 248

Creating Conditional Number Formats 251

Converting Actual Values to Displayed Values 255

Hiding Zeroes 256

14 Formatting with Styles for Less Effort 257

Applying a Built-In Style 258

Changing a Style Definition 259

Creating a Custom Style by Example 262

Copying Styles from Other Workbooks 264

Deleting a Style 265

IV Sorting, Filtering, and Summarizing Data

15 Sorting Lists 269

Sorting a List by a Single Column 270

Sorting a List by Two or Three Columns 272

Sorting a List by More Than Three Columns 275

Sorting According to a Custom List 277
Sorting a List Randomly 279
Undoing a Sort and Returning the List to Its Former Arrangement 281

16 **Filtering Lists 283**

Filtering Records 284
- Filtering a List on a Single Criterion 284
- Filtering a List on Multiple Criteria 286

Calculating Filtered Records 295

The Query Wizard: A Better Filter 298
- Using the Query Wizard to Extract Data 298
- Saving and Reusing a Query 307
- Querying a Web Page 309

17 **Finding Answers and Making Decisions 311**

Goal Seeking for Answers 312
- Goal Seeking an Answer to a Simple Question 312
- Goal Seeking in a More Complex Problem 316

Creating and Comparing Scenarios 318

18 **Summarizing Details with Consolidation or Subtotals 327**

Understanding Consolidations and Subtotals 328

Consolidating a Table 328
- Updating a Consolidation 332
- Selecting Consolidation Source Areas 332

Subtotaling a Table 333
- Hiding Subtotal Levels 336
- Showing Subtotal Levels 338
- Removing Subtotaling 338

Outlining a Table Manually 339

Summarizing Details with PivotTables and PivotCharts 343

Working with PivotTables 344

PivotTable Terms 344

Creating a PivotTable 346
- Using the PivotTable and PivotChart Wizard 347
- Changing the Data Source Range 351
- Refreshing Data 355

The PivotTable Toolbar 355

Changing PivotTable Arrangement 356
- Grouping Items in a Field 357
- Pivoting the Table 358
- Adding Fields 360
- Showing and Hiding Inner Field Details 360
- Creating Page Fields 361
- Creating Separate Pages 362
- Removing Fields 364

Changing PivotTable Calculations 365

Showing Underlying Details 367

Formatting a PivotTable 367
- Formatting Numbers 368
- Formatting Tables 368
- Changing Label Text 370

Working with PivotCharts 370

PivotCharts Versus Normal Charts 371

Creating PivotCharts 372
- Creating a PivotChart from Raw Data 372
- Creating a PivotChart from a PivotTable 376
- Creating a Normal Chart from a PivotTable 377

Rearranging PivotCharts 378

Formatting PivotCharts 379
- Embedding a PivotChart on a

Worksheet 381
Formatting Colors and Fonts 382

V Charts

20 Creating a Chart 385

Creating a Chart with the Chart Wizard 386

Types of Charts 390

The Chart Toolbar 393

Changing the Chart Type 394

Changing Chart Data 395
Adding More Data to a Source Range 395
Changing the Data Source Range 397

Changing Chart Orientation 397

Moving and Resizing a Chart 398

Changing the Chart Location 399

21 Formatting a Chart 403

Formatting Chart Colors, Lines, and Fonts 404

Deleting a Chart Element 405

Changing Axis Scale 406

Reordering the Series 408

Resizing and Exploding a Pie Chart 410
Making the Pie Bigger 410
Exploding the Pie 411

Changing 3D Perspective 413
Changing Perspective by Dragging 413
Changing Perspective Using a Dialog Box 414

Adding a Trendline 415
Adding a Trendline to Scientific Data 415
Adding a Moving Average to Business Data 418

Adding a Secondary Axis 419

Adding Data Labels 422

Creating Picture Markers 423

Saving and Reusing Your Custom Chart Format 427

22 Putting Data on a Map 431

Introducing Microsoft Map 432

Creating a Geographical Data Map 433

Adding Features to Your Map 436

Labeling Map Items 437

Repositioning and Enlarging a Map 439

Using the Map Control 440

Creating Custom Pin Maps 442

VI Printing

23 Deciding What to Print 449

Previewing Printed Pages 450

Printing a Quick Copy of a Worksheet 452

Printing Part of a Worksheet 452
Setting a Print Area 453
Removing a Print Area 454
Printing a Selected Range 454
Printing Specific Pages 455

Printing a Chart 456
Printing a Chart Sheet 457
Printing a Chart Object 457

Printing an Entire Workbook 459

24 Formatting the Printed Page 461

Changing Page Breaks 462
Changing Page Breaks in the Worksheet 462
Using Page Break Preview 464

Changing the Page Layout 465

Changing the Page Orientation 465
Changing the Paging Order 466
Changing the Centering 468
Changing Page Margins 468

Printing a Worksheet on a Specific Number of Pages 470

Printing Row and Column Labels on Every Page 471

Creating a Custom Header or Footer 472

Printing Worksheet Gridlines 474

Printing in Black and White 475

Formatting Printed Charts 475
Resizing a Printed Chart 475
Printing Data Markers in Black and White 478

VII Sharing Data with Other Users and Other Applications

25 Sharing a Workbook with Other Users 481

Sharing a Workbook 482

Who's Using a Shared Workbook? 484

Saving a Shared Workbook 484

Reviewing Changes in a Shared Workbook 486
Resolving Conflicts in a Shared Workbook 486

Tracking Changes in a Shared Workbook 487

Accepting and Rejecting Tracked Changes 488

Merging Shared Workbooks 490

Printing a History of Changes 491

Unsharing a Workbook 493

Saving a Workbook as Read-Only (the Opposite of Sharing) 493

Protecting Workbooks and Worksheets 494

26 Sharing Data Between Applications 499

Sharing Data: Pasting, Embedding, and Linking Objects 500

Sending Data from Excel to Word 501
Copying and Pasting Data 501
Embedding an Object 502
Linking to the Source File 505

Bringing Data from Word into Excel 507
Copying and Pasting Word Text to Excel 507
Embedding a Word Object in Excel 508
Linking a Word Object into Excel 509

Changing a Link's Source 509

Dragging a Hyperlink or Shortcut Icon into Excel 511

Pasting Excel Data to a PowerPoint Slide 512

VIII Customizing and Automating

27 Customizing Your Excel Screen 517

Customizing Screen Elements 518

Changing Your Screen Display 518
Using the Full Screen 519
Zooming In and Out 520

Personalizing Your Toolbars 522
Moving Toolbars 523
Hiding and Showing Toolbars 524
Changing Buttons in Built-In Toolbars 526
Creating Personal Toolbars 528

Customizing Your Menu Bar 530

28 Automating Repetitive Work with Macros 535

Introducing Macros 536

Recording a Macro **536**

Running a Macro **539**

Editing a Macro **540**

Attaching a Macro to a Toolbar Button or Menu Command **543**

Creating a Toggle Macro **545**

29 Using Excel's Built-In Templates 549

Working with Templates **550**

Installing the Template Wizard Add-In **550**

Entering Automated Information in the Template **551**

Setting Up the Collection Database **553**
- Setting Up a Database While You Set Up a New Template **553**
- Setting Up a Database for an Existing Template **555**

Saving Copies of the Template to Collect Summary Data **558**

Using the Collection Database **559**

IX Creative Excel

30 Drawing Objects 563

Basic Drawing **564**

Creating AutoShapes **567**

Drawing Text Boxes **568**

Converting Objects to 3D **570**

Creating WordArt Objects **571**

31 Creative Worksheets 575

Creative Approaches to Worksheet Applications **576**

Kurt's Invoice—a Creative Invoice Solution **576**
- How Kurt's Invoice Works **576**
- Setting Up the Invoice Worksheet **578**
- Automating the Invoice with Macros **581**
- Editing the Macro **583**
- Making the Macros Handy **584**

Theatre Seating **587**
- How the Seating Chart Works **587**
- Creating the Seating Chart Workbook **588**

32 Creative Charts 593

Creative Approaches to Charting **594**

Giff's Chart **594**

Stacked Columns **600**

Dynamic Chart Display **601**

Glossary 615

Index 629

Dedication

To God: You are awesome. Thanks for everything.

And to Creed, Ian, Conal, and Genny, because you are wonderful and I love you.

Acknowledgments

As with all computer books, this one was a team effort, and I want to thank all the team members at Que who made the process smooth and successful. In particular, thanks to my terrific agent, Margot Maley at Waterside Productions.

About the Author

Julia Kelly, cybergirl in cowspace, ex-jet jockey, and former mad scientist, has also done time as a stable cleaner, hardware-store cashier/barrista, theme park candy girl, veterinary cat-holder, Caribbean pilot, and teacher of diverse topics.

She currently lives on her farm in north Idaho, where she writes books, teaches classes, builds databases, chops wood, and shovels snow.

INTRODUCTION

So you have Excel 2000. Or perhaps your workplace is upgrading its computers and software and acquiring Office 2000, and you're wondering how to make sense of the new software. Well, you've come to the right place; my goal with *Using Microsoft Excel 2000* is to get you comfortable with Excel 2000.

I'll be honest with you: I won't gush over Excel or Microsoft software or computers in general, or tell you I love them or that I think they're the greatest thing since sliced bread, because for me they're just tools. They're useful, multifunctional tools, and for many businesses, they've become very important tools, but the sun doesn't rise and set according to a computer program. Most of us only need to know how to use our software tools efficiently, as an aid to our work, and then get back to our real jobs (which might be teaching, designing ad campaigns, training horses, selling real estate, running a department store, creating pottery, or whatever).

With that in mind, I'll teach you how to carry out various business tasks as easily and efficiently as possible; I'll show you which of Excel's features are most efficient for a given task, and when you'd want to use one technique instead of another.

All the Office 2000 programs give you several ways to accomplish nearly everything (I can think of six ways to copy the contents of one cell to another), but I'm not going to inundate you with every possible way to do everything. Instead, I'll show you the most efficient ways to do things. I'll teach you how to use

Excel as if I were sitting next to you at your computer (which is how I usually teach), and I won't bend your ear or waste your time with theory or extraneous details; I'll just show you how to do what you need to do.

The changes between Excel 2000 and Excel 97 are not spectacular, and for most people, there's no need to upgrade from Excel 97 to Excel 2000—but if you've just bought a new computer, you'll have Excel 2000 and its new goodies. Some of the new features are pretty cool, such as interactive Web pages, drag-and-drop data between Excel and Access, and the new PivotCharts, but perhaps not essential enough to be worth upgrading. My aim is to make Excel 2000 easy, comfortable, and efficient for you, and to that end, I'll share my honest opinions with you throughout the book.

Why This Book?

Using Microsoft Excel 2000 is a simple, practical approach to learning your software, designed to reflect the changing needs of today's computer users. This book's streamlined, conversational approach to painless productivity includes these features:

- **An improved index:** I want to help you find information the first time you look. If you're new to Excel, you can't be expected to know intuitively which words or feature names to look up; for example, if you wanted to find information about *built-in equations*, would you think to look up *functions*? In addition to the official Excel terms, the index contains all the other words and names that the Que team thought you might look up.
- **Real-life solutions:** Throughout the book, I've used real-life examples to demonstrate how to accomplish a task or solve a problem. My examples are drawn from my own work, my clients' problems, and my students' questions. I'll tell you when using a wizard is easier than doing something yourself, and when doing it yourself is faster and less confusing—and I'll tell you when the best way is a

combination of the wizard's work and your own tweaking. I'll also tell you when I think something is silly (which I couldn't do if Microsoft was publishing this book).

- **Relevant information written just for you:** This book is not a "doorstop" book (those encyclopedic tomes that tell you every esoteric detail about a software program). I've focused on the tasks that normal folks with real jobs need to do on a computer, and on the most efficient means of accomplishing those tasks.

  I realize that most folks will not use most of Excel, but everyone will use different parts of it; and the one-size-fits-all approach to modern software design means that each one of you will find some, but not all, of this book's information useful. My goal is for each of you to find all the information you *do* need, without having to waste time on information you *don't* need.

- **A reference orientation:** Every task and procedure is self-contained, so if you need to learn a new task, or just need a quick reminder about a task you haven't performed in several months, you can find the instructions you need quickly. General procedures are written out step-by-step and illustrated with real-life examples for clarity. Cross-references point you to related information that you might need to look up.

- **A wise investment:** Pay the right price for the right book. I won't waste your bookshelf space or budget on redundant or irrelevant material or assume that you want or need to know everything there is to know about Excel. This book is the meat (or soyburger) without the parsley or the pickle slices or the fancy toothpicks.

- **Easy-to-find procedures:** Every step-by-step procedure in the book begins with a short title explaining exactly what the procedure does (no clever titles that make you guess what's in the procedure). This saves you time by making it easier to find the procedure you need right away.

- **Cross-referencing to additional related information:** I've cross-referenced all the topics and tasks related to each procedure. If you need to look up information that leads up to what you're working on, or if you want to build further on your skills, you have the references to quickly guide you to related information.
- **Sidenote elements with quick-read headlines:** Extra information and helpful tips are in the margins, with titles that help you locate a specific sidenote that you read last month and want to find again quickly.

Who Should Use This Book?

This book is for anyone who uses Excel and needs to accomplish a specific task or solve a problem, or who wants to learn a better technique for something he needs to do. Basically, it suits anyone who

- Has basic Windows 95/98 skills but is new to Excel
- Uses Excel but wants to become more proficient
- Uses Excel at work
- Uses Excel at home
- Needs to create special spreadsheet files, such as invoices or expenses lists
- Wants to learn more efficient ways to manage flat-file databases such as contact lists or mailing lists
- Wants to learn how to use Excel's mathematical capabilities more efficiently
- Wants to learn how to combine data in Excel files with other Office programs such as Word and Access

This book is *not* for you if you have never used a Windows-based computer program. In that case, I recommend you read *Easy Windows 98* or *Using Windows 98* (Que, 1998). This book is also not for you if your goal is to learn everything there is to know about Excel 2000; in that case, I recommend you read *Special Edition Using Excel 2000*.

How This Book Is Organized

Using Microsoft Excel 2000 has task-oriented, easy-to-navigate reference information presented in a logical progression from simple to complex tasks, with related tasks grouped together. It covers features of the program you use in your daily work, and the examples are real-life issues drawn from real client, student, and personal situations, questions, and problems. You can work through the book chapter by chapter if you're just learning Excel, or you can look up specific procedures when you need to perform a task quickly.

Using Microsoft Excel 2000 is divided into nine parts.

Part I: Workbook Basics

Stuff you absolutely must know to work in Excel includes how to start and quit Excel, how to find what you need in Excel's help files, and what all the gadgets and doo-dads in the Excel environment are. You'll find that information in this section, along with how to open, save, and close files, how to search for specific files, how to move around in a worksheet and in a workbook, and how to change the Excel windows to see data in different worksheets and in different workbooks at the same time. You'll also learn how to connect different files with hyperlinks to make them instantly and easily accessible, and how to save workbooks and worksheets as Web pages to post on your company intranet or an Internet Web site.

Part II: Building Worksheets

Excel's raison d'être is to hold data so you can calculate it and arrange it until it's meaningful. This section contains procedures for getting data into a worksheet and then editing, rearranging, and calculating that data.

Part III: Formatting

Formatting is a worksheet frill; you don't *have to* format the data in a worksheet, but it's sure a lot easier to read and understand if you do. This section covers procedures for formatting the worksheet cells with colors, borders, and so forth and for formatting the data you enter into those cells. You'll also find procedures for working with styles, which are packages of formatting characteristics that make formatting repeatedly or on a large scale much faster.

Part IV: Sorting, Filtering, and Summarizing Data

To make a sea of numbers meaningful to most readers, you'll need to organize it. Organization includes sorting lists into a useful order so you can find individual items quickly, filtering lists to hide data you're not interested in so you can focus attention on the specific data you *are* interested in, and summarizing detailed data so you can see the big picture. One very useful method of summarizing data is PivotTables, and now you can create PivotCharts for a graphical, flexible presentation of PivotTable data.

Part V: Charts

Charts are an effective means of communicating an idea because they present data visually and allow instantly understandable comparisons between quantities. This part presents basic procedures for creating and formatting charts (both normal worksheet charts and PivotCharts) to achieve a custom look. You'll also find procedures for using Microsoft Map to create geographical maps that display geographically related data.

Part VI: Printing

Everything in a worksheet is printable, and you have a lot of control over what your printed pages look like. Moreover, formatting printed pages is important if you want to create a professional, highly readable printed presentation. In this part, you'll find procedures for controlling what gets printed and how it looks on the page.

Part VII: Sharing Data with Other Users and Other Applications

Sharing data might mean sharing a workbook with other users *at the same time* so that nobody has to wait his turn to open and use a workbook; it might also mean sharing data between programs, such as using a picture of an Excel chart in a Word report or using Access to create a professional report from an Excel table. All these procedures are covered in this part, as well as procedures for protecting your work when you have to share it (but don't want others to make changes).

Part VIII: Customizing and Automating

Here you'll learn how to make your Excel screen efficient for *you*, and how to create macros, your own personal bits of VBA programming, to make your repetitive work go faster. None of this information is absolutely necessary to know, but all of it contributes to a more efficient work environment for you (and it's fun!).

Part IX: Creative Excel

This part is about being creative in Excel. You'll find real-life examples of inventive solutions to business problems, all of which combine different Excel features in original ways. I don't expect that many of you will need these specific sample projects, but I want to light a fire in your imagination so you can figure out ingenious solutions to your own real-life business problems. You'll also find procedures for using Excel's graphical-arts tools, which you can use to liven up your worksheets and charts while you vent your artistic inclinations.

Conventions Used in This Book

This book defines various conventions to make it easier to use.

- **Menu and dialog box commands and options:** You can easily find the onscreen **menu and dialog box commands** by looking for bold text: Open the **File** menu and click **Save**.

- **Hotkeys for commands:** The underlined keys onscreen that activate commands and options are also underlined in the book as shown in the preceding example.
- **Graphical icons with the commands they execute:** Look for icons like [icon] in text and steps. These indicate buttons onscreen that you can click to accomplish the procedure.
- **Cross references:** If there's a related topic that is prerequisite to the section or steps you are reading, or a topic that builds further on what you are reading, you'll find the cross reference to it after the steps or at the end of the section:

SEE ALSO

➤ *To see how to format cells, see page xx.*

- **Glossary terms:** For all the terms that appear in the glossary, you'll find the first appearance of that term in the text in *italic* followed by its definition.

Your screen might look slightly different from some of the examples in this book. This is due to various options during installation and because of the hardware setup.

PART

I

Workbook Basics

1 Starting, Quitting, and Getting Help 11

2 Opening, Searching For, and Closing Files 29

3 Saving Files and Using Templates 45

4 Saving Excel Data as a Web Page 59

5 Selecting and Navigating Worksheets 79

6 Changing Your View of the Worksheet 95

CHAPTER

1

Starting, Quitting, and Getting Help

- Starting Excel
- Quitting Excel
- The Excel environment
- Getting help in Excel
- Using the Office Assistant

Starting and Quitting Excel

If you're a new Excel user, check out this chapter for details about starting, exiting, and getting onscreen help when you're using Excel.

Starting Excel is the same as starting any other program in Windows 95 or Windows 98; you click the Start button and look for Excel in the Start button's nested menus. Perhaps a faster or more efficient way to start Excel, if you use Excel often, is to put a shortcut icon for Excel on your desktop; if the Office shortcut bar is installed, you might find a button for Excel there. The following three sections show you how to start Excel with these three handy methods.

Start Excel from the Start menu

1. Click the Windows **Start** button.
2. Point to **Programs**.
3. Click **Microsoft Excel**.

Your copy of Excel might be stored with other Office programs in a Microsoft Office folder, in which case you need to point to Microsoft Office and then click Microsoft Excel.

When Excel starts, a new, blank *workbook* (an Excel file) opens.

Can't Find the Desktop?

If your desktop is currently cluttered with open windows, it might be hard to get to the desktop itself. Right-click the taskbar and then click **Minimize All Windows** to minimize all open programs at once.

Where's the Icon?

When you create a new shortcut on the desktop, the **Create Shortcut** dialog box may hide the New Shortcut icon. Drag the dialog box by its title bar to move it out of the way.

Start Excel from a shortcut icon the Windows desktop

1. Minimize or resize any open program windows so that you can see the Windows desktop.
2. Right-click the desktop.
3. On the shortcut menu, point to **New**, and click **Shortcut**.

   A new icon appears on the desktop, and the Create Shortcut dialog box appears (as shown in Figure 1.1).
4. In the dialog box, click the **Browse** button.

   The Browse dialog box appears, and the **Files of type** box reads `Programs` (which means you see only folders and executable program files, such as Excel, listed).

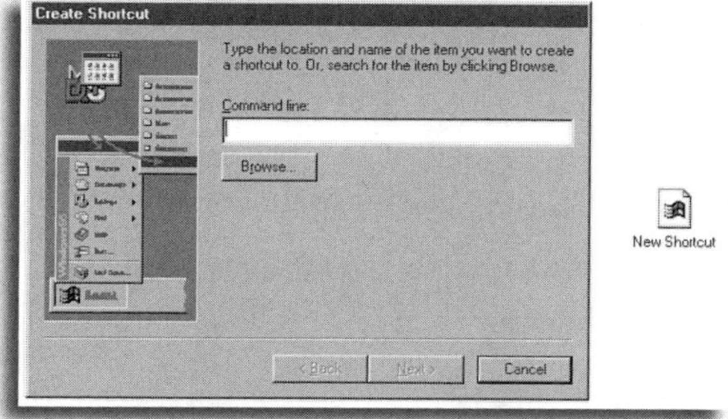

FIGURE 1.1
Browsing for the file is the easiest way to enter a path in the **Command line** box.

5. In the Browse dialog box, navigate to the folder that contains a file called Excel. This usually appears in the folder `C:\Program Files\Microsoft Office\Office`, but you may need to look elsewhere.
6. Double-click the Excel filename (shown in Figure 1.2).

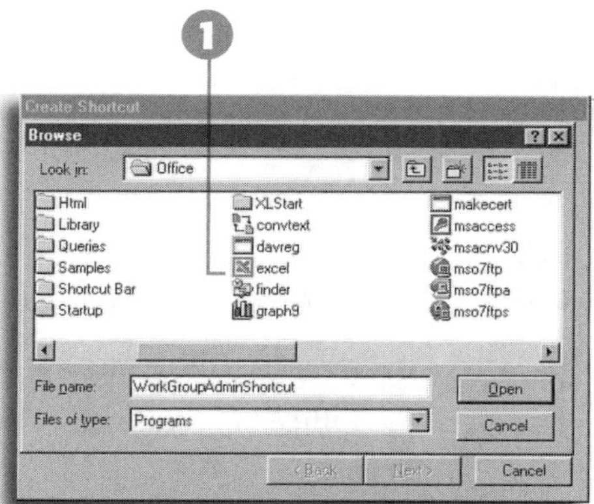

FIGURE 1.2
Double-click the filename, or click it once and then click **Open**.

1 Look for this icon.

The entire path to the file appears in the Create Shortcut dialog box.

7. Click **Next**.

Take a Shortcut to a Shortcut

A faster way to create a shortcut is to use the right mouse button. Drag a program name from the **Start** menu, or drag a file's icon from a My Computer window, onto the desktop. When you drop the icon, click **Create Shortcut(s) Here** on the shortcut menu.

8. Rename the shortcut icon if you want. (The name Excel is fine, but if your system is set up to show the file extension, `.exe`, you can delete the extension).
9. Click **Finish**. A new shortcut icon, like the one in Figure 1.3, is created on your desktop.

To start Excel, double-click the new icon.

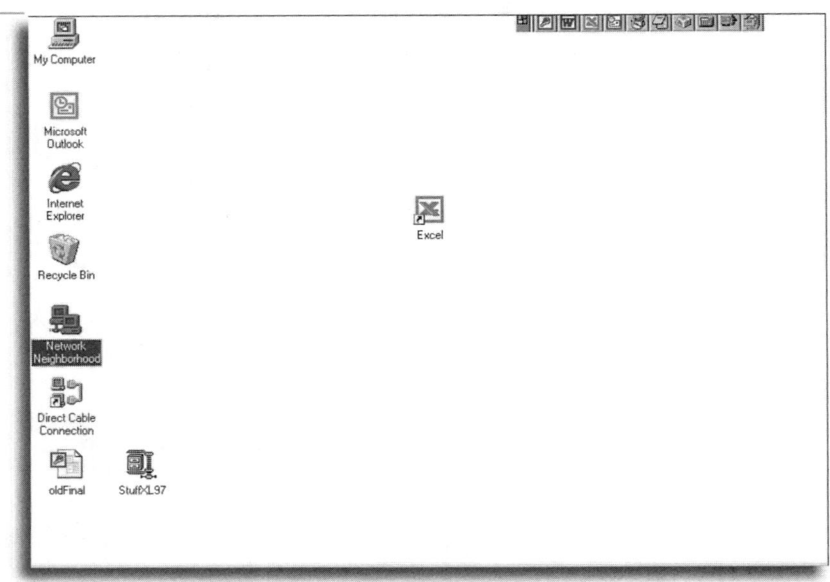

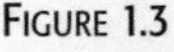

FIGURE 1.3

Double-click the shortcut icon to start Excel.

Your Windows Settings May Differ

If you see the filename `Excel.exe`, it means Windows is set up to display file extensions, which identify the file type (`.exe` identifies an executable file, which starts a program). If you find a file called `Microsoft Excel` (or `Microsoft Excel.lnk`) in your Microsoft Office folder, that's a shortcut to Excel, and you can create your desktop shortcut from that shortcut, if you like, rather than from the executable Excel icon in the Office folder. Either way, the result is the same.

Start Excel from the Office Shortcut bar

1. If the Office Shortcut bar is displayed, click the **Excel** button (shown in Figure 1.4).

FIGURE 1.4

If you don't have an Office Shortcut bar on your desktop, you can reinstall Office 2000 to install the Shortcut bar and then customize it to suit yourself.

1 Excel button

2. If you don't see an **Excel** button, add one. It may be hidden—see the sidenote to customize your Office shortcut bar.

Quitting Excel

When you've finished using Excel, you might want to exit the program to free your system resources for other programs. Follow this procedure to exit (quit) Excel.

Exit Excel

1. Click the **Close** button in the upper-right corner of the Excel window (shown in Figure 1.5).

   Be sure you click the **Close** button in the Excel window, not the one in the workbook window.

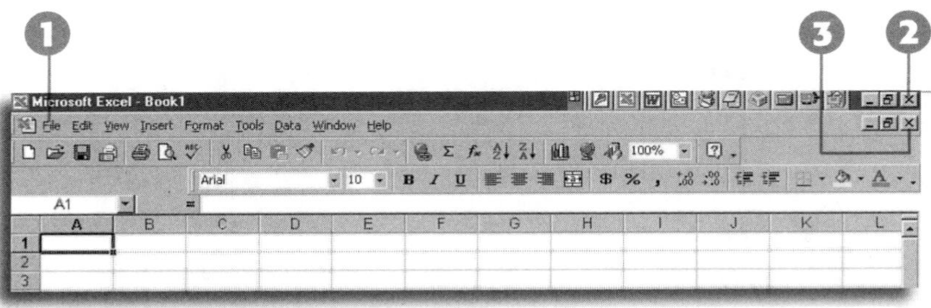

FIGURE 1.5

Click the **Close** button to quit in a single click, or use the **File, Exit** command to quit in two clicks.

1 File menu

2 Excel's Close button

3 Workbook Close button

2. If any open workbooks need saving before you close them, Excel asks you with a message box. Click **Yes** to save the workbook or **No** if you don't want to save the changes.

The Excel Environment

If you're new to Excel, you'll find a lot of unfamiliar terms and objects in the Excel landscape. Figure 1.6 shows many of the terms and objects I'll refer to in procedures throughout the book.

The two toolbars that appear when you first start Excel are the Standard and Formatting toolbars. You use these two toolbars more than any others.

Don't Like the Icon Name?

Click the name twice (not a double-click), type a new name, and press Enter. If you find yourself accidentally double-clicking, click the label once, then move the mouse a hair, then click the label again.

Do You Have a MOM?

The Office Shortcut bar, which used to be called the MOM (Microsoft Office Manager), is in the upper-right corner of your screen if it's installed and started. If it's missing an Excel button, you can add one: Right-click the left end of the Shortcut bar under the small Microsoft icon and then click **Customize**. On the Buttons tab, click the **Microsoft Excel** check box (and clear check boxes for any buttons that you don't want), and then click **OK**.

FIGURE 1.6

Part names and terms in the Excel environment.

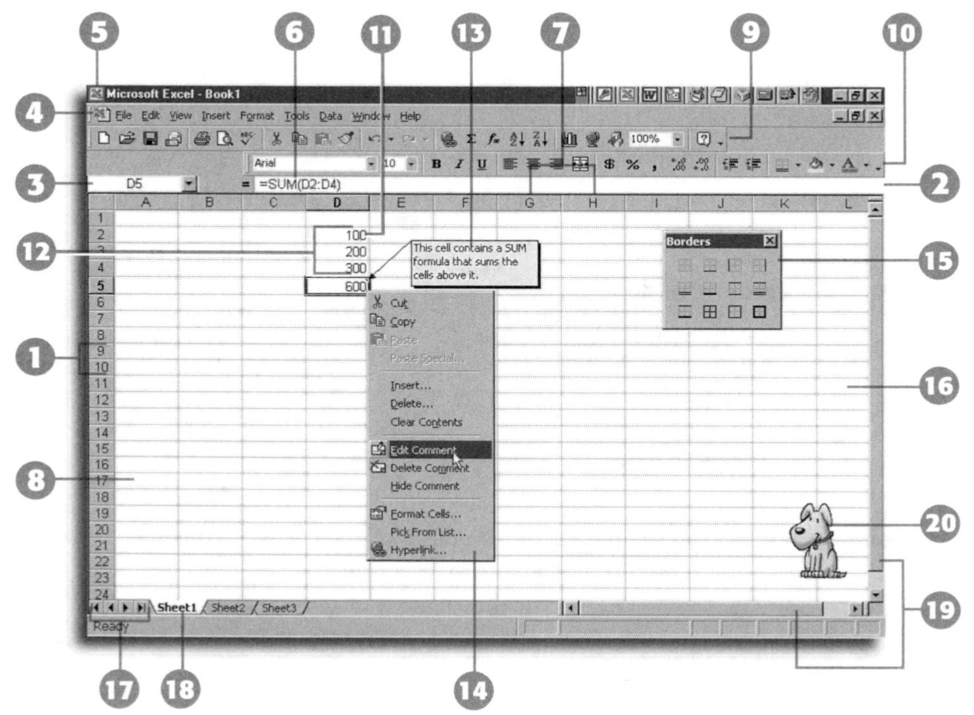

1. Rows
2. Formula bar
3. Name box
4. Menu bar
5. Title bar
6. Formula
7. Columns
8. Cell
9. Standard toolbar
10. Formatting toolbar
11. Cell contents
12. Range
13. Comment
14. Shortcut menu
15. Floating palette
16. Worksheet
17. Sheet tab scroll buttons
16. Sheet tab
19. Scrollbars
20. Office Assistant

Tables 1.1 and 1.2 help you sort out the buttons on these two toolbars, and in Chapter 27, "Customizing Your Excel Screen," you'll find procedures for customizing your toolbars to get rid of button clutter.

Which Is the Button I Want?

All those buttons are a bit mysterious until you get to know them, but if you place your mouse pointer over a button, after a moment, a **ScreenTip** (the name of the button—sometimes called a **ToolTip**) appears. If you click the down arrow at the right end of a toolbar, you'll see more buttons that aren't displayed on the toolbar for lack of space.

TABLE 1.1 **Standard toolbar buttons**

Button Face	Button Name	Function
	New	Opens a new workbook
	Open	Opens an existing workbook
	Save	Saves the active workbook
	Email	Turns workbook or worksheet into an email message
	Print	Prints the active worksheet
	Print Preview	Previews the printed page
	Spelling	Opens the spell-checker
	Cut	Cuts selected data for pasting
	Copy	Copies selected data for pasting
	Paste	Pastes cut or copied data
	Format Painter	Copies formatting from one area to another
	Undo	Undoes previous actions
	Redo	Reverses Undo actions
	Insert Hyperlink	Inserts a hyperlink
	AutoSum	Writes a SUM formula
	Paste Function	Opens the Function dialog boxes
	Sort Ascending	Sorts table in ascending order
	Sort Descending	Sorts table in descending order
	Chart Wizard	Starts the Chart Wizard
	Map	Creates a map based on the selected cells
	Drawing	Displays the Drawing toolbar
100%	Zoom	Changes worksheet magnification
	Office Assistant	Calls up the Office Assistant for help

The Buttons Change

Every time you use a toolbar button, it moves up to the toolbar, and the other toolbar hides buttons in its **More Buttons** drop-down palette to make room. The idea is that the buttons you use most will be displayed, and the buttons you rarely use will be out of your way. All the while, you have more screen space because the toolbars aren't stacked on top of each other. If you prefer your toolbars stacked on top of each other (with all buttons visible), right-click a toolbar, then click **Customize**. On the Options tab, clear the **Standard and Formatting toolbars share one row** check box and click **OK**.

TABLE 1.2 Formatting toolbar buttons

Button Face	Button Name	Function
Arial	Font	Displays list of available fonts
16	Font Size	Displays list of font sizes
B	Bold	Boldfaces selected data
I	Italic	Italicizes selected data
U	Underline	Underlines selected data
	Align Left	Aligns data to left in selected cells
	Center	Centers data in selected cells
	Align Right	Aligns data to right in selected cells
	Merge and Center	Combines adjacent cells into a single cell
$	Currency Style	Formats numbers in currency style
%	Percent Style	Formats numbers in percent style
,	Comma Style	Formats numbers in comma style
+.0 .00	Increase Decimal	Increases number of decimals displayed
.00 +.0	Decrease Decimal	Decreases number of decimals displayed
	Decrease Indent	Decreases indent (moves entry left)
	Increase Indent	Increases indent (moves entry right)
	Borders	Applies borders or displays a palette of border options
	Fill Color	Applies cell color or displays color palette
A	Font Color	Applies font color or displays color palette

Getting Help

The best way to get help is to look it up in a good book (like this one), but if someone else is using the book, or you want the answer to an obscure question that's not covered in your book, you can look up a topic in Excel's help files.

Several ways to get onscreen help from Excel are

- Office Assistant—An animated helper
- Contents, Index, and Answer Wizard—Access to all of Excel's help files
- What's This?—Context-sensitive help in dialog boxes
- The ? button—Context-sensitive help in dialog boxes

Using the Office Assistant

Some people love the Office Assistant, and some hate it. I personally find the default gyrating paper clip very irritating, but there's a new Office Assistant, a little dog named Rocky, and because I have a little dog named Rocky, I sort of like that one. The Office Assistant moves around on your screen and tries to stay out of the way, but remains there in case you need help. I'll tell you how to use it, how to change the character, and how to get rid of it (or at least hide it until you need it).

The Office Assistant has several alter egos, as shown in Figure 1.7.

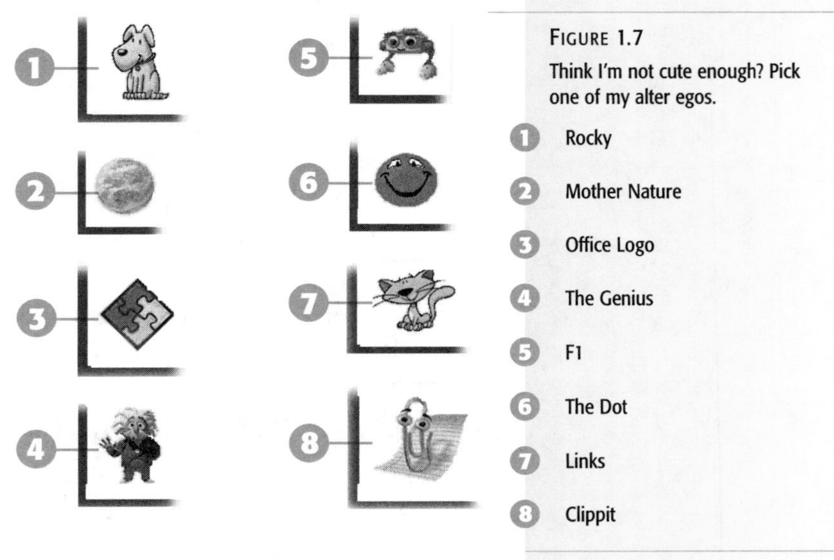

FIGURE 1.7
Think I'm not cute enough? Pick one of my alter egos.

1. Rocky
2. Mother Nature
3. Office Logo
4. The Genius
5. F1
6. The Dot
7. Links
8. Clippit

Get help from the Office Assistant

1. On the Standard toolbar, click the **Office Assistant** button [?].

   The Office Assistant appears on your screen, as shown in Figure 1.8.

FIGURE 1.8
Ask me anything; I know everything.

Keep It Short

A few well-chosen words yield better results than complete sentences or questions.

2. In the **Type your question here** box, type a word, a phrase, or an entire question.

   If you want to see him, but don't have a question, click away from the question balloon and it will disappear; click your Assistant to make the balloon reappear.

3. Click **Search**.

   The Office Assistant attempts to sort out what you really want to know and gives you a list of possible topics. (If it clearly doesn't understand what you're looking for, type a new word or phrase.)

4. Click an option button for a topic that looks useful.

The Help window opens. To show the two-pane Help window, with Contents, Answer Wizard, Index, and help files side-by-side (as shown in Figure 1.9), click the **Show/Hide** button.

Using the Contents, Index, and Answer Wizard

If the Office Assistant is installed, you have to go through him to get to the Help window; but if the Office Assistant isn't installed, click the **Help** button on the toolbar to open the Help window.

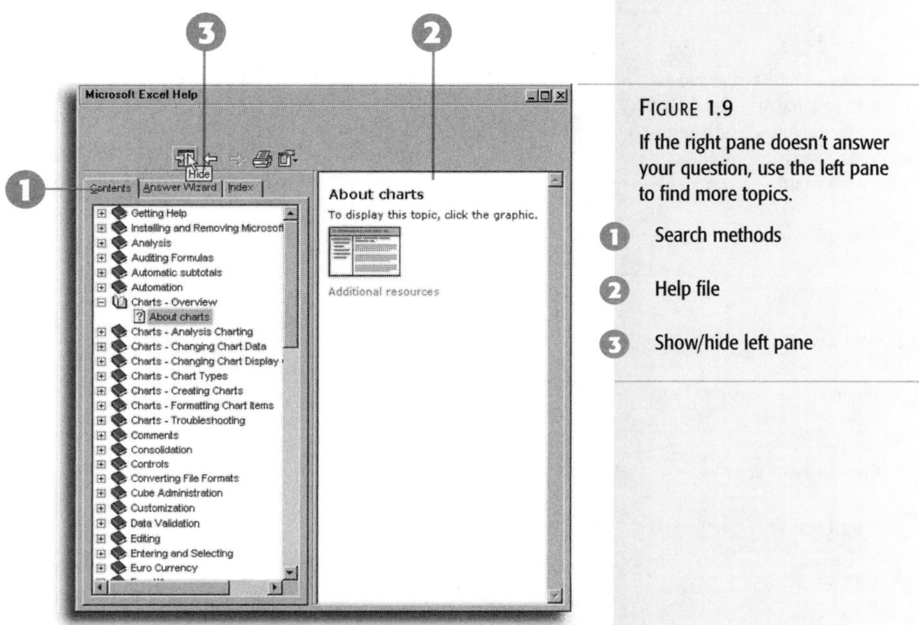

FIGURE 1.9

If the right pane doesn't answer your question, use the left pane to find more topics.

1. Search methods
2. Help file
3. Show/hide left pane

The Help window is an updated version of the old Microsoft help workhorse. It's not context-sensitive like the Office Assistant; rather, it's a general table of contents, an index to all Excel's help files, and a conversational Answer Wizard.

Use the Contents and Index help files

1. On the **Help** menu, click **Microsoft Excel Help** (or click a topic in the Assistant's question balloon).
2. Click the **Show** button in the window's upper-left corner to open the full Help window, as shown in Figure 1.10. The Show button becomes a Hide button when the full window is open.
3. Click the appropriate tab at the top of the left pane for the way you want to search.

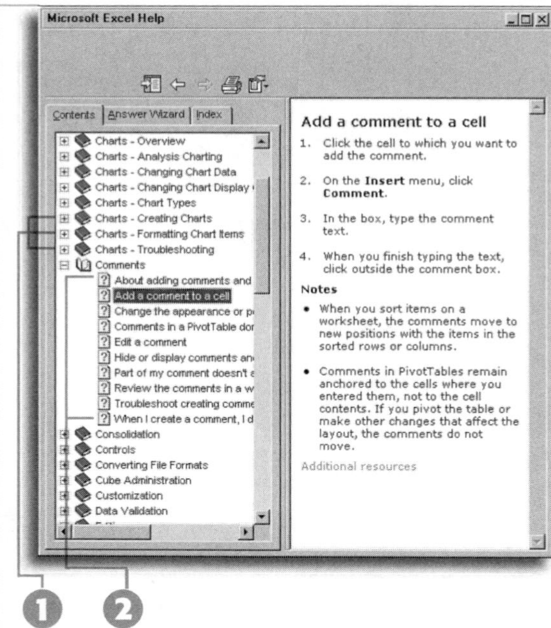

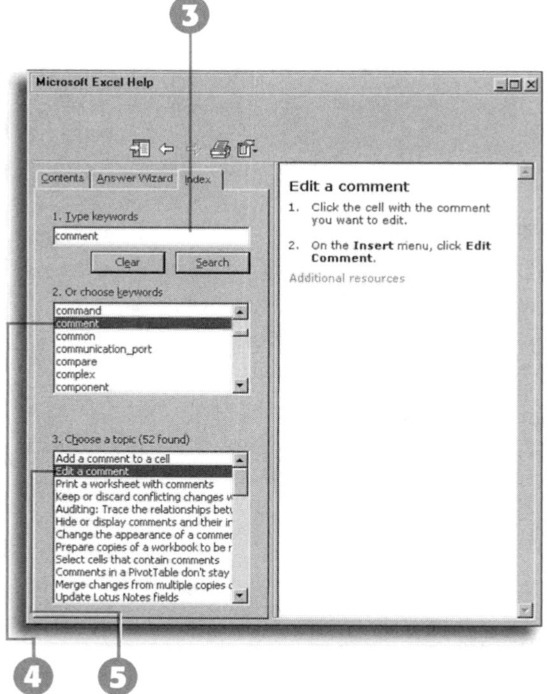

FIGURE 1.10

Three tabs in the Help window provide a table of contents, an alphabetical index, and a conversational search engine called the Answer Wizard.

1. Plus symbols
2. Topics
3. Type a word or words.
4. Double-click a general topic.
5. Click a specific topic.
6. Type a phrase or question.
7. Click a topic.
8. Hyperlink

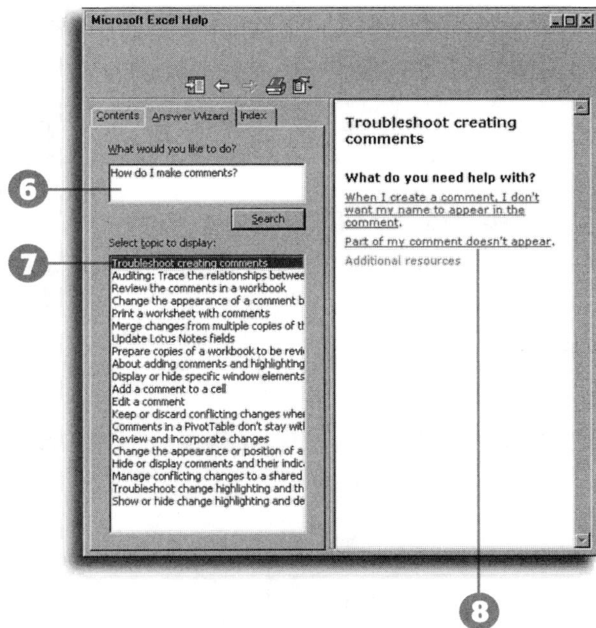

- On the **Contents** tab, click the plus symbol next to topic headings until you locate a topic that might be useful; then, click that topic to open the help file in the right pane.
- On the **Index** tab, in the box for step 1, type a word that you'd look up in an index. Or, in the box for step 2, scroll through the index list and double-click various words until one of them locates a list in the step 3 box that has a useful topic. Click the useful topic, and read the help file in the right pane.
- On the **Answer Wizard** tab, in the upper box, type a search word, phrase, or question, then click **Search**. In the **Select Topic to display** box, click a likely topic and read the information in the right pane.

  The right pane often has lots of hyperlinks (blue, underlined words and phrases) that lead to more help files; click one to read its file.

To return to a previous help file in the right pane, click the **Back** button at the top of the help window. The files in the right pane back up one-by-one through the files you previously opened (and the **Forward** button moves forward one-by-one through the files you previously opened).

Help and the Workbook Window

To keep the Help window open while you work in the workbook, click in the workbook window. The Help window hides behind the workbook.To see the help file again, click the help button on the taskbar.

Changing the Office Assistant's Behavior (a Bit)

If you click **Options** in the Office Assistant's initial dialog box, you can activate or deactivate other behaviors, such as making sounds, responding to the F1 key, moving out of the way, and displaying keyboard shortcuts.

Switch Office Assistants

1. Right-click the **Office Assistant**, and then click **Choose Assistant.**
2. On the **Gallery** tab (shown in Figure 1.11), scroll through the various characters by clicking the **Next** and **Back** buttons.

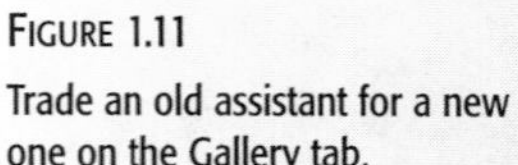

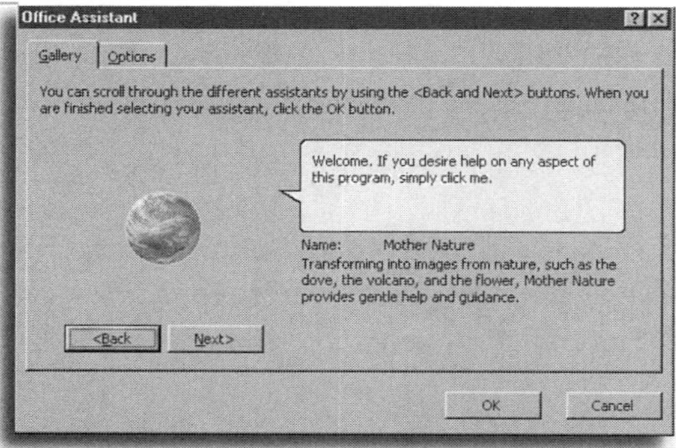

FIGURE 1.11
Trade an old assistant for a new one on the Gallery tab.

3. When you find an assistant you like, click **OK**.

   You can find more Assistants at the Microsoft Web site. Click **Help**, then click **Office on the Web**, and follow the instructions on the Web page to find more Assistants.

Hide the Office Assistant

1. Right-click the **Office Assistant.**
2. Click **Hide**.

You can recall the Assistant by clicking the Office Assistant button or by pressing F1.

You can also drag it out of your way, off to the side of your screen.

Getting Rid of the Office Assistant Permanently

To remove the Office Assistant completely, uninstall it with the **Add/Remove Programs** feature in the Windows Control Panel.

Remove the Office Assistant from your computer

1. Put your Office 2000 CD-ROM in your computer's CD-ROM drive. (If your CD-ROM drive window opens, click its **Close** button to close it.)
2. Click **Start**, point to **Settings**, and then click **Control Panel**.
3. In the Control Panel window, double-click **Add/Remove Programs.**
4. Select **Microsoft Office 2000 Premium Edition**, and then click **Add/Remove**. If instructed to insert the CD-ROM, click **OK**. If Setup advises you to close open applications, do so and then click **OK.**
5. In the Microsoft Office 2000 Maintenance Mode dialog box, click **Add or Remove Features**.
6. In the next dialog box, click the **plus** symbol next to Office Tools, then the icon next to Office Assistant, and click **Not Available** on the drop-down list.
7. Click **Update Now**.

Are You Sure You Want It Removed?

If you uninstall the Office Assistant, it disappears from all Office 2000 programs.

8. When you see a message telling you that the setup was completed successfully, click **OK**.
9. Close the **Add/Remove Program Properties** dialog box, and then close the **Control Panel** dialog box.

To reinstall the Office Assistant, repeat these steps but click **Run from My Computer** in the drop-down list in step 6. Click the **plus** symbol next to Office Assistant, check that the Assistant you want isn't marked X, and then finish steps 7 through 9.

Asking What's This?

What's This? help is context-sensitive help for those occasions when an item in a dialog box is a mystery.

Don't See the What's This Button?

Right-click the mysterious item, and click the **What's This?** button that appears.

Get What's This? help in a dialog box

1. Click the small button with the question mark in the upper-right corner of the dialog box, next to the Close button (as shown in Figure 1.12).

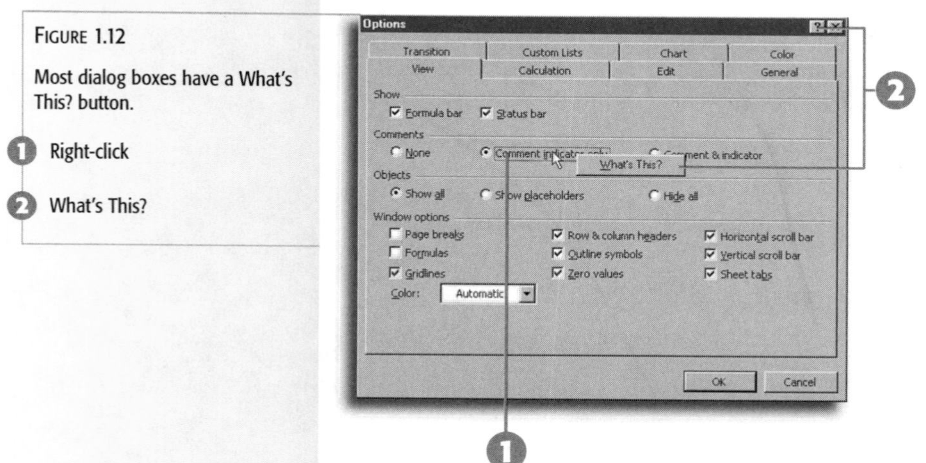

FIGURE 1.12

Most dialog boxes have a What's This? button.

1 Right-click

2 What's This?

2. Click the mysterious item.

   A quick answer appears (shown in Figure 1.13).

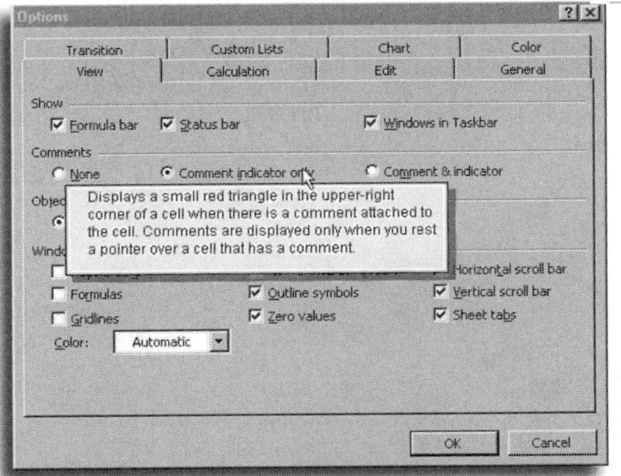

FIGURE 1.13
Quick solutions to the mysteries of dialog boxes.

What's This Other Thing?

To inquire about items that aren't in dialog boxes, use the **What's This?** command on the **Help** menu. For example, toolbar buttons are sometimes mysterious, and the button names that show up in ScreenTips may not help; however, the **What's This?** command can explain what the button does. (It works on most parts of the Excel screen, not just toolbar buttons.)

Get What's This? help in the Excel window

1. On the **Help** menu, click **What's This?**.

   The mouse pointer becomes a question-mark pointer (shown in Figure 1.14).

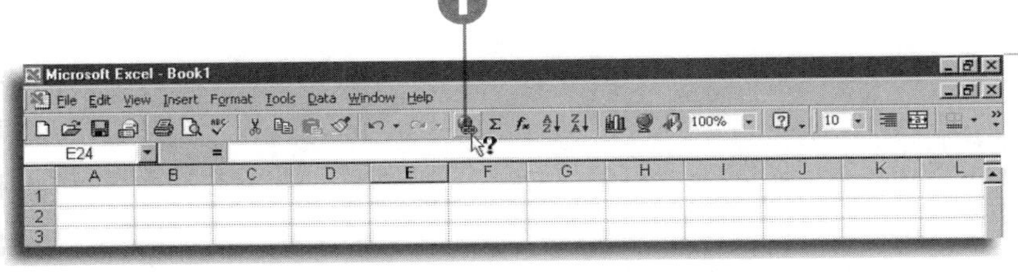

FIGURE 1.14
What does this button do?

1 Click a workbook item.

2. Click the mysterious item.

   An explanation of the item appears in a ScreenTip (see Figure 1.15).

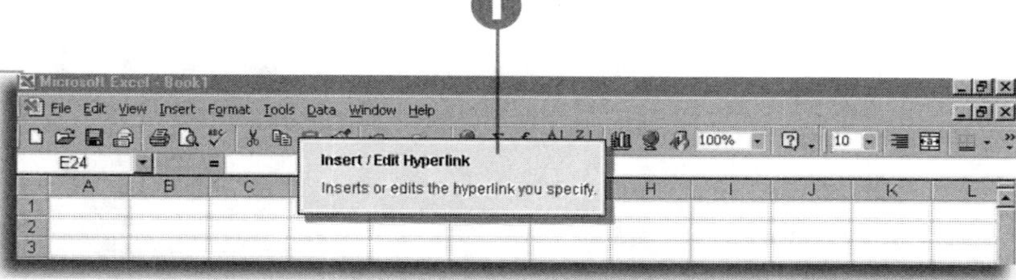

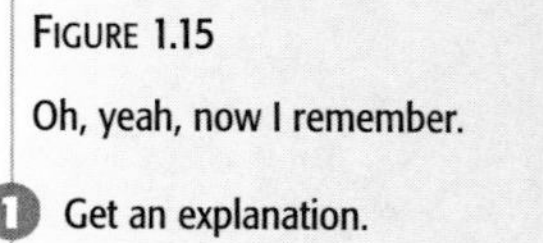

FIGURE 1.15

Oh, yeah, now I remember.

1 Get an explanation.

BURSAR PAYMENT RECEIPT
FOR LRC

Patron Name : Featherston (Last) James (First)

CWID: 10

Stamp Paid Here

computer won't print receipts
-[illegible]

Amount Due : 2.25

110010-570001-00 Fine ____ 310010-812205-250099 Copy Card ____

Amount Paid : ____

Cash ____ Check ____ Charge ____

Invalid without both signatures.

____ (Bursar)

[illegible] (LRC)

Date: 8/19/03

CHAPTER

2

Opening, Searching For, and Closing Files

- Opening a workbook
- Opening a workbook from a template
- Opening a workbook file while starting Excel
- Opening non-Excel files in Excel
- Opening multiple files
- Finding a file
- Connecting and opening files with hyperlinks
- Closing a workbook

Opening Files

More Than One Workbook

You can have as many workbooks open simultaneously as you like, until you run out of system resources. All workbooks that you open remain open until you close them.

This chapter is all about different techniques for opening, finding, and closing files.

Opening a single Excel workbook file is a common, straightforward procedure; but we'll look at other useful procedures and efficiency tricks that fall under the topic of opening files, such as opening several files at once, opening a non-Excel file in Excel, finding a file you've lost, and opening other files by clicking a hyperlink in your workbook.

You can open a new default workbook, a copy of a custom template, or an existing workbook in which you want to make changes.

Open a new, blank *default* workbook (the same as the workbook that opens when you start Excel)

1. On the Standard toolbar, click the **New** button. 

A new, blank workbook opens, as shown in Figure 2.1.

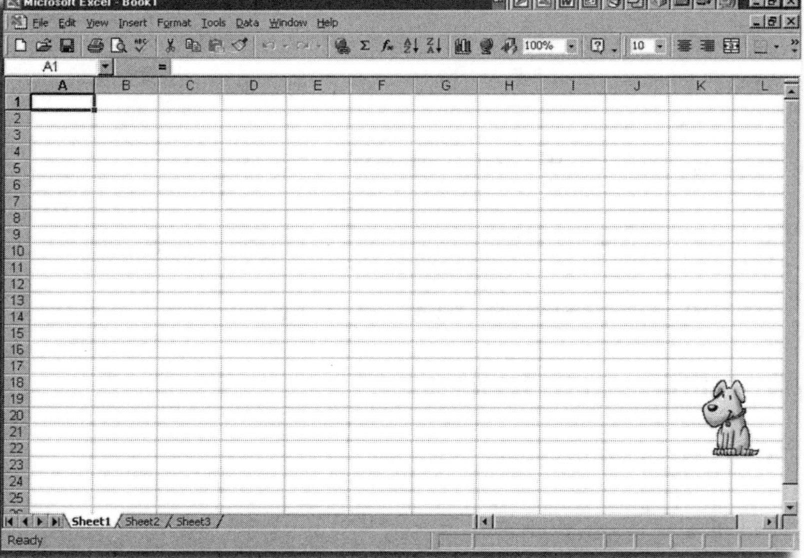

FIGURE 2.1

The **New** button opens a copy of Excel's default workbook template.

1 Unsaved workbook name

A *template* is like a printed pad of invoices or sales receipts: Each copy is preprinted with standard labels and formatting, and you tear off copies. A template, like a stationery pad, saves you work because you don't have to re-create the same labels, formatting, and formulas over and over again; you just open a copy of the workbook template, and all the labels, formatting, and formulas are already in place.

Open a new workbook from a template

1. Open the **File** menu, and choose **New**.

   The New dialog box appears (shown in Figure 2.2). In the New dialog box, you find Excel's default workbook template, named Workbook, and any custom workbook templates that are saved in the Templates folder.

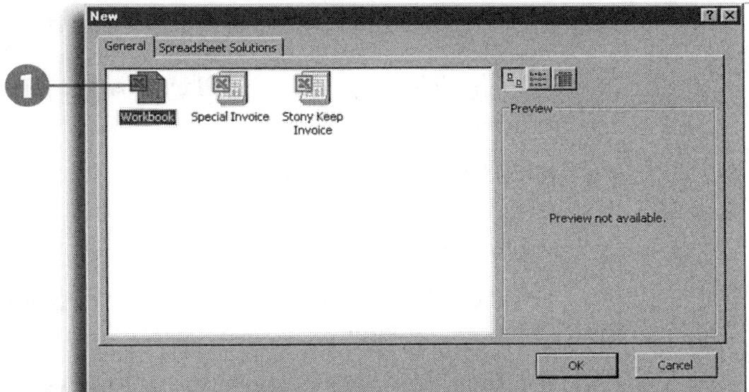

FIGURE 2.2

The New command on the File menu enables you to select from any custom templates in your Templates folder.

1 Excel's default workbook

2. Double-click the icon for the workbook you want to open.

   A copy of the template that you double-clicked opens.

SEE ALSO

➤ *To learn how to save a workbook as a template, see page 5.*

Open an existing workbook file (a file you saved previously).

1. On the Standard toolbar, click the **Open** button.

   The Open dialog box appears, as shown in Figure 2.3.

Recently Used Files

If the file you want is one of the last few Excel files you've opened, you'll probably find its name at the bottom of Excel's **File** menu (which saves time spent navigating to the folder where it's stored). Click **File**, and then click the name of the file.

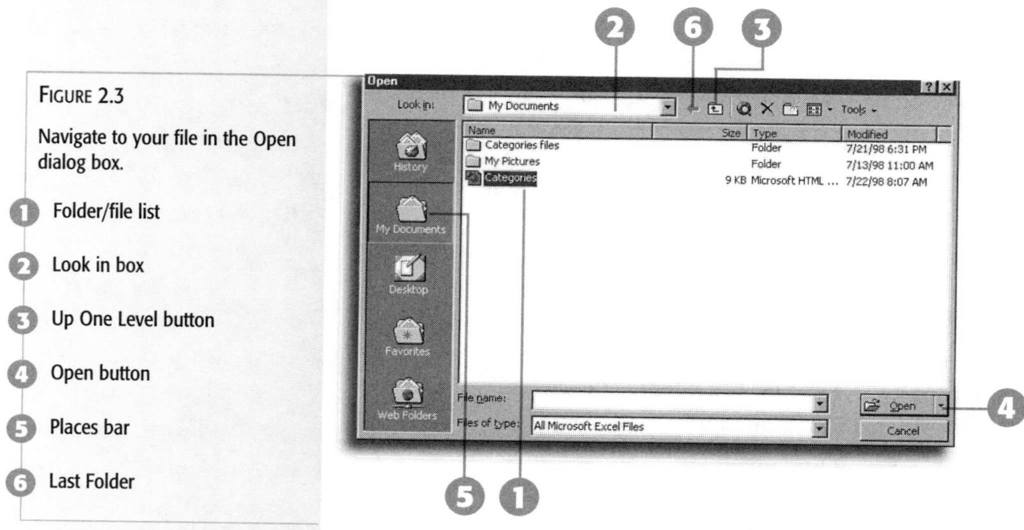

FIGURE 2.3

Navigate to your file in the Open dialog box.

1. Folder/file list
2. Look in box
3. Up One Level button
4. Open button
5. Places bar
6. Last Folder

I'm Tired of All This Clicking

To make Excel's Open dialog box always open to a specific folder (not the default Personal or My Documents folders), open the **Tools** menu and choose **Options.** In the Options dialog box, click the **General** tab. In the **Default file location** box, type the path to your folder and click **OK**. Files can be located on a local hard drive or on a network drive.

Quick–How Do I Create a Web Folder?

If you already have a Web server, you can create Web folders to hold your Web files. Click the **Web Folders** button in the Places bar, then click the Create New Folder button, and follow the steps in the Web Folder Wizard to add a new Web folder.

2. In the Open dialog box, use the Places bar to jump to one of five commonly used folders:
   - The **History** button opens the Recent folder, which holds shortcuts to a long list of recently opened files and folders.
   - The **My Documents** button opens the My Documents folder, the default folder for saving files.
   - The **Desktop** button opens the Windows desktop.
   - The **Favorites** button opens the Favorites folder, which holds Web favorites links and any files you choose to save there.
   - The **Web Folders** button opens the Web Folders folder, which holds shortcuts to your Web servers and any Web files and Web folders you've saved to Web servers.
3. In the Open dialog box, you can also use the **Look in** box to navigate to the folder where your file is saved.
   - Click the **Up One Level** button to navigate backwards through folders.

- Double-click folder names in the folder/file list to navigate forward through folders.
- Click the **Last Folder** button to jump back to the last folder that was open.
- Click the down-arrow button on the **Look in** box to drop a file-tree list (shown in Figure 2.4); then, you can select a folder or hard drive several levels back up the file tree.
- To navigate to a network drive, click the down-arrow button on the **Look in** box to drop a file-tree list; then, click **Network Neighborhood** and navigate to the drive and folder that you want.

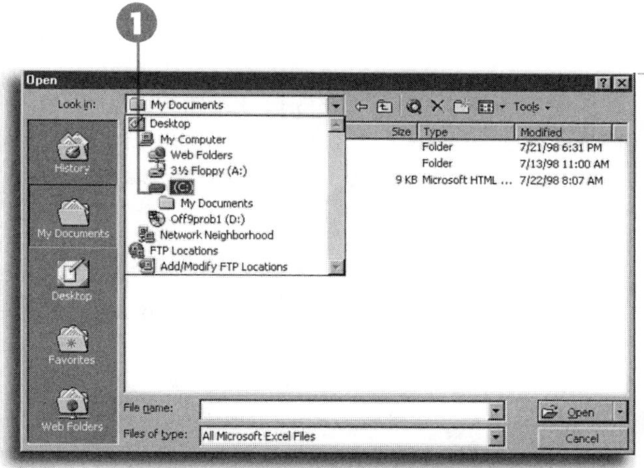

FIGURE 2.4
Drop the **Look in** box list to jump backwards several levels.

1 Click here to go to the hard-drive level.

4. When you see the filename you want in the folder/file list, click the filename, and then click **Open** (or just double-click the filename). The file opens, and the Open dialog box closes.

Take a Shortcut to the File

To create a desktop shortcut icon that opens your file and starts Excel for you, use the right mouse button to drag the filename out of the My Computer or Windows Explorer window and drop it on the desktop, and then click **Create Shortcut(s) Here**.

Start Excel and open a file at the same time

1. In the My Computer or Windows Explorer window, locate the folder where your file is stored (as shown in Figure 2.5). Excel files display an Excel icon, which makes the file easier to find.

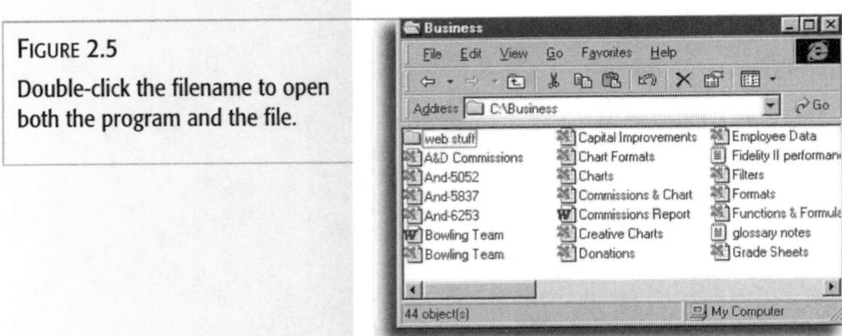

FIGURE 2.5

Double-click the filename to open both the program and the file.

2. Double-click the filename.

   Excel starts, and your file opens in Excel.

Opening Non-Excel Files in Excel

You Can Always Find a Way to Get the Data

If the data is in a file format for which you don't have an Excel converter, you get a message indicating that Excel can't read the file format. To get around that problem, have whoever sent the data save it as a text file and send that file to you.

Sometimes the data you need is not in an Excel file; it's saved in a file of a different type (for example, a text file, or a Lotus 1-2-3, Quattro Pro, Works, or dBASE file). You can open many of these file types in Excel—sometimes directly, and sometimes with the help of the Text Import Wizard.

Open a non-Excel file in Excel

1. On the Standard toolbar, click the **Open** button.

   The Open dialog box appears (shown in Figure 2.6).

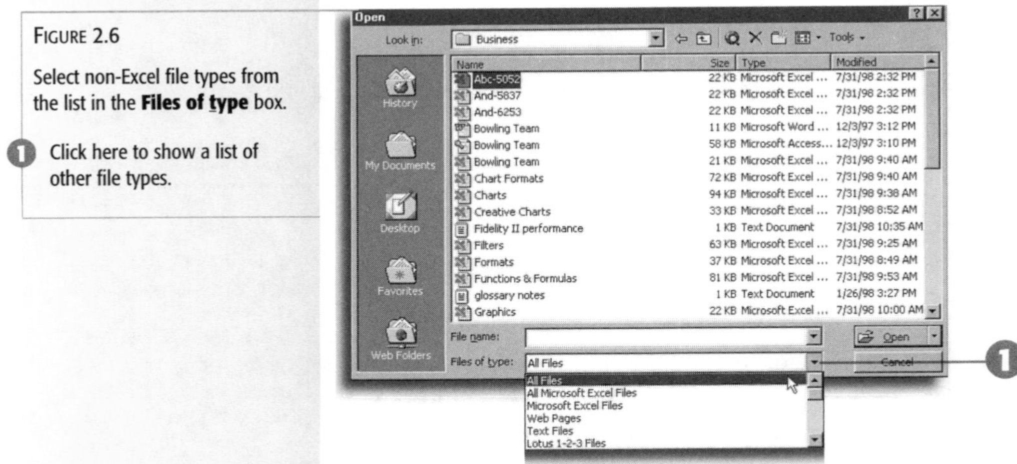

FIGURE 2.6

Select non-Excel file types from the list in the **Files of type** box.

1 Click here to show a list of other file types.

2. In the Open dialog box, use the **Look in** box to navigate to the folder where your file is saved.
3. In the **Files of type** box, click the file type (if you know it) or click **All Files** to display all the files in the folder.
4. When you see the filename that you want listed in the dialog box, click the filename, and then click **Open**.

   The file opens, and the Open dialog box closes.

If the Text Import Wizard starts, follow the procedure in Chapter 8, "Copying and Importing Data from Other Files," in the section "Importing a Text File," to bring the data into an Excel workbook.

SEE ALSO

➤ *To learn how to save files as a specific file format, see page 47.*
➤ *To learn how to import a text file, see page 129.*

I Don't Want to Mess Up My Colleague's Workbook

To guard against inadvertently changing and saving a workbook, you can open it as "read-only." Read-only means you can read what's in the file but only save changes to a copy of the file, not the file itself. To open a file as read-only, click the arrow next to the **Open** button, then click **Open Read-only**; to open a copy for yourself that you can freely save changes in, click **Open as Copy**. If you want to save changes that can be integrated back into the original file, see Chapter 25, "Sharing a Workbook with Other Users."

Opening More Than One File at a Time

Often, you may need to open several Excel files at the same time (for example, if you're copying data from one workbook to another or comparing several workbooks to each other). Instead of opening the files one-by-one, you can save time and mouse clicks by opening them all at once.

Open multiple files at once

1. On the Standard toolbar, click the **Open** button.
2. Navigate to the folder where the files are located.
3. Click the first of the filenames you want to open.
4. For filenames that are located next to each other in the dialog box (*adjacent* filenames), press and hold down the Shift key and click the last file you want. All files between the first and last are selected.

   For filenames that are *nonadjacent* (not next to each other), press and hold down the Ctrl key, and click to select each of the remaining filenames you want (see Figure 2.7).
5. Click **Open**.

   The Open dialog box closes, and all the files open.

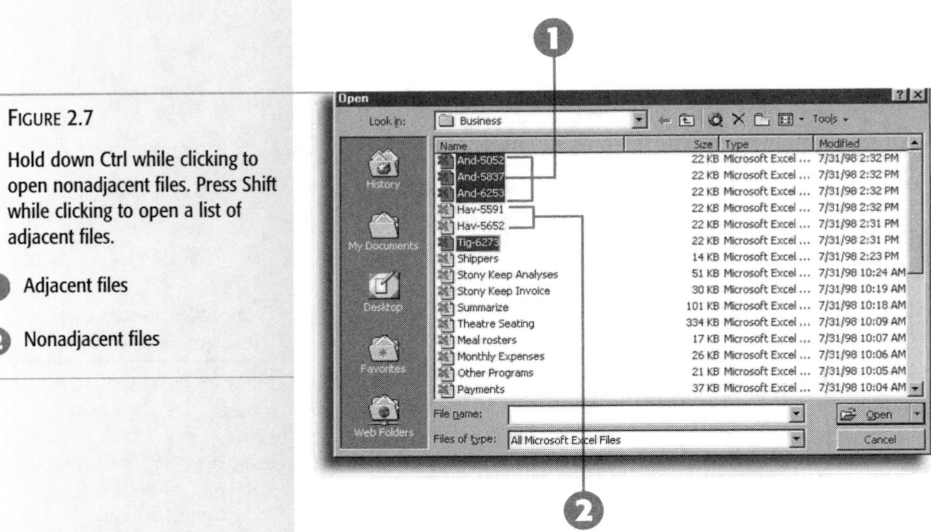

FIGURE 2.7

Hold down Ctrl while clicking to open nonadjacent files. Press Shift while clicking to open a list of adjacent files.

1 Adjacent files

2 Nonadjacent files

Searching for a File

If you've forgotten where you saved a file, or what you named it, you can search for it. When you've located a number of likely possibilities (for example, several invoices you sent last week), you can quick-view each file's contents to locate the one you want rapidly.

Finding a File by Searching for File Properties

If you've saved a file with specific file properties such as author name or keywords (which are explained later), you can search for those properties to find the file—even when you can't remember the filename or the folder where you saved it. Although you can search for a file using only the boxes in the Open dialog box, you won't often find what you're looking for, and you don't have much control over the search. You make a better search when you use the Advanced Find dialog box.

Search for a file with isolated details

1. On the Standard toolbar, click the **Open** button.

   The Open dialog box appears (shown in Figure 2.8).

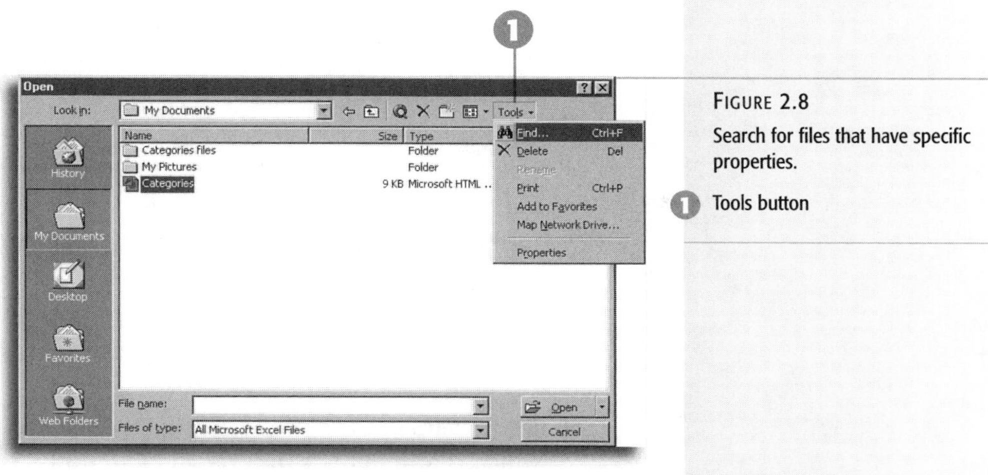

FIGURE 2.8

Search for files that have specific properties.

1 Tools button

2. In the Open dialog box, click the **Tools** button, then click **Find**.

   The Find dialog box appears (shown in Figure 2.9).

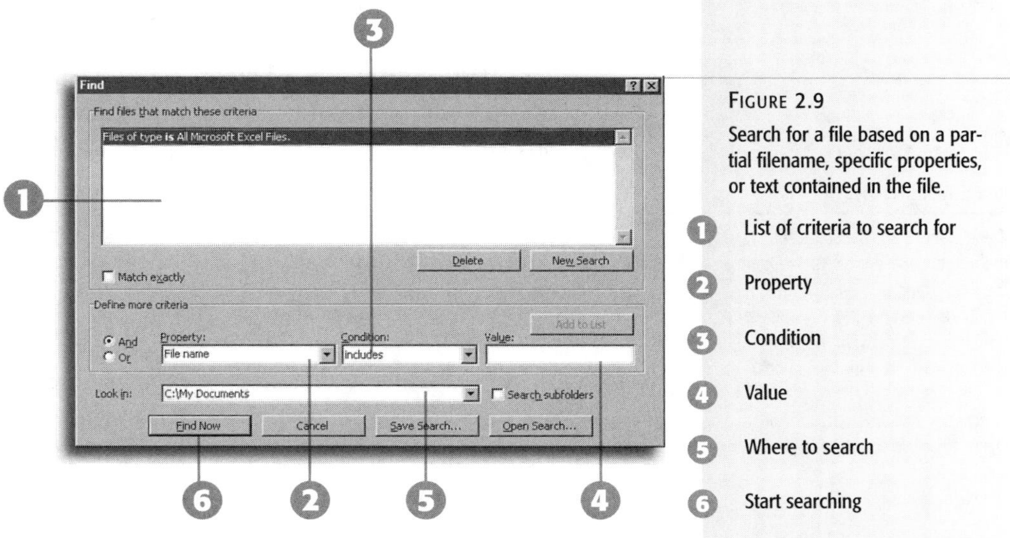

FIGURE 2.9

Search for a file based on a partial filename, specific properties, or text contained in the file.

1 List of criteria to search for

2 Property

3 Condition

4 Value

5 Where to search

6 Start searching

3. In the Find dialog box, click the down-arrow button in the **Property** box, and click a property for which you want to search (such as **Author**, **File names**, **Text**, or **Keywords**).

The **Text** property is any word or phrase contained anywhere in the file, such as a worksheet label or the word `total`. **Keywords** are properties you can set when you save a file.

4. In the **Condition** box, click the down arrow and click a phrase that describes what you're looking for.

   For example, the **Keywords** condition **includes words** narrows the search to specific keywords that you saved. The **File names** condition **begins with** narrows the search to filenames that have specific starting characters such as `inv` or `cr`.

5. In the **Value** box, type the words, characters, or dates for which to search the **Property** and **Condition**.

6. Click the **Add to List** button.

   The criteria are added to the **Find files that match these criteria** list.

7. In the **Look in** box, set the path to the area that you want to search, and click the **Search subfolders** check box to search all subfolders in the path you set. (For example, to search every folder on your hard drive—which could take a while—set the path to **C:** and check the **Search subfolders** check box.)

8. Check to see that the **Find files that match these criteria** list contains all your criteria and nothing extra that might unnecessarily limit your search (such as extra criteria that you didn't mean to set).

9. Click **Find Now** to start the search.

   Be patient while Excel searches. If you start the search from your hard drive, the search can take a few seconds or longer.

   Excel searches all folders in the path that you set and eventually returns a list of folders matching your criteria.

Figure 2.10 shows the results of a search of my hard drive for Excel files I saved with the keyword *invoice*.

Reuse Your Searches

If you want to use the same search in the future, save the search. Open the Find dialog box again, and click the **Save Search** button. Name the search and click **OK**. In the future, you can open the Find dialog box, click the **Open Search** button, select your saved search, and click **Open** to set up all the search criteria.

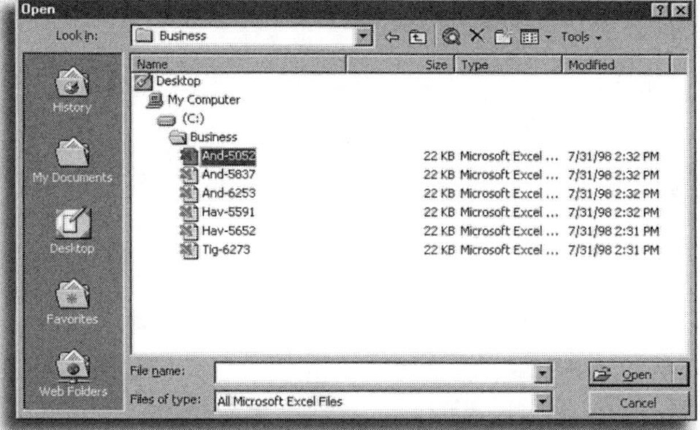

FIGURE 2.10
The results of a search include the path to each found file.

SEE ALSO

➤ *To learn how to save files with specific properties, see page 47.*

Locating the File You Want with Quick View

Quick View displays the contents of a file without opening the file, which can save you considerable time if you've just searched for files and you're not sure which of several files is the one you want.

Check the contents of files without opening them

1. On the Standard toolbar, click the **Open** button.
2. Conduct the search, or navigate to the folder where the files in question are stored.
3. Right-click a filename.
4. Click **Quick View**.

   A Quick View window opens, displaying the contents of the first worksheet in the workbook (shown in Figure 2.11). You can't edit a workbook in the Quick View window, but you can open the file by clicking its **Open File for Editing** button.

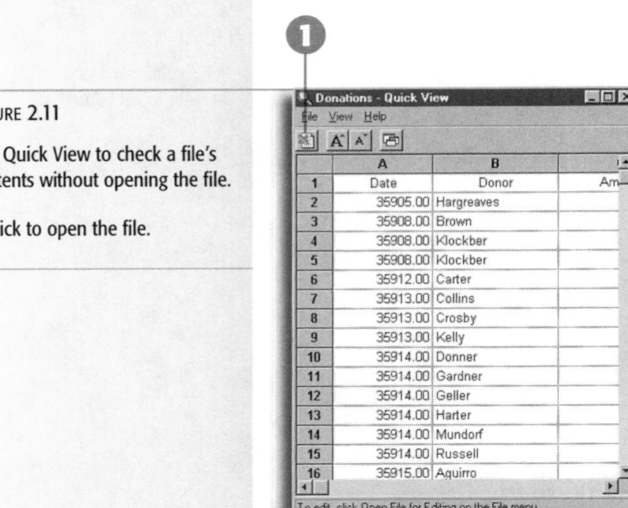

FIGURE 2.11

Use Quick View to check a file's contents without opening the file.

1 Click to open the file.

No Quick View?

If your computer is running Windows 98, you'll be able to Quick View all Office files; but if you're using Windows 95, you'll only be able to Quick View files saved as Office 95 or earlier versions. If you're using Windows 95 and want to be able to Quick View a specific Excel 2000 file, open that file and save it with the file type **Microsoft Excel 97-2000 & 5.0/95 Workbook**. The saved file will be bigger, but you'll be able to Quick View it.

Using Hyperlinks

A quick and fun way to navigate in Excel 2000 is by creating *hyperlinks* to other files on your computer or network. Hyperlinks to other files work just like hyperlinks in Internet Web pages, but they open other files in your computer or network instead of Web sites on the Internet.

You're not limited to Excel files; for example, you can use a hyperlink in a worksheet to open background information that's in a Word document or open a splashy, motivational PowerPoint slide.

Connecting Files with a Hyperlink

You can create a hyperlink to another file on your computer and then use the hyperlink to open the hyperlinked document.

Add a hyperlink to a file

1. Click the cell where you want to place the hyperlink.
2. On the Standard toolbar, click the **Insert Hyperlink** button.

   If Excel asks you to save your workbook, click **Yes**. The Insert Hyperlink dialog box appears (shown in Figure 2.12).

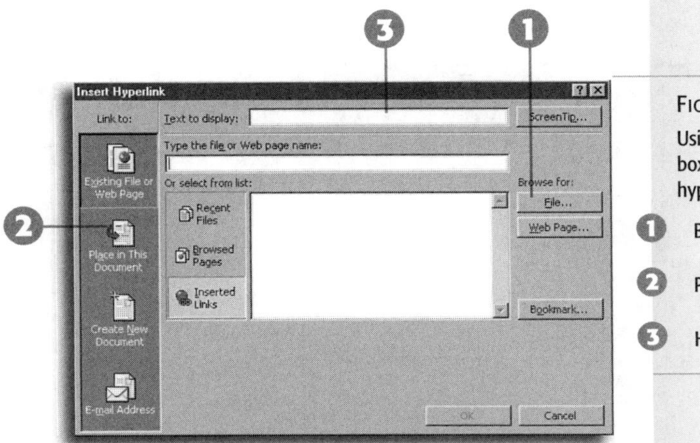

FIGURE 2.12
Using the Insert Hyperlink dialog box is the easy way to create a hyperlink to another file.

1. Browse to the hyperlinked file
2. Places bar
3. Hyperlink text

3. In the Places bar, click the sort of file or chunk of data to which the hyperlink will link. (**Existing File or Web Page** will create a link to another file.)
4. In the **Text to display** box, type a friendly, understandable label for the hyperlink.
5. Below **Browse for**, click the **File** button to navigate to the file you want.

   The Link to File dialog box appears.
6. In the Link to File dialog box, navigate to the file to which you want to hyperlink.
7. Click the filename, and then click **OK**.

   The name of the hyperlinked file appears in the **Type the file or Web page name** box.
8. In the Insert Hyperlink dialog box, click **OK**.

   The name of the hyperlinked file appears as a blue, underlined hyperlink in the worksheet cell, as shown in Figure 2.13. (This is a hyperlink to a Word document on my hard drive. When I click it, Word opens, and the document opens in Word.)

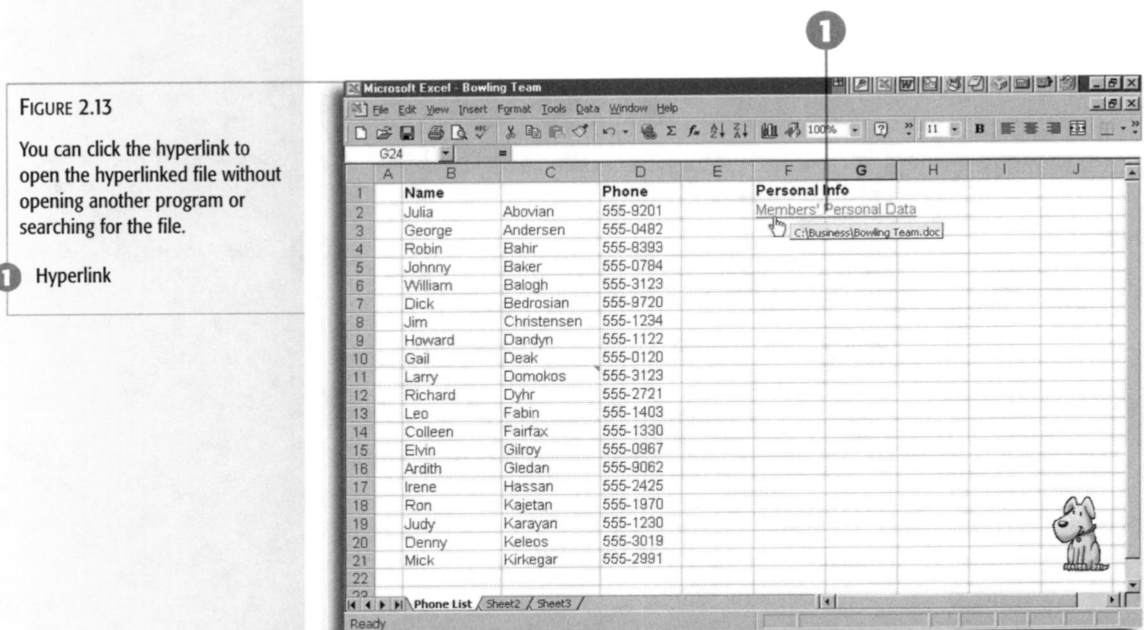

FIGURE 2.13

You can click the hyperlink to open the hyperlinked file without opening another program or searching for the file.

1 Hyperlink

Opening Files Using Hyperlinks

Using hyperlinks to open files enables you to open other files much more quickly. To open a hyperlinked file, click the hyperlink. After you've used the hyperlink to open the linked file, the hyperlink turns purple to indicate that you've used it.

Closing Workbook Files

When you're finished using a workbook but you want to continue working in Excel, close the open workbook to save system resources. You can close workbooks in a couple of ways.

To close a single workbook, use one of these techniques:

- Click the workbook window's **Close** button (in the upper-right corner of the workbook window, as shown in Figure 2.14).
- Open the **File** menu and choose **Close**.

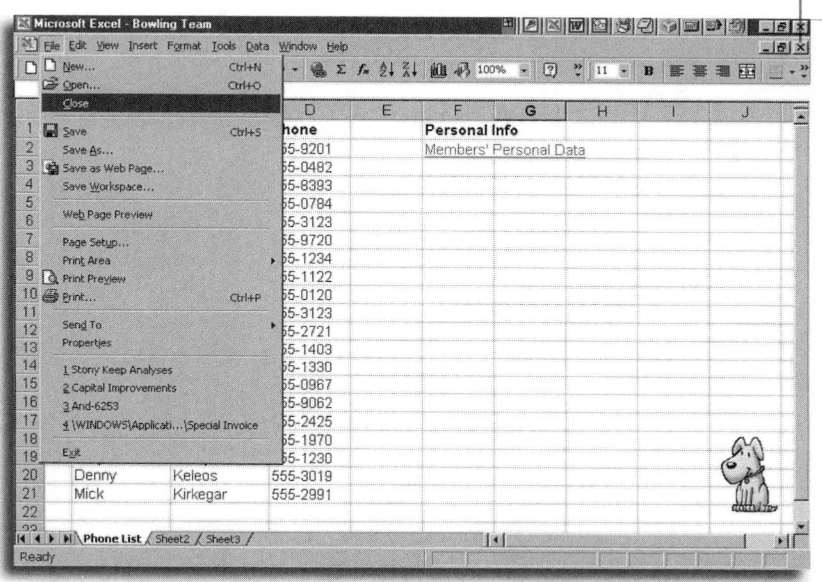

FIGURE 2.14

You can close a workbook with a single click, two clicks, or the keyboard. (On the keyboard, press Alt+F and then C.)

1. Close button

Close all open workbooks with a single command

1. Press Shift as you click the **File** menu.

   When you press Shift, the **Close** command changes to a **Close All** command.

2. Click **Close All**.

   All open, saved workbooks are closed. You are asked whether you want to save any unsaved workbooks, and then they're closed, too.

CHAPTER

3

Saving Files and Using Templates

Performing simple saves

Saving with specific file properties

Saving as different file types

Saving custom templates, opening custom templates

Editing custom templates

Using Excel's built-in templates

Saving Files as Workbooks

This chapter is all about the many different and useful ways you can save Excel files. Saving an Excel 2000 file can be as simple as clicking the Save button on the Standard toolbar; however, as with everything else in Excel, you can choose from many other efficient ways to save your files. For example, you can save a file as an Excel 5.0/95 Workbook so that someone who's using Excel 5 or 95 can open it, or you can save it as an Excel 97-2000 & 5.0/95 Workbook so that someone who's using any version of Excel 5 or higher can open it, or you can save it as a text file so that you can send the unformatted data to someone working in an incompatible program.

Saving a File

When you save a file for the first time (first time for the file, not the first time for you), you give the file a name and indicate to Excel where to store the file. After the file has been saved initially, one click of the Save button on the Standard toolbar saves any changes you make.

Save a new file

1. On the Standard toolbar, click the **Save** button.

   The Save As dialog box appears (shown in Figure 3.1).

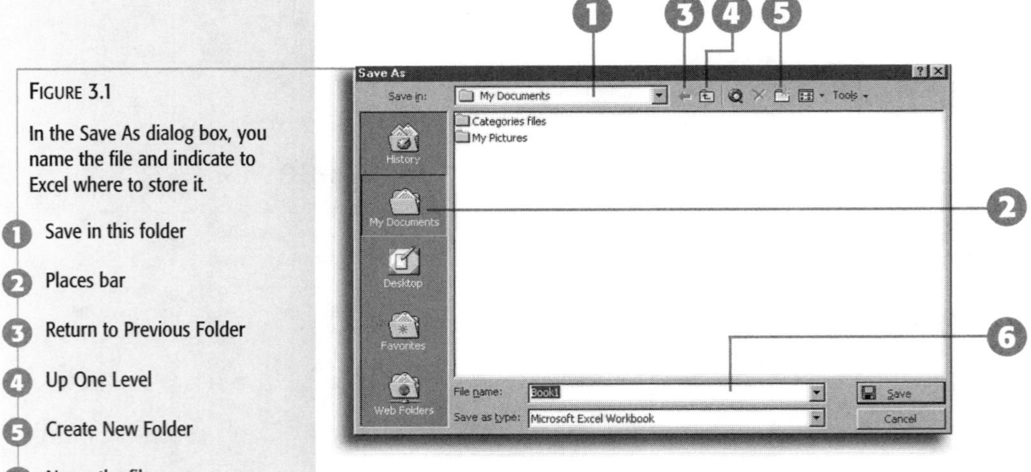

FIGURE 3.1

In the Save As dialog box, you name the file and indicate to Excel where to store it.

1. Save in this folder
2. Places bar
3. Return to Previous Folder
4. Up One Level
5. Create New Folder
6. Name the file

2. In the **Save in** box, navigate to the folder where you want to store the file.
3. In the **File name** box, select the default filename (to highlight it) and type your own filename.
4. Click **Save**.

   The file is named and saved in your designated folder, and the Save As dialog box disappears.

Can't I Go Straight to My Own Folder?

To make Excel's Save dialog box always open to a specific folder (not the default Personal or My Documents folders), open the **Tools** menu and choose **Options**. In the Options dialog box, click the General tab. In the **Default file location** box, type the path to your folder and click **OK**.

Save Effort with Templates

File properties saved in a workbook template are included in all copies of the template.

Saving File Properties

Searching for a file that you can't find is easier if you've saved it with specific file properties, such as category, subject, or keywords. For example, if you save all invoices with the keyword *invoice*, you can find all your invoices, no matter where you saved them, when you search for the keyword.

SEE ALSO

➤ *To learn how to search for files with specific properties, see page 36.*

Give a file specific properties

1. Open the file in which you want to save file properties.
2. Open the **File** menu and choose **Properties**.

   The File Properties dialog box appears (shown in Figure 3.2.)

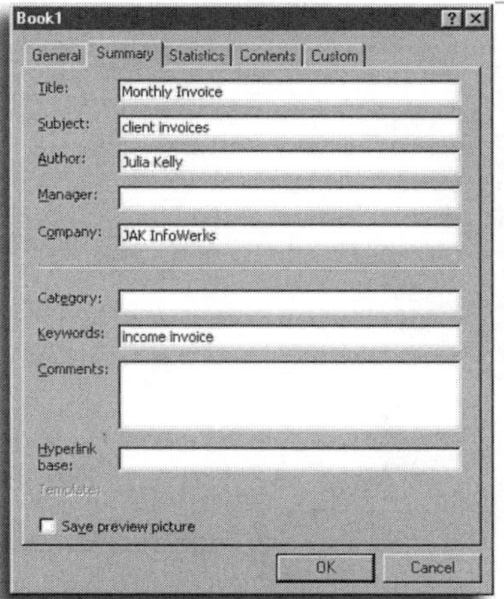

FIGURE 3.2

File properties can save you time and frustration when you attempt to find a file, or a group of files, later.

Use Multiple Keywords

If you save a file with more than one keyword, you can use any of those keywords to find the file in a search, so save a file with all the keywords you might think of years from now, when you can't remember much about the file any more. Be sure you spell keywords correctly, or at least consistently, so you can find them again in a search.

Everyone Gets What They Want

Some features in Excel 2000 aren't supported in other file types or in some earlier Excel versions; if you save a file as a different type, you lose those features. If you don't want to mess with your Excel file but need to send it to someone as a different file type, save the file with a new name as well as a different file type. (If you save it as **Microsoft Excel 97-2000 & 5.0/95 Workbook**, most of your colleagues who have Excel will be able to open it.)

3. On the Summary tab, enter any file properties that might be useful in a later search.

   Author and **Company name** are usually filled in automatically with information that you provide when you install Excel; however, you can change them (for example, if your accountant sent a file for you to use).

4. Click **OK**.

Saving a File in a Different Format

If you need to send a file to a colleague who doesn't have Excel 2000, you can save the file in a format he does have (such as an earlier version of Excel or as a Works, Lotus 1-2-3, Quattro Pro, or dBASE file). You can also save a workbook as a text file, which can be opened by virtually any program, including DOS programs. Also, text files are much smaller than formatted files, so they move through the email system faster.

Save a file as a different file type

1. Open the **File** menu and choose **Save As**.
2. Click the down-arrow button in the **Save as type** box, and click the file type you want (see Figure 3.3).
3. Click **Save**.

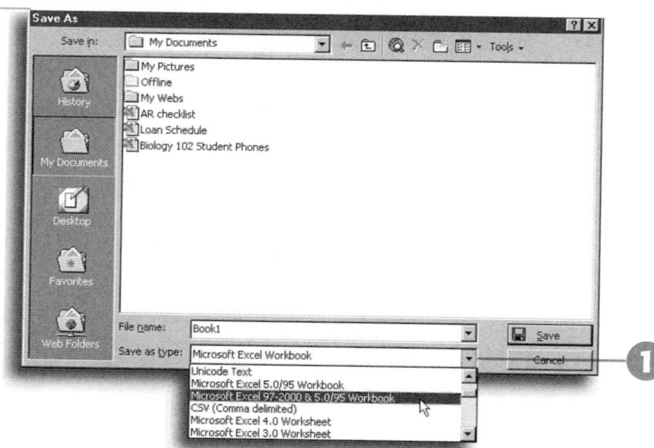

FIGURE 3.3

If you need to send a workbook to someone who doesn't have Excel 2000, you can save it instead as a file type that they can open.

1 Choose a different file type here.

4. You probably see a message box indicating that some formatting or features in your workbook will be lost because the file type you're saving to doesn't support certain Excel 2000 features. Because you can do nothing except be aware of it, click **OK**.

   When you close the file, you get another message box about losing changes; it's your last chance to think about what you're doing before you lose features in your workbook.

Saving an Identical Copy of a Workbook

Sometimes, you might want to create an identical copy of a workbook so that you can make changes to the workbook without affecting the original file.

Save a copy of the workbook

1. Open the **File** menu and choose **Save As**.
2. Give the workbook a new name and click **Save**.

   An identical copy of the workbook, with a different name, is saved in the same folder as the original file.

Copy a workbook without opening the workbook or Excel

1. Open a My Computer window and navigate to the folder where the file is stored.
2. Right-click the filename and click **Copy**.
3. To paste the copy, right-click a blank spot in the window and click **Paste**.
4. Click the new filename to highlight it (see Figure 3.4), type a new name, and press Enter.

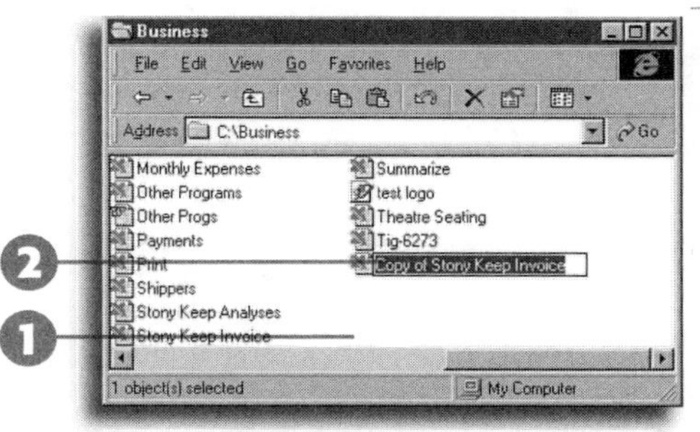

FIGURE 3.4

Create an identical copy of any file without opening either the file or the program.

1. Right-click to paste a copy.
2. Click name to highlight it for renaming.

Creating and Using Templates

A *template* is like a pad of preprinted paper: Every time you open a copy of the template, it's like tearing off a new sheet of paper from the pad. You can save a lot of time by using templates, and you can either use templates that Microsoft has built for you or build your own (which is probably a lot more useful).

Templates are an efficiency tool. If you repeatedly set up workbooks with identical formatting, labels, formulas, and so forth, you can save a lot of work by setting up the workbook one time and saving it as a template. When you open a copy of that template, all your formatting, formulas, labels, and such are already in place.

Save a workbook as a template

1. Set up your workbook the way you want new copies to be set up.

   You can include text, numbers, cell names, formulas, formatting, file properties, worksheet names, number of worksheets, hyperlinks, print areas, worksheet headers and footers—anything you want to have in place when you open a new copy of the workbook.

2. Open the **File** menu and choose **Save As**.

   The Save As dialog box appears.

3. In the **Save As Type** box, click **Template** (see Figure 3.5).

   The folder in the **Save in** box changes to show your computer's Templates location. Later, when you open the **File** menu and choose **New** to open a copy of the template, Excel automatically looks for it in the Templates folder.

4. Give the template a filename.

5. Click **Save**.

   The template is saved in the Templates folder.

Use the Default Templates Folder to Save Time

You can save the template elsewhere, but Excel won't remember where to look for it.

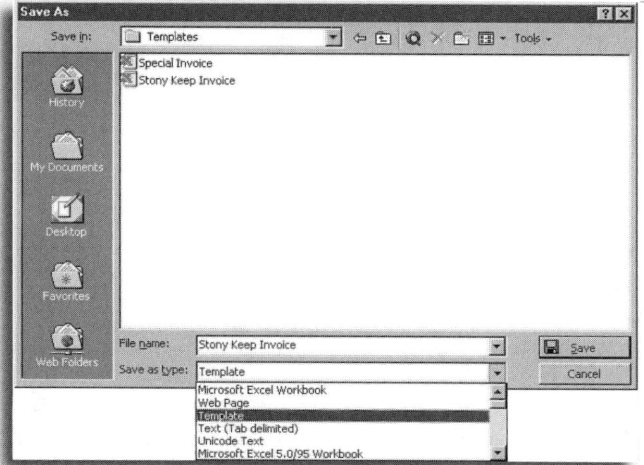

FIGURE 3.5

Select Template in the **Save As Type** box.

Opening a Copy of a Custom Template

Assuming that you had Excel save your template in the Templates folder, after you've created a custom template, you've saved yourself a lot of time.

Open a copy of a custom template

1. Open the **File** menu and choose **New**.

   After you've saved a custom template, the **New** command on the **File** menu opens the New dialog box (shown in Figure 3.6.)

Replace Excel's Default Workbook with Yours

To make a custom template replace Excel's default template (so that all new workbooks will be based on your custom template), give the template the name `Book.xlt` and save it in the XLStart folder (usually in `C:\Program Files\Microsoft Office\Office\XLStart` or you can search for the XLStart folder). Exit Excel and start it again for the new default template to work.

To return to Excel's default workbook template, delete the Book.xlt template you created, or rename it and move it to the Templates folder. When you delete your Book.xlt template, Excel reverts to its built-in default template.

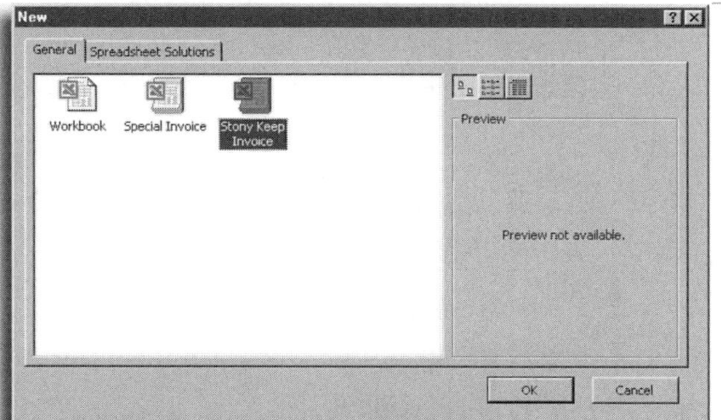

FIGURE 3.6

The icon named Workbook is the default Excel workbook; custom workbook templates are displayed with the names you give them.

2. Double-click the icon for the template you want to open.

   A new copy of your custom template opens. It's temporarily named with your template name and a copy number—you need to give it a new filename when you save it (see Figure 3.7).

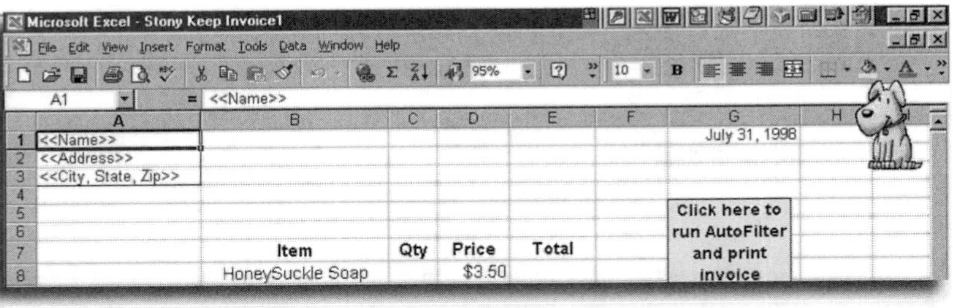

FIGURE 3.7
The title bar shows the template name and copy number until you save the new workbook with a new name.

Editing a Template

Often, a custom template needs to be tweaked—perhaps you need to add another column to a table, rewrite a formula, or change a few borders. To make these changes, you can open and edit the template itself.

Open and edit a template

1. On the Standard toolbar, click the **Open** button.
2. Navigate to your Templates folder (probably in `C:\Windows\Application Data\Microsoft\Templates`).
3. Double-click the name of the template you want to edit (see Figure 3.8).

   The template opens, and if your system is set to show filename extensions, the title bar shows the name of the template with the extension `.xlt` as shown in Figure 3.9. If your system is set to hide extensions, you see the filename without an extension.
4. Make the changes you want.
5. On the Standard toolbar, click the **Save** button.
6. Close the template.

Fast Template Setup

A quick way to set up a template for a workbook that you use a lot is to copy an existing workbook that contains all the formatting and formulas you want in your template, instead of setting up a fresh copy of the workbook to create the template. In the copy, remove all the existing client-specific data and save the workbook as your template. (Even if the workbook formatting isn't exactly what you want, this method is faster than starting from scratch.)

You Can't Get There from Here

The New button on the Standard toolbar won't take you to the Templates folder; you must use the menu command instead.

Open a Custom Template by Default

Do you want Excel to open a copy of your custom template, instead of the default workbook template, when you start Excel? Name your custom template Book.xlt and place it in Excel's XLStart folder. When you place a custom Book.xlt template in the XLStart folder, not only does your custom template open when you start Excel, but it also opens every time you click the New button on the Standard toolbar.

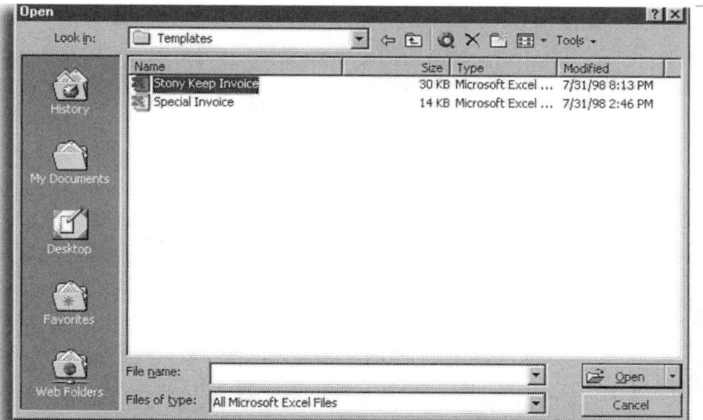

FIGURE 3.8
Opening a template in this way opens the template itself, rather than a copy of the workbook.

No Such Folder?

If you can't find the Templates folder, search for the filename `*.xlt`.

FIGURE 3.9
If the title bar shows the extension `.xlt`, you know you have the template open (but the title bar won't show the extension if your system is set to hide file extensions).

1 Filename extension

Using Excel's Built-In Templates

SEE ALSO

➤ *To learn more about templates, see page 549.*

Excel comes with a few built-in templates, called *Spreadsheet Solutions templates*, that you might (or might not) find useful: Invoice, Purchase Order, and Expense Statement are included in a typical installation of Excel. These templates contain macros that automate the process of filling in data.

Customize a Spreadsheet Solutions template

1. Open the **File** menu and choose **New**.
2. In the New dialog box (shown in Figure 3.10), click the **Spreadsheet Solutions** tab.

What Kind of File Am I?

To find out what kind of file you have open in Excel, choose **File**, **Save As**. The type of file is displayed in the **Save as type** box.

I Want to See the File Extensions

To turn file extensions on or off, click **Start**, **Settings**, **Folder Options**; click the **View** tab, and clear or mark the **Hide file extensions for known file types** check box. After you exit and restart Excel, the file extensions are changed.

3. Double-click the icon for the workbook you want to open. In the Office 2000 modular approach to installation, the Spreadsheet Solutions templates won't be installed until you want to use one (when you double-click the icon, the template installs itself).

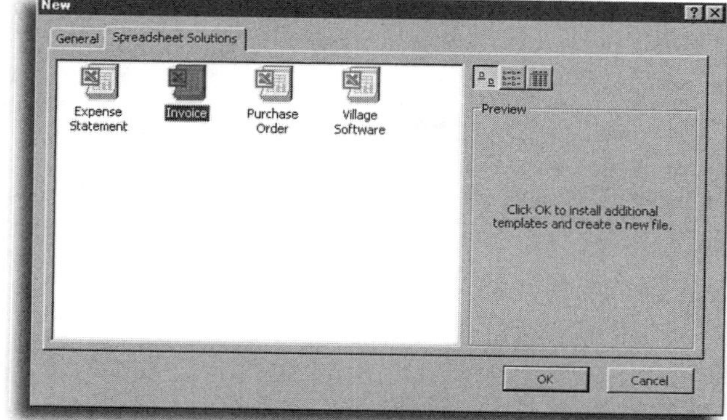

FIGURE 3.10
The Spreadsheet Solutions tab appears if you've installed any of the Spreadsheet Solutions templates.

A message warning you about viruses appears any time you open a file that contains macros because some annoying viruses travel around in the form of Excel and Word macros. Excel doesn't know whether a macro has a virus, so it warns you about every macro.

Because the Spreadsheet Solutions templates rely on macros for automation, you'll want to enable the macros. The first time you use a Spreadsheet Solutions template, click the **Yes** button to open a fully functional workbook. After the first time, just click the **Enable Macros** button.

Some of the templates require a Numbering add-in (a small, extra software program that runs in Excel) to enable their automatic-numbering features. If you see a message telling you to load an add-in, click **OK**. You can use the template without the Numbering add-in; to load it, click **Tools**, **Add-Ins**, then mark the **Template Utilities** check box and click **OK**. After the add-in loads, your template is automated.

4. Click the **Customize** button (see Figure 3.11).

   The customizing worksheet appears (see Figure 3.12).

How to Get Even More Templates

You can find more Spreadsheet Solutions templates at the Microsoft Office Web site, `http://office.microsoft.com`. The quickest way to get there is to open the **Help** menu and click **Office on the Web**. When your browser opens the Microsoft Office home page, click links that take you to more Spreadsheet Solutions templates.

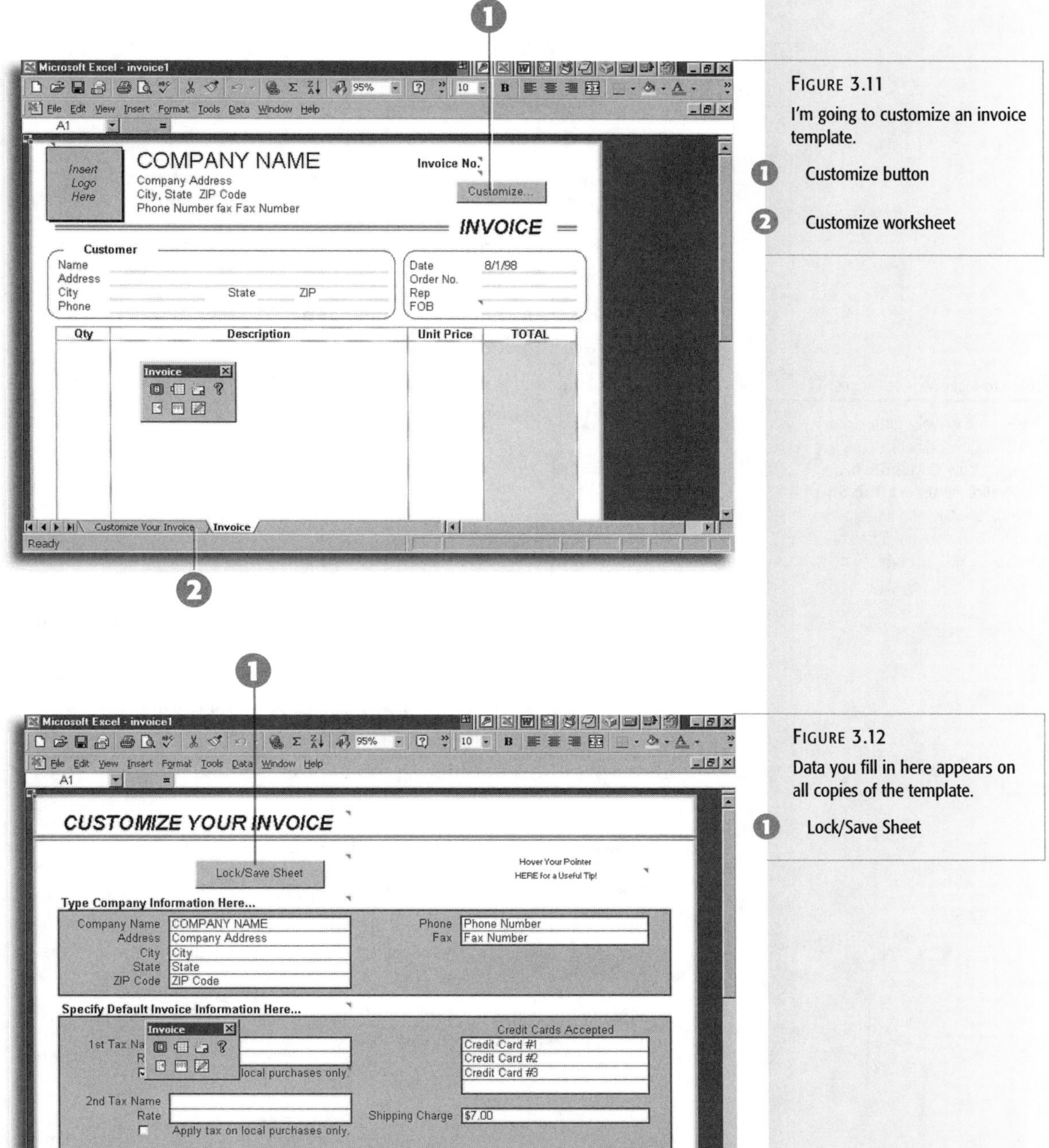

FIGURE 3.11
I'm going to customize an invoice template.

1. Customize button
2. Customize worksheet

FIGURE 3.12
Data you fill in here appears on all copies of the template.

1. Lock/Save Sheet

5. Fill in any company and other standard information that you want to appear in all copies of the workbook and then scroll to the bottom of the Customize worksheet to import a logo or format fonts.
6. Click the **Lock/Save Sheet** button.
7. In the Lock/Save Sheet dialog box, leave the **Lock and save Template** option selected, and click **OK**.
8. In the Save Template dialog box, give the template a name, and click **Save**.

   Your Spreadsheet Solutions template is saved, and a copy of the workbook opens.
9. You may see a message indicating where your template is saved; if so, read the message and then click **OK**.

Need to Make More Changes?

If you want to make further changes to either the workbook or the template, click the **Customize** button again, click the **Unlock This Sheet** button, click **OK**, and repeat steps 5 through 8. If not, your Spreadsheet Solutions workbook is ready to use.

The workbook and its worksheets work just like any other workbook or worksheet; the only difference is that they are preformatted and they contain some macros for automation.

When you open a Spreadsheet Solutions workbook, a special toolbar for the template/workbook appears. Like all other toolbars, if you point to a button, the name of the button appears in a ScreenTip. But unlike other toolbar buttons, if you open the **Help** menu and choose **What's This?** to find out what the button does, you get nothing useful or even correct. Table 3.1 explains what each button in the Invoice toolbar does, and the other Spreadsheet Solutions toolbars are similar.

TABLE 3.1 **Spreadsheet Solutions toolbar buttons**

Icon	This Button	Does This
	Size to Screen/ Return to Size	Zooms the page magnification out so that you can see the whole page, and zooms it in again to 100%.
	Hide Comments/ Display Comments	Hides and shows the small red comment indicators.

Icon	This Button	Does This
	New Comment	Adds a new comment to the selected cell (you can also add a comment in the normal way).
	Template Help	Opens a help file for the specific Spreadsheet Solutions template.
	Display Example/ Remove Example	Enters sample data in the worksheet so that you can see what goes where, and removes the sample data.
	Assign a Number	Assigns a nonrepeating, consecutive number to each worksheet you create from the template. (You find the number in a cell labeled something like "Invoice Number.")
	Capture Data in a Database	Saves the total from the worksheet in another workbook that's created to collect the totals from all worksheets based on the template.

SEE ALSO

➤ *For more on using the What's This? feature, see page 26.*

You can also

- Change the worksheet fonts.
- Change worksheet shading.
- Change or delete drawing objects (like the rounded boxes around the customer information).
- Fill in or delete the Fine Print and Farewell Statement at the bottom.

CHAPTER

4

Saving Excel Data as a Web Page

- Saving Excel data as static Web pages
- Saving Excel data as interactive Web pages
- Editing Web pages
- Using interactive Excel Web pages

Saving a Worksheet as a Web Page

It's easy to turn worksheet data, charts, PivotTables, and even entire workbooks into Web pages that can be posted on an Internet Web site or on your company network. When you create a Web page from Excel data, it can be read and used by folks who don't have Excel on their computers; all they need is a Web browser to open the Web page. (To use interactive Web pages, they need Internet Explorer Version 4.01 or later and Office Web Components, which are part of Office 2000.)

If you create a *static* Web page, the page can include an entire workbook, including separate worksheets with sheet tabs. Anyone with any browser can open the page and read the workbook and can copy information from the Web page to another program if she wants to work with the data.

If you create an *interactive* Web page, another user can open the page in his browser (provided the browser is Internet Explorer 4.01 or later) and manipulate the data within the Web page (provided he has Office Web Components installed). He can sort, filter, format, cut and paste, add and delete data, and adjust formulas without ever moving it into another program. He can also pivot published PivotTables and change the source data for published charts. None of the Web page manipulation affects your source workbook because the data in the workbook and the Web page are not linked. (If the data in the workbook changes, you need to update the data in the Web page by republishing it.)

Saving a Static Web Page

You can save a worksheet, selected cells on a worksheet, an entire workbook, or a chart as a static Web page. In a static Web page, embedded charts are included on their worksheets. Workbooks include all their worksheets and have sheet tabs and sheet tab scroll buttons for worksheet navigation.

You can easily republish the Web page when data in the workbook changes, and you can easily change the Web page from static to interactive by republishing. If you don't like the data layout in the Web page, you can edit the Web page within the browser.

Save a static Web page

1. Open the workbook that contains the data you want to save as a static Web page.
2. Select the data you want on the Web page:
   - For a range of cells or single table, select the cells.
   - For a chart, select the chart.
   - For an entire worksheet, select a single cell in the worksheet.
   - For an entire workbook, select a single cell in the workbook.
3. Click **File**, then click **Save as Web Page**.
4. In the Save As dialog box, in the **Save in** box, navigate to the folder where you want to save the Web page (and its associated folder of supporting HTML files).

   If you're posting the page on an Internet Web site, save the Web page where you save all pages for the Web site; if you're posting it to the company intranet, be sure it's in the appropriate public file so everyone on the network can find it.
5. The **Save** options (shown in Figure 4.1) vary depending on what you selected in step 2. Click the appropriate option. (In this example, I'm going to save the entire workbook as a Web page.)
6. To give the page a title, click **Change** (which is optional).

   In the Set Page Title dialog box, type a **Page title**, and then click **OK**.
7. In the **File name** box, give the Web page a suitable filename.
8. Click **Save**.

The Web page is created and saved. You can open it from your browser or by double-clicking its icon in the folder where you saved it.

Where Are My Sheet Tabs?

If you save a workbook, only those worksheets that have entries in at least one cell are included in the Web page.

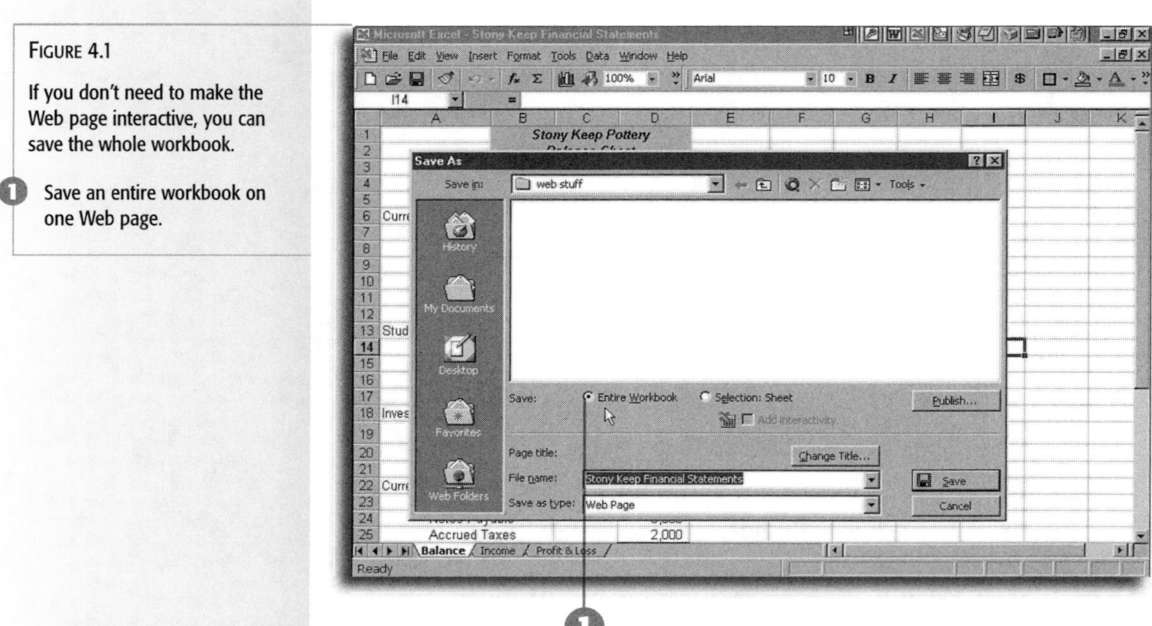

FIGURE 4.1

If you don't need to make the Web page interactive, you can save the whole workbook.

1 Save an entire workbook on one Web page.

Open a static Web page in your browser

1. Double-click the **My Computer** icon on your computer's desktop.
2. Navigate to the folder where you saved the Web page.
3. Double-click the icon for the Web page (as shown in Figure 4.2).

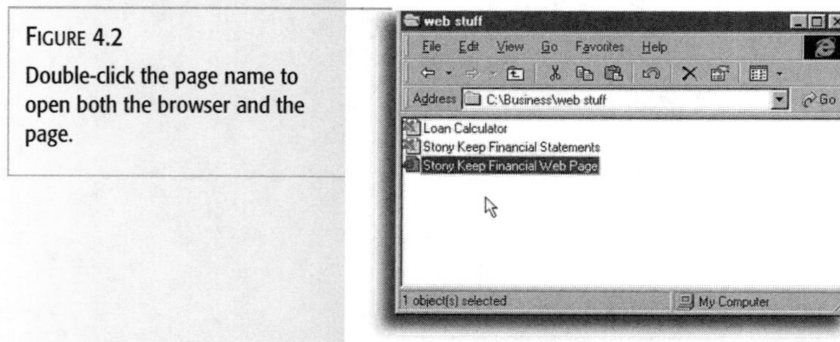

FIGURE 4.2

Double-click the page name to open both the browser and the page.

Your browser opens, and the Web page opens in the browser (shown in Figure 4.3).

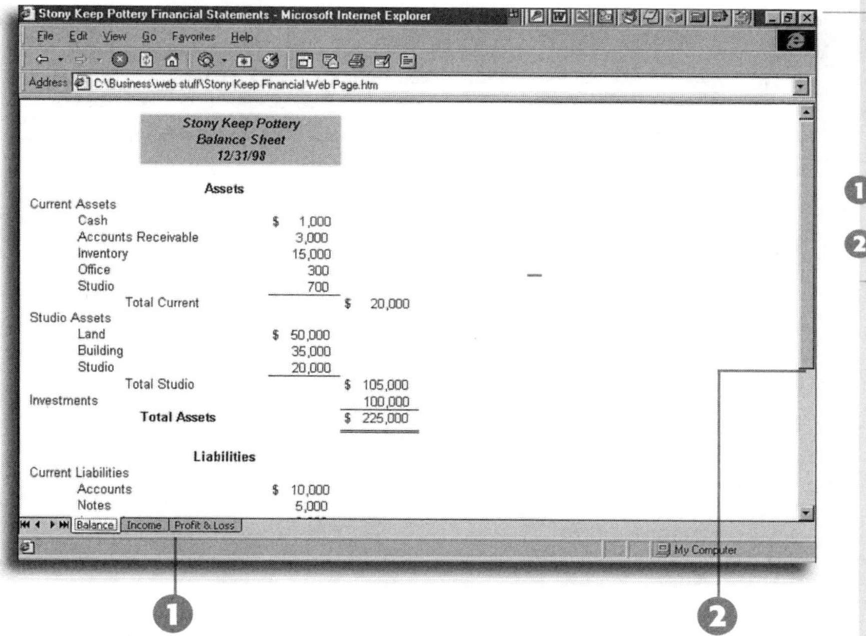

FIGURE 4.3
Click the sheet tabs to see the other worksheets on the page; use the scrollbar to see the rest of a long page.

1 Sheet tabs

2 Scrollbar

I saved an entire workbook as a static Web page, and I can show any worksheet in the Web page by clicking its sheet tab. If the worksheet is long or wide, I can see the rest of it by scrolling in the scrollbars; if the worksheet isn't larger than the browser screen, it won't have any scrollbars.

In a static Web page, any embedded charts are included on their worksheets, and worksheet formatting (colors, fonts, column widths, and so forth) all appear just as they do in the worksheet.

If you want to change anything on the Web page (such as widen a column or change a value), you can edit it from the browser. Either Word or Excel will open so you can edit the file.

Naming Web Page Files

I've included spaces in the filename for my Web page, Stony Keep Financial Web Page.htm, but some browsers don't handle spaces in filenames very well. If your Web page is going to be posted on a company intranet where everyone is using Internet Explorer 4.01 (or later) as a browser, spaces are fine. If you're going to post the page publicly, either leave out the spaces or use underscores instead of spaces.

Edit a static Web page

1. Open the Web page in your browser (shown in Figure 4.4).

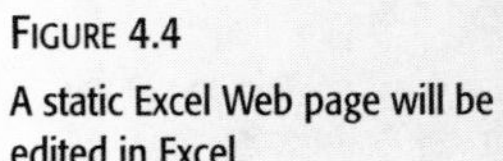

FIGURE 4.4
A static Excel Web page will be edited in Excel.

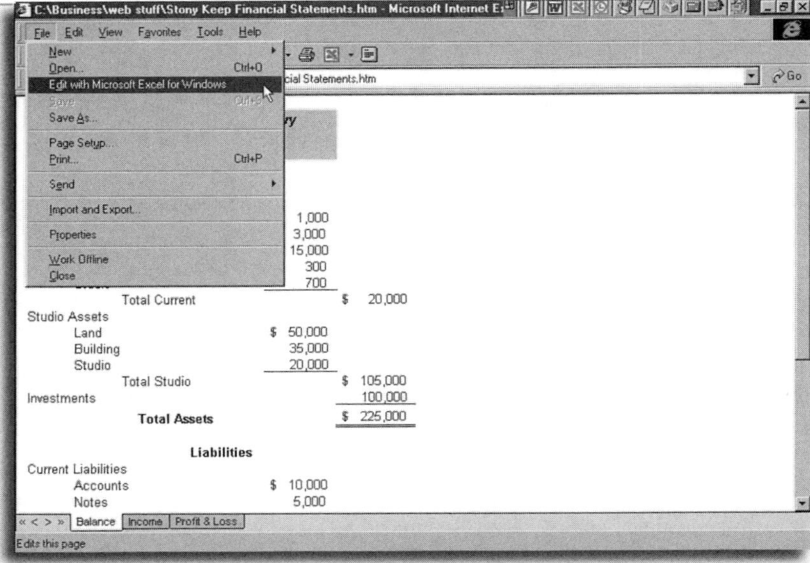

2. Click **File**, and then click **Edit with Microsoft Excel for Windows**.

   For a static Web page, Excel opens, and the source workbook appears. Because this is a static Web page, folks who don't have Office 2000 and access to your source workbook file cannot edit the workbook data.

3. Make changes in the page (shown in Figure 4.5), and then save and close the page and Excel.

   The Web page in the browser won't show your changes until you refresh the page.

4. In the browser toolbar, click the **Refresh** button (shown in Figure 4.6).

   The page refreshes to show your changes.

When you make changes in the workbook, you can republish the page to update it with your changes.

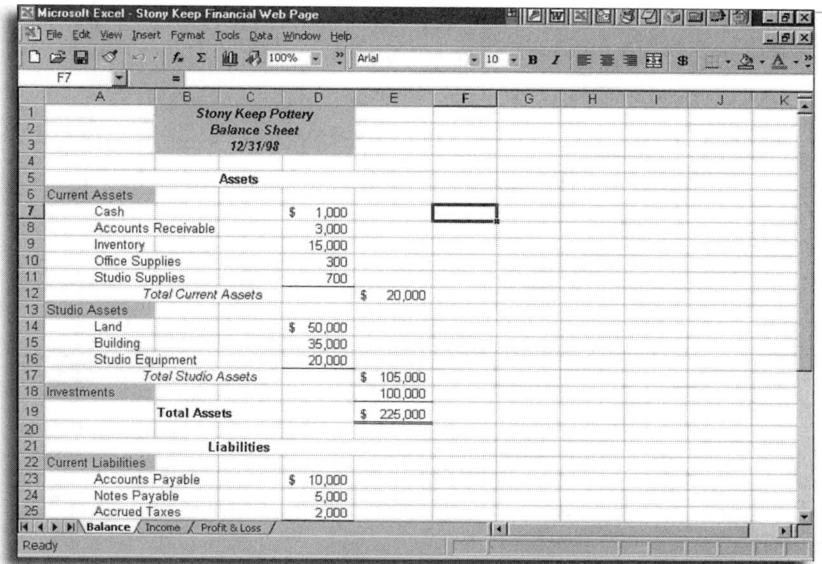

FIGURE 4.5
I changed some cell colors and font formatting using normal Excel formatting methods.

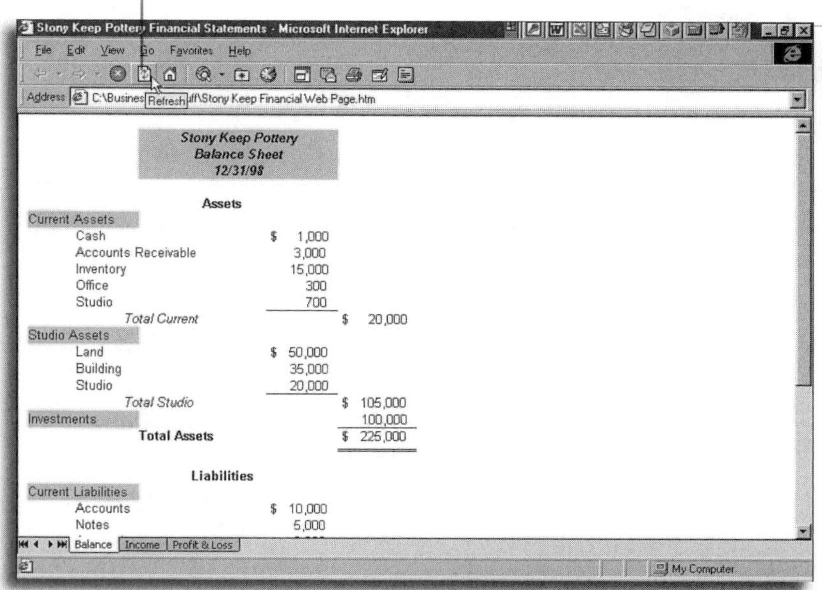

FIGURE 4.6
The page won't show editing changes until you refresh it.

1 Refresh button

Update a static Web page

1. Open the updated workbook and show the changed worksheet.
2. Click **File**, then click **Save as Web Page**.
3. In the Save As dialog box (shown in Figure 4.7), click the previous Web page name.

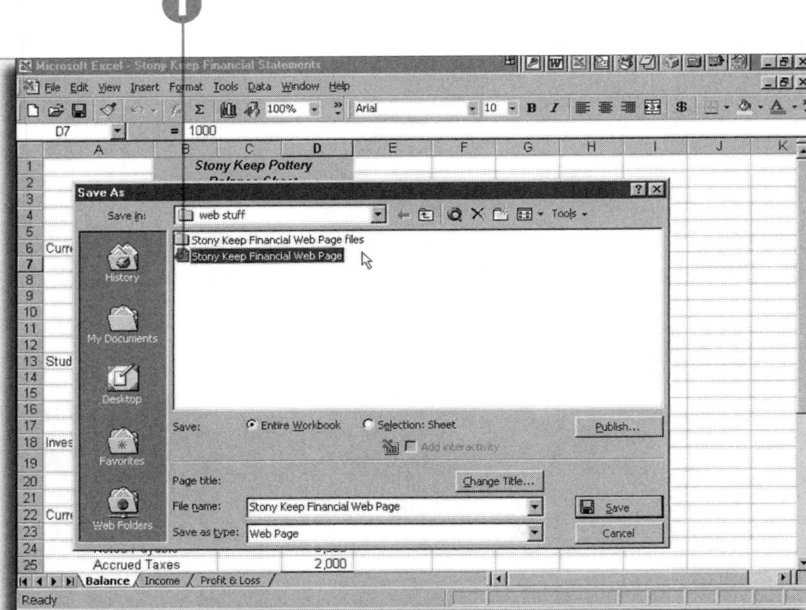

FIGURE 4.7

To update a static Web page, replace the old file by saving it again with the same filename.

1 Click the existing filename.

4. Click **Save**.

   When asked if you want to replace the existing file, click **Yes**.

   The Web page is updated with the most current worksheet data. You can check it by opening the Web page in your browser.

Saving an Interactive Web Page

You can save a single worksheet, chart, or PivotTable as an interactive Web page. In an interactive Web page, embedded charts are *not* included on their worksheets and must be published separately. You can open an interactive Web page in a browser and manipulate the data by filtering, sorting, changing values, changing formulas, and adding or deleting data. In an interactive chart page, you can change the source data on the Web page, and in an interactive PivotTable page, you can pivot the PivotTable. Changes made in the Web page won't affect the Excel files from which the Web page was created.

When data in the workbook changes, you can easily republish the Web page. You can also change the Web page from interactive to static by republishing. If you don't like the data layout in the Web page, you can edit the Web page from the browser.

Save an interactive Web page

1. Open the worksheet that contains the data you want to save as a Web page. (You cannot save an entire workbook as an interactive Web page.)
2. Select the data you want on the Web page:
    - For a range of cells or single table, select the cells.
    - For a chart, select the chart.
    - For an entire worksheet, select a single cell in the worksheet.
    - For a PivotTable, select the entire PivotTable.
3. Click **File**, and then click **Save as Web Page**.
4. In the Save As dialog box, in the **Save in** box, navigate to the folder where you want to save the Web page (and its associated folder of supporting HTML files).

    If you're posting the page on an Internet Web site, save the Web page where you save all the pages for the Web site; if you're posting it to the company intranet, be sure it's in the appropriate public file so everyone on the network can find it.

5. Click the **Selection** option (shown in Figure 4.8). The option will show the cells, chart, or PivotTable you selected on the worksheet.

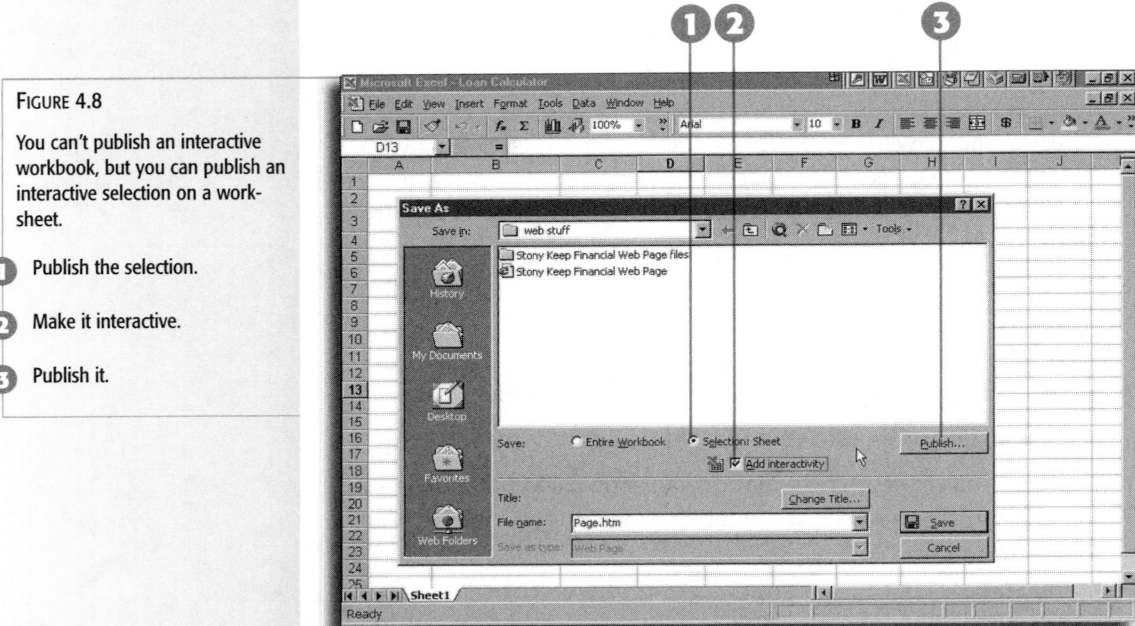

FIGURE 4.8

You can't publish an interactive workbook, but you can publish an interactive selection on a worksheet.

1. Publish the selection.
2. Make it interactive.
3. Publish it.

6. Click the **Add interactivity** check box.
7. Click **Publish**.

   The Publish as Web Page dialog box appears, shown in Figure 4.9.
8. The **Choose** boxes contain several items in the workbook available for publishing; be sure that the worksheet, range of cells, chart, or PivotTable you want to publish is shown in the **Choose** boxes.
9. Click the **Add interactivity with** check box, and select the appropriate functionality in the drop-down list.

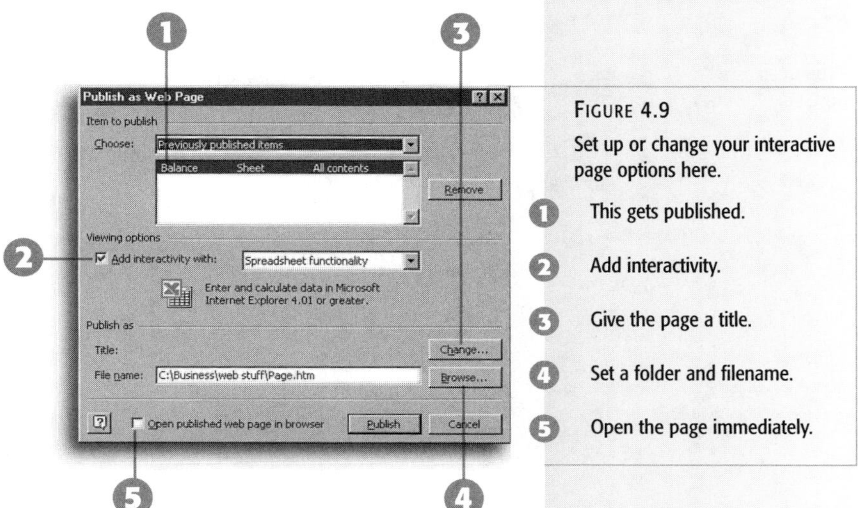

FIGURE 4.9

Set up or change your interactive page options here.

1. This gets published.
2. Add interactivity.
3. Give the page a title.
4. Set a folder and filename.
5. Open the page immediately.

The default functionality is usually appropriate; if you're publishing a PivotTable, you want PivotTable functionality, and if you're publishing a worksheet range or chart, you want spreadsheet functionality.

10. To give the page a title, click **Change** (which is optional).

    In the Set Page Title dialog box, type a title, and then click **OK**.

11. In the **File name** box, give the Web page a suitable filename. Click the **Browse** button to navigate to a folder, drive, or Web site address where you want to save the Web page. (This is easier than typing a path in the box.)

12. Click the **Open published web page in browser** check box so you can see it immediately in your browser.

13. Click **Publish**.

    The new Web page opens in your browser (shown in Figure 4.10).

If you want to make changes to the page layout (perhaps to add instructions for users), you can edit the Web page.

FIGURE 4.10
This interactive Web page could use a few instructions for users.

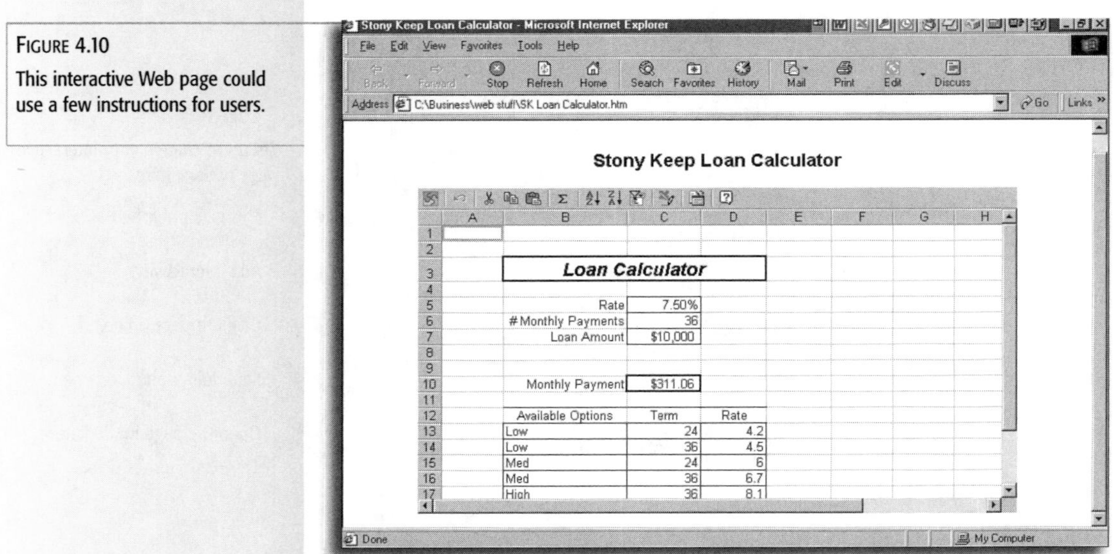

Edit an interactive Web page

1. Open the Web page in your browser (shown in Figure 4.11).

FIGURE 4.11
An interactive Web page with spreadsheet functionality will be edited in FrontPage.

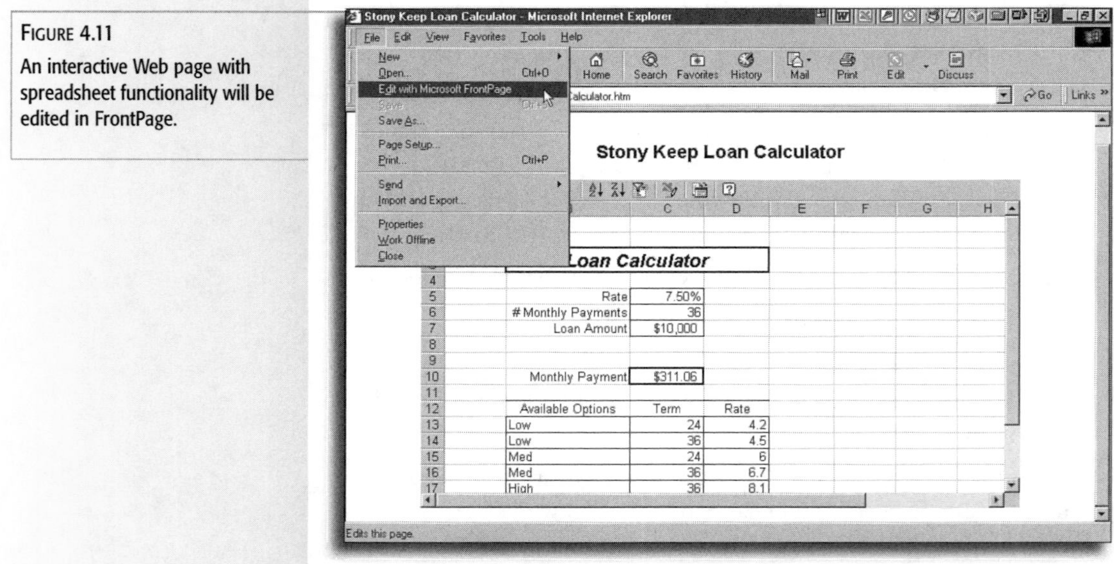

2. Click **File**, and then click **Edit with FrontPage** (shown in Figure 14.12).

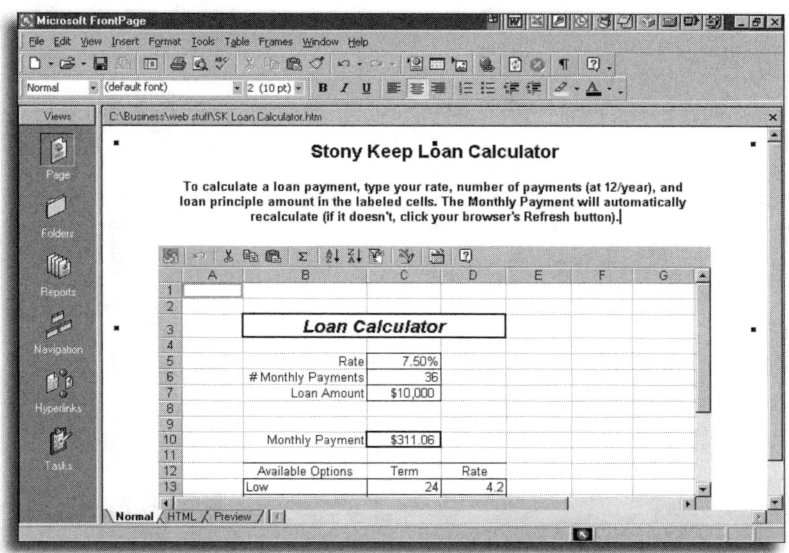

FIGURE 4.12
Using FrontPage 2000, I added instructions to the Web page, below the page title.

Click the Normal tab to edit the Web page; click the Preview tab to see the resulting page. If FrontPage is a mysterious program, use the book *Special Edition Using FrontPage 2000* to learn more about it.

3. When you finish making changes in the Web page layout, click the **Save** button on the FrontPage toolbar, and then close FrontPage. If you're asked to save changes (again), click **Yes**.

   Your changes won't appear in the Web page in the browser until you refresh the page (see Figure 4.13).

Editing a Web page changes the layout and text on the Web page, but opening and using a Web page interactively is how you'll discover the fun and usefulness of interactivity.

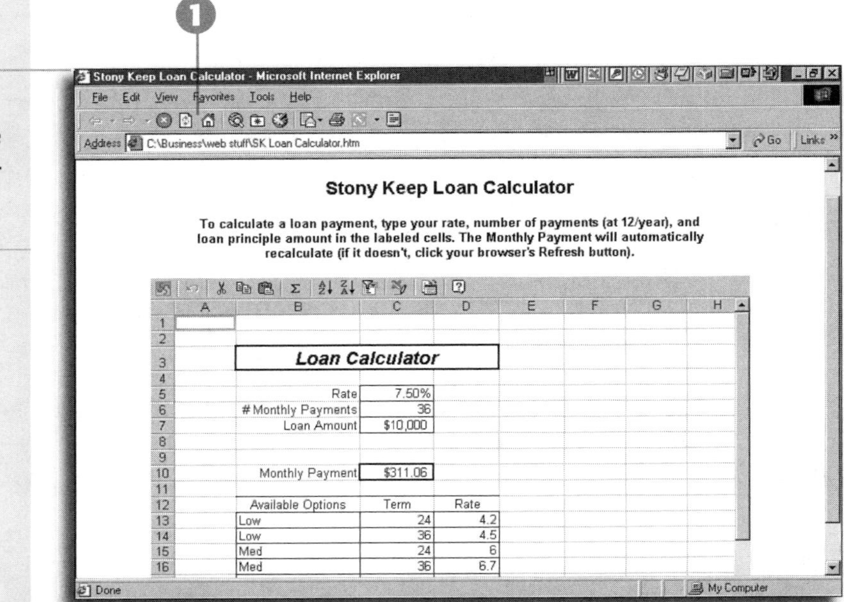

FIGURE 4.13

Back in the browser, refresh the page to see the editing changes.

1 Refresh button

Using an Interactive Web Page

To use an interactive Web page, open it in your browser. Working with the data in an interactive Web page is similar to working with an actual worksheet. If you don't recognize a toolbar button, point to it; you'll see its name in a ScreenTip.

Use the toolbar

1. Use the Cut, Copy, Paste, and AutoSum buttons just like in a normal worksheet.
2. To sort the list, click any cell in the list; then, click the **Sort Descending** or **Sort Ascending** button. A list of all the column names appears (shown in Figure 4.14); click the name of the column you want to sort by.

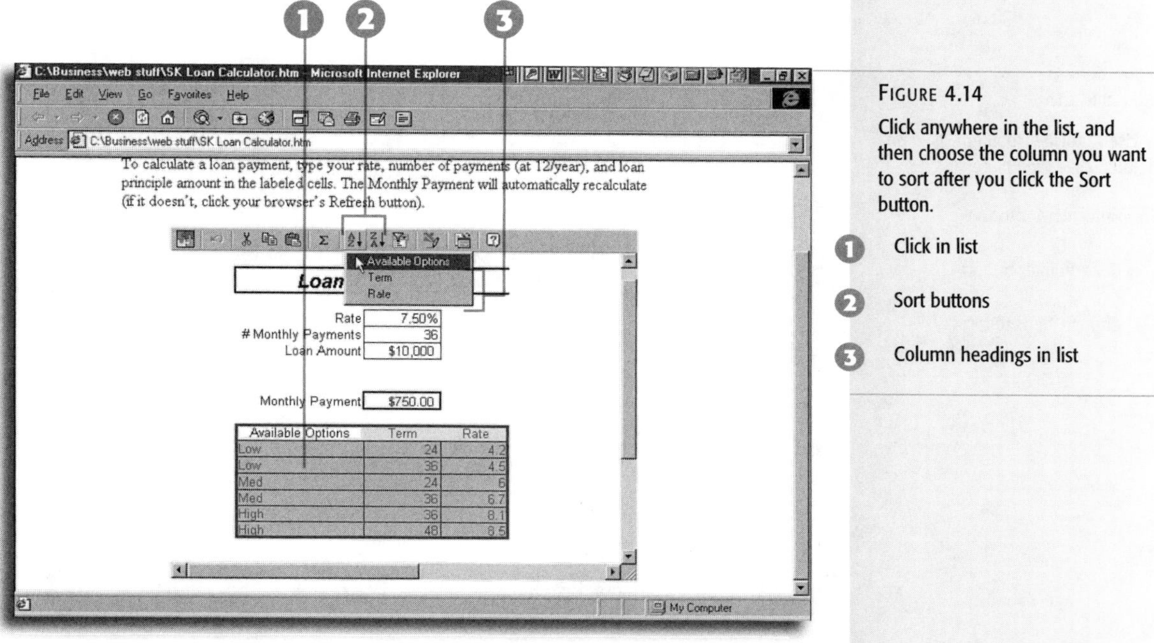

FIGURE 4.14
Click anywhere in the list, and then choose the column you want to sort after you click the Sort button.

1. Click in list
2. Sort buttons
3. Column headings in list

3. To filter the list, click any cell in the list; then, click the **AutoFilter** button. Filter arrows appear on each column heading (shown in Figure 4.15). Click the filter button in the column you want to filter, mark and clear check boxes until only the items you want to display are marked, and click **OK**.

   Click the **AutoFilter** button again to remove all filters.

4. To copy the data to an Excel worksheet, click the **Export to Excel** button. All the data in the interactive Web page is copied to a new Excel workbook.

   The new workbook is read-only, so you'll have to save it with a new name. Click **File**, click **Save As**, navigate to the folder you want to save it in, give the workbook a name, and select Microsoft Excel Workbook in the **Save as type** box; then, click **Save**.

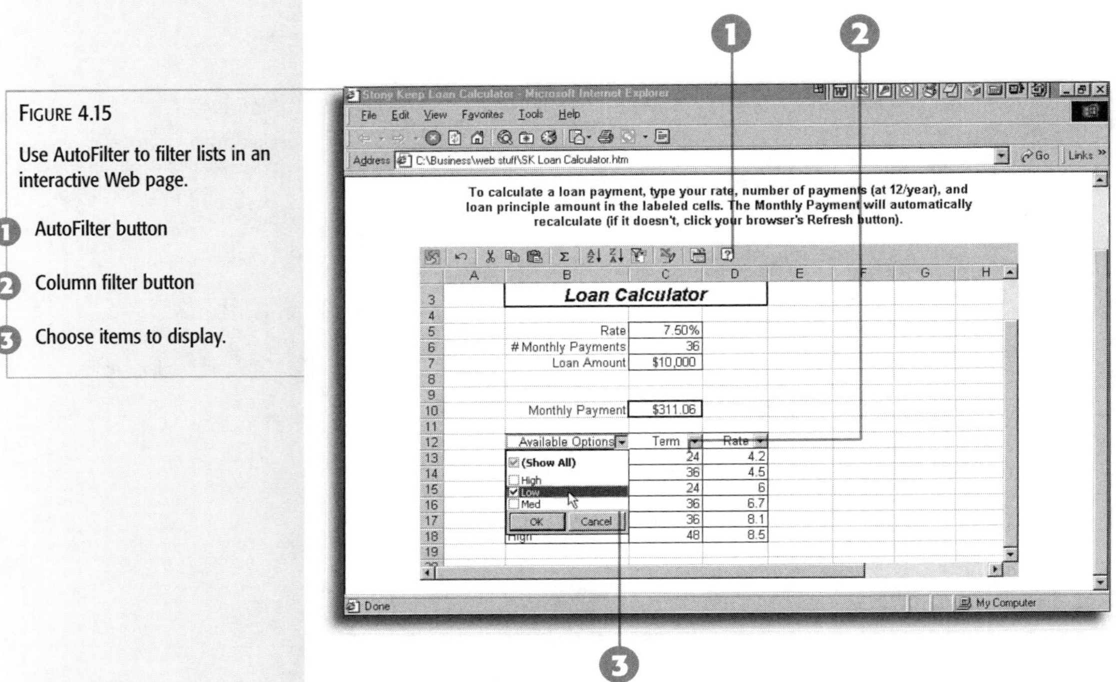

FIGURE 4.15

Use AutoFilter to filter lists in an interactive Web page.

1. AutoFilter button
2. Column filter button
3. Choose items to display.

5. To change formatting in the Web page, show and hide row and column headers, gridlines, and the toolbar, and to search for values, click the **Property Toolbox** button.

The Spreadsheet Property Toolbox appears, shown in Figure 4.16.

Each of the five bars in the toolbox opens a menu when you click the bar. (Figure 4.17 shows the **Format** and **Show/Hide** menus opened.)

With the toolbox menus open, you can click cells in the object and make formatting changes, apply borders, change column width and row height, and so on.

To close the toolbox, click the **X Close** box in the upper-right corner.

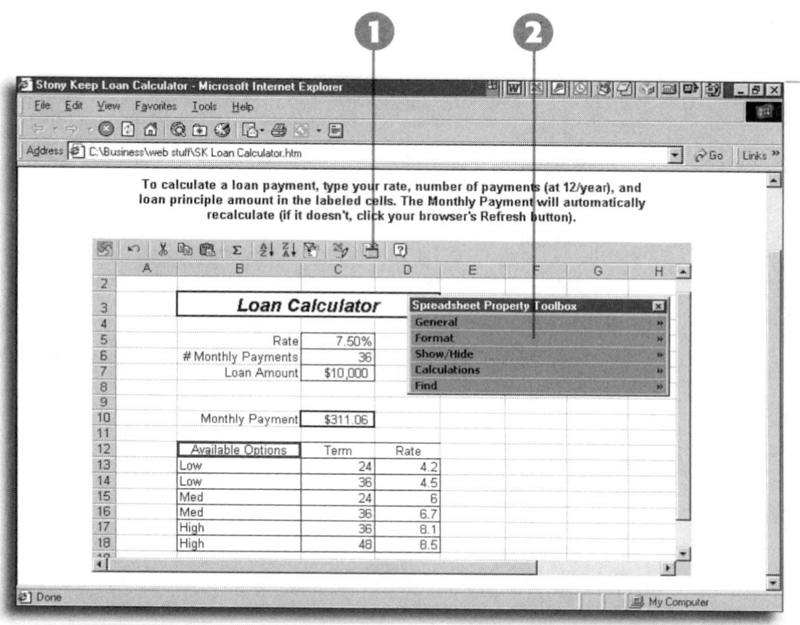

FIGURE 4.16

Formatting tools are in the Property Toolbox.

1. Property Toolbox button
2. Property Toolbox

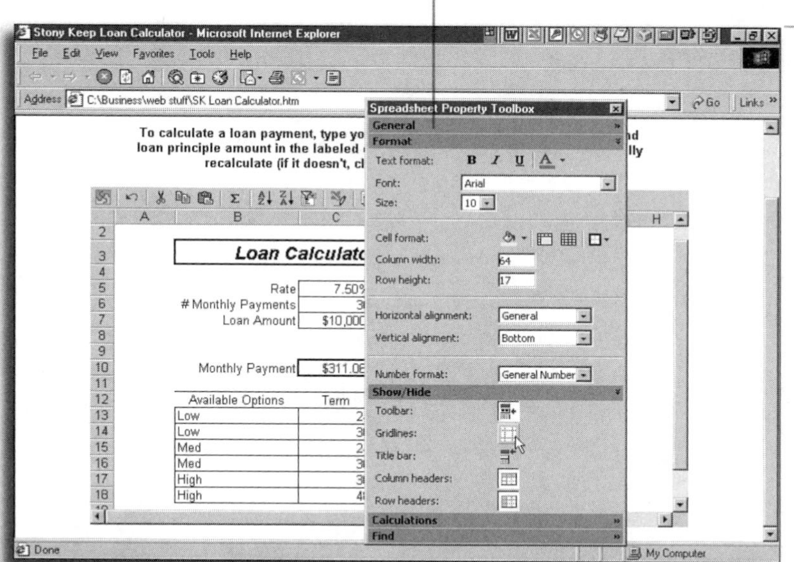

FIGURE 4.17

Click a bar in the Property Toolbox to open the tools in that category; click the bar again to hide its tools.

1. Click the bar to show or hide tools.

Because the Web page is interactive, you can change values and the formulas will recalculate; you can also change formulas or write new ones. There isn't a Function Wizard in the Web page, so you need to write your formulas yourself (but you can always look them up in a book; you'll find useful ones in Chapter 11, "Complex Calculations").

Change calculations

1. To calculate new values, select a cell, type a new value, and press Enter. Formulas should recalculate automatically.

   If formulas don't recalculate automatically, click the **Refresh** button on the browser toolbar.

2. To change an existing formula (perhaps you want to change a SUM formula to an AVERAGE formula or change a range in the formula), double-click the formula cell. The cell opens for editing (shown in Figure 4.18), and the formula appears; make your changes to the formula, and then press Enter.

3. To write a new formula in the worksheet, use normal worksheet procedures. Click a cell, type **=**, type the formula, drag to select ranges of cells, and press Enter to finish.

   To write a quick SUM formula, use the **AutoSum** button on the interactive toolbar.

You can add and delete data in the interactive Web page and insert and delete rows and columns, just like in a normal worksheet.

Add or delete data

1. To add new data to a list, click an empty cell, type the entry, and press Enter.

   To delete data, select the cells and press Delete.

2. To insert rows or columns, right-click a cell where you want to insert the row or column. New rows are inserted above the selected cell, and new columns are inserted left of the selected cell.

   On the shortcut menu, point to **Insert**, then click **Rows** or **Columns**.

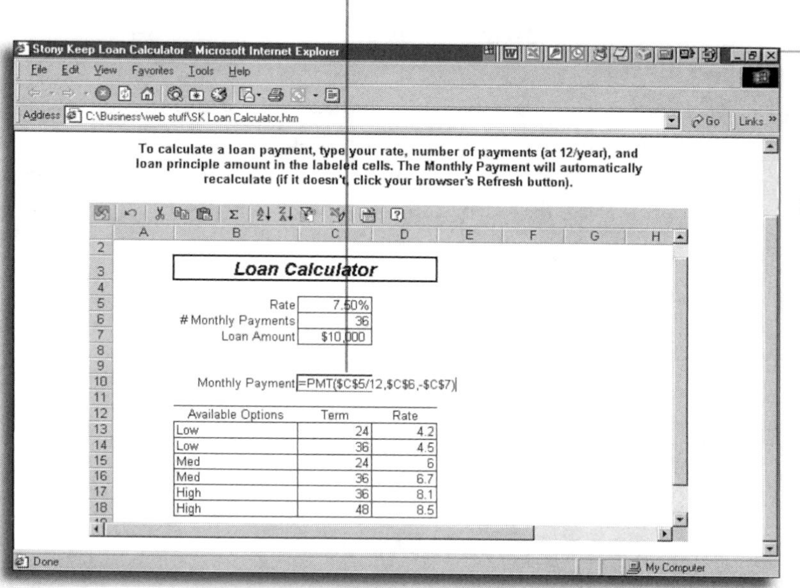

FIGURE 4.18

You can write and edit formulas in an interactive Web page just like in a worksheet.

1 Double-click the cell to open the formula for editing.

3. To delete rows or columns, right-click a cell in the row or column you want to delete.

   On the shortcut menu, point to **Delete**, then click **Rows** or **Columns**.

If you make changes in the Web page's source workbook and you want to post the changed data in the Web page, you can republish the Web page to update it.

Update an interactive Web page

1. Open the workbook from which the Web page was originally published and make any updates or changes to the worksheet.
2. Click **File**, and then click **Save as Web Page**.
3. In the Save As dialog box, click **Publish**.

4. In the Publish as Web Page dialog box, select the item you want to republish in the **Choose** boxes, and then click **Publish**.

   If you want to make any changes, such as removing interactivity, changing the Web page title, or publishing a different sheet in the workbook, make those changes in the Publish as Web Page dialog box before you click **Publish**.

5. Close the workbook and Excel.

6. If the Web page was open in your browser while you changed the workbook, it won't automatically show the changes; click the **Refresh** button on the browser toolbar to update the open page.

Selecting and Navigating Worksheets

- Naming and selecting worksheets
- Moving among worksheets in a workbook
- Moving from cell to cell within a worksheet
- Adding and deleting worksheets in a workbook
- Rearranging worksheets within a workbook
- Moving and copying worksheets to other workbooks

Naming Worksheets

Worksheets Versus Sheets

Worksheets are referred to as both "worksheets" and "sheets."

In this chapter, you'll learn procedures for finding your way around in workbooks and worksheets. In Excel, a workbook can contain one or more worksheets. The default worksheet names—Sheet1, Sheet2, and so forth—are decidedly unhelpful when you're looking for a specific sheet in a workbook, but you can name your worksheets anything you want and rename them whenever you need to.

Change the name of a worksheet

1. Double-click the sheet tab for the worksheet you want to name (or rename).

   The existing sheet tab name is highlighted, as shown in Figure 5.1.

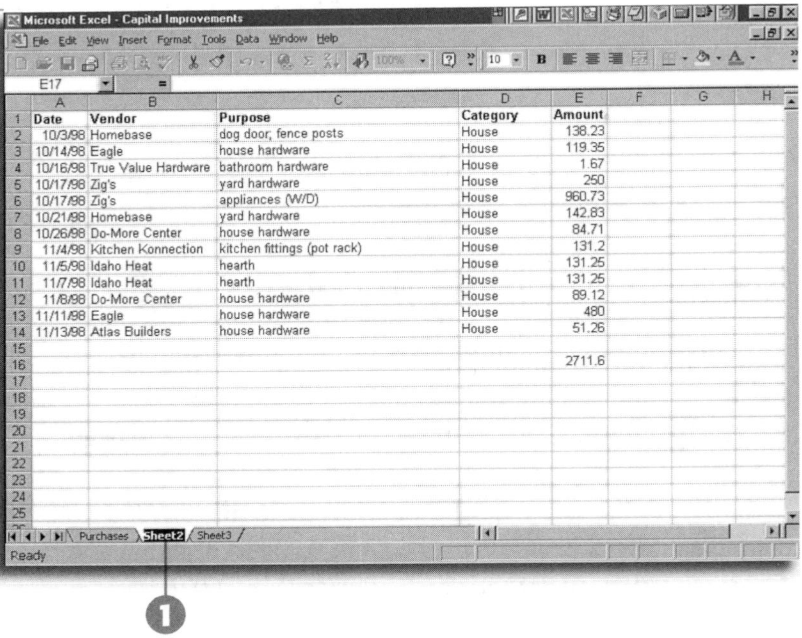

FIGURE 5.1

Giving sheets descriptive names makes workbook navigation easier.

1 Highlighted sheet tab

2. Type your new sheet name.
3. Press Enter.

Selecting Worksheets

Workbooks can contain a single worksheet or a huge number of worksheets, limited only by your system memory. Multiple worksheets make a workbook more useful because you can store related information together in a single workbook. You can use the sheet tabs at the bottom of the worksheet to select one or more sheets.

Selecting a Single Worksheet

Select a single worksheet in a workbook

1. Click the sheet tab for the worksheet you want, as shown in Figure 5.2.

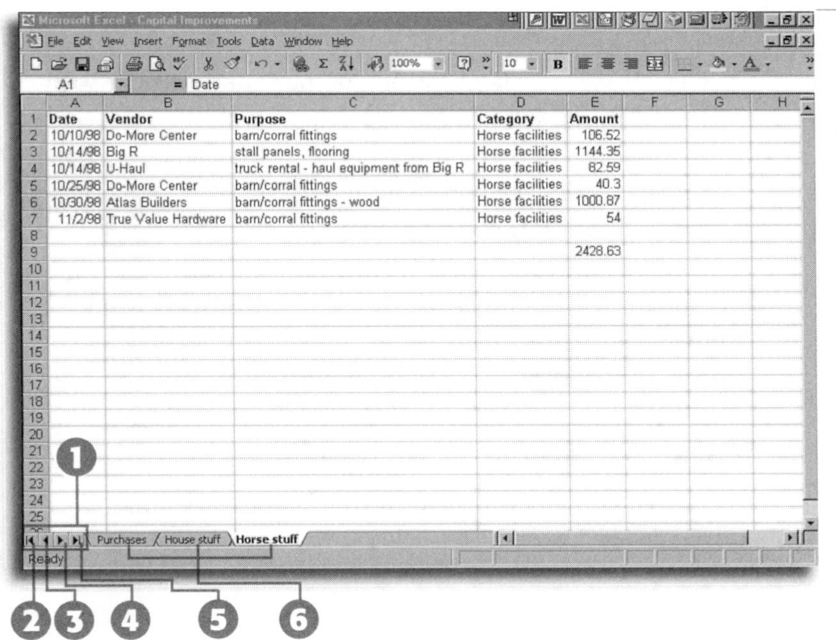

FIGURE 5.2

Display a specific worksheet by clicking its sheet tab.

1. Sheet tab scroll buttons
2. First
3. Previous
4. Next
5. Last
6. Sheet tabs

The sheet you clicked appears "on top" of the other sheets in the workbook.

2. If you can't see the sheet tab for the sheet you want, click the sheet tab scroll buttons to scroll more sheet tabs into view; then, click the sheet tab you want.

Where Did That Sheet Go?

If a workbook has several worksheets, scrolling through sheet tabs can be time-consuming. Instead, right-click the tab scroll buttons to see a list of all the sheet names; then, click the name of the sheet you want.

Selecting Several Sheets at Once

Sometimes, it's helpful to be able to select a group of sheets instead of a single sheet; for example, when you want to format a group of sheets in an identical manner, delete several sheets, or copy or move a group of sheets within a workbook or to another workbook.

When you've selected a group of worksheets, any entries you make on one sheet in the group are made on all the sheets in the group. This is one way to save yourself a lot of work: If you need to create several identical worksheets (for example, monthly expense worksheets or teachers' grade sheets for several classes), you can select a group of worksheets and do the worksheet setup just once.

Did You Forget to Group Your Worksheets?

If you forget to select a group of worksheets before you set up the worksheet, you can create identical copies of the finished worksheet by copying it. (See "Copying Worksheets Within a Workbook" later in this chapter.)

Select a group of worksheets in a workbook

1. Click the sheet tab for the first of the worksheets you want to select.
2. For nonadjacent worksheets, press and hold down the Ctrl key; then, click the remaining sheet tabs you want to include in the group, as shown in Figure 5.3.

   If you want to select a group of adjacent sheets, press and hold down the Shift key; then, click the last sheet you want to include in the group. All the sheets between the tabs you clicked are selected, as shown in Figure 5.4.

Deselecting a Group of Worksheets

To deselect a group of worksheets so that you can resume work on an individual worksheet, click another worksheet in the workbook—one that's not part of the selected group.

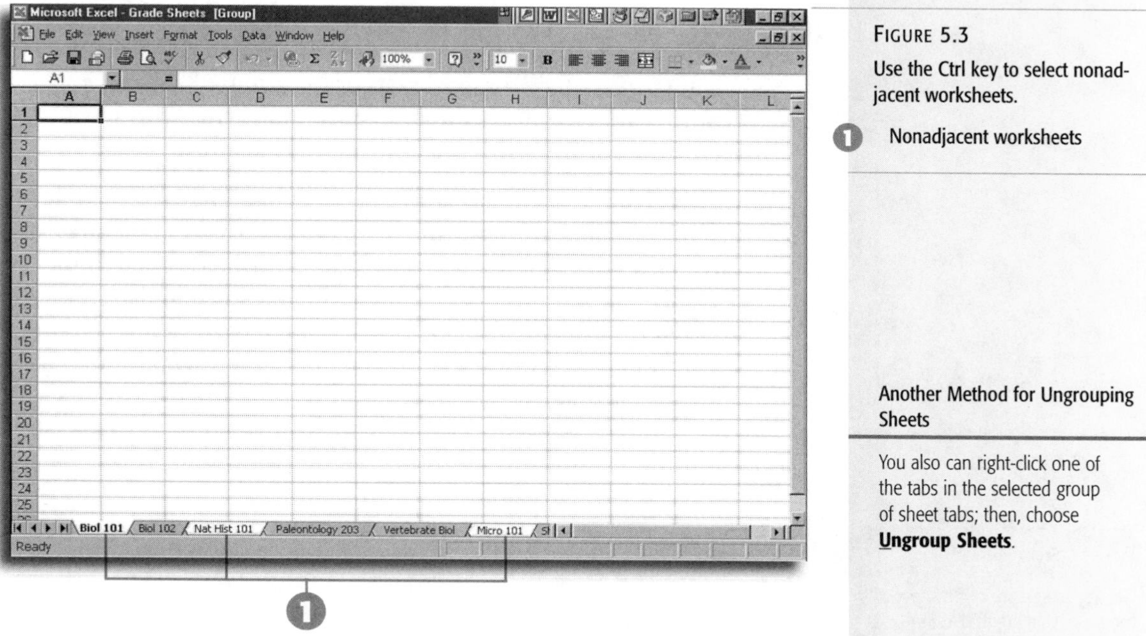

FIGURE 5.3
Use the Ctrl key to select nonadjacent worksheets.

1 Nonadjacent worksheets

Another Method for Ungrouping Sheets

You also can right-click one of the tabs in the selected group of sheet tabs; then, choose **Ungroup Sheets**.

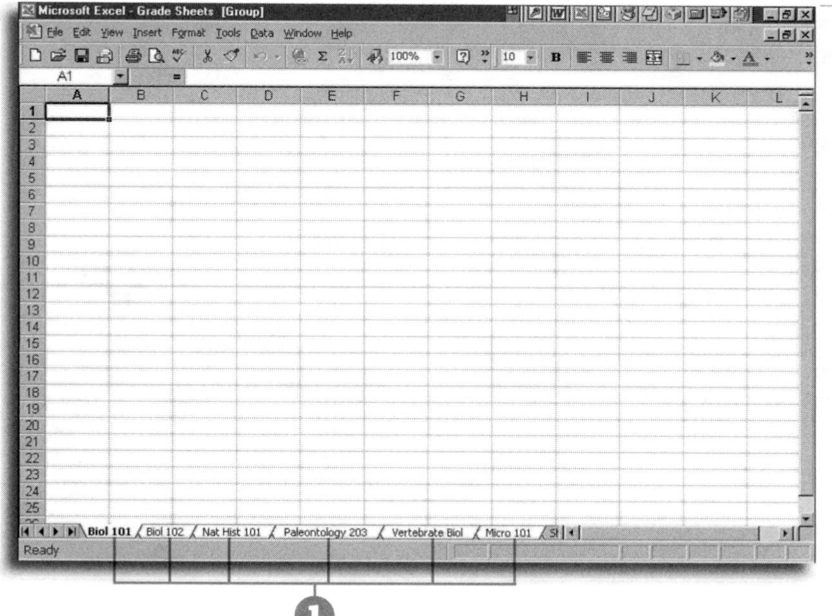

FIGURE 5.4
Use the Shift key to select adjacent worksheets.

1 Adjacent worksheets

Moving Around in a Worksheet

When you've selected the worksheet (or group of sheets) you want to work in, you need to move around in that worksheet to get to the cells or ranges of cells you want to select.

A *cell* is the intersection of a row and a column in a worksheet. A rectangular block of two or more cells is referred to as a *range* of cells. A *cell address* or *cell reference* is the position of a cell in the worksheet, in terms of its column letter and row number. (See Chapter 10, "Simple Calculations," to learn more about cell references.) Figure 5.5 shows the different methods you can use to move among worksheet cells.

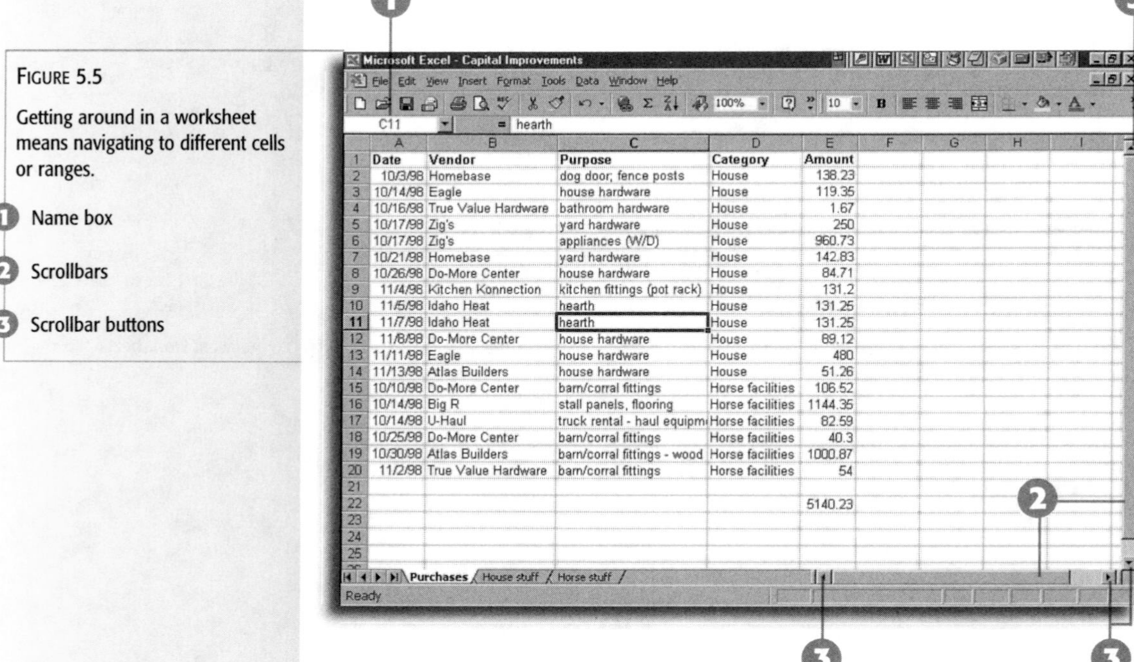

	A	B	C	D	E
1	Date	Vendor	Purpose	Category	Amount
2	10/3/98	Homebase	dog door, fence posts	House	138.23
3	10/14/98	Eagle	house hardware	House	119.35
4	10/16/98	True Value Hardware	bathroom hardware	House	1.67
5	10/17/98	Zig's	yard hardware	House	250
6	10/17/98	Zig's	appliances (W/D)	House	960.73
7	10/21/98	Homebase	yard hardware	House	142.83
8	10/26/98	Do-More Center	house hardware	House	84.71
9	11/4/98	Kitchen Konnection	kitchen fittings (pot rack)	House	131.2
10	11/5/98	Idaho Heat	hearth	House	131.25
11	11/7/98	Idaho Heat	hearth	House	131.25
12	11/8/98	Do-More Center	house hardware	House	89.12
13	11/11/98	Eagle	house hardware	House	480
14	11/13/98	Atlas Builders	house hardware	House	51.26
15	10/10/98	Do-More Center	barn/corral fittings	Horse facilities	106.52
16	10/14/98	Big R	stall panels, flooring	Horse facilities	1144.35
17	10/14/98	U-Haul	truck rental - haul equipm	Horse facilities	82.59
18	10/25/98	Do-More Center	barn/corral fittings	Horse facilities	40.3
19	10/30/98	Atlas Builders	barn/corral fittings - wood	Horse facilities	1000.87
20	11/2/98	True Value Hardware	barn/corral fittings	Horse facilities	54
21					
22					5140.23

FIGURE 5.5

Getting around in a worksheet means navigating to different cells or ranges.

1. Name box
2. Scrollbars
3. Scrollbar buttons

There are several ways to move from cell to cell in a worksheet. Table 5.1 lists the commonly used methods. Try different methods and use the ones that are most convenient for you.

TABLE 5.1 Ways to move around in a worksheet

To	Do This
Move down one cell	Press Enter
Move up one cell	Press Shift+Enter
Move right one cell	Press Tab
Move left one cell	Press Shift+Tab
Move one cell in the arrow direction	Press the arrow keys
Move to the beginning of a row	Press Home
Move to the beginning or end of a data range	Press End+arrow key
Move to the upper-left corner of a worksheet	Press Ctrl+Home
Move to the lower-right corner of a worksheet	Press Ctrl+End
Move the view up or down by one row	Click the vertical scrollbar buttons
Move the view right or left by one column	Click the horizontal scrollbar buttons
Move the view by several rows or columns	Drag the scrollbars up, down, right, or left
Move the view back to the selected cell	Press Ctrl+Backspace
Move to a specific cell address	Type the cell address in the Name box

Selecting Cells in a Worksheet

When you're ready to enter data, you need to select a cell or range of cells. Figure 5.6 shows some different kinds of ranges you can select.

Table 5.2 shows some convenient ways to select cells and ranges of cells in a worksheet.

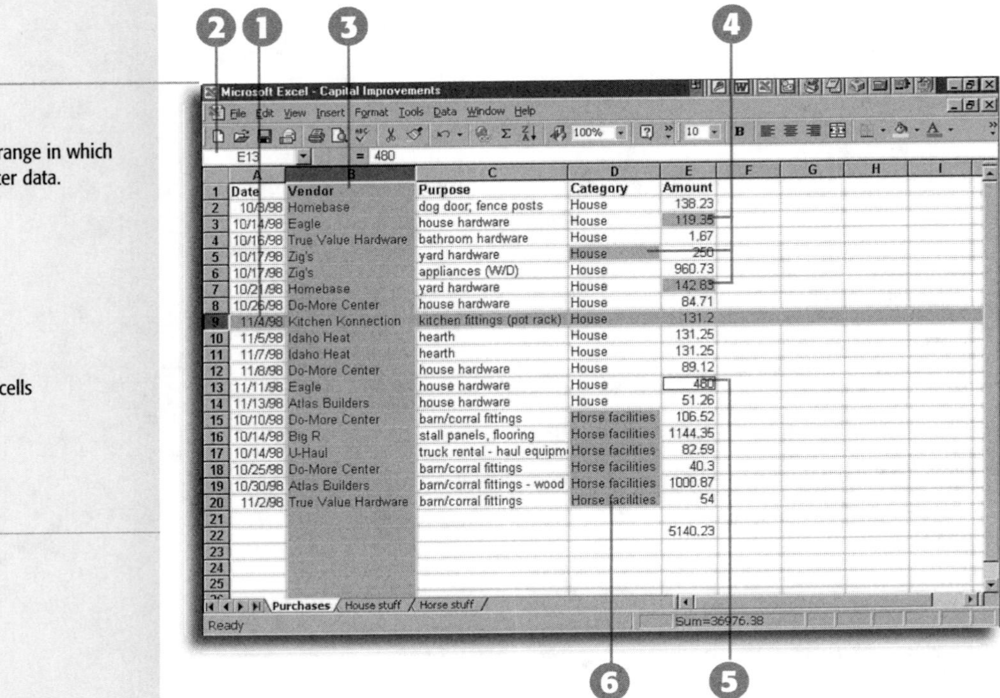

FIGURE 5.6

Select a cell or range in which you want to enter data.

1. Row
2. Name box
3. Column
4. Nonadjacent cells
5. Cell
6. Range

TABLE 5.2 Ways to select a cell or range in a worksheet

To	Do This
Select a cell	Click the cell
Select a range of cells	Click and drag over the cells
Increase the selection one cell, row, or column in the arrow direction	Hold down Shift and press arrow keys
Select an entire column	Click the column letter
Select an entire row	Click the row number
Select a nonadjacent range	Select one cell or range; then, hold down Ctrl while you select more cells or ranges
Select a range of adjacent cells	Select the cell at the beginning of the range; then, hold down Shift while you select the cell at the end of the range

Adding and Deleting Worksheets

New workbooks have three worksheets by default. They used to have 16, but Microsoft finally figured out that you and I found that annoying! You can delete worksheets you don't want or are finished using and insert new worksheets in a workbook.

Deleting Worksheets

If you don't need all three worksheets or if you've created a worksheet you want to throw away, you can delete the worksheet.

Delete a worksheet from a workbook

1. Right-click the sheet tab for the sheet you want to delete, as shown in Figure 5.7.

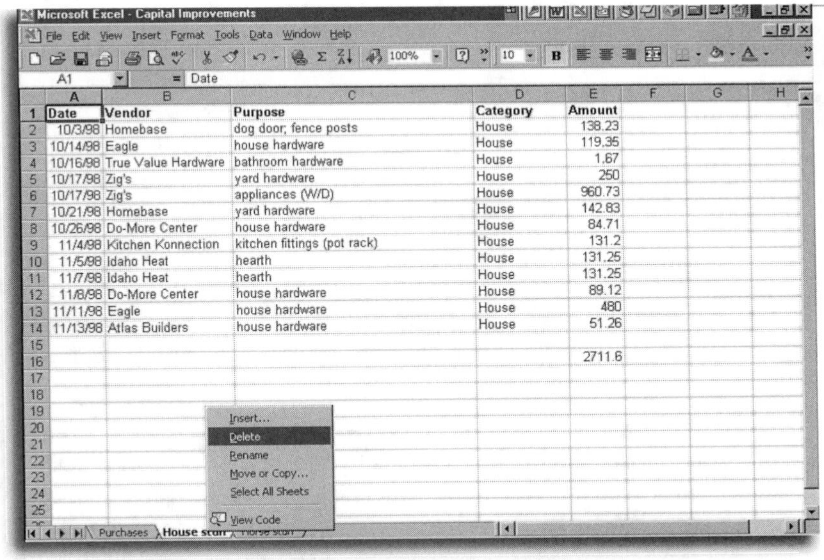

FIGURE 5.7
The sheet tab shortcut menu is the easiest way to delete a worksheet.

2. Choose **Delete**.

   A message box confirms that you want to delete the worksheet. (When it's gone, it's gone; there's no Recycle Bin for worksheets.)

3. In the message box, choose **OK**.

Adding More Worksheets

If three worksheets are not enough for your project, you can add more. You can add as many worksheets as you want, limited only by your system resources.

Insert a blank worksheet in a workbook

1. Right-click any sheet tab in your workbook, as shown in Figure 5.8.

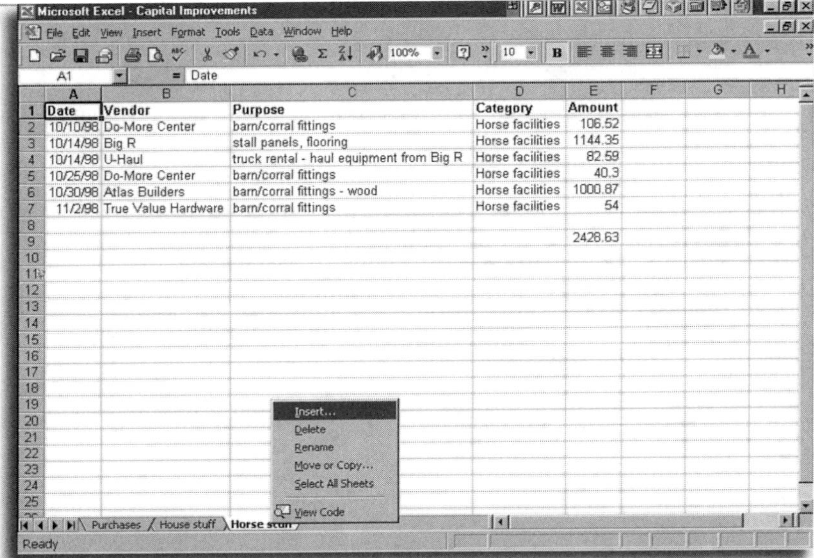

FIGURE 5.8
You can use the sheet tab shortcut menu to add more worksheets.

2. Choose **Insert**.

   The Insert dialog box appears, with a choice of worksheet types available (including any custom worksheet templates you've created).

3. Double-click the **Worksheet** icon to add a new default worksheet.

   The new worksheet is added to the left of the sheet tab you right-clicked. You can move and rename the new worksheet to make your workbook more efficient.

SEE ALSO

➤ *To learn more about creating custom worksheet templates, see page 53.*

Changing the Default Number of Sheets in a New Workbook

All new workbooks open with 3 worksheets, but if you routinely use only 2 worksheets, or 23 worksheets, you can save a lot of effort by changing the default number of worksheets in new workbooks.

Change the default number of worksheets

1. Open the **Tools** menu, and choose **Options**.
2. Click the **General** tab.
3. Enter a different number in the **Sheets in new workbook** box.
4. Choose **OK**.

All new workbooks will now contain the new default number of worksheets. The maximum number of default new worksheets you can set is 255, but you can add thousands (if you really want to) by adding them individually. I can't imagine why anyone would want to add this many worksheets to a single workbook, but some people like to know these things.

Rearranging Worksheets

Having a lot of worksheets in a workbook is like having a lot of files in a file drawer: A little organization makes the mess more efficient. You can easily move worksheets around within a workbook to rearrange them, create copies of worksheets in a workbook to duplicate work you've already done once, and move or copy worksheets to other workbooks.

Moving Worksheets to Rearrange a Workbook

Like papers in a folder or files in a filing cabinet, worksheets in a workbook are easier to find if you arrange them in a logical order.

Rearrange worksheets in a workbook

1. Click the sheet tab for the sheet you want to move.

2. Drag the sheet tab right or left, to its new position, and drop it (release the mouse button) when the position triangle is where you want to place the worksheet, as shown in Figure 5.9.

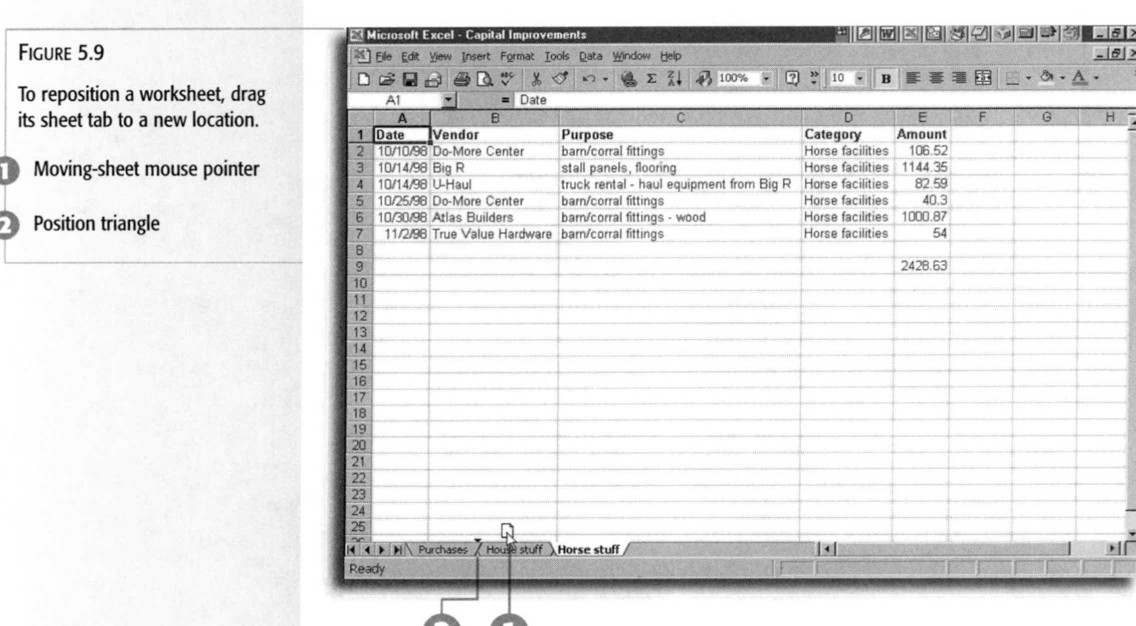

FIGURE 5.9

To reposition a worksheet, drag its sheet tab to a new location.

1 Moving-sheet mouse pointer

2 Position triangle

Copying Worksheets Within a Workbook

Copying a worksheet is one of several ways you can make identical copies of a worksheet. You can also select a group of worksheets to set up identical worksheets, and you can create workbook and worksheet templates to create identical new worksheets.

Oops, I Forgot to Press Ctrl First

You don't have to hold down Ctrl while you drag, but you *do* have to be holding down Ctrl when you drop the sheet tab.

Create an identical copy of a worksheet

1. Click the sheet tab for the sheet you want to copy.
2. Drag the sheet tab right or left to where you want to position the copy; then, press and hold down Ctrl.

When you press Ctrl, the mouse pointer displays a tiny plus symbol on the tiny sheet symbol. The tiny plus symbol indicates that you're creating a copy.

3. Drop the sheet tab (release the mouse button) when the little triangle is where you want to place the copy, as shown in Figure 5.10; then, release the Ctrl key.

   A copy of the worksheet is created, with the same sheet name and the number (2) next to it. (You'll probably want to rename the new worksheet.)

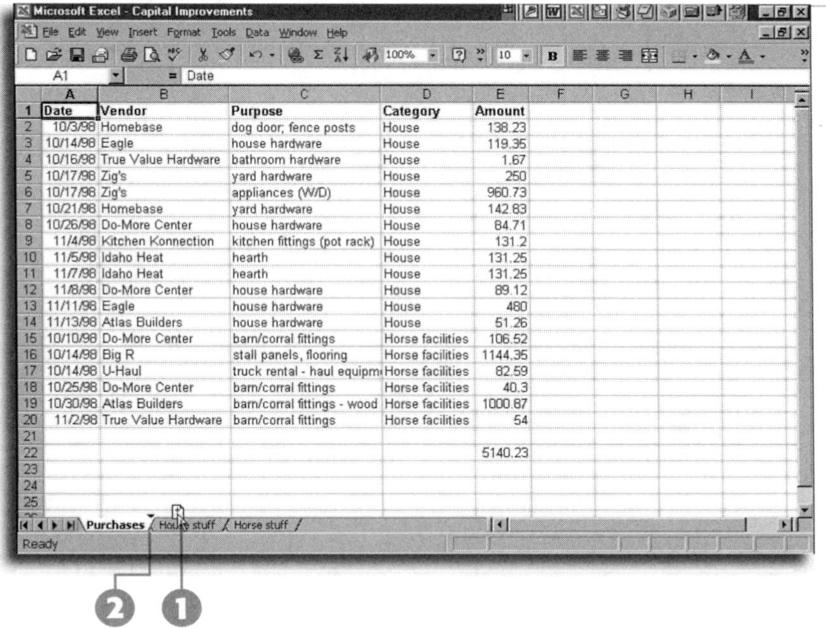

	A	B	C	D	E
1	Date	Vendor	Purpose	Category	Amount
2	10/3/98	Homebase	dog door, fence posts	House	138.23
3	10/14/98	Eagle	house hardware	House	119.35
4	10/16/98	True Value Hardware	bathroom hardware	House	1.67
5	10/17/98	Zig's	yard hardware	House	250
6	10/17/98	Zig's	appliances (W/D)	House	960.73
7	10/21/98	Homebase	yard hardware	House	142.83
8	10/26/98	Do-More Center	house hardware	House	84.71
9	11/4/98	Kitchen Konnection	kitchen fittings (pot rack)	House	131.2
10	11/5/98	Idaho Heat	hearth	House	131.25
11	11/7/98	Idaho Heat	hearth	House	131.25
12	11/8/98	Do-More Center	house hardware	House	89.12
13	11/11/98	Eagle	house hardware	House	480
14	11/13/98	Atlas Builders	house hardware	House	51.26
15	10/10/98	Do-More Center	barn/corral fittings	Horse facilities	106.52
16	10/14/98	Big R	stall panels, flooring	Horse facilities	1144.35
17	10/14/98	U-Haul	truck rental - haul equipm	Horse facilities	82.59
18	10/25/98	Do-More Center	barn/corral fittings	Horse facilities	40.3
19	10/30/98	Atlas Builders	barn/corral fittings - wood	Horse facilities	1000.87
20	11/2/98	True Value Hardware	barn/corral fittings	Horse facilities	54
21					
22					5140.23

FIGURE 5.10

To copy a worksheet, drag its sheet tab to a new location and press Ctrl when you drop it.

1. Copying-sheet mouse pointer
2. Position triangle

SEE ALSO

➤ *For information on using templates to create identical new worksheets, see page 49.*

Moving and Copying Worksheets Between Workbooks

There are a couple of ways to move and copy worksheets between two workbooks. One way is to display both workbooks on your screen and drag sheet tabs from one workbook to the other in the same way that you move or copy a worksheet within the same workbook. Another way is to use the following procedure, which relies on the Move or Copy dialog box.

SEE ALSO

➤ *To learn more about arranging multiple windows so that you can see several workbooks or worksheets at once, see page 101.*

Moving or Copying a Worksheet to Another Workbook

1. Open both workbooks (the workbook that contains the worksheet and the workbook that you want to move or copy the worksheet into).
2. Right-click the sheet tab for the worksheet you want to move or copy.
3. Choose **Move or Copy**.

   The Move or Copy dialog box appears, as shown in Figure 5.11.
4. In the **To book** drop-down list, select the workbook you want to move or copy the worksheet into.
5. In the **Before sheet** list box, click the name of a worksheet where you want to position the moved or copied worksheet. (Don't worry if you pick the wrong worksheet; you can easily move the worksheet to reposition it later.)
6. If you want to copy the worksheet to the new workbook, click the **Create a copy** check box; if you want to move the worksheet without creating a copy, leave the check box blank.

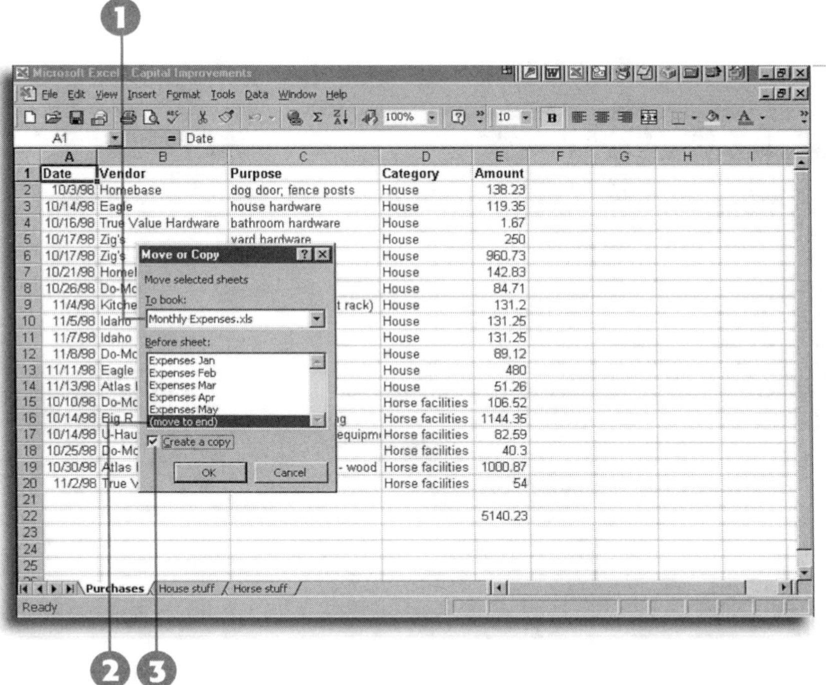

FIGURE 5.11

The Move or Copy dialog box lets you move or copy worksheets between workbooks when you're using a single window.

1. Select the workbook.
2. Select a position in the new workbook.
3. Copy instead of move.

7. Choose **OK**.

   The worksheet is moved or copied (depending on whether you checked the **Create a copy** check box) into the new workbook.

Moving or Copying a Worksheet to Another Workbook by Dragging It

The easiest way I know to move and copy worksheets from one workbook to another is to drag them.

Move or copy a worksheet by dragging it

1. Open both workbooks (the workbook that contains the worksheet and the workbook that you want to move or copy the worksheet into).

2. Arrange the two windows so you can see the sheet tabs in both workbooks, as shown in Figure 5.12.

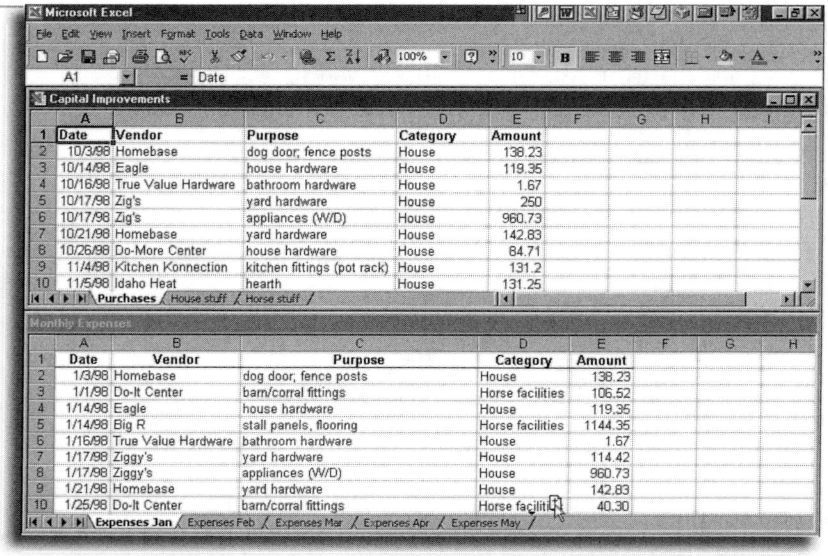

FIGURE 5.12

Use multiple windows to drag a worksheet from one workbook to another.

3. To move a worksheet without copying it, drag the sheet tab from one workbook and drop it among the sheet tabs in the other workbook.

   To copy a worksheet to another workbook, drag the sheet tab as if you're moving the worksheet; then, hold down Ctrl when you drop the sheet tab. A plus symbol appears with the mouse pointer to show that you're dropping a copy of the worksheet.

SEE ALSO

➤ *To learn more about arranging multiple windows so that you can see several workbooks or worksheets at once, see page 101.*

Start a New Workbook with an Existing Worksheet

To create a new workbook from an existing worksheet quickly, reduce the window size of the active workbook so you can see part of the Excel desktop as well as the active workbook's sheet tabs; then, drag the worksheet's sheet tab out of the workbook and drop it on the Excel desktop. A new workbook that contains the dragged worksheet is created.

CHAPTER

6

Changing Your View of the Worksheet

Freezing and unfreezing worksheet panes

Splitting worksheet panes and removing split panes

Arranging multiple worksheet windows

Arranging multiple workbook windows

Closing extra windows

Arranging windows manually

Freezing Worksheet Panes to Keep Rows or Columns in View

You have a few different ways to change your view of your worksheet or workbook, and each different view is useful in specific circumstances. When adding items to the bottom of a long list or filling in a column on the far right side of a worksheet table, the important row and column headings in the top rows and leftmost columns are scrolled out of view. If you lose track of the row and column headings in your list, you may inadvertently enter data in the wrong row or column. To keep a row of headings in view at the top of your worksheet while you scroll down to the bottom of a long list, you can *freeze* the heading row in its own pane. To see two distant parts of a worksheet side-by-side, you can *split* the worksheet into panes and scroll around in each pane separately. If you want to see the contents of two or more worksheets or workbooks at the same time, which makes it easy to move and copy cells and worksheets by dragging them from one window to another, you can arrange them in *multiple windows*.

Freezing Panes

To keep the headings in view while you work in a distant part of your list, you can freeze the heading rows or columns using the following procedure. You can edit cells in frozen rows and columns just like other cells; freezing just keeps them in view while you scroll around.

Which Rows or Columns Do You Want to Freeze?

Select the row below the rows you want to freeze and the column to the right of the columns you want to freeze. To freeze both row 1 and column A, for example, click cell B2.

Freeze worksheet panes

1. To freeze the top row of a worksheet, click the row selector for row 2 (shown in Figure 6.1).

   To freeze the leftmost column, click the column selector for column B.

2. On the **Window** menu, click **Freeze Panes**.

   The frozen panes remain in view no matter where you scroll in your worksheet (shown in Figure 6.2).

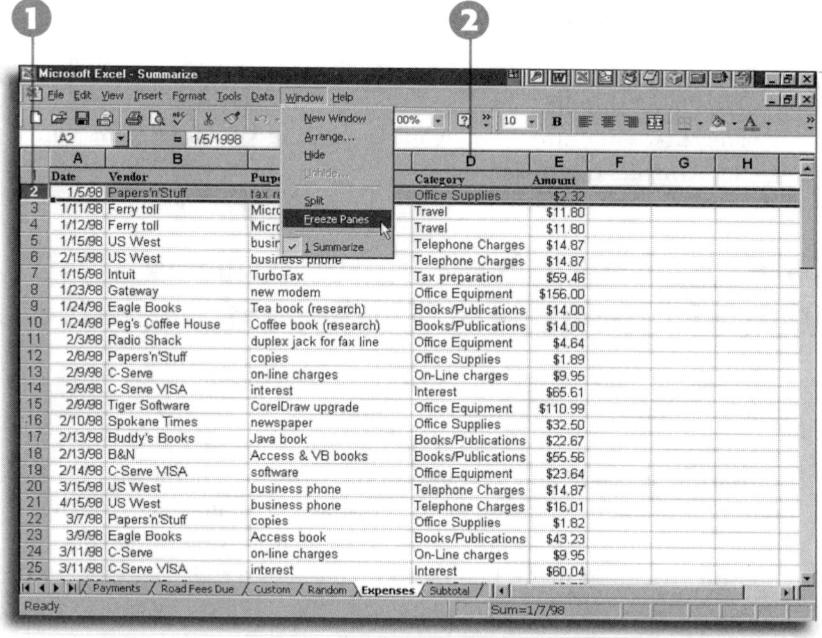

FIGURE 6.1

Select row 2 if you want to freeze row 1.

1. Row selector
2. Column selector

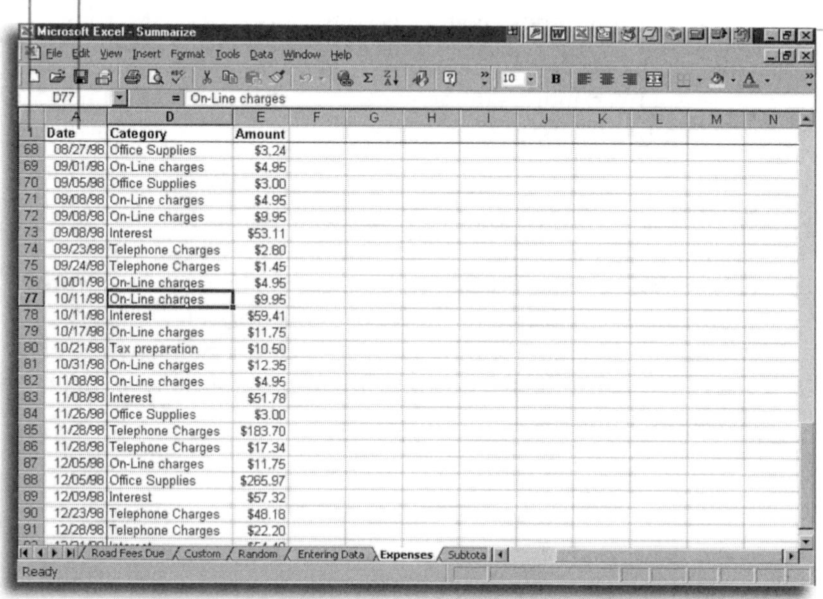

FIGURE 6.2

Even though the active cell is to the far right and bottom of the worksheet list, the top row and left column headings are still visible.

1. Frozen row
2. Frozen column

Unfreezing Panes

You can leave frozen panes in place for as long as you want, but if you need to split panes in a window, you have to unfreeze the panes first. To unfreeze the panes, open the **Window** menu and click **Unfreeze Panes**.

Splitting Worksheet Panes to View Multiple Areas in a Worksheet

In a really long or wide table of data, visually comparing data from distant parts is difficult. If, however, you split the table into two or four panes, you can scroll in each pane separately and view the far right and left sides of the table, or the top and bottom of the table, at the same time. Splitting is different from freezing panes because frozen panes remain in view; you can't scroll around in them, but all split panes are scrollable.

Unfreeze Panes Before You Split Them

You cannot split panes in a worksheet with frozen panes. To unfreeze panes, open the **Window** menu and click **Unfreeze Panes**.

The Panes Are the Wrong Size

To adjust the sizes of split panes, drag the split bar with the mouse. To adjust the sizes of four panes at once, drag the intersection of the horizontal and vertical split bars.

Split panes in a worksheet

1. Position the mouse pointer over the vertical or horizontal split box (as shown in Figure 6.3).
2. When your mouse pointer becomes a two-headed arrow, drag the split box into the worksheet.

   A split bar appears in the worksheet where you drop the split box (as shown in Figure 6.4).

You can scroll in each pane separately with that pane's scroll bars. Scrolling to see what you want takes a little practice. Just keep in mind that split panes are just two (or four) different windows onto the same worksheet. Changes you make in one worksheet pane are reflected in all worksheet panes. (Figure 6.5 shows four different panes.) When you select a cell, only the one cell is selected, although you may see it in all (or none) of your split-pane windows.

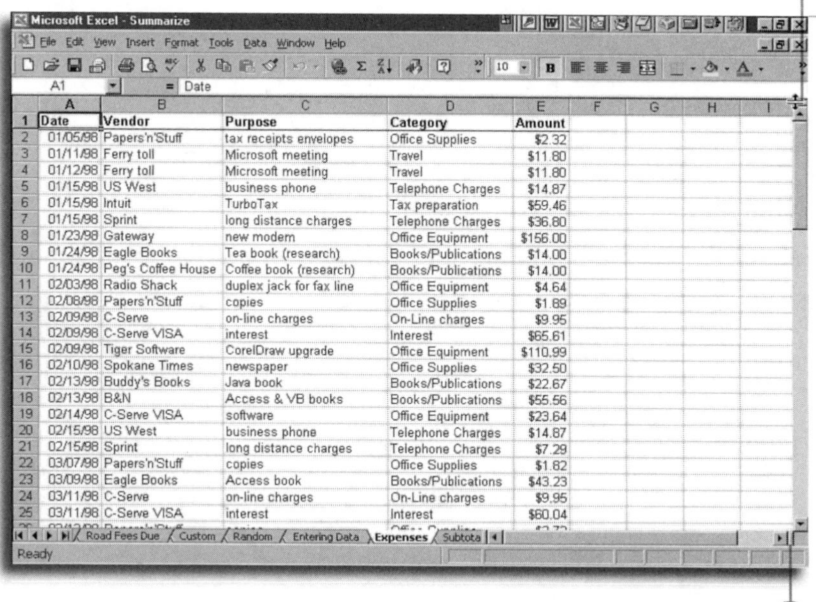

FIGURE 6.3

Use the vertical or horizontal split box to quickly split worksheet panes using the mouse.

1. Horizontal split box
2. Vertical split box

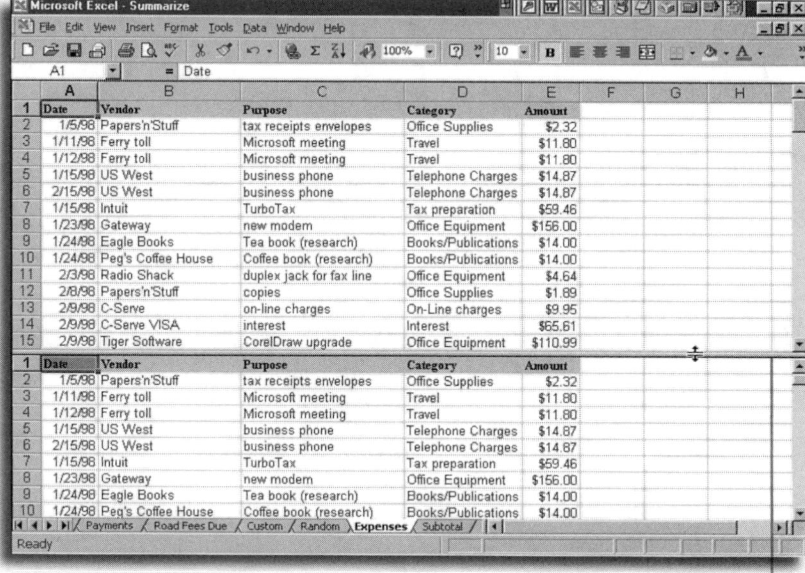

FIGURE 6.4

You can split the worksheet into two panes with one split bar.

1. Split bar

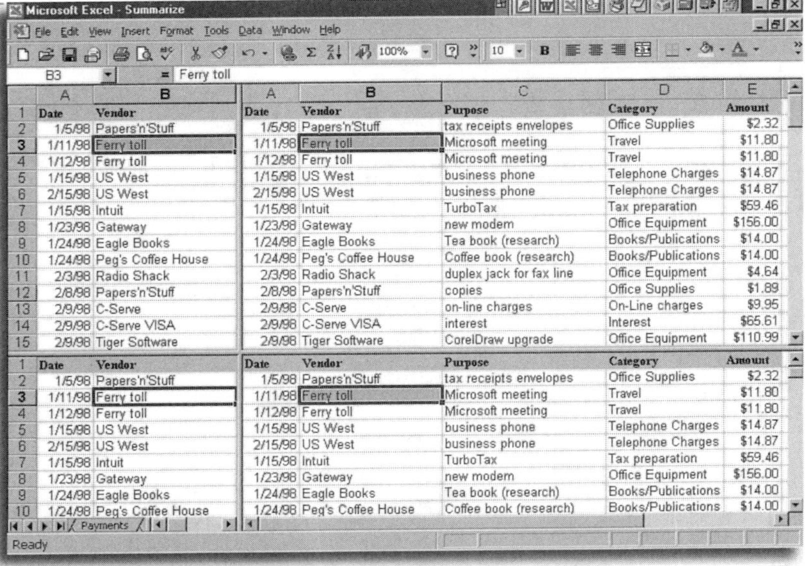

FIGURE 6.5

Four split panes provide four different views of the same selected cell.

Remove split panes

1. Position the mouse pointer over the split bar (shown in Figure 6.6).

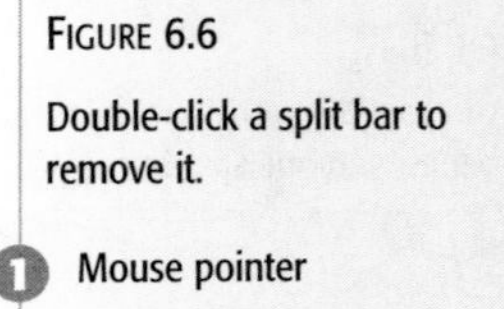

FIGURE 6.6

Double-click a split bar to remove it.

1 Mouse pointer

2. When the mouse pointer becomes a two-headed arrow, double-click the split bar.

   The split bar is removed.

Using Multiple Windows

If you're working in two or more worksheets (or workbooks) at the same time, you often can switch more quickly between them by arranging them in multiple windows. The windows can be arranged in a variety of layouts: vertical windows, side-by-side; horizontal windows, top-to-bottom; tiled windows, laid out in a grid; and cascading windows, like a deck of cards. Excel arranges the windows neatly to fit within the Excel desktop, but I find that after I've arranged my windows, I like to further arrange them by dragging the window borders to change their sizes.

Arranging Multiple Windows to See Several Worksheets at Once

If you want to move or copy cells to a different worksheet, the easiest way is to open multiple windows and drag the cells from one window to another.

Display worksheets from a single workbook in separate windows

1. On the **Window** menu, click **New Window**.

   A new window is created for the same worksheet, but you can't see it yet because both windows are full-sized.

2. On the **Window** menu, click **Arrange**.

   The Arrange Windows dialog box appears. (The arrangement options are shown in Figures 6.7 through 6.10.)

3. Click the arrangement option you want—**Tiled**, **Horizontal**, **Vertical**, or **Cascade**.

4. Click the **Windows of active workbook** check box.

   This check box limits the windows to the active workbook instead of opening windows on all the open workbooks.

5. Click **OK**.

I Want More Windows

To open more windows, repeat step 1 for each additional window.

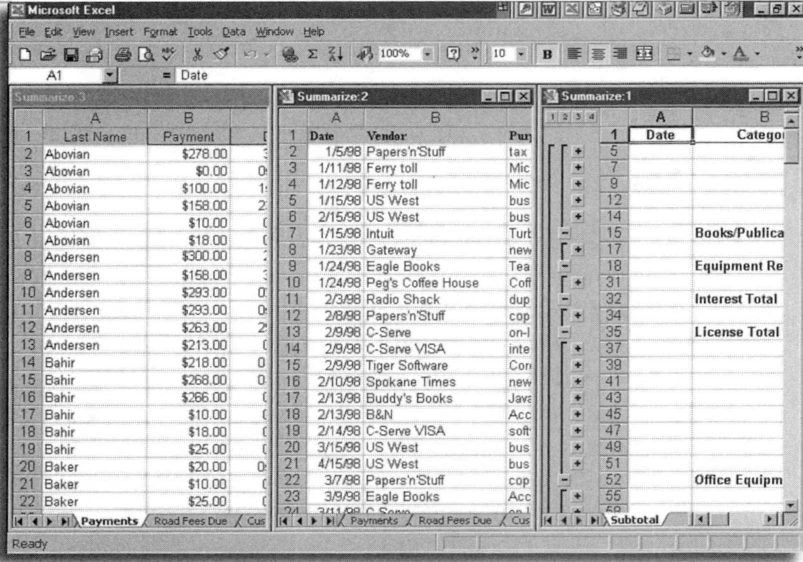

FIGURE 6.7
Vertical windows are good for comparing data on two or more different worksheets.

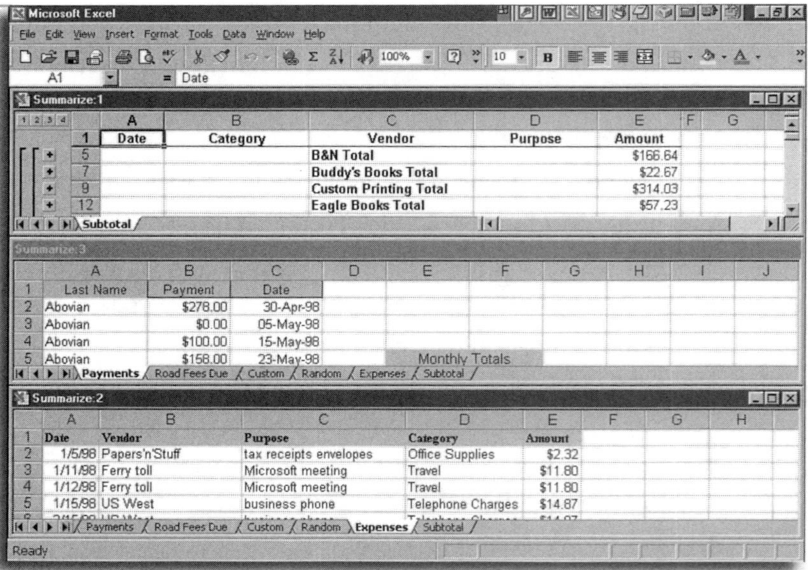

FIGURE 6.8
Horizontal windows are good for dragging sheet tabs between windows.

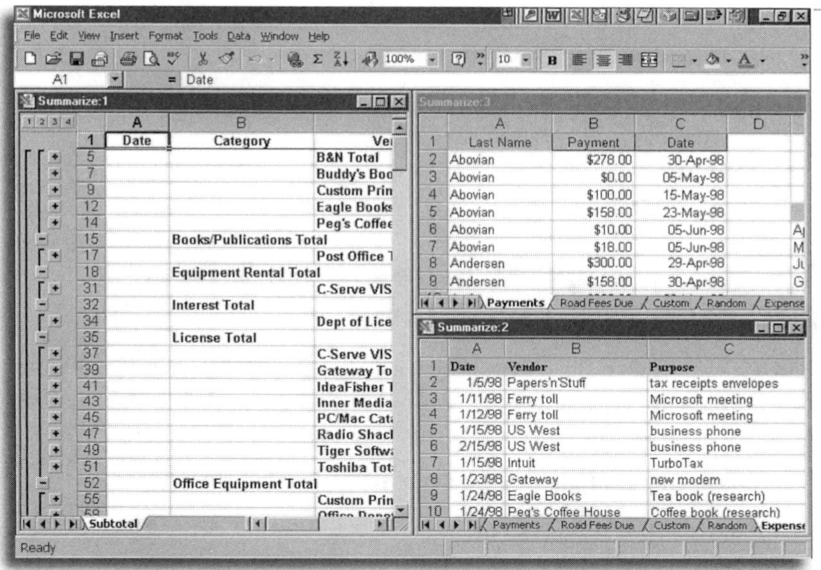

FIGURE 6.9
Tiled windows give you a view of all three worksheets at once.

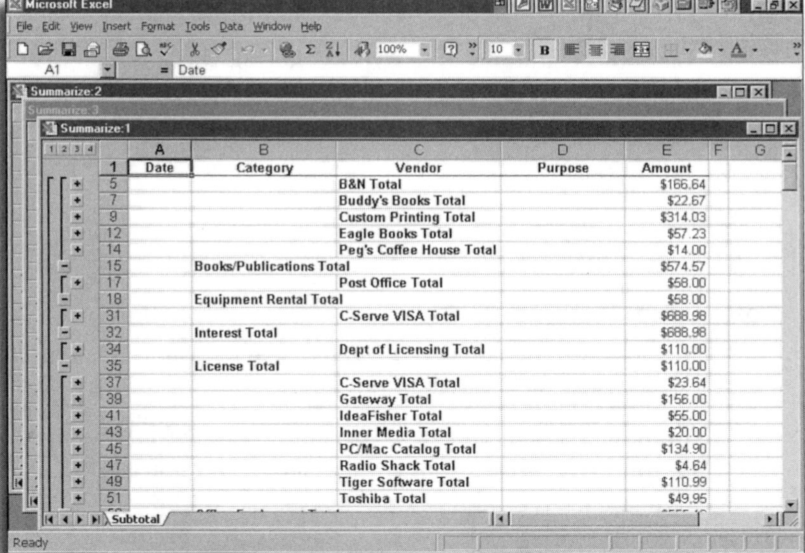

FIGURE 6.10
Cascaded windows enable you to see more data in each window but also keep them all within easy reach.

Look at Your Taskbar

In Excel 2000, every open window has its own button on the taskbar, which makes navigating between open windows a lot faster. Click the window's button to bring that window to the top of the stack.

Two Windows, Same Worksheet?

It might seem obvious, but be sure to select different sheets in each window (the sheet to copy or move *from* and the sheet to copy or move *to*) before you move or copy cells between windows.

Your windows are arranged so that you can select a different worksheet in each window. You can then drag cells between windows to move or copy them from one worksheet to another.

SEE ALSO

➤ *For more information on moving and copying cell data between worksheets, see page 144.*

Arranging Multiple Windows to See Several Workbooks at the Same Time

If you want to move or copy worksheets to a different workbook, the easiest way is to open multiple windows and drag your worksheets from one window to another window.

Displaying multiple workbooks in separate windows

1. Open the workbooks with which you want to work.
2. On the **Window** menu, click **Arrange**.
3. Click a window arrangement—**Tiled**, **Horizontal**, **Vertical**, or **Cascade**.
4. Clear the **Windows of active workbook** check box so that all the open workbooks are displayed in separate windows (shown in Figure 6.11).
5. Click **OK**.

SEE ALSO

➤ *To learn more about moving and copying worksheets between workbooks, see page 92.*

Close windows in the workbook

1. To close extra windows, click the **Close** button in the upper-right corner of each window.
2. To maximize the remaining window, click the **Maximize** button in the upper-right corner (shown in Figure 6.12), or double-click the window's title bar.

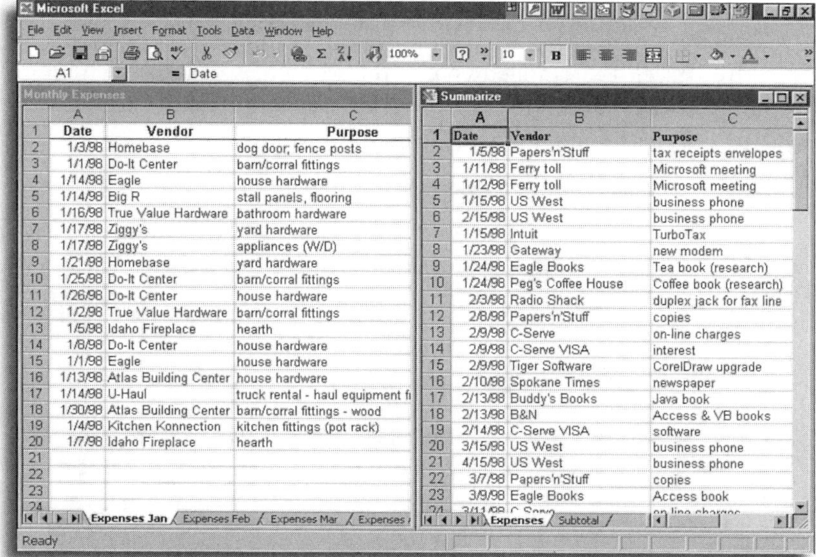

FIGURE 6.11

You can easily move or copy worksheets between workbooks if you drag sheet tabs from one window to another.

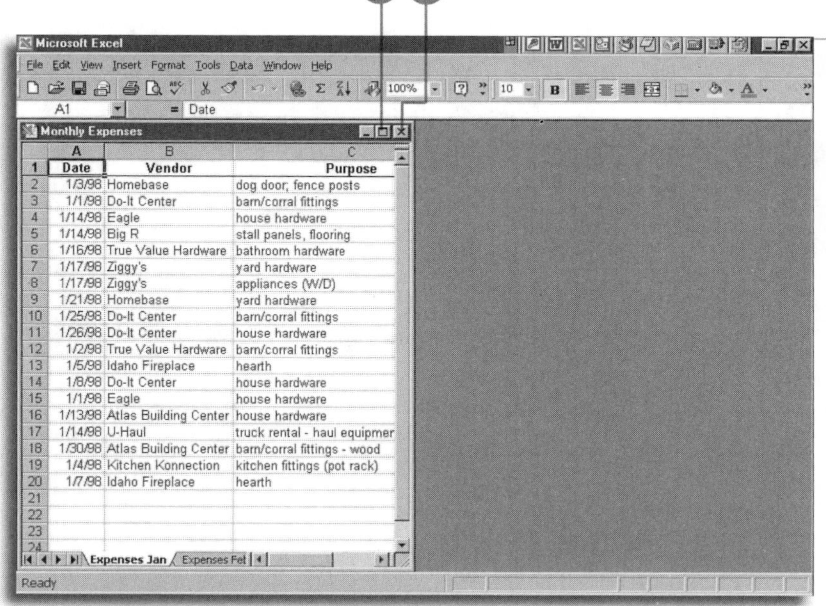

FIGURE 6.12

Close the extra windows and maximize the remaining window.

1. Maximize button
2. Close button

Arranging Multiple Windows Manually

After Excel has arranged your windows so that you can see them all, you can further arrange them by dragging window borders to resize them or dragging title bars to move them.

Resize and move windows manually

1. To resize a window, point to a window border or corner until the mouse pointer becomes a two-headed arrow (as shown in Figure 6.13).

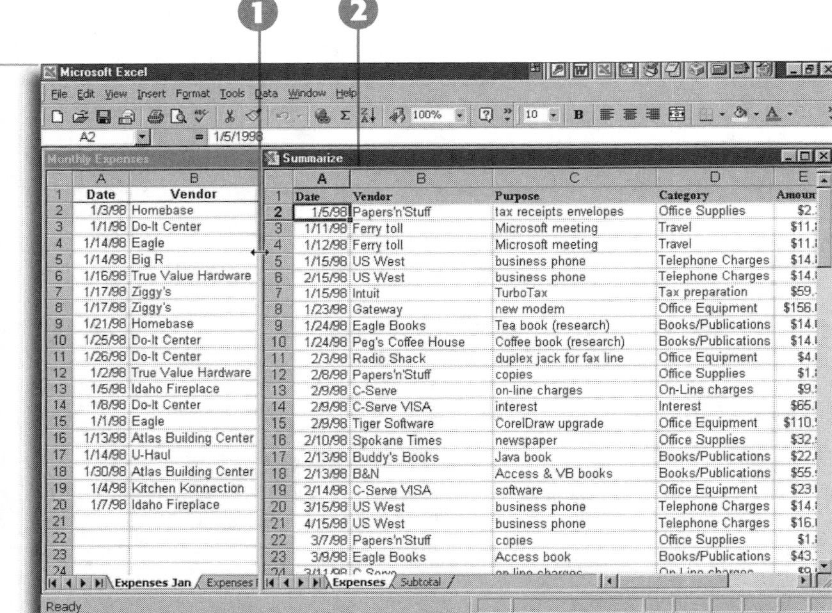

FIGURE 6.13

I like to tweak my multiple-window arrangement manually until it works well for me.

1 Drag a border to resize.

2 Drag the title bar to move.

2. Drag a window border to resize or reshape a window.
3. To move an entire window, drag its title bar.

PART II

Building Worksheets

7 **Entering Data 109**

8 **Copying and Importing Data from Other Files 121**

9 **Editing Data 133**

10 **Simple Calculations 159**

11 **Complex Calculations 175**

CHAPTER 7

Entering Data

Entering data directly into a cell

Using AutoFill to quickly enter text and number series

Repeating cell entries

Entering data with a data entry form

Setting up and removing data validation

Raw data is what you type into a cell—in other words, values rather than formulas. Data might be text, as in a list of names or days of the week, or numbers, as in expense-account amounts or hours worked, dates, or column labels. In short, data is anything you type into a cell other than a *formula* (which performs mathematical calculations using the data you enter).

Excel has a number of tools that make data entry quicker: AutoComplete, AutoFill, and some old standby keystrokes are all very handy. You can also set up *data validation* for individual cells to make sure accurate data is entered.

If the data you need to enter is already in electronic format (for example, in a text file, an Access database, or even a Word document), it's unnecessary to retype it; instead, you can import the data straight into your worksheet.

SEE ALSO

➤ *To learn more about writing formulas in Excel, see pages 165 and 177.*

Entering Data Directly in a Worksheet

The basic procedure for entering data in Excel is straightforward: Click a cell, type something, and press Enter.

The magic of computers is that they let you do less work (usually) than a typewriter—and, sure enough, Excel has easy tricks for making repetitive entries less work. In addition to entering data one cell at a time, you can

- Enter a series of numbers or repeated text entries into several cells by dragging the mouse across the worksheet (with AutoFill).
- Repeat the entry in the cell above with a keystroke.
- Enter identical data in several cells after typing it once.
- Repeat entries in a long list by typing the first one or two letters (with AutoComplete).

Entering Data in a Single Cell

The most common way to enter data is one cell at a time because most data is not repetitive.

Enter data in a cell

1. Click a cell.
2. Type your data.
3. Press Enter.

   The active cell (the selected cell) moves to the next cell down when you press Enter.

There's Always Another Way

You can also press Tab, press an arrow key, or click another cell to complete the entry. If you press Tab to move across the bottom of a table and then press Enter, the active cell moves down one row and returns to the left side of the table.

AutoFilling a Text Entry

To enter identical text entries or a built-in or custom list of different text entries, you can use AutoFill. If AutoFill recognizes your initial text entry as part of a built-in or custom list, it fills the list, but if AutoFill doesn't recognize your entry, it copies the entry to fill cells. For example, you can set up a table quickly by using AutoFill to enter month names across the top, or you can fill several cells with the word "North." In the next procedure, I'll show you how to use AutoFill to enter a list of day names.

Is It a Number, or Is It Text?

To enter a number that's really text (such as a ZIP code), type an apostrophe first. For example, the entry `'07623` is displayed as `07623` in the cell; it retains its leading zero and is not calculable. To learn how to format the cell to take care of this for you, see Chapter 12, "Formatting Cells."

Use AutoFill to enter text

1. Click a cell.
2. Type a day of the week (either the three-letter abbreviation or the full name).
3. Place your mouse pointer over the lower-right corner of the selected cell until it becomes a small black cross (see Figure 7.1), and drag to the right.

   The cells you drag over are filled with a series of day names, in correct order.

AutoFill Lists

Excel has built-in AutoFill lists for day names and month names, both full and abbreviated. If you start an AutoFill list with a day or month name, you'll fill cells with the built-in list instead of a repeated entry.

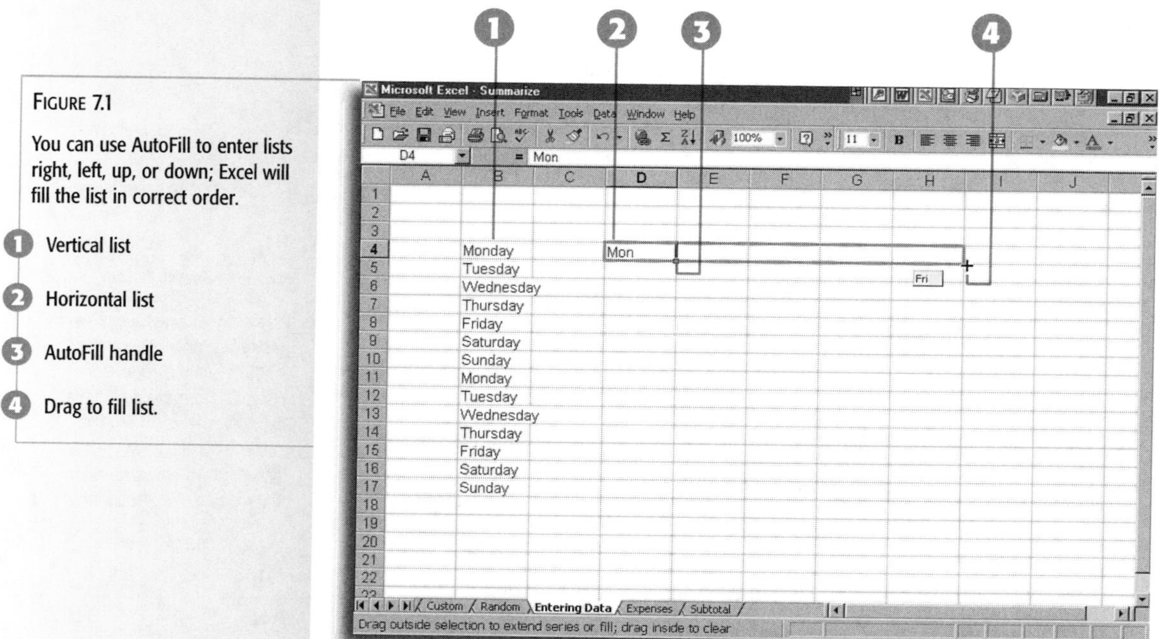

FIGURE 7.1

You can use AutoFill to enter lists right, left, up, or down; Excel will fill the list in correct order.

1. Vertical list
2. Horizontal list
3. AutoFill handle
4. Drag to fill list.

Creating Your Own Custom List

You can create your own custom lists (for example, a custom list of coworker or product names); then, when you enter any one of those names, you can use AutoFill to enter the rest of the list.

The easiest way to create a custom list is to first enter the list in a worksheet.

Create a custom AutoFill list

1. Select the list in the worksheet.
2. On the **Tools** menu, click **Options**.
3. Click the **Custom Lists** tab.

   The list range you selected is already entered in the **Import list from cells** box.
4. Click **Import.**

   The list is added to Excel's AutoFill lists.
5. Click **OK** to save the new list and close the Options dialog box.

AutoFilling a Number Series

You also can use AutoFill to enter a series of numbers that increases or decreases by a constant value (such as 1, 2, 3, 4 or 2, 4, 6, 8).

Use AutoFill to enter a series of numbers

1. Click a cell.
2. Type a number (for example, 1); then, press Enter.

   The active cell moves to the next cell down.
3. Type the next number in the series (for example, 2); then press Enter.
4. Select both cells.
5. Drag the AutoFill handle (the small black box in the lower-right corner of the selected range) down to fill the series, as shown in Figure 7.2.

Change the Active Cell Location

To change the direction in which the active cell moves when you press Enter, open the **Tools** menu, and click **Options**. On the **Edit** tab, next to **Move selection after Enter**, select a direction from the **Direction** drop-down list. (You can also clear the **Move selection after Enter** check box to prevent the active cell from moving anywhere when you press Enter.)

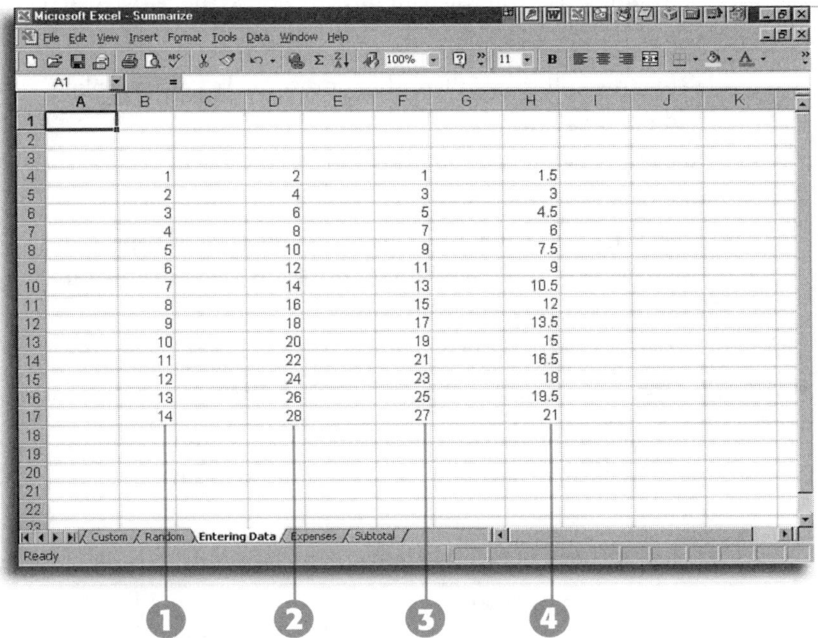

FIGURE 7.2

A number series is filled based on the cells you selected to begin the series.

1. Began with 1, 2
2. Began with 2, 4
3. Began with 1, 3
4. Began with 1.5, 3

AutoFilling a Growth Series

Instead of a *linear* series (such as 1, 2, 3, 4), you might want to use AutoFill to enter a *growth* series (a series that grows by a multiplication factor, such as 2, 4, 8, 16, 32).

Use AutoFill to enter a growth series

1. Enter the first two numbers in the series.
2. Drag the AutoFill handle with the *right* mouse button.

   When you release the mouse button, a shortcut menu is displayed.
3. Click **Growth Trend**.

   Excel guesses the multiplication factor based on your initial entries and fills the list with the series.

Repeating the Entry in the Cell Above

To repeat an entry from the cell directly above the active cell, use any of these methods:

- Select the cell to be filled; then, press Ctrl+' (apostrophe) and press Enter.
- Select the cell containing the entry you want to repeat; then drag the AutoFill handle.
- Select the cell containing the entry you want to repeat and the new cells to be filled; then, press Ctrl+D, as shown in Figure 7.3.

Entering the Same Data in Several Cells

To enter identical entries (text, numbers, dates, and so on) in several cells at one time, you can use an old standby keystroke, Ctrl+Enter.

Enter duplicate data in multiple cells

1. Select all the cells you want to enter the data in. (To select nonadjacent cells, click one cell; then, hold down Ctrl and select the remaining cells.)
2. Type your entry.

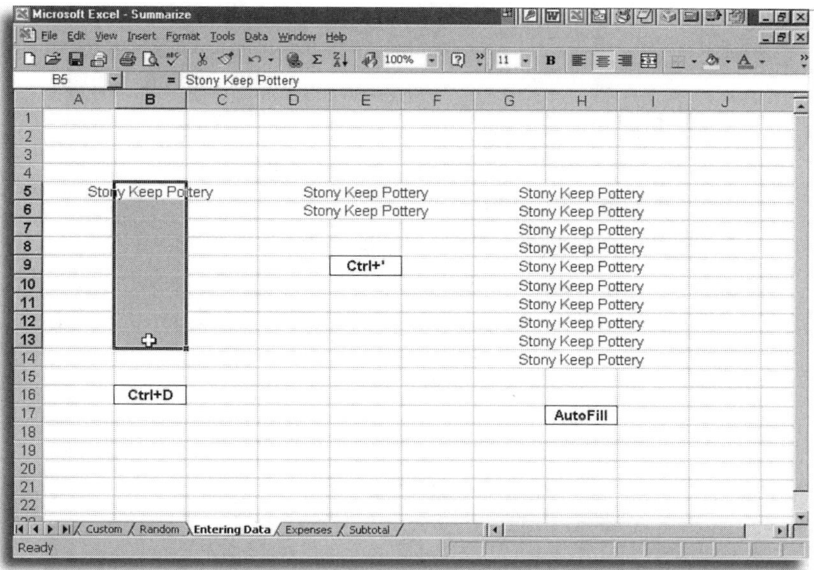

FIGURE 7.3

The easiest method for repeating cell entries to the cell below depends on what you want to accomplish.

3. Press Ctrl+Enter.

   The identical entry is entered in all selected cells, as shown in Figure 7.4.

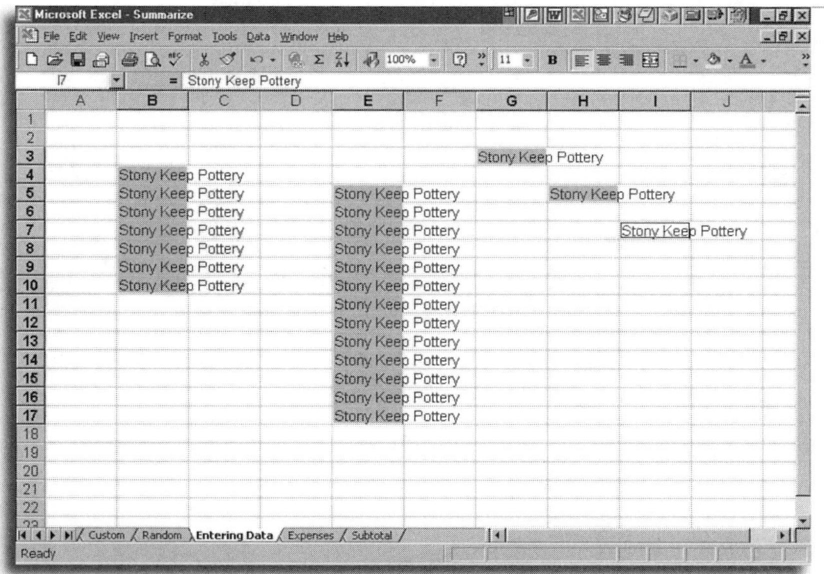

FIGURE 7.4

To enter the same data in several cells, use the Ctrl key to select nonadjacent cells; then type the entry and press Ctrl+Enter.

Repeating an Entry in a Text List with AutoComplete

To quickly enter an item in a list of repeated items (such as an expenses list), you can use AutoComplete.

Use AutoComplete to repeat entries in a list

1. Begin typing an entry at the bottom of a list.
2. If the characters you type are identical to an existing entry in the list, the rest of the entry is filled in for you (see Figure 7.5).

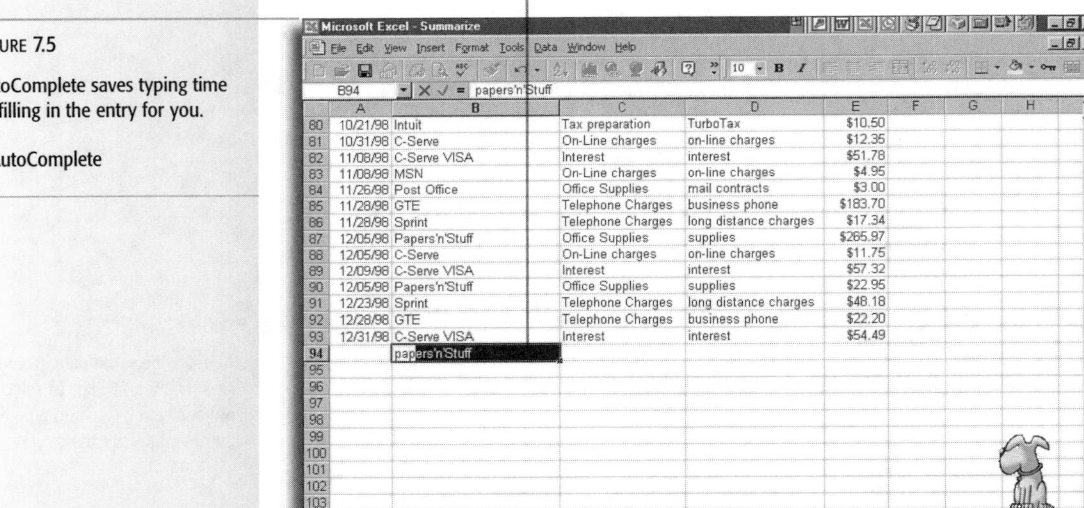

FIGURE 7.5

AutoComplete saves typing time by filling in the entry for you.

1 AutoComplete

3. If your entry is different from the previous list entry, keep typing. (The AutoComplete entry will disappear.)

If there are two or more similar entries in the list, right-click the cell where you want to enter data; then, click **Pick From List**. Click the entry you want from the list of existing entries.

AutoComplete Bothers Me

To turn off AutoComplete, open the **Tools** menu, and click **Options**. On the **Edit** tab, clear the **Enable AutoComplete for cell values** check box.

Entering Data with a Data Entry Form

Some folks find entering data in a form to be less confusing than entering data in a big table. You can create a data entry form instantly, as long as you have entered column headings for your table.

Create a data entry form for a worksheet

1. Be sure your table has column headings and at least one row of data already entered.
2. Click any cell within the table.
3. On the **Data** menu, click **Form**.

   A data form is created for the table, as shown in Figure 7.6.

   - Click the **New** button to start a new record.
   - Press Tab and Shift+Tab to move from field to field in the displayed record.
   - Press Enter to move to the next record in the table or to start a new record if the last record in the table is displayed.

4. Click the **Close** button to close the data form. New records are displayed at the end of the table.

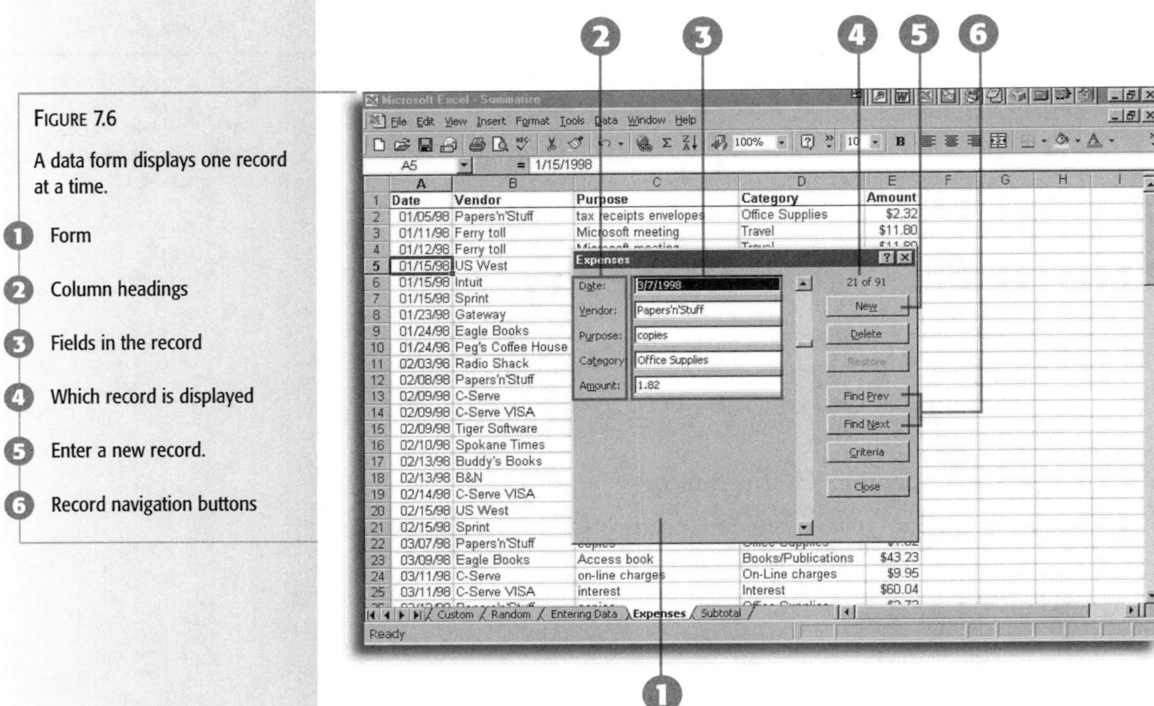

FIGURE 7.6

A data form displays one record at a time.

1. Form
2. Column headings
3. Fields in the record
4. Which record is displayed
5. Enter a new record.
6. Record navigation buttons

Validating Data During Entry

It's all too easy to inadvertently enter inaccurate data, which renders the data worthless. You can prevent some inaccuracies by setting up data validation, which displays an error message in response to data that doesn't meet standards you set, such as "text length equal to 16" or "date greater than =TODAY()."

Set up data validation

1. Select the cell or range where you want to validate the entries.
2. On the **Data** menu, click **Validation**. The Data Validation dialog box is displayed, as shown in Figure 7.7.
3. On the **Settings** tab, select a type of data in the **Allow** drop-down list.

Can I Specify the Allowable Entries?

To limit entries to those on a specific list, in the **Allow** drop-down list, select **List**. In the **Source** box, type the allowable entries (separated by commas) or drag to select a worksheet range that lists the allowable entries.

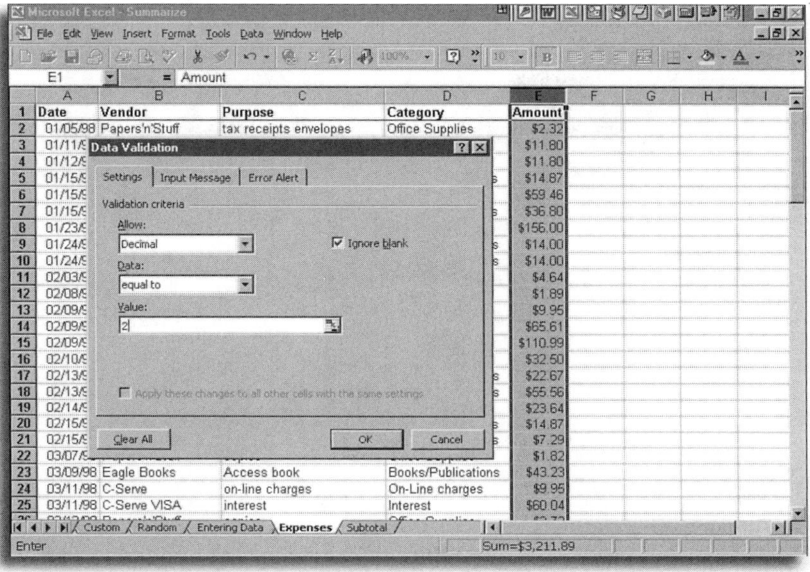

FIGURE 7.7
Use data validation to specify what type of data is allowable in selected cells and to display messages when data is entered.

4. In the **Data** drop-down list (if it's available), select any value-limiting criteria you want, such as "between" or "greater than."
5. In the boxes that are displayed below the **Data** drop-down list, set criteria such as **Minimum** and **Maximum** allowable values. (The criteria you can set are determined by the choices you make in the **Allow** and **Data** drop-down lists.)
6. To require an entry in the cell, clear the **Ignore blank** check box.
7. On the **Input Message** tab, type a title and message that display when one of the validated cells is selected (if you don't want a message when a cell is selected, clear the **Show input message when cell is selected** check box). An input message is shown in Figure 7.8.
8. On the **Error Alert** tab, choose an icon, type a title, and type an error message that displays when invalid data is entered (if you don't want a message but merely want invalid data entry refused, clear the **Show error alert after invalid data is entered** check box).

Different Warning Levels

The **Information** and **Warning** error styles allow invalid data to be entered after warnings appear, but the **Stop** error style prohibits invalid data entry.

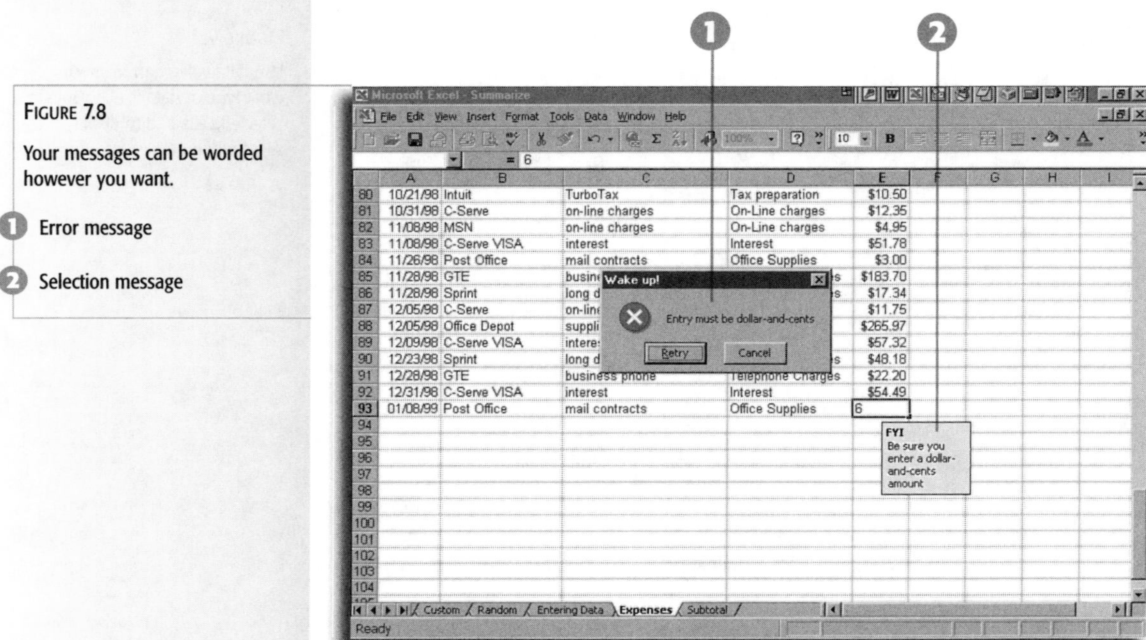

FIGURE 7.8

Your messages can be worded however you want.

1 Error message

2 Selection message

Which Cells Are Validated?

To locate validated cells on a worksheet, open the **Edit** menu and click **Go To**. Click the **Special** button. In the Go To Special dialog box, click **Data validation** and **All**; then click **OK**. All cells with validation rules are highlighted.

9. Click **OK**.

Invalid data that already exists on the worksheet won't show error messages, but you can locate it with Excel's auditing tools.

SEE ALSO

➤ *To learn more about finding invalid data, see page 211.*

Remove data validation

1. Select a cell where data validation is in place.
2. On the **Data** menu, click **Validation**.
3. Click the **Clear All** button.
4. To remove the same validation settings from all cells where they're enforced, click the **Settings** tab; then click the **Apply these changes to all other cells with the same settings** check box.
5. Click **OK**.

Copying and Importing Data from Other Files

- Trading data between Excel and other programs
- Copying data from Word to Excel
- Sending data from Access to Excel
- Sending data from Excel to Access
- Importing a text file into Excel

Trading Data with Other Programs

Typing is not the only way to get data into a spreadsheet. If the data already exists in electronic form (for example, in a Word document, an Access table, a text file, or a dBASE table), you don't need to reenter it. Instead, copy it or import it; you save time and you reduce retyping errors. To copy data from another file, use the other file's copy procedures and Excel's paste procedures. To import data from another file type, open the file in Excel using the procedures outlined later in this chapter in the section "Importing a Text File."

As you can see from the following list, you can open or import data directly from most common file types:

- Earlier versions of Excel
- Lotus 1-2-3
- Quattro Pro
- Text
- DOS
- Microsoft Works 2.0
- dBASE II, III, IV
- SYLK (Symbolic Link)
- DIF (Data Interchange Format)

SEE ALSO

➤ *To learn more about sharing data between software programs, see page 499.*

Copying Data from Word

If the data you need is already in a Word file, it's easy to copy and paste it into Excel. For example, if someone has kept a list of names and phone numbers in a Word document, you can start setting up a list of contacts in Excel quickly by copying and pasting the list from Word. To copy a list from Word to Excel, use the following procedure.

Copy data from Word to Excel

1. Open the Word document, and select the list of data (as shown in Figure 8.1).

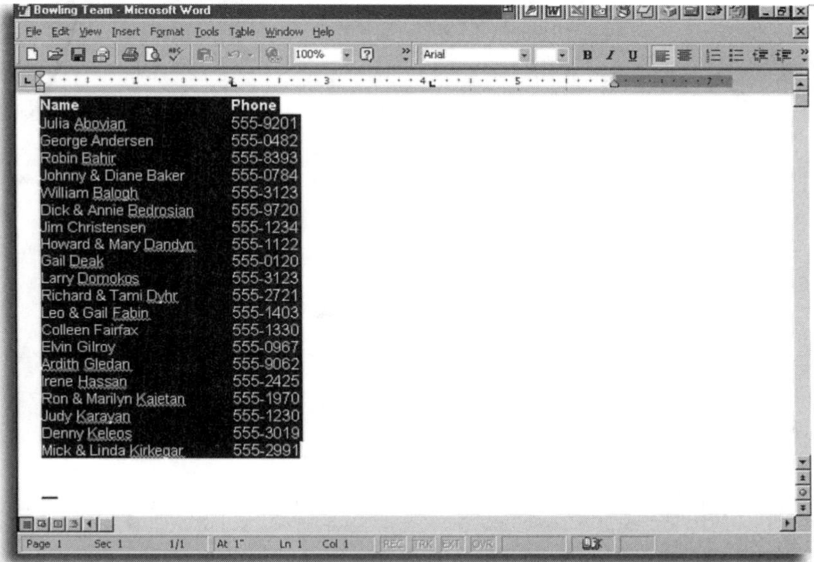

FIGURE 8.1
The two columns in Word are separated by tab characters.

2. Copy the data by clicking the **Copy** button (or use whatever copy method you prefer).

   Data you copy or cut is kept in a temporary file called the Windows *Clipboard*, and you can paste the copied or cut data repeatedly.

3. Switch to the Excel worksheet.
4. Click the cell in which you want to paste the upper-left corner of the list.
5. Open the **Edit** menu, and click **Paste**.

   The list is pasted into your worksheet (as shown in Figure 8.2). The data is separated, or *parsed*, into columns according to how it was separated in the Word document. (Parsing means Excel uses tab characters in the Word text to separate

The New Office 2000 Clipboard

The new Office 2000 Clipboard holds up to 12 cut or copied items. If you've cut or copied only one item, that item is pasted when you use any Paste command. If you've cut or copied more than one item, a Clipboard toolbar appears when you use a Paste command, and you can choose which item to paste. The item icons on the toolbar are identical. To tell which is which, hold the mouse pointer over an icon; the first several characters of the item appear in a ScreenTip. Click the icon for the item you want to paste.

the text into columns in the worksheet.) As you can see in Figures 8.1 and 8.2, data that's copied and pasted by this method doesn't bring its formatting into the worksheet. You need to format the data and widen the worksheet columns to make it look nice again.

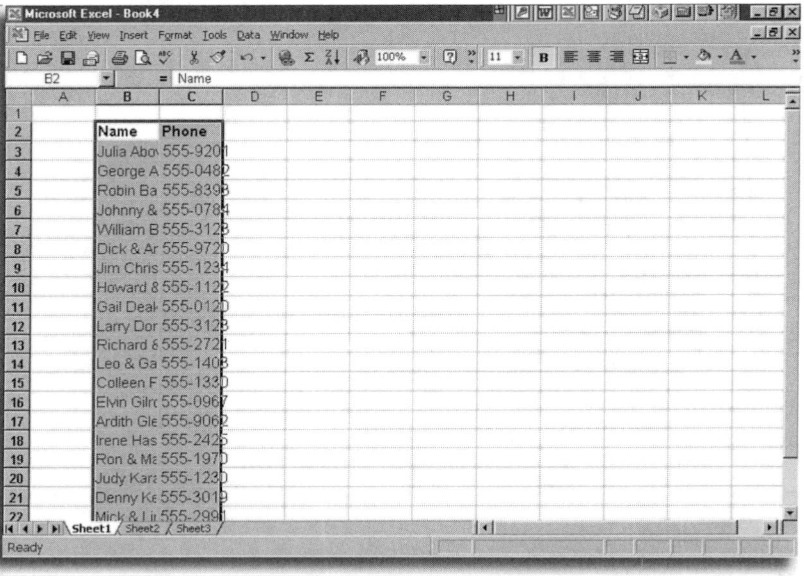

FIGURE 8.2
When you paste them into your worksheet, the columns are parsed with the tab characters that separated the columns in the Word document.

What Files Can I Copy from?

You can also copy data from WordPerfect, Works, and other Windows-based word processing files. You can also copy from any OLE-capable program, including IE, Navigator, and many other programs.

SEE ALSO

➤ *To learn more about formatting worksheet cells, see page 215.*

Sending Data Over from Access

The biggest difference between an Excel worksheet and an Access table is that Excel is designed to maneuver, manipulate, calculate, and crunch numbers, whereas Access is designed to store and retrieve data. I don't mean that you can't do calculations in an Access database; I only mean that Excel is far more flexible and easier to crunch numbers in.

That being said, if you have a table of data in Access in which you want to do some serious calculating, you can easily send the table of data to an Excel worksheet using the following procedure.

Send data from Access to Excel

1. Open the Access database.
2. In the database window, click the **Tables** button, and then click the name of the table you want to send to Excel (but don't open the table).
3. Open the **Tools** menu, point to **Office Links**, and then click **Analyze It with MS Excel** (as shown in Figure 8.3).

   Excel starts (if it's not already started), and a new workbook opens. The new workbook contains a single sheet, and both the worksheet and the workbook are named with the name of the Access table (shown in Figure 8.4).

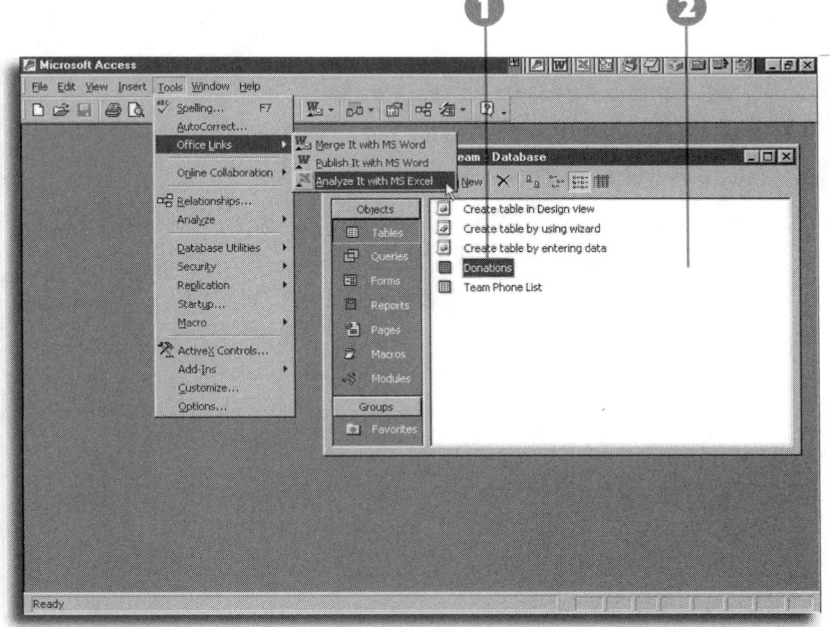

FIGURE 8.3
Send an Access table to Excel to perform calculations more easily.

1. Selected table name
2. Tables group

An even easier way to get Access data into Excel is to drag it and drop it. You can drag and drop Access tables or queries into an Excel worksheet.

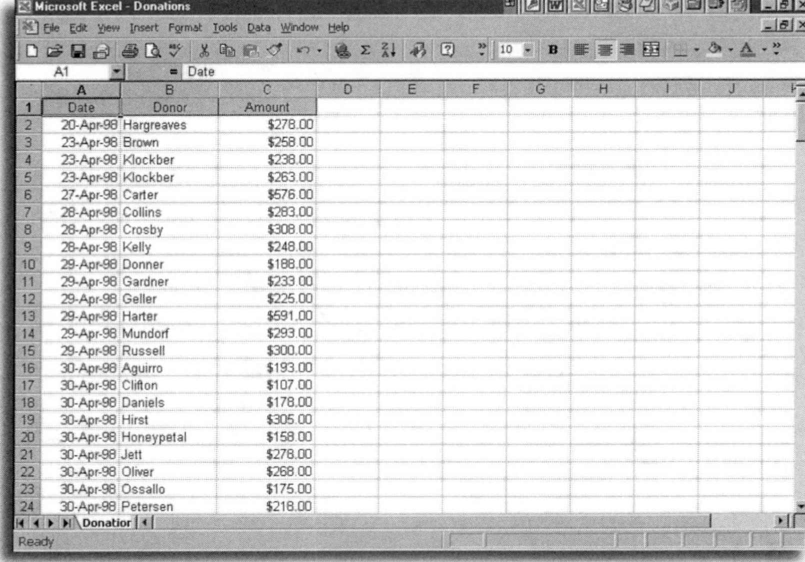

FIGURE 8.4

After you have moved Access data into Excel, the data becomes even more usable because you can calculate, chart, and analyze data more easily in Excel.

Drag and drop data from Access into Excel

1. Open the Access database.
2. Open the Excel workbook.
3. Resize the Access window so it's smaller, on top of the Excel window (as shown in Figure 8.5).

   You can also right-click the taskbar and click **Tile Windows Vertically**.
4. Drag the name of a table or a query from the Access database window, and drop it in the worksheet grid (as shown in Figure 8.6).
5. The Access data appears in the worksheet, as shown in Figure 8.7 (you'll need to resize the columns).

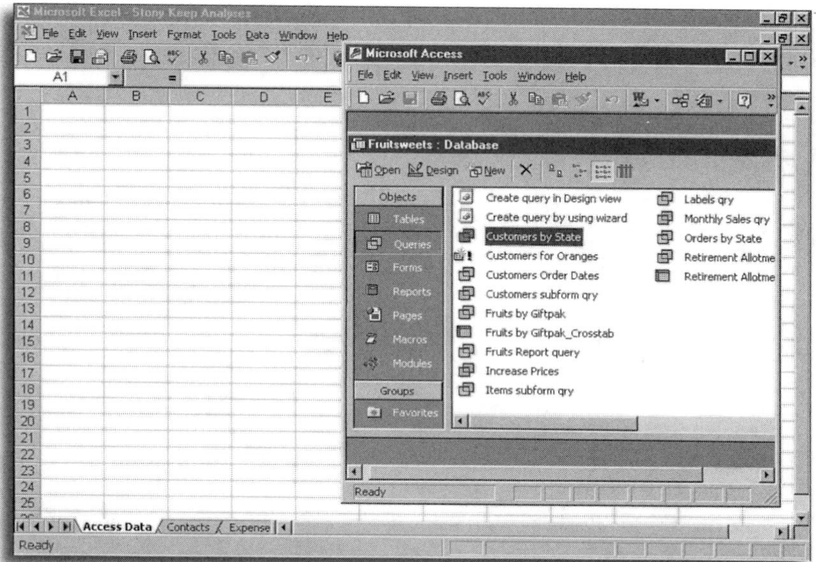

FIGURE 8.5
Resize the Access window so you can see the Excel window next to it.

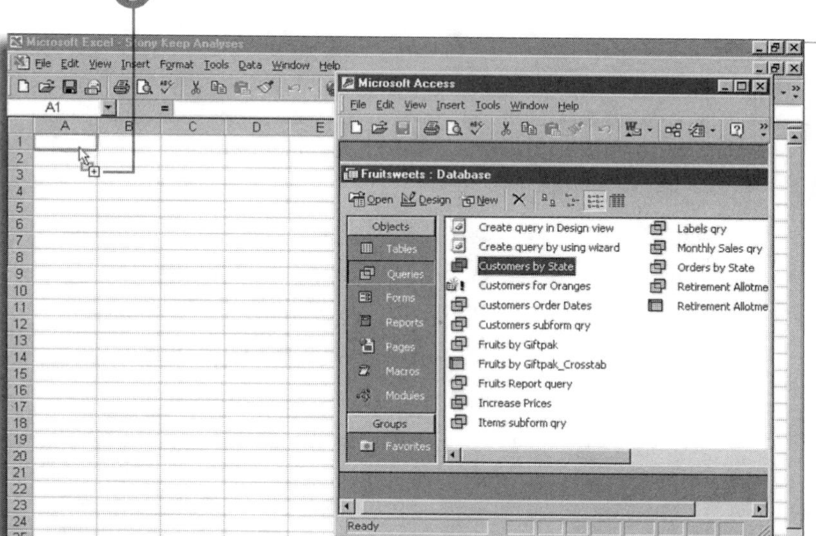

FIGURE 8.6
Drag a table or query from Access, and drop it in an Excel worksheet.

1 Drop the table or query name.

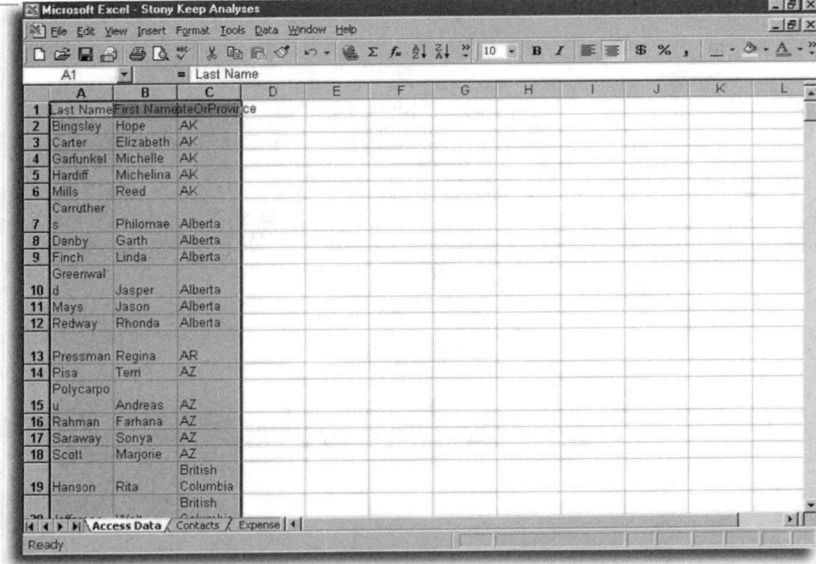

FIGURE 8.7
This is the fastest way to get Access data into Excel.

Sending Excel Data to Access

If you've been keeping a list in Excel, you can easily convert the Excel worksheet into an Access table, in either a new or existing Access database. From an Access database, you can create professional, easy-to-read reports out of the data (which you can't do in Excel).

Send Excel data to an Access table

1. Open the worksheet you want to send to Access, and click a cell within the list of data.
2. Open the **Data** menu, and click **Convert to MS Access**.

   The Convert to Microsoft Access dialog box appears.
3. If you want to create a new database with the Excel worksheet, leave the **New database** option selected. If you want to make the worksheet into a table in an existing database, click the **Existing database** option, and then click the **Browse** button to navigate to the existing database file and double-click the filename.

Do You Have Access?

For this procedure to work—for the **Convert to MS Access** command to appear on the **Data** menu—you must have Microsoft Access installed, and you must install Excel's AccessLinks add-in program. To install the add-in, click **Tools**, **Add-Ins**; then, mark the **AccessLinks** check box, and click **OK**.

Clean Up the Data First

To make this process easy, be sure there are no entries in the worksheet other than the table of data you want to convert to an Access table.

4. In the Convert to Microsoft Access dialog box, click **OK**.

   Access starts, an Access window opens, and the Import Spreadsheet Wizard (shown in Figure 8.8) guides you through the process of creating the Access table. Your worksheet column headings are the field names in the new Access table. If this part gets confusing, consult a good Access book, or the Access help files, for help.

   Your worksheet isn't affected except for the text box that tells you the list has been converted to Access; you can delete the text box by selecting its border and pressing Delete.

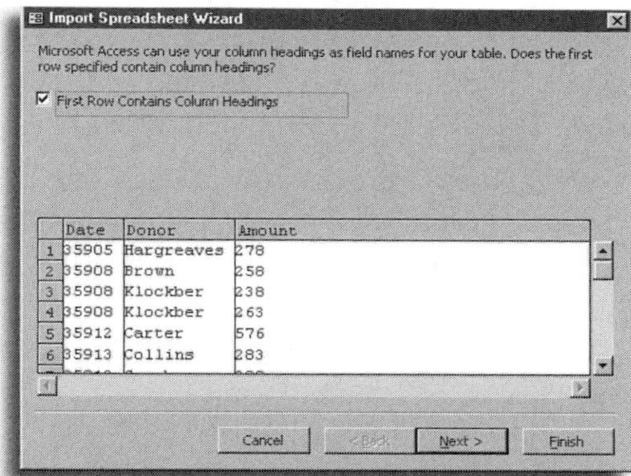

FIGURE 8.8
If you need to use Excel data in an Access database, converting the worksheet to an Access table is one of several ways to do it.

Importing a Text File

If a colleague has data you need in an obscure file format you can't open in Excel, you can get around that obstacle by asking your colleague to save the data as a text file and then opening the text file in Excel. To import a text file to Excel, use the following procedure:

Import a text file

1. On the Standard toolbar in Excel, click **Open**.
2. In the **Files of type** box, select **All Files (*.*)**.
3. Double-click the name of the text file.

   The Text Import Wizard starts (shown in Figure 8.9).

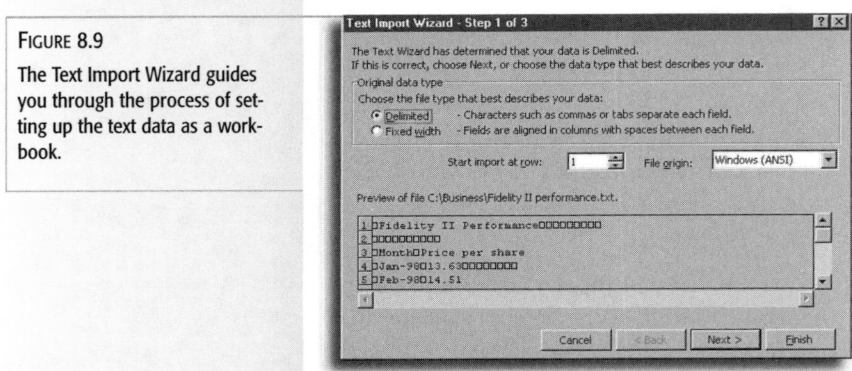

FIGURE 8.9

The Text Import Wizard guides you through the process of setting up the text data as a workbook.

4. In Step 1 of the Text Import Wizard, be sure the **Delimited** option button is selected and then click **Next**.
5. In Step 2 of the wizard (Figure 8.10), mark the **Tab** check box. If the data isn't parsed into neat columns in the **Data preview** window, mark other delimiters until you get good column separation. Then click **Next**.

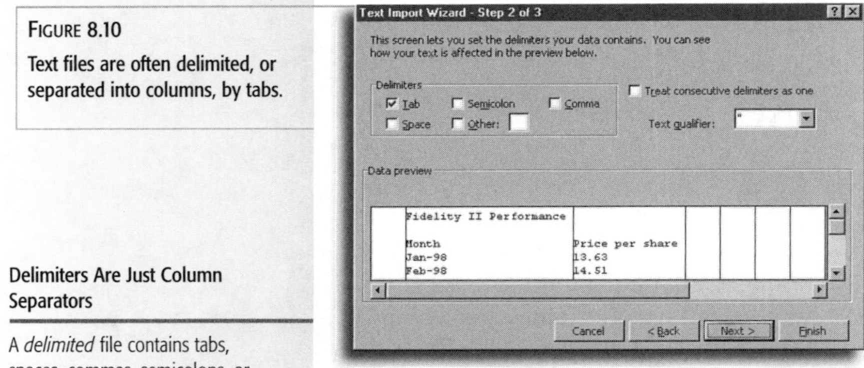

FIGURE 8.10

Text files are often delimited, or separated into columns, by tabs.

Delimiters Are Just Column Separators

A *delimited* file contains tabs, spaces, commas, semicolons, or some other consistent method of separating the data into columns of information. The Text Import Wizard is pretty good at guessing where the data should be divided, but you might need to do some adjusting to put everything into the right columns after the import process is finished.

6. In Step 3 (see Figure 8.11), you can set preliminary data formatting. Click the heading in the **Data preview** window for the column you want to format. If the column contains numbers, leave the formatting in the **Column data format** section set to **General**; if the column contains dates, select the **Date** option instead, and so on.

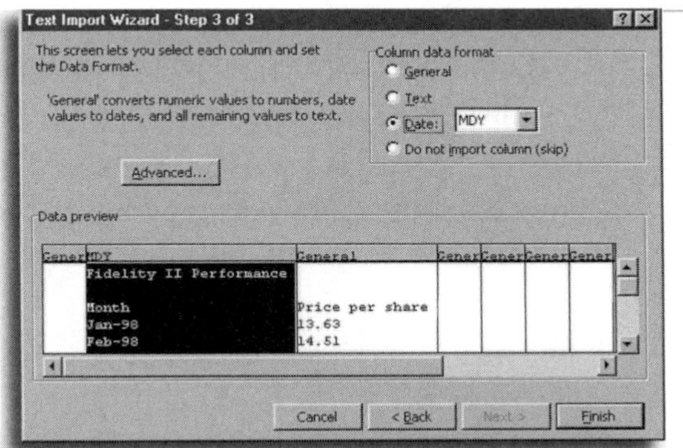

FIGURE 8.11
Leave columns of numbers as **General**, but set columns of dates to a **Date** format.

7. Click **Finish**.

The text file data is imported into your worksheet and placed properly into columns (as in Figure 8.12).

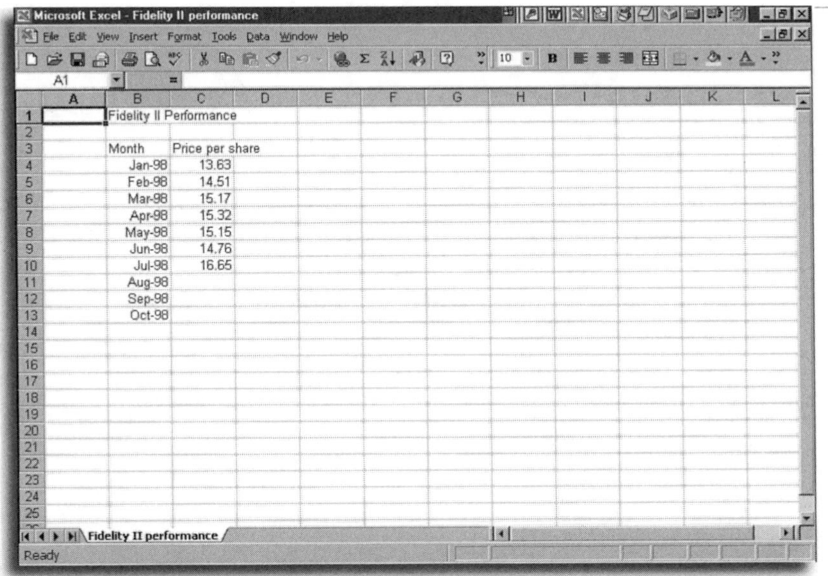

FIGURE 8.12
Now you can use the data in Excel.

When you save the workbook, the Save As dialog box appears and tries to save the data as a text file. If you just click **Save**, the file is saved as a text file, and every time you open the file, you have to use the Text Import Wizard again. To stop the endless Text Import Wizard cycle, you need to save the file as a workbook instead of a text file.

To save the data as a workbook, select **Microsoft Excel Workbook** in the **Save as type** box in the Save As dialog box.

CHAPTER

9

Editing Data

- Editing an entry to change a number, word, or formula
- Finding and replacing data
- Deleting data
- Undoing mistakes
- Moving or copying data to another location
- Inserting and deleting rows, columns, and cells
- Separating one column into two or more columns
- Adding extra worksheet information with comments
- Using AutoCorrect to do some of your work for you

Editing Cell Entries

No matter how you decide to get data into your worksheet, you can't get away from errors. Whether it's a typo, data that changed later, or a file you imported that had someone else's errors in it, inevitably something requires changing.

You can open a cell and edit data directly in the cell, or you can select a cell and edit its contents in the Formula bar.

Can't Open the Cell?

If you cannot open a cell for editing, the *in-cell editing* feature is probably not activated. Open **Tools**, select **Options**, and click the **Edit** tab; click the check box for **Edit directly in cell**, and click **OK**.

Replacing Cell Contents Is Quick

To completely replace the contents of a cell, select the cell and type the new contents, and then press Enter.

Edit data directly in the cell

1. Double-click the cell.
2. Edit the contents of the cell:
   - Use the Backspace key to erase characters to the left.
   - Use the Delete key to erase characters to the right.
   - Use the mouse to select characters and replace, delete, or format them individually (see Figure 9.1).
3. Press Enter.

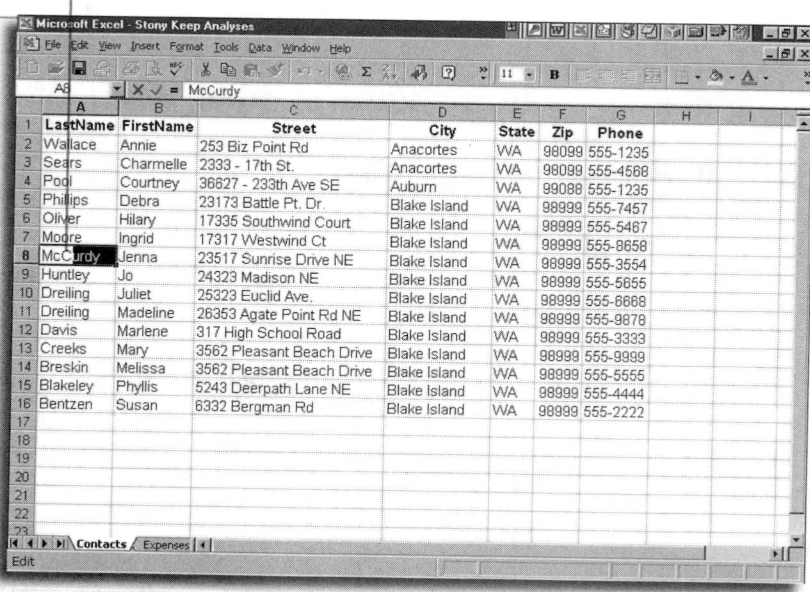

	A	B	C	D	E	F	G
1	LastName	FirstName	Street	City	State	Zip	Phone
2	Wallace	Annie	253 Biz Point Rd	Anacortes	WA	98099	555-1235
3	Sears	Charmelle	2333 - 17th St.	Anacortes	WA	98099	555-4568
4	Pool	Courtney	36827 - 233th Ave SE	Auburn	WA	99088	555-1235
5	Phillips	Debra	23173 Battle Pt. Dr.	Blake Island	WA	98999	555-7457
6	Oliver	Hilary	17335 Southwind Court	Blake Island	WA	98999	555-5467
7	Moore	Ingrid	17317 Westwind Ct	Blake Island	WA	98999	555-8658
8	McCurdy	Jenna	23517 Sunrise Drive NE	Blake Island	WA	98999	555-3554
9	Huntley	Jo	24323 Madison NE	Blake Island	WA	98999	555-5655
10	Dreiling	Juliet	25323 Euclid Ave.	Blake Island	WA	98999	555-6668
11	Dreiling	Madeline	26353 Agate Point Rd NE	Blake Island	WA	98999	555-9878
12	Davis	Marlene	317 High School Road	Blake Island	WA	98999	555-3333
13	Creeks	Mary	3562 Pleasant Beach Drive	Blake Island	WA	98999	555-9999
14	Breskin	Melissa	3562 Pleasant Beach Drive	Blake Island	WA	98999	555-5555
15	Blakeley	Phyllis	5243 Deerpath Lane NE	Blake Island	WA	98999	555-4444
16	Bentzen	Susan	6332 Bergman Rd	Blake Island	WA	98999	555-2222

FIGURE 9.1

You can edit a cell's contents directly in the cell.

 1 Select characters with the mouse.

Edit data in the Formula bar

1. Select the cell you want to edit.

   The cell's contents appear in the Formula bar (see Figure 9.2).

2. Click the Formula bar.

3. Use the following to edit the contents of the Formula bar:
   - Use the Backspace key to erase characters to the left.
   - Use the Delete key to erase characters to the right.
   - Use the mouse to select characters and replace, delete, or format them individually.

4. Press Enter.

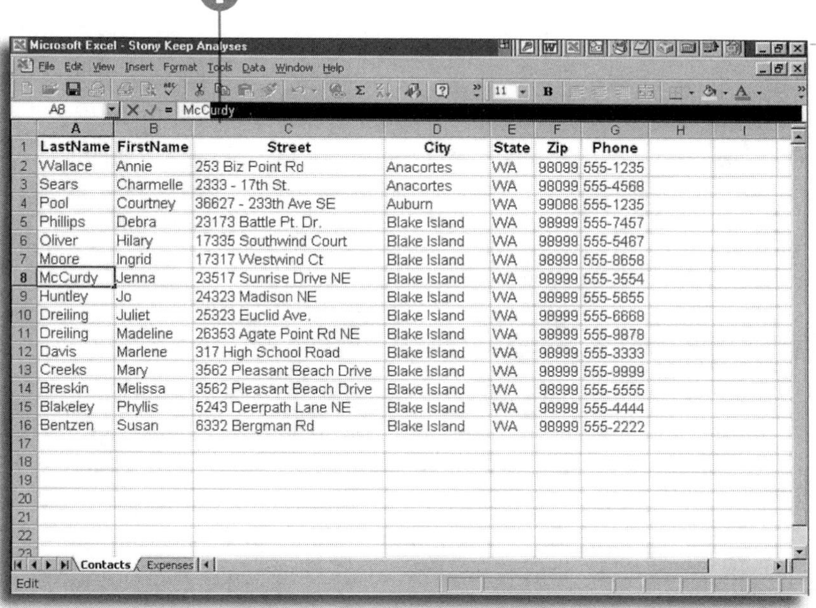

	LastName	FirstName	Street	City	State	Zip	Phone
2	Wallace	Annie	253 Biz Point Rd	Anacortes	WA	98099	555-1235
3	Sears	Charmelle	2333 - 17th St.	Anacortes	WA	98099	555-4568
4	Pool	Courtney	36627 - 233th Ave SE	Auburn	WA	99088	555-1235
5	Phillips	Debra	23173 Battle Pt. Dr.	Blake Island	WA	98999	555-7457
6	Oliver	Hilary	17335 Southwind Court	Blake Island	WA	98999	555-5467
7	Moore	Ingrid	17317 Westwind Ct	Blake Island	WA	98999	555-8658
8	McCurdy	Jenna	23517 Sunrise Drive NE	Blake Island	WA	98999	555-3554
9	Huntley	Jo	24323 Madison NE	Blake Island	WA	98999	555-5655
10	Dreiling	Juliet	25323 Euclid Ave.	Blake Island	WA	98999	555-6668
11	Dreiling	Madeline	26353 Agate Point Rd NE	Blake Island	WA	98999	555-9878
12	Davis	Marlene	317 High School Road	Blake Island	WA	98999	555-3333
13	Creeks	Mary	3562 Pleasant Beach Drive	Blake Island	WA	98999	555-9999
14	Breskin	Melissa	3562 Pleasant Beach Drive	Blake Island	WA	98999	555-5555
15	Blakeley	Phyllis	5243 Deerpath Lane NE	Blake Island	WA	98999	555-4444
16	Bentzen	Susan	6332 Bergman Rd	Blake Island	WA	98999	555-2222

FIGURE 9.2
You can also edit a cell in the Formula bar.

1 Formula bar

Changed Your Mind?

If you discover that you're changing the data in the wrong cells or the correction is turning into a hopeless mess, press Esc to return to the original cell contents and start over with your changes.

Sometimes menu and keyboard methods are faster than mouse methods. If you've been using Windows a while, for example, you may be used to pressing Ctrl+X to cut text to the Clipboard, and that may be faster for you than grabbing the mouse and finding the right button to click. Table 9.1 shows a quick list of editing methods you can use in Excel to edit and rearrange your data. These methods work in addition to those described throughout this chapter.

TABLE 9.1 **Quick methods for editing data**

Task	Shortcut Method	Menu Method
Cut the selection	Ctrl+X	Open the **Edit** menu and select **Cut**.
Copy the selection	Ctrl+C	Open the **Edit** menu and select **Copy**.
Paste the selection	Ctrl+V	Open the **Edit** menu and select **Paste**.
Remove cell contents		Right-click the cell or selected range, and click Clear Contents.
Delete selected rows/columns		Open the **Edit** menu and select **Delete**.
Undo the last change	Ctrl+Z	Open the **Edit** menu and select **Undo**. Note that the **Undo** option on the menu changes to show the last action you took that can be undone.
Redo your last undo	Ctrl+Y	Open the **Edit** menu and select **Redo**. Note that the **Redo** option on the menu changes to show the last undone action that can be redone.

Finding and Replacing Data

If you've entered a worksheet full of data correctly, but later learn that a word (perhaps someone's name) was misspelled, you can have Excel find and replace every instance of the misspelling.

You can also find or replace data (for example, cell references or names) in formulas. You can find, but *not* replace, data in comments. (See the later section "Adding Worksheet Comments" for details on using comments.)

Find specific data, such as a word or number

1. From **Edit**, choose **Find**.

   The Find dialog box appears (shown in Figure 9.3).

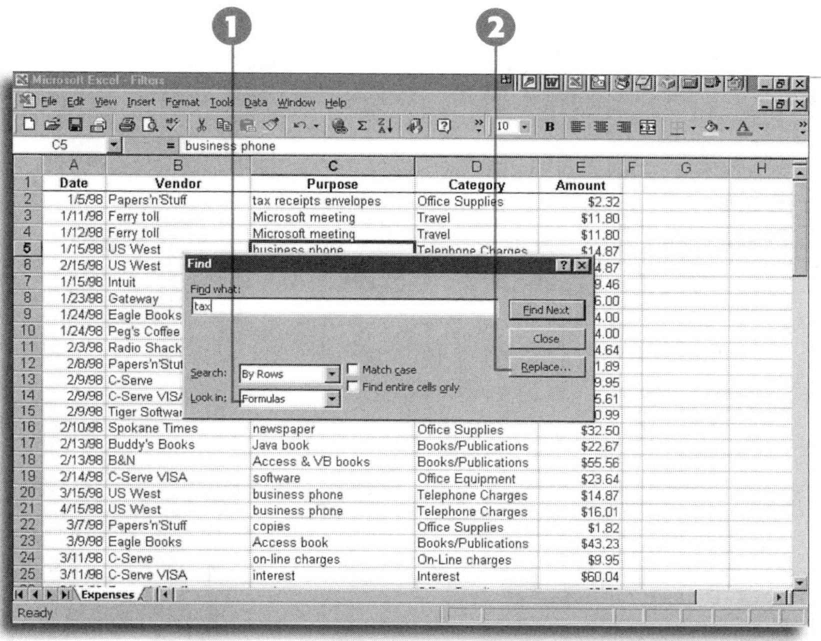

FIGURE 9.3
Use the Find dialog box to locate text strings, such as words, cell references, or values that are the results of formulas.

1. Select Formulas, Values, or Comments.

2. Switch to the Replace dialog box.

2. In the **Find what** box, type the text string you want to locate.
3. In the **Look in** box, select **Formulas**, **Values**, or **Comments**.
   - *Formulas*—Finds text strings entered in cells (such as the word `tax`) and formulas (such as `=subtotal+tax`).
   - *Values*—Finds text strings entered in cells and those displayed as the results of formulas.
   - *Comments*—Finds text strings in worksheet comments.
4. If capitalization counts (such as when you want to find `Tax` but not `tax`), click the **Match case** check box. To locate complete matches (such as `tax` but not `taxable`), click the **Find entire cells only** check box.
5. Click **Find Next**.

   Excel searches the worksheet and stops at the first instance of your text string. To find the next instance, click **Find Next** again.

If you want to replace the text string you've found, click the **Replace** button and follow the next procedure. If, on the other hand, you want to replace entries without finding each one first, follow the next procedure.

Replace one text string with another (For example, replace `expenses` **with** `expenditures`**)**

1. Open **Edit** and select **Replace**.

   The Replace dialog box appears, as shown in Figure 9.4. (The Replace dialog box also appears if you click the **Replace** button in the Find dialog box.)

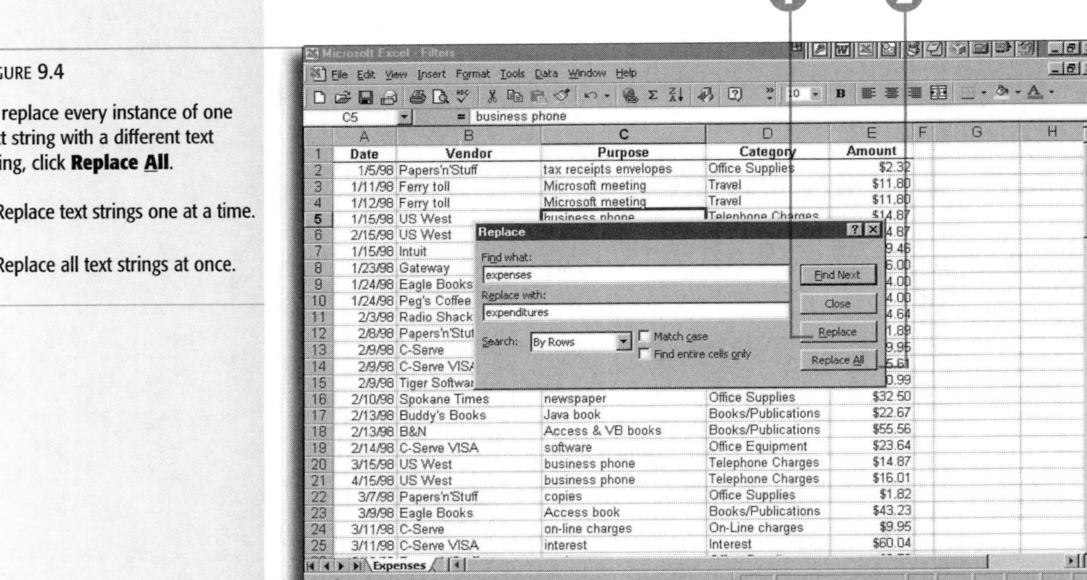

FIGURE 9.4

To replace every instance of one text string with a different text string, click **Replace All**.

1. Replace text strings one at a time.
2. Replace all text strings at once.

2. In the **Find what** box, type the characters you want to change.
3. In the **Replace with** box, type the new characters.

If you don't want to replace all instances of the text string, you can find and replace individual occurrences, or you can replace all the occurrences at once.

- To find and replace individual occurrences, click **Find Next** until you locate an occurrence that you want to replace and then click **Replace**.
- To replace all occurrences, click **Replace All**.

Deleting Data

When you need to remove data from a worksheet (for example, if you've been practicing entering data or typing formulas or you change your mind about a table you entered), you can quickly delete the contents of cells. Deleting cell contents doesn't remove formatting, however, so you find your cell shading and borders still in place after the cell contents are gone.

Completely remove the contents of a cell or range

1. Select the cell or select the range.
2. Press Delete.

Clean It All Off

To erase everything in a cell or range, including data, formatting, and comments, select the range you want to erase, open the **Edit** menu, and select **Clear**, **All**.

SEE ALSO

➤ *To learn about inserting and deleting cells, see page 148.*

Undoing Mistakes

Undo and redo are frustration solvers. Sometimes, I do specific things in a worksheet and then want to undo everything I just did. Sometimes, I click the wrong spot on a worksheet, something completely unintended happens, and I don't know how I did it or how to fix it. The easy way out is to have Excel *undo* what you did by clicking the Undo button. If, moreover, you undo something and then change your mind about having undone it, you can *redo* what you undid by clicking the Redo button.

Undo what you did

1. To undo the last single thing you did, click the **Undo** button on the Standard toolbar.
2. To undo the last several things you did, click the down arrow on the side of the Undo button and then select the number of actions you want to undo (see Figure 9.5).

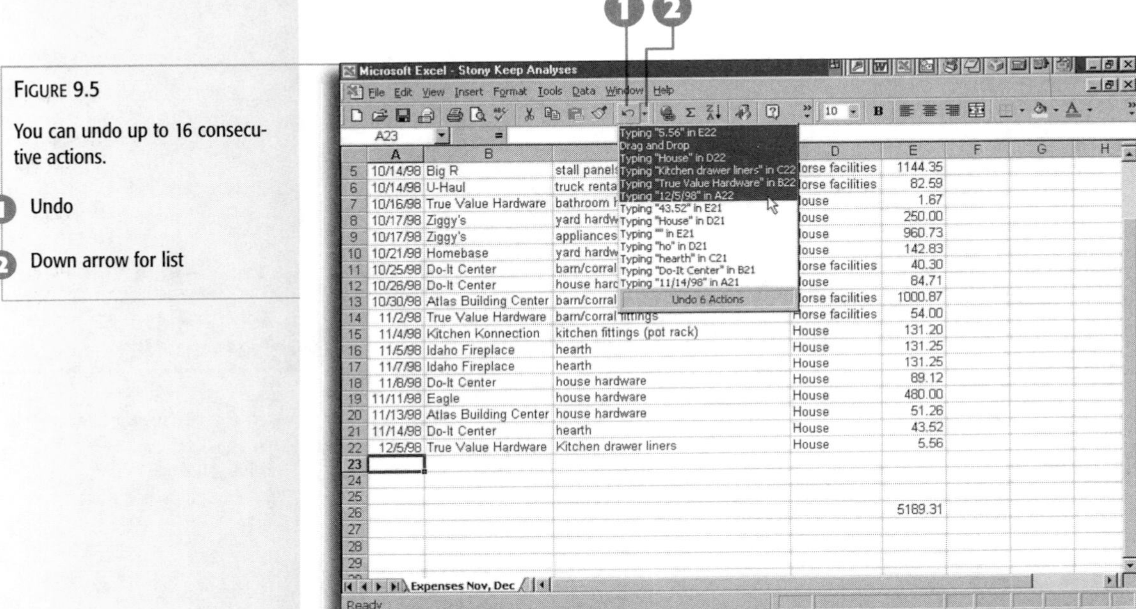

FIGURE 9.5

You can undo up to 16 consecutive actions.

1. Undo
2. Down arrow for list

Redo what you undid

1. To redo the last single thing you undid, click the **Redo** button on the Standard toolbar.
2. To redo the last several things you undid, click the down arrow on the side of the Redo button, and select the number of undone actions you want to redo.

   Only actions you've undone appear on the Redo list.

Moving and Copying Cells on the Same Worksheet

The easiest way to move or copy cell contents to new locations on a worksheet is to drag the cells and drop them where you want them.

Can't Drag and Drop?

If you cannot drag and drop cells, *drag-and-drop cell editing* is probably turned off. Open **Tools**, select **Options**, click the **Edit** tab, click the check box for **Allow cell drag and drop**, and click **OK**.

Do the Cells Really Move?

Although you often hear or read the phrase "move or copy cells," what you're really doing is moving or copying the contents of the cells, not the cells themselves.

Move cells by dragging them to another location

1. Select the cell or range of cells you want to move.
2. Position the mouse pointer on one of the cell or range borders (see Figure 9.6).

   When the mouse pointer is over a border, it becomes an arrow.

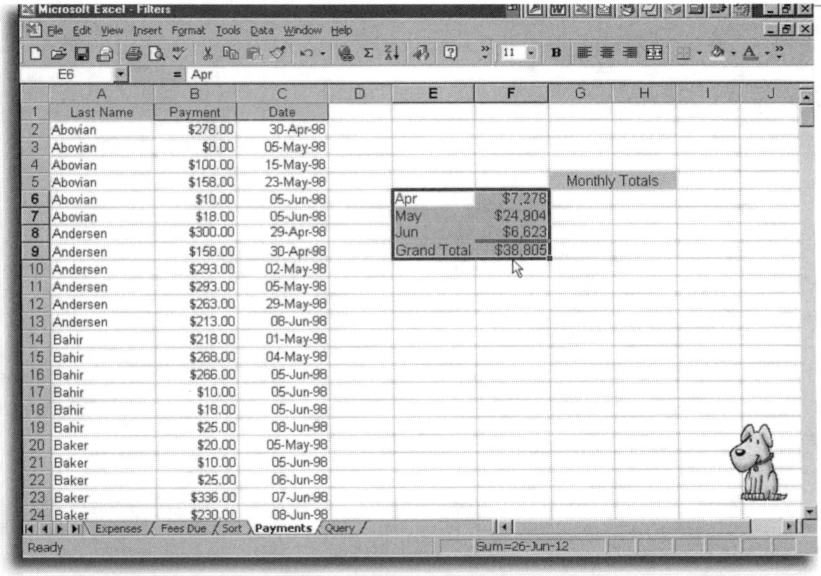

FIGURE 9.6

Position the mouse pointer on a border so that it becomes an arrow.

3. Drag the border to a new location.
4. When the cell or range border is positioned (see Figure 9.7), drop the cells by releasing the mouse button.

Where Do These Cells Drop?

When you drag cells, a *range tip* indicates exactly where you have positioned them.

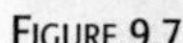

FIGURE 9.7

A border shadow shows where you're moving the range.

1 Range tip

Try the Right Mouse Button for More Options

If you drag a range with the right mouse button, you can select a **Move** or **Copy** command from a shortcut menu after you drop the range.

Copy cells by dragging them to another location

1. Select the cell or range of cells you want to copy.
2. Position the mouse pointer on one of the cell or range borders (see Figure 9.8).

   When the mouse pointer is over a border, it becomes an arrow.
3. Drag the border to a new location.
4. When the cell or range border is positioned, press and hold the Ctrl key and then drop the cells by releasing the mouse button.

   When you press Ctrl while dragging cells to copy them, a small plus symbol next to the mouse pointer indicates that you're dragging a copy (see Figure 9.9).
5. After you drop a copy of the range, release the Ctrl key.

Microsoft Excel - Filters

A1 = Last Name

	A	B	C
1	Last Name	Payment	Date
2	Abovian	$278.00	30-Apr-98
3	Abovian	$0.00	05-May-98
4	Abovian	$100.00	15-May-98
5	Abovian	$158.00	23-May-98
6	Abovian	$10.00	05-Jun-98
7	Abovian	$18.00	05-Jun-98
8	Andersen	$300.00	29-Apr-98
9	Andersen	$158.00	30-Apr-98
10	Andersen	$293.00	02-May-98
11	Andersen	$293.00	05-May-98
12	Andersen	$263.00	29-May-98
13	Andersen	$213.00	08-Jun-98
14	Bahir	$218.00	01-May-98
15	Bahir	$268.00	04-May-98
16	Bahir	$266.00	05-Jun-98
17	Bahir	$10.00	05-Jun-98
18	Bahir	$18.00	05-Jun-98
19	Bahir	$25.00	08-Jun-98
20	Baker	$20.00	05-May-98
21	Baker	$10.00	05-Jun-98
22	Baker	$25.00	06-Jun-98
23	Baker	$336.00	07-Jun-98
24	Baker	$230.00	08-Jun-98

Monthly Totals	
Apr	$7,278
May	$24,904
Jun	$6,623
Grand To	$38,805

Expenses / Fees Due / Sort / Payments / Query

Ready

FIGURE 9.8

Position the mouse pointer on a border so that it becomes an arrow.

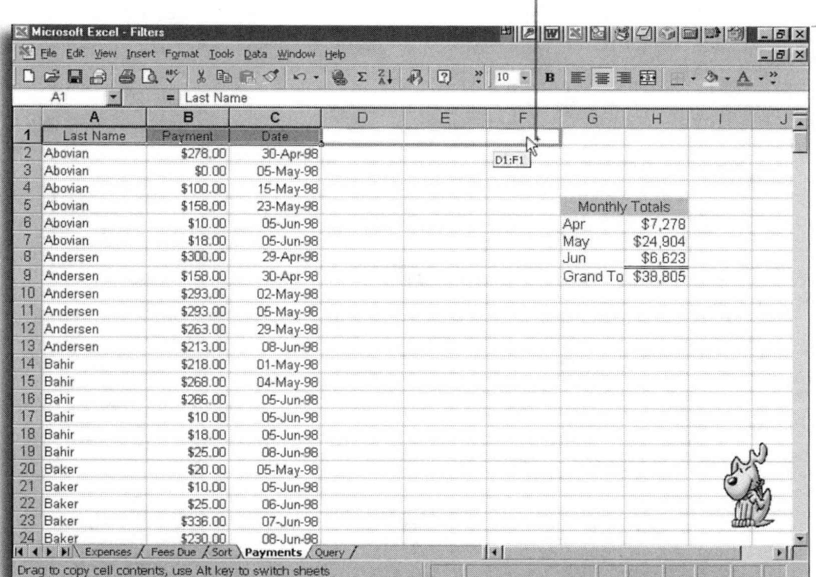

FIGURE 9.9

A small plus symbol indicates that you're copying, instead of moving, cells.

1 Plus symbol

Moving and Copying Cells to a Different Worksheet

Cutting and pasting cells (or copying and pasting) is an alternative to dragging and dropping, and it is the easier method if you're moving or copying the cells to another worksheet (or another workbook).

In Excel 2000, you can move or copy several items at a time. Each item you cut or copy is saved to a temporary storage area called the Office Clipboard, and the new Clipboard can hold up to 12 items at once (when you cut or copy a thirteenth item, you lose the first item you cut or copied). From the Office Clipboard toolbar, you can paste any or all of the items as often as you like.

Move cells to a different worksheet

1. Select the cells you want to move.
2. On the toolbar, click **Cut**.

   The cells you cut are surrounded by a moving border.
3. On the worksheet on which you want to paste the cells, select the cell on which you want to paste the upper-left corner of the range.
4. On the toolbar, click **Paste**.

   The cells move from their previous location to wherever you pasted them. If the Office Clipboard toolbar appears, see the step by step exercise "Paste with the Office Clipboard toolbar."

Copy cells to a different worksheet

1. Select the cells you want to copy.
2. On the toolbar, click **Copy**.
3. On the worksheet on which you want to paste the cells, select the cell on which you want to paste the upper-left corner of the range.
4. On the toolbar, click **Paste**.

   You can paste the copied cells as often as you like. If the Office Clipboard toolbar appears, see the step by step exercise "Paste with the Office Clipboard toolbar."

Special Drag-and-Drop Techniques

Want to drop selected cells *between* existing cells on the worksheet? If you're copying the selection, hold down Shift+Ctrl as you drag the cells. Moving the cells? Hold down Shift as you drag. The edges of the existing cells are shaded, indicating where the new cells are to be inserted. Going to a different worksheet? Hold down the Alt key and drag the selection over the sheet tab.

The Status Bar Tells Me to Press Enter

If you press Enter to paste the selection, you only get one paste, and the Windows Clipboard is cleared. If, therefore, you want to paste repeatedly, use a method other than pressing Enter.

Paste with the Office Clipboard toolbar

1. Click in the cell where you want to paste a cut or copied item.
2. Right-click any toolbar, then click **Clipboard**.

   The Office Clipboard toolbar appears (see Figure 9.10).
3. Point to each icon in the toolbar to identify the item you want; when you point to an icon, the first several characters of the item appear in a ScreenTip.
4. Click the icon you want to paste:
   - Click the **Paste All** button to paste all the items, one right after the other.
   - Click the **Clear Clipboard** button to clear all cut or copied items from the Clipboard.
   - Click the Office Clipboard toolbar's **X** close box to close it. (All items will remain in the Office Clipboard.)

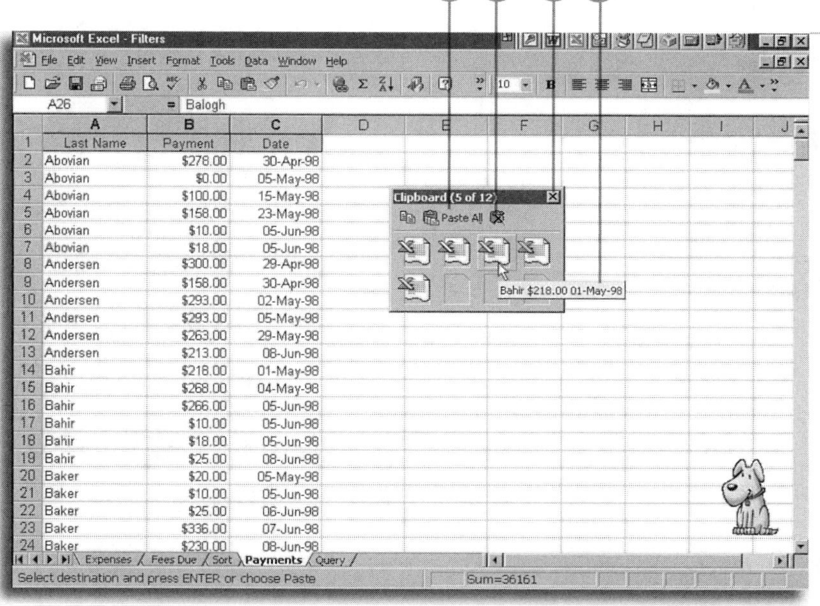

FIGURE 9.10

The Office Clipboard toolbar.

1. Identifying ScreenTip
2. Paste All
3. Clear Clipboard
4. Close the toolbar.

Inserting and Deleting Rows and Columns

Sometimes, you have entire rows or columns of information in a worksheet that you want to remove, but if you only delete the contents of the cells, you have blank rows or columns in the middle of a table. What you really need to do is delete the entire row or column from the worksheet and leave no empty spaces. At other times, you need to insert new rows or columns into a table because you need to add new data into the middle of an existing layout. Use the following procedures to delete or insert rows and columns.

Delete rows or columns

1. Click the *row header* (the row number) or the *column header* (the column letter) to select the entire row or column, as shown in Figure 9.11.

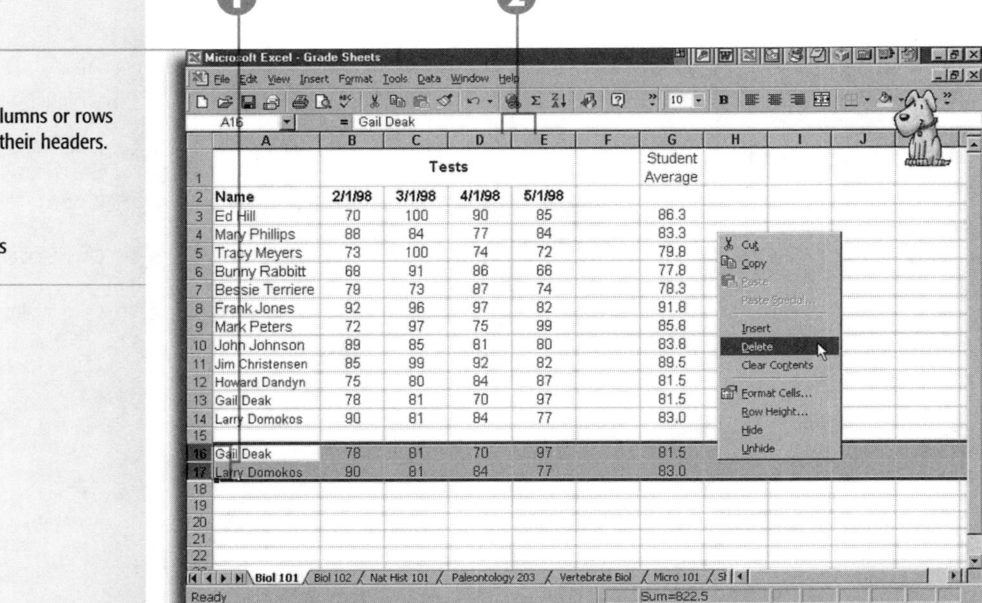

FIGURE 9.11

Select multiple columns or rows by dragging over their headers.

1 Row headers

2 Column headers

2. Right-click in the selection and then click **Delete** on the shortcut menu.

   The selected rows or columns disappear, and the remaining rows or columns are renumbered (or relettered).

Insert rows or columns

1. Click the row header below or the column header to the right of where you want to insert rows or columns.
2. Right-click in the selection and then open **Insert** on the shortcut menu.

   Rows or columns are inserted (see Figure 9.12), and the original rows or columns are renumbered (or relettered).

If you find that a formula gives incorrect results after you insert or delete rows or columns, you might need to correct the formula's cell reference types.

SEE ALSO

➤ *To learn more about cell reference types, see page 162.*

The Shrinking Worksheet

Deleting rows and columns won't reduce the size of your worksheet; you always have 256 columns and 65,536 rows. When you delete a row or column, Excel adds a new row at the bottom or a new column at the right side of the worksheet and changes the row numbers and column letters so that they remain consecutive.

All formulas that rely on cell references are updated with their new row and column references within the workbook. If, however, you have linked formulas in another workbook and that workbook is closed when you delete the rows or columns, you must relink those linked formulas to their new cell references the next time you open that other workbook.

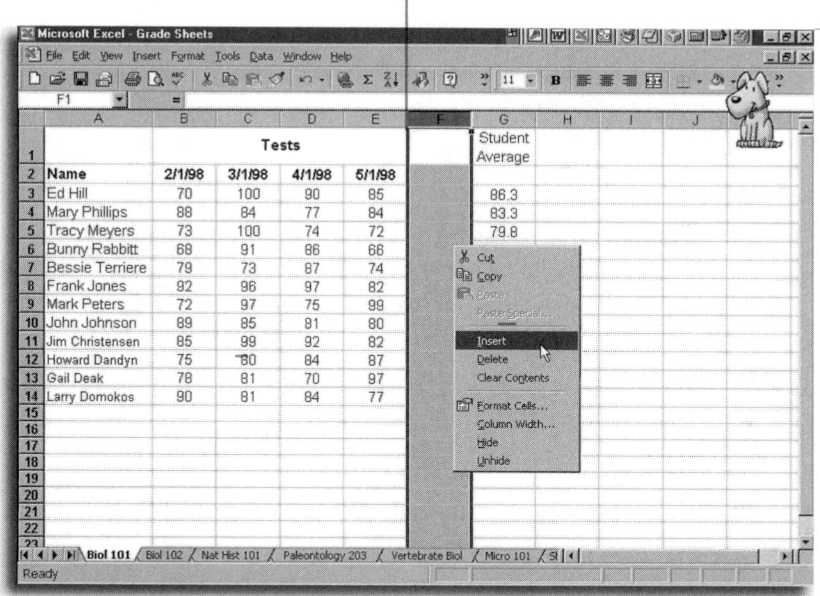

FIGURE 9.12

To insert more than one row or column, select a number of rows or columns equal to the number of rows or columns you want to insert.

1 Columns are inserted here.

Sometimes This Is Faster

Alternatively, click a cell, and then open the **Insert** menu and choose either **Rows** or **Columns**.

Inserting and Deleting Cells

If you need to delete or insert individual cells into a table, you can delete existing cells or insert new ones. (If the table of data is large, this method can be faster than moving a range of data to make room for new data or fill in for deleted data.) The surrounding cells in the worksheet move in the direction you specify to make room or fill in for cells you insert or delete. This method is really useful if you have two tables of data on a worksheet, and inserting or deleting rows or columns in one table would disrupt the other table. You can insert or delete cells in one table without affecting the other table.

When you insert new cells, the surrounding cells move down or to the right to make room, depending on what you choose in the Insert dialog box. When you delete cells, the surrounding cells move up or left, depending on what you choose in the Delete dialog box. (This description makes sense after you've tried it on a worksheet.)

Insert cells

1. Select the cells that are to be moved below or right of where you want to insert the cells.

   The cells you select will be moved to make room for an equal number of new cells.

2. Right-click the selected cells and then click **Insert**.

   The Insert dialog box appears (see Figure 9.13).

3. Click the **Shift cells right** option to move your selected cells to the right to make room for the new cells. Click the **Shift cells down** option to move your selected cells down to make room for the new cells.

4. Click **OK**.

Delete cells

1. Select the cells that you want to delete.

2. Right-click the selected cells and then click **Delete**.

   The Delete dialog box appears (see Figure 9.14).

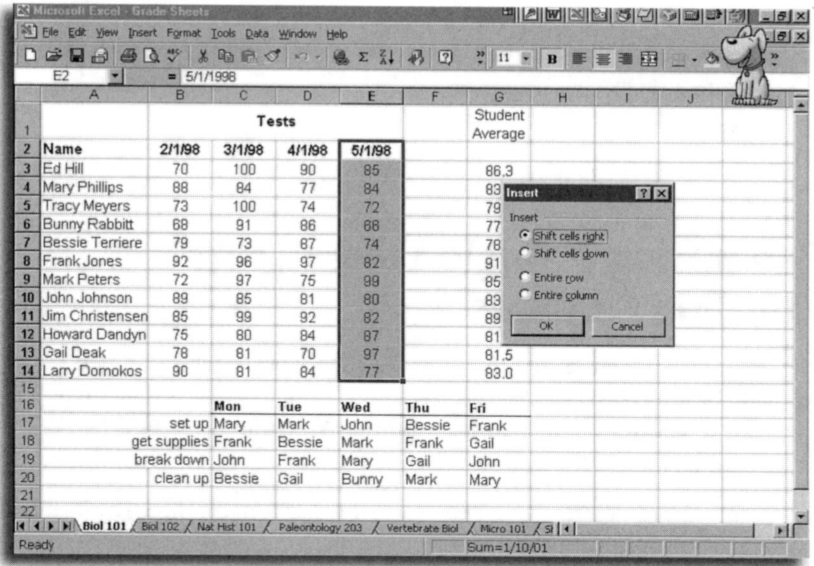

FIGURE 9.13
Insert cells into one table without affecting other tables on the worksheet.

3. Click the **Shift cells <u>l</u>eft** option to fill in the space by moving existing cells to the left. Click the **Shift cells <u>u</u>p** option to fill in the space by moving existing cells up.
4. Click **OK**.

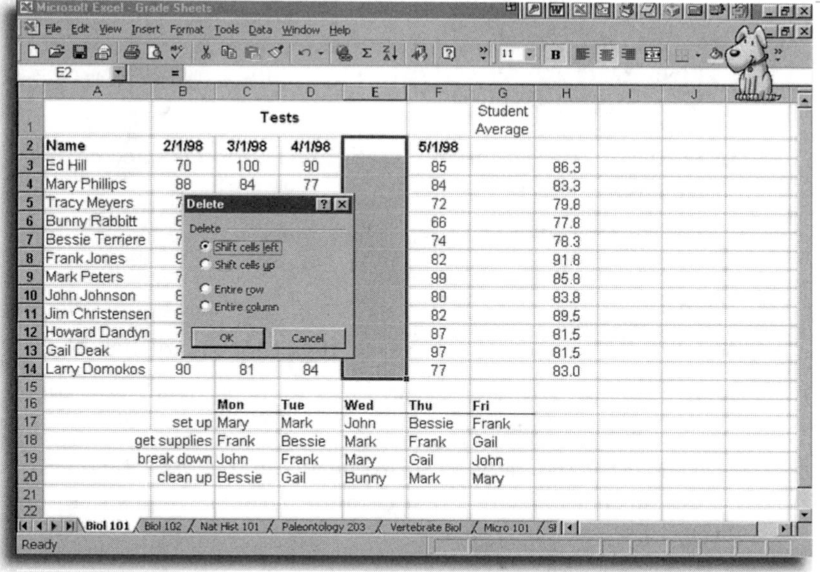

FIGURE 9.14
Delete cells from one table without affecting other tables on the worksheet.

If you find that a formula gives incorrect results after you insert or delete cells, you might need to correct the formula's cell reference types.

SEE ALSO

➤ *To learn more about cell reference types, see page 162.*

Separating a Single Column into Multiple Columns

Often, I've entered a list of names in a worksheet and typed both first and last names in the same cell. Later, I realize that I need to separate the full-name column into a column for first names and a column for last names.

Instead of deleting and retyping all the last names, cell-by-cell, Excel can separate, or *parse*, each full-name cell into two separate name cells for me. If you need to do something similar, use the following procedure.

Parse cell contents

1. Select the cells you want to parse.

   Leave an empty column on the right of the column you're parsing so that the new column you're going to create has somewhere to be pasted.

2. Open **Data** and select **Text to Columns**.

   The Convert Text to Columns Wizard starts.

3. In Step 1 of 3, be sure the **Delimited** option is selected and click **Next** (see Figure 9.15).

   In Step 2 of 3, you choose a delimiter. In a case like this, the names are separated by a space character, so the delimiter is a space.

4. Click the **Space** check box (see Figure 9.16) and click **Next**.

5. In Step 3 of 3, you don't need to set any particular data format, so click **Finish**.

   Your list is separated into two neat columns (like the one in Figure 9.17) with a new column started at each space character.

Do I Need to Clear the Tab Check Box?

You can clear the **Tab** check box if you want to, but it won't matter if you have no tab characters in your list.

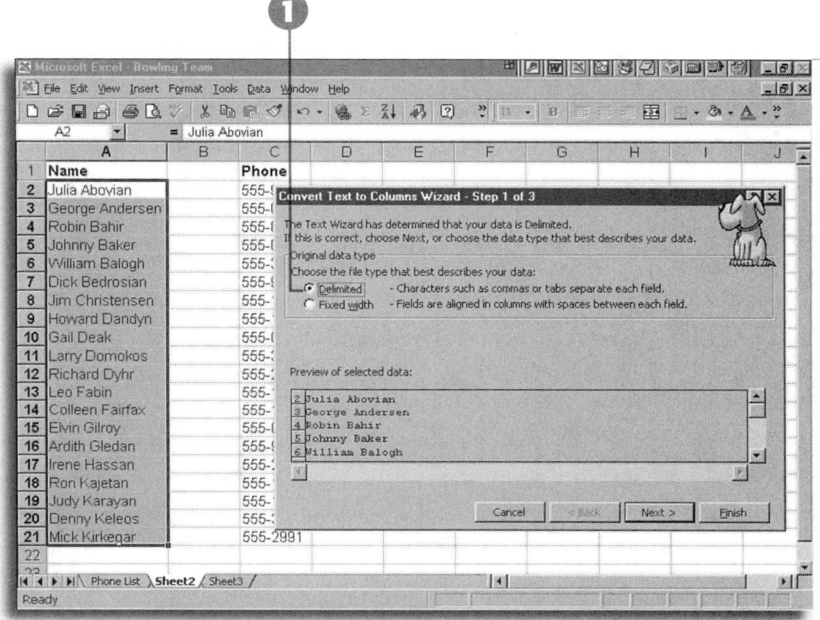

FIGURE 9.15
Let the Convert Text to Columns Wizard separate your column into separate columns.

1 Delimited option

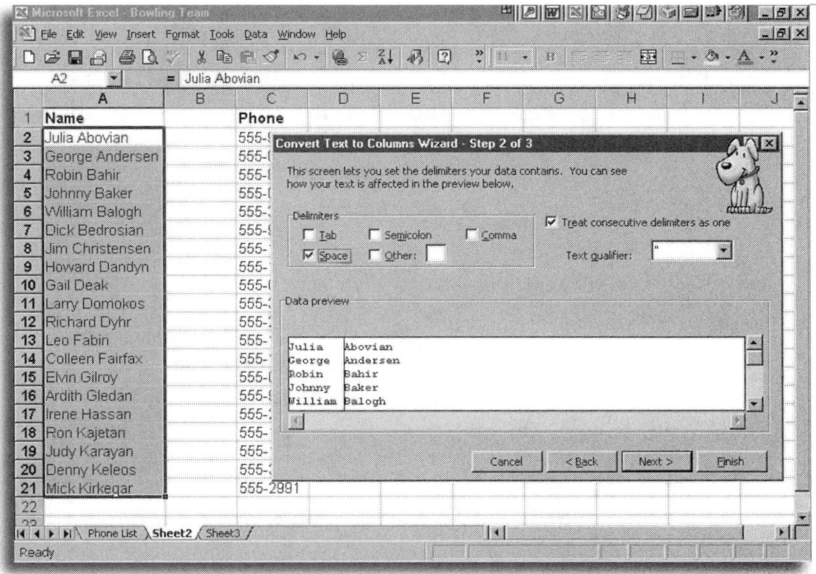

FIGURE 9.16
You know you've selected the correct delimiter when the Data preview window shows your list separated into columns.

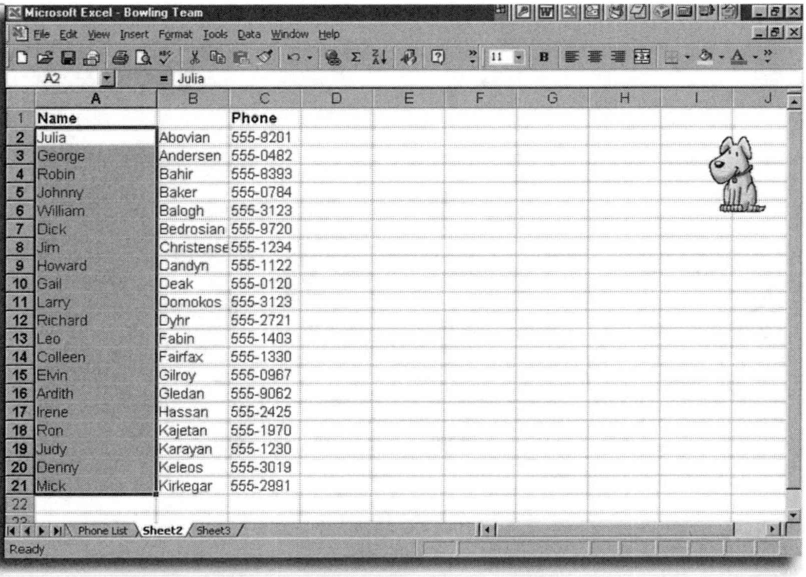

FIGURE 9.17
The wizard pastes the newly separated column of data into the column that you left empty.

I Got Three Columns Instead of Two

A cell that has two spaces in it (for example, Mary A. Jones) is separated into three columns. You can fix those cells with individual cell editing.

Adding Worksheet Comments

The meaning of information in a worksheet is not always obvious to someone who didn't create the worksheet, or to the worksheet's creator a year or three later. If you want to add extra information about data in the worksheet (perhaps an explanation of the formula or the name of the contact who gave you the information), you can add a *comment* that floats on top of the worksheet rather than taking up a cell in the worksheet. Comments also help to prevent inaccurate data entry by adding extra on-the-spot instructions for data entry.

A small, red triangle in the upper-right corner of the cell indicates a comment. When you point to a cell that has a comment indicator, its comment appears. Use the following procedures to add, edit, and delete comments:

Add extra information with a comment

1. Right-click the cell to which you want to add the comment.
2. Click **Insert Comment**.

A new comment frame appears on the worksheet, with your computer's user name filled in (as shown in Figure 9.18). You can select and delete the user name; format the font, point size, and so on for the comment text; and change the size and shape of the comment by dragging resizing handles.

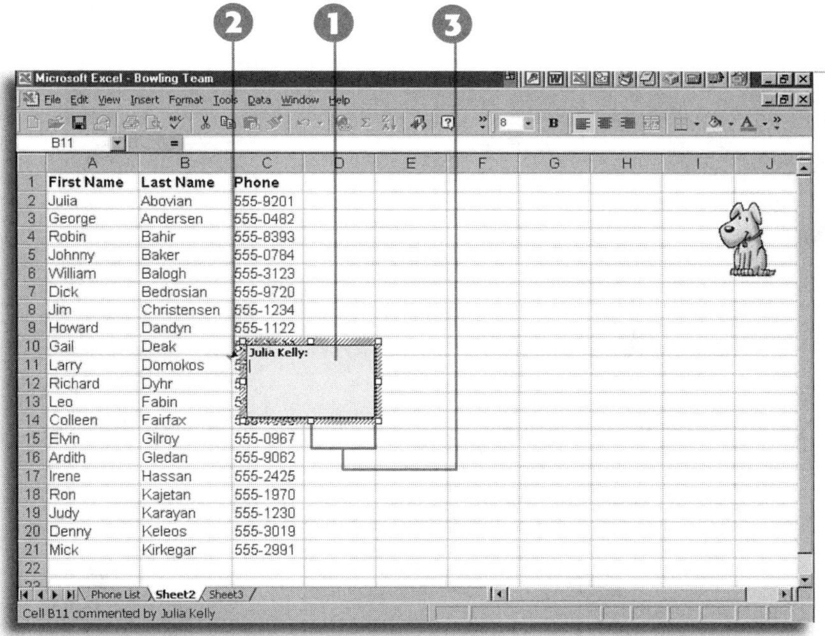

FIGURE 9.18
You can select and delete the user name if you want to.

1 New comment

2 Comment indicator

3 Resizing handles

3. Type your comment.
4. Click another cell on the worksheet.

   Your finished comment closes. To see the comment, position the mouse pointer over the cell, as in Figure 9.19.

Edit a comment

1. Right-click the cell with the comment.
2. Click **Edit Comment**.

   The comment opens with a hatched border and resizing handles, like a new comment.
3. Edit the comment. If desired, drag resizing handles to change the shape or size of the comment.

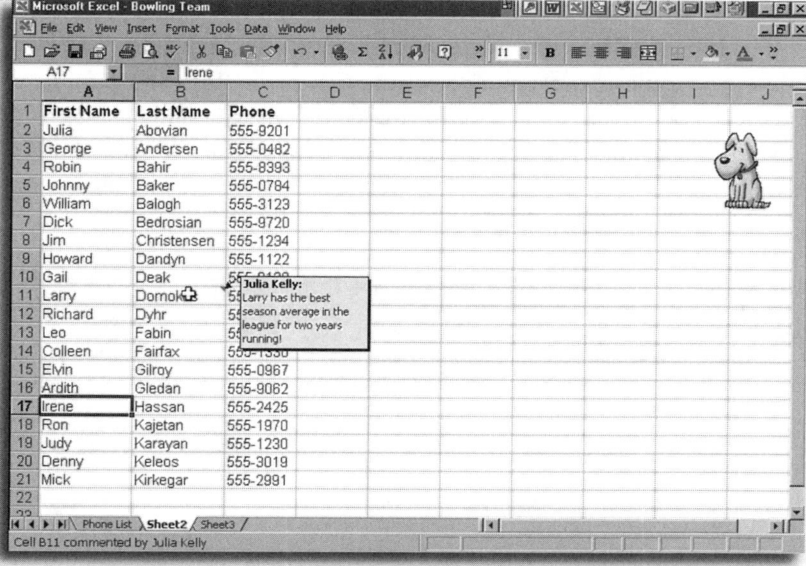

FIGURE 9.19

Comments are a good way to add extra information to a table without interfering with the table layout.

4. When the comment is complete, click another cell in the worksheet.

   Your finished comment closes.

Delete a comment

1. Right-click the cell with the comment.
2. Click **Delete Comment**.

   The comment is deleted.

Using AutoCorrect

AutoCorrect corrects your spelling as you type, which prevents a great many errors before anyone catches them. It recognizes many common misspellings, such as *teh* (*the*) and *adn* (*and*), and corrects them before you notice the misspelling.

You can personalize AutoCorrect by adding your own personal common misspellings to AutoCorrect's list (I tend to type *tabel* for *table*), and you can make AutoCorrect do a lot of repetitive typing for you. For example, if your job requires you to type *Lake City High School Alumni* often, you can make this an

AutoCorrect task so that when you type the acronym **lch**, AutoCorrect replaces it with the entire five words.

Make AutoCorrect help do your work

1. Open **Tools** and select **AutoCorrect**.

   The AutoCorrect dialog box appears (shown in Figure 9.20).

2. In the **Replace** box, type what you'll type in the worksheet (either a misspelling or an acronym you want replaced).
3. In the **With** box, type what AutoCorrect is to enter in place of your misspelling or acronym.
4. Click **OK**.

Delete an AutoCorrect Entry

To delete an AutoCorrect entry, select the entry in the AutoCorrect dialog box, click **Delete** and then click **OK**.

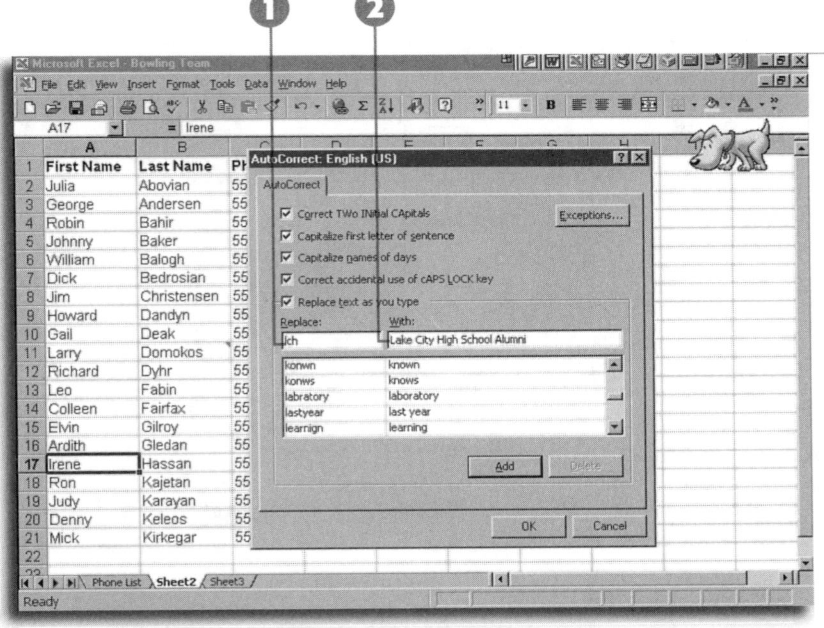

FIGURE 9.20

AutoCorrect can make even the sloppiest typist more efficient.

1 What you type

2 What AutoCorrect enters

Undo an AutoCorrect

If occasionally you don't want AutoCorrect to correct a word or acronym you've typed, press Ctrl+Z immediately after AutoCorrect corrects the spelling. The AutoCorrect action is undone and your original typing remains unchanged. This works when you are still typing in the cell and AutoCorrect corrects your spelling when you type a space; however, if you've pressed Enter before pressing Ctrl+Z, the whole cell entry is undone and erased.

Letting Excel Check Your Spelling

Adding spelling corrections to the AutoCorrect list works well for words you know you consistently misspell, but when you aren't aware that a word is misspelled, or flying fingers on the keyboard inadvertently misspell a word that's not in the

AutoCorrect list, Excel can find those errors by checking your spelling for you.

Use the Spelling Checker

1. Click any cell in the worksheet.

   To check the entire worksheet, click a single cell. To check a specific set of cells, select those cells.

2. On the Standard toolbar, click the **Spelling** button.

3. When the Spelling Checker finds a word that's not in its dictionary, you'll see a dialog box like the one shown in Figure 9.21.

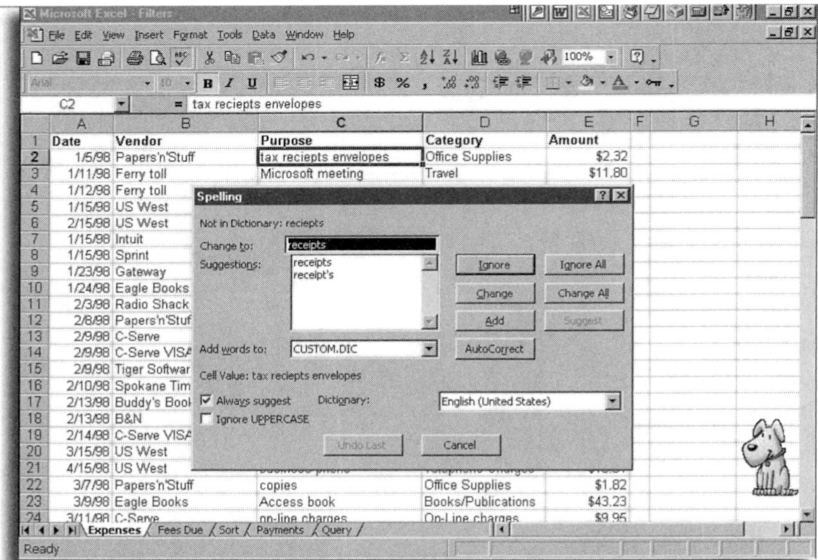

FIGURE 9.21
Excel thinks this word is misspelled.

4. Suggestions for spelling are listed in the **Change to** and **Suggestions** boxes.

   - If the suggestion in the **Change to** box is the spelling you want, click **Change** to change the word in the selected cell; click **Change All** to change every instance of the misspelling in the worksheet.
   - If the spelling you want is shown in the **Suggestions** list, click it, then click **Change** to change the word in

Sheet Tab Names Are Not Checked

You're on your own for sheet tab names, because the Spelling Checker doesn't check them. This can be embarrassing if the header for the printed worksheet is the worksheet name, so check your sheet tabs visually for proper spelling.

the selected cell; click **Change All** to change every instance of the misspelling in the worksheet.

- If the word is correctly spelled but Excel doesn't recognize it, and you plan to use it again, click **Add** to add it to the Office 2000 dictionary so it won't go unrecognized in the future. Examples of words you want to add to your Office 2000 dictionary are personal names, brand names, and industry-specific terms.
- If the word is abbreviated or otherwise oddly spelled, you may want it spelled that way in *this* worksheet, but don't want to add it to the dictionary. Click **Ignore** to ignore this one instance, or **Ignore All** to ignore every instance of the spelling in this worksheet.
- If the word is misspelled but the correct spelling isn't in the **Suggestions** list, type the correct spelling in the **Change to** box, then click **Change**. When you're asked if you really want to change the spelling, click **Yes**. The new spelling is accepted throughout this worksheet, but not added to the dictionary.
- If the word is misspelled but the correct spelling isn't in the **Suggestions** list, type the correct spelling in the **Change to** box, then click **Add**. The new spelling is added to the dictionary.
- If the word is misspelled, and you want to add the misspelling to your AutoCorrect list so it's automatically corrected as you type, be sure the correct spelling is shown in the **Change to** box, then click **AutoCorrect**.

Where's the Dictionary?

The default Office 2000 dictionary is the file named CUSTOM.DIC, shown in the **Add words to** box in the Spelling dialog box. If you accidentally add a misspelled word to the dictionary, you can open its file (`in C:\Windows\Application Data\Microsoft\Proof`) and delete the word.

CHAPTER

10

Simple Calculations

- Calculating without using formulas
- Writing simple formulas
- Using cell references
- Copying formulas
- Linking workbooks with formulas
- Editing formulas
- Auditing formulas

Can't Find the Status Bar?

If your status bar is missing, open the **Tools** menu, and click **Options**. On the **View** tab, click the **Status bar** check box; then, click **OK**.

I Don't See My AutoCalculate Box

AutoCalculate appears in the status bar only when a function is selected *and* calculable cells are selected. (For example, if the selected function is SUM but no cells with numbers are selected, AutoCalculate is hidden.)

Simple Calculations, Quick Answers

Calculations are why Excel exists. To perform calculations in a worksheet, you write formulas; to perform complex calculations, you use functions in your formulas. (*Functions* are built-in mathematical equations that save you time and effort.)

This section contains lots of procedures that make simple calculations easier and more useful, and you don't have to write any formulas yourself.

To get really quick answers without writing a formula yourself, you have two options: AutoCalculate, which calculates cells you select but doesn't write a formula in the worksheet, and AutoSum, which writes a SUM formula for you in the worksheet.

Quickly Calculating Numbers Without a Formula

To calculate selected cells "on-the-fly" without writing a formula, you can use AutoCalculate.

Use AutoCalculate to perform quick calculations

1. Select the cells you want to add (or average or count).

   Look at the AutoCalculate box in the status bar of Figure 10.1.

2. To change the calculation function, right-click the AutoCalculate box; then, click a different function.

   You can select from six functions (sum, average, count entries, count numbers, minimum, or maximum), or you can select **None** to turn off the feature.

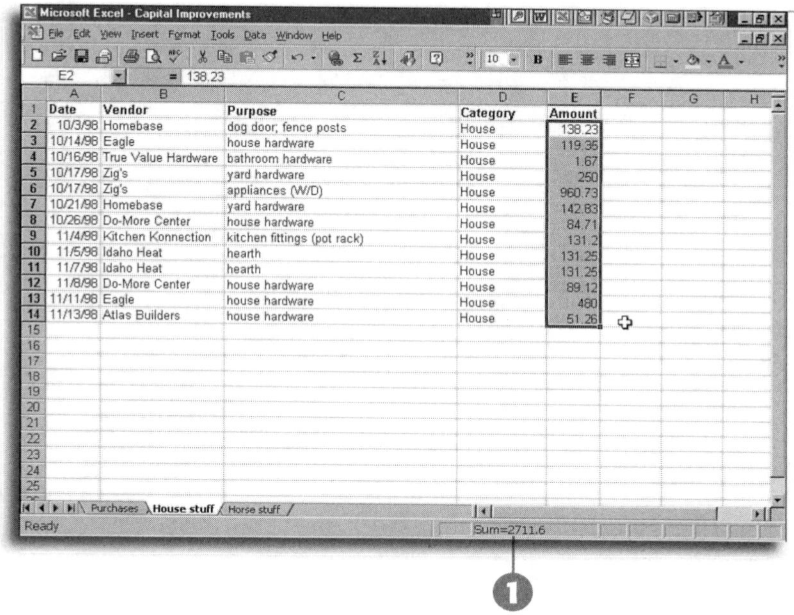

FIGURE 10.1

AutoCalculate calculates all selected cells according to the function you select.

1 AutoCalculate

Using AutoSum to Enter a Formula

To enter a formula that sums a group of numbers without actually writing the formula yourself, use the AutoSum button on the Standard toolbar.

Use the AutoSum button to enter a SUM formula

1. Click a cell at the bottom of a column of numbers you want to sum, as shown in Figure 10.2.
2. On the Standard toolbar, click the **AutoSum** button. Σ

   A SUM formula is written, and the cells Excel thinks you want to sum are surrounded by a moving border. If you want to sum different cells, drag to select them on the worksheet.
3. Press Enter.

AutoSum Is Versatile

You can sum a row of numbers by placing the AutoSum formula at the end of the row, or you can place the AutoSum formula anywhere on the worksheet, and then drag to select the cells you want to sum.

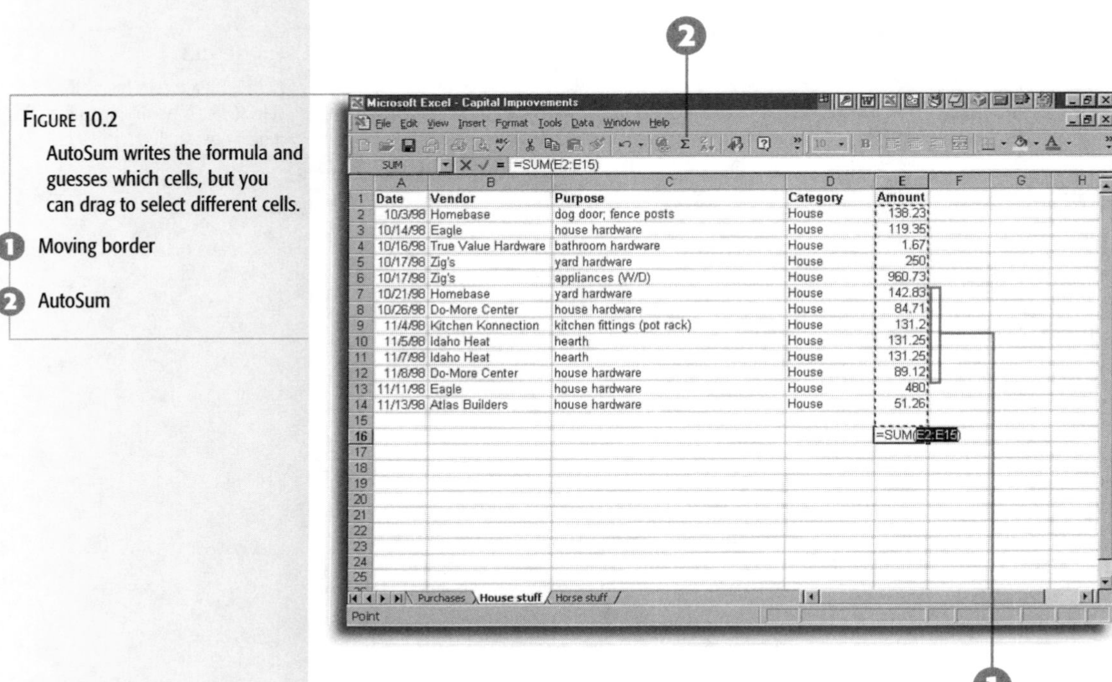

	A	B	C	D	E
1	Date	Vendor	Purpose	Category	Amount
2	10/3/98	Homebase	dog door, fence posts	House	138.23
3	10/14/98	Eagle	house hardware	House	119.35
4	10/16/98	True Value Hardware	bathroom hardware	House	1.67
5	10/17/98	Zig's	yard hardware	House	250
6	10/17/98	Zig's	appliances (W/D)	House	960.73
7	10/21/98	Homebase	yard hardware	House	142.83
8	10/26/98	Do-More Center	house hardware	House	84.71
9	11/4/98	Kitchen Konnection	kitchen fittings (pot rack)	House	131.2
10	11/5/98	Idaho Heat	hearth	House	131.25
11	11/7/98	Idaho Heat	hearth	House	131.25
12	11/8/98	Do-More Center	house hardware	House	89.12
13	11/11/98	Eagle	house hardware	House	480
14	11/13/98	Atlas Builders	house hardware	House	51.26
15					
16					=SUM(E2:E15)

FIGURE 10.2

AutoSum writes the formula and guesses which cells, but you can drag to select different cells.

1. Moving border
2. AutoSum

About Cell References

A *cell reference* is the cell's address on the worksheet in terms of its column letter and row number. You can tell what a cell's reference is by either looking at the row and column that intersect at the cell or selecting the cell and looking at the Name box (see Figure 10.3).

If you click in the upper-left corner of a worksheet, the Name box reads A1, which is that cell's reference: a combination of the column letter, A, and the row number, 1.

When you write formulas that include cells, the cells in the formula are identified by their references; for example, the formula =A1+B1 adds together the values stored in cells A1 and B1.

About Cell Reference Types

Cells can have different types of references, depending on how you want to use them in a formula. First, I'll explain the

	A	B	C	D	E
1	Date	Vendor	Purpose	Category	Amount
2	10/3/98	Homebase	dog door, fence posts	House	138.23
3	10/14/98	Eagle	house hardware	House	119.35
4	10/16/98	True Value Hardware	bathroom hardware	House	1.67
5	10/17/98	Zig's	yard hardware	House	250
6	10/17/98	Zig's	appliances (W/D)	House	960.73
7	10/21/98	Homebase	yard hardware	House	142.83
8	10/26/98	Do-More Center	house hardware	House	84.71
9	11/4/98	Kitchen Konnection	kitchen fittings (pot rack)	House	131.2
10	11/5/98	Idaho Heat	hearth	House	131.25
11	11/7/98	Idaho Heat	hearth	House	131.25
12	11/8/98	Do-More Center	house hardware	House	89.12
13	11/11/98	Eagle	house hardware	House	480
14	11/13/98	Atlas Builders	house hardware	House	51.26
16					2711.6

FIGURE 10.3

This cell's reference is A1: It's at the intersection of column A and row 1.

1. Name box
2. Cell A1 selected

terminology and how to create the different types; then, I'll show you how they work with actual examples (at which point they'll make more sense).

For any cell, there is only one reference but four reference types: relative, absolute, and two mixed types. Dollar signs ($) in the reference determine the type:

- A1 is called *relative*.
- A1 is called *absolute*.
- $A1 and A$1 are called *mixed*.

An *absolute* cell reference is a fixed geographical point, like a street address, such as "123 Cherry Street."

A *relative* cell reference is a relative location, as in "one block west and two blocks south."

A *mixed* cell reference is a mixture of absolute and relative locations, as in "three blocks east on Hampton Avenue." A mixed cell reference can have an absolute column and relative row, as in $A1, or a relative column and absolute row, as in A$1.

The dollar signs designate the row and/or column as absolute, or unchanging, within a reference. When you write formulas, the meanings of absolute, relative, and mixed become more clear.

Changing References to Relative, Absolute, or Mixed

If you need to change a cell reference type in a formula, there's a much faster way than typing in the dollar signs ($).

Cycle through the cell reference types

1. Double-click the cell containing the formula.
2. Within the formula, click in the cell reference you want to change (see Figure 10.4).
3. Press F4 until the reference changes to the type you want.

   Pressing F4 repeatedly cycles through all the possible reference types.
4. Press Enter to complete the change.

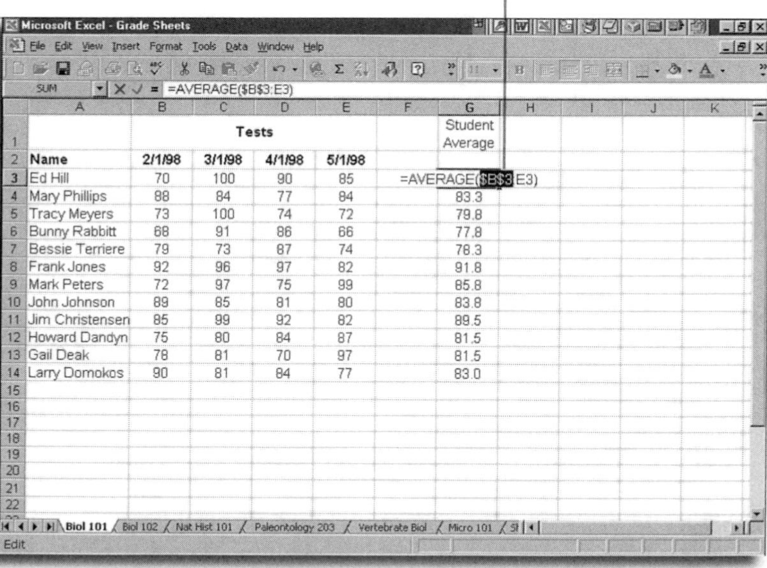

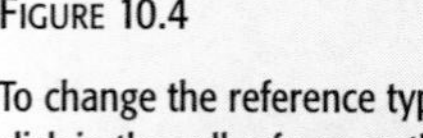

FIGURE 10.4

To change the reference type, click in the cell reference; then, press F4.

1 Click in the cell reference.

Writing Your Own Formulas

Starting a Formula in Excel

All Excel formulas begin with an equal sign (=).

You'll probably need to do more calculations in your workbooks than AutoSum can do for you, which means learning how to write formulas.

A simple formula might consist of adding, subtracting, multiplying, and dividing cells. Excel's arithmetic operators are detailed in Table 10.1.

TABLE 10.1 **Arithmetic operators**

Operator	Description
+ (plus sign)	Addition
– (minus sign)	Subtraction
* (asterisk)	Multiplication
/ (forward slash)	Division
^ (caret)	Exponentiation

All formulas can calculate cells in the same worksheet, on different worksheets, and even in different workbooks (which link the workbooks and worksheets together).

Writing a Simple Formula

You can write a simple formula that adds the values of two cells; to write a simple formula with other arithmetic operators, type another operator in place of the plus sign.

Write a formula that sums the values in two cells

1. Click a cell where you want to display the results of the formula.
2. Type an equal sign (=).
3. Click one of the cells you want to add.
4. Type a plus sign (+).
5. Click the other cell you want to add (as shown in Figure 10.5).
6. Press Enter.

The formula is complete.

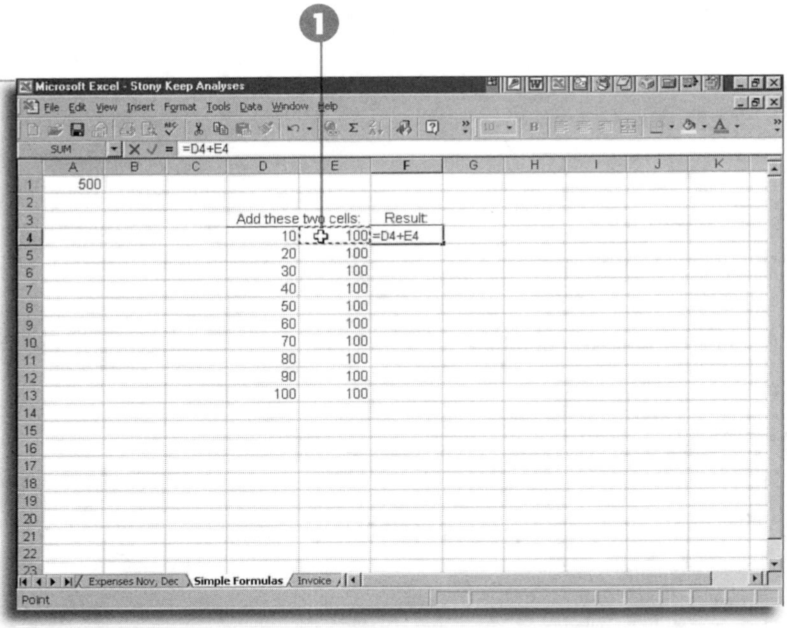

FIGURE 10.5

Start with an equal sign; then build the formula by clicking the cells you want and typing the arithmetic operators between them.

1 Click a cell to add it.

The Symbols in the Formula Bar

When you write a formula, three symbols appear in the Formula bar: an **X** (the cancel button), a check mark (the confirm button), and an equal sign (**=**). These symbols are for the keyboard-challenged and mouse-addicted among us. Click the **=** to start the formula; then, write your formula, and click the check mark to complete it. If you change your mind, you can delete the formula by clicking the **X**.

When you build a formula by clicking cells and ranges (as in the previous exercise), the cells have relative references. What the formula in Figure 10.5 really does is add the cell *two cells left* and the cell *one cell left* of the current cell because the references are relative. The advantage of using relative references will become clear in the next exercise, when you use AutoFill to copy the formula.

Using AutoFill to Copy a Formula

When you write a formula that uses relative references, the references adjust themselves when you copy the formula. They do this because the formula is calculating cells that are located relative to the formula on the worksheet.

Understand the concept of relative references

1. Write a formula that adds the cell left of the formula and the cell left of that cell (as in Figure 10.6, where the formula in F4 adds cells D4 and E4).

2. Position the mouse pointer over the AutoFill handle (the small black box in the lower-right corner of the selected cell). Then drag down to fill the formula down the right side of the table.

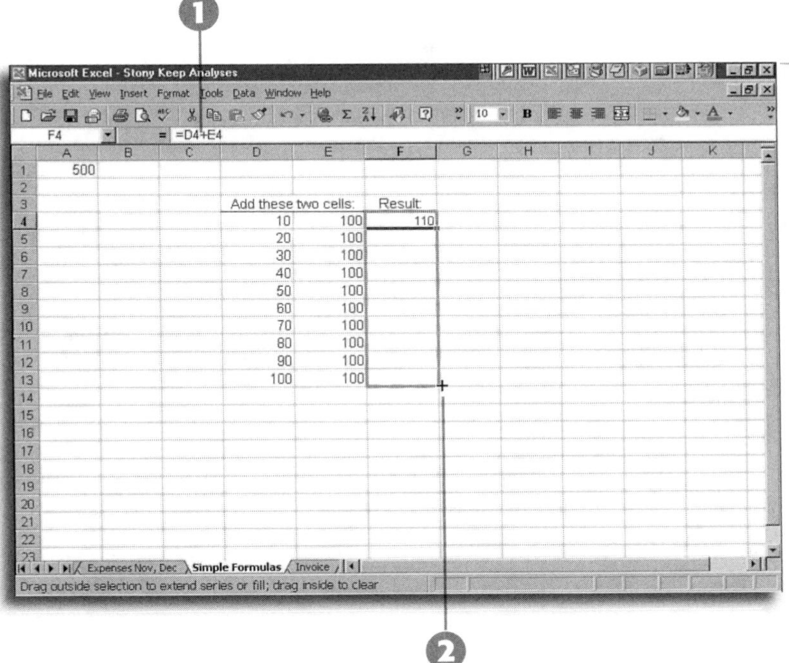

FIGURE 10.6

Copy a formula quickly by dragging the AutoFill handle.

1. Formula in cell F4
2. AutoFill

Sideways, Too

AutoFill also works horizontally to copy formulas across a row.

3. Release the mouse button after you've dragged to AutoFill all the cells down the side of the table.

   The formula is copied to all the cells you dragged across, as shown in Figure 10.7.

The formulas you copied using AutoFill have adjusted themselves so that every formula adds the two cells left of it. The formulas are self-adjusting because they contain relative references.

In Figure 10.8, the same formula has been copied down the side of the table, but the formula contains absolute references. The references add cells D4 and E4 all the way down the column—which in this example is quite useless.

FIGURE 10.7

Relative references are self-adjusting when you use AutoFill to copy a formula.

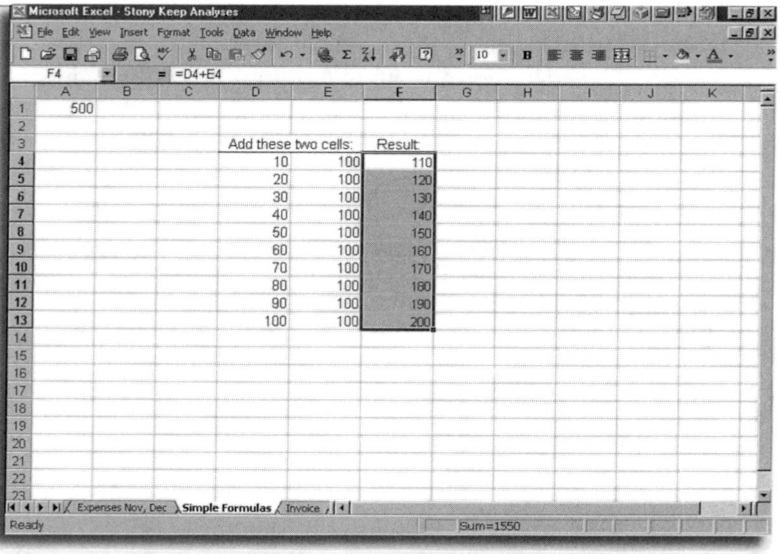

FIGURE 10.8

Absolute references do not adjust when you copy a formula; they always calculate the same cells.

1 Absolute references in the selected cells

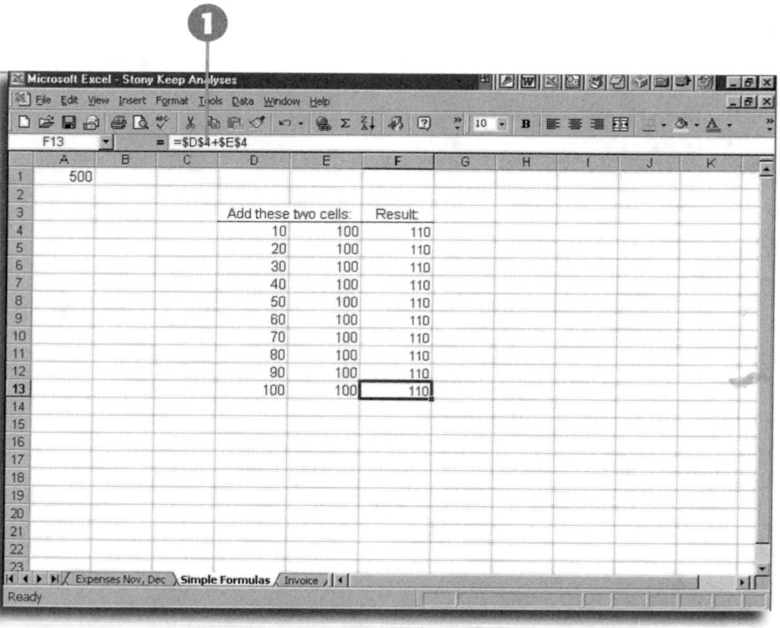

Suppose you want every formula to add the two cells left of it (relative references) to the value in cell A1 (an absolute reference). In this case (see Figure 10.9), an absolute reference for cell A1 ensures that the correct values are calculated in every copy of the formula.

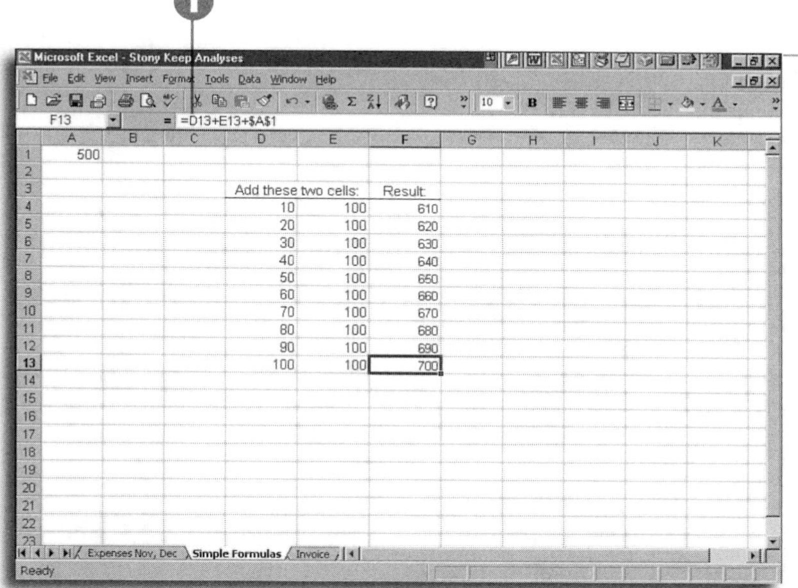

FIGURE 10.9

In these formulas, the relative references adjust, and the absolute reference always refers to the same cell.

1 Two relative references, one absolute reference

Mixed references allow a formula to refer to cells that have relative row references within an absolute, or unchanging, column (as in $A1) or relative column references within an absolute row (as in A$1).

Writing a Formula That Links Workbooks

A formula that *links* workbooks is a formula that refers to cells in more than one workbook. (You can also link worksheets in the same workbook.) For example, if you have two workbooks that represent sales from two districts, you can write a formula that sums values from both workbooks.

Write a formula that adds the values of cells in two workbooks

1. Open both workbooks (and a third workbook, if that's where you want to write the formula).

2. Begin the formula by typing =.
3. Click in one of the source workbooks (the workbooks with values you want to sum), and click the cell you want to include in the formula.

   The cell reference is added to the formula, but because it's in another workbook, the reference includes the workbook name and worksheet name, too (see Figure 10.10). The workbook name is in square brackets and is followed by the worksheet name; the worksheet name is separated from the cell reference by an exclamation point, like this:

   ```
   [workbook name]worksheet name!cell reference
   ```

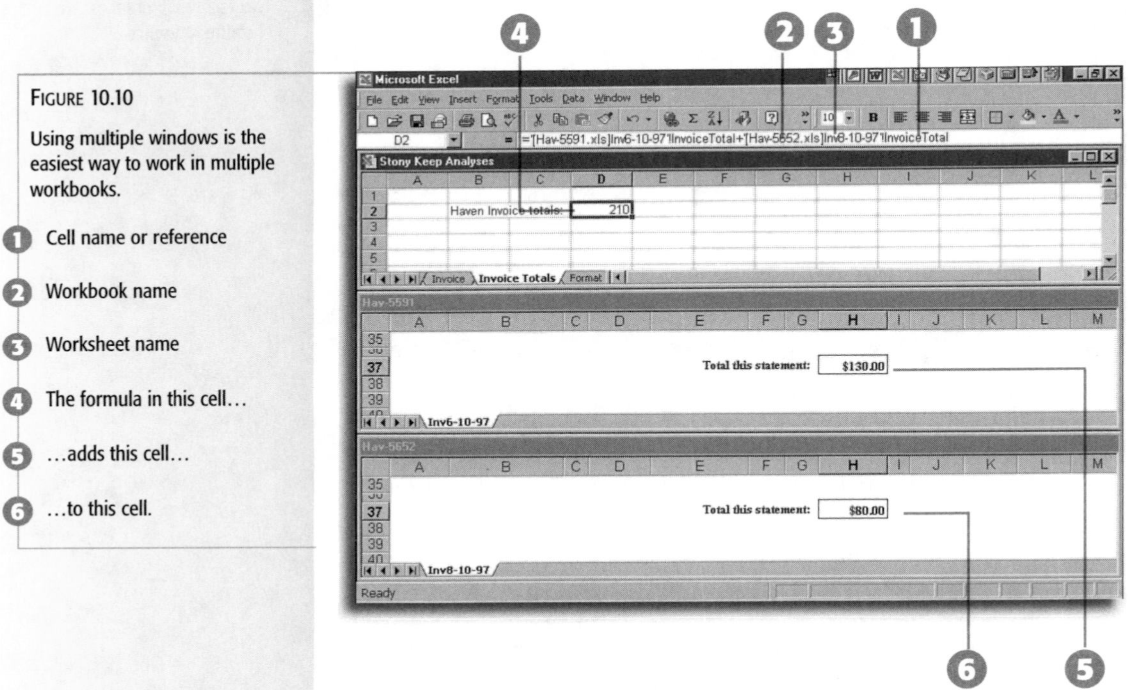

FIGURE 10.10

Using multiple windows is the easiest way to work in multiple workbooks.

1. Cell name or reference
2. Workbook name
3. Worksheet name
4. The formula in this cell...
5. ...adds this cell...
6. ...to this cell.

4. Type a plus sign (+).
5. Click in the other source workbook, and click the cell you want to include in the formula.
6. Press Enter.

   The formula calculates the sum of the cells in the two source workbooks, and all three workbooks are linked by the formula (refer to Figure 10.10).

The next time you open the workbook containing the formula, called the *dependent* workbook, you'll be asked if you want to update all linked information:

- If you click **Yes**, the formula is updated with current values in the source workbooks, even if those values have changed.
- If you click **No**, the formula won't be updated with current values but will retain its previous values, which saves you time spent waiting for a large workbook to recalculate.
- If you open one of the source workbooks, the formula will automatically recalculate with the values in the open source workbook.

SEE ALSO

➤ *To learn more about opening and arranging multiple windows on your screen, see page 101.*

How Can I Break This Link?

If you don't want the formula to recalculate, ever, you can save the current formula result as a value; see the procedure in Chapter 11, "Complex Calculations," in the section "Converting Formula Results to Values."

Editing a Formula

You can easily change an existing formula in any way (change the function, arithmetic operators, cells, or constant values).

Edit an existing formula in the worksheet

1. Double-click the cell to open it for editing.

   As shown in Figure 10.11, the cell references and names are colored, and the colors correspond to colored cell borders on the worksheet (which makes it easy to see at a glance which cells the formula refers to).

Another Way

You might find it easier to click the cell and edit it in the Formula bar.

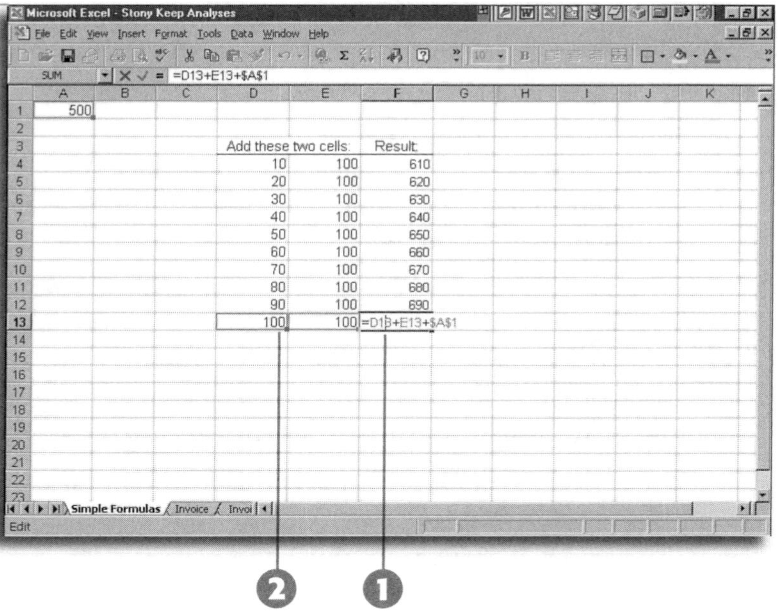

FIGURE 10.11

To replace one cell reference with another, double-click the reference in the formula; then, click the replacement cell on the worksheet.

1 The color of this reference...

2 ...matches the color of its cell border.

2. Select and replace whatever you want to change:
   - To replace a referenced or named cell, double-click to select it; then, in the worksheet, click the replacement cell.
   - To replace a range, double-click and drag over both references (to select them). Then, in the worksheet, drag the replacement range.
   - To replace a constant value or an arithmetic operator, select it and type the replacement characters.
3. Press Enter.

I Want to See All My Formulas

To show all the formulas in a worksheet, press Ctrl+` (the grave accent, left of the 1 on your keyboard). To hide the formulas again, press Ctrl+` again.

Auditing a Formula

If you've previously created a worksheet with formulas, you might want some help tracing how you built your formulas (especially if the worksheet is a complicated one).

Auditing, or tracing, a formula is a way to see at a glance where the referenced cells (the *precedent* cells) are in the worksheet; you can also trace a formula's *dependent* cells—those cells where other formulas use the results of the formula you're tracing.

Find a formula's precedent (or source) cells

1. Click the cell containing the formula.
2. On the **Tools** menu, point to **Auditing**; then, click **Trace Precedents**.

   Lines are displayed on the worksheet that trace source cells to the formula cell, as shown in Figure 10.12.

   If the precedent cells are on another worksheet or in another workbook, you see a dashed line and an other-workbook symbol (see Figure 10.12).

Are There Toolbar Buttons for Auditing?

To trace precedent and dependent cells with toolbar buttons, you can use the Auditing toolbar. On the **Tools** menu, point to **Auditing**; then, click **Show Auditing Toolbar**.

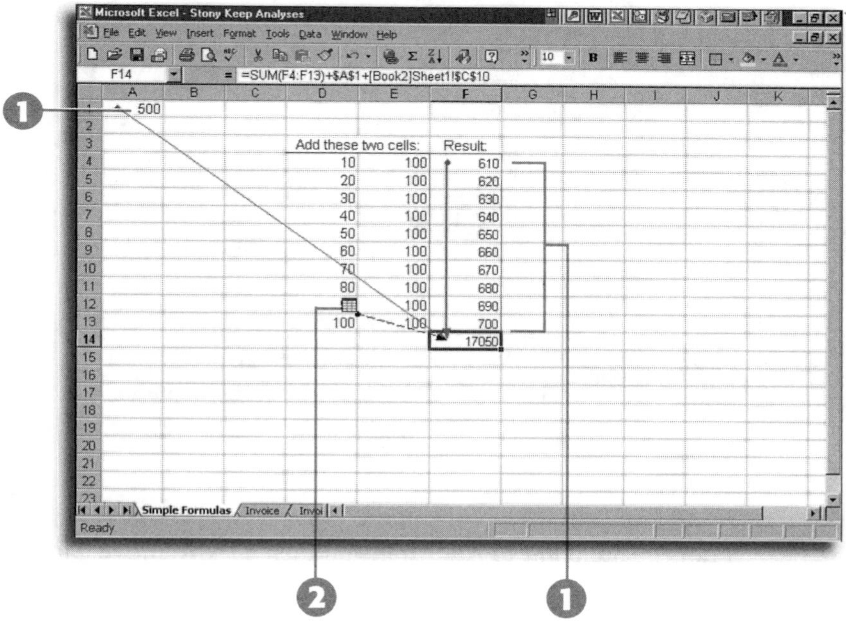

FIGURE 10.12
Double-click the other-workbook symbol to see which workbooks are referred to.

1. Precedent cells on this worksheet
2. Other-workbook symbol

3. To remove all trace lines from the worksheet, open the **Tools** menu, point to **Auditing**, and then click **Remove All Arrows**.

Find a formula's dependent cells

1. Click the cell containing the formula.
2. On the **Tools** menu, point to **Auditing**; then, click **Trace Dependents**.

Lines are displayed on the worksheet that trace the formula to its dependent cells, as shown in Figure 10.13.

If the dependent cells are on another worksheet or in another workbook, you see a dashed line and another other–workbook symbol (see Figure 10.13).

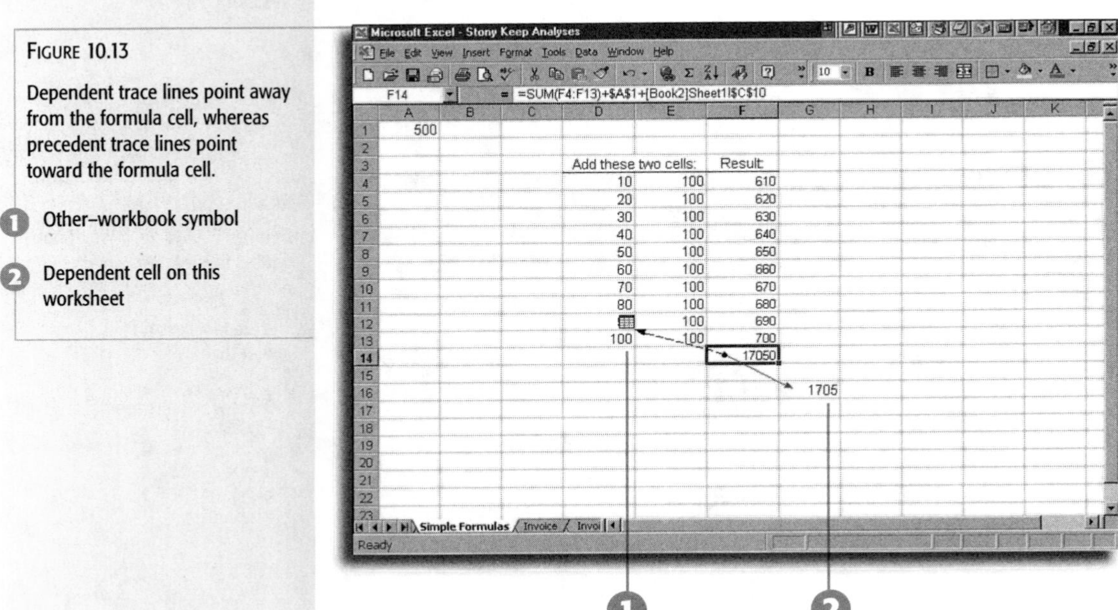

FIGURE 10.13

Dependent trace lines point away from the formula cell, whereas precedent trace lines point toward the formula cell.

1. Other–workbook symbol
2. Dependent cell on this worksheet

3. To remove all trace lines from the worksheet, open the **Tools** menu, point to **Auditing**, and then click **Remove All Arrows**.

CHAPTER

11

Complex Calculations

Understanding functions

Writing formulas that use functions

Using cell names and labels

Converting formula results to values

Finding errors in worksheets

Understanding Functions

Not all calculations are simple. Fortunately, Excel can handle tremendously complex calculations for you.

Functions are built-in formulas that perform complex math for you. You enter the function name and any *arguments* (extra information) the function requires, and Excel performs the calculations. SUM and AVERAGE are examples of simple, straightforward functions, and PMT and VLOOKUP are examples of common but more complex functions that I will show you how to use.

Any formula is easier to read and understand if you use cell *names* and *labels* in place of cell references (for example, the formula `=tax+subtotal` is easier to understand than `=H32+H33`). After you create cell names or labels, Excel automatically uses the cell name instead of the reference when you use the cell in a formula. A cell name can be anything you create. A cell label is similar to a cell name but is a row or column label that Excel automatically uses to identify cells in a formula. In this chapter, I show you how to create and use cell names and labels to make your formulas easier to understand.

Errors and invalid data always seem to find their way into worksheets, especially when you're working with complex calculations; however, they're easier to locate and correct when you have the proper tools. In this chapter, I show you some helpful tools for ferreting out problems.

Using Functions

Excel comes with a slew of functions—some you'll use all the time, and some you'll only be interested in if you're an electrical engineer or nuclear physicist. Functions have specific names, like SUM or AVERAGE or BETADIST, and function names must be spelled correctly or Excel won't recognize them; however, Excel provides dialog boxes that do the spelling for you and help you fill in the arguments each function requires.

Where Are the Advanced Functions?

The more advanced (and less commonly used) functions are found in the Analysis Toolpak add-in. If you don't see the Analysis Toolpak add-in listed in the Add-Ins dialog box (open the **Tools** menu and select **Add-Ins**), you need to install the add-in from your Office 2000 or Excel 2000 CD-ROM.

Writing a Formula Using Functions

Use the Paste Function dialog box to write a formula

1. Click the cell in which you want the results of the formula to appear.
2. On the toolbar, click the **Paste Function** button.

   The Paste Function dialog box appears (shown in Figure 11.1).

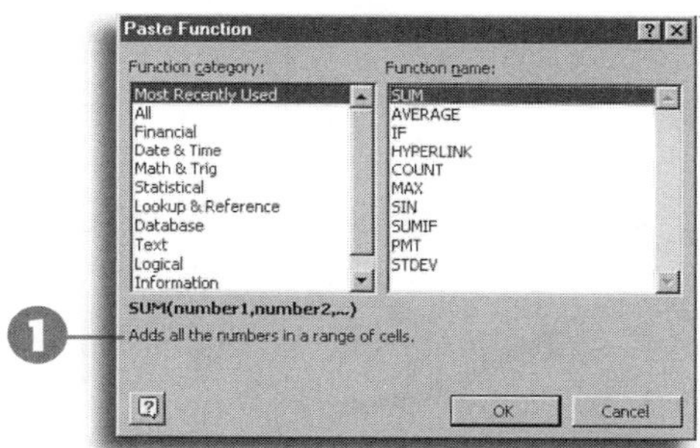

FIGURE 11.1
The Paste Function dialog box briefly explains the selected function.

1 Function explanation

3. Click a category of functions and double-click the function you want.

   The Formula Palette opens to help you complete the function (shown in Figure 11.2).

This Formula Thing Is in My Way

You can drag the *Formula Palette*—the dialog box in which you supply arguments for the formula—elsewhere on the worksheet to move it out of your way.

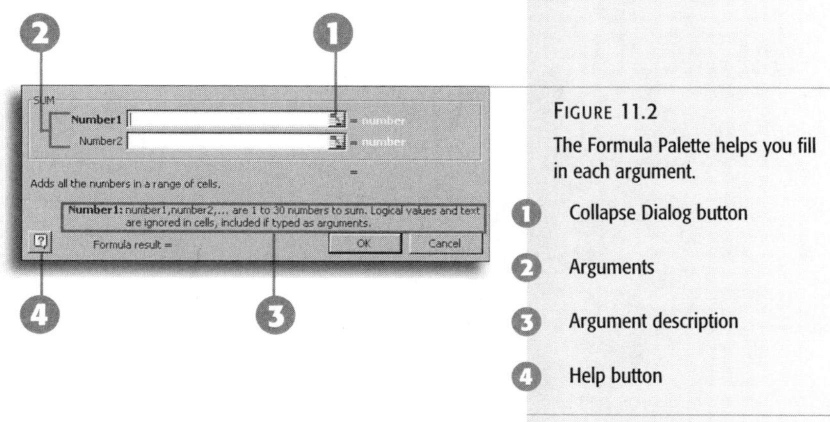

FIGURE 11.2
The Formula Palette helps you fill in each argument.

1 Collapse Dialog button
2 Arguments
3 Argument description
4 Help button

4. Click the argument box and read the description of the argument to figure out what information is needed. Click the Help button for more information about the function.
5. Click or drag worksheet cells to fill in arguments (if the arguments call for cell references).

   To shrink the Formula Palette so that it doesn't cover worksheet cells you want to select, click the **Collapse Dialog** button at the right end of the argument, select the worksheet cells, and click the **Expand Dialog** button (at the right end of the collapsed argument box) to display the Formula Palette again and continue building your function.
6. Click **OK**.

   The function is built and the formula is completed.

This is the basic procedure. Now I show you how to use it to write the specific, common, and useful worksheet formulas (shown in Table 11.1).

Writing Your Own Formulas

After you get comfortable with formulas, you can often write them faster yourself, but you must spell the function name correctly. Try this tip: Type the function name in lowercase letters. If it's spelled correctly, Excel converts it to uppercase after you press Enter. (For example, sum is converted to SUM.) If it's spelled incorrectly, Excel won't convert it to uppercase; that's your clue that it's misspelled.

TABLE 11.1 **Common and useful worksheet functions**

Function	Purpose
SUM	Add together the values in a selected range
MIN	Find the minimum value in a selected range
MAX	Find the maximum value in a selected range
AVERAGE	Average the values in a selected range
COUNTIF	Count all values that meet specific criteria
SUMIF	Add together all values that meet specific criteria
VLOOKUP and HLOOKUP	Find a value in a table
IF	Display a value that depends on criteria you set
PMT	Calculate the payment for specific loan terms
NOW	Return current date and time
TODAY	Return the current date
CONCATENATE	Join cell values together in a single cell
LEFT and RIGHT	Return a specific number of characters from the left (or right) end of a cell's value

Some Common and Useful Functions

In this section, I'll show you examples of the functions in Table 11.1, with suggestions about where they're useful in real life. This short list of functions is just a few of the hundreds of functions available in Excel. If you explore the list of functions in the Paste Function dialog box, you'll find functions that calculate sine, cosine, tangent, the actual value of pi, and functions for a lot of accounting and engineering equations, logarithms, and binomials. It's nearly endless, but I'm only showing you the functions that you'll most likely want to use.

SUM

The SUM function is universally useful: It adds all the numbers in a selected range. A good place for the SUM function is at the end of a list of numbers, such as the list in Figure 11.3.

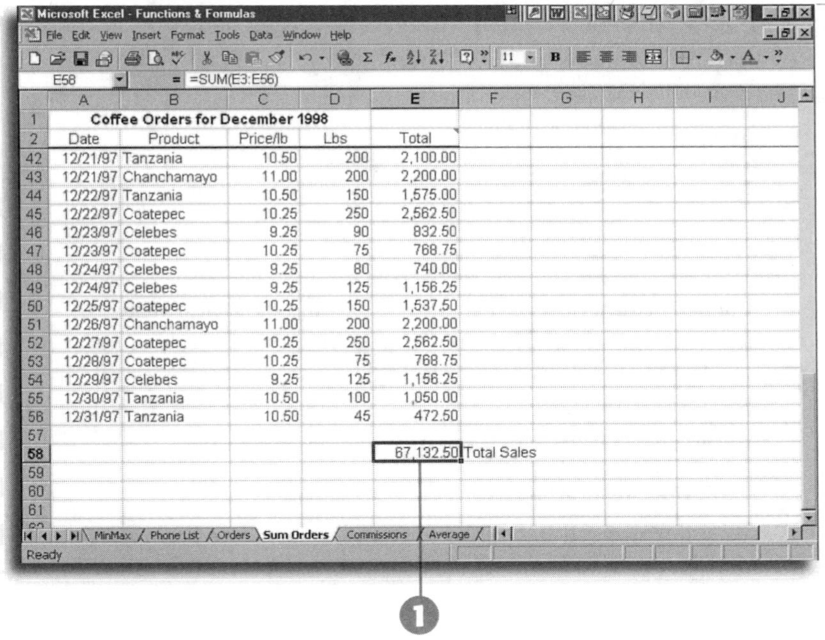

Use Mock Data

When you first write a formula, you want to test it to be sure that it's calculating properly (that is, you want to be sure you entered all the arguments correctly and the results are accurate). To test your formulas, enter *mock data* (phony numbers) in the worksheet. Use mock data that's simple: short text that's quick to type and round numbers so that you can do the math in your head and know quickly whether the results are accurate.

Microsoft Excel - Functions & Formulas

E58 = =SUM(E3:E56)

	A	B	C	D	E	F
1	Coffee Orders for December 1998					
2	Date	Product	Price/lb	Lbs	Total	
42	12/21/97	Tanzania	10.50	200	2,100.00	
43	12/21/97	Chanchamayo	11.00	200	2,200.00	
44	12/22/97	Tanzania	10.50	150	1,575.00	
45	12/22/97	Coatepec	10.25	250	2,562.50	
46	12/23/97	Celebes	9.25	90	832.50	
47	12/23/97	Coatepec	10.25	75	768.75	
48	12/24/97	Celebes	9.25	80	740.00	
49	12/24/97	Celebes	9.25	125	1,156.25	
50	12/25/97	Coatepec	10.25	150	1,537.50	
51	12/26/97	Chanchamayo	11.00	200	2,200.00	
52	12/27/97	Coatepec	10.25	250	2,562.50	
53	12/28/97	Coatepec	10.25	75	768.75	
54	12/29/97	Celebes	9.25	125	1,156.25	
55	12/30/97	Tanzania	10.50	100	1,050.00	
56	12/31/97	Tanzania	10.50	45	472.50	
57						
58					67,132.50	Total Sales

MinMax / Phone List / Orders / Sum Orders / Commissions / Average

Ready

FIGURE 11.3

Although below the list is a convenient place, you can put the formula anywhere you want on the worksheet.

❶ The new formula

Write a SUM formula

1. Click the cell in which you want to place the formula.
2. Type `=`.
3. Type **`sum(`**.
4. On the worksheet, drag to select the cells you want to add together (in this example, the range E3:E56).
5. Type `)`.
6. Press Enter.

   The formula is complete. If you spelled the function name, SUM, correctly, Excel converted it to uppercase letters.

Change the Reference Type

To quickly change the cell reference type, click the reference, press F4 until the type cycles to the type you want, and then press Enter.

When you drag cells to insert them in a formula, Excel uses relative references by default; if you copy this formula to another cell, the results change because the relative references adjust themselves. If, however, you drag the cell to *move* it elsewhere on the worksheet, Excel retains the original references and the results remain accurate. If this gets confusing and you want to be sure the references remain the same, you can change the references to absolute types.

SEE ALSO

➤ *To learn more about cell references, see page 162.*
➤ *To learn how to use the AutoSum button to quickly sum ranges, see page 161.*

MIN

The MIN function returns the minimum, or lowest, value in a range of numbers. Of course, if your range is a single column of numbers, you can also find the smallest value by sorting or filtering the list. If your range is a large table of numbers, like the one in Figure 11.4, the MIN function comes in handy.

Write your own formula with the MIN function

1. Click the cell in which you want to place the formula.
2. Type `=`.
3. Type **`min(`**.

Microsoft Excel - Functions & Formulas

D15 = =MIN(B3:M11)

	A	B	C	D	E	F	G	H	I	J	K	L	M
1	Commissions for 1998												
2		January	Februai	March	April	May	June	July	August	Septem	Octobe	Noveml	Decemb
3	Marcia	4913	3194	3650	2592	1330	3002	4166	4324	2906	2571	1777	1221
4	Fred	3554	1006	4029	2430	1635	4508	4472	1616	3260	4941	1282	2168
5	Lila	3098	4820	1032	2628	4213	1951	2099	4451	3939	1409	2450	4207
6	Armelle	1894	4237	3333	3256	2382	2486	1818	1064	3292	2178	3649	4918
7	Jamie	3423	4609	3707	2441	2896	1327	1429	3714	2940	2687	3512	4565
8	Tracy	3266	1621	2873	3526	2622	2148	2094	3449	2420	3600	4588	2776
9	Susannah	2366	2445	4514	4753	4505	4934	3523	4179	3055	1854	3378	3738
10	Tina	4578	2963	2982	1522	2067	3944	2605	4621	2510	3634	1462	3798
11	Diane	3217	1248	4004	3449	4563	4542	4668	3612	1345	2205	2752	4930
15		Lowest single month		1006									

MinMax / Phone List / Orders / Sum Orders / Commissions / Average

Ready

FIGURE 11.4
The MIN function finds the minimum value in the selected table of data.

4. On the worksheet, drag to select the cells you want to search for a minimum value (in this example, the range B3:M11, all the numbers in the table).
5. Type).
6. Press Enter.

   The minimum value in the table is 1006, and it would have taken a bit more time to find it yourself.

Because the minimum value is the result of a formula, it continues to find the minimum value automatically, even if you change the numbers in the table.

SEE ALSO

➤ *To learn more about saving workbooks as templates, see page 50.*

Save Time with a Template

If your business requires monthly worksheets like the one in Figure 11.4, you could save yourself time by creating a template and including the MIN formula in it. When you open a copy of the template, the formula is already in place, and as you enter numbers, the formula finds the minimum value automatically.

MAX

The MAX function is the opposite of the MIN function and works exactly the same way. It finds the largest value in a selected range of cells. To write your own formula with the MAX function, you can follow the preceding procedure for the MIN function.

Write a formula with the MAX function using the Paste Function dialog box

1. Click the cell in which you want to enter the formula.
2. Click the **Paste Function** button.

   The Paste Function dialog box appears (shown in Figure 11.5).

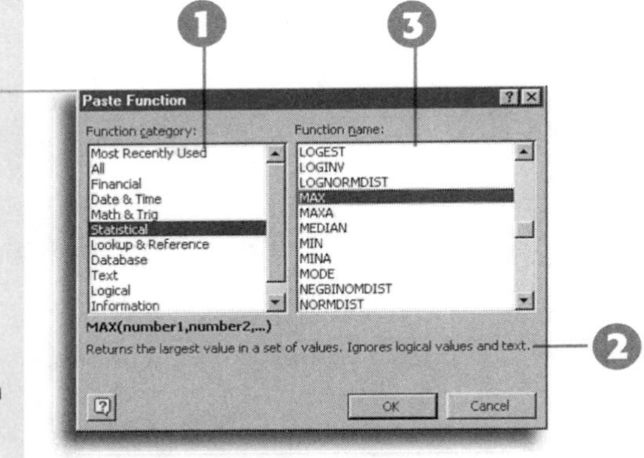

FIGURE 11.5

The Paste Function dialog box helps you select and write a formula using any of Excel's myriad functions.

1. Function categories
2. Description of selected function
3. Functions

Make the MAX and MIN Functions More Useful

When you use the MAX or MIN function to determine the highest or lowest value in a large table, you still have to search to find that value among all those numbers. You can make it jump out visually by combining the MAX or MIN function with conditional number formatting, which formats the number in the table with any formatting you choose.

3. To narrow your range of choices, click a function category in the **Function category** list. (If you know the name of the function you want but don't know in which category to find it, click **All**.)
4. Scroll through the list of functions on the right side of the dialog box and double-click the function you want. (In this example, I've looked up the **MAX** function in the **Statistical** category.)
5. The Formula Palette appears for the function you double-clicked (in this case, the MAX function, as shown in Figure 11.6).
6. Highlight or delete any value in the Number1 argument and enter the entire table range by dragging to select the cells. In this example, the table range is A2:M11 (but I previously named this range Commissions, so when I select the range, Excel inserts the range name, shown in Figure 11.7).

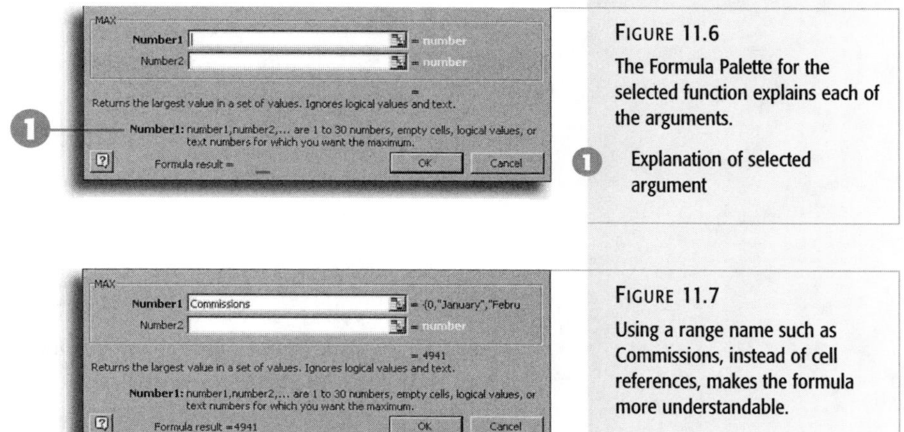

FIGURE 11.6
The Formula Palette for the selected function explains each of the arguments.

1 Explanation of selected argument

FIGURE 11.7
Using a range name such as Commissions, instead of cell references, makes the formula more understandable.

7. Click **OK**.

The formula is complete, and the maximum value in the range, 4941, is displayed (see Figure 11.8).

SEE ALSO

➤ *To learn more about conditional number formatting, see page 251.*

Microsoft Excel - Functions & Formulas

D14 =MAX(Commissions)

	A	B	C	D	E	F	G	H	I	J	K	L	M
1	Commissions for 1998												
2		January	Februa	March	April	May	June	July	August	Septem	Octobe	Noveml	Decemb
3	Marcia	4913	3194	3650	2592	1330	3002	4166	4324	2906	2571	1777	1221
4	Fred	3554	1006	4029	2430	1635	4508	4472	1616	3260	4941	1282	2168
5	Lila	3098	4820	1032	2628	4213	1951	2099	4451	3939	1409	2450	4207
6	Armelle	1894	4237	3333	3256	2382	2486	1818	1064	3292	2178	3649	4918
7	Jamie	3423	4609	3707	2441	2896	1327	1429	3714	2940	2687	3512	4565
8	Tracy	3266	1621	2873	3526	2622	2148	2094	3449	2420	3600	4588	2776
9	Susannah	2366	2445	4514	4753	4505	4934	3523	4179	3055	1854	3378	3738
10	Tina	4578	2963	2982	1522	2067	3944	2605	4621	2510	3634	1462	3798
11	Diane	3217	1248	4004	3449	4563	4542	4668	3612	1345	2205	2752	4930
12													
13													
14		Highest single month		4941									
15		Lowest single month		1006									

MinMax / Phone List / Orders / Sum Orders / Commissions / Average /

Ready

FIGURE 11.8
Whether you use the Paste Function dialog box or write the formula yourself, the result is the same.

AVERAGE

The AVERAGE function is another common and easy-to-use function. It's as simple to write as the SUM, MIN, and MAX functions, so I demonstrate it without using any dialog boxes.

The important thing to know about the AVERAGE function is that it gives a more correct result than you get by adding cells and dividing by the number of cells. When I first began using Excel, I didn't know about functions. I calculated averages by adding the cells together and then dividing by the number of cells. Occasionally, however, I got wrong answers because if a cell didn't have a value in it, my method averaged that cell as a zero! The AVERAGE function, however, adds the cells in the selected range and then divides the sum by the number of values; so any blank cells are left out of the calculation. (The comparison is shown in Figure 11.9. Cell comments show the formulas for each cell.)

FIGURE 11.9

Adding and dividing doesn't always give the correct average, but the AVERAGE function does.

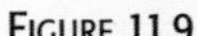

1 Ed Hill was excused from this test.

2 His resulting add-and-divide average is wrong.

	A	B	C	D	E	F	G	H
1			Tests				Student Average	Average (the wrong way)
2	Name	2/1/98	3/1/98	4/1/98	5/1/98			
3	Ed Hill	70	100		85		85.0	63.8
4	Mary Phillips	88	84	77	84		83.3	83.3
5	Tracy Meyers	73	100	74	72		79.8	79.8
6	Bunny Rabbitt	68	91	86	66		77.8	77.8
7	Bessie Terriere	79	73	87	74		78.3	78.3
8	Frank Jones	92	96	97	82		91.8	91.8
9	Mark Peters	72	97	75	99		85.8	85.8
10	John Johnson	89	85	81	80		83.8	83.8
11	Jim Christensen	85	99	92	82		89.5	89.5
12	Howard Dandyn	75	80	84	87		81.5	81.5
13	Gail Deak	78	81	70	97		81.5	81.5
14	Larry Domokos	90	81	84	77		83.0	83.0
15	Richard Dyhr	79	73	68	78		74.5	74.5
16	Leo Fabin	86	69	68	96		79.8	79.8
17	Colleen Fairfax	76	82	93	85		84.0	84.0
18	Elvin Gilroy	70	80	80	74		76.0	76.0
19	Ardith Gledan	76	85	65	89		78.8	78.8
20	Irene Hassan	100	78	89	79		86.5	86.5

=(B3+C3+D3+E3)/4

=AVERAGE(B3:E3)

Write a formula using the AVERAGE function

1. Click the cell in which you want to place the formula.
2. Type `=AVERAGE(`.
3. In the worksheet, drag the range of cells you want to average (or type the range name or label).
4. Type a closing parenthesis, `)`.
5. Press Enter.

SUMIF

In the table in Figure 11.10, I want to know how much of the product named Celebes was sold in December.

To find the answer, I use a SUMIF function, which sums values if they correspond to my criterion. (In this case, I write a formula that sums values in the Total column if they correspond to the value Celebes in the Product column.) A SUMIF formula can be written one of two ways. You can use the Conditional Sum Wizard, an add-in which, in my opinion, wastes a whole lot of time if you want to sum by a single criterion and only serves to make the function more mysterious. The other way is to use the Formula Palette, which is simpler and faster for single-criterion sums. I show you both ways, and you can decide for yourself which is easier.

Why Bother with the Conditional Sum Wizard?

If you want to use more than one criterion in your conditional sum formula (for example, how much Celebes was sold in quantities greater than 200 pounds), using the wizard is easier.

B:B Doesn't Look Like a Cell Reference

My range entry, B:B, designates the entire column B as the range containing my criteria. It's important that there not be any other entries on the worksheet below this table, or the formula calculates with those entries and gets messed up. Also, the range reference B:B is a relative reference. If I wanted an absolute reference to column B, I'd type $B:$B.

Use the Paste Function dialog box to write a SUMIF formula

1. Click the cell in which you want to place the formula.
2. Click the **Paste Function** button. [fx]
3. In the **All** or **Math & Trig** category, double-click **SUMIF**.

   The Formula Palette for SUMIF appears (see Figure 11.11).
4. In the **Range** box, enter the range of cells that contains the criterion (in this example, the Product column, because it contains the Celebes criterion).

   You can drag the cells in column B (B3:B56), or you can enter the entire column (B:B) as I've done.

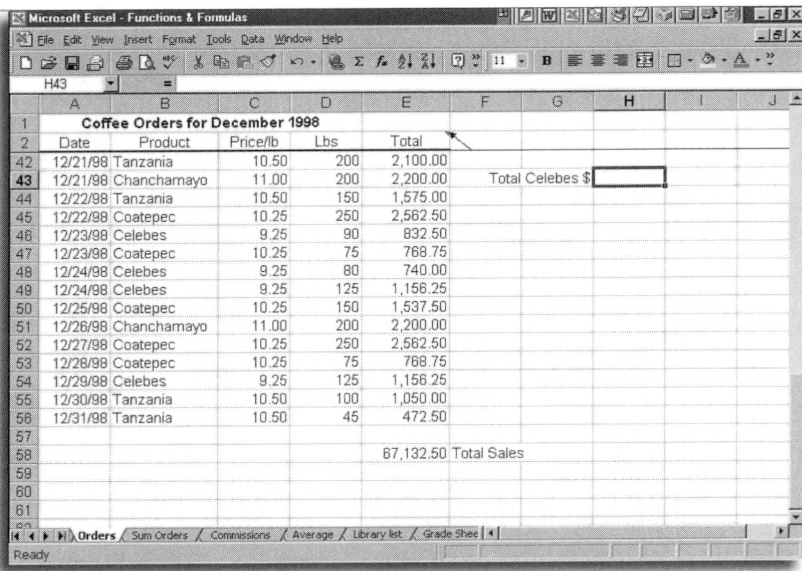

FIGURE 11.10

For these December sales figures, I want to know the total revenues just for orders of Celebes coffee.

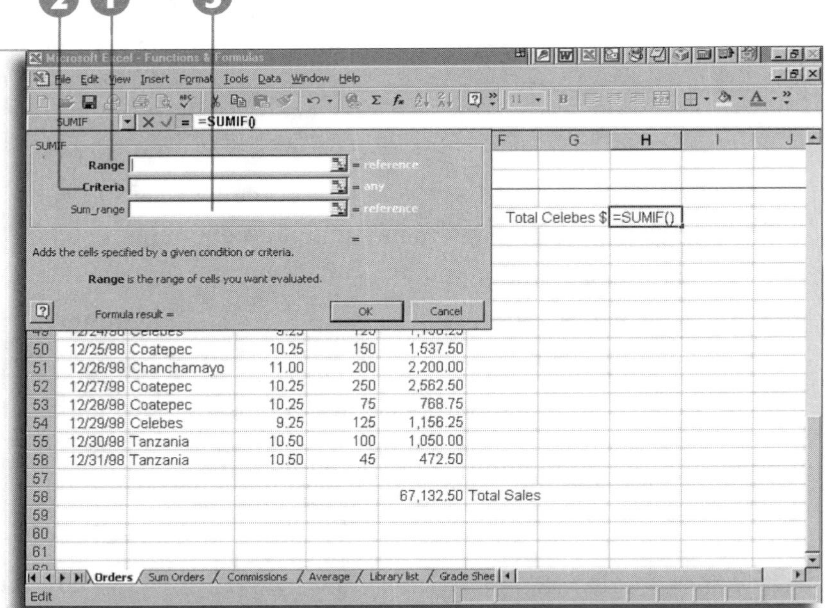

FIGURE 11.11

The Formula Palette makes the SUMIF function reasonably easy to write.

1. Range containing criteria (Product column)
2. Criteria (Celebes)
3. Range containing values to sum (Total column)

5. In the **Criteria** box, enter the criteria you want to sum values for.
   - If it's a text string, as "Celebes" is, be sure to type quotation marks around it.
   - Alternatively, you can click a cell containing the entry Celebes, instead of typing the text string and quotation marks.
6. In the **Sum_range** box, enter the range of values you want to sum (in this example, column E, entered as the range `E:E`).

   Your SUMIF dialog box should look similar to the one in Figure 11.12.

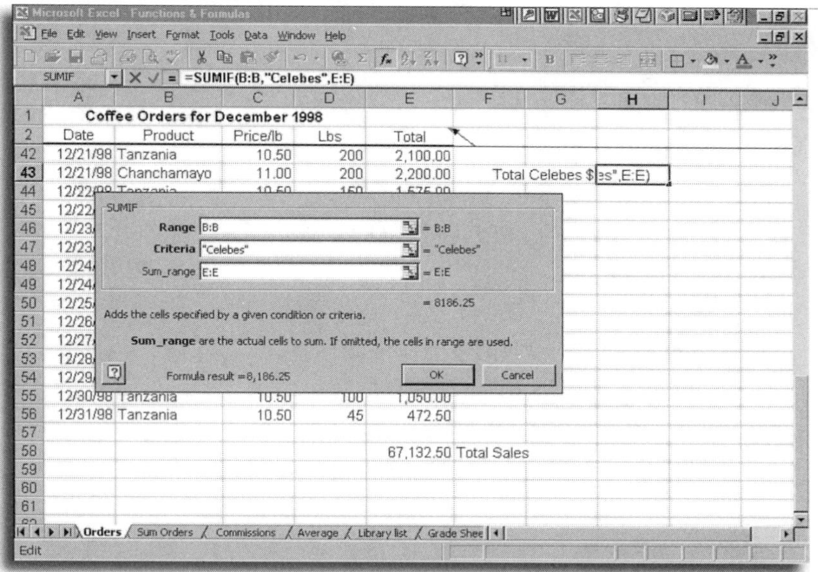

FIGURE 11.12
The SUMIF dialog box, ready to sum only Celebes orders.

7. Click **OK**.

   The SUMIF formula is complete (shown in Figure 11.13). To find the total for Tanzania, open the cell and edit the formula: Change "Celebes" to "Tanzania" and press Enter.

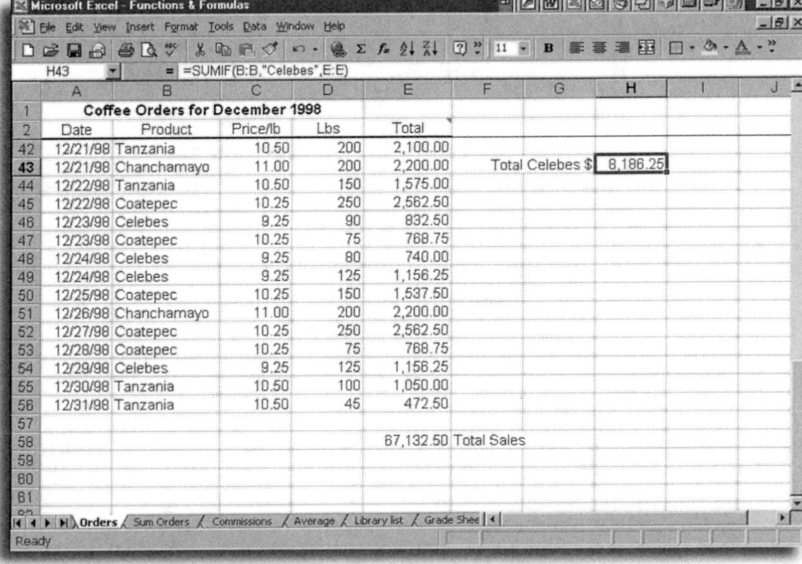

FIGURE 11.13
Celebes orders totaled $8186.25 in December.

The Conditional Sum Wizard is a long, roundabout way of getting the same result for a single criterion but is better than SUMIF if you want to write a conditional sum for multiple criteria.

SEE ALSO

➤ *To learn more about reference types, see page 162.*

SEE ALSO

➤ *To learn about AutoCalculate, see page 160.*

➤ *To learn about filters, see page 283.*

Is There a Faster Way?

Another way to get a quick answer to this question is to filter the table to show only Celebes and then take a count of the orders by using AutoCalculate.

COUNTIF

The COUNTIF function counts the number of values in a range that meet a specific criterion, such as "How many orders were there for Celebes coffee in December?"

The COUNTIF function works like the SUMIF function but without a wizard alternative (nor any need for one).

Use the COUNTIF function

1. Click the cell in which you want to place the result.

2. Click the **Paste Function** button. *fx*
3. In the **All** or **Statistical** categories, double-click the **COUNTIF** function.

   The COUNTIF dialog box appears (shown in Figure 11.14).

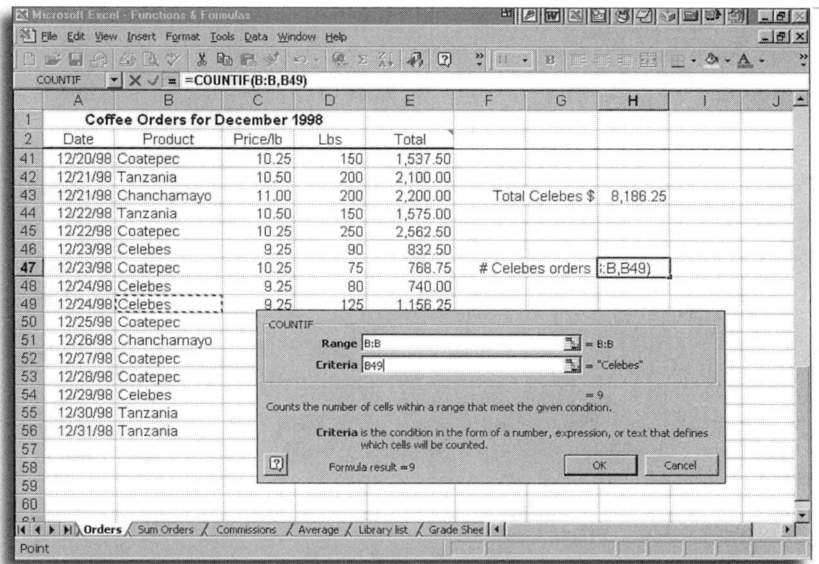

FIGURE 11.14
COUNTIF requires only a range to search and what to count in that range.

4. In the **Range** box, enter the range of cells to search (in this case, I've entered column B).
5. In the **Criteria** box, enter the criteria for counting cells (in this case, I've clicked cell B49, a Celebes entry, so the function counts all identical entries).
6. Click **OK**.

   The formula is complete as shown in Figure 11.15. I can find the average Celebes order by dividing the sum by the count.

SEE ALSO

➤ *To learn more about AutoFilter, see page 284.*

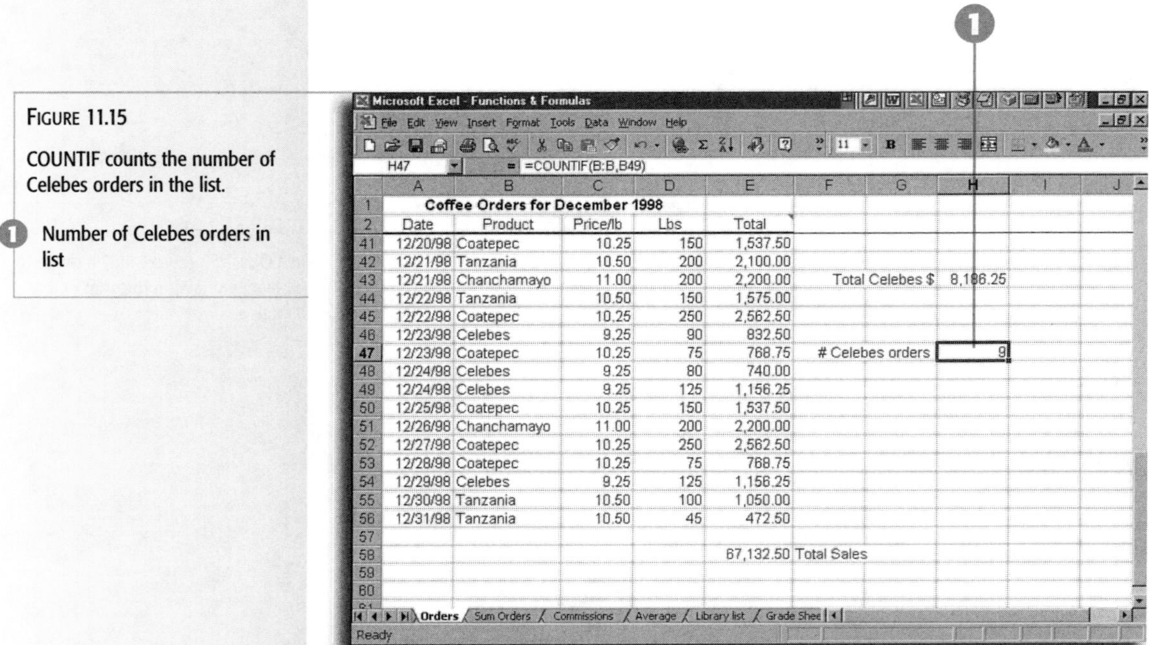

	A	B	C	D	E	F	G	H
1	Coffee Orders for December 1998							
2	Date	Product	Price/lb	Lbs	Total			
41	12/20/98	Coatepec	10.25	150	1,537.50			
42	12/21/98	Tanzania	10.50	200	2,100.00			
43	12/21/98	Chanchamayo	11.00	200	2,200.00	Total Celebes $		8,186.25
44	12/22/98	Tanzania	10.50	150	1,575.00			
45	12/22/98	Coatepec	10.25	250	2,562.50			
46	12/23/98	Celebes	9.25	90	832.50			
47	12/23/98	Coatepec	10.25	75	768.75	# Celebes orders		9
48	12/24/98	Celebes	9.25	80	740.00			
49	12/24/98	Celebes	9.25	125	1,156.25			
50	12/25/98	Coatepec	10.25	150	1,537.50			
51	12/26/98	Chanchamayo	11.00	200	2,200.00			
52	12/27/98	Coatepec	10.25	250	2,562.50			
53	12/28/98	Coatepec	10.25	75	768.75			
54	12/29/98	Celebes	9.25	125	1,156.25			
55	12/30/98	Tanzania	10.50	100	1,050.00			
56	12/31/98	Tanzania	10.50	45	472.50			
57								
58					67,132.50	Total Sales		
59								
60								

FIGURE 11.15

COUNTIF counts the number of Celebes orders in the list.

1 Number of Celebes orders in list

VLOOKUP and HLOOKUP

Sometimes, you need to look up a value in another table. For example, in an invoice, you might want Excel to look up the state tax rate for the shipping address, or if you're a teacher keeping grade sheets, you might want Excel to look up the letter grades corresponding to your students' test score averages.

A good function for looking up values in another table is VLOOKUP (or its transposed equivalent, HLOOKUP). These two functions are quite similar, the only difference being that one works vertically (VLOOKUP) and the other works horizontally (HLOOKUP) in the table. I demonstrate VLOOKUP, and when you understand VLOOKUP, you'll be able to figure out HLOOKUP if you ever need it.

Write a VLOOKUP formula

1. Create a lookup table that contains the values you want to look up (such as a state tax rate table or the letter grades table I use in this example).

The table needs to be set up so that the values you are looking up (in this example, the test averages) are in the leftmost column (as shown in Figure 11.16) and sorted in ascending order. The table can have several columns in it, as long as the values you look up are on the left.

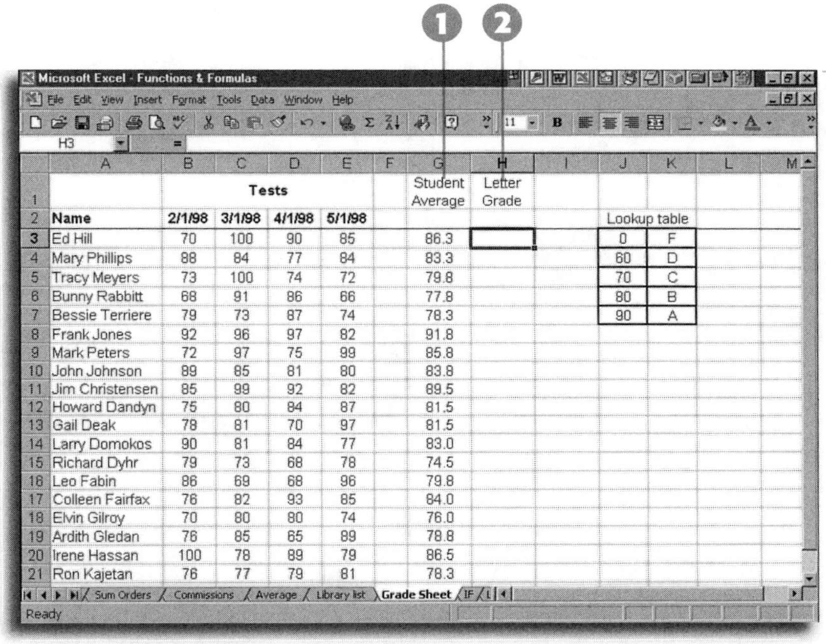
1
2
Microsoft Excel - Functions & Formulas
File Edit View Insert Format Tools Data Window Help
H3
Tests
Student Average
Letter Grade
Name 2/1/98 3/1/98 4/1/98 5/1/98
Lookup table
Ed Hill 70 100 90 85 86.3
Mary Phillips 88 84 77 84 83.3
Tracy Meyers 73 100 74 72 79.8
Bunny Rabbitt 68 91 86 66 77.8
Bessie Terriere 79 73 87 74 78.3
Frank Jones 92 96 97 82 91.8
Mark Peters 72 97 75 99 85.8
John Johnson 89 85 81 80 83.8
Jim Christensen 85 99 92 82 89.5
Howard Dandyn 75 80 84 87 81.5
Gail Deak 78 81 70 97 81.5
Larry Domokos 90 81 84 77 83.0
Richard Dyhr 79 73 68 78 74.5
Leo Fabin 86 69 68 96 79.8
Colleen Fairfax 76 82 93 85 84.0
Elvin Gilroy 70 80 80 74 76.0
Ardith Gledan 76 85 65 89 78.8
Irene Hassan 100 78 89 79 86.5
Ron Kajetan 76 77 79 81 78.3
0 F
60 D
70 C
80 B
90 A
Sum Orders / Commissions / Average / Library list / Grade Sheet / IF
Ready

FIGURE 11.16

In my lookup table, the values I want to look up (test scores) are in the leftmost column (column J), and the table is sorted in ascending order.

1. What I look up
2. What the formula returns

For greater convenience, you can name the table and refer to it by name in the formula.

2. Click the cell in which you want the result to appear.
3. Click the **Paste Function** button. *fx*
4. In the **All** or **Lookup & Reference** categories, double-click the **VLOOKUP** function.

   The VLOOKUP dialog box appears (shown in Figure 11.17).

One Lookup Table, a Lot of Lookups

A lookup table can be on the same worksheet, another worksheet, or in another workbook. For example, if you need several identical worksheets that all look up values in the same table, you can create one table on its own worksheet and use that table in the VLOOKUP formulas on all the other worksheets.

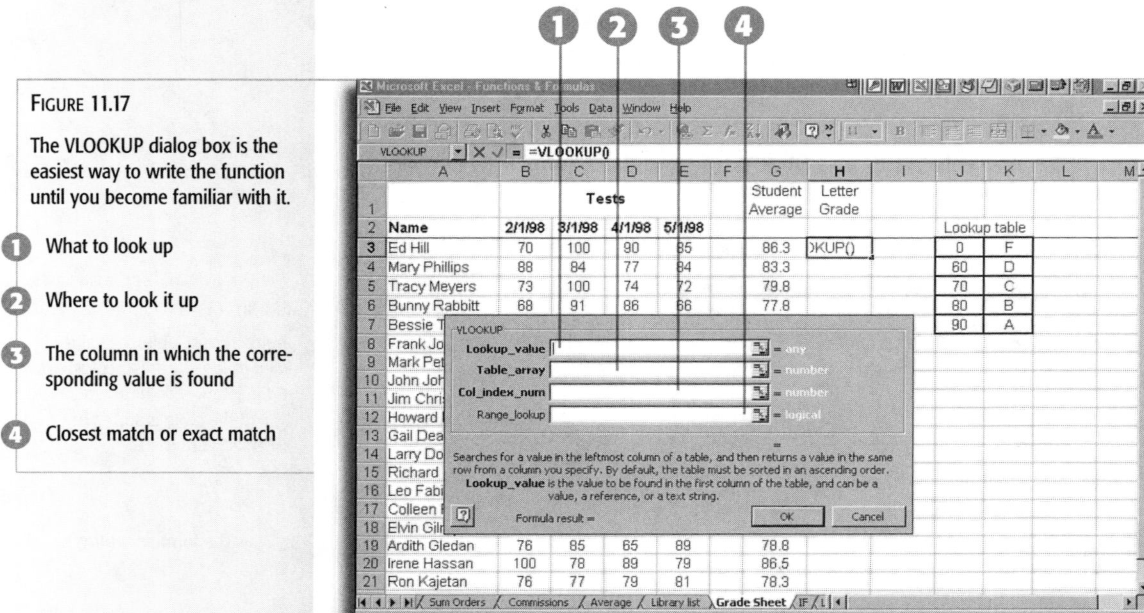

FIGURE 11.17

The VLOOKUP dialog box is the easiest way to write the function until you become familiar with it.

1. What to look up
2. Where to look it up
3. The column in which the corresponding value is found
4. Closest match or exact match

Watch Your Reference Types

If you're using a range reference instead of a range name, be sure you change the range reference types to absolute (as I've done in Figure 11.18); otherwise, the lookup table range adjusts incorrectly in every copy of the formula. To change the reference type, open the formula, click the reference, press F4 to cycle through types, and press Enter to finish the formula.

5. Click the **Lookup_value** box and click the cell that contains the value you want to look up (in this case, the test average).
6. Click the **Table_array** box and drag to select the lookup table (or enter the range name if you named the table).
7. In the **Col_index_num** box, type the number of the lookup table column in which Excel is to find a corresponding value.

   Think of the table columns as numbered left to right, starting with 1. In this example, the corresponding values (the letter grades) are in Column 2 of the lookup table.
8. In the **Range_lookup** box, decide whether you want to find the closest match or an exact match. For the closest match, leave the box empty. For an exact match, type `false`.

   In this case, each score you look up has a closest match, but probably not an exact match. The lookup table is sorted in ascending order, and VLOOKUP looks down the column for the closest match that's less than the test score value that it looks up.

For this example, the VLOOKUP dialog box should look like the one in Figure 11.18.

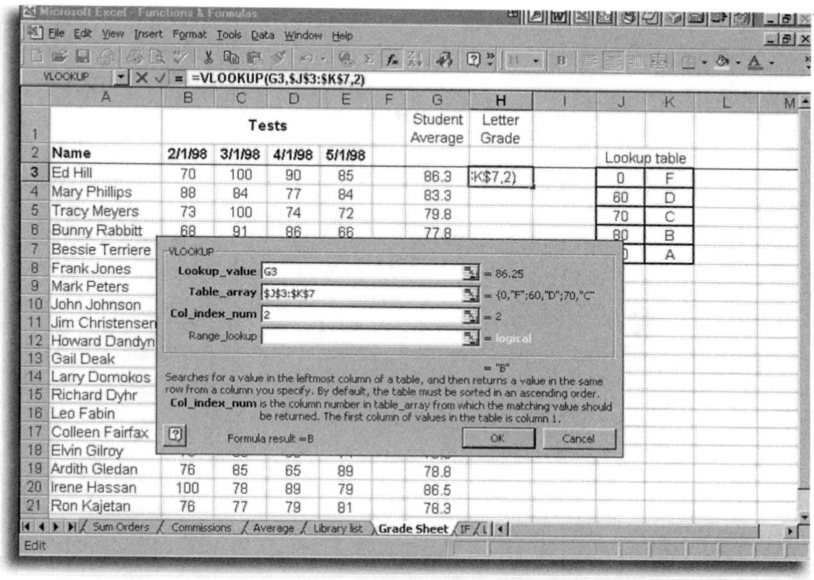

FIGURE 11.18
The VLOOKUP dialog box is ready to look up a letter grade for the test score average.

9. Click **OK**.

   The VLOOKUP function looks up the score in the lookup table, finds the closest match, and returns the letter grade in the second column.

10. To copy the formula quickly down the side of the table, position the mouse pointer over the AutoFill handle and double-click.

    Double-clicking the AutoFill handle works if the column is adjacent to the table, as shown in Figure 11.19. The formula is copied down the length of the table.

FIGURE 11.19

AutoFill is the fastest way to copy the formula down the length of the table.

1 AutoFill handle and pointer

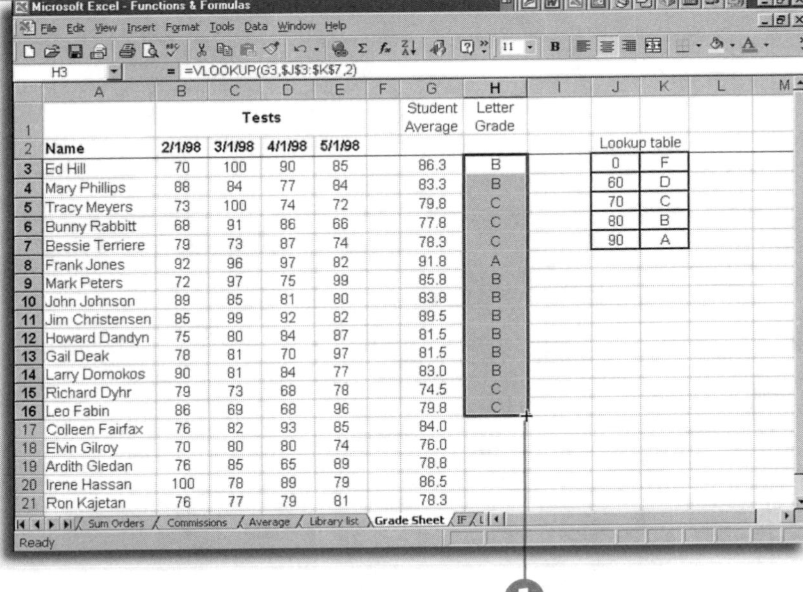

	A	B	C	D	E	F	G	H	I	J	K	L
1		Tests					Student Average	Letter Grade				
2	Name	2/1/98	3/1/98	4/1/98	5/1/98					Lookup table		
3	Ed Hill	70	100	90	85		86.3	B		0	F	
4	Mary Phillips	88	84	77	84		83.3	B		60	D	
5	Tracy Meyers	73	100	74	72		79.8	C		70	C	
6	Bunny Rabbitt	68	91	86	66		77.8	C		80	B	
7	Bessie Terriere	79	73	87	74		78.3	C		90	A	
8	Frank Jones	92	96	97	82		91.8	A				
9	Mark Peters	72	97	75	99		85.8	B				
10	John Johnson	89	85	81	80		83.8	B				
11	Jim Christensen	85	99	92	82		89.5	B				
12	Howard Dandyn	75	80	84	87		81.5	B				
13	Gail Deak	78	81	70	97		81.5	B				
14	Larry Domokos	90	81	84	77		83.0	B				
15	Richard Dyhr	79	73	68	78		74.5	C				
16	Leo Fabin	86	69	68	96		79.8	C				
17	Colleen Fairfax	76	82	93	85		84.0					
18	Elvin Gilroy	70	80	80	74		76.0					
19	Ardith Gledan	76	85	65	89		78.8					
20	Irene Hassan	100	78	89	79		86.5					
21	Ron Kajetan	76	77	79	81		78.3					

IF

The IF function is another way to determine a cell value based on criteria you set. The IF function works like this: IF *a statement is true*, THEN *return this first value;* OTHERWISE *return this second value*. (Figure 11.20 shows several examples of the IF function in action.)

As you can see in Figure 11.20, IF functions can be *nested* or combined within other IF functions to make them even more useful. In fact, any function can be nested in another function, up to seven levels deep, which enables you to be creative with worksheet calculations.

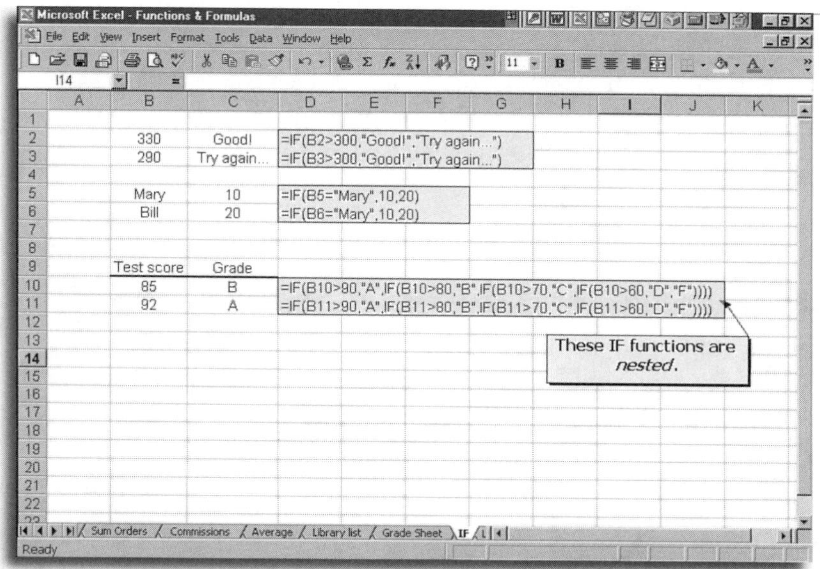

FIGURE 11.20
You can use the IF function in a lot of creative ways.

PMT

If you're shopping for a house, car, boat, or anything else that's expensive enough to require a loan, a key bit of information you want to know is the monthly payment. The PMT function figures it out for you quickly if you provide the annual interest rate, number of monthly payments, and total loan amount. (Figure 11.21 shows the PMT formula—in the Formula bar—filled out with the appropriate cells in the worksheet.) If you use cell references or named cells in the formula instead of numerical values, then you can experiment with the formula results by simply changing the input values on the worksheet.

Two things to be aware of when you use the PMT function are

- Match the rate to the terms
- The function calculates a negative payment

If the interest rate is annual (as most are), and your payments are monthly, you need to divide the rate by 12 to make the rate and terms equivalent. It's easiest to divide the function argument by 12 (as shown in Figure 11.21), so you can enter an annual rate in the rate cell.

The PMT function calculates a negative payment for a positive amount, or a negative amount for a positive payment. To make the figures in the worksheet positive (which is what folks are accustomed to seeing), make the function's pv argument negative in the formula (as shown in Figure 11.21).

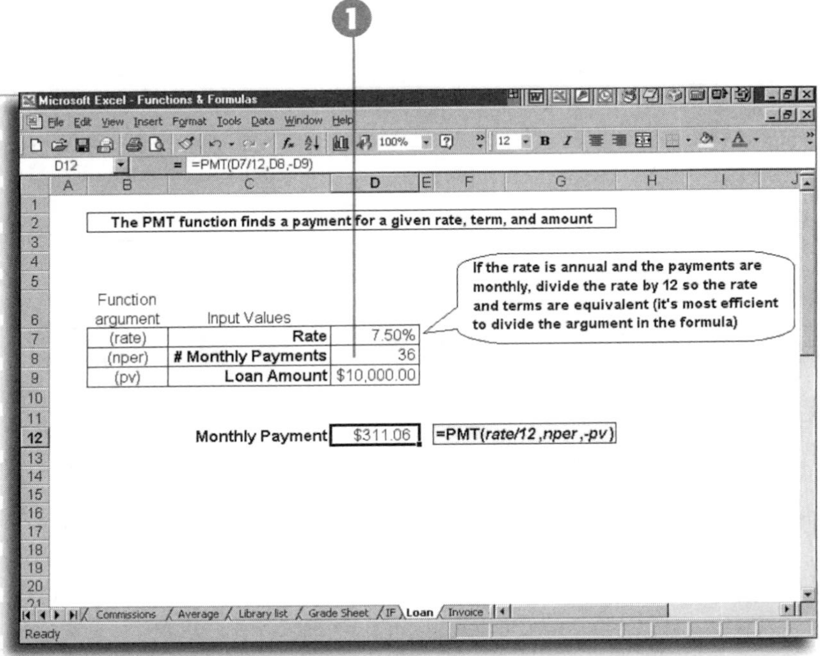

FIGURE 11.21

Use the PMT function to calculate how much of a loan you can afford.

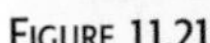
Name cells with **Insert**, **Name**, **Create**.

How Can I See the Serial Number?

If you want to see the serial number for a date, enter the date, then format the cell as General. The serial numbers for dates begin with the number 1 on January 1, 1900; the serial number 100,000 corresponds to the date October 14, 2173. Time is determined by numbers on the right side of the decimal point in the serial number. For example, the decimal .5 corresponds to 12:00:00 noon.

How Do I Know if I Spelled It Wrong?

Remember, typing a function name in lowercase letters is a good way to catch spelling errors. If the function name is spelled correctly, Excel converts it to uppercase when you complete the formula.

SEE ALSO

➤ *To learn more about scenarios, see page 318.*

NOW and TODAY

The NOW function returns the current date and time. The TODAY function returns the current date. They're useful to have in the corner of a worksheet so that you can always tell how current (or old) the information in a printed page is.

NOW and TODAY have no arguments; to write them, you type `=now()` or `=today()`, and press Enter. (Be sure you include the parentheses and don't type anything in between the parentheses.)

The resulting value is actually a serial number for the number of days since January 1, 1900. It's displayed as a date or time because the cell has a date or time format.

SEE ALSO

➤ *To learn more about formatting numbers, see page 243.*

LEFT and RIGHT

Text functions such as LEFT and RIGHT seem rather pointless unless you have a real-life use for them; then, they're amazingly useful.

One of my students is a school librarian. She wants to use Excel to keep a list of the library's books with author names, call numbers, ISBN numbers, and so forth. After typing in a long list of book titles and author names (like the list in Figure 11.22), she was going to type in the call numbers for each name. The call number, however, is composed of the first three letters of the author's last name, and she'd already done all that typing.

At this point the LEFT function saved her a lot of redundant typing.

How Can I Combine the Call# Letters and ISBN Numbers?

To combine the extracted letters in the Call# column with the numbers in the ISBN column, combine the text function with a CONCATENATE function. In Figure 11.23, enter this formula in cell B4 and AutoFill it down the column: `=LEFT(C4,3)&E4`.

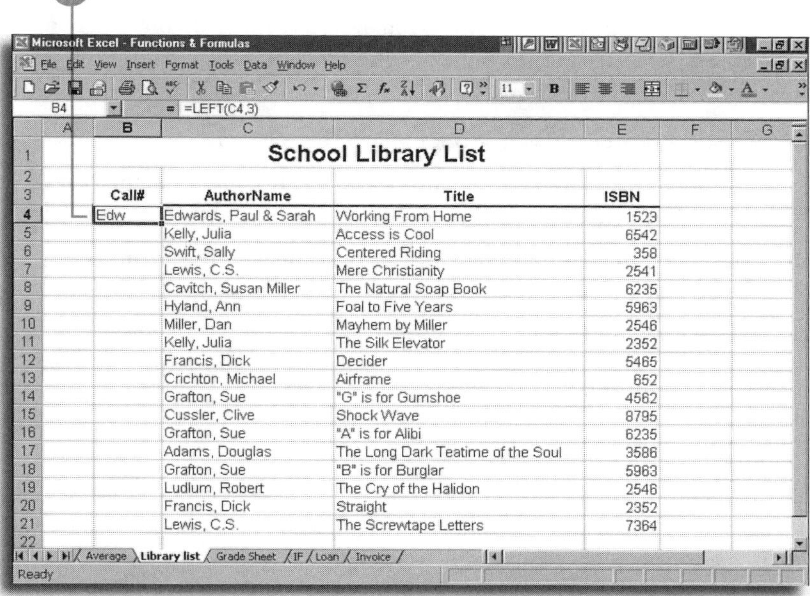

Call#	AuthorName	Title	ISBN
Edw	Edwards, Paul & Sarah	Working From Home	1523
	Kelly, Julia	Access is Cool	6542
	Swift, Sally	Centered Riding	358
	Lewis, C.S.	Mere Christianity	2541
	Cavitch, Susan Miller	The Natural Soap Book	6235
	Hyland, Ann	Foal to Five Years	5963
	Miller, Dan	Mayhem by Miller	2546
	Kelly, Julia	The Silk Elevator	2352
	Francis, Dick	Decider	5465
	Crichton, Michael	Airframe	652
	Grafton, Sue	"G" is for Gumshoe	4562
	Cussler, Clive	Shock Wave	8795
	Grafton, Sue	"A" is for Alibi	6235
	Adams, Douglas	The Long Dark Teatime of the Soul	3586
	Grafton, Sue	"B" is for Burglar	5963
	Ludlum, Robert	The Cry of the Halidon	2546
	Francis, Dick	Straight	2352
	Lewis, C.S.	The Screwtape Letters	7364

FIGURE 11.22

The LEFT function saves typing all the call numbers for this long list of books.

1. The call number is the first three letters of the author's name.

Write a formula using the LEFT function

1. Click the cell where you want the result of the function (in this case, the call number) to appear.
2. Type **=left(**.
3. Click the cell containing the value from which you want to extract characters (in this case, the AuthorName cell next to the formula).
4. Type a comma (,), and then type the number of characters you want to extract (in this case, **3**, for the leftmost three characters).
5. Type **)** and press Enter.

   The formula is complete, and it extracts the three leftmost characters in the AuthorName cell next to it.
6. Use AutoFill to copy the formula down the length of the list.

   As you can see in Figure 11.23, this saves a lot of typing.

The LEFT and RIGHT functions are also useful for creating an invoice numbering system, like the one in my invoice in Figure 11.24.

To create this unique-numbering system for my invoices, I combined the date serial number in the Date cell with the LEFT and RIGHT functions.

Create a unique-number invoice numbering system

1. Create a Date cell (in this case, cell H5) and a Client Name cell (in this case, cell A3).
2. Click the cell in which you want to display the formula result (in this case, the labeled Invoice No cell).
3. Enter the following formula:

```
=LEFT(A3,3)&"-"&RIGHT(H5,4)
```

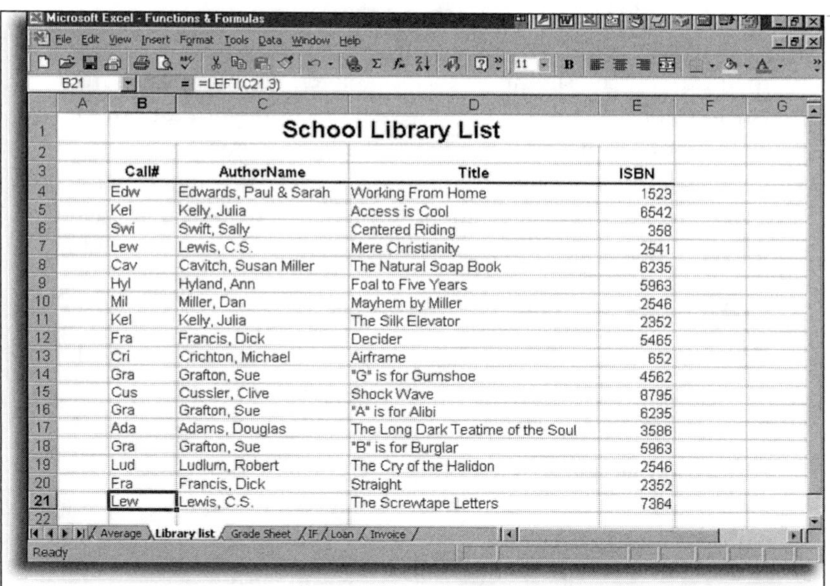

FIGURE 11.23

After the formula is written using relative references, AutoFill copies the formula down the length of the table.

Concatenate Is a LONG Name

Unlike most other functions, the CONCATENATE function name can be either spelled out (CONCATENATE) or abbreviated to an ampersand (&), which is much easier.

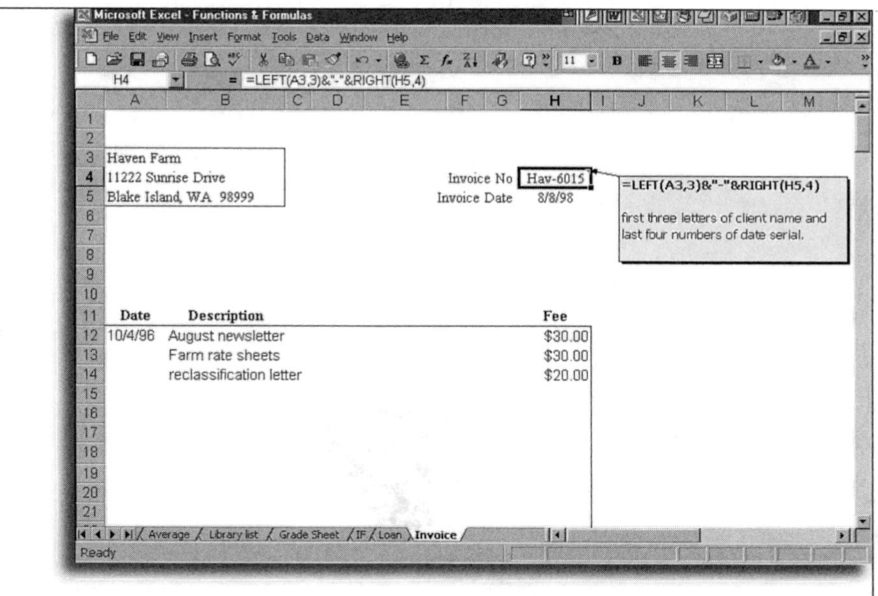

FIGURE 11.24

The text functions work with the date serial number to help me create unique invoice numbers for good record keeping.

Where Did These #REF! Values Come From?

If you later want to delete the original cells (in this case, the FirstName and LastName columns), convert the CONCATENATE formulas to values first, or you get a column full of #REF! errors because the cells to which the formulas refer are gone.

A Lot of Uses for &

You can also join a text string such as Mr. to each cell value. To join, or concatenate, Mr. to the LastName values in Figure 11.26, click cell F2 and enter the formula `="Mr."&" "&C2` (this formula joins Mr. and a space and the last name). Then use AutoFill to copy the formula down the list. (Of course, you'd have to edit the women's titles in this example, but it still saves time.)

This formula extracts the leftmost three characters from the Client Name cell (A3), joins or *concatenates* a dash character, and then extracts the rightmost four characters from the serial number in the Date cell (H5). (In the next section, you learn more about concatenation.) This makes the invoice number for each invoice unique. Because I save invoices using the invoice number as a filename, I get a clue about how ancient or recent an invoice file is when I scan a list of filenames in a My Computer window.

CONCATENATE (&)

The CONCATENATE function joins together the displayed values in two or more cells. It can also join a text string to the displayed value in a cell.

A situation where the CONCATENATE function comes in handy is shown in Figure 11.25. I want to join the first and last name columns into a single column of full names. I could do this slowly and inefficiently by laboriously copying and pasting every name, or I can write a single CONCATENATE formula and AutoFill copies it down the length of the FullName column.

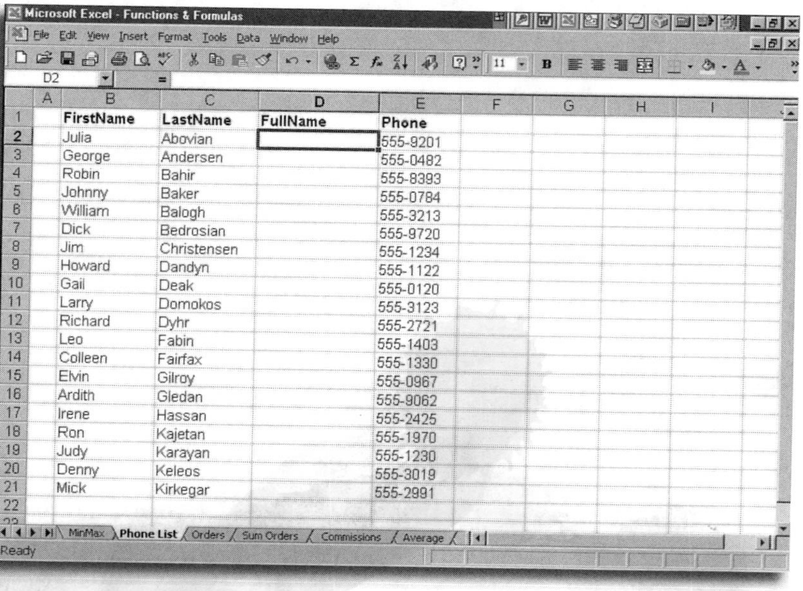

FIGURE 11.25

To join each pair of names into a single cell, use the CONCATENATE function.

	FirstName	LastName	FullName	Phone
2	Julia	Abovian		555-9201
3	George	Andersen		555-0482
4	Robin	Bahir		555-8393
5	Johnny	Baker		555-0784
6	William	Balogh		555-3213
7	Dick	Bedrosian		555-9720
8	Jim	Christensen		555-1234
9	Howard	Dandyn		555-1122
10	Gail	Deak		555-0120
11	Larry	Domokos		555-3123
12	Richard	Dyhr		555-2721
13	Leo	Fabin		555-1403
14	Colleen	Fairfax		555-1330
15	Elvin	Gilroy		555-0967
16	Ardith	Gledan		555-9062
17	Irene	Hassan		555-2425
18	Ron	Kajetan		555-1970
19	Judy	Karayan		555-1230
20	Denny	Keleos		555-3019
21	Mick	Kirkegar		555-2991

Join the values of two cells in a single cell

1. Create a column where the joined value will be displayed (in this case, the FullName column).
2. Type **=g** and click the first cell to be joined (in this case, the FirstName cell in the same row).
3. Type **&**.
4. Insert a space between the two names by typing " " (two quote marks with a space between them).
5. Type **&** again.
6. Click the second cell to be joined (in this case, the LastName cell in the same row).
7. Press Enter to complete the formula.

   The final formula is shown in Figure 11.26 in the Formula bar. The formula has been copied down the column.

SEE ALSO

➤ *To learn more about converting formula results to values, see page 208.*

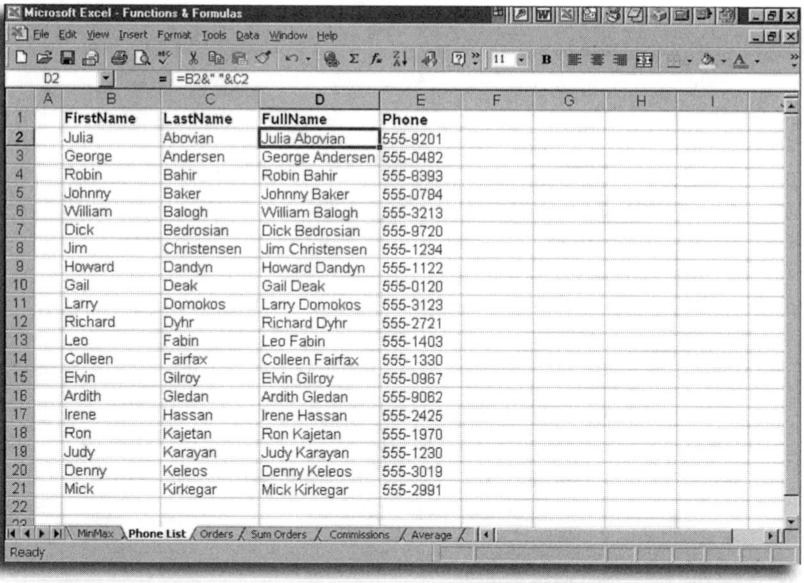

Microsoft Excel - Functions & Formulas

D2 = =B2&" "&C2

	A	B	C	D	E
1		FirstName	LastName	FullName	Phone
2		Julia	Abovian	Julia Abovian	555-9201
3		George	Andersen	George Andersen	555-0482
4		Robin	Bahir	Robin Bahir	555-8393
5		Johnny	Baker	Johnny Baker	555-0784
6		William	Balogh	William Balogh	555-3213
7		Dick	Bedrosian	Dick Bedrosian	555-9720
8		Jim	Christensen	Jim Christensen	555-1234
9		Howard	Dandyn	Howard Dandyn	555-1122
10		Gail	Deak	Gail Deak	555-0120
11		Larry	Domokos	Larry Domokos	555-3123
12		Richard	Dyhr	Richard Dyhr	555-2721
13		Leo	Fabin	Leo Fabin	555-1403
14		Colleen	Fairfax	Colleen Fairfax	555-1330
15		Elvin	Gilroy	Elvin Gilroy	555-0967
16		Ardith	Gledan	Ardith Gledan	555-9062
17		Irene	Hassan	Irene Hassan	555-2425
18		Ron	Kajetan	Ron Kajetan	555-1970
19		Judy	Karayan	Judy Karayan	555-1230
20		Denny	Keleos	Denny Keleos	555-3019
21		Mick	Kirkegar	Mick Kirkegar	555-2991

MinMax | Phone List | Orders | Sum Orders | Commissions | Average

Ready

FIGURE 11.26
CONCATENATE, or &, makes it easy to join cell values.

Using Cell Names and Labels

Cell names and labels make formulas easier to read because the cells to which they refer are quickly and easily identified.

A cell *name* is an identifying name you create; it can be almost anything, as long as it's not an existing cell reference. (For example, you can name a cell rate or January or Fred, but not FY1998 because that's the intersection of column FY and row 1998.) Cell names use absolute cell references for identification, so using a name in a formula is just like an absolute reference but easier to read.

The rules for cell names follow:

- Cell names must start with a letter or an underscore (_).
- Don't use spaces; use an underscore or, better yet, use initial capitals to separate words, as in FirstName. (Names are not case-sensitive, so you don't have to remember to type the capital letters; however, the initial capitals make the name easier to read.)
- Don't use periods (.). They're allowed but can interfere with VBA programming code, which uses periods to identify objects.
- Keep the names shorter than 255 characters (but really, that's way too long to be practical, anyway).
- Don't use hyphens or other punctuation marks. (If Excel won't let you create the name, a punctuation mark may be the problem.)

Naming Cells

You can use a few different methods for naming cells: the Name box, the Create Names dialog box, and the Define Name dialog box. Each is more convenient in particular situations. I will show you how and when to use each procedure.

Using the Name Box

The Name box is the fastest way to name a cell or range if you're only creating one name or if the name is not already a label or table heading on the worksheet. For example, on my

Phone List worksheet, I'm going to name the entire table Contacts so that I can get to it quickly from anywhere in the workbook (see Figure 11.27).

Name cells or ranges using the Name box

1. Select the cell or range you want to name.
2. Click the **Name** box (shown in Figure 11.28).
3. Type the name and press Enter.

   When the named range is selected, the name appears in the Name box (as shown in Figure 11.29). To select the range, click the down arrow in the Name box and then click the range name.

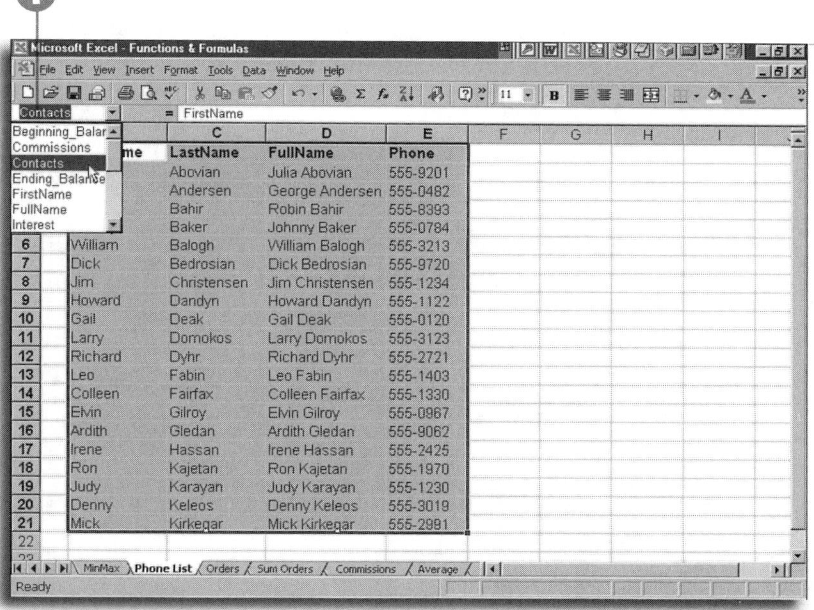

FIGURE 11.27
After the range is named, I can select it quickly by clicking its name on the Name box list.

1 Name box

B1

FIGURE 11.28
Click the Name box once to highlight it for naming.

FIGURE 11.29

When a named range or cell is selected, the name appears in the Name box.

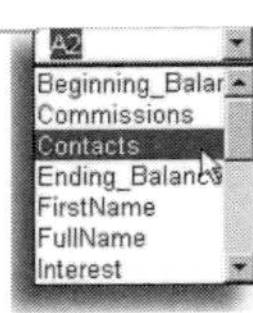

Using the Create Names Dialog Box

The Create Names dialog box is the quickest method if the names you want to use are already in place on the worksheet as row or column labels. For example, on my Phone List worksheet, I'm going to name each column in my Contacts range with its column heading. The Create Names dialog box creates all four names at once.

Create names using the Create Names dialog box

1. Select the range you want to name, including the headings on the top, left, bottom, or right edges of the range (as shown in Figure 11.30).

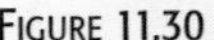

FIGURE 11.30

To create names, select the range and include the headings or labels.

1 These headings become range names.

2. From the **Insert** menu, point to **Name** and then click **Create**.
3. In the Create Names dialog box, mark or clear check boxes as needed so that only the appropriate check boxes are checked. (In this example, only the **Top row** check box should be marked.)
4. Click **OK**.

   The names are created, and you can select any of the ranges by clicking its name in the Name box list (as shown in Figure 11.31).

What's a Constant?

A *constant value* is an unchanging number value, such as 135 or 7.5%. Where would you use it? If the local sales tax rate is 8.17%, you can name the value TaxRate and not have to remember the exact numerical value. When the city raises the tax rate next year, you just redefine the name instead of changing it in all the cells or formulas where the number appears

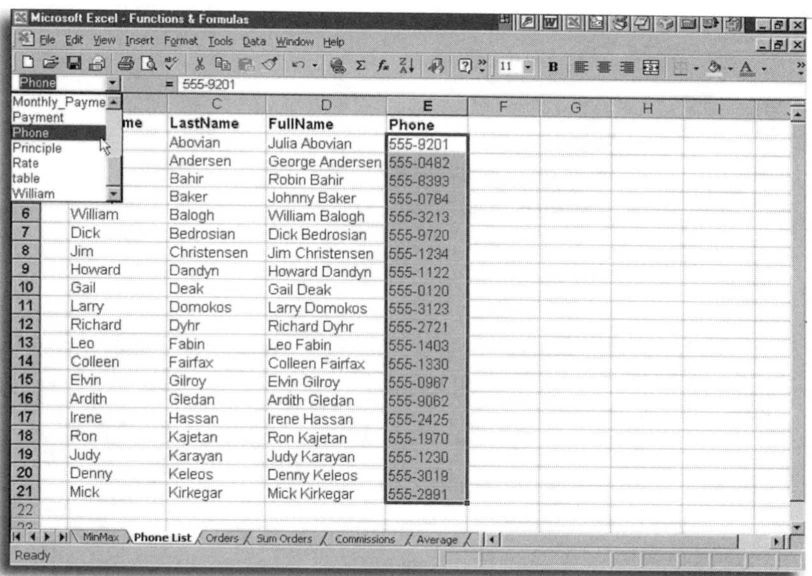

FIGURE 11.31
You can select a range name from wherever you are in the workbook.

Using the Define Name Dialog Box

The Define Name dialog box is another way to create cell and range names, although not the quickest. It is, however, the only way to name formulas or constant values. Instead of repeatedly writing, or even copying, a long and complex formula, you can write the formula once, give it a name, and then simply write the formula name instead of the formula.

I Don't See My Formula and Constant Names

Formula names and constant value names don't appear on the Name box list, but you can type them into cells or other formulas.

Name a formula or a constant value with the Define Name dialog box

1. From the **Insert** menu, point to **Name** and then click **Define**.

   The Define Name dialog box appears.

2. In the **Names in workbook** box, type the name for your formula, range, or constant value.
3. In the **Refers to** box, type **=** followed by the formula or value. (Figure 11.32 shows a Define Name dialog box that names a constant value.)
4. Click **OK**.

   Figure 11.33 shows a named constant in use.

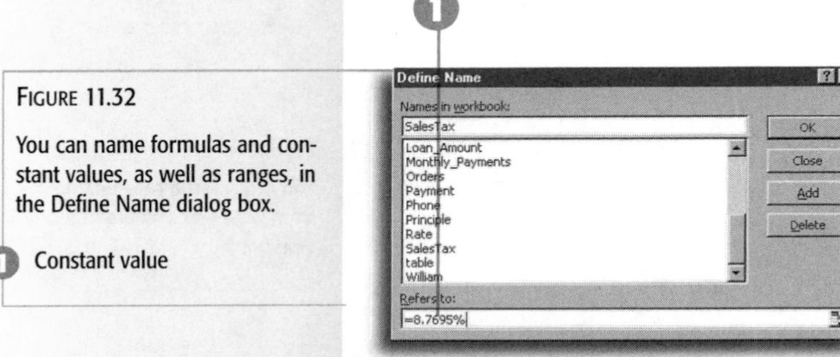

FIGURE 11.32

You can name formulas and constant values, as well as ranges, in the Define Name dialog box.

1 Constant value

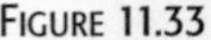

FIGURE 11.33

Naming a constant value makes it easier to use repeatedly.

1 Named constant value

Microsoft Excel - Functions & Formulas

E59 = =E58*SalesTax

	A	B	C	D	E	F
1	Coffee Orders for December 1998					
2	Date	Product	Price/lb	Lbs	Total	
49	12/24/98	Celebes	9.25	125	1,156.25	
50	12/25/98	Coatepec	10.25	150	1,537.50	
51	12/26/98	Chanchamayo	11.00	200	2,200.00	
52	12/27/98	Coatepec	10.25	250	2,562.50	
53	12/28/98	Coatepec	10.25	75	768.75	
54	12/29/98	Celebes	9.25	125	1,156.25	
55	12/30/98	Tanzania	10.50	100	1,050.00	
56	12/31/98	Tanzania	10.50	45	472.50	
57						
58					67,132.50	Total Sales
59					5,887.18	Tax
60					73,019.68	Total Charge

MinMax / Phone List / Orders / Sum Orders / Commissions / Average

Ready

Writing Formulas with Named Cells

Using cell and range names in a formula is easy and makes the formula easier to read and understand.

Use cell and range names in a formula

1. Click the cell in which you want to display the result of the formula.
2. Type your formula, beginning with an =.
3. Where you need to insert a name, type the name, or on the **Insert** menu, point to **Name**, click **Paste**, and then click the name in the list.
4. Complete the formula by pressing Enter. (A formula with cell names instead of references might look like the one in the Formula bar in Figure 11.34.)

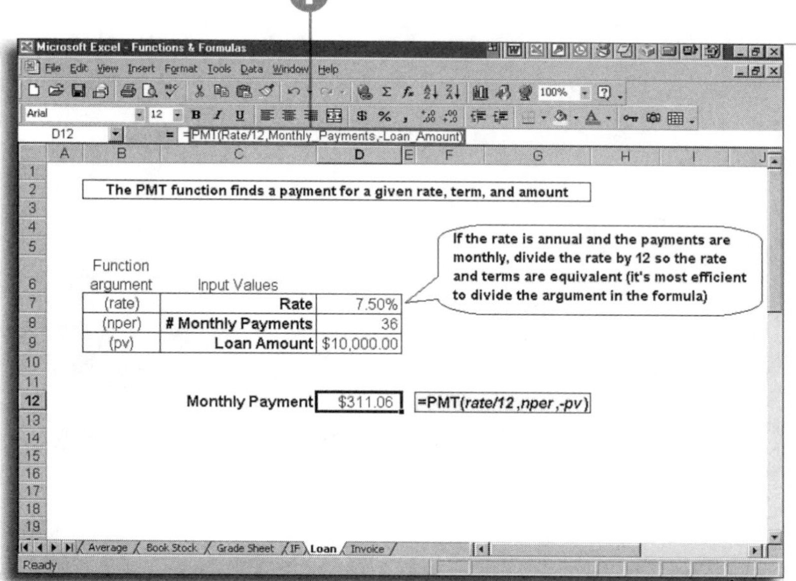

FIGURE 11.34
Names make formulas easier to understand.

1. Names instead of cell references

It Was Better in the Old Days

Popping names into formulas used to be a lot easier; you could select names from the Name box. Microsoft, however, replaced that functionality with the altogether less useful list of functions in the Name box. Personally, I hope they return the Name box functionality in future versions of Excel.

Should I Use Labels or Names?

Labels are convenient as long as the formulas are positioned close to the table so that Excel knows to which labels the formula refers. If, however, the formula is not lined up with the columns or rows the labels identify, then the labels don't work and you need to create names instead.

Writing Formulas with Labels

If your data has row and column labels, you can use them in formulas just like names but without first creating names.

(In Figure 11.35, the table has column headers that I can use in formulas without first creating names with them.)

Write a formula with labels

1. Click a cell in line with the labeled columns and rows you want to use in the formula.
2. Type your formula, and type labels where the cell references are needed (as shown in Figure 11.35).

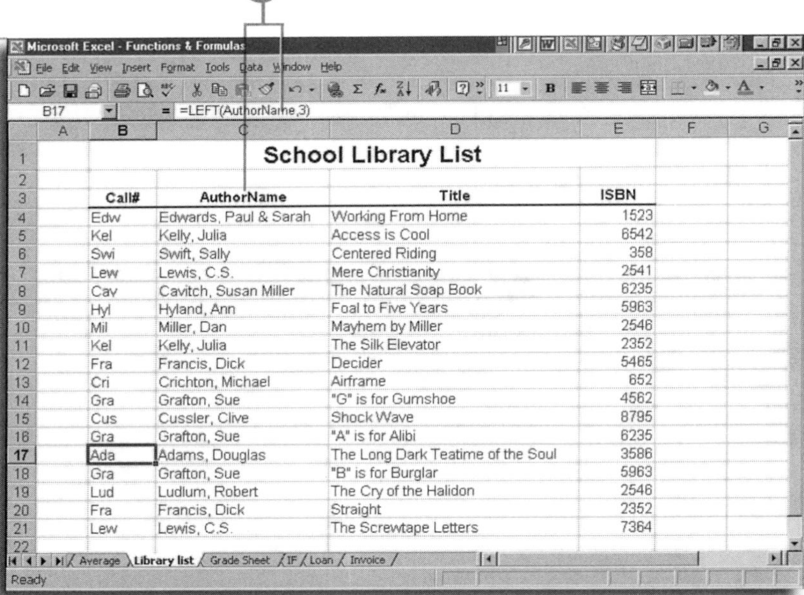

School Library List

Call#	AuthorName	Title	ISBN
Edw	Edwards, Paul & Sarah	Working From Home	1523
Kel	Kelly, Julia	Access is Cool	6542
Swi	Swift, Sally	Centered Riding	358
Lew	Lewis, C.S.	Mere Christianity	2541
Cav	Cavitch, Susan Miller	The Natural Soap Book	6235
Hyl	Hyland, Ann	Foal to Five Years	5963
Mil	Miller, Dan	Mayhem by Miller	2546
Kel	Kelly, Julia	The Silk Elevator	2352
Fra	Francis, Dick	Decider	5465
Cri	Crichton, Michael	Airframe	652
Gra	Grafton, Sue	"G" is for Gumshoe	4562
Cus	Cussler, Clive	Shock Wave	8795
Gra	Grafton, Sue	"A" is for Alibi	6235
Ada	Adams, Douglas	The Long Dark Teatime of the Soul	3586
Gra	Grafton, Sue	"B" is for Burglar	5963
Lud	Ludlum, Robert	The Cry of the Halidon	2546
Fra	Francis, Dick	Straight	2352
Lew	Lewis, C.S.	The Screwtape Letters	7364

FIGURE 11.35

Labels are quick and convenient when your formulas are lined up with labeled rows and columns.

1 Column label

Converting Formula Results to Values

If you write a formula, such as a CONCATENATE formula, then delete the referenced cells that you no longer need on the worksheet, the formulas won't work any more. You can, however, convert the formula results to values so that you can delete the unnecessary source cells without changing the results that the formulas produced.

Convert formula results to values

1. Select the formulas.

2. Click the **Copy** button (or use your favorite Copy method).
3. From the **Edit** menu, click **Paste Special**.
4. In the Paste Special dialog box (shown in Figure 11.36), click the **Values** option.

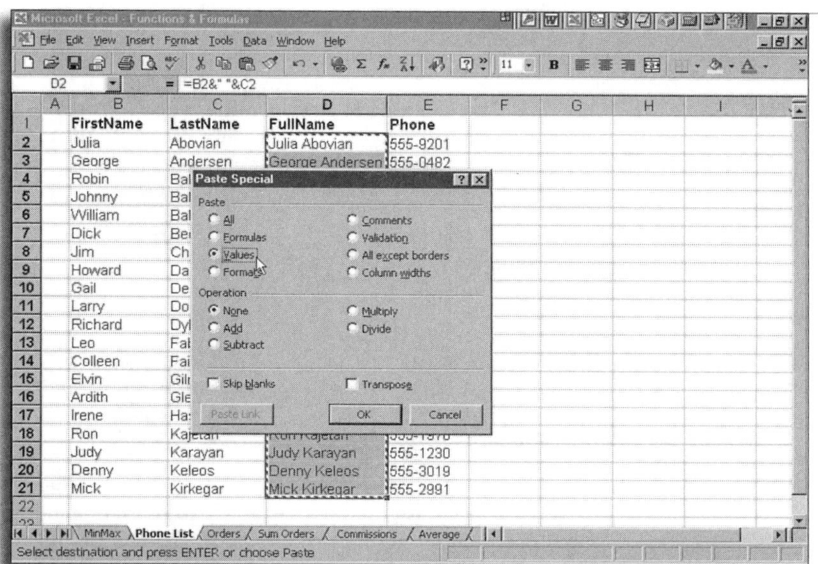

FIGURE 11.36
Use the Paste Special dialog box to convert formulas to values; then you can delete the source cells without affecting the formula results.

5. Click **OK**.

   The formulas are replaced by their resulting values, and you can delete the source cells. If the moving border bothers you, you can remove it by pressing Escape.

Will I Need the Last Name Column?

In a worksheet like Figure 11.36, you might want to leave the last name column in place so that you can continue to sort the list by last name.

Locating Worksheet Errors

Errors and invalid data seem to sneak into the most scrupulously designed worksheets, but you can find and fix them with the help of a few Excel tools. If an error appears in a formula, you can use the Auditing tools to find the source of the error. (Table 11.2 provides a list of errors and what they mean.) If someone has entered invalid data in a worksheet where data validation is in effect, you can locate and edit the inaccuracies by using the Circle Invalid Data button on the Auditing toolbar.

TABLE 11.2 **Error values**

This Error	Means This	To Fix It, Do This
#####	The column isn't wide enough to display the value.	Widen the column.
#VALUE!	Wrong type of argument or operand (for example, calculating a cell with the value #N/A).	Check operands and arguments; make sure references are valid.
#DIV/0!	Formula is attempting to divide by zero.	Change the value or cell reference so that the formula doesn't divide by zero.
#NAME?	Formula is referencing an invalid or nonexistent name.	Make sure the name still exists or correct the misspelling.
#N/A	Most commonly means no value is available or inappropriate arguments were used.	In a lookup formula, be sure the lookup table is sorted correctly.
#REF!	Excel can't locate the referenced cells. (For example, referenced cells were deleted.)	Click Undo immediately to restore references and then change formula references or convert formulas to values.
#NUM!	Incorrect use of a number (such as SQRT(-1)), or formula result is a number too large or too small to be displayed.	Make sure that the arguments are correct, and that the result is between $-1*10^{307}$ and $1*10^{307}$.
#NULL!	Reference to intersection of two areas that do not intersect.	Check for typing and reference errors.
Circular	A formula refers to itself, either directly or indirectly.	Click OK and then look at the status bar to see which cell contains the circular reference.

Locating Errors in Formulas

To locate the source of an error in a formula, begin by checking the formula itself for typing and spelling mistakes.

Find the source of an error

1. Right-click a toolbar and click **Customize** to display the Auditing toolbar. In the Customize dialog box, on the **Toolbars** tab, mark the **Auditing** check box and click **Close**.
2. Click the cell containing the error.
3. On the Auditing toolbar, click the **Trace Errors** button.

   Tracing arrows appear and guide you visually to possible sources of error. Blue trace lines show referenced cells, and red trace lines lead to the cell that caused the error value.

Finding Invalid Data in a Worksheet

If you've set up data validation in such a way that invalid data can be entered by ignoring the validation messages, or if you apply data validation rules to an existing table of data, you can locate cells containing data that doesn't meet the validation rules.

Look for invalid data

1. Make sure Data Validation has been set up for the cells you want to check. If not, go ahead and set up validation rules.
2. Right-click a toolbar and click **Customize** to display the Auditing toolbar. In the Customize dialog box, on the **Toolbars** tab, mark the **Auditing** check box and then click **Close**.
3. Select the range you want to check for invalid data.
4. On the Auditing toolbar, click the **Circle Invalid Data** button.

   All cells containing data that doesn't meet validation rules are circled in red (shown in Figure 11.37).

   To remove the circles, click the **Clear Validation Circles** button.

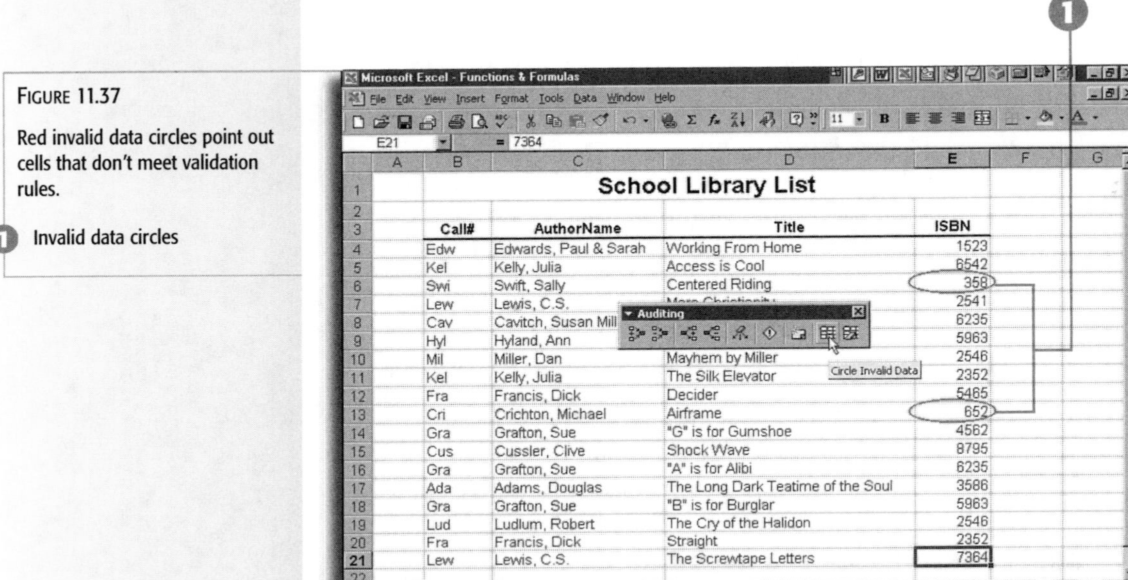

FIGURE 11.37

Red invalid data circles point out cells that don't meet validation rules.

1 Invalid data circles

SEE ALSO

➤ *To learn more about validating data during entry, see page 118.*

PART III

Formatting

12 Formatting Cells 215

13 Formatting Numbers 243

14 Formatting with Styles for Less Effort 257

CHAPTER

12

Formatting Cells

- Using the Formatting toolbar
- Making entries bold or italic, changing font size
- Controlling how entries are displayed in a cell
- Transposing table orientation
- Merging multiple cells into one cell
- Applying cell borders
- Changing colors
- Copying formatting to other cells
- Formatting tables with built-in formats
- Adding graphics to a worksheet

Save at Each Step

If you make many formatting changes at once, it might be difficult to reverse all those changes if you don't like the result. Instead, save the workbook at each stage where you like the look. If the next set of changes makes things worse instead of better, close the workbook without saving and reopen the saved version.

The Formatting Toolbar

Formatting dresses up a worksheet and makes it look nice, but more than that, formatting can make data more meaningful by visually segregating data into groups and highlighting summary information.

The Formatting toolbar, shown in Figure 12.1, holds buttons for the most commonly used formatting choices. It's usually displayed at the top of your Excel window, but if it isn't, you can display it.

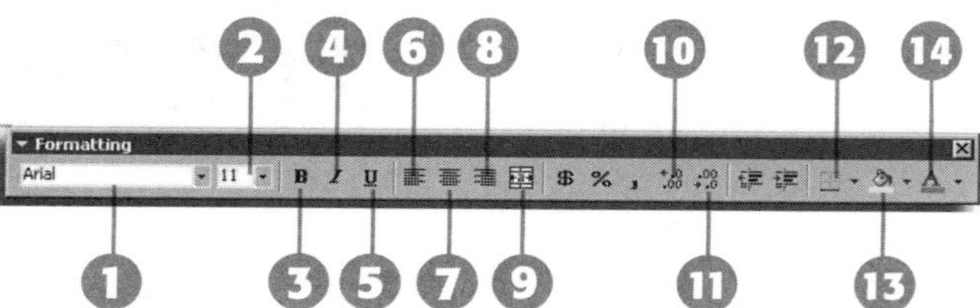

FIGURE 12.1

The default Formatting toolbar.

1. Font
2. Font size
3. Bold
4. Italic
5. Underline
6. Align left
7. Center
8. Align right
9. Merge and Center
10. Increase Decimal
11. Decrease Decimal
12. Borders
13. Fill Color
14. Font Color

Display the Formatting toolbar

1. Right-click any toolbar or menu bar.
2. On the shortcut menu, click **Formatting**.

If your toolbar options are set so that the Standard and Formatting toolbars share one row, both toolbars will appear at the top of your screen side-by-side, and neither will display a complete set of buttons. (The buttons are all there, but some are hidden until you use them.) To find the hidden buttons, display the drop-down buttons palette.

Find the hidden buttons

1. Click the small down arrow at the right end of the toolbar. The ScreenTip says **More Buttons**.
2. Click the button you want to use. After you click a button, it appears on the toolbar and another button is hidden.

   If you want your toolbars to be fully displayed, one below the other, right-click any toolbar. Click **Customize**, and on the **Options** tab, clear the **Standard and Formatting toolbars share one row** check box.

If your Formatting toolbar is missing any of the buttons shown in Figure 12.1, someone might have accidentally (or purposely) removed them. You can restore the default configuration to any built-in toolbar (all the default buttons are restored, and any extra buttons you added are removed).

Restore the Formatting toolbar to its default configuration

1. In the Customize dialog box, in the **Toolbars** tab, click the **Formatting** toolbar name; then, click the **Reset** button.

   When asked if you're sure you want reset, click **OK**.

2. Click **Close**.

SEE ALSO

➤ *To learn more about customizing toolbars, see the section "Create a Personal Toolbar," page 529.*

Hey! Where'd My Button Go?

Every time you use a "hidden" button, that button remains in view on the toolbar and a different button (one you haven't used recently) is hidden; and every time you change the length of one of the toolbars, more buttons are revealed on the lengthened toolbar and hidden on the shortened toolbar. There isn't much rhyme or reason to it, but the idea is that the buttons you use least are hidden.

Formatting the Font

Formatting the font means changing the look of the characters in a cell. You can change the format of all the characters in a cell, or you can select individual characters within a cell and format them differently. (For example, you can use subscript formatting to write a chemical name, use superscript formatting to write an exponent, or make the first letter of a name bold and red.) Table 12.1 shows some of the ways you can format the characters in an entry.

TABLE 12.1 Font formatting possibilities

Format	Notes
Font	Typeface. Any font installed on your computer, including symbol fonts, is available in a worksheet.
Size	Size of characters, measured in points (72 points per inch).
Font Style	Bold, italic, or bold and italic together.
Underlines	Several underline styles are available in the Format Cells dialog box on the Font tab. Accounting underlines leave space between the characters and the underline (which makes characters more legible because their descending tails aren't hidden by the underline).

continues...

TABLE 12.1 Continued

Format	Notes
Effects	Effects include superscript (10^3), subscript (H_2O), and ~~strikethrough~~; available in the Format Cells dialog box.
Align Left	Pushes the entry against the left side of the cell.
Center	Centers the entry in the cell.
Align Right	Pushes the entry against the right side of the cell.
Merge and Center	Merges selected adjacent cells into a single cell, and centers the entry across the merged cells.
Increase Decimal	Adds one decimal place to displayed value.
Decrease Decimal	Reduces the number of displayed decimal places by one (and rounds displayed value).
Borders	Lots of border options are available on the Borders toolbar, and there are more in the Format Cells dialog box.
Fill Color	Cell shading (background color in cell). Patterns are available in the Format Cells dialog box.
Font Color	Character color.

Apply formatting with toolbar buttons

1. Select the cells or characters where you want to apply the formatting.
2. Click the toolbar buttons for the formats you want.

Apply formatting with the Format Cells dialog box.

1. Select the cells or characters where you want to apply the formatting.
2. Right-click the selection; then, click **Format Cells**.
3. Click tabs and select the desired formatting; when you're finished, click **OK**.

These are the basic procedures. Figure 12.2 shows a worksheet with lots of data but desperately in need of a makeover, so I'll go through individual formatting procedures in more detail (with pictures).

I'll start by making the worksheet and column headings bold.

	A	B	C	D	E	F	G	H	I	J
1	Accoutrement & Deshabille, Inc. Employee Commissions									
2		1998								
3	Dept/Empl	January	February	March	April	May	June	July	August	Septembe
4	Accessories									
5	Marcia	4913	3194	3650	2592	1330	3002	4166	4324	2906
6	Fred	3554	1006	4029	2430	1635	4508	4472	1616	3260
7	Lila	3098	4820	1032	2628	4213	1951	2099	4451	3939
8	Lingerie									
9	Armelle	1894	4237	3333	3256	2382	2486	1818	1064	3292
10	Jamie	3423	4609	3707	2441	2896	1327	1429	3714	2940
11	Tracy	3266	1621	2873	3526	2622	2148	2094	3449	2420
12	Hats									
13	Susannah	2366	2445	4514	4753	4505	4934	3523	4179	3055
14	Tina	4578	2963	2982	1522	2067	3944	2605	4621	2510
15	Diane	3217	1248	4004	3449	4563	4542	4668	3612	1345
16	Bags									
17	Kurt	1104	2936	2296	1051	2310	3746	2918	3473	3675
18	Jill	1373	1246	2861	3949	1111	3683	1756	1954	1574
19	Elaine	3622	3486	1654	3092	1313	4869	3819	1757	1913
20	Jewelry									
21	Albert	3105	1886	2433	2325	3842	4861	2460	3008	4268
22	Ruby	4855	2797	4422	2312	4336	2969	3630	1064	4850

FIGURE 12.2

Good data, but a thoroughly dull presentation.

Make the text boldface

1. Select the cells with the worksheet titles and month names (in this case, A1:M3).
2. On the Formatting toolbar, click **Bold**. **B**

All the month names are formatted bold, as shown in Figure 12.3.

I want to make the worksheet title, "Accoutrement & Deshabille, Inc. Employee Commissions," italic.

Italicize text

1. Select the cells you want to format (in this case, A1).
2. On the Formatting toolbar, click **Italic**. *I*

I also want to make the worksheet title much larger.

Increase or decrease font size

1. Select the cells you want to format (in this case, A1).
2. On the Formatting toolbar, click the down arrow on the Font Size box; then, click **18**.

   Figure 12.4 shows the Commissions worksheet with a large, italic title.

Select a Block of Data Fast

To select to the end of a block of data, click the first cell (B3); then, hold down the Shift key and double-click the right border of the selected cell.

Format Only the Cells That Need It

You can select and format the entire row, all the way across the worksheet, but it wastes system resources to apply formatting to cells you aren't going to use.

FIGURE 12.3
This is a bold beginning to a better presentation. (I couldn't resist the pun!)

	A	B	C	D	E	F	G	H	I	J
1	**Accoutrement & Deshabille, Inc. Employee Commissions**									
2		**1998**								
3	**Dept/Empl**	**January**	**February**	**March**	**April**	**May**	**June**	**July**	**August**	**Septembe**
4	Accessories									
5	Marcia	4913	3194	3650	2592	1330	3002	4166	4324	2906
6	Fred	3554	1006	4029	2430	1635	4508	4472	1616	3260
7	Lila	3098	4820	1032	2628	4213	1951	2099	4451	3939
8	Lingerie									
9	Armelle	1894	4237	3333	3256	2382	2486	1818	1064	3292
10	Jamie	3423	4609	3707	2441	2896	1327	1429	3714	2940
11	Tracy	3266	1621	2873	3526	2622	2148	2094	3449	2420
12	Hats									
13	Susannah	2366	2445	4514	4753	4505	4934	3523	4179	3055
14	Tina	4578	2963	2982	1522	2067	3944	2605	4621	2510
15	Diane	3217	1248	4004	3449	4563	4542	4668	3612	1345
16	Bags									
17	Kurt	1104	2936	2296	1051	2310	3746	2918	3473	3675
18	Jill	1373	1246	2861	3949	1111	3683	1756	1954	1574
19	Elaine	3622	3486	1654	3092	1313	4869	3819	1757	1913
20	Jewelry									
21	Albert	3105	1886	2433	2325	3842	4861	2460	3008	4268
22	Ruby	4855	2797	4422	2312	4336	2969	3630	1064	4850

FIGURE 12.4
Larger font and italics make the worksheet title stand out.

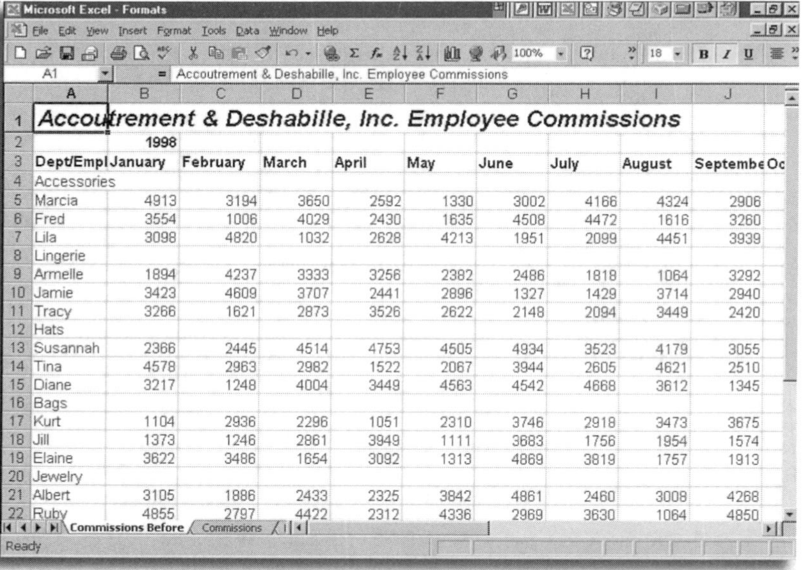

	A	B	C	D	E	F	G	H	I	J
1	***Accoutrement & Deshabille, Inc. Employee Commissions***									
2		**1998**								
3	**Dept/Empl**	**January**	**February**	**March**	**April**	**May**	**June**	**July**	**August**	**Septembe**
4	Accessories									
5	Marcia	4913	3194	3650	2592	1330	3002	4166	4324	2906
6	Fred	3554	1006	4029	2430	1635	4508	4472	1616	3260
7	Lila	3098	4820	1032	2628	4213	1951	2099	4451	3939
8	Lingerie									
9	Armelle	1894	4237	3333	3256	2382	2486	1818	1064	3292
10	Jamie	3423	4609	3707	2441	2896	1327	1429	3714	2940
11	Tracy	3266	1621	2873	3526	2622	2148	2094	3449	2420
12	Hats									
13	Susannah	2366	2445	4514	4753	4505	4934	3523	4179	3055
14	Tina	4578	2963	2982	1522	2067	3944	2605	4621	2510
15	Diane	3217	1248	4004	3449	4563	4542	4668	3612	1345
16	Bags									
17	Kurt	1104	2936	2296	1051	2310	3746	2918	3473	3675
18	Jill	1373	1246	2861	3949	1111	3683	1756	1954	1574
19	Elaine	3622	3486	1654	3092	1313	4869	3819	1757	1913
20	Jewelry									
21	Albert	3105	1886	2433	2325	3842	4861	2460	3008	4268
22	Ruby	4855	2797	4422	2312	4336	2969	3630	1064	4850

Making the Cell Fit the Text (and Vice Versa)

When you start a new worksheet, you probably won't devote much time initially to thinking about how the data will look; after all, the point of a worksheet is usually formulas and calculations, not presentation. A default worksheet has millions of cells for data entry—all the same size. As you type entries, Excel pops them into these cells and displays only what will fit. Although the worksheet will work just fine that way, it isn't very helpful for you as you read the cell entries or for anyone else who tries to read the reports you print from this default setup.

When your data is entered and ready to use—or anywhere along the way—you can use Excel's many formatting features to help make the worksheet and its contents fit together.

Aligning Entries

When you enter data, Excel automatically aligns text on the left side of the cell and numbers on the right, but you can easily change alignment to make your data easier to read. I want to center the month names in my column headings.

Change cell alignment

1. Select the cells you want to align (in this case, B3:M3).
2. On the Formatting toolbar, click an alignment button (in this case, the Center button).

   Figure 12.5 shows the results of centering the month names. The names are *truncated*, cut off at the right to fit in the cell, but I'll fix that later by rotating the entries and changing the column widths.

In column A, I have department names and employee names in the same column; to differentiate them, I'll leave the department names aligned on the left but indent the employee names by four characters.

FIGURE 12.5

Month names are centered but they're also truncated.

	A	B	C	D	E	F	G	H	I	J
1	Accoutrement & Deshabille, Inc. Employee Commissions									
2		1998								
3	Dept/Empl	January	February	March	April	May	June	July	August	Septembe
4	Accessories									
5	Marcia	4913	3194	3650	2592	1330	3002	4166	4324	2906
6	Fred	3554	1006	4029	2430	1635	4508	4472	1616	3260
7	Lila	3098	4820	1032	2628	4213	1951	2099	4451	3939
8	Lingerie									
9	Armelle	1894	4237	3333	3256	2382	2486	1818	1064	3292
10	Jamie	3423	4609	3707	2441	2896	1327	1429	3714	2940
11	Tracy	3266	1621	2873	3526	2622	2148	2094	3449	2420
12	Hats									
13	Susannah	2366	2445	4514	4753	4505	4934	3523	4179	3055
14	Tina	4578	2963	2982	1522	2067	3944	2605	4621	2510
15	Diane	3217	1248	4004	3449	4563	4542	4668	3612	1345
16	Bags									
17	Kurt	1104	2936	2296	1051	2310	3746	2918	3473	3675
18	Jill	1373	1246	2861	3949	1111	3683	1756	1954	1574
19	Elaine	3622	3486	1654	3092	1313	4869	3819	1757	1913
20	Jewelry									
21	Albert	3105	1886	2433	2325	3842	4861	2460	3008	4268
22	Ruby	4855	2797	4422	2312	4336	2969	3630	1064	4850

Formatting Nonadjacent Cells

To select nonadjacent cells for formatting, select the first cell or range; then, hold down Ctrl and select the remaining cells or ranges.

Indent entries

1. Select the cells you want to indent (in this case, all the employee name cells in column A).
2. On the **Format** menu, click **Cells**.
3. On the **Alignment** tab, set a number in the **Indent** box, as shown in Figure 12.6; then, click **OK**. (The Indent number is a number of character widths.) Later, I'll fix the column widths to fully display the entries.

The columns are too wide to fit conveniently on my screen or on a printed page, but only because the month names are so wide. I can make the columns narrower without abbreviating the month names by rotating the month name entries.

Rotate cell entries

1. Select the cells you want to rotate (in this case, B3:M3).
2. On the **Format** menu, click **Cells**.
3. On the **Alignment** tab, under **Orientation**, click in the half-circle to set a rotation angle, as shown in Figure 12.7; then, click **OK**.

   The cell entries are rotated.

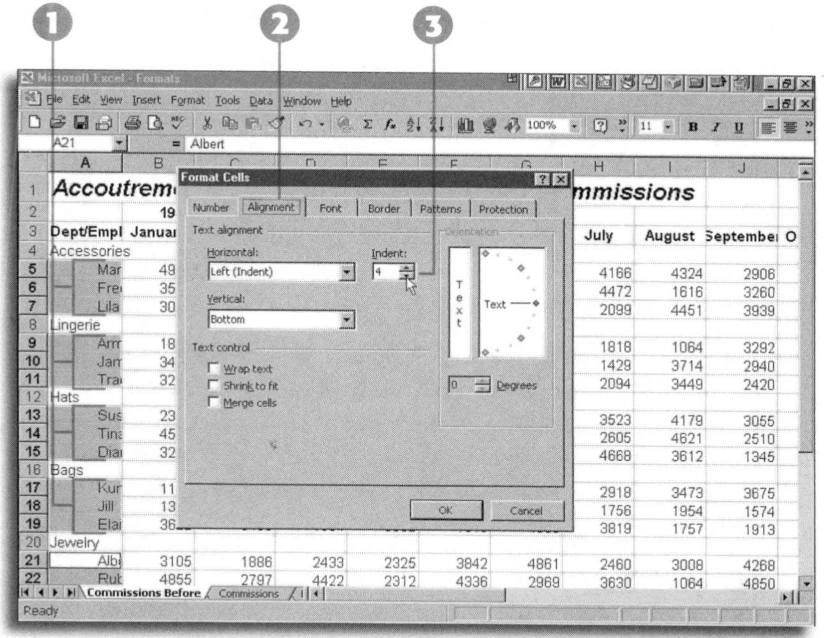

FIGURE 12.6
Indenting entries leaves them aligned on the left but sets them apart visually.

1. Entries indented by four characters
2. Alignment tab
3. Indent box

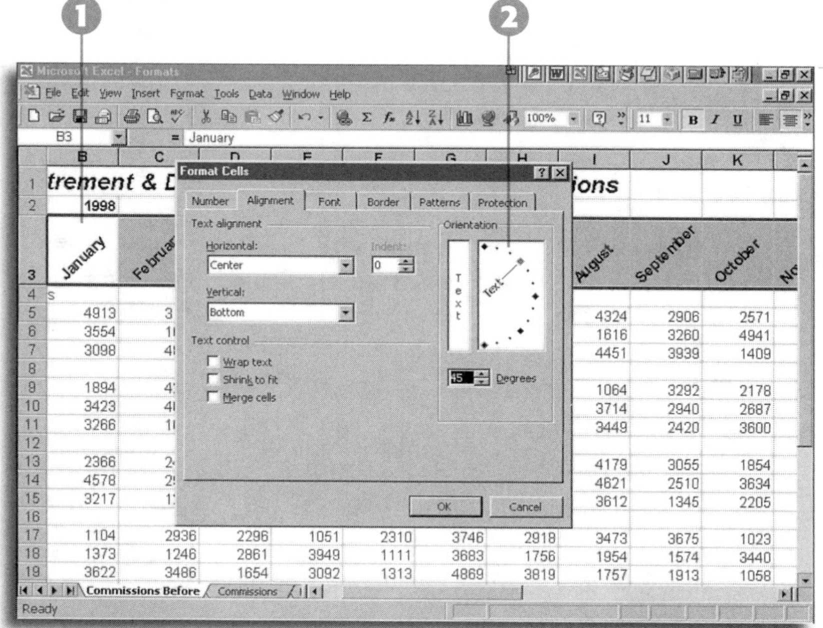

FIGURE 12.7
Row height automatically increases to accommodate the angle you set.

1. Rotated entries
2. Click an angle.

Changing Column Width and Row Height

Most worksheets must have columns resized, and often, row heights need adjusting, too. There are several ways you can resize rows and columns:

- Drag the borders of row and column selectors.
- Set a precise width or height in a dialog box.
- "Best-fit" a row or column to accommodate the tallest or widest entry.

You can also hide rows and columns. This is useful, for example, if you have a lookup table on a worksheet, and you want worksheet formulas to reference the lookup table but don't want the table to be in view. Hiding items is also useful when you want to print a worksheet but don't want some of the rows or columns in a table printed.

Resize a column visually

1. Position the mouse pointer over the right border of the column selector for the column you want to resize.
2. When the mouse pointer becomes a two-headed arrow (as shown in Figure 12.8), drag the border to resize the column.

To resize rows, follow the same procedure, but drag the bottom border of the row selector for the row you want to resize.

Resize Several Columns at Once

To make several columns (adjacent or nonadjacent) the same width, select all of the columns; then, drag the border of one of the column selectors. They'll all become precisely the same width.

Change *All* the Columns or *All* the Rows

To change the column width or row height for the entire worksheet, click the gray rectangle at the upper-left corner of the worksheet, where the row selectors and column selectors intersect (this selects the entire worksheet); then, change row height or column width by any method.

Best-Fit Several Columns at Once

To make several columns (adjacent or nonadjacent) all best-fit their entries, select all the columns; then, double-click the border of one of the column selectors. They'll all best-fit their own entries.

Best-Fitting

Sometimes when you drag a column to resize it, it looks great—until you scroll down the worksheet and find a longer entry that's still truncated. You can save yourself the aggravation of guessing the appropriate width by "best-fitting" the column width (this works with row heights, too).

Best-fit a column width

1. Position the mouse pointer over the right border of the column selector for the column you want to best-fit.
2. When the mouse pointer becomes a two-headed arrow (as shown in Figure 12.8), double-click the border to best-fit the column.

   In Figure 12.9, I've best-fitted all the month columns.

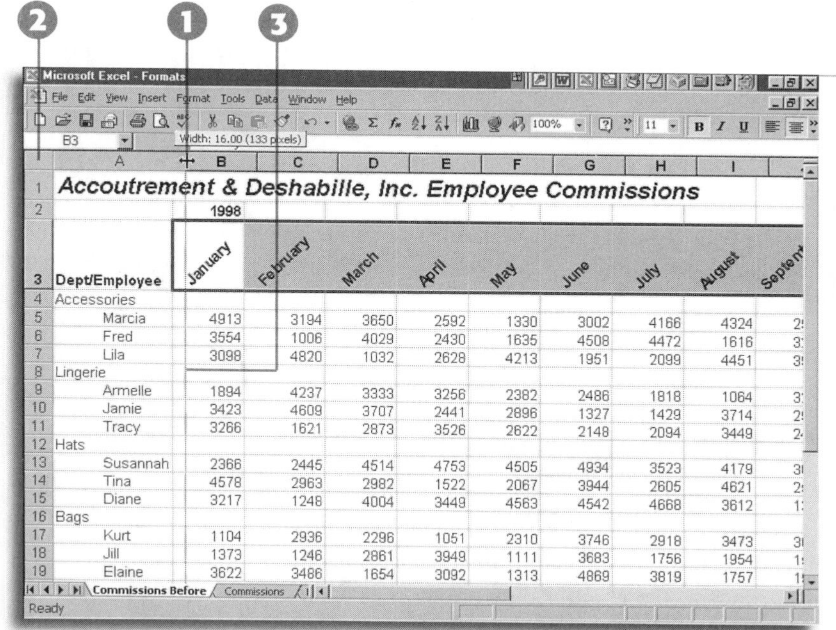

FIGURE 12.8

Resize columns and rows the same way: Drag header borders.

1. Two-headed arrow mouse pointer
2. Click here to select the entire worksheet.
3. Dragging to resize

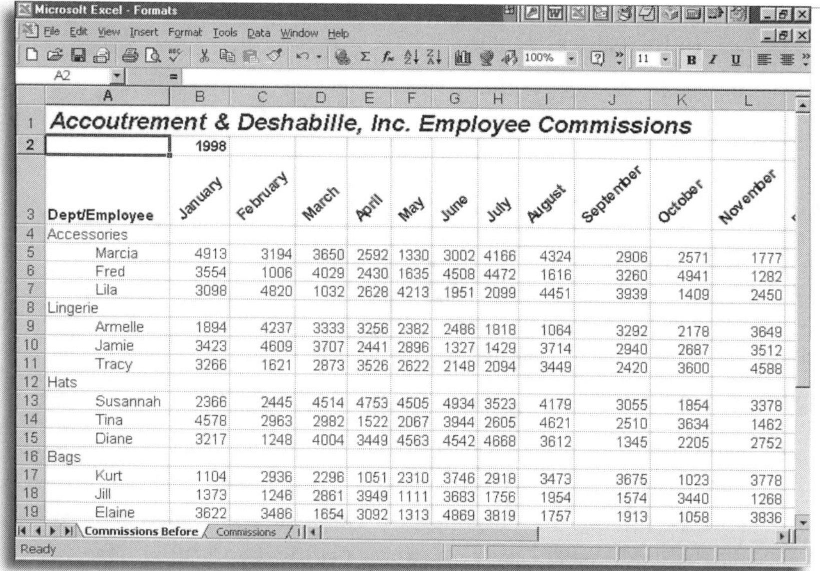

FIGURE 12.9

The month columns were best-fitted, but the Dept/Employee column was dragged to fit because a best-fit would have widened the column to fit the worksheet title.

Remember, the worksheet title only *looks* like it's typed in cells A1 through L1. The entire title—all 52 characters—is actually entered in cell A1, and I certainly wouldn't want column A to be best-fit to 52 characters wide.

To best-fit rows, follow the same procedure, but double-click the bottom border of the row selector for the row you want to resize. Best-fitting row heights becomes most useful when you've applied or removed wrap-text formatting somewhere in a row.

SEE ALSO

➤ *To learn more about fitting entries into cells by wrapping the text, see the section "Wrapping Text to Multiple Lines in a Cell," page 229.*

Matching Precise Width or Height

If you want to match the measurements of rows and columns that are far apart in a worksheet or in different worksheets, you can set precise measurements for the columns and rows you want to match, and they'll match exactly.

To set a precise column width or row height, follow this procedure.

Someone Always Wants to Know

The column width number is the number of characters in the default worksheet font that will fit in the cell. (For example, a column width of 8.43 means that 8.43 characters in the worksheet's default font can be displayed in the cell.) Row height is measured in points, which is a standard typeface unit of measure. (There are 72 points per inch.)

Set precise width or height

1. Right-click a column or row selector.
2. Click **Column Width** or **Row Height** (whichever is applicable).
3. Enter a new measurement; then, click **OK**.

To set the same precise measurement for multiple rows or columns, select all the rows or columns; then, right-click in the selection, enter a new measurement, and click **OK**.

Hiding and Unhiding Rows and Columns

It's not uncommon to have formula "machinery," such as lookup tables and referenced values, that you don't want visible in the worksheet. You can hide these important but messy cells by hiding the columns and/or rows; the worksheet still functions properly, but you don't see what's going on behind the scenes.

Hide rows or columns

1. Right-click the selector for the column or row you want to hide.

   To hide several columns or rows, select all the columns or rows; then, right-click in the selection.

2. Click **Hide**.

   The selected columns or rows are hidden. You can tell columns (or rows) are hidden because there's a gap in the selector letters (or numbers), as shown in Figure 12.10.

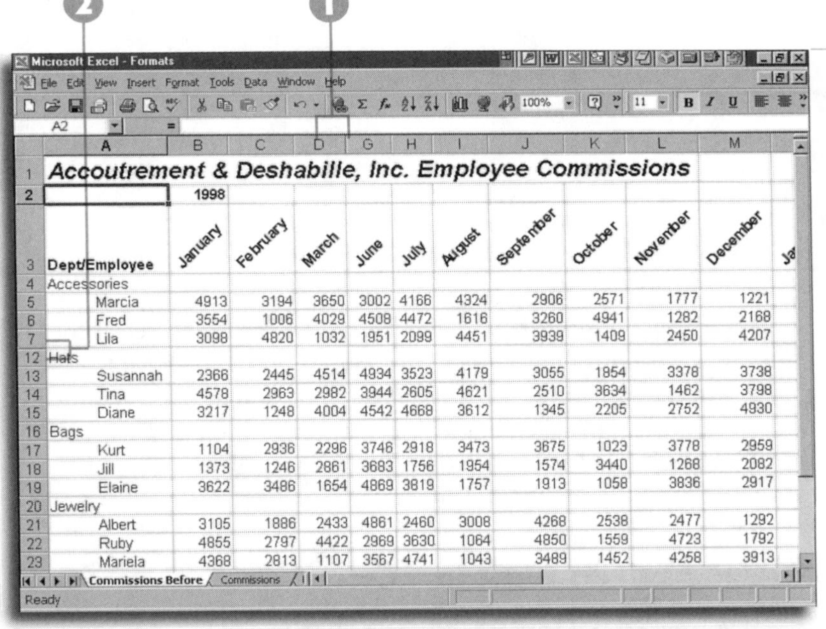

Microsoft Excel - Formats

	A	B	C	D	G	H	I	J	K	L	M
1	Accoutrement & Deshabille, Inc. Employee Commissions										
2		1998									
3	Dept/Employee	January	February	March	June	July	August	September	October	November	December
4	Accessories										
5	Marcia	4913	3194	3650	3002	4166	4324	2906	2571	1777	1221
6	Fred	3554	1006	4029	4508	4472	1616	3260	4941	1282	2168
7	Lila	3098	4820	1032	1951	2099	4451	3939	1409	2450	4207
12	Hats										
13	Susannah	2366	2445	4514	4934	3523	4179	3055	1854	3378	3738
14	Tina	4578	2963	2982	3944	2605	4621	2510	3634	1462	3798
15	Diane	3217	1248	4004	4542	4668	3612	1345	2205	2752	4930
16	Bags										
17	Kurt	1104	2936	2296	3746	2918	3473	3675	1023	3778	2959
18	Jill	1373	1246	2861	3683	1756	1954	1574	3440	1268	2082
19	Elaine	3622	3486	1654	4869	3819	1757	1913	1058	3836	2917
20	Jewelry										
21	Albert	3105	1886	2433	4861	2460	3008	4268	2538	2477	1292
22	Ruby	4855	2797	4422	2969	3630	1064	4850	1559	4723	1792
23	Mariela	4368	2813	1107	3567	4741	1043	3489	1452	4258	3913

Commissions Before / Commissions

Ready

FIGURE 12.10

Columns E and F and rows 8 through 11 are hidden.

1. Letter gap
2. Number gap

Unhide hidden rows or columns

1. Select the rows or columns on *both* sides of the gap, as shown in Figure 12.11.
2. Right-click the selection.
3. Click **Unhide**.

   The hidden rows or columns are unhidden.

How Can You Find Hidden Columns and Rows?

When columns or rows are deleted, there's a gap in the letters or numbers; the gap is how you can locate hidden columns and rows.

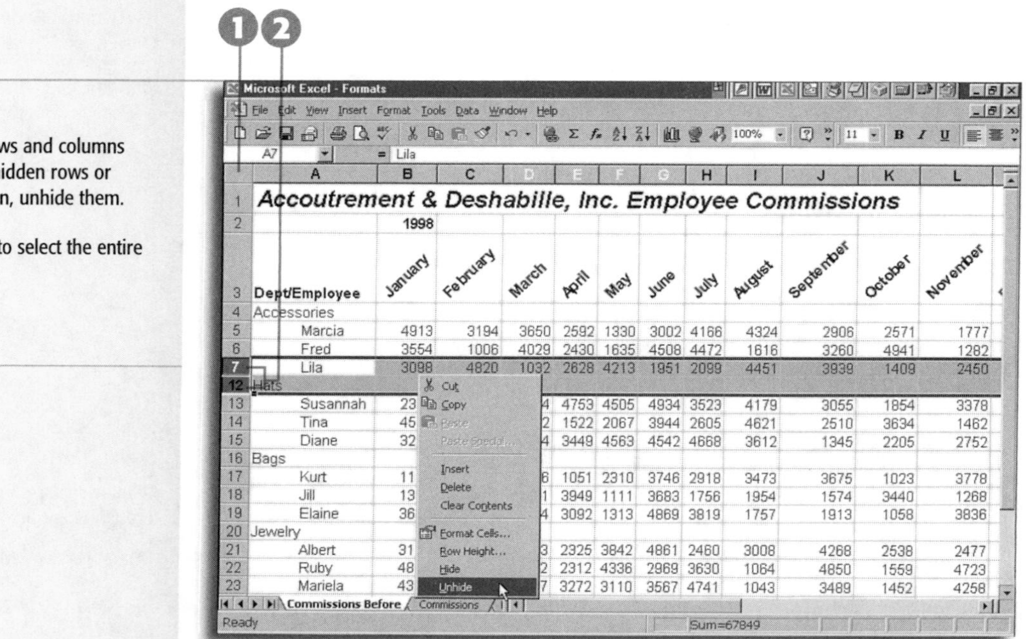

FIGURE 12.11

Select the rows and columns around the hidden rows or columns; then, unhide them.

1. Click here to select the entire worksheet.
2. Gap

If you can't find the elusive hidden rows or columns, select the entire worksheet (click the gray rectangle in the upper-left corner of the worksheet, where the row and column selectors intersect); then, right-click in the selected worksheet, and click **Unhide**. All hidden rows and columns in the worksheet are unhidden.

Shrinking Entries to Fit in a Cell

If you have a cell entry that doesn't quite fit and you don't want to widen the column for it, you can shrink the entry so it fits within the column width and stays neatly fitted, even if you resize the column.

Shrink an entry to fit the column width

1. Select the cells where you want to shrink entries.
2. On the **Format** menu, click **Cells**.
3. On the **Alignment** tab, click the **Shrink to fit** check box.
4. Click **OK**.

Wrapping Text to Multiple Lines in a Cell

Another way to fit long entries into a narrow column width is to wrap them onto multiple lines. Wrapping text makes the row taller but keeps the characters large and the column narrow. (It's practical only when the entry is two or more words.)

Wrap an entry to multiple lines

1. Select the cells where you want to wrap entries.
2. On the **Format** menu, click **Cells**.
3. On the **Alignment** tab, click the **Wrap text** check box.
4. Click **OK**.

You might need to resize the row and column after you apply wrapped-text formatting. To do so, drag the column to the width you want; then, best-fit the row to fit the entry.

SEE ALSO

➤ *To learn about resizing rows and columns, see the section "Changing Column Width and Row Height," page 224.*

Don't Like Where Excel Places the Breaks?

To break a long entry where you want, rather than where the column width breaks it, click between the characters where you want the entry to break; then, press Alt+Enter.

Transposing a Range from Vertical to Horizontal (or Vice Versa)

Why Won't This Work?

You can't paste the transposed table over the copied table (Excel won't let you); you must paste it outside the area of the copied table.

Sometimes, I start a table like the one in Figure 12.12 and realize after it's gotten fairly large that it would be more practical if the orientation of the table were flipped, or *transposed*.

Transpose a table or list

1. Select the entire table or list.
2. Right-click the selection.
3. Click **Copy**.
4. Right-click the cell where you want to paste the upper-left corner of the transposed table. (In Figure 12.12, I'll paste the transposed table to cell A9.)
5. On the shortcut menu, click **Paste Special**.
6. In the Paste Special dialog box, click the **Transpose** check box; then, click **OK**.

The result will be similar to Figure 12.13.

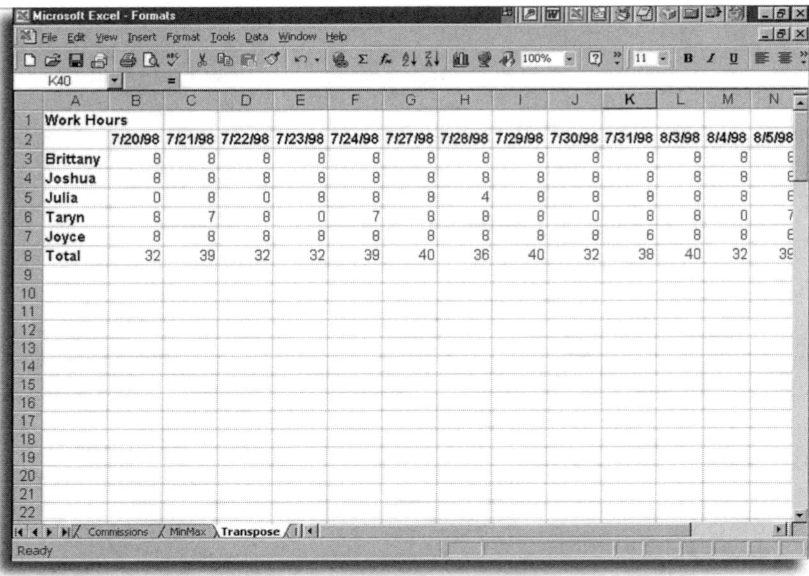

FIGURE 12.12

This table would be more practical if the dates ran down column A and the names were across the top.

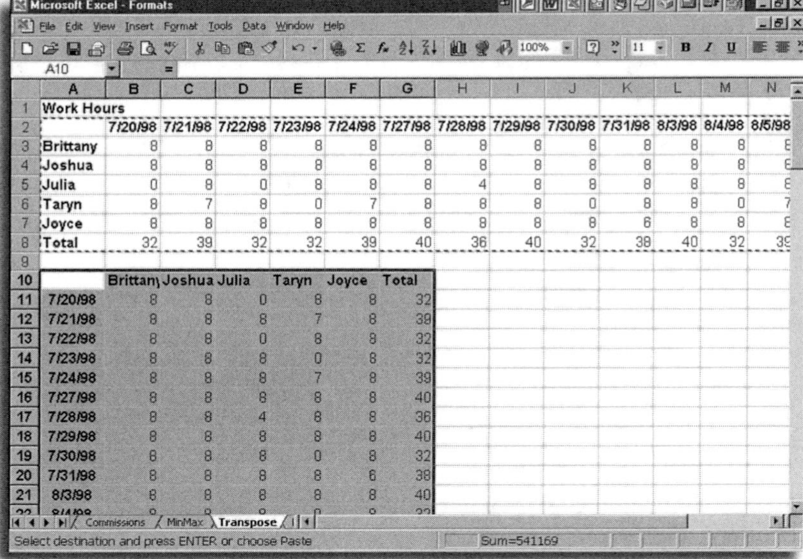

FIGURE 12.13

A transposed copy of the table is pasted, and I can delete the original.

Next, I'll select and delete rows 2 through 8, and the worksheet is ready to use again.

Merging Several Cells into a Single Cell (and Unmerging)

On a worksheet like the one in Figure 12.14, the worksheet title would look better if it were centered in a single cell over the length of the table.

Accoutrement & Deshabille, Inc. Employee Commissions

1998

Dept/Employee	January	February	March	April	May	June	July	August	September	October	November
Accessories											
Marcia	4913	3194	3650	2592	1330	3002	4166	4324	2906	2571	1777
Fred	3554	1006	4029	2430	1635	4508	4472	1616	3260	4941	1282
Lila	3098	4820	1032	2628	4213	1951	2099	4451	3939	1409	2450
Lingerie											
Armelle	1894	4237	3333	3256	2382	2486	1818	1064	3292	2178	3649
Jamie	3423	4609	3707	2441	2896	1327	1429	3714	2940	2687	3512
Tracy	3266	1621	2873	3526	2622	2148	2094	3449	2420	3600	4588
Hats											
Susannah	2366	2445	4514	4753	4505	4934	3523	4179	3055	1854	3378
Tina	4578	2963	2982	1522	2067	3944	2605	4621	2510	3634	1462
Diane	3217	1248	4004	3449	4563	4542	4668	3612	1345	2205	2752
Bags											
Kurt	1104	2936	2296	1051	2310	3746	2918	3473	3675	1023	3778
Jill	1373	1246	2861	3949	1111	3683	1756	1954	1574	3440	1268
Elaine	3622	3486	1654	3092	1313	4869	3819	1757	1913	1058	3836

FIGURE 12.14
The title should be centered neatly over the table.

Merge several cells into a single cell and center the entry in the new big cell

1. Select all the adjacent cells you want to merge. (In this example, I merged and centered cells A1 through M1 and then repeated the procedure to merge and center cells A2 through M2.)

   After cells are merged, you can use the Align Left, Center, and Align Right buttons to align the contents in the merged cell.

2. On the Formatting toolbar, click **Merge And Center.**

   The cells are merged into a single cell, as shown in Figure 12.15.

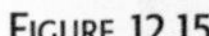

FIGURE 12.15

The title looks more professional, centered in one wide cell.

1. The title is merged, centered, and text wrapped.

Unmerge with a Toolbar Button

If you merge and unmerge cells often, add the Unmerge Cells button to a toolbar; it's in the Format category, on the Commands tab of the Customize dialog box. See Chapter 27 to learn more about customizing toolbars.

If you want to change the worksheet's formatting, you can unmerge the merged cells.

Unmerge a merged cell

1. Right-click the merged cell.
2. Click **Format Cells**.
3. On the **Alignment** tab, clear the **Merge cells** check box; then, click **OK**.

Formatting Borders

Borders are important, not only for dressing up a worksheet, but also for segregating information so it's quickly understood. Also, if you're printing a worksheet, you need to supply your own borders because Excel doesn't print worksheet gridlines by default.

To apply cell borders quickly, use the Borders palette.

Apply borders with the Borders toolbar

1. On the Formatting toolbar, click the down arrow on the **Borders** button.
2. Drag the palette of Borders buttons away from the toolbar to "float" on the worksheet. Drag it by its thin title bar, as shown in Figure 12.16.

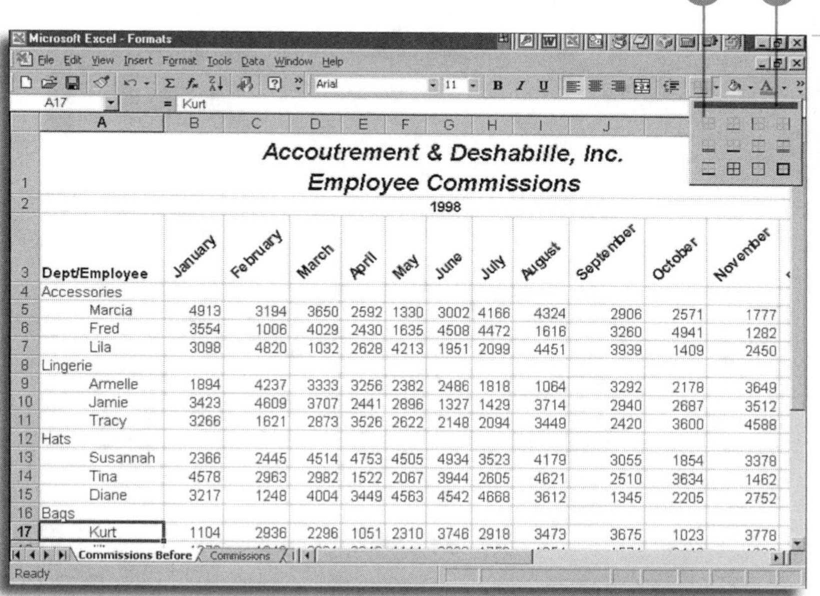

FIGURE 12.16
Floating palettes are convenient ways to apply borders and colors.

1. No Border button
2. Drag by the title bar.

3. Select the cells you want to apply a border to; then, click the border you want. Repeat until all your cells have borders.

   You can apply lots of borders; if it gets messy, select all the cells, click the **No Border** button, and start over.

To apply a wider variety of cell borders and change border colors, use the Borders tab in the Format Cells dialog box.

Apply borders with the Format Cells dialog box

1. Select the cells where you want to apply the border.
2. On the **Format** menu, click **Cells**.

What If I Want Gridlines?

I think Microsoft realized that most of us were turning off the printed gridlines and making more professional layouts using borders; you can turn on the printed gridlines, if you want to, by opening the **File** menu, clicking **Page Setup**, and checking **Gridlines** on the **Sheet** tab.

3. In the Format Cells dialog box, shown in Figure 12.17, click the **Border** tab.

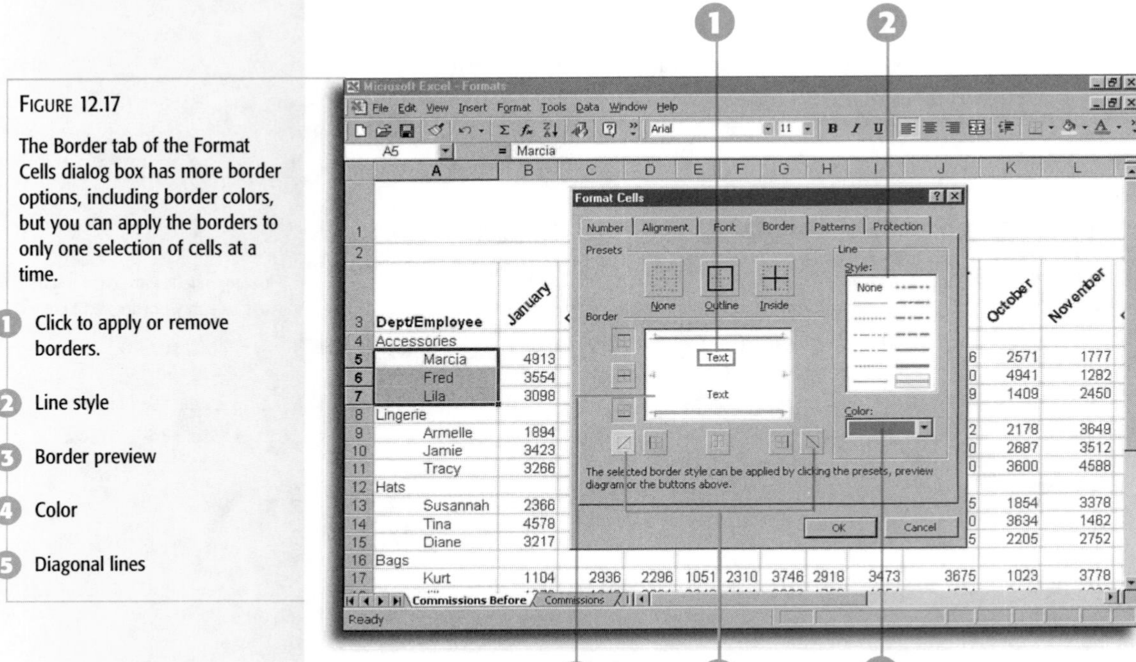

FIGURE 12.17

The Border tab of the Format Cells dialog box has more border options, including border colors, but you can apply the borders to only one selection of cells at a time.

1 Click to apply or remove borders.

2 Line style

3 Border preview

4 Color

5 Diagonal lines

4. Set the borders you want; then, click **OK**.

The Border tab takes a bit of exploration; here are some tips for using it:

- Click a color first, then a line style; then, click in the border preview to place the line you've chosen.
- You can make each border line a different color and style to add flair to your worksheet.
- The diagonal lines serve to "X" out cells visually but don't affect the cell entries. (You might find this handy for something like marking off completed tasks in a list.)

Get Rid of the Gridlines on a Worksheet

To hide the gridlines on a worksheet (so your borders look more attractive), click **Tools**, **Options**. On the **View** tab, clear the **Gridlines** check box, then click **OK**.

Formatting Colors

There are two sources of color in cells: the characters (*font color*) and the background (*fill color*). The only difference between using the floating palettes and the Format Cells dialog box to set colors is that background patterns appear in the Format Cells dialog box—but the floating palettes are quicker to use because they remain ready on the worksheet.

Set the text color (font color)

1. On the Formatting toolbar, click the down arrow on the **Font Color** button.
2. Drag the Font Color palette away from the toolbar to float on the worksheet (as shown in Figure 12.18).

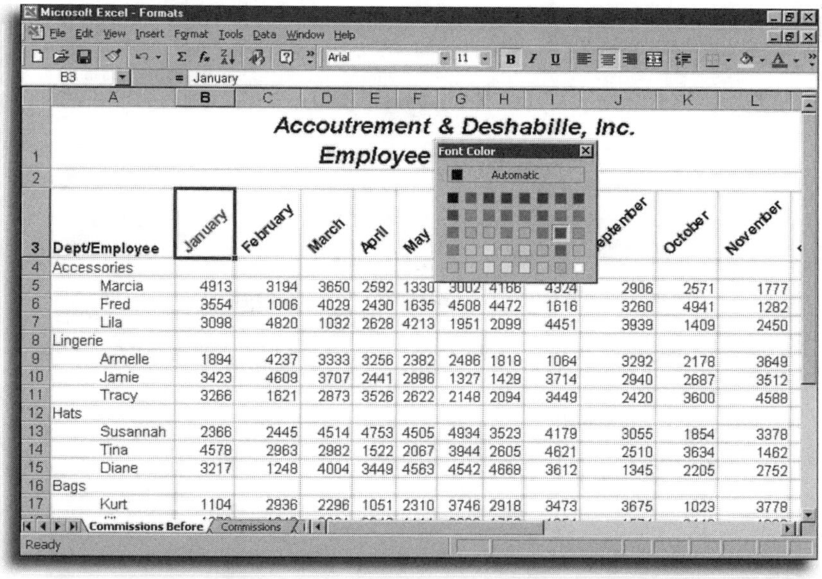

Lots of Formatting Buttons

There are floating palettes and buttons for almost everything in the Format Cells dialog box, but there isn't room for all of them on the Formatting toolbar; so, only the most commonly used buttons are built in. You can, however, add any buttons you want by customizing your toolbars. (See Chapter 27, "Customizing Your Excel Screen," to learn how to do this.)

FIGURE 12.18
Floating palettes make worksheet artistry easy.

3. Select the cells or individual characters you want to color.
4. Click the color you want in the floating palette.
5. When you're finished, click the floating palette's **Close** button to close it.

Set the cell color (fill color)

1. On the Formatting toolbar, click the down arrow on the **Fill Color** button.
2. Drag the Fill Color palette away from the toolbar to float on the worksheet (as shown in Figure 12.19).

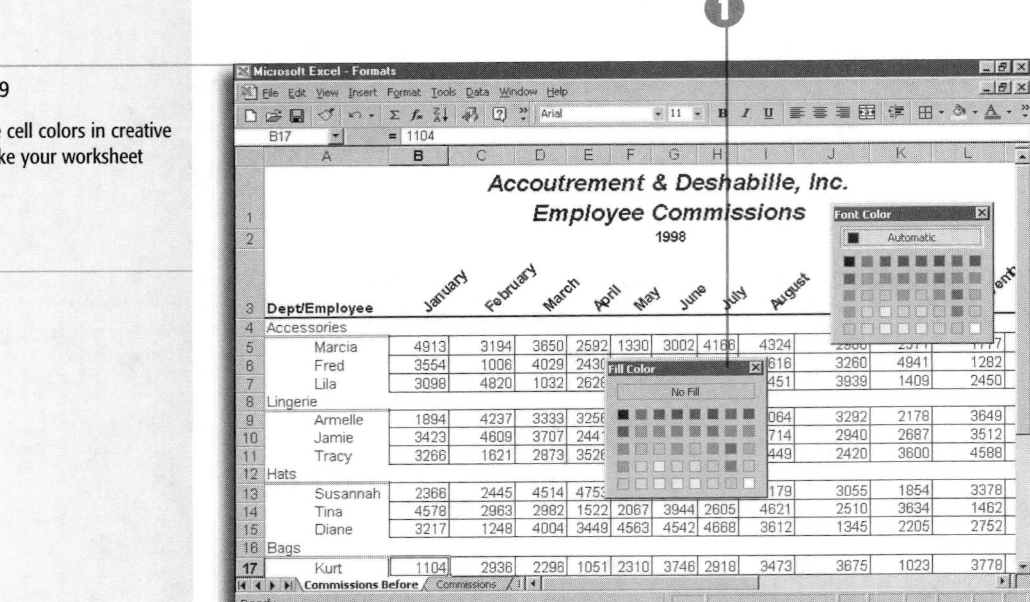

FIGURE 12.19

You can use cell colors in creative ways to make your worksheet look great.

1 Fill Color

3. Select the cells you want to color.
4. Click the color you want in the floating palette.
5. When you're finished, click the floating palette's Close button to close it.

Here's a trick professionals use to make worksheets look special (you'll find a bit of this in Excel's Spreadsheet Solutions templates): Use narrow rows and columns of color around a table to create custom borders, the way I've done in Figure 12.20.

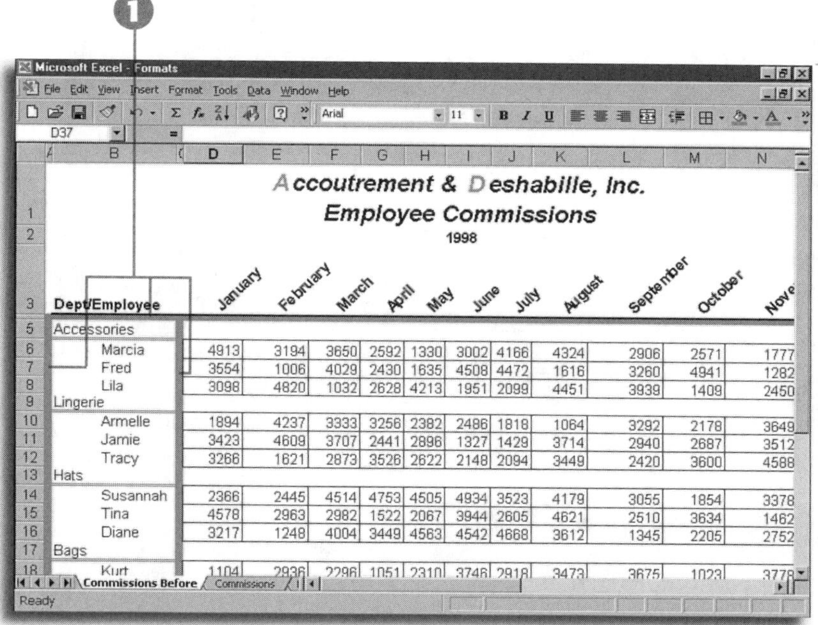

FIGURE 12.20
Create custom borders around a table by resizing and coloring cells.

1 These lines are colored cells, not cell borders.

To create these custom borders, insert and resize rows or columns; then, select and color the cells that form a border around the table.

Copying Formatting with Format Painter

When you've formatted a cell or group of cells with several formats (for example, you might have applied a cell color, font color, font size, alignment, and number format), it's daunting to think you have to repeat all that work to format other cells similarly. Well, you don't! You can copy the whole set of formats by painting them to other cells with the Format Painter.

You can copy the formatting from a single cell or a group of cells to a similar group of cells.

In Figure 12.21, I want to make the table easy to read across by coloring the rows.

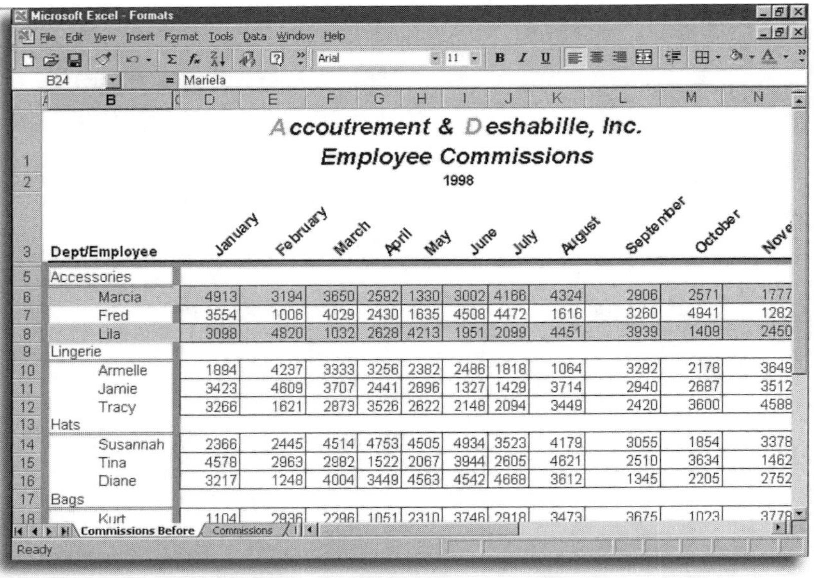

FIGURE 12.21
Select all the cells that have formatting you want to copy.

Microsoft Excel - Formats

Accoutrement & Deshabille, Inc.
Employee Commissions
1998

Dept/Employee	January	February	March	April	May	June	July	August	September	October	Nove
Accessories											
Marcia	4913	3194	3650	2592	1330	3002	4166	4324	2906	2571	1777
Fred	3554	1006	4029	2430	1635	4508	4472	1616	3260	4941	1282
Lila	3098	4820	1032	2628	4213	1951	2099	4451	3939	1409	2450
Lingerie											
Armelle	1894	4237	3333	3256	2382	2486	1818	1064	3292	2178	3649
Jamie	3423	4609	3707	2441	2896	1327	1429	3714	2940	2687	3512
Tracy	3266	1621	2873	3526	2622	2148	2094	3449	2420	3600	4588
Hats											
Susannah	2366	2445	4514	4753	4505	4934	3523	4179	3055	1854	3378
Tina	4578	2963	2982	1522	2067	3944	2605	4621	2510	3634	1462
Diane	3217	1248	4004	3449	4563	4542	4668	3612	1345	2205	2752
Bags											
Kurt	1104	2936	2296	1051	2310	3748	2918	3473	3675	1023	3778

After I've colored one set of rows, I can paint the row formatting to the rest of the table.

Paint a Format Repeatedly

You can make the Format Painter "hot" by double-clicking it; it will continue to paint the same formatting until you click the Format Painter button again.

Use the Format Painter to copy formatting

1. Select the cells that contain the formatting you want to copy.

   In this case, I've selected all the cells in rows 5 through 8 so I can copy the pattern of the colors.

2. On the Standard toolbar, click **Format Painter.**

3. Drag the Format Painter mouse pointer over all the cells you want to paint the format to.

   Painting the row formatting to the rest of the table results in the table shown in Figure 12.22.

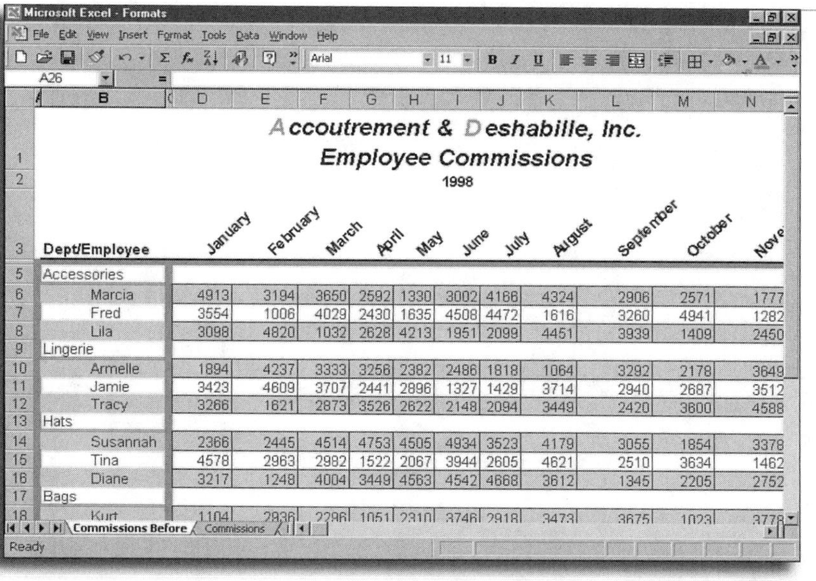

FIGURE 12.22

Coloring rows makes a wide table easier to read across (like old-fashioned computer paper).

Using AutoFormat to Create a Table with Built-In Formats

If you need to format a table in a hurry, you can apply a built-in AutoFormat to the entire table more quickly than you can apply all the individual formatting elements.

AutoFormat a table

1. Click in the table.
2. On the **Format** menu, click **AutoFormat**.

   The AutoFormat dialog box is displayed, as shown in Figure 12.23.
3. Scroll through the different table formats in the list until you see one you like, and click it to select it.

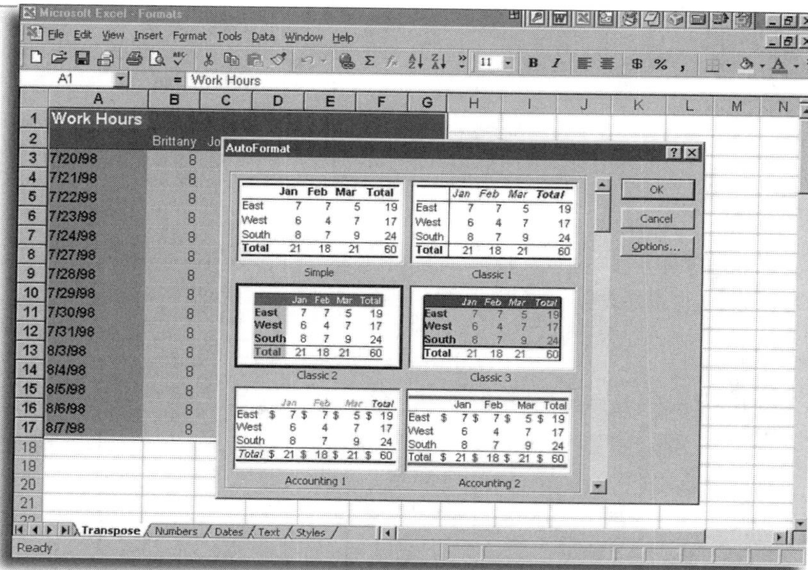

FIGURE 12.23

Choose a built-in table format in the AutoFormat dialog box.

4. Click **OK**.

The table format is applied to the entire contiguous table, as in Figure 12.24.

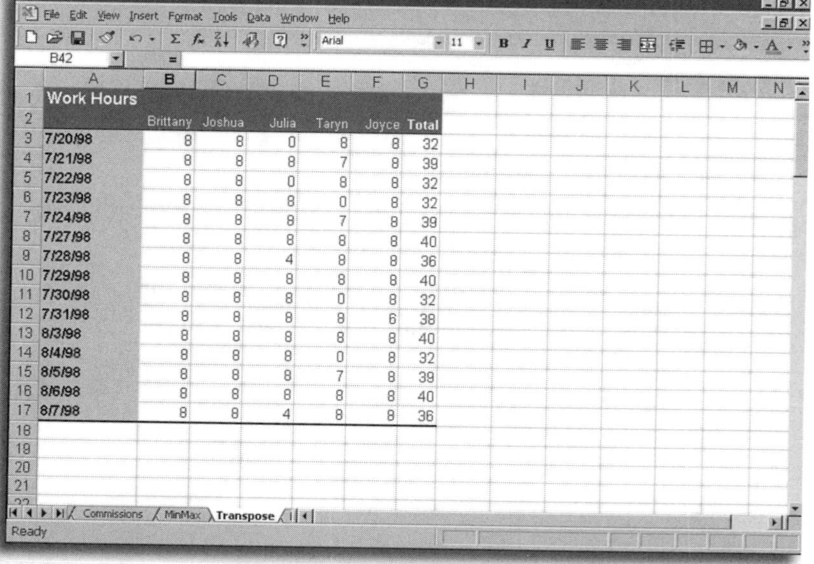

FIGURE 12.24

A table formatted using AutoFormat.

Adding a Graphic Image to a Worksheet

A logo or graphic image can really jazz up a worksheet.

Paste a graphic image into a worksheet

1. Make room in the worksheet for the image.

   Either insert several rows or insert a single row and resize it tall enough to make room on the worksheet for the image.

2. Click in the cell where you want to paste the upper-left corner of the picture (and you can always move it later if you need to).

3. On the **Insert** menu, point to **Picture**; then, click **From File**.

4. In the Insert Picture dialog box, navigate to the folder where your graphic image is saved, and double-click the image file.

   The image is pasted into your worksheet, like the one in Figure 12.25. Click the image to select it; then, drag it by its center to move it, or drag a handle to resize it.

Add a Logo to a Template

Placing a logo in a workbook template can tie together a company's image because the logo will automatically appear in every new workbook.

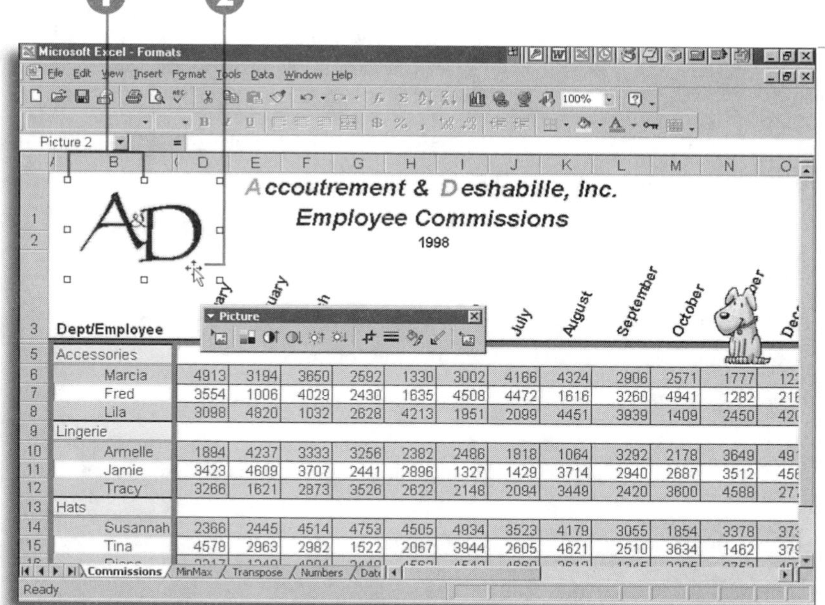

FIGURE 12.25

You can paste a graphic image into a worksheet.

1. Handles
2. Move pointer

You can

- Move the graphic to reposition it.
- Drag the handles around its edges to resize it.
- Press Ctrl or Shift while dragging a corner handle to resize it without stretching it out of shape.
- Press Ctrl while dragging a side handle to resize it equally from the center.
- Use the buttons in the Picture toolbar that is displayed, or close the toolbar by clicking its Close button. (Table 12.2 shows what the buttons do.)
- To display the Picture Toolbar quickly, right-click the picture, and then click **Show Picture Toolbar**.

TABLE 12.2 **Picture toolbar buttons**

Icon	Button Name	Button Function
	Insert Picture From File	Opens the Insert Picture dialog box so you can insert another picture.
	Image Control	Select from Automatic (displays the image's original colors), Gray Scale (converts to shades of gray), Black and White (converts to black and white), or Watermark (converts to a bright, low-contrast watermark).
	More Contrast	Increases the intensity of the colors in the image.
	Less Contrast	Reduces the intensity of the colors in the image.
	More Brightness	Adds white to lighten the image colors.
	Less Brightness	Adds black to darken the image colors.
	Crop	Trims the image when you drag a handle.
	Line Style	Sets the style of line used in an image border.
	Format Picture	Opens the Format Picture dialog box.
	Set Transparent Color	Makes a color transparent. (Click the button; then, click the color that you want to change in the image.)
	Reset Picture	Undoes the image manipulation.

CHAPTER

13

Formatting Numbers

Applying number formats to cells

Formatting dates and times

Formatting text entries

Creating conditional number formats

Converting actual values to displayed values

Hiding zeroes

The Numbers Don't Add Up!

If the calculation on the worksheet appears to be incorrect, it's because the *actual* cell values are calculated, not the rounded-off, *displayed* values. You might want to add a label telling others who see the table that numbers might appear inaccurate because they've been rounded.

Applying Number Formats to Cells

What you see in a cell is not necessarily the value entered in the cell (or the value calculated by Excel). The actual value of an entry in a selected cell is shown in the Formula bar, but what you see in the cell is the *displayed value*, the format of which you can control with number formatting.

Some of the many ways you can change a displayed value with formatting are shown in Figure 13.1. All the numbers in Column B were entered as 12345 with a variety of formats applied.

FIGURE 13.1

All these cells contain the actual value 12345, but clever formatting changes the meaning entirely.

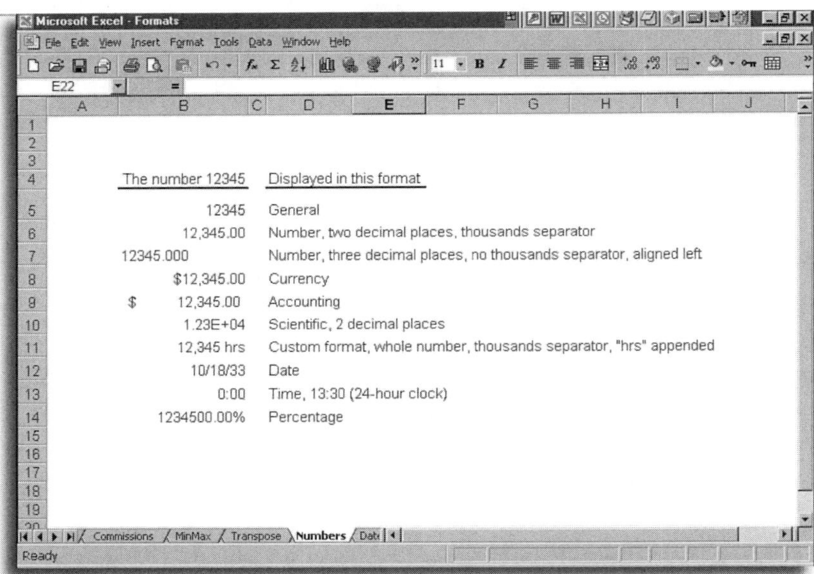

The number displayed in a cell is seldom the actual calculating value, especially if the value is the result of a formula. You can display a number in many ways by changing its format, as shown in Table 13.1.

TABLE 13.1 **Number formatting possibilities**

This Number	In This Format	Looks Like This
1.2345	Number, zero decimal places	1
	Number, two decimal places	1.23
	Currency	$1.23
	Fraction, up to one digit	1 1/4
	Fraction, up to two digits	1 19/81
12345	Number, two decimals, thousands separator	12,345.00
	Currency	$12,345.00
	Scientific, one decimal place (E indicates that 04 is an exponent)	1.2E+04
	Special, Social Security number	000-01-2345
.0012345	General	0.0012345
	Number, three decimal places	.001
	Percentage, two decimal places	.12%
	Fraction, up to three digits	1/810

Format a number value to display the way you want it

1. Select the cell or range you want to format.
2. On the **Format** menu, click **Cells**.

   The Format Cells dialog box is displayed, as shown in Figure 13.2.
3. On the **Number** tab, select a format category.

   Each category has specific options that customize the format further.
4. Select and set the options available for the format category.

   The Sample area shows what your number looks like with the formatting options applied.

Can I Use Yen or Pounds?

If you select the **Currency** category, you can choose a different currency symbol from the **Symbol** drop-down list that is displayed in the dialog box.

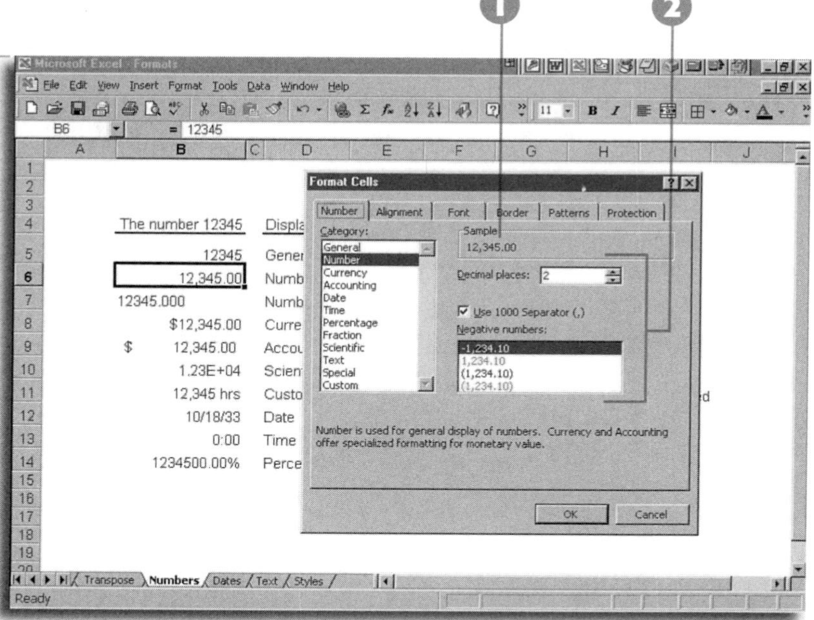

FIGURE 13.2

Number formatting is set on the **Number** tab in the Format Cells dialog box.

1. What your number looks like in the selected format

2. Options vary with the selected format.

Some Formatting Tips

You can also paint number formatting to other cells by using the Format Painter toolbar button. Apply number formatting to nonadjacent cells and ranges by using the Ctrl key to select them. You can also make a number format part of a custom style.

5. When the sample looks the way you want it, click **OK**.

   The format is applied to all selected cells.

SEE ALSO

➤ *To learn more about using the Format Painter, see the section "Copying Formatting with Format Painter," page 237.*

➤ *To learn more about selecting nonadjacent cells, see the section "Selecting Cells in a Worksheet," page 85.*

➤ *To learn more about formatting with styles, see page 257.*

Formatting Dates and Times

Dates and times are recognized by Excel, and as such, are formatted, sorted, and calculated as dates and times rather than plain old number values. Excel can calculate dates in formulas because, although you see a date or time displayed, Excel's actual value is a serial number that corresponds to the specific date and time of day.

A serial number that's an integer (no fractions) indicates the time 12 a.m. (midnight) on the serial number's day; a serial number with a fraction indicates a date and a time of day. You can most easily learn what time a fraction indicates by entering the fraction and applying the Time formats.

Some of the many date and time formatting options are shown in Table 13.2.

Hey! Where's My Number?

Occasionally you might enter a number, such as `12345`, and be surprised to see it transformed into a date. This happens because Excel recognizes the number as a date serial number, and the cell was already formatted with date/time formatting. To change the display to a number, change the formatting of the cell to Number or General.

TABLE 13.2 **Date and time formatting possibilities**

This Date or Time	In This Format	Looks Like This
1/7/56	Date, 14-Mar	7-Jan
	Date, March 14, 1998	January 7, 1956
	3/14/98 1:30 PM	1/7/56 12:00 AM
12345	Date, March 14, 1998	October 18, 1933
	Time, 1:30 PM	12:00 AM
.75	Time, 13:30	18:00
	Time, 13:30:55	18:00:00
	Time, 1:30 PM	6:00 PM

Change the format of a date or time

1. Select the cell or range of dates (or times) you want to format.
2. On the **Format** menu, click **Cells**.

   The Format Cells dialog box is displayed, as shown in Figure 13.3.
3. On the **Number** tab, select the **Date** or the **Time** category.
4. Select a format from the **Type** list.

   The Sample area shows what your date or time looks like with the selected type applied.
5. When the sample looks the way you want it, click **OK**.

   The format is applied to all selected cells.

Get All the Dates at Once

If you want all the date or time cells in the worksheet to have the same format, hold down the Ctrl key and then click or drag across each cell or range of cells. When you apply the date format, all the selected cells will be formatted simultaneously.

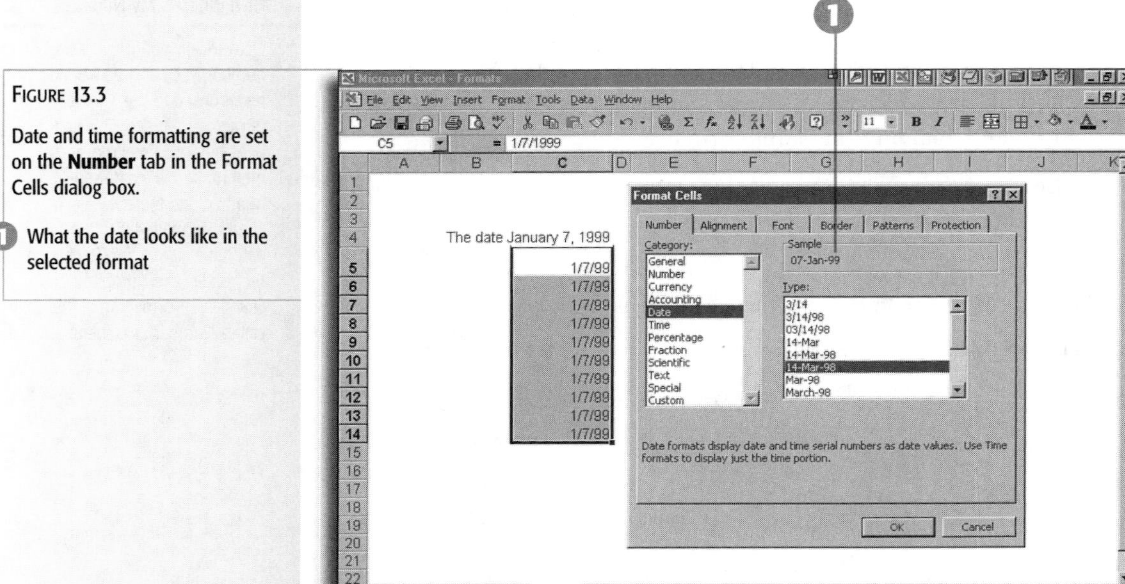

FIGURE 13.3

Date and time formatting are set on the **Number** tab in the Format Cells dialog box.

1. What the date looks like in the selected format

Formatting Text Entries

Text entries (like labels, part numbers, and ZIP codes) might be composed of number characters but are different from number values in that they must

- Retain any leading zeroes
- Not be included in calculations

If an entry has any character other than numbers in it (for example, the Social Security number 555-55-5555, which has hyphens in it), Excel sees the entry as text and the format is not a problem. Format becomes a problem when the entry is supposed to be text but contains no letters or punctuation marks to indicate to Excel that it's text.

A Quick Trick for Text

You can enter a number as text without changing the formatting by typing an apostrophe (') first; the apostrophe will be hidden in the cell display, but Excel will treat the entry as text.

Format cells as text so that numbers you enter will be treated as text characters

1. Select the cells that should be text.
2. On the **Format** menu, click **Cells**.

3. On the **Number** tab, click the **Text** category (as shown in Figure 13.4).
4. Click **OK**.

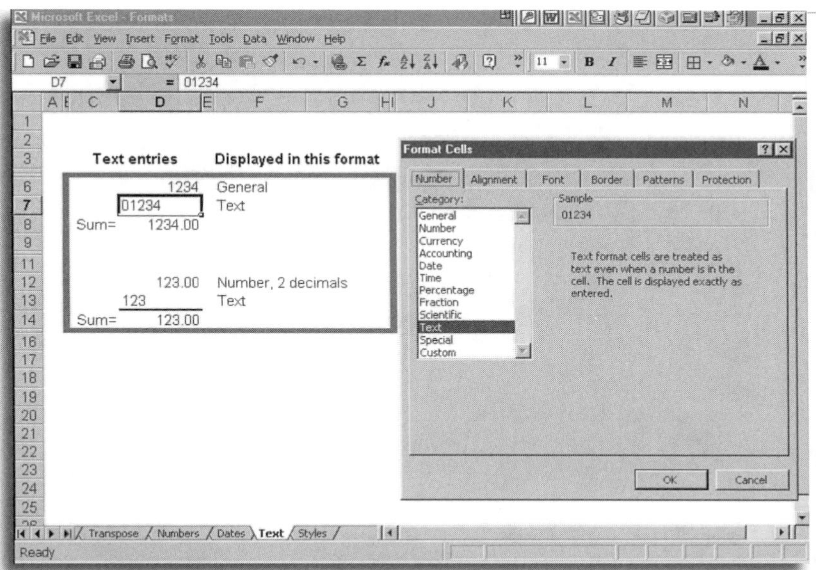

FIGURE 13.4
Text-formatted entries are left-aligned and not calculated.

Occasionally, you might want to enter calculable numbers but show text characters in the cell. This is a different problem.

One of my students wanted to create a timesheet and wanted to show the time entries with the suffix `hrs`, as in `8 hrs`. If you enter `8 hrs` in a cell, Excel treats the entry as text, and if you concatenate the letters to the number, as in `=H13&" hrs"`, Excel again treats the entry as text. If, however, you make the text characters part of the format rather than part of the entered value, Excel treats the entry as a number, whereas you view it in the worksheet as text.

I Want My Numbers Centered

When you apply number or text formatting, a default alignment is part of the format, but you can change the alignment in selected cells by clicking one of the alignment buttons on the Formatting toolbar.

Include text in a number format by creating a custom number format

1. Select the cells you want to custom format.
2. On the **Format** menu, click **Cells**.
3. On the **Number** tab, click the **Custom** category.

4. In the **Type** box, type the format code **`#,##0 "hrs"`** (as shown in Figure 13.5).

5. Click **OK**.

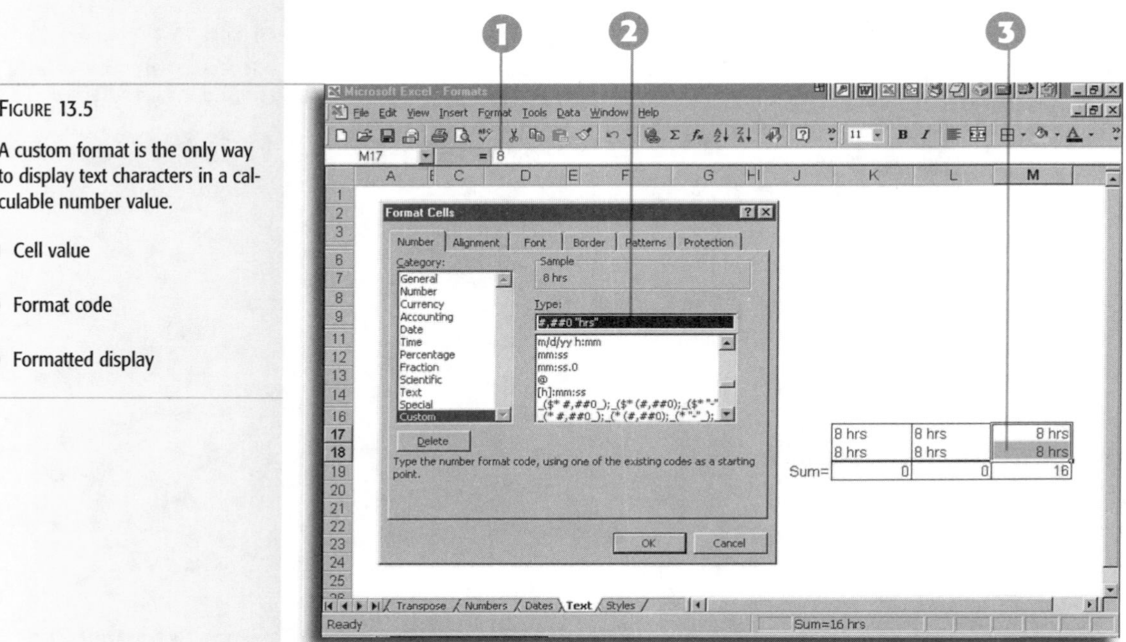

FIGURE 13.5

A custom format is the only way to display text characters in a calculable number value.

1. Cell value
2. Format code
3. Formatted display

Table 13.3 shows more useful custom format codes.

TABLE 13.3 Custom format codes

This Code	Gives This Result	Example (Value 01234.333)
`#,###0`	Rounds to a whole number; comma separates thousands; no leading zeroes	`1,234`
`# ?/?`	Displays decimal portion as a fraction	`1234 1/3`
`0.00`	Rounds to two decimal places; no thousands separator	`1234.33`

This Code	Gives This Result	Example (Value 01234.333)
`00000`	Displays all digits, including leading zeroes to five places (like ZIP codes)	`01234`
`000-00-0000`	Placeholders for all nine digits in a Social Security number; inserts hyphens after you press Enter	123-45-6789
`000-0000`	Placeholders for all seven digits in a phone number; inserts hyphen automatically after you press Enter	555-1234
`(000) 000-0000`	Placeholders for area code and telephone number; inserts parentheses and hyphen after you press Enter	(800)-555-1234
`000"."000 "."0000`	European-style placeholders for digits in a phone number; inserts periods automatically after you press Enter (quotes distinguish period from decimal point)	999.555.1234

Some Special Format Codes Are Ready-Made

If you want to use custom format codes for ZIP codes, phone numbers, and Social Security numbers (such as those in Table 13.3), you can create them yourself or find them built in under the Special category. Use the codes to learn how to build unique number formats that aren't in the Special category.

For more information about custom format codes, look it up in Excel's help files.

Get help on custom format codes

1. In the Office Assistant's question ballon, type "custom number format codes."
2. Click the **About number formats** option.
3. Use the Help file's hyperlinks to find information about format codes.

SEE ALSO

➤ *To learn more about concatenating cell values, see the section "Concatenate (&)," page 199.*

➤ *To learn more about locating Excel's help files, see the section "Using the Contents and Help Files," page 21.*

Creating Conditional Number Formats

If you have a sea of data and want specific values to visibly leap forward from the surrounding numbers, you can create a *conditional number format*, a display format that depends on the value in the formatted cell.

For example, Figure 13.6 has a lot of numbers and formulas (MIN and MAX) that look up the minimum and maximum values in that morass of numbers. But knowing what the minimum and maximum values are doesn't make it any easier to find when and by whom they were earned.

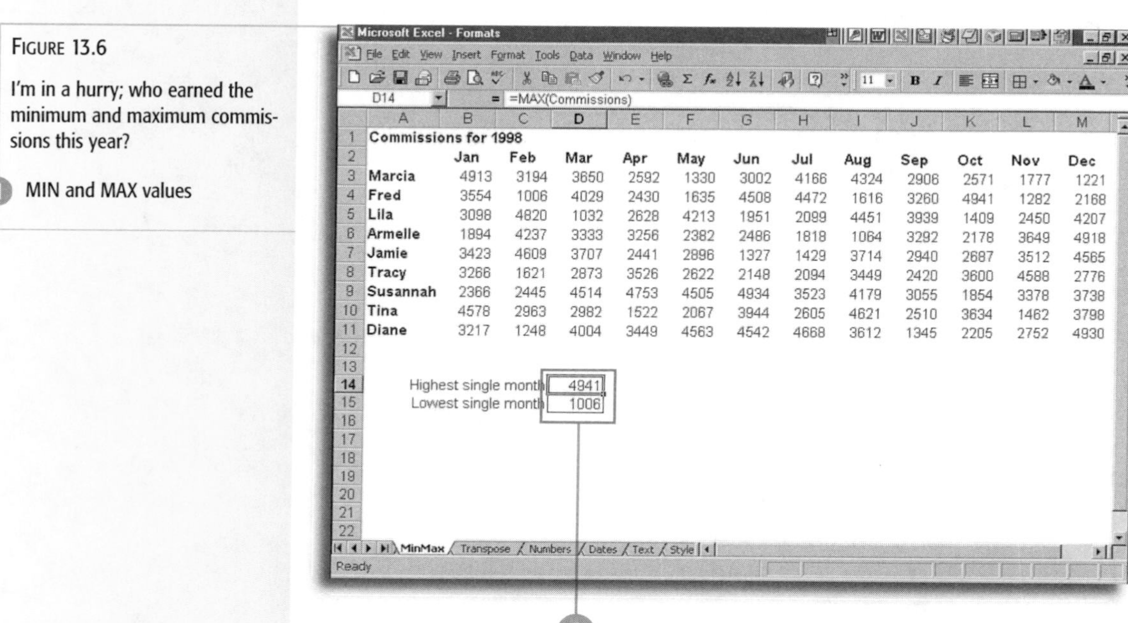

FIGURE 13.6

I'm in a hurry; who earned the minimum and maximum commissions this year?

1 MIN and MAX values

To make the minimum and maximum values easy to locate visually, I can apply color, bold formatting, and borders to the minimum and maximum values in the worksheet.

Apply conditional formatting

1. Select the range where you want to apply the conditional formats (in this case, cells B3:M11).
2. On the **Format** menu, click **Conditional Formatting**.

   The Conditional Formatting dialog box is displayed, as shown in Figure 13.7.
3. Select options from the boxes, starting with the **Condition 1** box on the left.

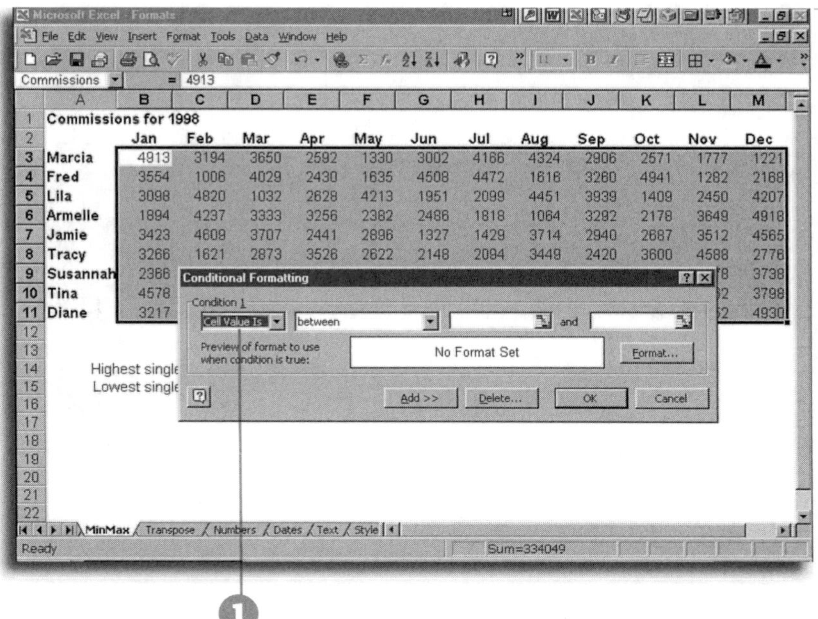

FIGURE 13.7
Use the Conditional Formatting dialog box to create cell formatting that responds to cell values.

1 Start here.

The options you choose in each box determine which options display in the remaining boxes.

In Figure 13.8, I've set the condition as the cell value equal to the result displayed in cell D14. Even if the numbers in the table change, the MAX formula and the conditional format will still find the maximum value in the table.

4. Click the **Format** button.

   The Format Cells dialog box is displayed.

5. Set **Font**, **Border**, and **Patterns** formats; then, click **OK**.

6. If you want to add more conditions, click the **Add** button to add another conditional format. (In this case, I'm also going to format the minimum value in the table.)

7. When you finish creating conditional formats, click **OK**.

   Figure 13.9 shows the results of my two conditional formats: The minimum and maximum values are easy to see among all the numbers.

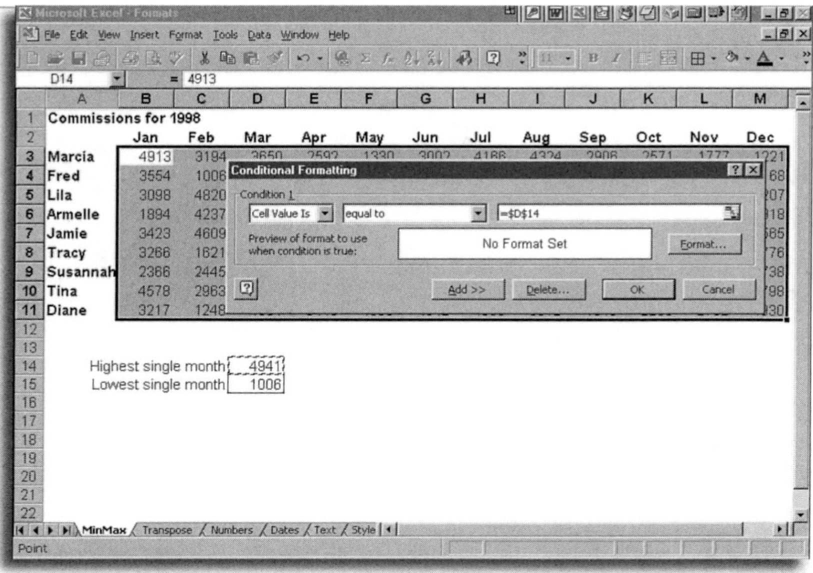

FIGURE 13.8

The conditional format will apply to any cell with the value displayed by the MAX formula.

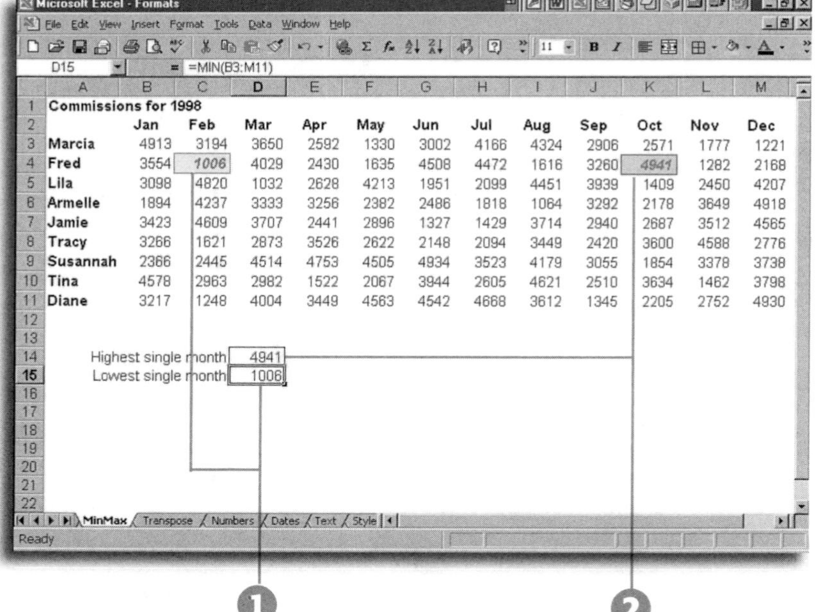

FIGURE 13.9

Looks like Fred was on a roller coaster this year.

1. MIN value
2. MAX value

SEE ALSO

➤ *To learn more about the MIN and MAX functions, see the sections "MIN" and "MAX," pages 180 and 181.*

Converting Actual Values to Displayed Values

If the results of your calculations end up with 11 or 12 decimal places and you want to reduce the values to whole numbers, you can permanently change the actual full-precision values to the formatted values you've displayed. For example, if you displayed `1.2345` as `1`, converting to displayed value changes the actual cell value to `1`, and you lose the `.2345` part of the value (often an audience appreciates data that's simple and straightforward, without lots of decimal points).

You cannot, however, change only a few cells; all constant values in the workbook are changed to their displayed values and lose accuracy in future calculations.

Convert actual values to displayed values

1. Format all values to the precision you want (for example, "Number, no decimals").
2. On the **Tools** menu, click **Options**.
3. On the **Calculation** tab, click the **Precision as displayed** check box.
4. Click **OK**. The message that you're about to lose data accuracy is your last chance to back out of the operation.

   All constant values in the workbook are permanently changed to the values that are displayed, and the change cannot be undone.

Hiding Zeroes

A worksheet full of zeroes is messy, and important values can be overlooked. Hiding unnecessary zeroes makes nonzero values more noticeable and makes the worksheet look more professional.

There are three ways to hide zeroes:

- Hide all zeroes on the worksheet by opening the **Tools** menu, clicking **Options**, and clearing the **Zero values** check box on the **View** tab.
- To hide zeroes that are the result of a formula, nest the formula in an IF function, as follows:
  `=IF(`*`formula`*`=0,"",`*`formula`*`)` says "If the result of the formula is zero, then display nothing; otherwise, display the result of the formula."
- Create a custom number format to hide all zero values in the cells where you apply it: `#,##0;(#,##0);`. (Be sure you type both semicolons.)

CHAPTER

14

Formatting with Styles for Less Effort

Applying a built-in style

Changing a style definition

Creating a custom style by example

Copying styles from other workbooks

Deleting a style

Applying a Built-In Style

If you've used styles in other programs (such as Microsoft Word), you already know how useful and time-saving they are, and you'll be pleased to know that styles work the same way in Excel. In case styles are new for you, I'll show you how easy it is to make formatting easy and fast by using styles.

A *style* is a complete package of formats that you can apply all at once. For example, a style might include red, bold Times New Roman font, size 12, centered alignment, a heavy green cell border, pale yellow cell shading, and currency number format. (That would be an eye opener!) You can create a custom style by including any cell and number formats you want, giving the style a name, and applying the style to cells anywhere in the worksheet or workbook. You save time because all the formats included in the style are applied at once.

You save time again if you need to change a format included in the style because you need to change only the style definition; every cell where the style is applied will automatically change to display the new style formats. For example, if you've applied a custom style to subtotal cells throughout eight worksheets in a workbook and you decide to change the font color to blue, all you need to do is change the font color in the style definition. Every subtotal cell in which you applied the style will change to blue font.

Excel comes with four built-in styles: Comma, Currency, Normal, and Percent. Normal is the default style that's applied to all cells until you apply a different style.

Currency, Percent, and Comma styles are built-in number formats with buttons on the Formatting toolbar for easy access. If you apply one of these styles, only the number formatting is applied. (No other cell formats are affected.)

Apply a built-in style

1. Select the cells where you want to apply the style.
2. On the Formatting toolbar, click the button for the built-in style you want to apply.

   The three number styles are demonstrated in Figure 14.1.

Where Can I Use Styles?

All styles are available throughout the workbook where they've been created or copied.

Reformat All Cells at Once

You can change the formats in every cell of a workbook by changing the definition of Normal style. For example, change Normal style to include pale blue cell shading, and every worksheet in the workbook will become entirely pale blue.

Money Can Be Deceiving

Although the button is named Currency Style, the number format it applies is actually accounting (which lines up decimal points and dollar signs in a column), not currency.

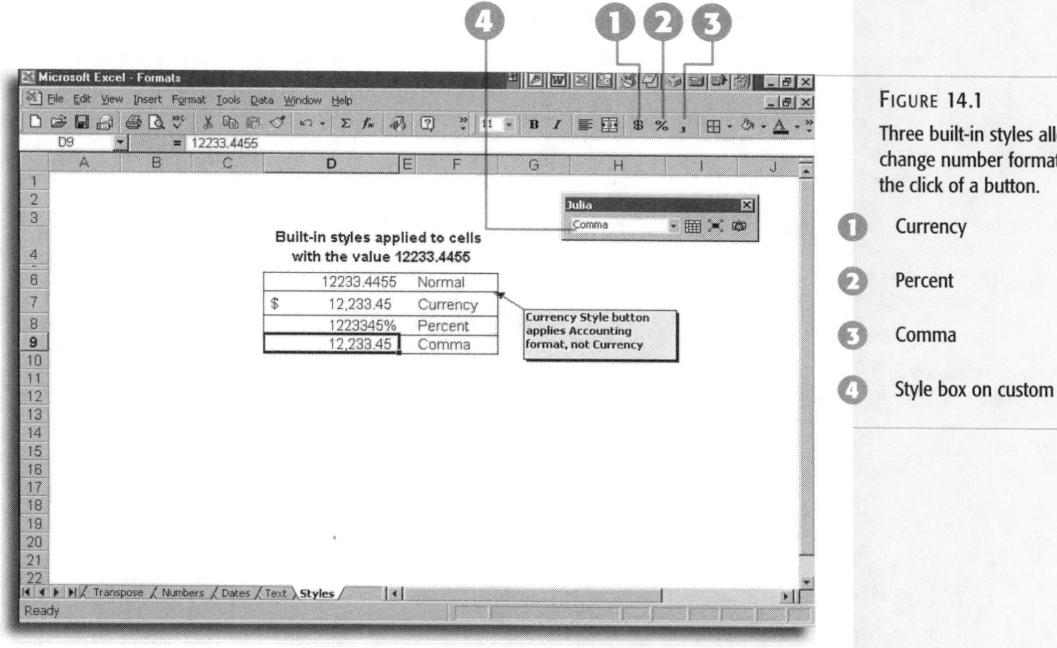

FIGURE 14.1

Three built-in styles allow you to change number formatting with the click of a button.

1. Currency
2. Percent
3. Comma
4. Style box on custom toolbar

Using styles is easier if you customize a toolbar to display the Style box, shown in Figure 14.1. The Style box is in the toolbar **Customize** dialog box, on the **Commands** tab, in the Format category.

SEE ALSO

➤ *To learn more about adding a new button to a toolbar, see the section "Create a Personal Toolbar" in Chapter 27, "Customizing Your Excel Screen," page 529.*

Changing a Style Definition

Applying a built-in style is quick and easy, but it might not be exactly what you want. For example, you might want the built-in Comma style to apply a red font as well as a comma number format, or you might want to make a workbook-wide change to the Normal style. You can change a style definition, including built-in styles, and all cells in the workbook where the changed style is applied will automatically change to reflect the new style definition.

Change a style definition

1. Select a cell where the style is applied. (In Figure 14.2, I'm going to change the Normal style.)
2. On the **Format** menu, click **Style**.

   The Style dialog box is displayed, as shown in Figure 14.2.

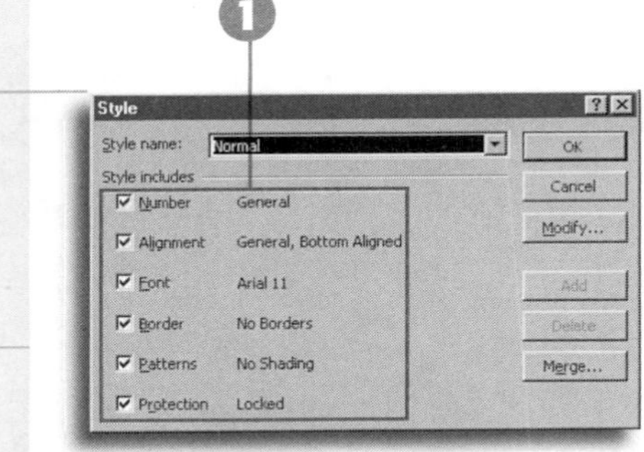

FIGURE 14.2

One way to change style definitions is in the Style dialog box.

1 Formats included in style

   If a format check box is cleared, the style has no effect on that characteristic of cell formatting.

3. Click the **Modify** button.

   The Format Cells dialog box is displayed, as shown in Figure 14.3.

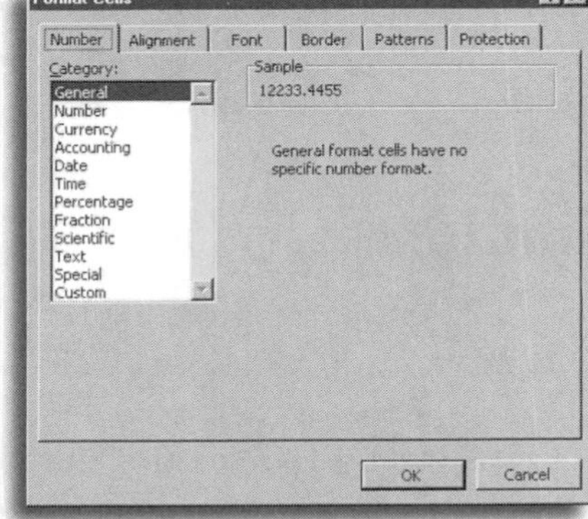

FIGURE 14.3

If you use the Style dialog box to change a style definition, you set and change the style's formats in the Format Cells dialog box.

4. In the Format Cells dialog box, set and change the formats you want the style to apply.
5. Click **OK** to close the Format Cells dialog box.

6. Click **OK** to close the Style dialog box.

   Every cell where the style was applied is changed to reflect the new style formats, as shown in Figure 14.4 (where I changed the Normal style).

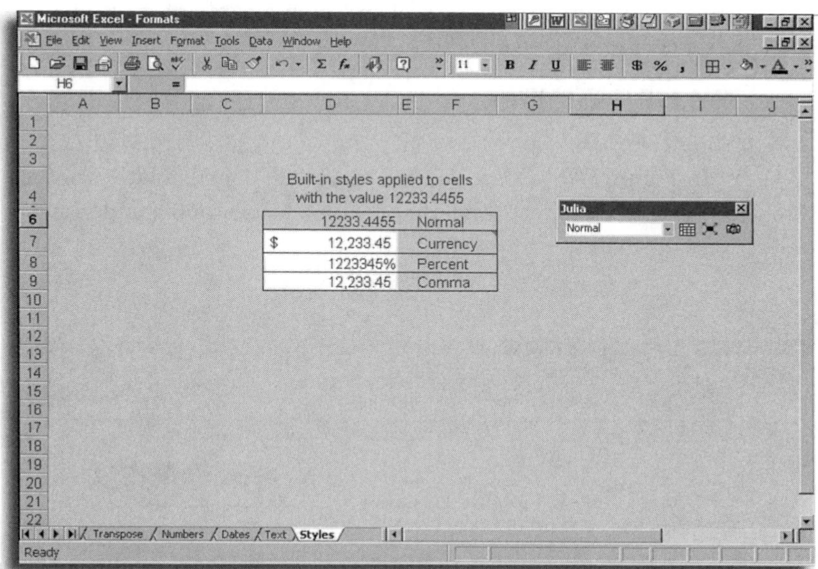

FIGURE 14.4
By changing the Normal style in this workbook, I made all the Normal cells in the entire workbook display the new formatting.

If you use the built-in Currency, Percent, or Comma style buttons to apply any of those number formats to cells, and then change workbook-wide formatting by changing the Normal style, you'll get a surprise: Cells in which the Currency, Percent, or Comma style is applied don't change because changes to the Normal style don't affect them. For this reason, I find it more efficient to apply Currency, Percent, or Comma formats by changing number formatting rather than using the toolbar buttons to apply styles.

Styles Can Be Overridden

If you change a specific format, such as cell color, in a cell where a style is applied, the formatting you apply overrides the format in the style definition for that cell. (It doesn't change the style definition; it just adds another format characteristic on top of the style.)

If you apply a specific number format often and you like the efficiency of applying it by clicking a button, you can create a macro and custom toolbar button that are just as quick to use as the built-in style button.

SEE ALSO

➤ *To learn how to create macros and attach them to custom toolbar buttons, see page 536 and 543 [Chapter 28, "Automating Repetitive Work with Macros"].*

Creating a Custom Style by Example

Creating and changing styles in the Style dialog box is sometimes the long way to go about it. It's usually faster to create and change custom styles *by example*, which means you apply all the formats you want to a single cell and then give that set of formats a custom style name.

Create a style by example

1. Format a cell.

   In Figure 14.5, I've formatted a cell to be blue, bold, Arial size 14, white font, and underlined with a black double underline.

Create a New Style the Detailed Way

If you want to, you can use this same procedure to create a new style in the detailed and time-consuming way: On the **Format** menu, click **Style**; in the Style dialog box, type a new **Style name** and then click **Modify**. Set all the formatting in the Format Cells dialog box, and click **OK** twice to close the dialog boxes.

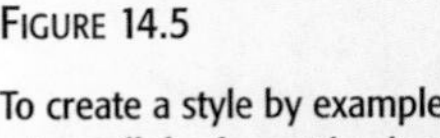

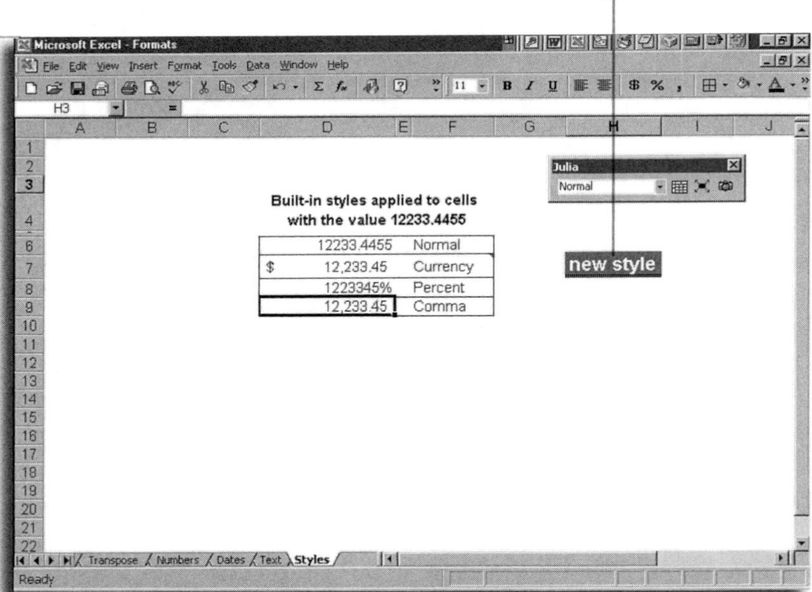

FIGURE 14.5

To create a style by example, first set up all the formatting in a cell.

❶ Formatted cell

2. Select the formatted cell.
3. On the **Format** menu, click **Style**.
4. In the Style dialog box, type a name for your new style in the **Style name** box (as shown in Figure 14.6).
5. Click **OK**.

   The style is ready to apply to other cells in the workbook.

The Toolbar Style Box Is Faster

If you have the Style box displayed on a toolbar, click in the box and type a name for the custom style; then, press Enter.

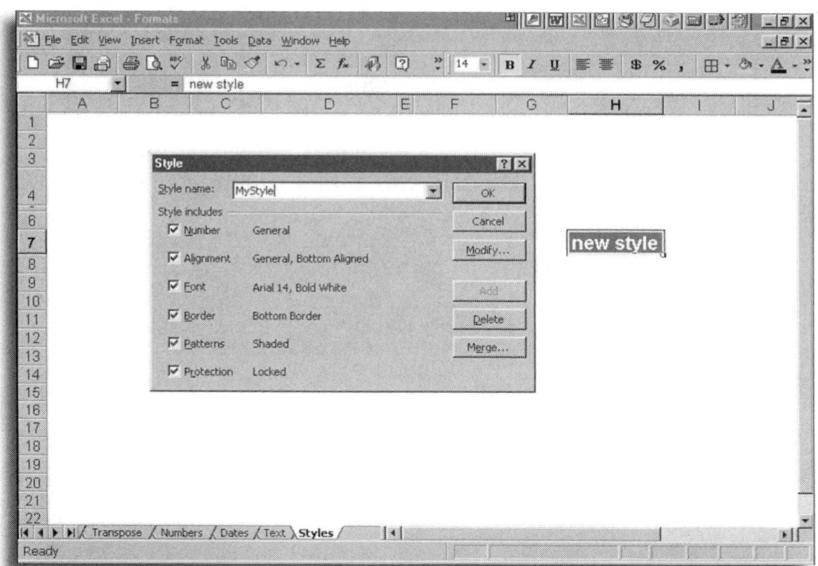

FIGURE 14.6
Type a name for your custom style, and it's ready to use.

In Figure 14.7, I've applied my new custom style by selecting a range and then clicking the custom style name on the drop-down list in the Style box on my custom toolbar.

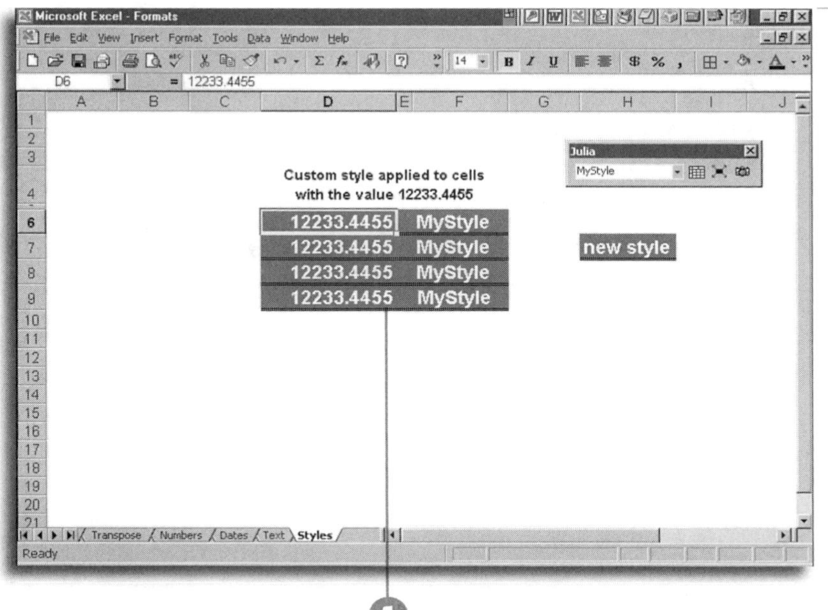

FIGURE 14.7
Custom styles can change a lot of formatting characteristics quickly.

1 Custom style applied

Copying Styles from Other Workbooks

Copying styles from other workbooks is especially helpful if you have several custom styles already set up in one workbook. (Maybe a colleague sent you a workbook with great formatting, and you want to duplicate the formatting without having to recreate it from scratch.)

You can copy a single style from one workbook to another or merge several styles at one time from one workbook to another.

Copy a style from one workbook to a second workbook

1. Open both workbooks.
2. Copy a cell that has the style applied.
3. Paste the cell into the second workbook.

   The copied-and-pasted cell carries its style with it into the second workbook, and the style name is added to the list of styles available there.

After you've pasted the cell with the custom style, you can delete the cell (or open the **Edit** menu, point to **Clear**, and click **All** to remove its contents and formatting); the custom style remains in the workbook even after you delete the cell that carried it in.

SEE ALSO

➤ *To learn about copying and pasting cells, see the section "Moving and Copying Cells to a Different Worksheet," page 144.*

Merge, or copy, several styles from one workbook to a second workbook

1. Open both workbooks.
2. In the second workbook (the workbook you want to copy styles *into*), open the **Format** menu; then, click **Style**.
3. In the Style dialog box, click the **Merge** button.
4. In the Merge Styles dialog box, click the name of the workbook that contains the styles; then, click **OK**.

   If there are styles in both workbooks with the same name but different formats, you'll see a message asking if you want to merge those styles.

If you click **Yes**, the styles you're merging will override the existing styles of the same name, and you can't Undo the style merger. (Be careful; if you're not sure, click **No**.)

The styles are merged, or copied, into the second workbook.

Deleting a Style

If you have a long list of styles in a workbook, it takes a long time to scan that list to find the style you want to apply. Styles you no longer need can be deleted. Another good reason to delete a style is that it's a quick way to clean up a workbook and start over. When you delete a style, all cells with that style applied are returned to Normal style.

Delete a style

1. Under the **Format** menu, click **Style**.
2. In the **Style name** box, select the style you want to delete.
3. Click **Delete**.

   The style is deleted from the workbook, and all cells with that style applied are returned to Normal style.

Return to Normalcy

If you accidentally override Normal style with an altered Normal style during a merge, here's a quick way to get your default Normal style back: Open a new workbook (it will have only the default Normal and built-in styles); then, merge styles from the new, unsaved workbook into the workbook where you accidentally over-rode the Normal style.

PART

IV

Sorting, Filtering, and Summarizing Data

15 Sorting Lists 269

16 Filtering Lists 283

17 Finding Answers and Making Decisions 311

18 Summarizing Details with Consolidation or Subtotals 327

19 Summarizing Details with PivotTables and PilotCharts 343

CHAPTER

15

Sorting Lists

Sorting lists by one column

Sorting lists by two or three columns

Sorting lists by more than three columns

Sorting by a custom list

Sorting a list randomly

Undoing a sort

Sorting Out the Terminology

In general, the terms *list* and *table* mean the same thing: a rectangular block of data that all pertains to a single subject (for example, contact information), in which each column, or *field*, contains the same kind of data (for example, last name or phone number).

What If I Just Want to Sort One Column?

To sort a single column in a table without sorting the attached data along with the column, select all the cells in the table column before sorting; only the selected column is sorted, and the other columns are unchanged.

Sorting a List by a Single Column

After you've entered or imported a sea of data into a worksheet, you need to organize it to render it useful or meaningful. Your first line of defense against a jumble of meaningless data is to sort it. Some data-organizing procedures, such as subtotaling (covered in Chapter 18, "Summarizing Details with Consolidation or Subtotals"), require that you sort the data first.

When you sort a list, you arrange a specific column, or *field*, in the list in an ascending or descending order. The field you sort on is also known as a *sort key*. All the attached data is sorted along with the specific column so that if you sort a contacts list in the Last Name column, the First Name, Phone, and Address columns are sorted along with the Last Names, and the data remains intact.

Any data in cells adjacent to the list is sorted with the records in the list, and data in cells separated from the list by a blank row or column is not included in the sort. This means that you can have two lists on a worksheet and sort them independently of one another, as long as they are separated by a blank row or column.

Sort a list quickly by a single key

1. Click in the table column (the field) you want to sort by. In Figure 15.1, I'm going to sort the list by Last Name.

   Don't select more than one cell; just click in the table column.

2. On the Standard toolbar, click a sort button:
   - To sort in an ascending order (1–10 or A–Z), click **Sort Ascending**.
   - To sort in a descending order (10–1 or Z–A), click **Sort Descending**.

   The list or table is sorted, as shown in Figure 15.2.

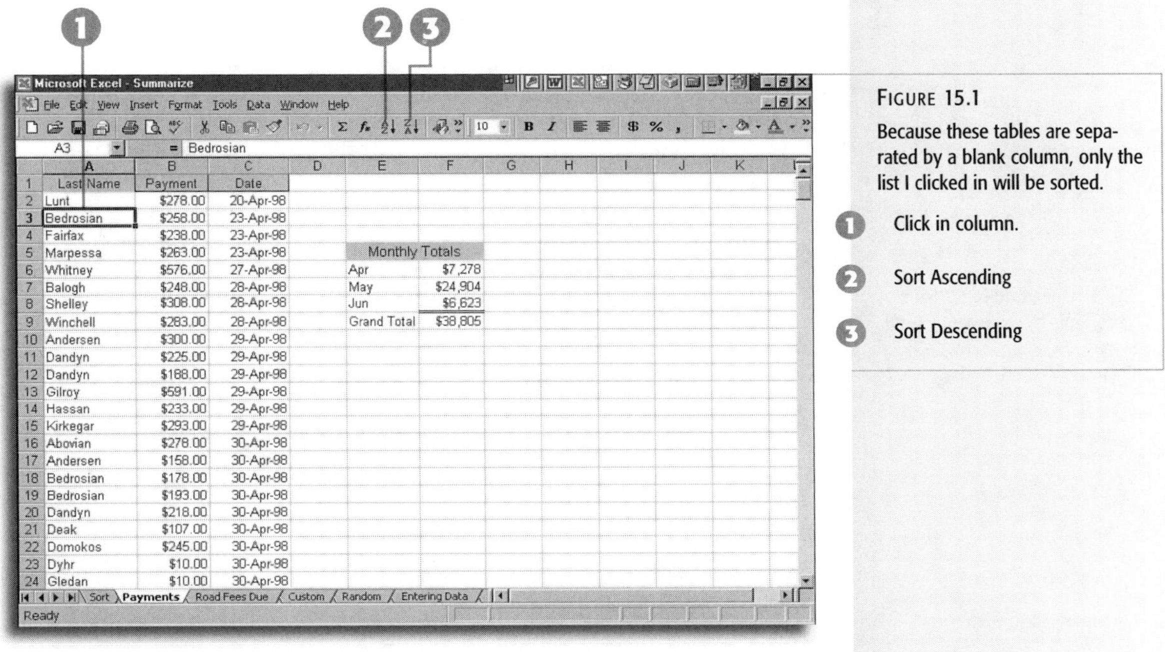

	Last Name	Payment	Date
1	Last Name	Payment	Date
2	Lunt	$278.00	20-Apr-98
3	Bedrosian	$258.00	23-Apr-98
4	Fairfax	$238.00	23-Apr-98
5	Marpessa	$263.00	23-Apr-98
6	Whitney	$576.00	27-Apr-98
7	Balogh	$248.00	28-Apr-98
8	Shelley	$308.00	28-Apr-98
9	Winchell	$283.00	28-Apr-98
10	Andersen	$300.00	29-Apr-98
11	Dandyn	$225.00	29-Apr-98
12	Dandyn	$188.00	29-Apr-98
13	Gilroy	$591.00	29-Apr-98
14	Hassan	$233.00	29-Apr-98
15	Kirkegar	$293.00	29-Apr-98
16	Abovian	$278.00	30-Apr-98
17	Andersen	$158.00	30-Apr-98
18	Bedrosian	$178.00	30-Apr-98
19	Bedrosian	$193.00	30-Apr-98
20	Dandyn	$218.00	30-Apr-98
21	Deak	$107.00	30-Apr-98
22	Domokos	$245.00	30-Apr-98
23	Dyhr	$10.00	30-Apr-98
24	Gledan	$10.00	30-Apr-98

Monthly Totals	
Apr	$7,278
May	$24,904
Jun	$6,623
Grand Total	$38,805

FIGURE 15.1

Because these tables are separated by a blank column, only the list I clicked in will be sorted.

1. Click in column.
2. Sort Ascending
3. Sort Descending

Microsoft Excel - Summarize

A3 = Abovian

	Last Name	Payment	Date
1	Last Name	Payment	Date
2	Abovian	$278.00	30-Apr-98
3	Abovian	$0.00	05-May-98
4	Abovian	$100.00	15-May-98
5	Abovian	$158.00	23-May-98
6	Abovian	$10.00	05-Jun-98
7	Abovian	$18.00	05-Jun-98
8	Andersen	$300.00	29-Apr-98
9	Andersen	$158.00	30-Apr-98
10	Andersen	$293.00	02-May-98
11	Andersen	$293.00	05-May-98
12	Andersen	$263.00	29-May-98
13	Andersen	$213.00	08-Jun-98
14	Bahir	$218.00	01-May-98
15	Bahir	$268.00	04-May-98
16	Bahir	$266.00	05-Jun-98
17	Bahir	$10.00	05-Jun-98
18	Bahir	$18.00	05-Jun-98
19	Bahir	$25.00	08-Jun-98
20	Baker	$20.00	05-May-98
21	Baker	$10.00	05-Jun-98
22	Baker	$25.00	06-Jun-98
23	Baker	$336.00	07-Jun-98
24	Baker	$230.00	08-Jun-98

Monthly Totals	
Apr	$7,278
May	$24,904
Jun	$6,623
Grand Total	$38,805

Sort Payments Road Fees Due Custom Random Entering Data

Ready

FIGURE 15.2

The whole list is sorted along with the column I clicked in (Last Name).

Sorting a List by Two or Three Columns

In Figure 15.3, I've got a table of nationwide sales results for baseball caps. I want to compare the sales for each color, red and black, and see if different target audiences have different cap color preferences.

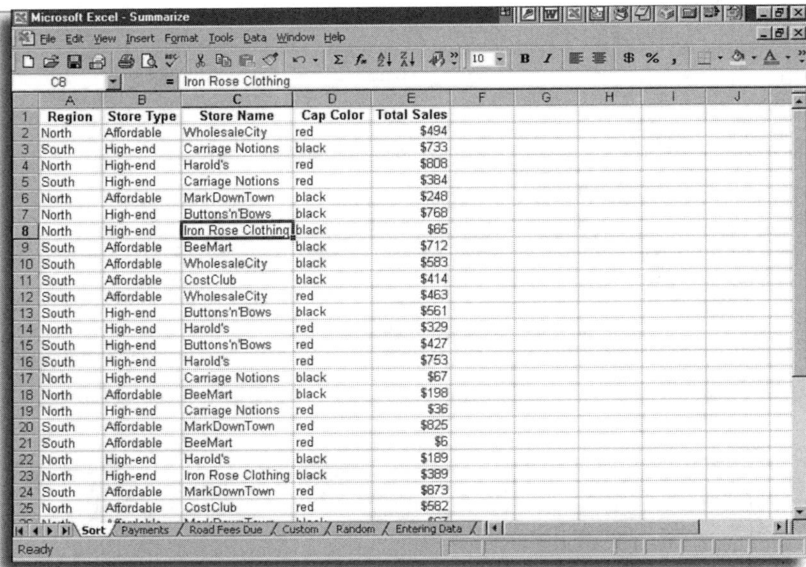

Region	Store Type	Store Name	Cap Color	Total Sales
North	Affordable	WholesaleCity	red	$494
South	High-end	Carriage Notions	black	$733
North	High-end	Harold's	red	$808
South	High-end	Carriage Notions	red	$384
North	Affordable	MarkDownTown	black	$248
North	High-end	Buttons'n'Bows	black	$768
North	High-end	Iron Rose Clothing	black	$65
South	Affordable	BeeMart	black	$712
South	Affordable	WholesaleCity	black	$583
South	Affordable	CostClub	black	$414
South	Affordable	WholesaleCity	red	$463
South	High-end	Buttons'n'Bows	black	$561
North	High-end	Harold's	red	$329
South	High-end	Buttons'n'Bows	red	$427
South	High-end	Harold's	red	$753
North	High-end	Carriage Notions	black	$67
North	Affordable	BeeMart	black	$198
North	High-end	Carriage Notions	red	$36
South	Affordable	MarkDownTown	red	$825
South	Affordable	BeeMart	red	$6
North	High-end	Harold's	black	$189
North	High-end	Iron Rose Clothing	black	$389
South	Affordable	MarkDownTown	red	$873
North	Affordable	CostClub	red	$582

FIGURE 15.3
This data needs to be sorted by Store Type, by Store Name within Store Type, and then by Cap Color within Store Name.

The data was entered in a random order, and now I need to sort it to make sense of it. I'll sort it by Store Type (High-end or Affordable), then by the actual Store Name, and then by Cap Color.

Sort a list by two or three keys

1. Click any cell in the table.
2. On the **Data** menu, click **Sort**.

   The Sort dialog box is displayed, as shown in Figure 15.4.

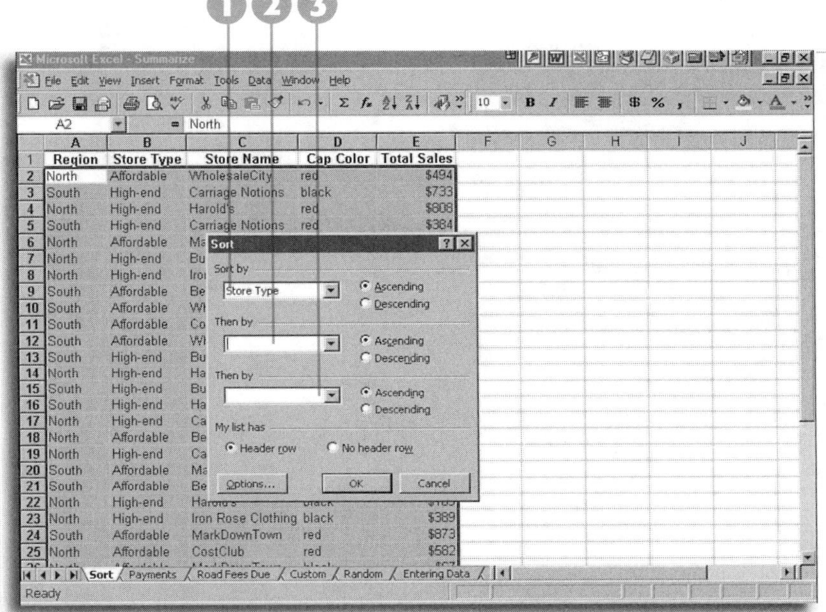

FIGURE 15.4

You can sort a table by three keys at a time in the Sort dialog box.

1. First key
2. Second key
3. Third key

3. In the **Sort by** box, click the down arrow; then click the top-level sort key (in this case, the Store Type field).
4. Click an option button for the sort order you want (in this case, **Ascending**).
5. In the first **Then by** box, choose the second-level sort key (in this case, Store Name) and a sort order.
6. In the second **Then by** box, choose the third-level sort key (in this case, Cap Color) and a sort order.

   The completed dialog box for this example is shown in Figure 15.5.
7. Click **OK**.

   The table is sorted by the keys you set in the Sort dialog box; in this example, my sorted table is shown in Figure 15.6.

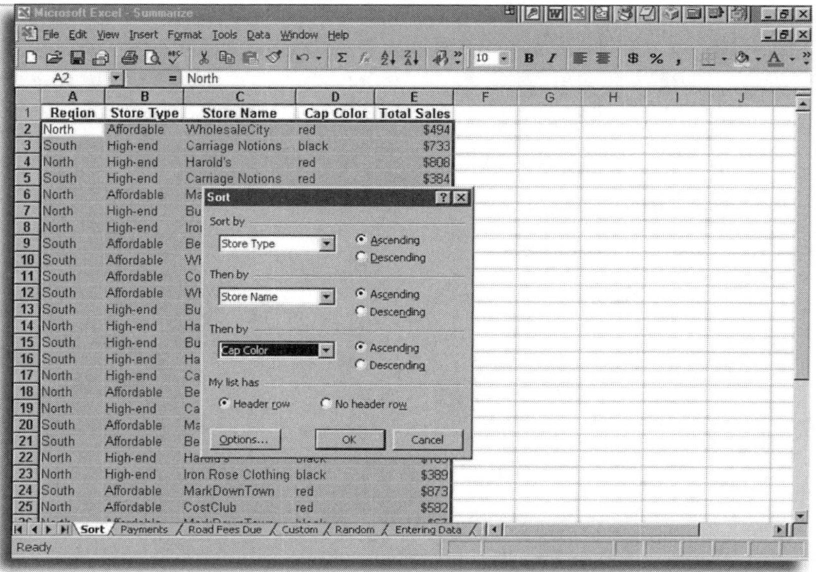

FIGURE 15.5

The Sort dialog box is ready to sort the table by three keys.

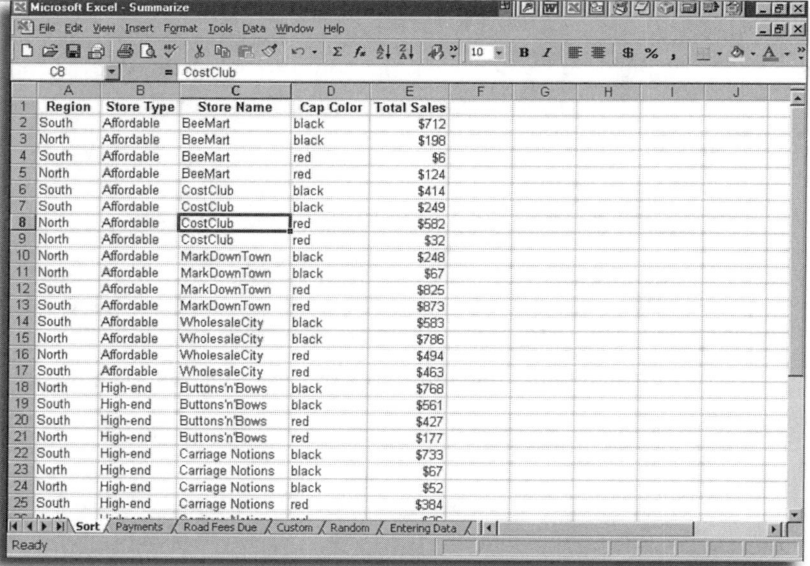

	Region	Store Type	Store Name	Cap Color	Total Sales
2	South	Affordable	BeeMart	black	$712
3	North	Affordable	BeeMart	black	$198
4	South	Affordable	BeeMart	red	$6
5	North	Affordable	BeeMart	red	$124
6	South	Affordable	CostClub	black	$414
7	South	Affordable	CostClub	black	$249
8	North	Affordable	CostClub	red	$582
9	North	Affordable	CostClub	red	$32
10	North	Affordable	MarkDownTown	black	$248
11	North	Affordable	MarkDownTown	black	$67
12	South	Affordable	MarkDownTown	red	$825
13	South	Affordable	MarkDownTown	red	$873
14	South	Affordable	WholesaleCity	black	$583
15	North	Affordable	WholesaleCity	black	$786
16	North	Affordable	WholesaleCity	red	$494
17	South	Affordable	WholesaleCity	red	$463
18	North	High-end	Buttons'n'Bows	black	$768
19	South	High-end	Buttons'n'Bows	black	$561
20	South	High-end	Buttons'n'Bows	red	$427
21	North	High-end	Buttons'n'Bows	red	$177
22	South	High-end	Carriage Notions	black	$733
23	North	High-end	Carriage Notions	black	$67
24	North	High-end	Carriage Notions	black	$52
25	South	High-end	Carriage Notions	red	$384

FIGURE 15.6

This table is sorted by Store Type, then by Store Name, and then by Cap Color.

Sorting a List by More Than Three Columns

The Sort dialog box lets you sort by up to three keys; if you need to sort by four or more, there's a trick you need to know: *Sort by the major, overall biggest key last*. Perform the sort on the smaller, more detailed keys first with the Sort dialog box; then, perform a second sort with the Sort dialog box, but *only* on the major sort key or keys (usually the leftmost fields in the table).

For example, in the table in Figure 15.6, I want to sort sales by Region as well as by Store Type, Store Name, and Cap Color.

Because I've already performed the sort in Figure 15.6 by the three *minor*, or more detailed, keys, I'm set up to sort on the major key: Region.

Sort a list with four keys

1. Be sure a single cell in the table is selected.
2. On the **Data** menu, click **Sort**.
3. In the **Sort by** box, select the major sort key (in this case, **Region**), and click a sort order option.
4. In the remaining **Then by** boxes, select **(none)**.

   The dialog box in Figure 15.7 is set up to perform the fourth-key sort.
5. Click **OK**.

   The fourth key becomes the top-level sort key in the table, as shown in Figure 15.8.

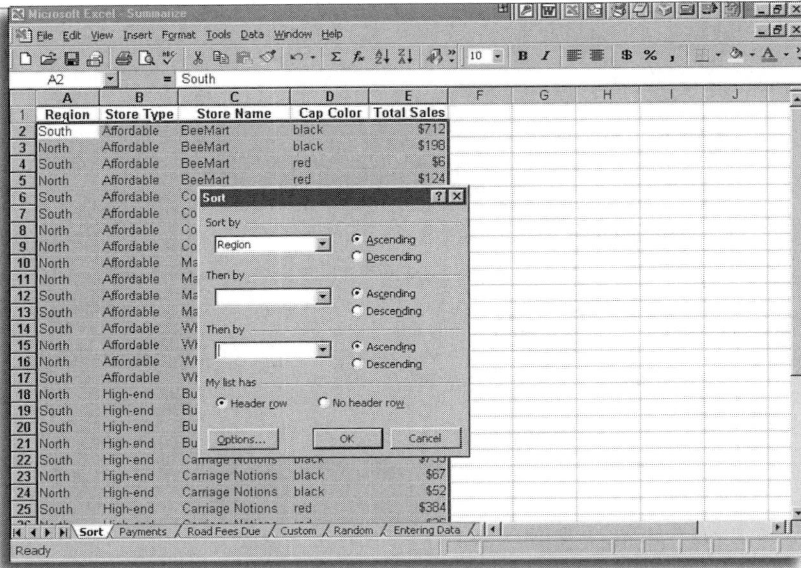

FIGURE 15.7
The second sort overlays a new sort order on top of the already sorted table.

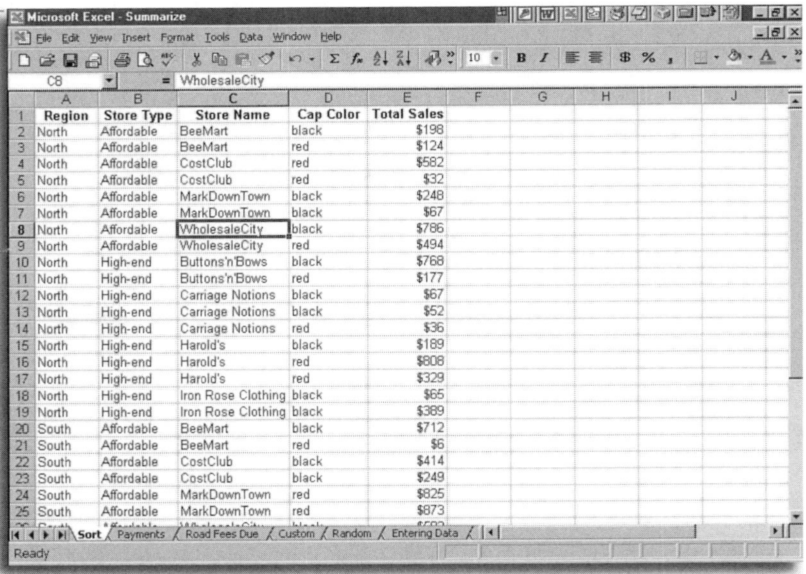

FIGURE 15.8
This table is sorted by four keys: Region, Store Type, Store Name, and Cap Color.

Sorting According to a Custom List

You can sort any key in ascending or descending order, but suppose you want to sort by a special order that's neither ascending nor descending. For example, you might want to sort a list of names of children from oldest to youngest.

Sort options let you sort according to an order in a custom list, which includes days, months, and any custom lists you've created and saved.

SEE ALSO

➤ *To learn how to create a custom list, see page 112.*

Sort a list according to a custom sort order

1. Make sure you've created and saved a custom list. (To see the custom lists, open the **Tools** menu and click **Options**; then click the **Custom Lists** tab.)
2. Click in the custom-list column in your table, also called the custom list *key*.
3. On the **Data** menu, click **Sort**.
4. In the Sort dialog box, shown in Figure 15.9, click **Options**. The list I created as a custom list retains its original sort order, whether I enter it with AutoFill or sort it with special sorting options.
5. In the Sort Options dialog box, shown in Figure 15.10, click the down arrow in the **First key sort order** drop-down list box; then, click the custom list you want to use as a sort order.
6. Click **OK**; then, click **OK** again to close the Sort dialog box.

The list is sorted according to the custom sort order.

Sorting Left to Right

To sort by a horizontal row, left to right, click the **Sort Left to Right** option in the Sort Options dialog box.

FIGURE 15.9

I previously created and saved this list of names as a custom list.

1. Custom list column
2. Options button

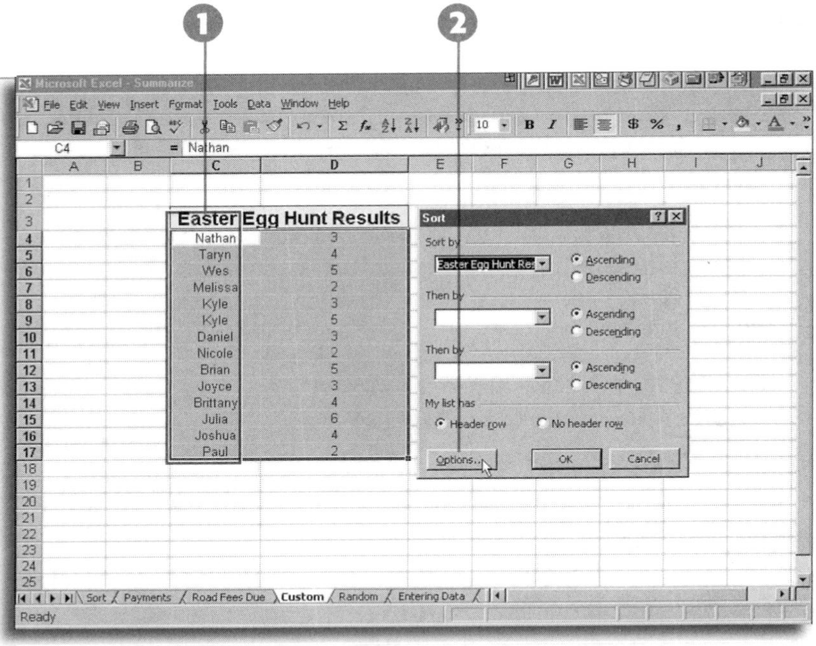

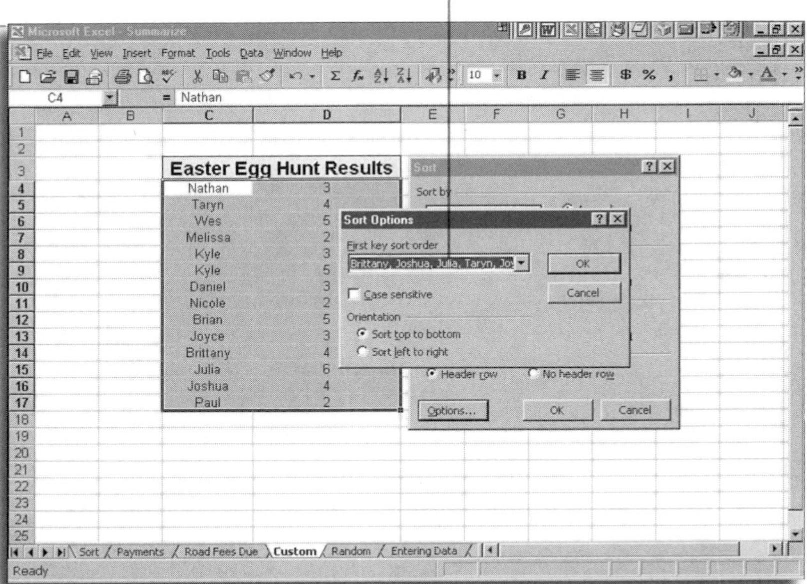

FIGURE 15.10

Choose a custom sort order in the Sort Options dialog box by selecting from previously saved custom lists.

1. Custom-list key

Sorting a List Randomly

Some situations call for a random assortment of items in a list, sometimes even repeated random sorting of the same list. For example, one of my students is a high school teacher, and he likes to thwart potential exam cheaters by creating several versions of the same exam. Each exam has the same long list of true/false questions in a different order. An easy way to create several random-order versions of the exam is to combine the RAND function, which returns random numbers, with repeated sorting.

Sort a list in random order

1. Create the table or list. (For my student's example, I've created a list of exam questions in a worksheet.)
2. Add to the table a column for random numbers, like the one shown in Figure 15.11.

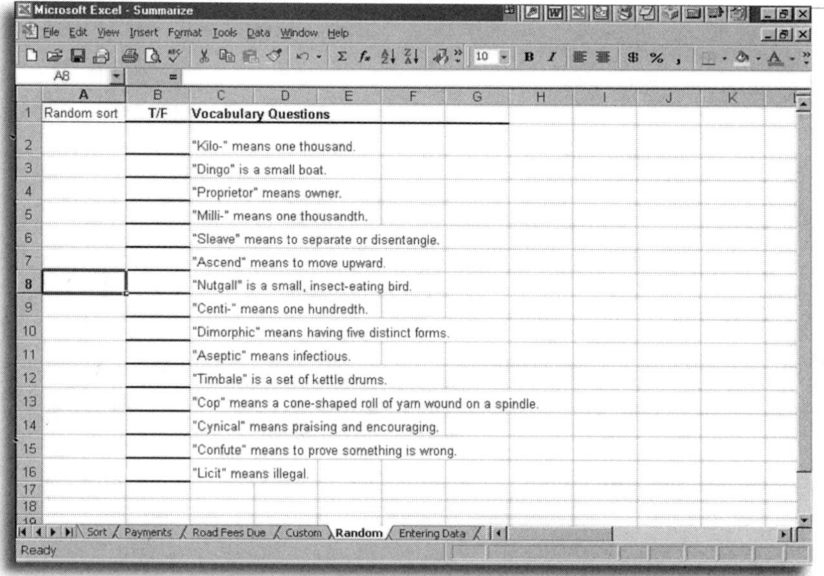

FIGURE 15.11
This table will be sorted at random every time the worksheet recalculates (which is more often than you'd think).

3. Select all the cells in the table's random number column, and type this formula:

```
=rand()
```

Generating Random Whole Numbers

To generate random numbers that are integers greater than 100, try this formula: `=int(rand()*100)`.

4. Press Ctrl+Enter to enter the formula in all the selected cells.

   A formula that generates random numbers to 15-digit precision is entered in the new column.

5. Click in the random number column; then click the **Sort Ascending** button on the Standard toolbar.

   Every time you click the Sort Ascending button, the RAND function recalculates, the list is resorted, and new random numbers are calculated, as shown in Figure 15.12.

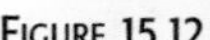

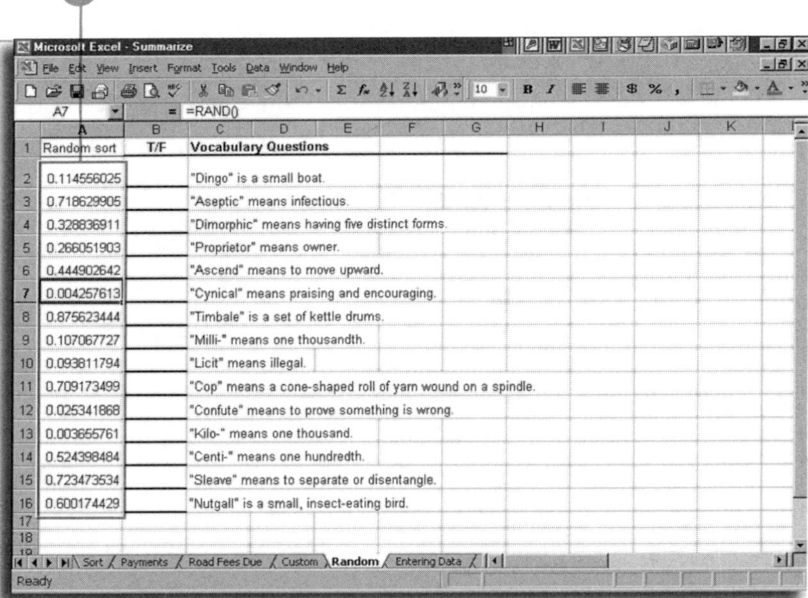

FIGURE 15.12

Random sorting is a good way to create nonidentical lists that contain the same information.

1. Random numbers for sort

Here are some ways to "freeze" and save randomly sorted lists to create several versions:

- Copy the list without the random number column and paste it into another worksheet.

- Copy the list without the random number column and paste it into a Word document.
- Freeze the randomly sorted list by deleting the random number formulas.

SEE ALSO

➤ *To learn more about copying data to another worksheet, see page 144.*

➤ *To learn more about copying data to a Word document, see page 501.*

Undoing a Sort and Returning the List to Its Former Arrangement

You might need to sort a list for temporary information but not want to keep that sort order. There are a couple of ways to return a sorted list to its original sort arrangement:

- To undo a sort and return the list to its former arrangement, click the **Undo** button on the Standard toolbar.
- To be able to return to a presort arrangement after performing a lot of data manipulation in a table, first insert a column of numbers, sorted in ascending order, somewhere in the table. (Insert a column and use AutoFill to enter the numbers.) Then, ignore the new column while you work with the table. When you need to return the initial sort order to the table, sort the number column you inserted.

CHAPTER

16

Filtering Lists

- Filtering a list with a single criterion
- Filtering a list with multiple criteria
- Calculating filtered records
- Complex filtering with Microsoft Query
- Saving and reusing queries

Filtering Records

New Terms

Field is the common term for a column of data in a table, and *record* is the common term for a row of data in a table. You see these terms a lot, both in this book and in Excel's help files.

If you have a large table of data and you want to focus on particular *records*, or rows, within the table, you can *filter* the table to show only those records and hide all others. You can also use filters to *extract*, or pull out, specific records and paste them onto another worksheet (or into another file, such as a Word document).

The easiest, fastest way to filter a list is by using *AutoFilter*. You can filter a list by looking for a specific entry in a single *field* (for example, a specific city in a City field) or by looking for multiple criteria (such as expense amounts greater than $100 in a specific expense category).

Filtering a List on a Single Criterion

I'm the treasurer for a local nonprofit organization, and the table in Figure 16.1 is similar to a table I use to keep track of who has paid their fees. It's a fairly long list, and I want to see at a glance who still owes a balance. I use AutoFilter to hide everyone who's paid and show only those who owe fees by filtering the nonblank cells in the Balance field.

Filter a table with AutoFilter

1. Click any cell in the table.
2. On the **Data** menu, point to **Filter** and then click **AutoFilter**.

   Small gray filter arrows appear at the top of every column in the table (shown in Figure 16.2).
3. Click a filter arrow in the field in which you want to set filter criteria (in this example, the Balance field, as shown in Figure 16.3).

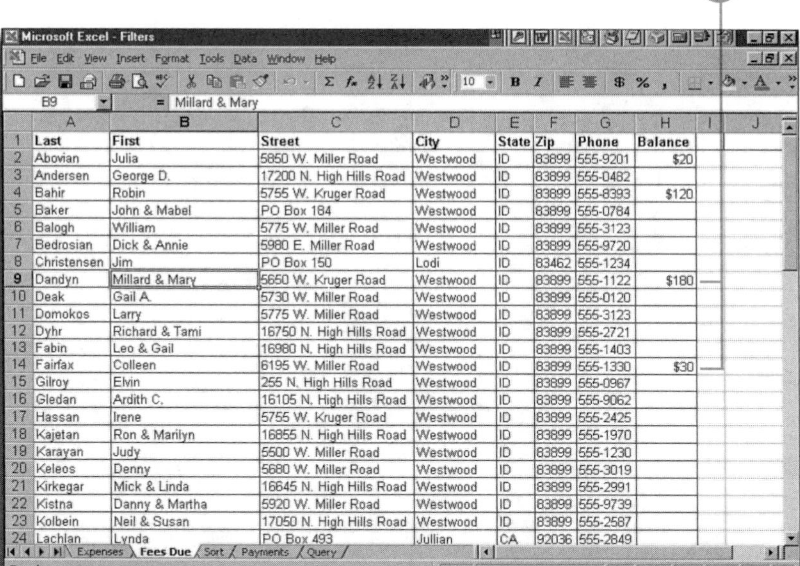

FIGURE 16.1
By hiding the records with blank cells in the Balance column, I can see a list of people who still owe money.

1 Filter non-blanks

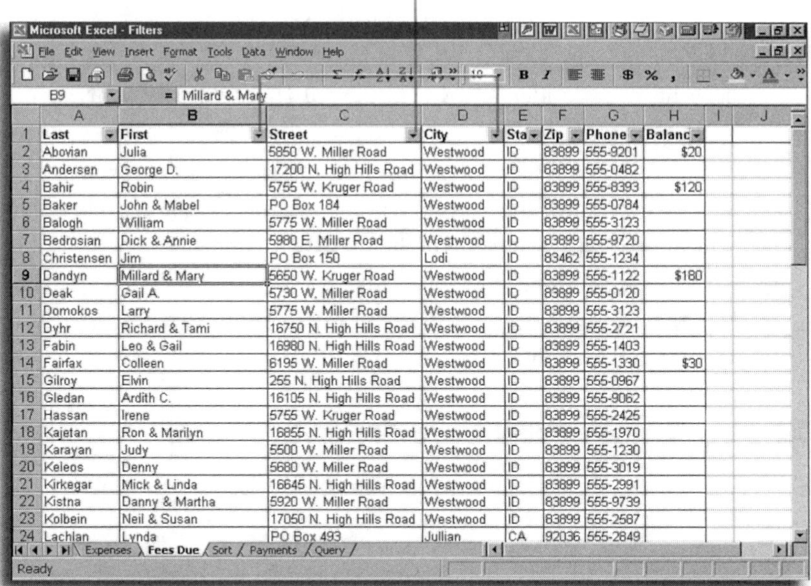

FIGURE 16.2
AutoFilter displays small gray filter arrows at the top of each column.

1 Filter arrows

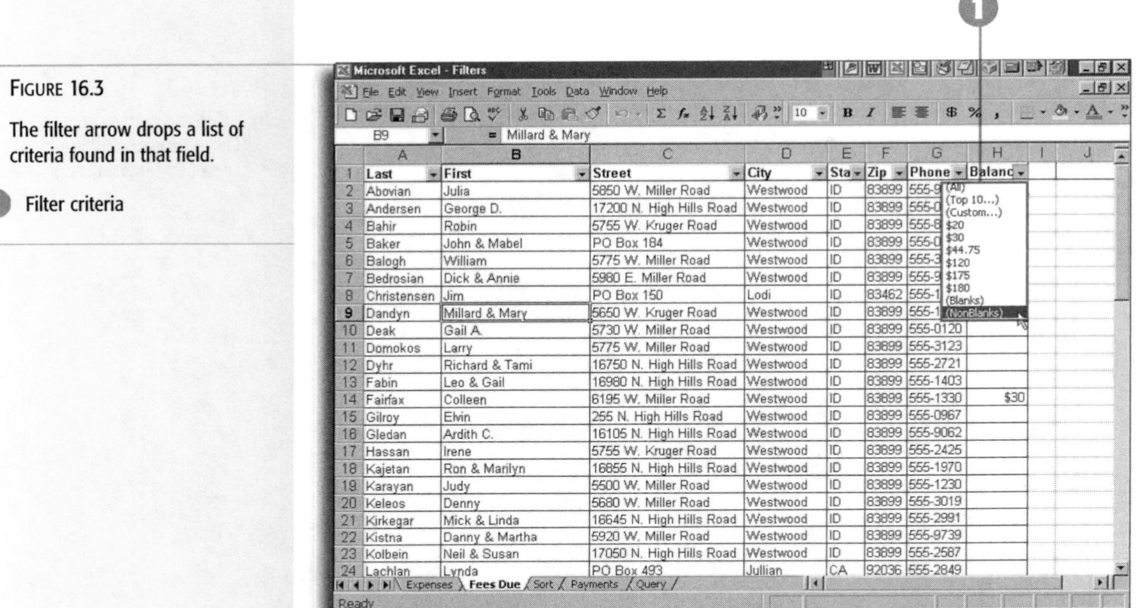

	A	B	C	D	E	F	G	H
1	Last	First	Street	City	Sta	Zip	Phone	Balanc
2	Abovian	Julia	5850 W. Miller Road	Westwood	ID	83899	555-9	
3	Andersen	George D.	17200 N. High Hills Road	Westwood	ID	83899	555-0	
4	Bahir	Robin	5755 W. Kruger Road	Westwood	ID	83899	555-8	
5	Baker	John & Mabel	PO Box 184	Westwood	ID	83899	555-0	
6	Balogh	William	5775 W. Miller Road	Westwood	ID	83899	555-3	
7	Bedrosian	Dick & Annie	5980 E. Miller Road	Westwood	ID	83899	555-9	
8	Christensen	Jim	PO Box 150	Lodi	ID	83462	555-1	
9	Dandyn	Millard & Mary	5650 W. Kruger Road	Westwood	ID	83899	555-1	
10	Deak	Gail A.	5730 W. Miller Road	Westwood	ID	83899	555-0120	
11	Domokos	Larry	5775 W. Miller Road	Westwood	ID	83899	555-3123	
12	Dyhr	Richard & Tami	16750 N. High Hills Road	Westwood	ID	83899	555-2721	
13	Fabin	Leo & Gail	16980 N. High Hills Road	Westwood	ID	83899	555-1403	
14	Fairfax	Colleen	6195 W. Miller Road	Westwood	ID	83899	555-1330	$30
15	Gilroy	Elvin	255 N. High Hills Road	Westwood	ID	83899	555-0967	
16	Gledan	Ardith C.	16105 N. High Hills Road	Westwood	ID	83899	555-9062	
17	Hassan	Irene	5755 W. Kruger Road	Westwood	ID	83899	555-2425	
18	Kajetan	Ron & Marilyn	16855 N. High Hills Road	Westwood	ID	83899	555-1970	
19	Karayan	Judy	5500 W. Miller Road	Westwood	ID	83899	555-1230	
20	Keleos	Denny	5680 W. Miller Road	Westwood	ID	83899	555-3019	
21	Kirkegar	Mick & Linda	16645 N. High Hills Road	Westwood	ID	83899	555-2991	
22	Kistna	Danny & Martha	5920 W. Miller Road	Westwood	ID	83899	555-9739	
23	Kolbein	Neil & Susan	17050 N. High Hills Road	Westwood	ID	83899	555-2587	
24	Lachlan	Lynda	PO Box 493	Jullian	CA	92036	555-2849	

FIGURE 16.3

The filter arrow drops a list of criteria found in that field.

1 Filter criteria

4. Click the criterion on which you want to filter. (In this example, I'm filtering on non-blanks.)

   Records with the criterion you choose are displayed, and all others are hidden (shown in Figure 16.4). The filter arrow in the active-filter field is blue, which helps you remember where you set criteria.

5. To keep AutoFilter on but remove the filter criteria, click the filter arrow and then click **(All)**.

   To remove the filter and display all the records, open the **Data** menu, point to **Filter**, and then click **AutoFilter** to turn off AutoFilter.

Filtering a List on Multiple Criteria

Sometimes you need more complex filter criteria, as I want in the expenses list in Figure 16.5.

Microsoft Excel - Filters

B9 = Millard & Mary

	Last	First	Street	City	Sta	Zip	Phone	Balanc
2	Abovian	Julia	5850 W. Miller Road	Westwood	ID	83899	555-9201	$20
4	Bahir	Robin	5755 W. Kruger Road	Westwood	ID	83899	555-8393	$120
9	Dandyn	Millard & Mary	5650 W. Kruger Road	Westwood	ID	83899	555-1122	$180
14	Fairfax	Colleen	6195 W. Miller Road	Westwood	ID	83899	555-1330	$30
26	Lawler	Karen L.	HCI 415	Spirit Mountai	ID	83869	555-3636	$120
27	Lunt	Thomas	17225 N. High Hills Road	Westwood	ID	83899	555-	$120
28	Marpessa	Ron & Rhonda	PO Box 3060	Hope	ID	83899	555-7890	$180
29	Munin	Joyce	16625 N. High Hills Road	Westwood	ID	83899	555-2731	$120
32	Rinaldo	John & Jean	6250 W. Miller Road	Westwood	ID	83899	555-	$180
35	Selyz	Dave & Mary	17155 N. High Hills Road	Westwood	ID	83899	555-0731	$120
36	Shelley	Gordon E.	5855 W. Miller Road	Westwood	ID	83899	555-0797	$120
38	Takeri	Fred & Betty	5800 W. Kruger Road	Westwood	ID	83899	555-0719	$44.75
45	Whitney	Doug & Wilma	16755 N. High Hills Road	Westwood	ID	83899	555-3033	$175
46	Winchell	Mickey	5565 W. Miller Road	Westwood	ID	83899	555-3587	$120
49								1629.75

Expenses / Fees Due / Sort / Payments / Query

14 of 45 records found

FIGURE 16.4

Filtering the table shows me at a glance who still owes what.

1 Active filter (blue arrow)

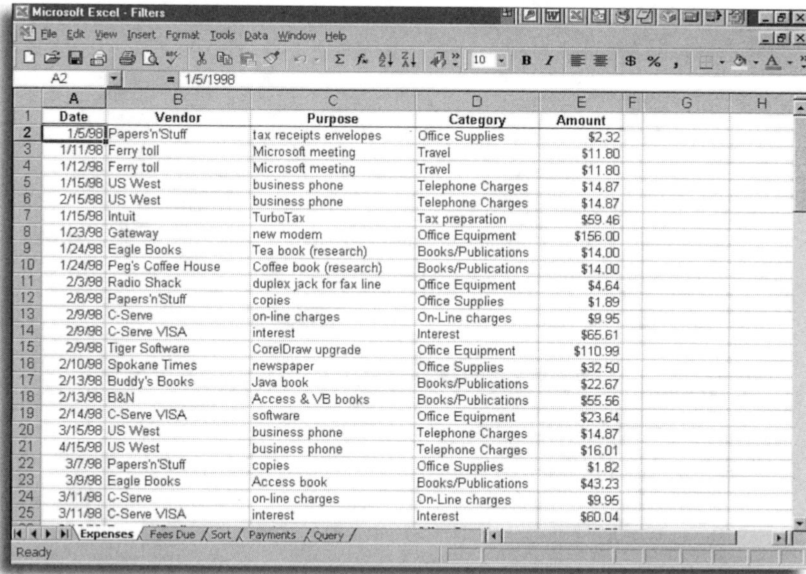

Microsoft Excel - Filters

A2 = 1/5/1998

	Date	Vendor	Purpose	Category	Amount
2	1/5/98	Papers'n'Stuff	tax receipts envelopes	Office Supplies	$2.32
3	1/11/98	Ferry toll	Microsoft meeting	Travel	$11.80
4	1/12/98	Ferry toll	Microsoft meeting	Travel	$11.80
5	1/15/98	US West	business phone	Telephone Charges	$14.87
6	2/15/98	US West	business phone	Telephone Charges	$14.87
7	1/15/98	Intuit	TurboTax	Tax preparation	$59.46
8	1/23/98	Gateway	new modem	Office Equipment	$156.00
9	1/24/98	Eagle Books	Tea book (research)	Books/Publications	$14.00
10	1/24/98	Peg's Coffee House	Coffee book (research)	Books/Publications	$14.00
11	2/3/98	Radio Shack	duplex jack for fax line	Office Equipment	$4.64
12	2/8/98	Papers'n'Stuff	copies	Office Supplies	$1.89
13	2/9/98	C-Serve	on-line charges	On-Line charges	$9.95
14	2/9/98	C-Serve VISA	interest	Interest	$65.61
15	2/9/98	Tiger Software	CorelDraw upgrade	Office Equipment	$110.99
16	2/10/98	Spokane Times	newspaper	Office Supplies	$32.50
17	2/13/98	Buddy's Books	Java book	Books/Publications	$22.67
18	2/13/98	B&N	Access & VB books	Books/Publications	$55.56
19	2/14/98	C-Serve VISA	software	Office Equipment	$23.64
20	3/15/98	US West	business phone	Telephone Charges	$14.87
21	4/15/98	US West	business phone	Telephone Charges	$16.01
22	3/7/98	Papers'n'Stuff	copies	Office Supplies	$1.82
23	3/9/98	Eagle Books	Access book	Books/Publications	$43.23
24	3/11/98	C-Serve	on-line charges	On-Line charges	$9.95
25	3/11/98	C-Serve VISA	interest	Interest	$60.04

Expenses / Fees Due / Sort / Payments / Query

Ready

FIGURE 16.5

Filtering helps me understand better where I spent my year's expenses.

The following are several ways to narrow a filter and make it even more specific (all are covered in the following sections):

- You can filter on two different fields. (For example, I want to see the expenses for Office Supplies, specifically for the Papers'n'Stuff vendor.)
- You can filter on two criteria in the same field. (For example, I want to see what I spent at Buddy's Books and at Eagle Books, both in the Vendor field.)
- You can filter on a criteria range. (For example, I want to see a filtered list of all my expenses in January.)
- You can filter on the highest or lowest numbers in a number field. (For example, I want to see the five highest expense amounts for the year.)

Filtering on Two Different Fields

I want to see the expenses for Office Supplies, specifically for the Papers'n'Stuff vendor.

Filter on two different fields

1. Click the table. On the **Data** menu, point to **Filter** and then click **AutoFilter**.
2. Click the filter arrow in the first field (in this case, Category), and then click the criterion you want (in this case, Office Supplies).
3. Click the filter arrow in the second field (in this case, Vendor), and then click the criterion you want (in this case, Papers'n'Stuff).

   Figure 16.6 shows the results of my two-field filter.

Filtering on Two Criteria in the Same Field

I want to see what I spent at Buddy's Books and Eagle Books, both in the Vendor field. This filter requires that I set up an OR criterion in the Vendor field to show every record where the vendor is either Buddy's Books or Eagle Books.

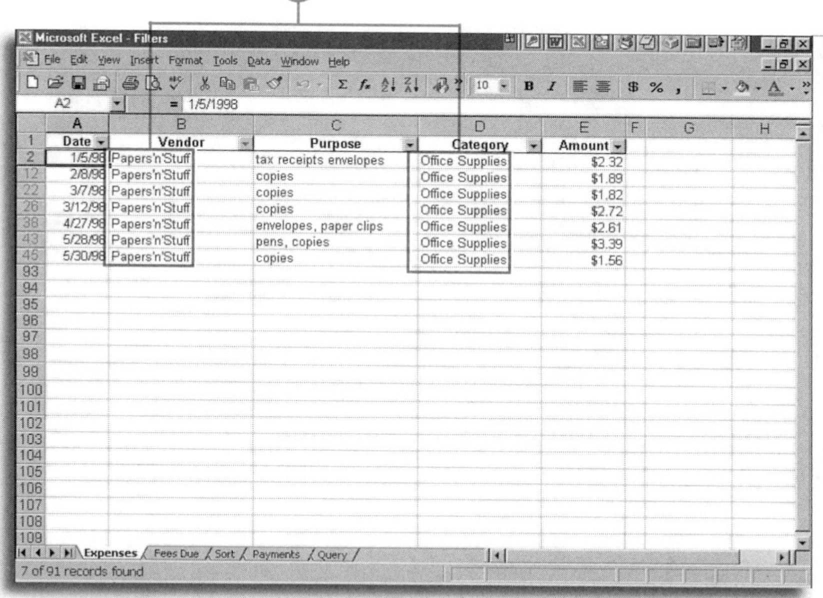

FIGURE 16.6
To filter on two fields, select a filter criterion in each field.

1 These two fields are filtered.

Filter on two criteria in the same field

1. Click the table. On the **Data** menu, point to **Filter** and then click **AutoFilter**.

   If AutoFilter is already turned on, be sure all other AutoFilter criteria are removed. (All AutoFilter arrows should be black.)

2. Click the filter arrow in the Vendor field and then click **(Custom...)**.

   The Custom AutoFilter dialog box appears (shown in Figure 16.7).

3. In the upper-left box, select a comparison operator from the list (in this example, **equals**).

4. In the upper-right box, select a value from the field (in this example, **Buddy's Books**).

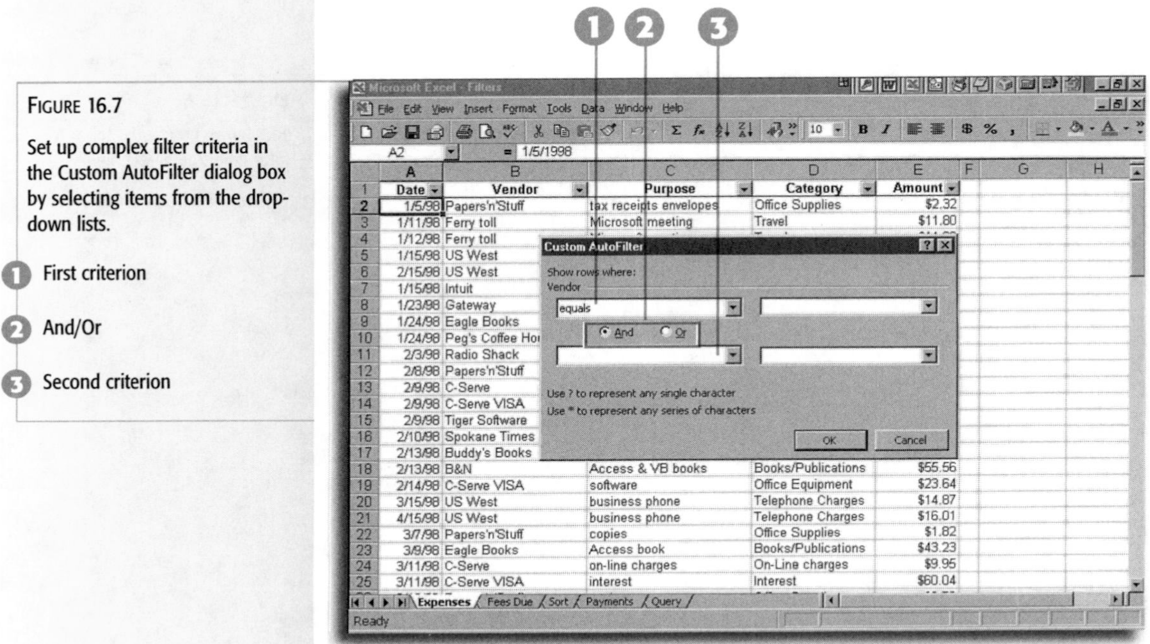

FIGURE 16.7

Set up complex filter criteria in the Custom AutoFilter dialog box by selecting items from the drop-down lists.

1. First criterion
2. And/Or
3. Second criterion

An OR Criterion or an AND Criterion?

An OR criterion displays records that meet either of the criteria; it reads "show me any entries that are X OR Y." An AND criterion displays records that meet both of the criteria; it reads "show me each entry that's both X AND Y." If you create an AND filter and get no records displayed, you probably want an OR filter instead.

5. Click the **Or** option button.
6. In the lower boxes, select a comparison operator and field value (in this example, **equals** and **Eagle Books**).

   The Custom AutoFilter dialog box in Figure 16.8 is set up to run this filter.
7. Click **OK**.

   The results of my filter are shown in Figure 16.9.

Filtering on a Criteria Range

I want to see a filtered list of all my expenses in January. This is an example of an AND filter: Show all records where the Date value is greater than or equal to 1/1/98 AND less than or equal to 1/31/98.

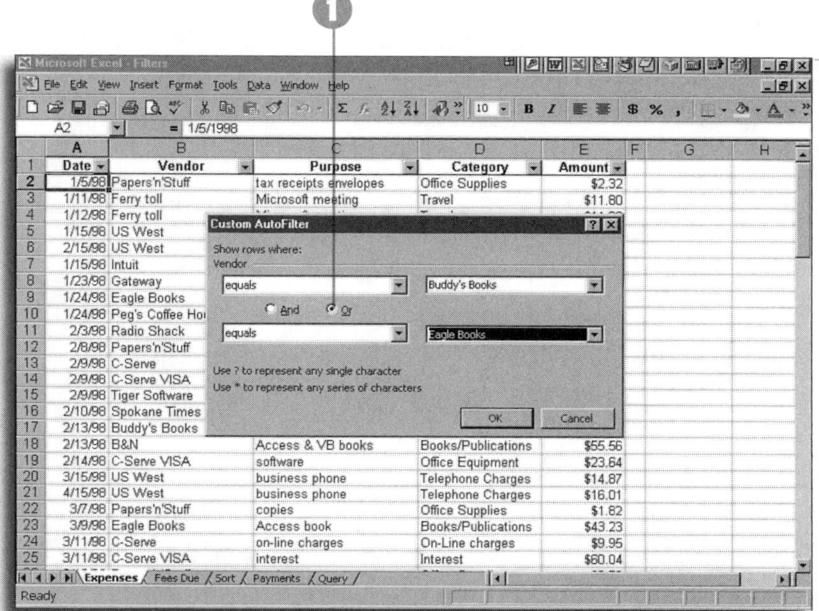

FIGURE 16.8
This OR filter displays records for both bookstores.

1 Or option

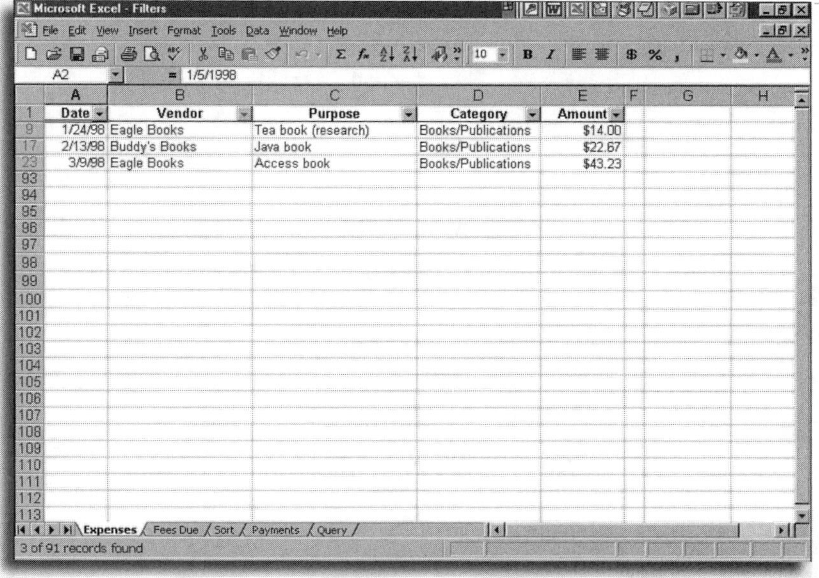

FIGURE 16.9
The results of my OR filter: all vendors that are Buddy's Books or Eagle Books.

Filter on a criteria range

1. Click the table. On the **Data** menu, point to **Filter** and then click **AutoFilter**.

   If AutoFilter is already turned on, be sure all other AutoFilter criteria are removed.

2. Click the filter arrow in the Date field and then click **(Custom...)**.

   The Custom AutoFilter dialog box appears.

3. In the upper-left box, select a comparison operator from the list (in this example, **is greater than or equal to**).
4. In the upper-right box, type the beginning date (in this example, **1/1/98**).
5. Be sure the **And** option button is selected.
6. In the lower boxes, select a comparison operator and field value (in this example, **is less than or equal to** and **1/31/98**).

   Figure 16.10 shows the Custom AutoFilter dialog box set up to run this filter.

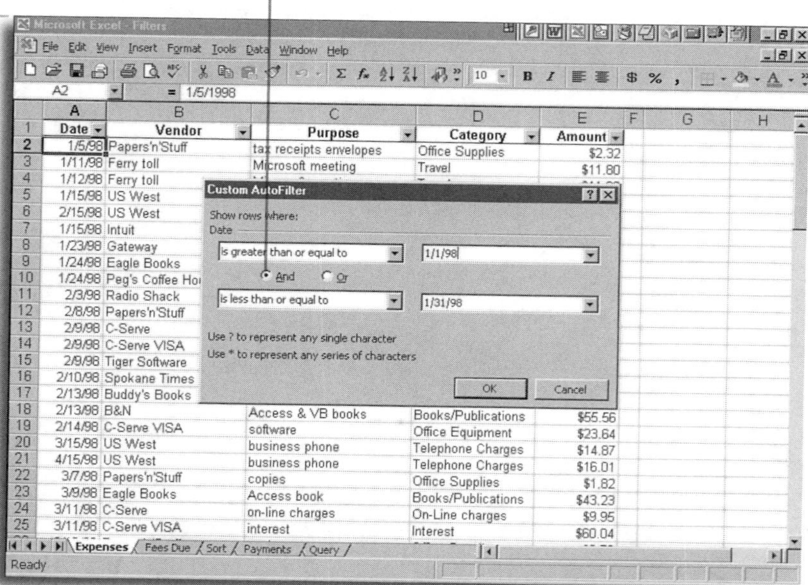

FIGURE 16.10

These complex criteria display records with values between two dates: greater than one date AND less than another.

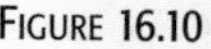
1 And option

7. Click **OK**.

   The results of my AND filter are shown in Figure 16.11.

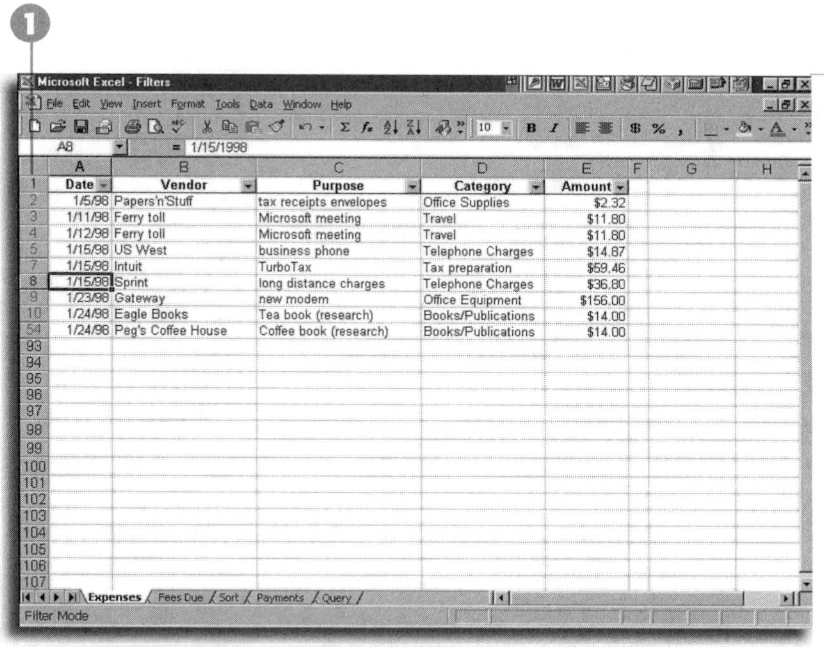

FIGURE 16.11

Blue row numbers indicate that the table is filtered and many rows are hidden.

1 Blue row numbers

SEE ALSO

➤ *To learn more about formatting dates and times, see page 246.*

Filtering on the Highest or Lowest Numbers in a Number Field

I want to see the five highest expense amounts for the year.

Filter on the highest or lowest numbers in a number field

1. Click the table. On the **Data** menu, point to **Filter** and then click **AutoFilter**.

   If AutoFilter is already turned on, be sure all other AutoFilter criteria are removed.

2. Click the filter arrow in a number field (in this case, the Amount field) and then click **(Top 10...)**.

   The Top 10 AutoFilter dialog box appears (shown in Figure 16.12).

Excel Sees Your Dates as Serial Numbers

If you open the Custom AutoFilter dialog box again, you see that Excel has converted the typed dates into date serial numbers.

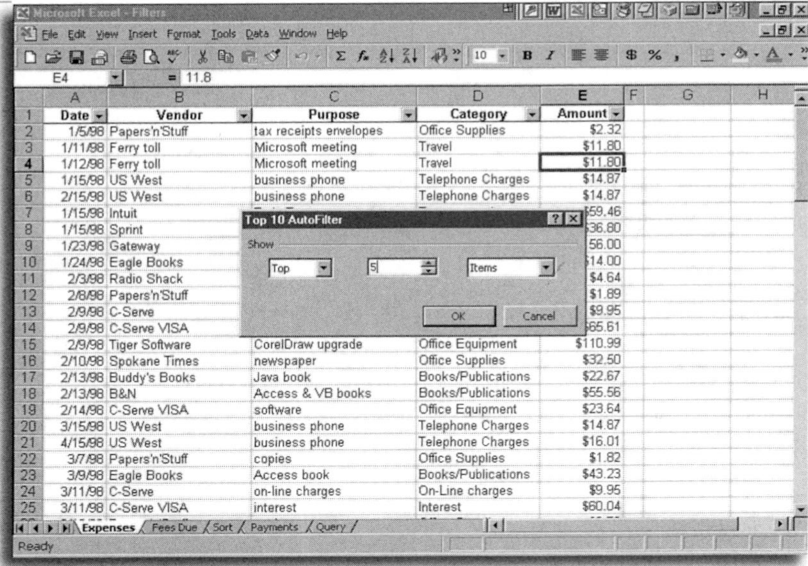

FIGURE 16.12
I've set up the Top 10 AutoFilter dialog box to show the 5 highest amounts in my expenses table.

3. In the leftmost box, select Top or Bottom. (For this example, I select **Top**.)
4. In the center box, type or scroll to the number of records you want to display (in this case, **5**).
5. In the rightmost box, select Items or Percent. I select **Items**; Percent shows me amounts that fall within the top five percent of the list, but I'm not interested in percentages.
6. Click **OK**.

   The results are shown in Figure 16.13. If I'd sorted by Amount before filtering, the results would be displayed in sorted order, too.

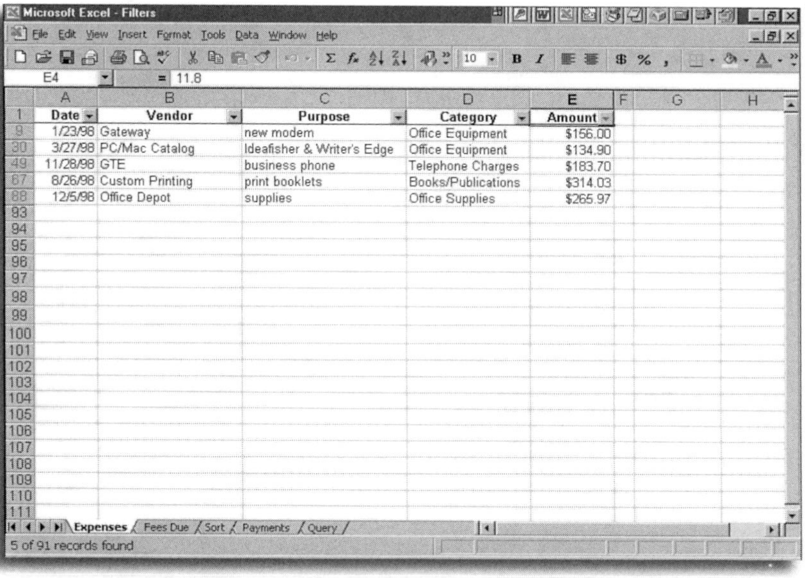

FIGURE 16.13
My top five individual expense items for the year.

Calculating Filtered Records

Viewing a filtered list is a good beginning, but calculations give you more information about the table. For example, I'd like to know my average telephone charge from Sprint. I can get that by using the SUBTOTAL function with my filtered list.

If I use the SUM or AVERAGE functions, the entire table is calculated rather than the records I display with a filter. If, however, I use the SUBTOTAL function, the formula calculates the filtered, displayed records only, rather than the entire table.

The SUBTOTAL function can calculate several different functions, depending on the arguments you enter. The function SUBTOTAL(*function_num,Ref1*) requires a number in the *function_num* argument that determines what specific calculation it performs. Table 16.1 shows the possible SUBTOTAL *function_num* arguments and their corresponding calculations.

Fast, Temporary Calculations

To get a quick, impermanent calculation of filtered records, use AutoCalculate. Filter the list, select the cells you want to sum (or average or whatever), and look at the AutoCalculate box on the status bar. AutoCalculate only calculates visible (non-hidden) cells.

AutoSUBTOTAL?

If you use the AutoSum button to create a SUM formula when the table is filtered, a SUBTOTAL formula is created instead of a SUM formula, but the new SUBTOTAL function calculates a sum. If you want the SUBTOTAL function to calculate an average instead of a sum, you need to change the calculation argument in the SUBTOTAL function.

TABLE 16.1 **SUBTOTAL arguments and calculations**

This Argument	Performs This Calculation
1	AVERAGE
2	COUNT
3	COUNTA
4	MAX
5	MIN
6	PRODUCT
7	STDEV
8	STDEVP
9	SUM
10	VAR
11	VARP

For this example, I'm going to set up a SUBTOTAL formula that averages the filtered values in the Amount field of my expenses list.

It Matters Where You Put the Formula

If you click a cell next to the list, the cell is probably hidden when you filter the list; a cell below the list is still visible during a filter.

It Could Be Easier

The only difficult part of the SUBTOTAL function is figuring out what calculation argument to use. Maybe in the next version of Excel, Microsoft will make the arguments available in the dialog box, instead of making us plow through the layers of help files to find them. In the meantime, refer to Table 16.1 to find the argument you need quickly.

Calculate a filtered list with the SUBTOTAL function

1. Click a cell below the list in which you want to display the result of the formula.
2. On the toolbar, click the **Paste Function** button. 
3. In the **All** or **Math & Trig** category, double-click **SUBTOTAL**.

   The SUBTOTAL dialog box appears (shown in Figure 16.14).
4. In the **Function_num** box, type `1`.

   The argument `1` tells SUBTOTAL to calculate an average. For a different calculation, look up the argument in Table 16.1.
5. In the **Ref1** box, enter the range to calculate (in this case, the range E2:E92, in the Amount column).
6. Click **OK**.

   The SUBTOTAL formula calculates an average for the Amount cells that are displayed. Figure 16.15 shows the SUBTOTAL formula and the list filtered for Sprint charges.

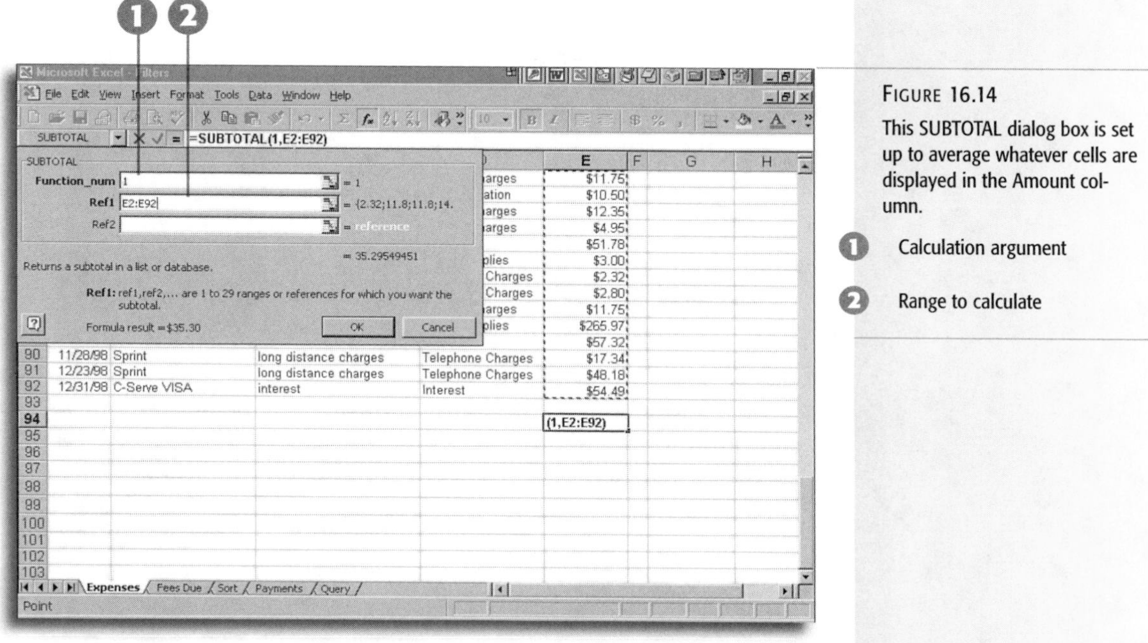

FIGURE 16.14
This SUBTOTAL dialog box is set up to average whatever cells are displayed in the Amount column.

1 Calculation argument

2 Range to calculate

Microsoft Excel - Filters

E94 =SUBTOTAL(1,E2:E92)

	A	B	C	D	E	F	G
1	Date	Vendor	Purpose	Category	Amount		
8	1/15/98	Sprint	long distance charges	Telephone Charges	$36.80		
56	2/15/98	Sprint	long distance charges	Telephone Charges	$7.29		
61	3/15/98	Sprint	long distance charges	Telephone Charges	$18.90		
63	4/15/98	Sprint	long distance charges	Telephone Charges	$27.62		
64	6/16/98	Sprint	long distance charges	Telephone Charges	$26.10		
74	7/16/98	Sprint	long distance charges	Telephone Charges	$14.19		
75	8/16/98	Sprint	long distance charges	Telephone Charges	$6.48		
85	8/23/98	Sprint	long distance charges	Telephone Charges	$2.32		
86	9/23/98	Sprint	long distance charges	Telephone Charges	$2.80		
90	11/28/98	Sprint	long distance charges	Telephone Charges	$17.34		
91	12/23/98	Sprint	long distance charges	Telephone Charges	$48.18		
93							
94					$18.91		Subtotal Average

Expenses / Fees Due / Sort / Payments / Query

11 of 91 records found

FIGURE 16.15
Every time I change the filter, the SUBTOTAL formula recalculates an average for the displayed cells.

SEE ALSO

➤ *To learn more about writing formulas, see page 165.*

➤ *To learn more about using functions, see page 176.*

The Query Wizard: A Better Filter

If you've used Access, you probably already know what queries are. If you don't know Access, however, I'll tell you what queries are and how and why you'd want to use them.

A query is like a *better* filter. When you use a filter, you can select specific records, but you get every field in the record. When you use a query, you can select specific records and specific fields within those records. (For example, in Figure 16.15, a query would enable me to extract just the Date and Amount fields for the Sprint charges.)

The Query Wizard in Excel helps you to pinpoint exactly the data you want to extract, and you can use the wizard to extract data from Excel lists, Access database tables and queries, and other database program files. The procedures for querying Excel, Access, and other database files are all similar; after you know how to query an Excel list, you're able to query other database files just as easily.

A new feature in Excel 2000 is the capability to query Web pages. Perhaps there's a Web page of basketball scores, racing results, or futures prices that you want to pull into a workbook to keep track of. If you query the Web page, you can import the data directly into your worksheet and then reuse the query daily to pull the new day's data into the worksheet.

Using the Query Wizard to Extract Data

One good reason to learn how to use the Query Wizard with Excel files is that you can extract data from closed workbooks, including workbooks that a colleague may have saved as read-only to prevent inadvertent changes. In this example, I pull data out of my expenses list in a closed workbook named Filters.

Before you run a query on an Excel table, name the range of data you're querying so that the wizard can find the data more easily. I named my expenses list Expenses before I began this procedure and then saved and closed the workbook.

The first time you run any query, it's a two-part process: First, you define a data source (tell Query Wizard where to look for data), and then, you run the Query Wizard and indicate exactly what data to extract from the data source. After you've defined a data source, the Query Wizard remembers it and you don't need to redefine it.

SEE ALSO

➤ *To learn more about naming cells and ranges, see page 202.*

Defining a Data Source

The procedure for defining a data source is similar whether the data source is an Excel workbook, an Access database, or another type of database file.

Create a new database query

1. Open the workbook in which you want to place the queried data.
2. On the **Data** menu, point to **Get External Data**, and then click **New Database Query**.

   Microsoft Query starts, and the Choose Data Source dialog box appears (shown in Figure 16.16).

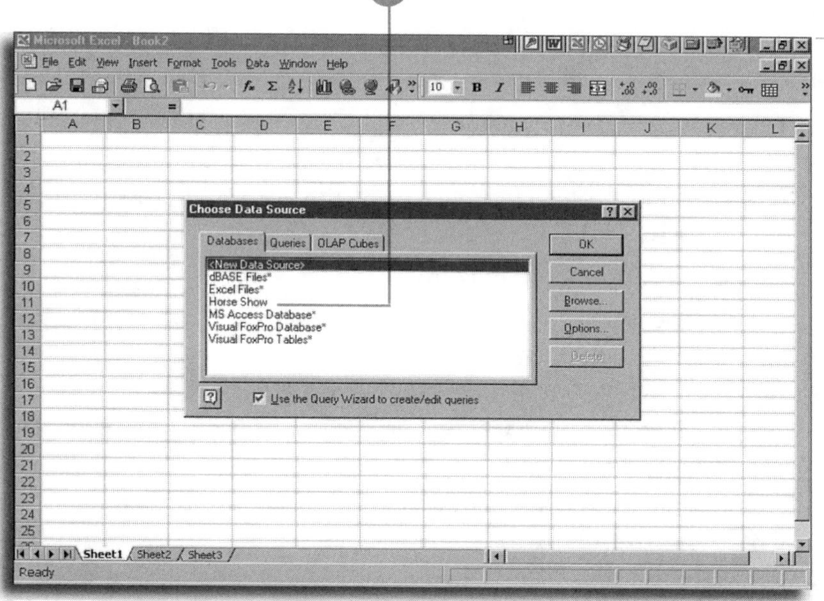

FIGURE 16.16

First, you need to define the data source you want to query.

1 Previously defined data source

3. On the **Databases** tab, double-click **<New Data Source>**.

The Create New Data Source dialog box appears (shown in Figure 16.17).

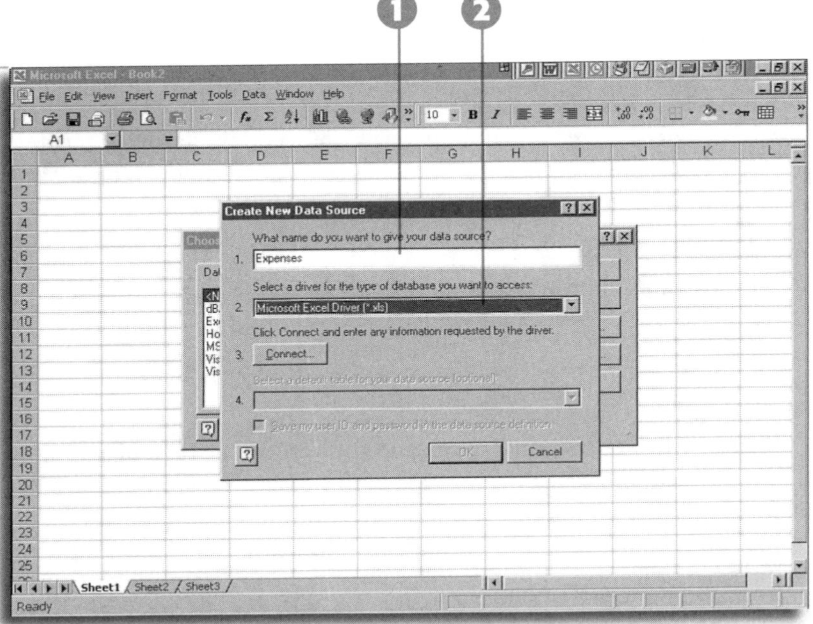

FIGURE 16.17

I've given the new data source a name and selected the proper driver for the Query Wizard to use.

1 Data source

2 Database driver

4. In Box 1, type a name for your data source. (In this example, I named the data source **Expenses**.)

5. In Box 2, click the down arrow and choose **Microsoft Excel Driver**.

6. Click the **Connect** button.

The ODBC Microsoft Excel Setup dialog box appears (shown in Figure 16.18), where you can select the workbook source from which you want to extract data.

7. Make sure the Excel version is correct for the workbook you are querying, and then click **Select Workbook**.

The Select Workbook dialog box appears (shown in Figure 16.19).

Deleting a Data Source Name

To delete a data source name from the list, use My Computer window to navigate to your Data Sources folder and delete the name. The data source name has the extension .dsn. (In my computer, the path is C:\Program Files\Common Files\ODBC\Data Sources.) You can also click Start, point to **Find**, click **Files or Folders**, and search for the data source name or files with the extension .dsn.

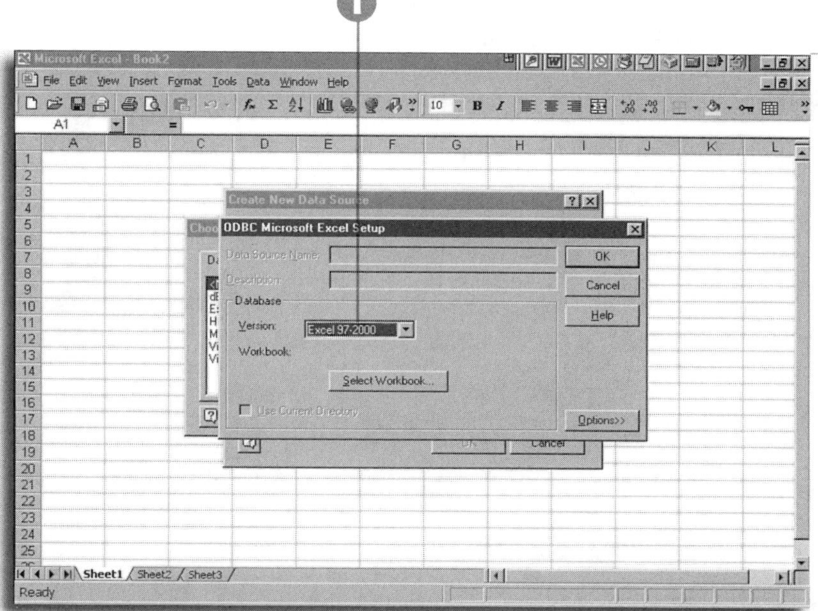

FIGURE 16.18

Make sure to indicate for the Query Wizard what version the Excel source is.

1 Excel version number

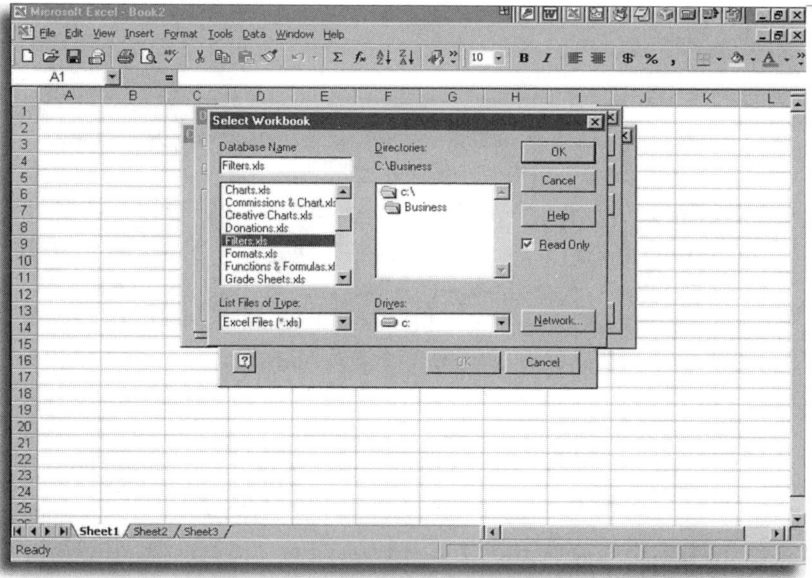

FIGURE 16.19

Select the workbook that contains your source data.

What Does ODBC Stand for?

ODBC means Open Database Connectivity; it's one of those computer jargon acronyms that you don't need to think about unless you want to impress members of your local hackers club.

8. In the Select Workbook dialog box, navigate to your workbook data source, and double-click the workbook name that contains your source data.

   The workbook name and path appear in the ODBC Microsoft Excel Setup dialog box (shown in Figure 16.20).

9. Click **OK**.

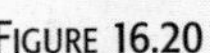

FIGURE 16.20

Make sure the workbook path and name are correct.

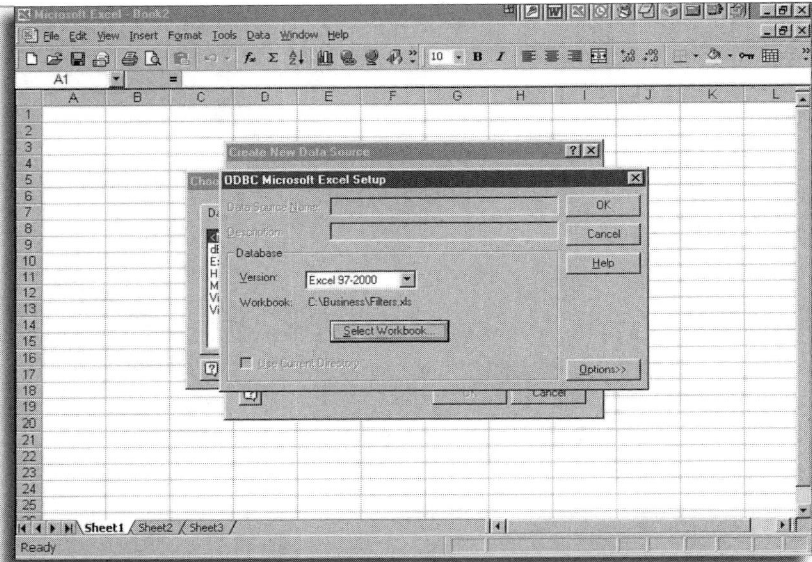

10. In the Create New Data Source dialog box, click **OK**.

    Your new data source (in this case, Expenses) appears in the Choose Data Source dialog box (shown in Figure 16.21). You can click **OK** to close the dialog box and come back to it later or continue with the Query Wizard in the next section.

Running the Query Wizard

After you define a data source, it appears in the Choose Data Source dialog box whenever you start the Query Wizard.

1. Click the **Use the Query Wizard to create/edit queries** check box, then double-click your named data source (in this case, Expenses).

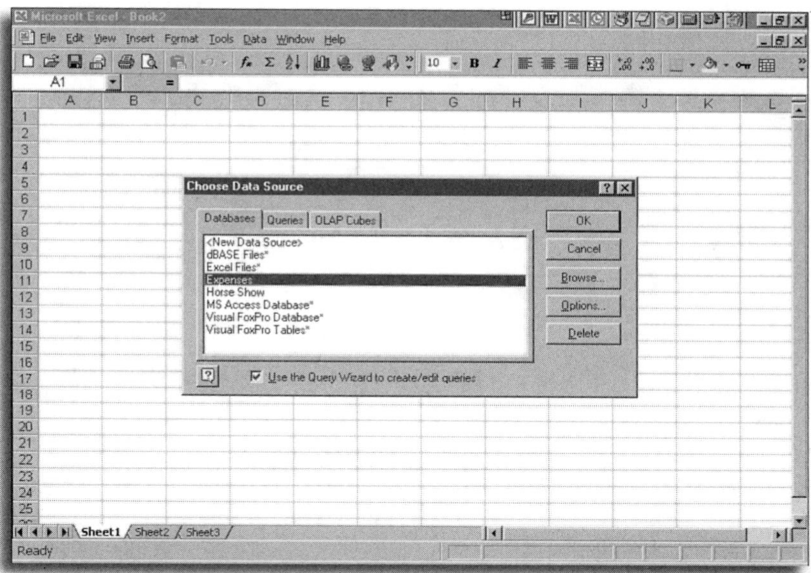

FIGURE 16.21
The Choose Data Source dialog box keeps a list of all data sources you define so you can use them repeatedly.

If the Choose Data Source dialog box isn't already open, you need to open it. On the **Data** menu, point to **Get External Data**, and then click **New Database Query.**

Shown in the list (see Figure 16.22) are any named ranges in the data source workbook. Click the small plus (+) symbol to display the column names in the named range.

2. Double-click the column names you want to include (in this example, I include Category and Amount) and then click **Next**.

   The second wizard step appears (shown in Figure 16.23).

3. In the second wizard step, you set up the filter that determines which records are extracted from the data source table. (In this case, I set the filter criterion "Category equals Office Equipment **Or** Category equals Office Supplies.") Click **Next**.

4. In the third wizard step (shown in Figure 16.24), you can select a sort key (I selected **Category** for a sort key and **Ascending** for a sort order) and click **Next**. You can sort on up to three keys.

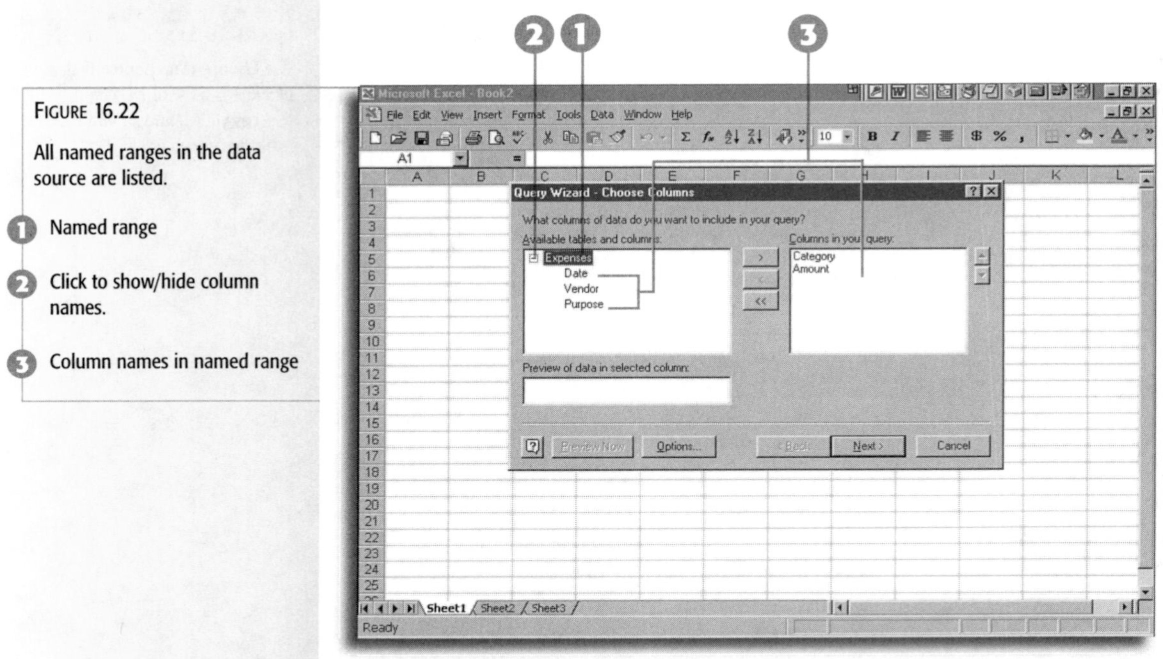

FIGURE 16.22

All named ranges in the data source are listed.

1 Named range

2 Click to show/hide column names.

3 Column names in named range

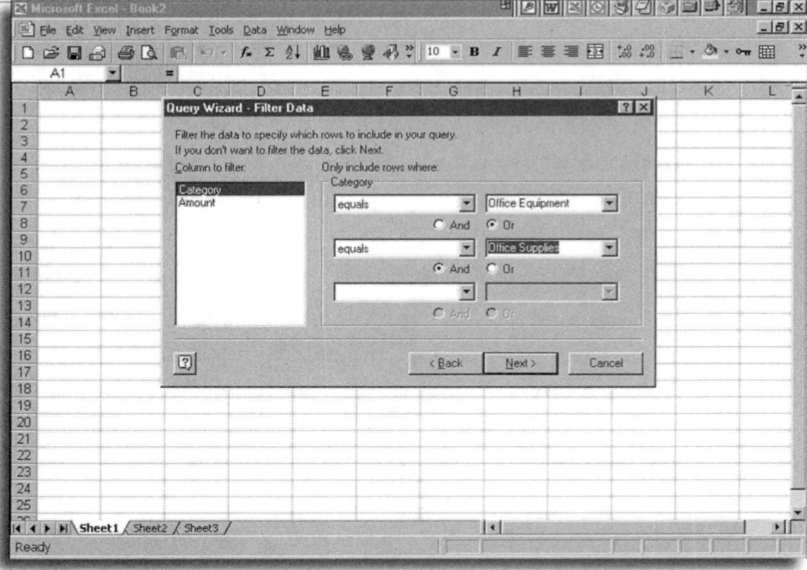

FIGURE 16.23

Set the filter criterion for the records you want to extract.

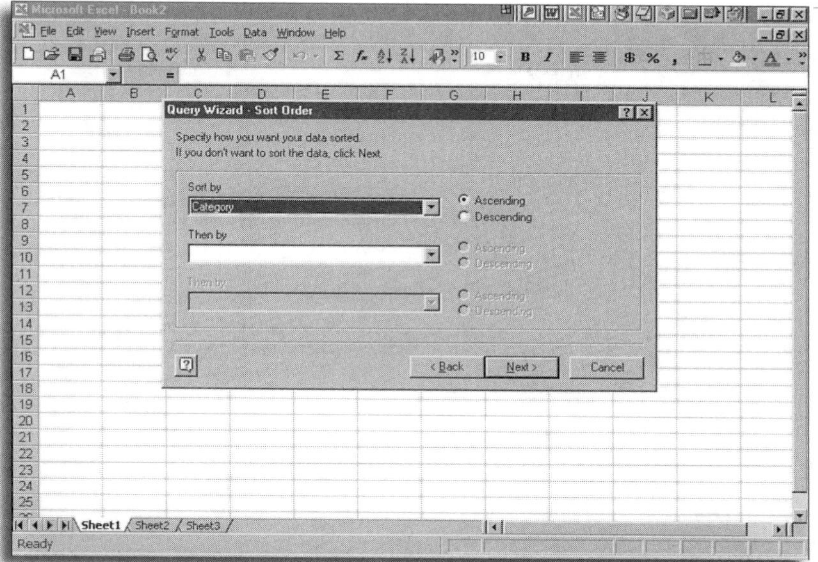

FIGURE 16.24
Selecting a sort order for the queried data saves you the time of sorting it after it's in the worksheet.

5. If you want to use this particular query again, click the **Save Query** button and follow the steps for saving and reusing a query in the next section. If you don't want to save and reuse this query, continue with step 6.
6. In the Query Wizard - Finish dialog box, click the **Return data to Microsoft Excel** option and then click **Finish**.
7. In the Returning External Data to Microsoft Excel dialog box (shown in Figure 16.25), click the **Existing worksheet** option button, click a cell on the worksheet in which you want to paste the upper-left corner of the extracted data, and click **OK**.

   Query revs its engines for a few seconds, and the extracted data appears in your worksheet (as shown in Figure 16.26). The cells still need to be formatted.

When queried data is pasted into a worksheet, the External Data toolbar appears (which makes some tasks quicker). If it doesn't appear, right-click any toolbar and click **External Data**. Table 16.2 describes the buttons in the External Data toolbar.

Update the Query with Fresh Data

To refresh a query with changed source data, you don't have to run the query again. Instead, click the **Refresh All** button on the External Data toolbar.

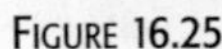

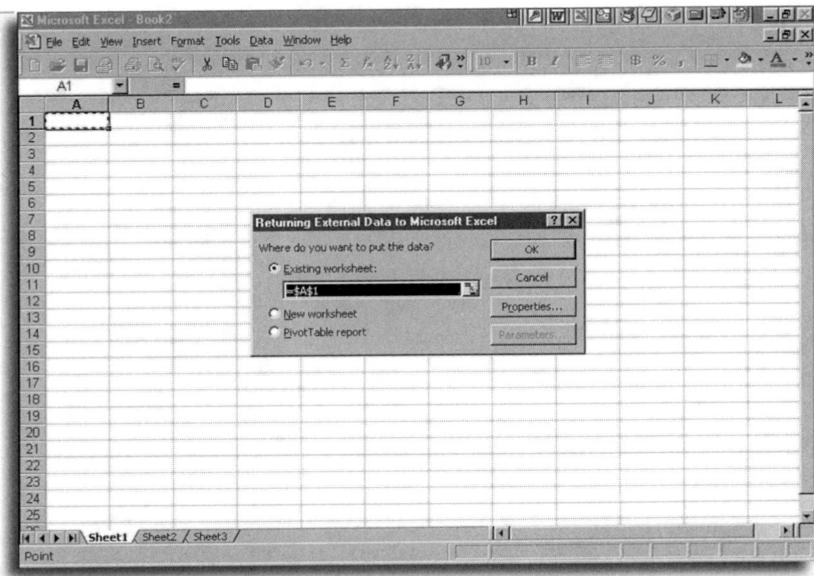

FIGURE 16.25
Indicate in the Query Wizard where you want the extracted data pasted.

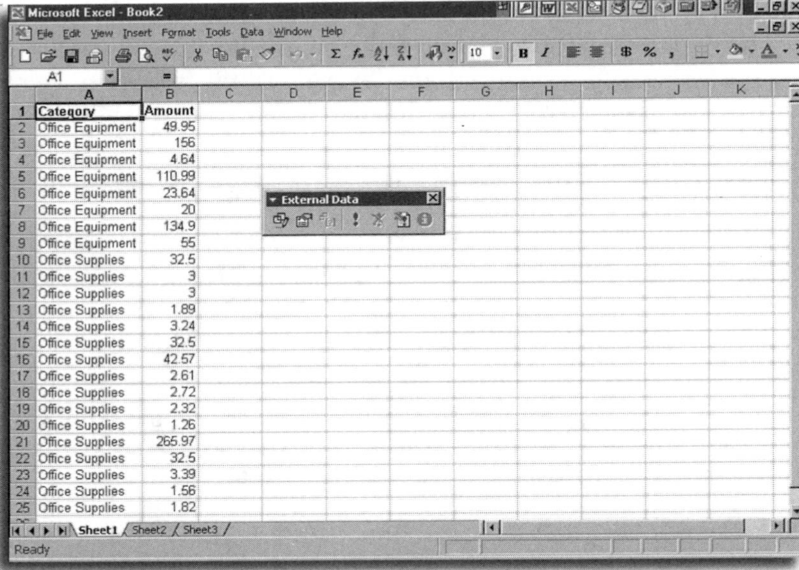

	A	B
1	Category	Amount
2	Office Equipment	49.95
3	Office Equipment	156
4	Office Equipment	4.64
5	Office Equipment	110.99
6	Office Equipment	23.64
7	Office Equipment	20
8	Office Equipment	134.9
9	Office Equipment	55
10	Office Supplies	32.5
11	Office Supplies	3
12	Office Supplies	3
13	Office Supplies	1.89
14	Office Supplies	3.24
15	Office Supplies	32.5
16	Office Supplies	42.57
17	Office Supplies	2.61
18	Office Supplies	2.72
19	Office Supplies	2.32
20	Office Supplies	1.26
21	Office Supplies	265.97
22	Office Supplies	32.5
23	Office Supplies	3.39
24	Office Supplies	1.56
25	Office Supplies	1.82

FIGURE 16.26
Raw data is extracted from the source.

TABLE 16.2 **Buttons in the External Data toolbar**

Icon	Button Name	Function
	Edit Query	Modifies an existing query: set different fields, filter criteria, and sort order.
	Data Range Properties	Sets advanced option on the data range or record set returned by a query.
	Query Parameters	Sets parameters that ask for criteria when you run the query. Parameter queries enable you to extract different data every time you run the query.
	Refresh Data	Updates data in a PivotTable. Use this button to refresh queried data if you've returned extracted data to a PivotTable rather than a worksheet range.
	Refresh All	Updates all queried data. Use this button to refresh queried data whether you've returned it to a worksheet range or a PivotTable.
	Refresh Status	Displays a dialog box that shows the status of a refresh procedure and how long it's taking.
	Cancel Refresh	Stops the refresh procedure if the refresh is going to take a long time and you don't want to wait for it.

Saving and Reusing a Query

If you want to run the same query repeatedly (for example, to extract the same data from an updated report every week), you can save yourself time and effort by saving and reusing the query. You need to save the query before you return the data to Excel (while the Query Wizard - Finish dialog box is open).

Save a query

1. In the Query Wizard - Finish dialog box (shown in Figure 16.27), click the **Save Query** button.
2. Navigate to the folder in which you want to save the query definition. The default Queries folder is a good choice because Excel looks there automatically when you run a saved query.

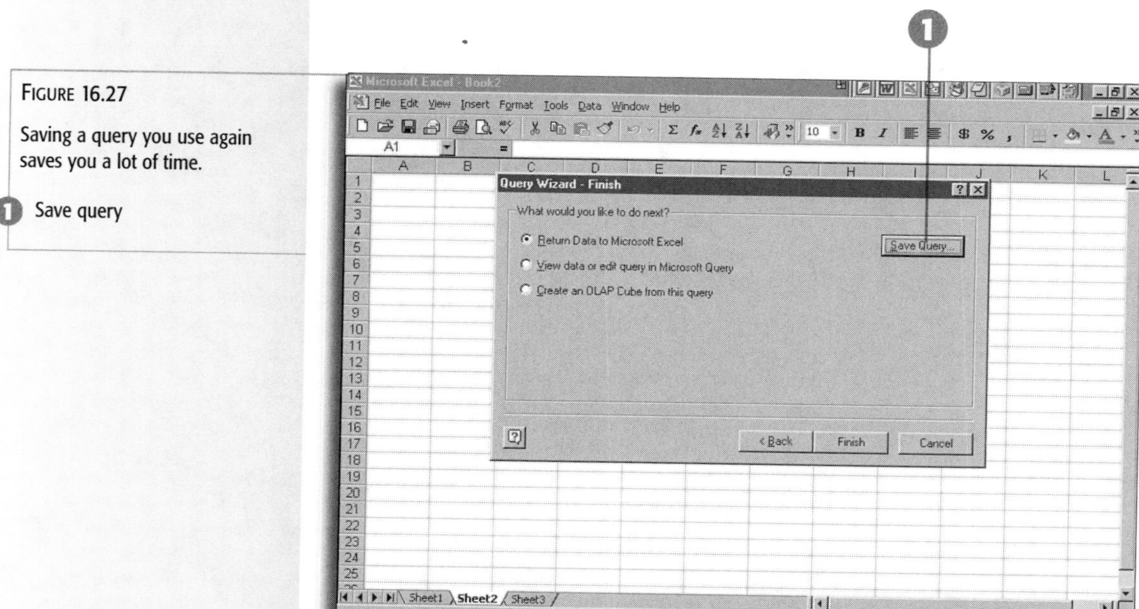

FIGURE 16.27

Saving a query you use again saves you a lot of time.

1 Save query

3. Give the query a memorable name and click **Save**.
4. Click **Finish** in the Query Wizard and continue with your query operation.

   Your saved query appears in the Choose Data Source dialog box on the **Queries** tab.

Reuse a saved query

1. Click a blank cell in the worksheet.
2. On the **Data** menu, point to **Get External Data**, and then click **Run Saved Query**.
3. In the Run Query dialog box (shown in Figure 16.28), navigate to the folder in which you saved the query definition.
3. Double-click the saved query name. (The extension of a query is .dqy.)

Does Saving a Query Fill Up My Hard Drive?

When you save a query, you don't save a ton of data; you save only the query definition, a SQL statement that contains instructions for which data to extract when the query runs.

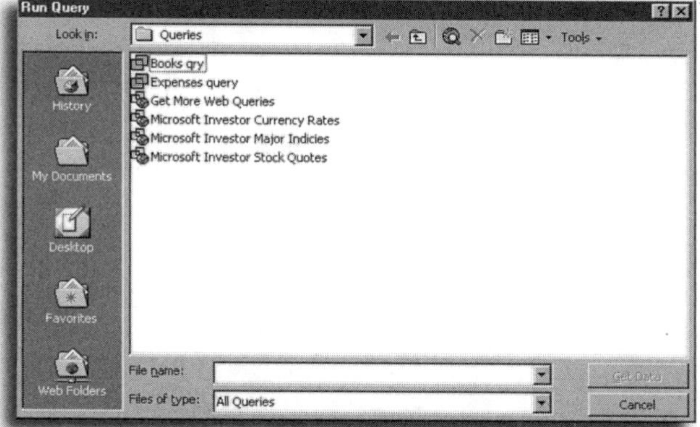

FIGURE 16.28

Excel 2000 comes with built-in saved Web queries to encourage you to go online with Microsoft. Your own saved queries are added to the list.

4. In the **Returning External Data to Microsoft Excel** dialog box, indicate to the Query Wizard where to put the queried data and then click **OK**.

   The query runs, and current data is extracted from the data source.

Querying a Web Page

Querying a Web page is a little simpler than querying a database because you don't have as many choices. You can pull in the entire Web page, only the tables on the page, or only specific tables on the page, but you can't choose records and fields.

On the **Data** menu, point to **Get External Data**, and then click **New Web Query**. In the New Web Query dialog box (shown in Figure 16.29), enter the URL (the Web page address, including the "http://" part), click options for the data you want to pull in, and click **OK**.

If you don't know the URL, click the **Browse Web** button to go online and find the page you want to query. After you locate the Web page, leave your browser open and switch back to Excel (the page URL appears in the Edit Web Query dialog box as long as the Web page is open). In the Edit Web Query dialog box, click **OK**.

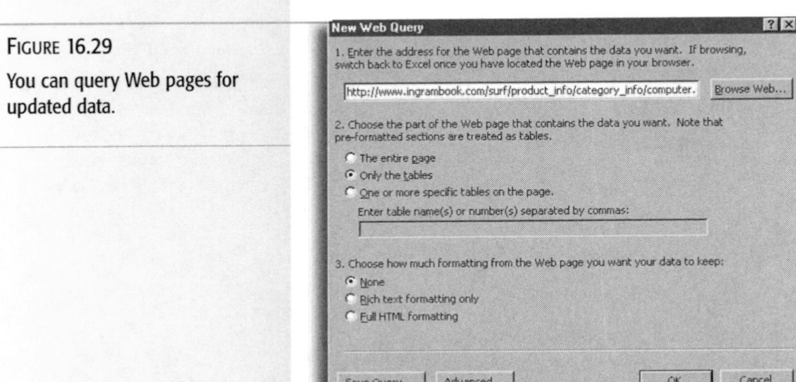

FIGURE 16.29
You can query Web pages for updated data.

Your browser finds the Web page and gets the data. If you want to run the query on a regular basis, save it by clicking the **Save Query** button and entering the appropriate information in the Save Query dialog box.

To reuse the saved query, click the **Data** menu, point to **Get External Data**, and then click **Run Saved Query**. Click the name of the query you want to run, then click **Get Data**. Along with your own saved Web queries, Excel 2000 includes several built-in saved Web queries, which you'll see in the Run Query dialog box when you choose **Run Saved Query**.

CHAPTER

17

Finding Answers and Making Decisions

- Using Goal Seek to find answers to simple questions
- Using Goal Seek to solve more complex problems
- Using Scenario Manager to create alternative scenarios
- Editing a scenario
- Summarizing multiple scenarios

Goal Seeking for Answers

One of a computer's most important functions is to help us make better decisions. The capability to calculate and summarize large quantities of data is a good beginning, but there are two more areas where Excel can help you make better decisions. If you have several possible situations, or scenarios, it's wise to compare the results of different courses of action before moving ahead with one of them. Excel's Scenario Manager can help you compare different scenarios. If you're working on a problem and you know what result, or solution, you want to arrive at, Excel can help you figure out what you need to do to get there. The Goal Seek tool will work problems "backwards" to figure out what input values will give you a specific answer.

Excel was designed to perform calculations, and if you know what input values a function or formula requires, Excel gives you an answer. But what if you know what answer you want but don't know what input values will give you that specific answer?

This chapter covers how to use Goal Seek to do "backwards" math: You know the answer you want, so you have Excel figure out what the input values should be to arrive at that answer.

For example, you can use the PMT function to figure out what a loan payment will be when you know the interest rate, number of payments, and loan amount; but suppose you want to know how large a loan amount you can get for a specific payment size. This question works the formula in reverse: You know what the answer should be (the payment), and you want to know how to get that answer (the loan amount).

Goal Seeking an Answer to a Simple Question

To demonstrate using Goal Seek to find a solution to the problem posed previously, I'm going to determine how big a loan I can get if I can afford a payment of $750 per month with an interest rate of 7.5 percent and monthly payments for three years (36 payments).

Use Goal Seek to determine a loan amount

1. Enter the formula and its input values (*arguments*) in a worksheet, as shown in Figure 17.1.

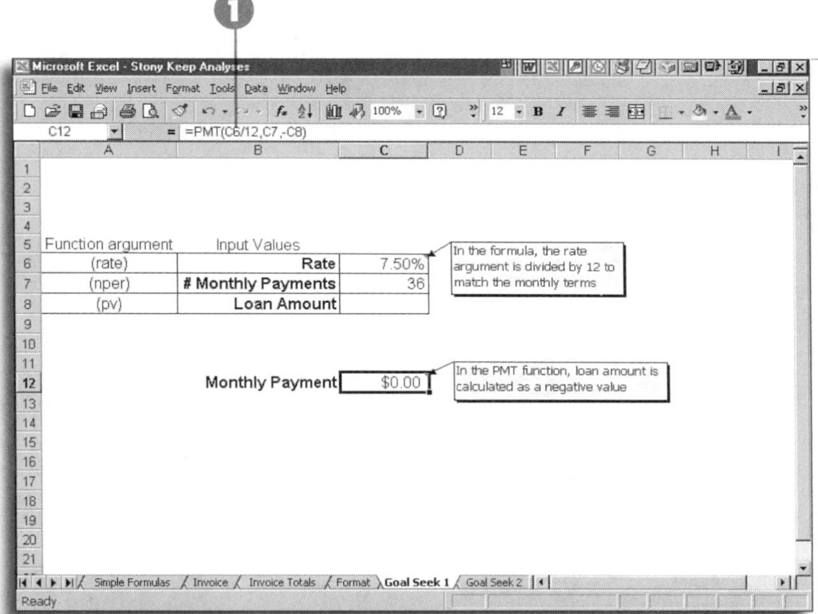

FIGURE 17.1
First, set up the equation; then, run Goal Seek to find new answers.

1 PMT formula

2. Fill in the input values that won't change (in this case, the interest rate and number of payments).
3. On the **Tools** menu, click **Goal Seek**.

   The Goal Seek dialog box is displayed, as shown in Figure 17.2. The currently active cell is displayed in the **Set cell** box; if you click the cell you want in the **Set cell** box before you start Goal Seek, steps 4 and 5 will already be done.
4. Be sure the value in the **Set cell** box is highlighted; if it's not, select it or delete it because you're going to replace it in the next step.

A PMT Function Idiosyncrasy

In the PMT formula, the loan amount argument is entered as a negative number so that your payments appear as positive values. You can enter either a negative value or the minus sign in the function argument, as I've done here; or you can enter the loan amount as a positive value and your payments will show up as negative values.

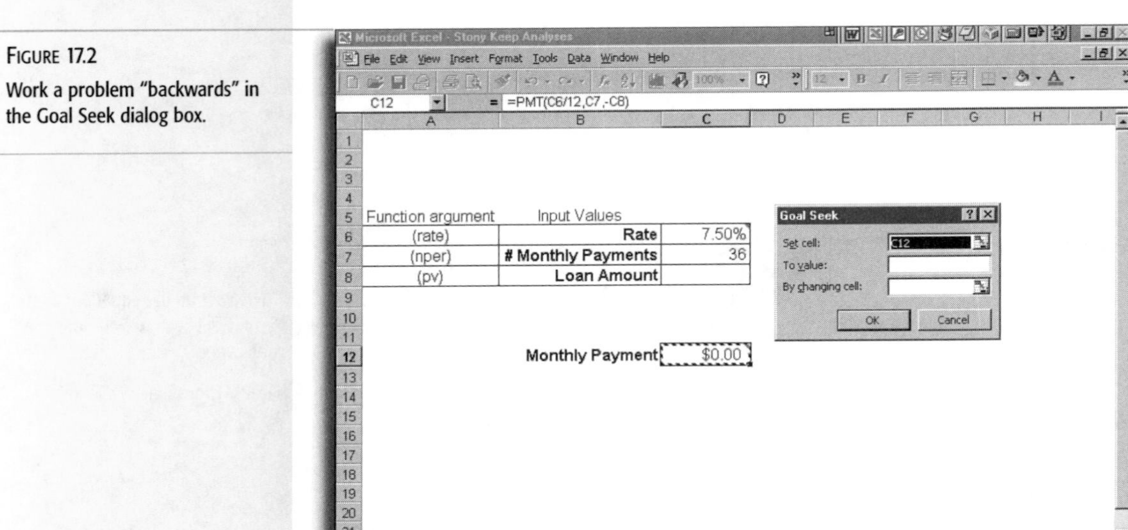

FIGURE 17.2
Work a problem "backwards" in the Goal Seek dialog box.

5. On the worksheet, click the cell you want to set a value in (in this case, cell C12, the PMT formula cell, because I want to calculate a specific payment value).
6. Click in the **To value** box, and type the value you want to arrive at (in this case, the payment I can afford, $750).
7. Click in the **By changing cell** box.
8. On the worksheet, click the cell that contains the input value that you want Excel to figure out (in this case, cell C8, the loan amount cell).

   In this example, the worksheet and Goal Seek dialog box resemble Figure 17.3.
9. Click **OK**.

   Excel finds an answer and changes the data on the worksheet, as shown in Figure 17.4.

   To keep the new worksheet data, click **OK**; to return the worksheet to its previous values (if you want to run Goal Seek again with different numbers), click **Cancel**.

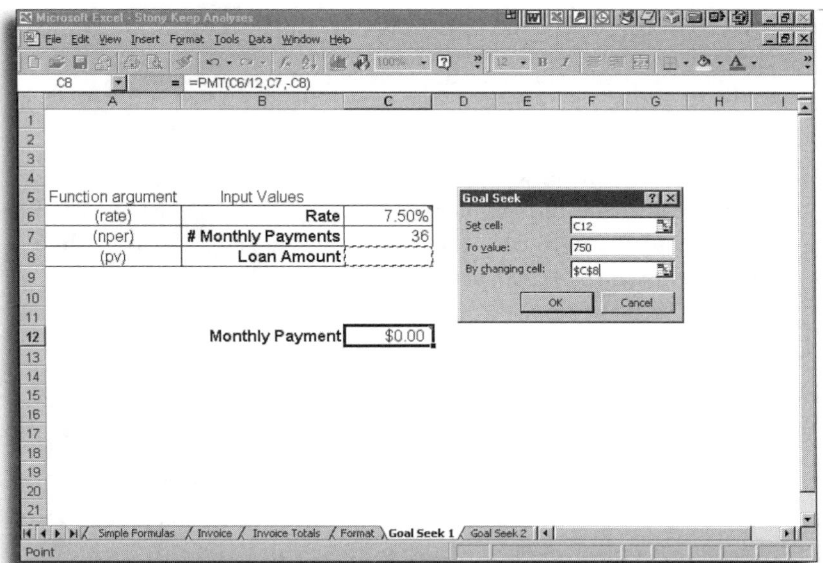

FIGURE 17.3
This Goal Seek dialog box is ready to calculate the loan that a specific payment will cover.

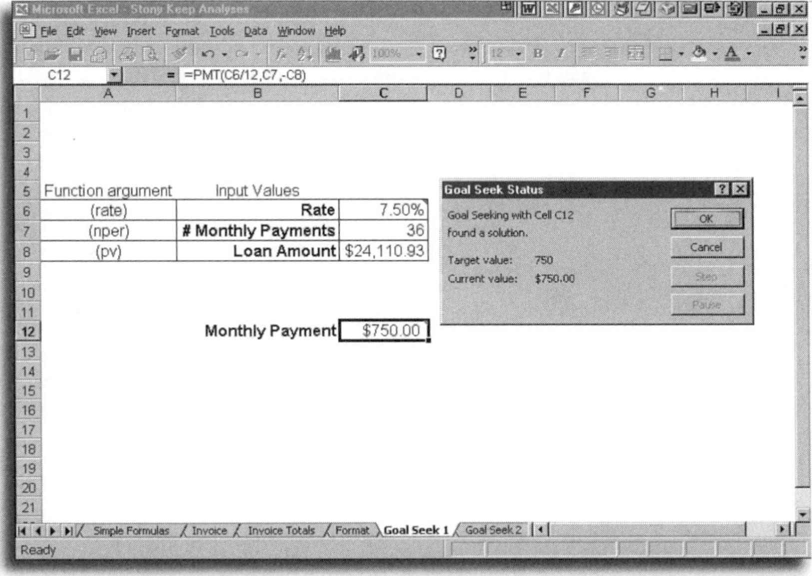

FIGURE 17.4
Goal Seek found the solution—a loan amount of $24,110.93, as shown in cell C8.

SEE ALSO

- *To learn more about writing formulas, see page 165.*
- *To learn more about using functions, see page 176.*

The Right-Triangle Equation

The mathematical formula for a right triangle, which this problem is based upon, is

$a^2+b^2=c^2$

Goal Seeking in a More Complex Problem

Although Goal Seek is limited to changing one variable at a time, you can use it to find answers to problems that involve many more cells. In this example, I'm working a right-triangle problem; I know how long the long side (Side b) is, and I know how long I want the hypotenuse (Side c) to be. What I want to know is how long should the short side (Side a) of the triangle be to give me the hypotenuse I need. Refer to the illustration in Figure 17.5 for a visual approach to the problem.

Use Goal Seek to solve a complex problem

1. Enter the input values and formula in your worksheet.

   The cells in the Length Squared column are named Asq (for A squared), Bsq, and Csq. The cells in the Length column are named a_, b_, and c_.

   I know what the length of Side b is, so I enter that length; then, I enter formulas in all the cells that calculate (as shown in Figure 17.5).

   Formulas are entered in Asq and Bsq to calculate the squares (a_*a_ and b_*b_); the right-triangle formula is entered in cell Csq; and the formula for the length of the hypotenuse, the square root of Csq, is entered in cell c_.

2. Click **Cell c_** (the cell with the formula for the length of the hypotenuse).

3. On the **Tools** menu, click **Goal Seek**.

   The Goal Seek dialog box is displayed, with the selected cell in the **Set cell** box.

4. In the **To value** box, type **35** (the length I want for the hypotenuse).

If You Don't Have This Decimal Display

I formatted these cells to display numbers with no decimal places. (See Chapter 13, "Formatting Numbers," to learn how.)

5. Click in the **By changing cell** box; then, click **Cell a_** (the side I want to know the length of).

   The dialog box should look similar to the one shown in Figure 17.6.

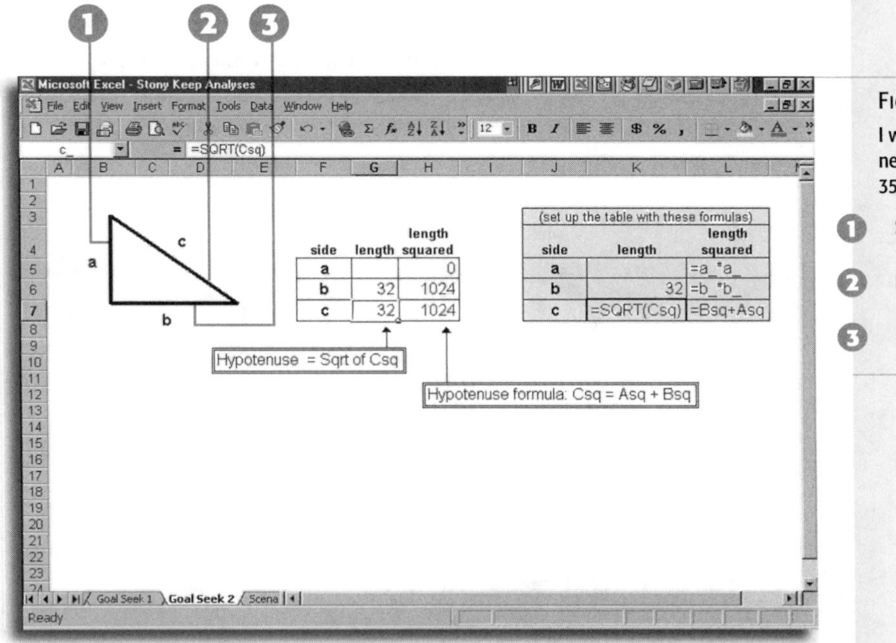

FIGURE 17.5
I want to know what value I need for Side a to get a value of 35 for the hypotenuse, Side c.

1. Short side
2. Hypotenuse
3. Long side

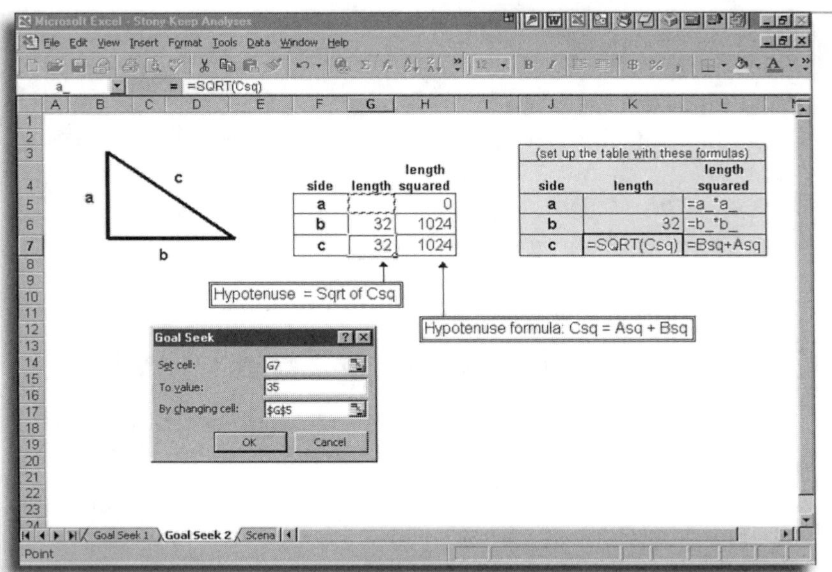

FIGURE 17.6
One click and I'll have my answer.

6. Click **OK**.

   If you watch closely, you'll see the numbers on your worksheet change rapidly as Excel tries different values and recalculates the formulas with each try. Your results should be similar to Figure 17.7.

7. To keep the new values, click **OK**.

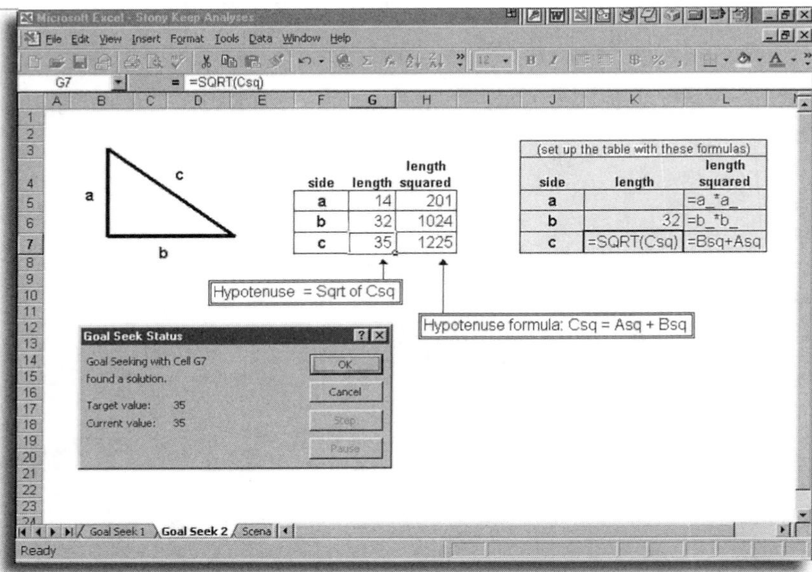

FIGURE 17.7
Goal Seek found the short-side length that gives me the hypotenuse length I want.

SEE ALSO

➤ *To learn more about naming cells, see page 202.*
➤ *To learn more about formatting cells, see page 215.*

Creating and Comparing Scenarios

Scenarios are alternative solutions to a business question; by comparing different scenarios, you can make well-informed decisions.

Scenario Manager is a tool for comparing alternative solutions to a question. You can set up a worksheet with formulas and values and then change and save different sets of values so that you can compare them at your leisure. As a simple example, you can set up alternative loan scenarios, edit them if you need to, and then summarize them for easier comparison.

Create alternative scenarios

1. Lay out your worksheet with formulas and input values, as shown in Figure 17.8.

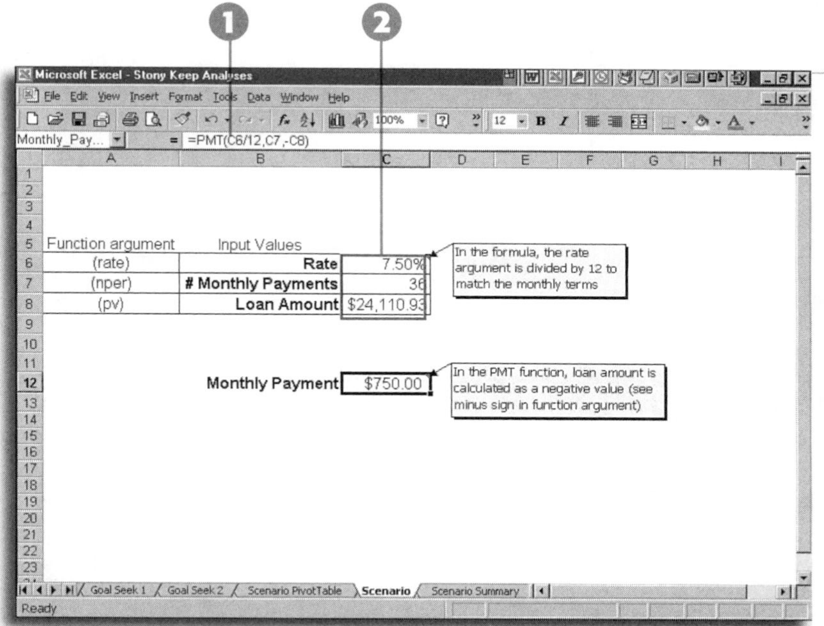

FIGURE 17.8

Start by setting up a worksheet with the first of the scenarios to be compared.

1 PMT formula

2 Input values for formula

2. On the **Tools** menu, click **Scenarios**.

   The Scenario Manager dialog box is displayed, as shown in Figure 17.9.

3. Click **Add**.

   The Add Scenario dialog box is displayed (shown in Figure 17.10).

4. In the **Scenario name** text box, type a name to identify the first scenario.

5. Click in the **Changing cells** box; then on the worksheet, click the cells where you want to change values to create different scenarios.

   In this example, I clicked Cells C6 and C7, the Rate and # Monthly Payments values. Your dialog box should look similar to Figure 17.11.

What's the Easiest Way to Name These Cells?

To name the cells used in these scenarios, I used the Create Names dialog box. Select the cells and their labels; then, open the **Insert** menu, point to **Name**, and then click **Create**. Click the check box that tells where the labels are (in this case, **Left column**), and click **OK**.

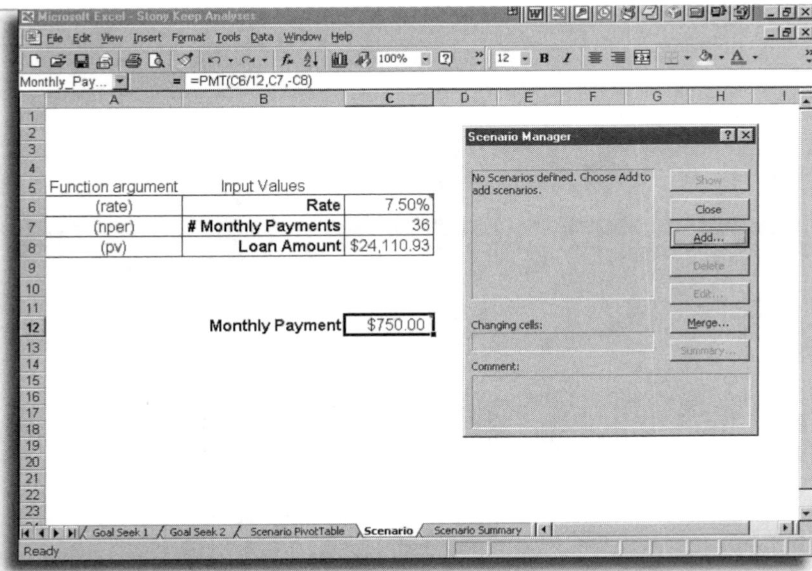

FIGURE 17.9
Use Scenario Manager to save, edit, and summarize scenarios.

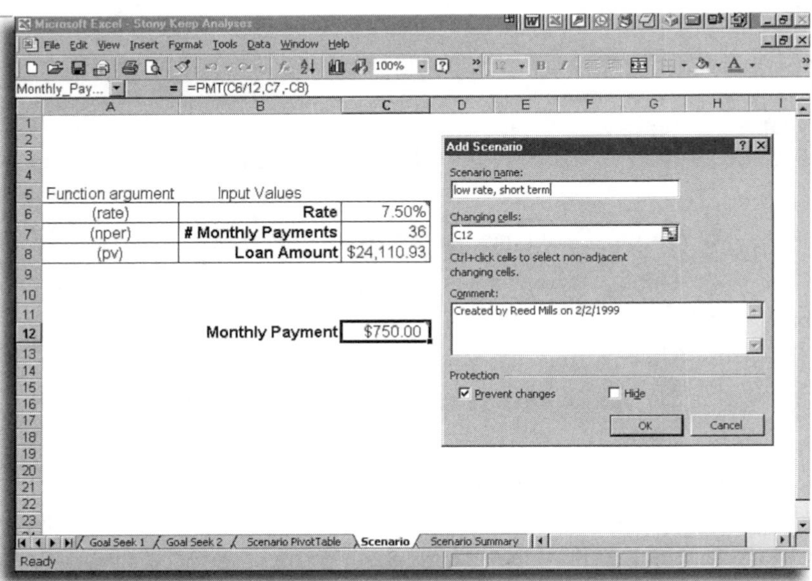

FIGURE 17.10
To add a scenario, name it and identify the cells that change in the different scenarios.

6. Click **OK**.

   The Scenario Values dialog box is displayed, as shown in Figure 17.12.

Use Cell Names for Easy Reading

To have the cell names display in your scenarios instead of references, name the changing cells first.

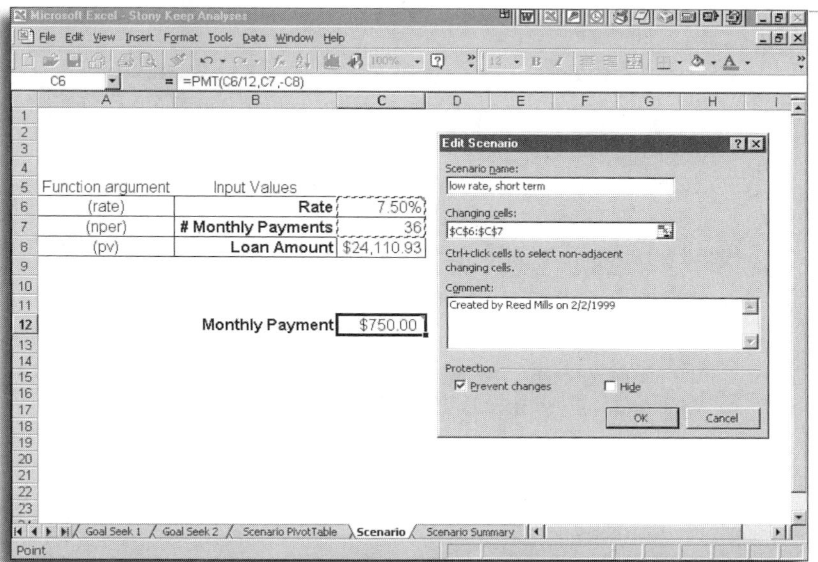

FIGURE 17.11

In this example, I'm going to create scenarios with interest rates and numbers of payments.

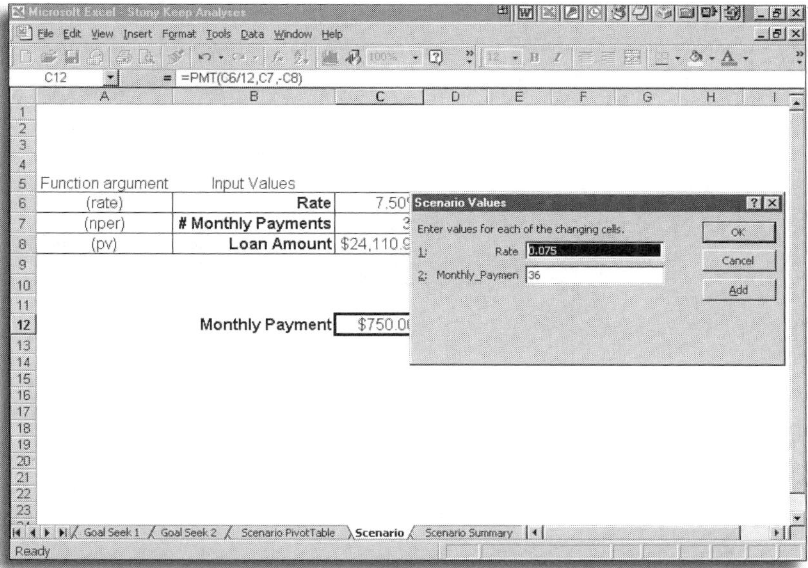

FIGURE 17.12

To save the first scenario, leave the values that are displayed; then, click **Add**.

To save your initial set of values, leave the values that are displayed.

7. Click **Add** to add a second scenario.
8. In the Add Scenario dialog box, type a name for the next scenario; then, click **OK**.
9. In the Scenario Values dialog box, type new scenario values that you want to compare to other scenarios; then, click **Add**.

   Repeat steps 8 and 9 to add more scenarios. When you've added all the scenarios you want, finish step 9 by clicking **OK** instead of **Add**.

   All your named scenarios are displayed in a list in the Scenario Manager dialog box, as shown in Figure 17.13.

   To show values for a specific scenario in the worksheet, click the Scenario name; then, click **Show**.

   To close the Scenario manager, click **Close**.

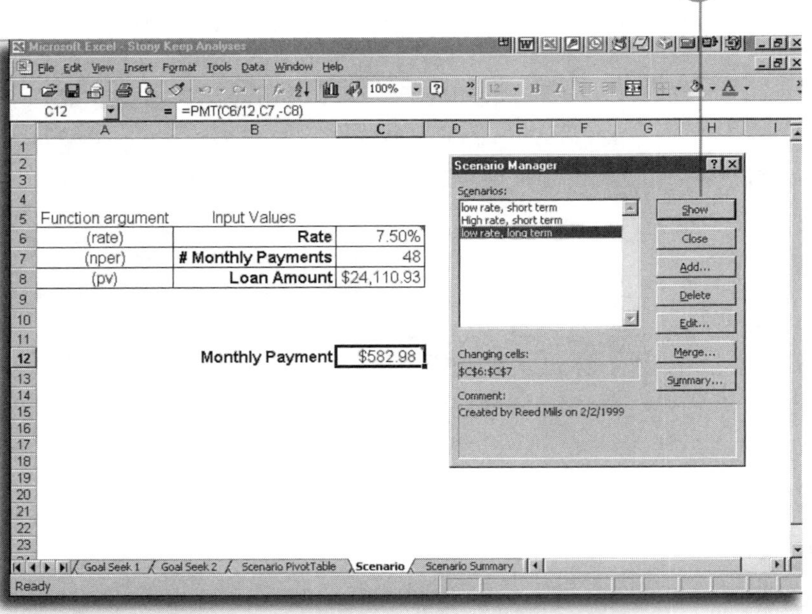

FIGURE 17.13

Click the scenario name you want to see; then, click **Show** to see the scenario on the worksheet.

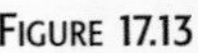
Show selected scenario on worksheet.

To change values in a specific scenario (or a misspelled scenario name), you can edit that scenario.

Edit a scenario

1. On the **Tools** menu, click **Scenarios**. In the Scenario Manager dialog box, click the name of the scenario you want to edit.
2. Click **Edit**.
3. In the Edit Scenario dialog box, change the scenario name or select new changing cells.
4. Click **OK**.
5. In the Scenario Values dialog box, set the values you want to use in the changing cells.
6. Click **OK**; then, click **Close** to close the Scenario Manager.

You can summarize the results of all scenarios in one place, which allows you to compare them more easily.

Summarize multiple scenarios

1. On the **Tools** menu, click **Scenarios**. In the Scenario Manager dialog box, click **Summary**.

   The Scenario Summary dialog box is displayed, as shown in Figure 17.14.
2. Be sure the **Result cells** box shows the cell that contains your formula.
3. Click **OK**.

   A new worksheet is added to your workbook (shown in Figure 17.15), and a table is created that shows the values and results for all your scenarios.

   If you click the Scenario PivotTable option before you click OK, you get a PivotTable like the one shown in Figure 17.16.

The summary table is outlined so you can show and hide details:

- To hide details in a section, click the small minus (–) button in the left or top margin.
- To show details in a section, click the small plus (+) button in the left or top margin.

To Delete a Scenario

To delete a scenario, select the scenario name in the Scenario Manager dialog box, and click **Delete**.

Did You Use Named Cells?

If you used named cells in your scenarios, the summary makes much more sense.

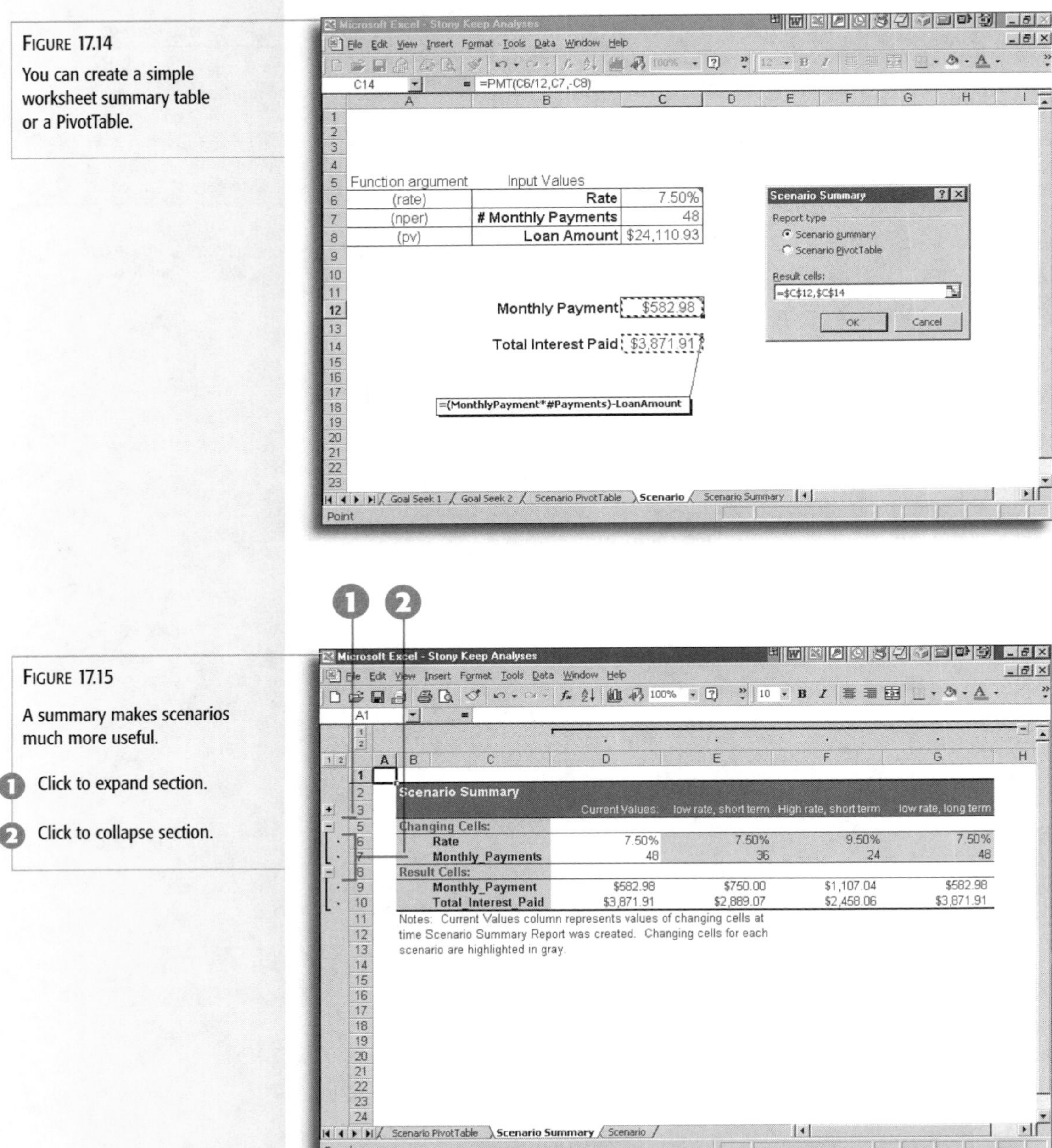

FIGURE 17.14

You can create a simple worksheet summary table or a PivotTable.

FIGURE 17.15

A summary makes scenarios much more useful.

1. Click to expand section.
2. Click to collapse section.

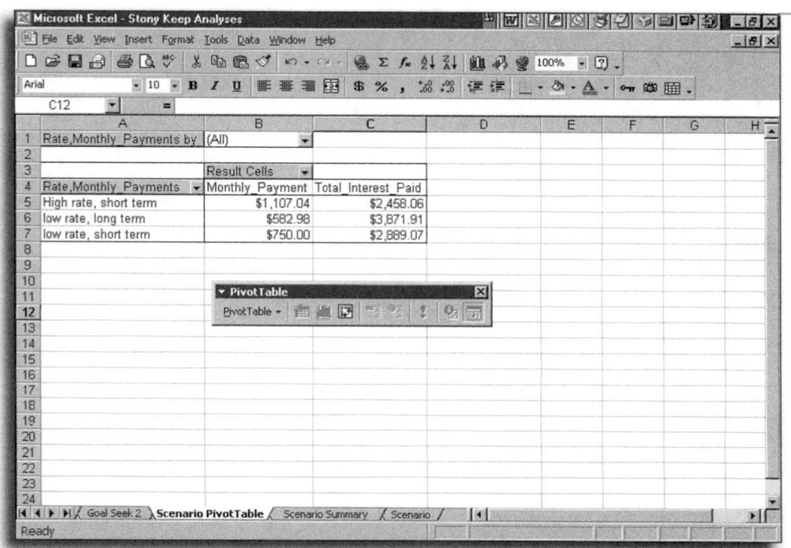

FIGURE 17.16

PivotTables are a different and more flexible way to summarize data.

SEE ALSO

➤ *To learn more about worksheet outlines, see page 339.*

➤ *To learn more about PivotTables, see page 343.*

CHAPTER

18

Summarizing Details with Consolidation or Subtotals

Understanding consolidations and subtotals

Consolidating a table and updating the consolidation

Selecting consolidation source areas

Subtotaling a table

Hiding and showing subtotal levels

Removing subtotals

Outlining a table manually

Understanding Consolidations and Subtotals

If you have a long list of data (like the expenses list in Figure 18.1), summarizing the data with subtotals makes it more meaningful. Three ways to summarize all the subcategories in a table at once are consolidation, subtotaling, and PivotTables.

Consolidation was Excel's early method of summarizing details with subtotals, and because Microsoft rarely throws away a functional feature, it's still available. Consolidation is quick and easy but inflexible: The result is a list of subtotals with no underlying detail data available (like the finished consolidation in Figure 18.4). Occasionally, however, that's exactly what you need, and it does enable you to consolidate the details of up to 255 source ranges.

Subtotaling goes one step beyond consolidation. It creates subtotals for each subcategory in the table but retains the detail items in the table and enables you to show or hide whichever subcategory details you want.

PivotTables are much more complex (and flexible and useful) than consolidation and subtotaling, so they're covered separately, in Chapter 19, "Summarizing Details with PivotTables and PivotCharts."

Make Sure Redundant Entries Are Identical

The list has no misspelled Vendor or Category entries because I used AutoComplete and Pick From List to make those entries. Accuracy like this is important when you want to filter, sort, consolidate, or subtotal a table. (See Chapter 7, "Entering Data," to learn about AutoComplete and Pick From List.)

Consolidating a Table

The expenses list in Figure 18.1 is a long enumeration of detailed expenses with repeated Vendor and Category entries.

I want to consolidate the details into a list of Vendor and Amount subtotals with no detail data included.

Consolidate a list

1. Select a *destination area*, where the consolidated list will be pasted. (For this example, I'll paste the consolidated list next to my detailed list with a blank column separating the two.)

   A destination area can be on the same worksheet or in a different worksheet or workbook.

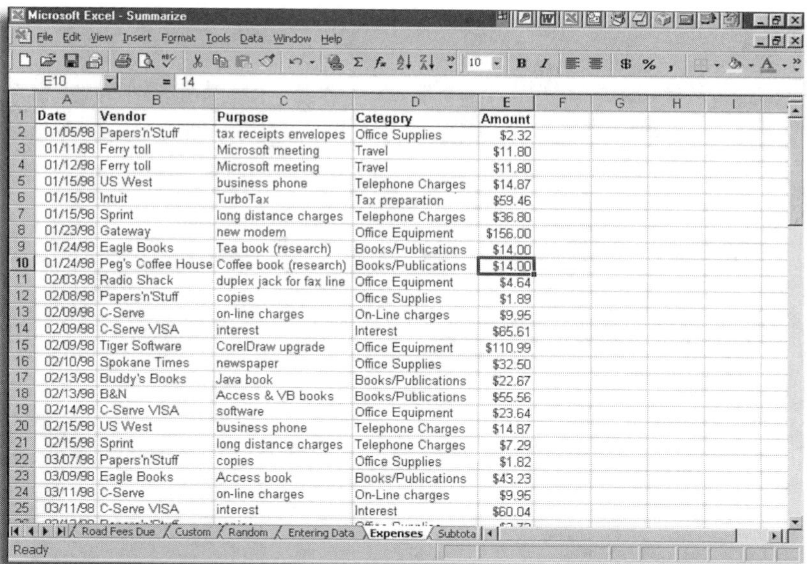

FIGURE 18.1

A detailed expenses list doesn't tell you much until it's summarized.

2. At the top of the destination area, enter (or better yet, copy) the headings of the label and number columns that will be used in the consolidation. For this example, I've copied the headings from the Vendor and Amount columns, shown in Figure 18.2.

3. Select the destination area column labels, as shown in Figure 18.2.

4. On the **Data** menu, click **Consolidate**.

   The Consolidate dialog box appears, as shown in Figure 18.3.

5. Select a function in the **Function** drop-down list box. (Although **Sum** is most common, you can consolidate using any of several functions.)

6. Click in the **Reference** box and enter the ranges you want to consolidate. In this case, I'll drag to select the expenses list, making the Vendor column the leftmost column in my source range. (I won't include the Date column because Excel is looking for subcategory labels in the left column of the source range.)

How Much of the Data Gets Consolidated?

Consolidation includes only one column of labels but can consolidate multiple columns of numbers.

Consolidation Is Easier with Named Ranges

To make source area selection easier, name the source ranges, and type the range names into the Consolidate dialog box. See Chapter 11, "Complex Calculations," to learn how to name ranges.

	Date	Vendor	Purpose	Category	Amount		Vendor	Amount
2	01/05/98	Papers'n'Stuff	tax receipts envelopes	Office Supplies	$2.32			
3	01/11/98	Ferry toll	Microsoft meeting	Travel	$11.80			
4	01/12/98	Ferry toll	Microsoft meeting	Travel	$11.80			
5	01/15/98	US West	business phone	Telephone Charges	$14.87			
6	01/15/98	Intuit	TurboTax	Tax preparation	$59.46			
7	01/15/98	Sprint	long distance charges	Telephone Charges	$36.80			
8	01/23/98	Gateway	new modem	Office Equipment	$156.00			
9	01/24/98	Eagle Books	Tea book (research)	Books/Publications	$14.00			
10	01/24/98	Peg's Coffee House	Coffee book (research)	Books/Publications	$14.00			
11	02/03/98	Radio Shack	duplex jack for fax line	Office Equipment	$4.64			
12	02/08/98	Papers'n'Stuff	copies	Office Supplies	$1.89			
13	02/09/98	C-Serve	on-line charges	On-Line charges	$9.95			
14	02/09/98	C-Serve VISA	interest	Interest	$65.61			
15	02/09/98	Tiger Software	CorelDraw upgrade	Office Equipment	$110.99			
16	02/10/98	Spokane Times	newspaper	Office Supplies	$32.50			
17	02/13/98	Buddy's Books	Java book	Books/Publications	$22.67			
18	02/13/98	B&N	Access & VB books	Books/Publications	$55.56			
19	02/14/98	C-Serve VISA	software	Office Equipment	$23.64			
20	02/15/98	US West	business phone	Telephone Charges	$14.87			
21	02/15/98	Sprint	long distance charges	Telephone Charges	$7.29			
22	03/07/98	Papers'n'Stuff	copies	Office Supplies	$1.82			
23	03/09/98	Eagle Books	Access book	Books/Publications	$43.23			
24	03/11/98	C-Serve	on-line charges	On-Line charges	$9.95			
25	03/11/98	C-Serve VISA	interest	Interest	$60.04			

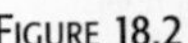

FIGURE 18.2

The destination area column labels tell Excel which columns to include in the consolidation.

1 Copied column labels, selected as the destination area

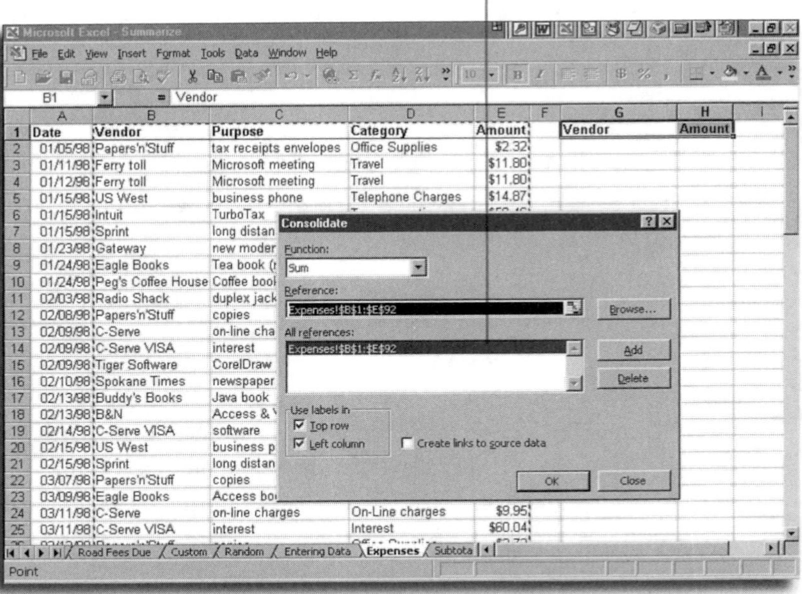

FIGURE 18.3

After the destination area is prepared, set up the Consolidate dialog box.

1 Areas in this list are consolidated.

7. Click the **Add** button to add the reference to the list of source areas to consolidate.

   If you are consolidating multiple ranges, add each new range to the source list by selecting it and then clicking **Add**. (See Table 18.1 for tips on selecting multiple ranges for consolidation.)

8. Click the **Top row** and **Left column** check boxes to enable Excel to look for labels in the source ranges.

9. When the Consolidate dialog box is set up, click **OK**.

   The range is consolidated, as shown in Figure 18.4. The subcategories are labeled with the labels from the Vendor column, the leftmost column of my source range, and Amounts are consolidated for each Vendor subcategory.

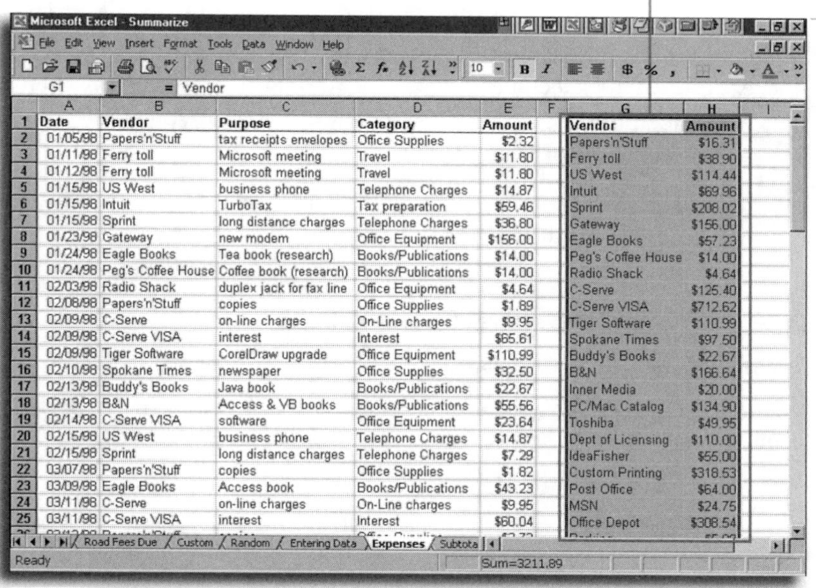

	A	B	C	D	E	F	G	H
1	Date	Vendor	Purpose	Category	Amount		Vendor	Amount
2	01/05/98	Papers'n'Stuff	tax receipts envelopes	Office Supplies	$2.32		Papers'n'Stuff	$16.31
3	01/11/98	Ferry toll	Microsoft meeting	Travel	$11.80		Ferry toll	$38.90
4	01/12/98	Ferry toll	Microsoft meeting	Travel	$11.80		US West	$114.44
5	01/15/98	US West	business phone	Telephone Charges	$14.87		Intuit	$69.96
6	01/15/98	Intuit	TurboTax	Tax preparation	$59.46		Sprint	$208.02
7	01/15/98	Sprint	long distance charges	Telephone Charges	$36.80		Gateway	$156.00
8	01/23/98	Gateway	new modem	Office Equipment	$156.00		Eagle Books	$57.23
9	01/24/98	Eagle Books	Tea book (research)	Books/Publications	$14.00		Peg's Coffee House	$14.00
10	01/24/98	Peg's Coffee House	Coffee book (research)	Books/Publications	$14.00		Radio Shack	$4.64
11	02/03/98	Radio Shack	duplex jack for fax line	Office Equipment	$4.64		C-Serve	$125.40
12	02/08/98	Papers'n'Stuff	copies	Office Supplies	$1.89		C-Serve VISA	$712.62
13	02/09/98	C-Serve	on-line charges	On-Line charges	$9.95		Tiger Software	$110.99
14	02/09/98	C-Serve VISA	interest	Interest	$65.61		Spokane Times	$97.50
15	02/09/98	Tiger Software	CorelDraw upgrade	Office Equipment	$110.99		Buddy's Books	$22.67
16	02/10/98	Spokane Times	newspaper	Office Supplies	$32.50		B&N	$166.64
17	02/13/98	Buddy's Books	Java book	Books/Publications	$22.67		Inner Media	$20.00
18	02/13/98	B&N	Access & VB books	Books/Publications	$55.56		PC/Mac Catalog	$134.90
19	02/14/98	C-Serve VISA	software	Office Equipment	$23.64		Toshiba	$49.95
20	02/15/98	US West	business phone	Telephone Charges	$14.87		Dept of Licensing	$110.00
21	02/15/98	Sprint	long distance charges	Telephone Charges	$7.29		IdeaFisher	$55.00
22	03/07/98	Papers'n'Stuff	copies	Office Supplies	$1.82		Custom Printing	$318.53
23	03/09/98	Eagle Books	Access book	Books/Publications	$43.23		Post Office	$64.00
24	03/11/98	C-Serve	on-line charges	On-Line charges	$9.95		MSN	$24.75
25	03/11/98	C-Serve VISA	interest	Interest	$60.04		Office Depot	$308.54

FIGURE 18.4
The consolidated data appears next to the source table.

1 Consolidated data

SEE ALSO

➤ *To learn more about AutoComplete and Pick From List to ensure accurate data entry, see pages 116–117.*

Do I Have to Open the Source to Update?

When updating a consolidation, you do not need to open closed source workbooks.

Updating a Consolidation

After you set up a consolidation, the settings are retained in the destination worksheet, and you can run the consolidation again to update it with changed source data.

Update a consolidation

1. Select the destination area column labels.
2. On the **Data** menu, click **Consolidate**.
3. Click **OK**.

   The same consolidation is run again and the subtotals are updated.

Selecting Consolidation Source Areas

Consolidation has great flexibility when it comes to choosing the data you want to consolidate. *Source areas*, the details you want to consolidate, can be on any worksheet, in any open or closed workbook, and on multiple worksheets (a *3D source area*). The easiest way to select a source area is to drag the range in an open worksheet; but you can use closed sources, too, if you enter the workbook and worksheet names.

Table 18.1 lists more ways to enter source ranges for consolidation in the Consolidate dialog box.

TABLE 18.1 **Consolidation source area possibilities**

To Add This Range	Do This
To consolidate a range from another workbook	Click the **Browse** button, navigate to the workbook you want, and double-click the workbook name. The path to the workbook is entered, and you need to type a range name or a worksheet name and range reference. The worksheet name is separated from the range name with an exclamation mark: *worksheet!range*.
To enter a range name from the active workbook	Type the range name.
To enter multiple ranges from different worksheets	Enter the first range and click **Add**. Then, click a different worksheet, enter the range there, and click **Add**. Continue until all source ranges are listed in the **All references** box.

Subtotaling a Table

Subtotaling a table provides different results than a consolidation:

- A subtotaled worksheet retains detail data.
- Subtotals and outlining are added to the table so that you can show or hide the details with a click of a button.
- Subtotaling includes several levels of label columns as well as number columns.
- Data must be sorted before you subtotal it.

I'm subtotaling my expenses list and creating subtotals by both Category and Vendor within Category. I'll start by arranging my columns and sorting them so that the subtotal outline is well organized, and then I'll apply the subtotaling.

Apply automatic subtotaling

1. Arrange your table so that the columns are logically organized, and sort the columns in the order that you want to apply subtotals.

   In Figure 18.5, I've rearranged the columns and sorted them by Category and then by Vendor.

Hide Columns You Don't Need

To remove the Date and Purpose columns from view without removing them from the table, you can hide them. Select the columns, right-click the selection, and click **Hide**.

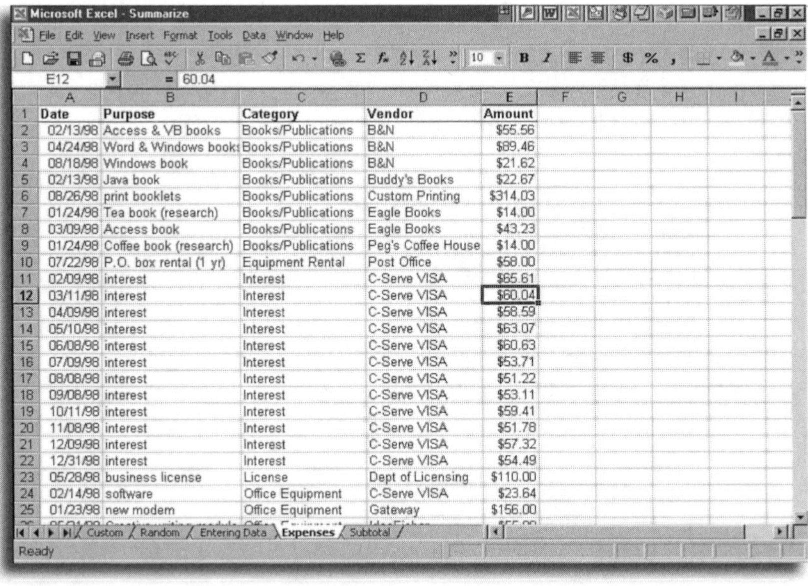

	A	B	C	D	E
1	Date	Purpose	Category	Vendor	Amount
2	02/13/98	Access & VB books	Books/Publications	B&N	$55.56
3	04/24/98	Word & Windows book	Books/Publications	B&N	$89.46
4	08/18/98	Windows book	Books/Publications	B&N	$21.62
5	02/13/98	Java book	Books/Publications	Buddy's Books	$22.67
6	08/26/98	print booklets	Books/Publications	Custom Printing	$314.03
7	01/24/98	Tea book (research)	Books/Publications	Eagle Books	$14.00
8	03/09/98	Access book	Books/Publications	Eagle Books	$43.23
9	01/24/98	Coffee book (research)	Books/Publications	Peg's Coffee House	$14.00
10	07/22/98	P.O. box rental (1 yr)	Equipment Rental	Post Office	$58.00
11	02/09/98	interest	Interest	C-Serve VISA	$65.61
12	03/11/98	interest	Interest	C-Serve VISA	$60.04
13	04/09/98	interest	Interest	C-Serve VISA	$58.59
14	05/10/98	interest	Interest	C-Serve VISA	$63.07
15	06/08/98	interest	Interest	C-Serve VISA	$60.63
16	07/09/98	interest	Interest	C-Serve VISA	$53.71
17	08/08/98	interest	Interest	C-Serve VISA	$51.22
18	09/08/98	interest	Interest	C-Serve VISA	$53.11
19	10/11/98	interest	Interest	C-Serve VISA	$59.41
20	11/08/98	interest	Interest	C-Serve VISA	$51.78
21	12/09/98	interest	Interest	C-Serve VISA	$57.32
22	12/31/98	interest	Interest	C-Serve VISA	$54.49
23	05/28/98	business license	License	Dept of Licensing	$110.00
24	02/14/98	software	Office Equipment	C-Serve VISA	$23.64
25	01/23/98	new modem	Office Equipment	Gateway	$156.00

FIGURE 18.5

This table has been arranged and sorted to prepare it for subtotaling.

2. Click a cell in the table.
3. On the **Data** menu, click **Subtotals**.

   The Subtotal dialog box appears, as shown in Figure 18.6.

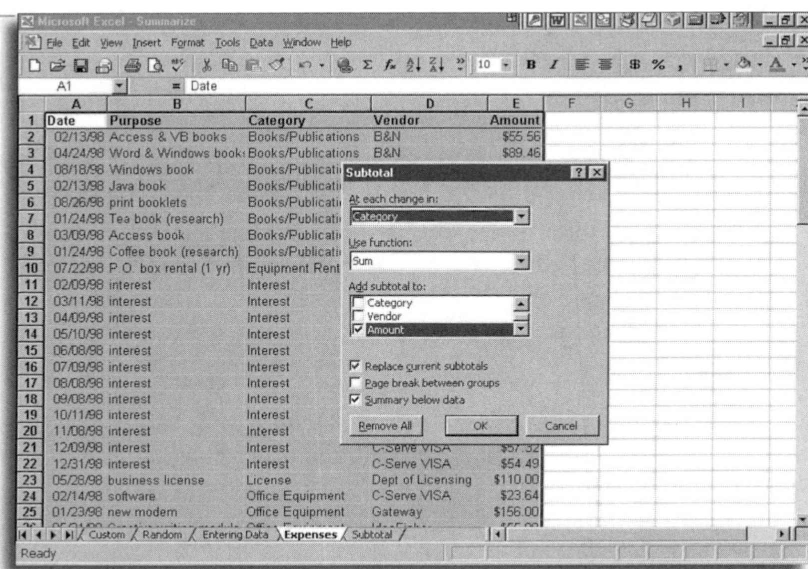

FIGURE 18.6
The Subtotal dialog box is set up to apply the first of my two levels of subtotals.

4. In the **At each change in** box, select the first category to which you want to add subtotals (the higher-level category—in this case, the Category field).
5. In the **Use function** box, select a function. (**Sum** is most common, but several functions are available.)
6. In the **Add subtotal to** list box, mark the check boxes for the number fields you want subtotaled. Clear the check boxes for any fields you don't want calculated.

   Only fields that contain numerical values should be included because only numerical values can be calculated.

   Use the scrollbar on the right side of the **Add subtotal to** list box to scroll through all the field check boxes.

7. Click **OK**.

   The first level of subtotals is applied to your table, as shown in Figure 18.7. If any of your subtotal labels are truncated, you can widen the column to display their full text.

   If you want to apply only a single level of subtotals, stop here; you're done.

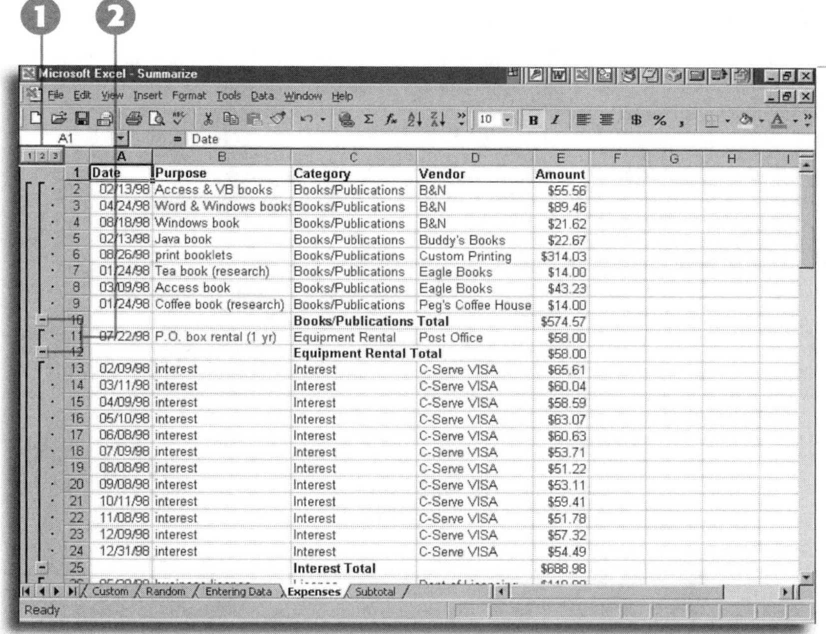

FIGURE 18.7

The Category field is subtotaled, and the worksheet is outlined so that you can show or hide details.

1. Outline levels
2. Hide buttons

For this example, I want to apply a second level of subtotals to the Vendor field.

8. On the **Data** menu, click **Subtotals**.
9. Select the second-level subtotal field (in this case, Vendor).
10. Clear the **Replace current subtotals** check box (because I want to add a second level of subtotals, not replace the existing subtotals).

    The Subtotal dialog box shown in Figure 18.8 is ready to apply the second level of subtotals.

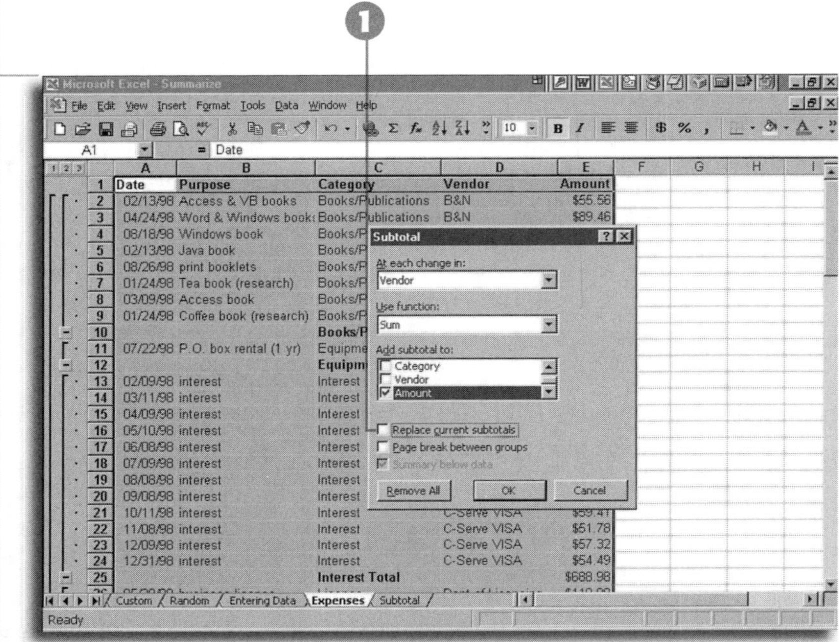

FIGURE 18.8

This Subtotal dialog box is ready to add a second level of subtotals.

1 Clear checkbox to add more subtotals.

11. Click **OK**.

    The additional subtotals and outline level are added to the table, as shown in Figure 18.9.

SEE ALSO

➤ *To learn more about sorting a list, see page 269.*

Hiding Subtotal Levels

Now, you learn the flexibility of subtotaling: You can hide and show the details. To hide an entire level of detail, click a level button (shown in Figure 18.10). To hide a section of details, click a Hide button (with the minus symbol) next to the subtotal row for which you want to hide details.

In Figure 18.10, I've shown all the details by clicking Level 4 and then hidden the details for Eagle Books by clicking the Hide button next to Row 12, the row with the Eagle Books subtotal.

	Date	Purpose	Category	Vendor	Amount
2	02/13/98	Access & VB books	Books/Publications	B&N	$55.56
3	04/24/98	Word & Windows book	Books/Publications	B&N	$89.46
4	08/18/98	Windows book	Books/Publications	B&N	$21.62
5				**B&N Total**	$166.64
6	02/13/98	Java book	Books/Publications	Buddy's Books	$22.67
7				**Buddy's Books Total**	$22.67
8	08/26/98	print booklets	Books/Publications	Custom Printing	$314.03
9				**Custom Printing Total**	$314.03
10	01/24/98	Tea book (research)	Books/Publications	Eagle Books	$14.00
11	03/09/98	Access book	Books/Publications	Eagle Books	$43.23
12				**Eagle Books Total**	$57.23
13	01/24/98	Coffee book (research)	Books/Publications	Peg's Coffee House	$14.00
14				**Peg's Coffee House Total**	$14.00
15			**Books/Publications Total**		$574.57
16	07/22/98	P.O. box rental (1 yr)	Equipment Rental	Post Office	$58.00
17				**Post Office Total**	$58.00
18			**Equipment Rental Total**		$58.00
19	02/09/98	interest	Interest	C-Serve VISA	$65.61
20	03/11/98	interest	Interest	C-Serve VISA	$60.04
21	04/09/98	interest	Interest	C-Serve VISA	$58.59
22	05/10/98	interest	Interest	C-Serve VISA	$63.07
23	06/08/98	interest	Interest	C-Serve VISA	$60.63
24	07/09/98	interest	Interest	C-Serve VISA	$53.71
25	08/08/98	interest	Interest	C-Serve VISA	$51.22

FIGURE 18.9

Now I have subtotals for each Category, and within each Category are subtotals for each Vendor.

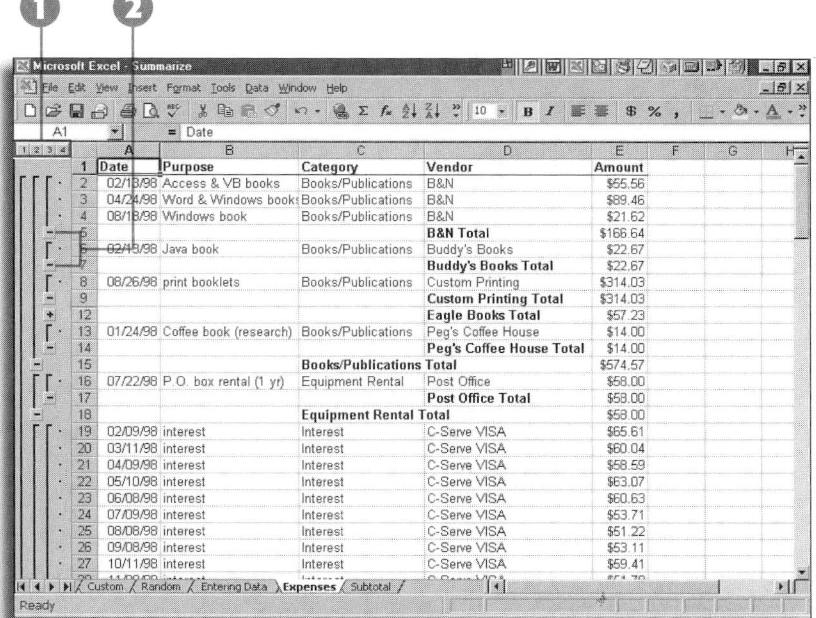

	Date	Purpose	Category	Vendor	Amount
2	02/13/98	Access & VB books	Books/Publications	B&N	$55.56
3	04/24/98	Word & Windows book	Books/Publications	B&N	$89.46
4	08/18/98	Windows book	Books/Publications	B&N	$21.62
5				**B&N Total**	$166.64
6	02/13/98	Java book	Books/Publications	Buddy's Books	$22.67
7				**Buddy's Books Total**	$22.67
8	08/26/98	print booklets	Books/Publications	Custom Printing	$314.03
9				**Custom Printing Total**	$314.03
12				**Eagle Books Total**	$57.23
13	01/24/98	Coffee book (research)	Books/Publications	Peg's Coffee House	$14.00
14				**Peg's Coffee House Total**	$14.00
15			**Books/Publications Total**		$574.57
16	07/22/98	P.O. box rental (1 yr)	Equipment Rental	Post Office	$58.00
17				**Post Office Total**	$58.00
18			**Equipment Rental Total**		$58.00
19	02/09/98	interest	Interest	C-Serve VISA	$65.61
20	03/11/98	interest	Interest	C-Serve VISA	$60.04
21	04/09/98	interest	Interest	C-Serve VISA	$58.59
22	05/10/98	interest	Interest	C-Serve VISA	$63.07
23	06/08/98	interest	Interest	C-Serve VISA	$60.63
24	07/09/98	interest	Interest	C-Serve VISA	$53.71
25	08/08/98	interest	Interest	C-Serve VISA	$51.22
26	09/08/98	interest	Interest	C-Serve VISA	$53.11
27	10/11/98	interest	Interest	C-Serve VISA	$59.41

FIGURE 18.10

To show all the details, click the Level 4 button.

1. Level buttons
2. Hide buttons

Showing Subtotal Levels

A subtotaled table is a convenient presentation when all the details are hidden, and you can show the specific details in which you're interested.

To show details in a hidden level, click the Show button (the button with the plus symbol) next to the subtotal row for which you want to show details; all the next-level details for that section are displayed on the worksheet. To show details for an entire level, click a level button; all the detail items for the level you clicked are displayed on the worksheet.

In Figure 18.11, I hid all details by clicking Level 3 and then clicking Level 2 (to consolidate the details level-by-level); all the Level 2 subtotals are displayed. Then, I displayed subtotals within the Office Supplies Total by clicking the Show button next to row 74, which displayed the Level 3 subtotals for the Office Supplies category. Next, I displayed the Level 4 details for the Papers'n'Stuff Total by clicking the Show button next to row 66.

If you find that more details are shown than you want, first collapse the outline sections backwards by clicking Level 4, Level 3, and then Level 2. Next, show the Level 2 subtotals you want (in this example, Office Supplies), and then show the Level 3 details you want (in this example, Papers'n'Stuff).

Removing Subtotaling

Return a table to details without subtotals

1. Click a cell in the table.
2. On the **Data** menu, click **Subtotals**.
3. Click **Remove All**.

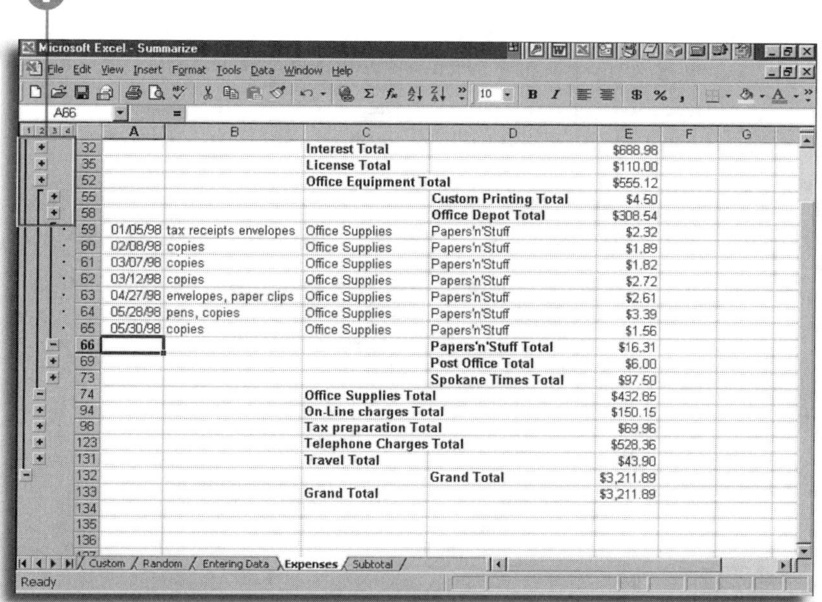

FIGURE 18.11
To hide all but the Grand Total, click the Level 1 button.

1 Show buttons

Outlining a Table Manually

To add the capability of showing and hiding rows in a table without adding subtotals to the table, you can outline the table manually. An outlined table has Show buttons and Hide buttons, just like a subtotaled table, but you determine which items are hidden or shown as groups.

You might want to use manual outlining if

- You've already added subtotals to a table by writing your own formulas, rather than using the Subtotals command.
- You want to group data into categories so that you can show and hide category details without adding subtotals to the categories.
- You want to outline only part of a table without outlining the entire table.

You Can Outline Columns, Too

You can also apply outlining to columns and then show or hide groups of columns. To outline columns, follow the same procedures as for outlining rows, but select groups of adjacent columns instead of groups of rows.

Outline a table manually

1. Select adjacent rows that you want to combine into a single show-or-hide group, as shown in Figure 18.12.

   If you have totals in your table, don't include them in the group or they'll be hidden when you hide the group.

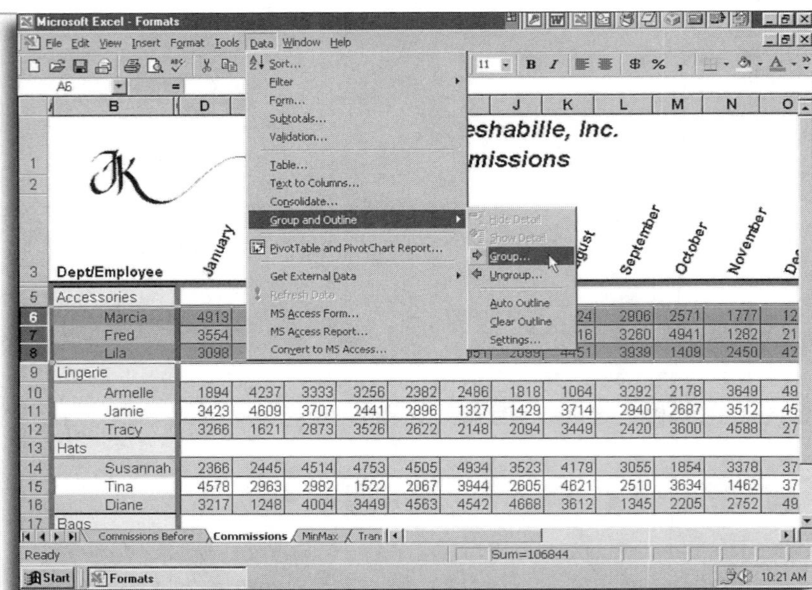

FIGURE 18.12
Select individual groups of detail rows or columns, and group them for hiding.

2. On the **Data** menu, point to **Group and Outline**, and click **Group**.

   Outlining is applied to the selected group of rows, and a Hide button appears at the left side of the group (just like in a Subtotaled table), as shown in Figure 18.13. To hide the group, click the **Hide** button. To show the group, click the **Show** button.

3. Repeat steps 1 and 2 for each set of adjacent rows you want to combine into a single show-or-hide group.

Remove manual outlining

1. Show the detail rows for the groups in which you want to remove outlining.

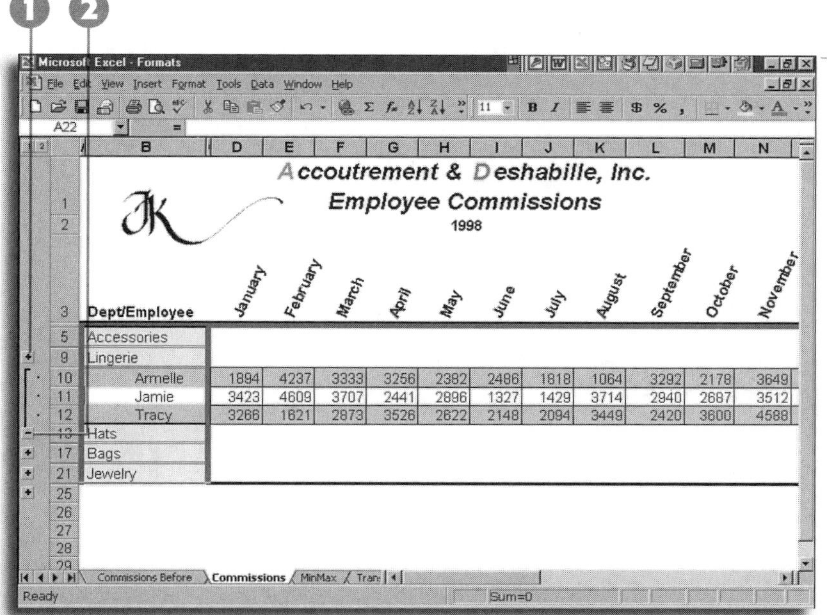

FIGURE 18.13
Outlining allows a reader to hide or show specific details in the table, and it makes a large table easier to study.

1. Click to show details.
2. Click to hide details.

2. Select the rows that you want to remove from the outline.

   You can remove a few rows from a larger outline group by selecting just those rows. You cannot, however, select nonadjacent rows; you can remove outlining from only one set of adjacent rows at a time.

3. On the **Data** menu, point to **Group and Outline**, and click **Ungroup**.

   Outlining is removed from the rows you selected.

   To remove all outline groups in the table, click in the table, open the **Data** menu, point to **Group and Outline**, and click **Clear Outline**.

Oops! I Ungrouped Without Showing Details First!

If you select the whole table and ungroup it without showing the detail rows first, the Show/Hide buttons disappear but the detail rows don't reappear. It's okay; they're just hidden. Select the group of rows that contains the hidden rows (look for the row-number gap), then right-click the selected rows and click **Unhide**.

CHAPTER

19

Summarizing Details with PivotTables and PivotCharts

Working with PivotTables and understanding the terminology

Creating a PivotTable with the PivotTable and PivotChart Wizard

Using the PivotTable toolbar

Changing the arrangement of a PivotTable

Changing calculations in a PivotTable

Displaying the underlying details and formatting PivotTables

Creating PivotCharts

Changing the arrangement of a PivotChart

Use PivotTables for Charts

PivotTables are a great data source for charts because when the PivotTable is changed, the chart changes automatically to display whatever is in the PivotTable. You can also create a PivotChart directly from the data, instead of a separate PivotTable and chart.

Working with PivotTables

PivotTables are an interactive and flexible presentation of data. You can change which data is presented and how it's laid out and summarized, even in the middle of an electronic presentation to a room full of people. PivotCharts are similar to PivotTables, but graphical; you'll learn how to create them later in this chapter.

When you use a PivotTable to summarize data, you can

- Summarize data from several sources: Excel lists, external databases, multiple worksheets, or other PivotTables.
- Pivot the table to change its orientation.
- Group items in a field (for example, group dates into months or quarters).
- Change the calculation function for a field.
- Show the details underlying a single summarized item.
- Format the PivotTable for a professional and reader-friendly presentation.

If you learned how to create PivotTables in an earlier version of Excel, you'll be relieved to know that you can still use the same methods to create PivotTables in Excel 2000. When you get to the PivotTable and PivotChart Wizard's Step 3, click the **Layout** button and arrange the PivotTable in the traditional PivotTable dialog box. On the other hand, you might like the new method in Excel 2000 better. The new method is what I demonstrate in this book.

PivotTable Terms

PivotTables use some terms that you can look up here if you get lost later in the chapter. Figure 19.1 and Table 19.1 show and define important PivotTable terms.

FIGURE 19.1
Terms associated with PivotTables.

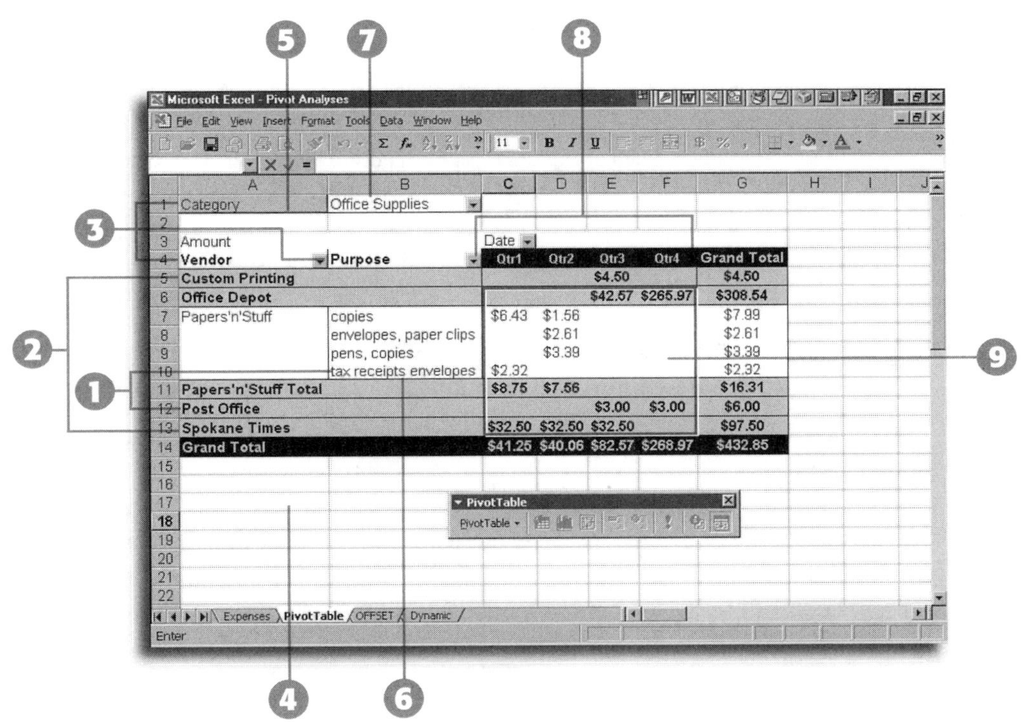

1. Items
2. Row field
3. Field labels
4. Outer field
5. Page field
6. Inner field
7. Page field item
8. Column fields
9. Data area

TABLE 19.1 PivotTable terms

Term	Definition
Page field	A field that displays one item at a time. (In Figure 19.1, Category is a page field.)
Page field item	The item displayed by the page field. (In Figure 19.1, Office Supplies is the page field item that's displayed.)
Row field	A field with data displayed in rows. (In Figure 19.1, Vendor and Purpose are row fields.)
Column field	A field with data displayed in columns. (In Figure 19.1, Date is the only column field.)
Item	A specific row or column heading. (In Figure 19.1, Custom Printing and Qtr2 are both items.)
Data area	Part of PivotTable where data and calculations are displayed.
Field label	Label that identifies a row or column field—also called *field heading* and *field button*.
Outer field	When more than one field is displayed in the row or column area, the outermost field is the outer field. Each outer field encompasses one or more inner field items.
Inner field	When more than one field is displayed in the row or column area, the innermost field is the inner field. Each inner field item is grouped within an outer field item.
Refresh data	Update the PivotTable with changed source data.

Creating a PivotTable

PivotTables are a bit more complex to create than subtotals or consolidations, but the PivotTable and PivotChart Wizard guides you through the process of creation. The wizard also guides you through editing a PivotTable if you need to change the data source (for example, if new records or fields are added to a source worksheet table). Editing a table to change the source ranges is not the same as updating a PivotTable with current data; that's a procedure called *refreshing*, and it doesn't require the assistance of the wizard.

Using the PivotTable and PivotChart Wizard

You can only create a PivotTable by using the PivotTable and PivotChart Wizard.

Create a PivotTable from a worksheet table

1. Click the worksheet source table from which you want to create a PivotTable.

   If you want to use an external data source (not a worksheet table), or create a PivotTable from another PivotTable, click anywhere in any worksheet.

2. On the **Data** menu, click **PivotTable and PivotChart Report**.

   The PivotTable and PivotChart Wizard starts (shown in Figure 19.2).

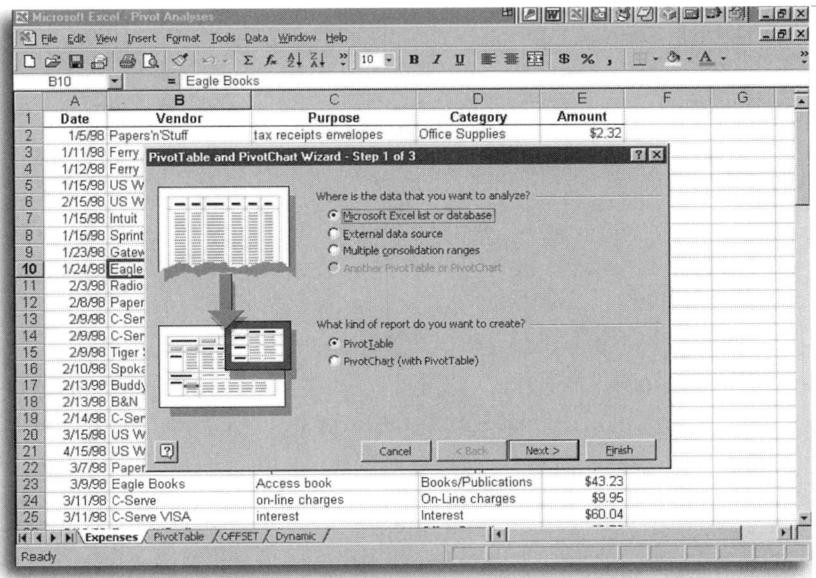

FIGURE 19.2
In the PivotTable and PivotChart Wizard Step 1, click the type of source data you're using.

3. In Step 1 of the wizard, click an option for the type of source data (in this case, a Microsoft Excel list or database).

4. Click **Next**.

   The Step 2 dialog box appears, and the worksheet table you clicked is defined as the source range. (The worksheet range is outlined with a moving border, as shown in Figure 19.3).

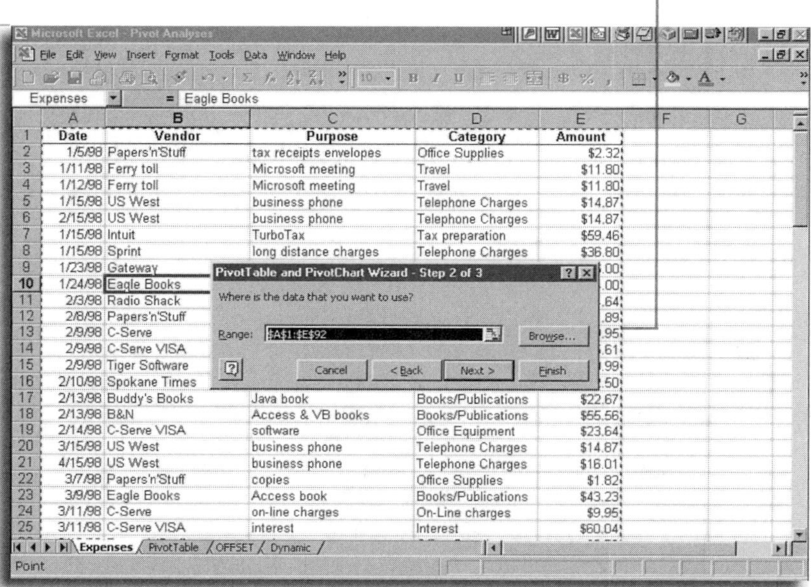

FIGURE 19.3

The range in the Range box is outlined with a moving border on the worksheet.

1 Moving border

5. If the range is correct, click **Next**.

   If you want to use a named range instead of a range reference, type the name in the **Range** box and click **Next**.

   The wizard Step 3 appears. At this point, you can construct your PivotTable the old way (in the dialog box layout diagram) by clicking the **Layout** button.

   You can change several options in the PivotTable, such as whether you want grand totals for your columns and/or rows or whether you want users to be able to drill down for details by double-clicking a PivotTable cell. You can set or change options now by clicking the **Options** button in Step 3 or later by clicking **Table Options** on the PivotTable menu (on the PivotTable toolbar).

6. If you have a worksheet set up to hold the PivotTable (as I do in this workbook), click the **Existing worksheet** option; then, click the sheet tab, and click a cell in the worksheet where you want the upper-left corner of the PivotTable to be located (shown in Figure 19.4).

   If you want Excel to insert a new worksheet for the PivotTable, leave the **New worksheet** option selected.

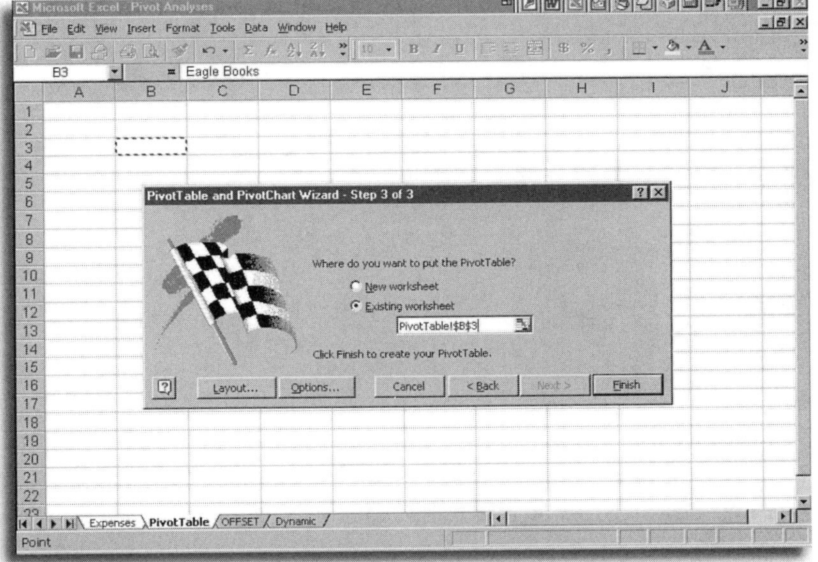

FIGURE 19.4
Tell Excel where to put the PivotTable (and change a few options while you're here).

7. Click **Finish**.

   A PivotTable area is created on the worksheet, and your source data headings appear in the PivotTable toolbar.

8. Drag the Field labels onto the PivotTable area to lay out the structure of the PivotTable.

   In this example, I'm creating a PivotTable that shows expenses by Category and Date and summarizes the Amount values with the SUM function. In Figure 19.5, Category is being dropped in the column area, so each category will appear in a column. Date was dropped in the row area, so each date will have its own row. Finally, the Amount field will be dropped in the data area to be calculated with the SUM function.

Hey! My PivotTable Went Blank!

You probably clicked outside the PivotTable, which changed your PivotTable toolbar and hid the PivotTable area guides. To return to PivotTable mode, click inside the PivotTable area. You can also hide or display the PivotTable area guides by clicking the **Hide Fields** button on the PivotTable toolbar while a PivotTable cell is selected.

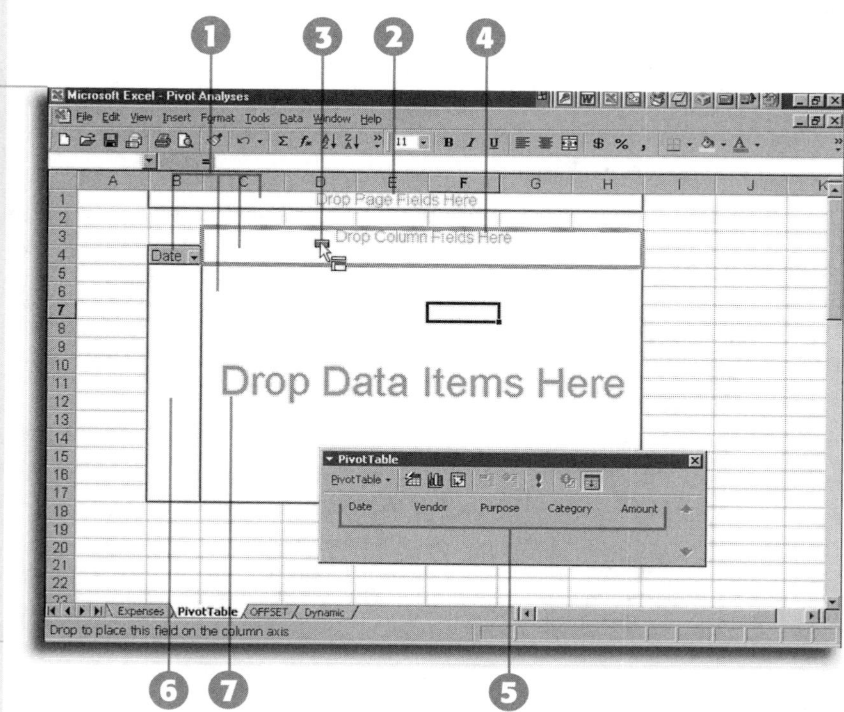

FIGURE 19.5

Lay out the PivotTable structure by dragging field labels to PivotTable areas.

1. PivotTable areas
2. Drag to here for a page field.
3. Drag label to area.
4. Drag to here for a column field.
5. Field labels from source range
6. Drag to here for a row field.
7. Drag data field to be calculated here.

Your PivotTable is created. (The resulting PivotTable in this example is shown in Figure 19.6.)

My initial PivotTable is messy and difficult to read because the data is too detailed. I'll make it more useful by grouping the dates into quarters and transposing the layout so that dates are across the top and categories are listed on the left.

What If I Want an Average Instead of a Sum?

To change the summary function at this step, double-click the **Field label** in the data area (in this case, the **Sum of Amount** label). In the PivotTable Field dialog box that appears, click a different function, click **OK**, and continue building the PivotTable with the wizard.

This PivotTable Doesn't Look Finished…

Whenever a cell within the PivotTable is selected, the PivotTable areas will be visible, the toolbar will show data labels, and you'll see ScreenTips wherever your mouse is hovered. To "finish" the PivotTable, click a cell outside of the PivotTable area.

Creating Several PivotTables from the Same Source Data

If you have more than one PivotTable in a workbook, and all are based on the same source data, it's more efficient to create the first PivotTable from the source data and create the rest of the PivotTables from the first PivotTable. This saves system resources, but more importantly, it saves you time. When you refresh data in any one of the related PivotTables, all the related PivotTables are refreshed at the same time. The alternative, creating each PivotTable directly from the source data, requires that you refresh each PivotTable separately.

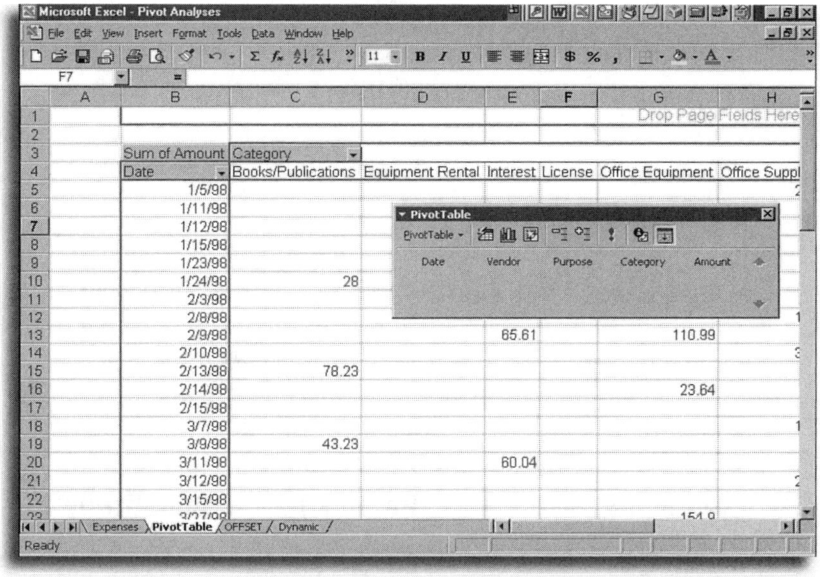

FIGURE 19.6
This PivotTable was placed on a new worksheet, and the page field area is still empty.

To create a PivotTable from another PivotTable, click the Another PivotTable or PivotChart option in Step 1 of the PivotTable and PivotChart Wizard and then continue with normal PivotTable construction procedures.

Changing the Data Source Range

If more rows or columns of data are added to a source range, you need to change the source range for the PivotTable to include the new data. You can add the new data two ways: the straightforward way that uses the PivotTable and PivotChart Wizard and the fast-and-clever way, by using a named formula to define the source range.

Changing the Source Range with the Wizard

The PivotTable and PivotChart Wizard is a reliable, straightforward method of updating a changed PivotTable source range.

I Closed My PivotTable Toolbar

To display the PivotTable toolbar, right-click any toolbar and click PivotTable.

Update a changed source range with the PivotTable and PivotChart Wizard

1. Click a cell in the PivotTable.
2. On the PivotTable toolbar, click the **PivotTable and PivotChart Wizard** button . (Alternatively, on the **Data** menu, click **PivotTable and PivotChart Report**.)

   Step 3 of the PivotTable and PivotChart Wizard appears, but you need to back up to Step 2 to change the source range.
3. Click the **Back** button.
4. In the wizard Step 2, drag a new source range or type new references in the **Range** box.
5. If you don't want to make any other changes using the PivotTable and PivotChart Wizard, click **Finish**.

   The PivotTable is updated to use the new source range.

Is This Only for PivotTables?

Defining a dynamic source range with the OFFSET function works well for charts and for print areas, too.

Creating a Source Range That Changes Automatically

The next method will amaze your friends and colleagues (at least, those who are not Excel experts themselves). It's a little harder to decipher at first, and if it leaves you really confused, don't bother with it. If, however, it works for you, you can create a PivotTable that updates its worksheet source ranges automatically when you refresh the PivotTable.

This method uses a named formula to define a *dynamic* worksheet source range, a range that automatically changes its defined size to include all adjacent rows and columns. The formula uses the OFFSET function, which defines a worksheet range by where it begins, how many rows it has, and how many columns it has. It uses the COUNTA function to indicate to the OFFSET function how many rows and columns to include.

A simple OFFSET formula looks like the one I've laid out in Figure 19.7. To select the range, click in the **Name** box, type the name of the formula, and press Enter; or open the **Edit** menu, select **Go To,** type the name of the formula in the **Reference** box, and click **OK**.

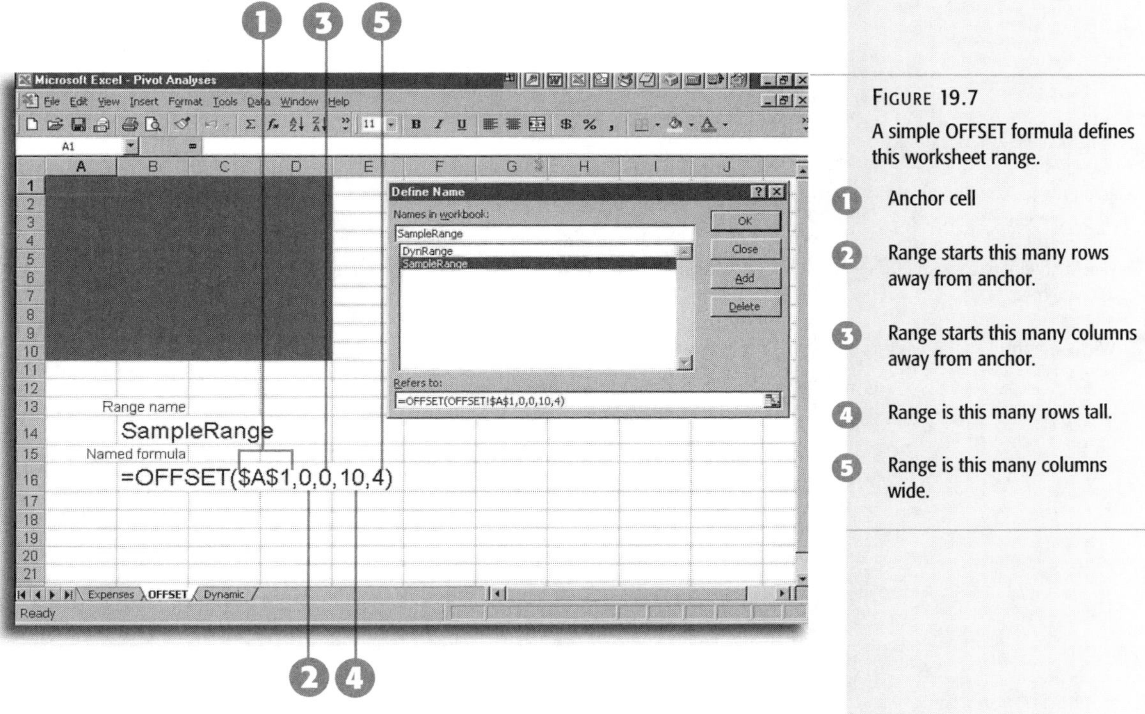

FIGURE 19.7

A simple OFFSET formula defines this worksheet range.

1. Anchor cell
2. Range starts this many rows away from anchor.
3. Range starts this many columns away from anchor.
4. Range is this many rows tall.
5. Range is this many columns wide.

In Figure 19.7, I created a named formula, SampleRange, that defines the range I've colored in. If I filled the range with numbers, the formula =SUM(SampleRange) would sum all the numbers in the range. This named formula is a simple example of the OFFSET function. The range it defines is not *dynamic*; it's always the same size and location, just like a named range.

To make the range *dynamic*, I'll change the fourth and fifth arguments in the formula so that instead of the range being 10 rows tall and 4 columns wide, the range is as many rows tall as there are entries in column A and as many columns wide as there are entries in row 1. To do this, the formula nests a couple of COUNTA functions in the OFFSET function. (Figure 19.8 shows the dynamic range formula named DynRange.)

If Your Dynamic Range Has Too Many Rows...

For a dynamic range to work correctly, make sure that you have no entries in column A or row 1 other than those in the table because the dynamic range counts all the entries in the entire column and row.

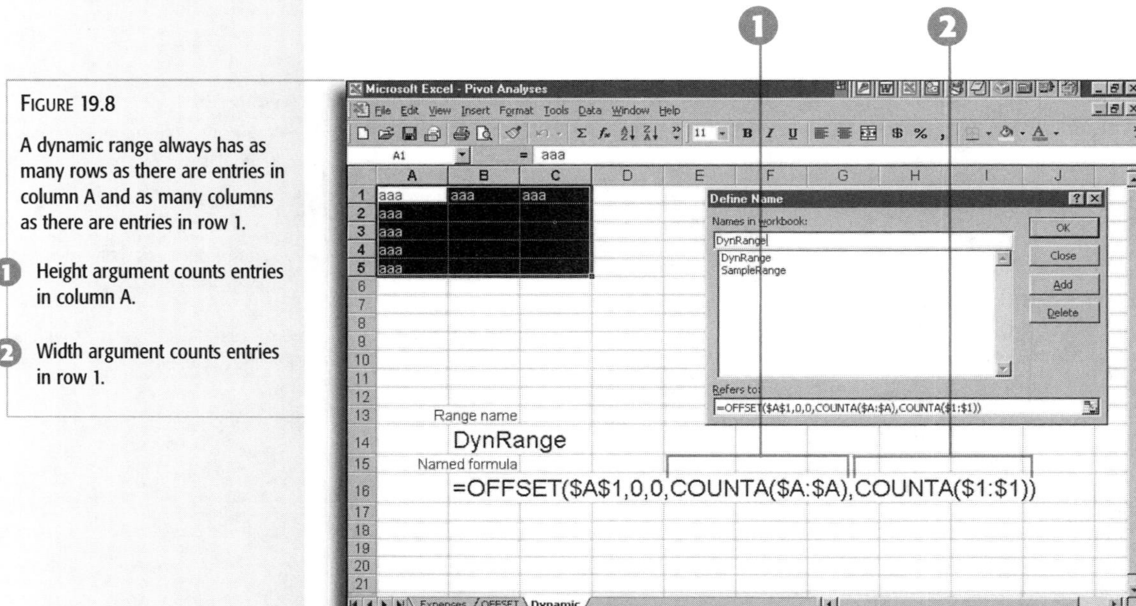

FIGURE 19.8

A dynamic range always has as many rows as there are entries in column A and as many columns as there are entries in row 1.

1. Height argument counts entries in column A.
2. Width argument counts entries in row 1.

Easier Formula Construction

When I write a long, complex formula like this, I find it easier to write it in a cell without an = because I can easily see and edit the entire formula and then copy the formula and paste it into the Define Name dialog box.

Where's My Named Formula?

The formula name won't appear in either the Name box list or the Go To dialog box; however, both recognize the name, so if you type it in either the Name box or the Go To dialog box, the dynamic range is selected.

Create a dynamic range with a named formula

1. On the worksheet where you want to create the named dynamic-range formula, open the **Insert** menu, point to **Name**, and click **Define**.
2. In the **Define Name** dialog box (shown in Figure 19.8), type a name for your dynamic-range formula under **Names in workbook**.
3. Type the OFFSET/COUNTA formula in the **Refers to** box.
4. Click **OK**.
5. To test your dynamic-range formula, click the **Name box** (left of the Formula bar), type the formula name, and press Enter. If the formula is written correctly, the dynamic range is selected. (Be sure there are entries in column A and row 1 for the formula to count.)

To use your dynamic range in a PivotTable, type the range name in the **Range** box in Step 2 of the PivotTable and PivotChart Wizard. When you click the **Refresh Data** button (see the following section), a dynamic-range PivotTable is updated with both changed data and newly added rows and columns.

SEE ALSO

➤ *To learn more about naming cells and ranges, see page 202.*

Refreshing Data

Refresh is the PivotTable term for updating a PivotTable with current data. When you refresh data, the PivotTable and PivotChart Wizard goes to the PivotTable's source range and looks for changed data.

Refresh data in a PivotTable

1. Click a cell in the PivotTable.
2. Click the **Refresh Data** button on the PivotTable toolbar [!].

   That's it. The PivotTable and PivotChart Wizard checks the source ranges for changed data and updates your PivotTable.

Save Time Refreshing Multiple PivotTables

If you create a PivotTable from another PivotTable, the two PivotTables are related to each other. When you refresh data in a PivotTable that's related to other PivotTables, all the related PivotTables are refreshed at the same time. (The alternative if PivotTables are unrelated is to refresh each PivotTable separately.)

The PivotTable Toolbar

Figure 19.9 shows the PivotTable toolbar, which appears whenever you display a PivotTable. Table 19.2 explains what the toolbar buttons do.

TABLE 19.2 PivotTable toolbar buttons

Icon	Button Name	Button Purpose
PivotTable ▾	PivotTable Menu	Shows a shortcut menu of PivotTable commands.
	Format Report	Opens AutoFormat dialog box.
	Chart Wizard	Creates automatic chart from PivotTable.
	PivotTable and PivotChart Wizard	Opens PivotTable and PivotChart Wizard Step 3.

continues...

TABLE 19.2 Continued

Icon	Button Name	Button Purpose
	Hide Detail	Hides selected data.
	Show Detail	Shows hidden data.
	Refresh Data	Updates PivotTable with current source data.
	Field Dialog	Displays the PivotTable Field dialog box.
	Hide/Display Fields	Hides or displays toolbar field buttons and PivotTable layout guides.

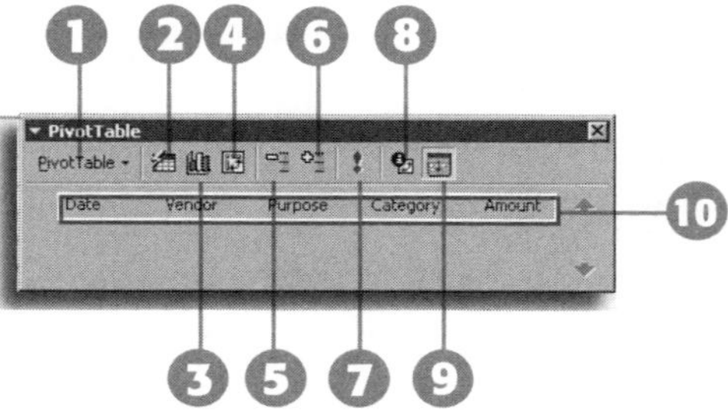

FIGURE 19.9

The PivotTable toolbar enables you to perform some common procedures more quickly.

1 PivotTable Menu
2 Format Report
3 Chart Wizard
4 PivotTable Wizard
5 Hide Detail
6 Show Detail
7 Refresh Data
8 Field Dialog
9 Hide Fields
10 Source data labels

If you click the toolbar's Close button to close the PivotTable toolbar, you can display it again by right-clicking any toolbar and clicking PivotTable on the shortcut menu.

Changing PivotTable Arrangement

The PivotTable I created in Figure 19.6 is messy, hard to read, and far too detailed. The following lists some of the changes I'll make to it:

- Group the dates into quarters.
- Pivot the table to put categories on the left (in row fields) and dates across the top (in column fields).
- Add the Vendor field.
- Create a page field for Category items.
- Create separate pages for each Category item.

Grouping Items in a Field

The dates in the PivotTable in Figure 19.6 are too detailed. I don't want to see each individual transaction, but I do want to see summaries of what expenses were in each quarter.

Group items in a field

1. Right-click any cell in the field that you want to group (in this example, any cell in the Date field).
2. On the shortcut menu, point to **Group and Outline** and then click **Group**.

   The Grouping dialog box appears. Because I selected a Date field in Figure 19.10, Excel guesses some appropriate grouping levels.
3. Click to select the group you want, and click to deselect any groups you don't want.

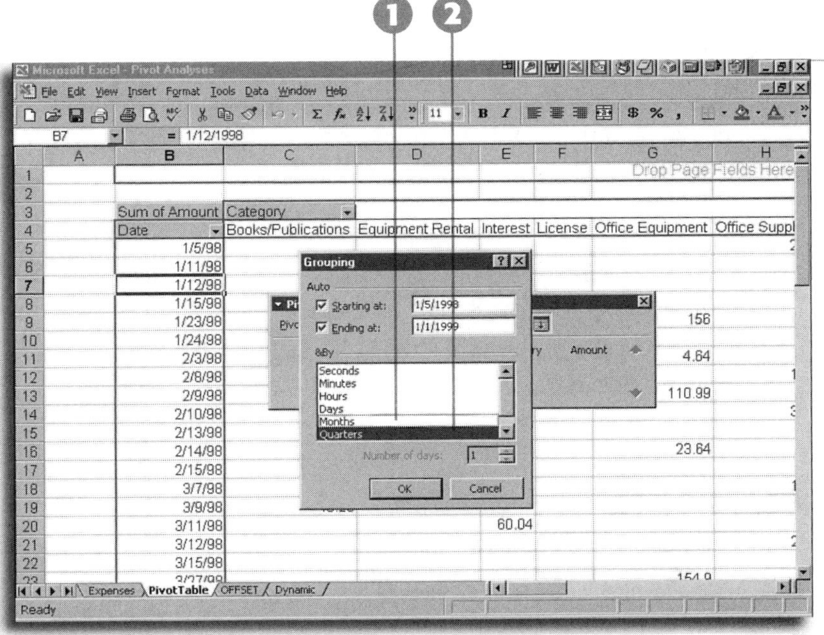

FIGURE 19.10
Use the Grouping dialog box to group items in a field.

1. Click Months to deselect.
2. Click Quarters to select.

4. Click **OK**.

   Figure 19.11 shows the result of my grouping by quarter.

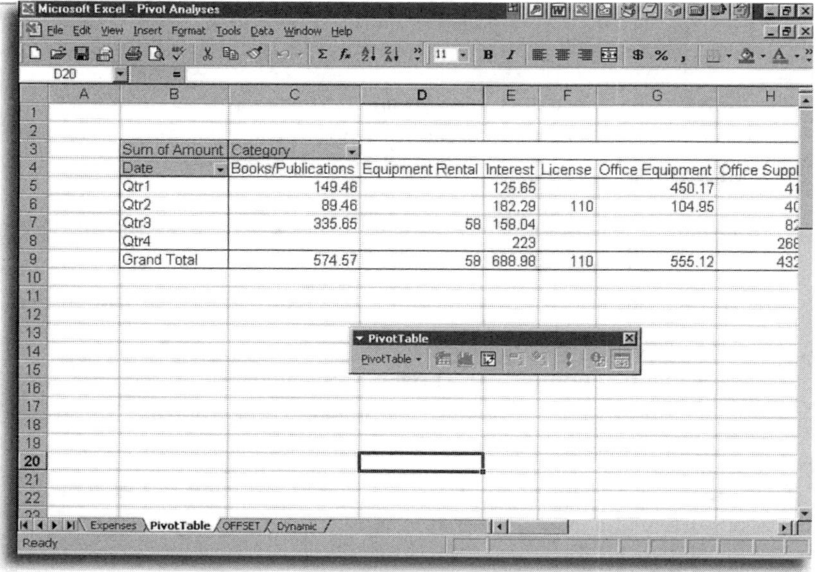

FIGURE 19.11
The PivotTable data is more meaningful now that I've grouped it into quarterly expenses.

Pivoting the Table

Pivoting a PivotTable layout is similar to transposing a worksheet table, but easier and with more options. I want to pivot the PivotTable in Figure 19.11 so that Category items are listed down the side and Date fields are across the top.

To pivot a PivotTable layout, you drag a field label to a different location in the PivotTable. When you drag field labels, the mouse pointer becomes various symbols, depending on where the dragged label is located in the PivotTable. Table 19.3 shows the different mouse pointer symbols you see when you drag field labels around the PivotTable.

I Dropped a Label in the Wrong Place

If you inadvertently drop a label in the wrong area (or out of the PivotTable entirely), click the **Undo** button on the Standard toolbar to undo the drop.

TABLE 19.3 **Symbols you see when you drag field labels**

Mouse Pointer Symbol	Meaning
	Dropped label becomes a column field.
	Dropped label becomes a row field.
	Dropped label becomes a page field.
	Dropped label is removed from PivotTable.

Change a row field to a column field

1. Drag the Date label to the column field area of the PivotTable. This moves Date to the top of the PivotTable.
2. When the mouse pointer changes to a column field symbol, drop the label.

Change a column field to a row field

1. Drag the Category label to the row field area of the PivotTable. This moves Category to the side of the PivotTable.
2. When the mouse pointer changes to a row field symbol, drop the label.

I pivoted the PivotTable in Figure 19.11 and got the results shown in Figure 19.12. The next time I create a PivotTable like this one, I'll lay it out this way when I first create it.

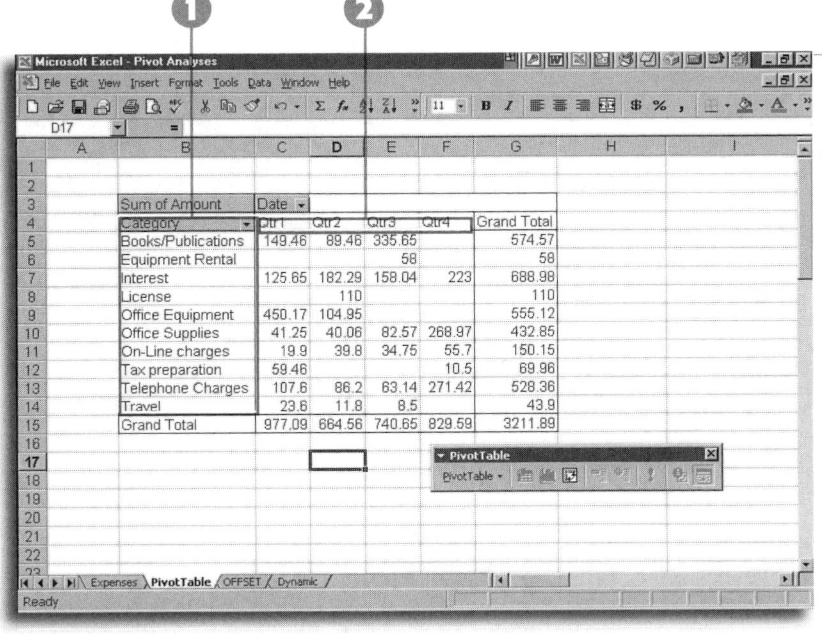

Sum of Amount	Date				
Category	Qtr1	Qtr2	Qtr3	Qtr4	Grand Total
Books/Publications	149.46	89.46	335.65		574.57
Equipment Rental			58		58
Interest	125.65	182.29	158.04	223	688.98
License		110			110
Office Equipment	450.17	104.95			555.12
Office Supplies	41.25	40.06	82.57	268.97	432.85
On-Line charges	19.9	39.8	34.75	55.7	150.15
Tax preparation	59.46			10.5	69.96
Telephone Charges	107.6	86.2	63.14	271.42	528.36
Travel	23.6	11.8	8.5		43.9
Grand Total	977.09	664.56	740.65	829.59	3211.89

FIGURE 19.12

This layout makes all the data easier to read.

1. Row field area
2. Column field area

Adding Fields

I want to add the Vendor field to my PivotTable so that I can show more of the details in my expenses list.

Add a field to a PivotTable

1. Click the PivotTable (so the data source labels appear in the PivotTable toolbar).
2. Drag the field you want to add to a PivotTable area.

   In Figure 19.13, I dragged the Vendor field to the row area.

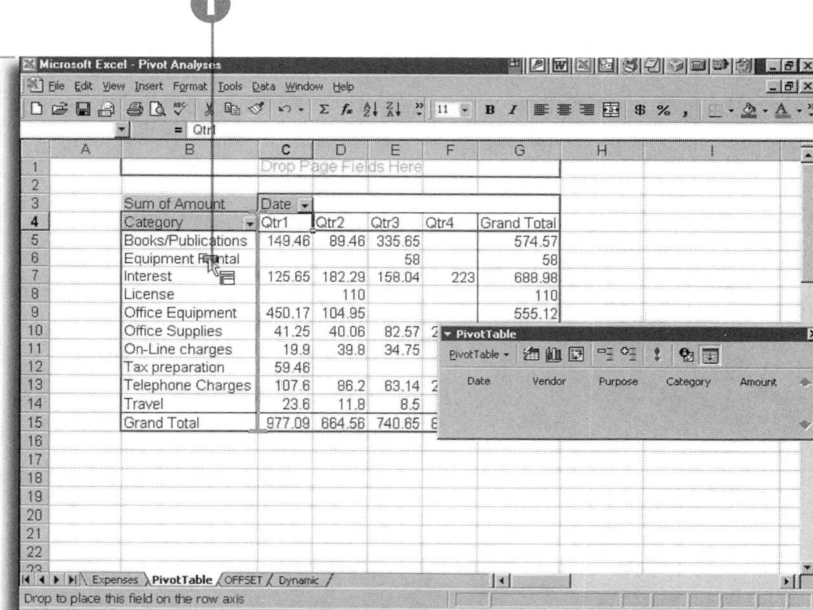

FIGURE 19.13

Dropping the Vendor field below the Category field makes the Vendor field an inner field in the PivotTable. (You see what that means in Figure 19.14).

1 Vendor field dropped here.

Figure 19.14 shows my PivotTable after I added the Vendor field.

Showing and Hiding Inner Field Details

The Vendor field I added to the row field area in Figure 19.14 is an *inner* row field, which means the Vendor items are subordinate to the Category items. I can show or hide the Vendor field items for each Category item. To show or hide inner field items, double-click the outer field where you want to show or hide inner field items. (In Figure 19.15, I hid the inner field items for all Category items, and then, I showed the inner field items for the Books/Publications category.)

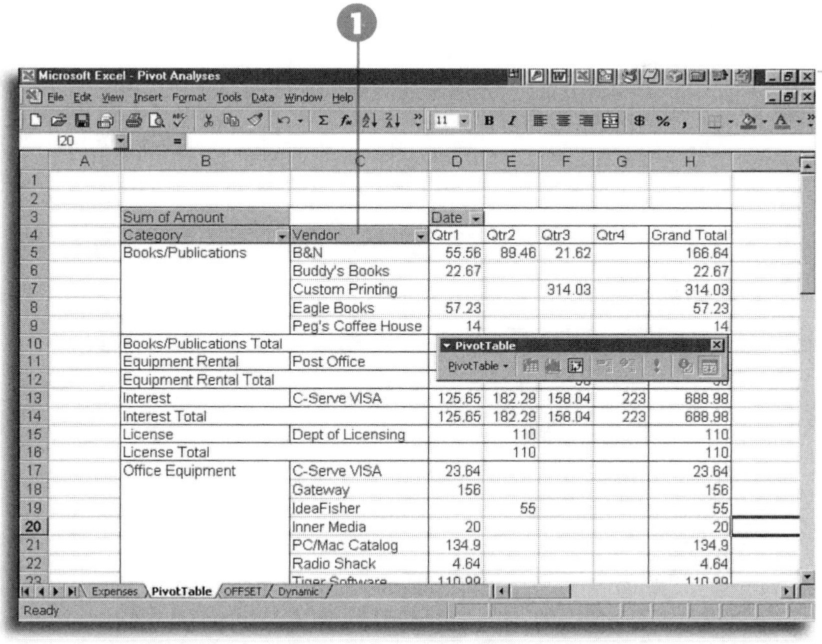

FIGURE 19.14

The Vendor field I added is an inner row field that I can hide or show.

1 Vendor field

Creating Page Fields

Another way I can make this PivotTable more useful is to make the Category field into a Page field. Then, I can show only the vendors in a specific category.

Change a row or column field to a page field

1. Drag the field label to the upper-left corner of the PivotTable.
2. When the mouse pointer changes to a page field symbol, drop the label.

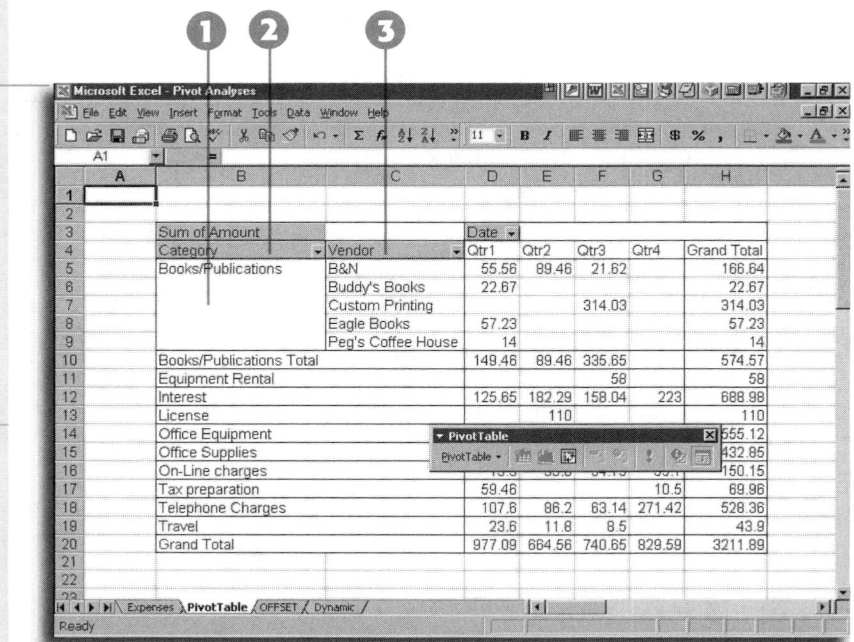

FIGURE 19.15

The Books/Publications vendors are shown; all other vendors are hidden.

1. Double-click to show or hide vendors in this category.
2. Outer field
3. Inner field

A page field is created for the field you dragged. To show data for a specific page field item, click the down arrow in the page field item box, select the item, and then click OK (as shown in Figure 19.16). I made my expenses category field into a page field and then selected the Books/Publications category. The data for the vendors in my Books/Publications category is displayed.

Creating Separate Pages

I want to create separate tables for each of my expense category items so that I can print them all at once.

Create separate page field tables

1. Click the PivotTable.
2. On the PivotTable toolbar, click the **PivotTable** menu, then click **Show Pages**.

   The Show Pages dialog box appears (shown in Figure 19.17).

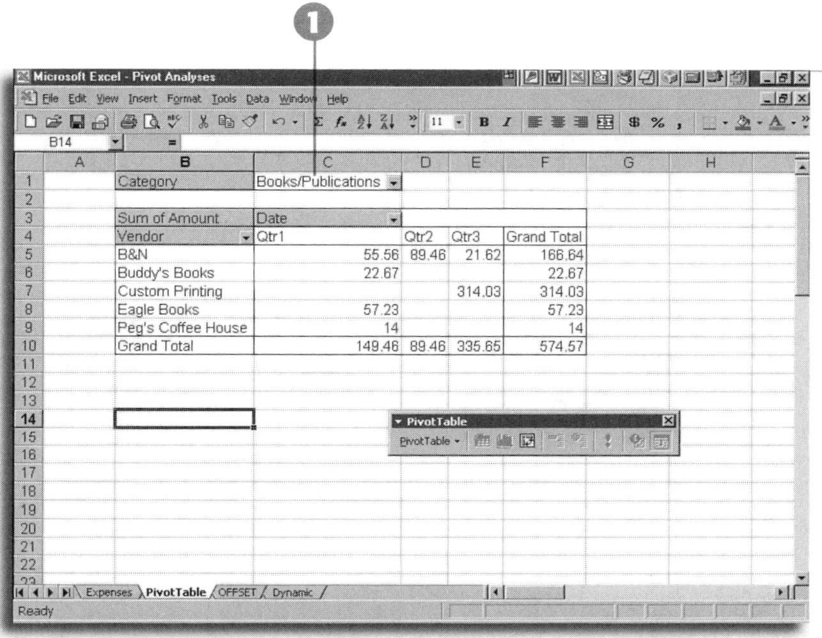

FIGURE 19.16

A Page field lets you display one category of data at a time.

1 Page field item box

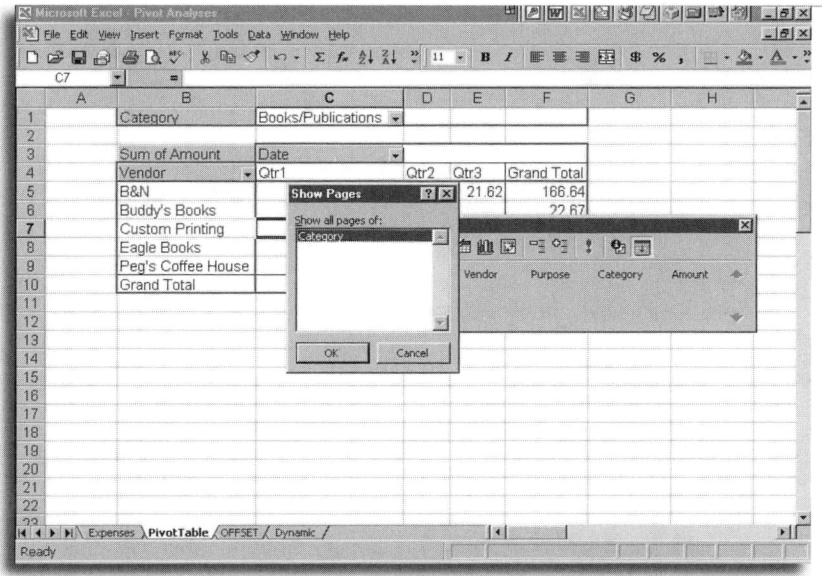

FIGURE 19.17

If I had more than one page field, they'd all be listed in the Show Pages dialog box.

Print All the New Worksheets

To print all the new worksheets with a single command, open the **File** menu, select **Print**, click the **Entire workbook** option, and click **OK**.

3. Double-click the field name for which you want to create pages (in this case, Category).

A new worksheet is created for each item in the field (as shown in Figure 19.18), and each worksheet has an identical PivotTable with the item's data displayed. The new worksheets are named with the names of the page field items, so you can navigate easily.

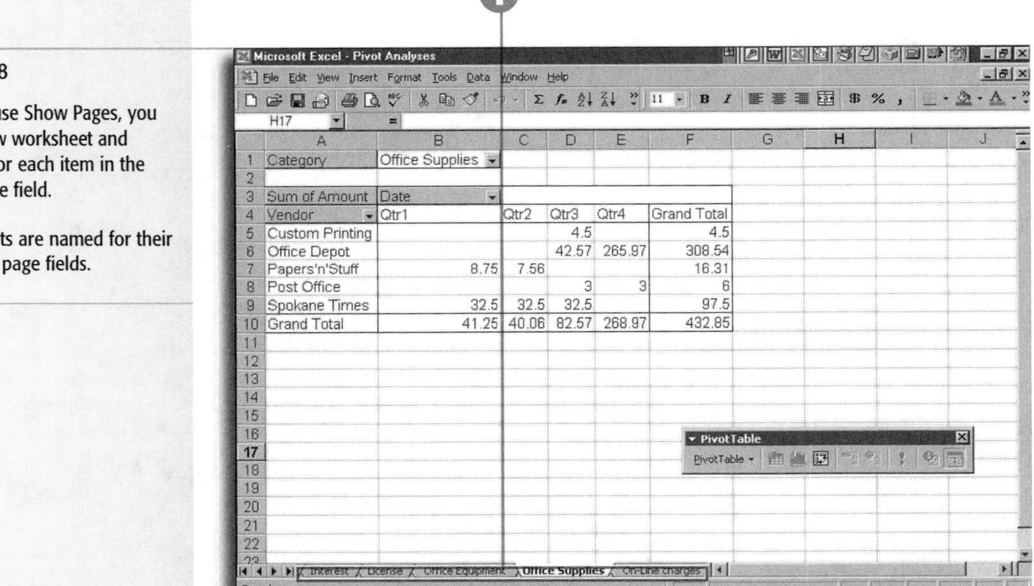

FIGURE 19.18

When you use Show Pages, you create a new worksheet and PivotTable for each item in the original page field.

1 Worksheets are named for their displayed page fields.

SEE ALSO

➤ *To learn more about printing worksheets, see page 449.*

Removing Fields

I want to remove the Vendor and Date fields from the PivotTable so that only the total expenses in each category are displayed.

Remove fields from a PivotTable

1. Drag the field label away from the PivotTable until it becomes a remove field symbol (shown in Figure 19.19).

2. Drop the field label.

   The field is removed from the PivotTable.

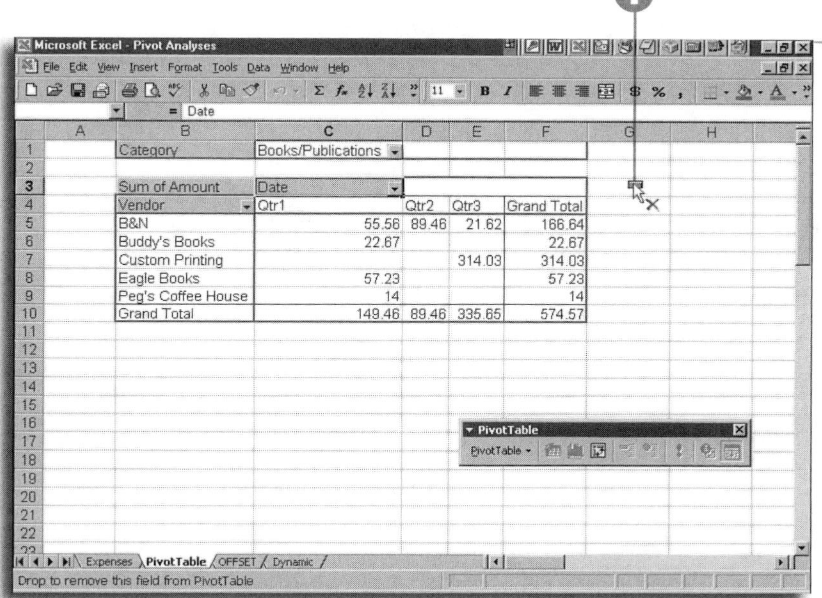

FIGURE 19.19

The X is your clue that you lose the field from the PivotTable if you drop it.

1 "Remove field" mouse pointer symbol

Changing PivotTable Calculations

Although SUM is the most common calculation used in data summaries, you can change the calculation in a PivotTable field to any of several functions, including AVERAGE, MIN, MAX, COUNT, and others.

Change the calculation function for a field

1. Click a field or data cell for the field in which you want to change the function.
2. On the PivotTable toolbar, click the **PivotTable Field** button.

   The PivotTable Field dialog box appears (shown in Figure 19.20).
3. In the **Summarize by** list, click the function you want.

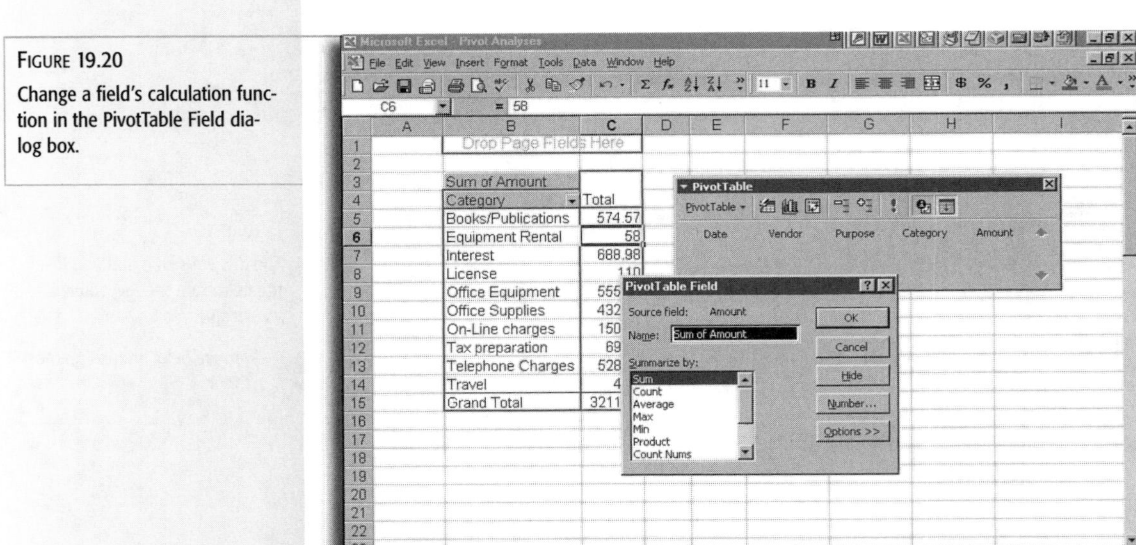

FIGURE 19.20
Change a field's calculation function in the PivotTable Field dialog box.

4. Click **OK**.

   In Figure 19.21, I've changed the Amount calculation to AVERAGE. The numbers still need to be formatted, however, to be displayed as dollar amounts.

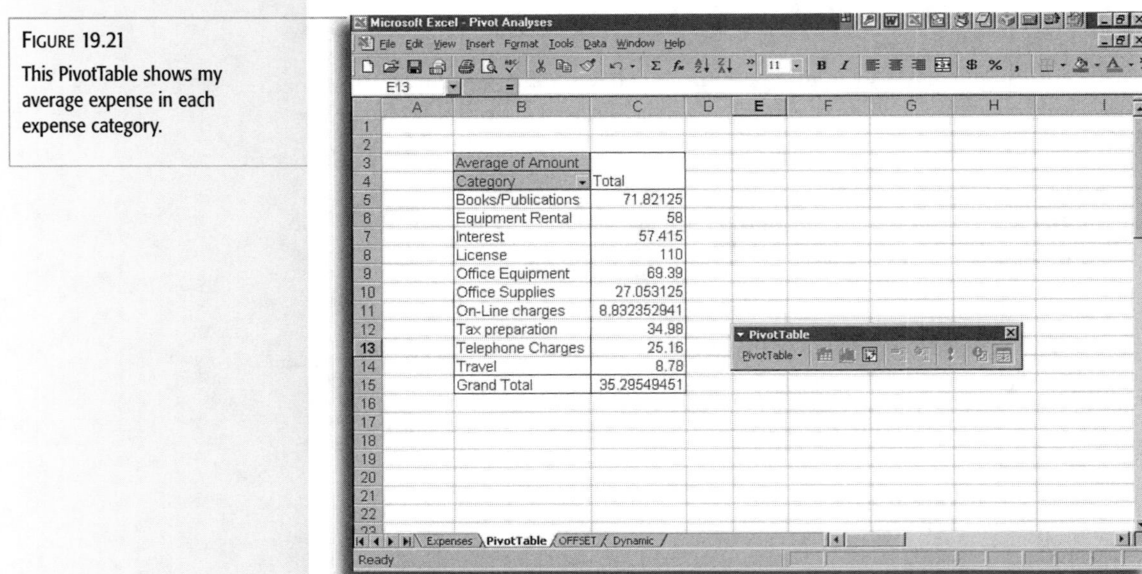

FIGURE 19.21
This PivotTable shows my average expense in each expense category.

Showing Underlying Details

I want to know what individual expenses make up the Books/Publications average shown in Figure 19.21.

To display the source data underlying a data cell in the PivotTable, double-click the data cell for which you want to see source data.

To show underlying data for the Books/Publications average in Figure 19.21, double-click its data cell in the Total column. This is called drilling down for the source data. A new worksheet is created (shown in Figure 19.22) with a table that shows all the source table entries that were calculated to produce the Books/Publications average.

Turn the Drilldown On or Off

Drilldown capability is on by default, but if you want to prevent readers of your workbook from drilling down to find the details, you can turn it off. Right-click the **PivotTable**, click **Table Options**, clear the **Enable** drilldown check box, and click **OK**.

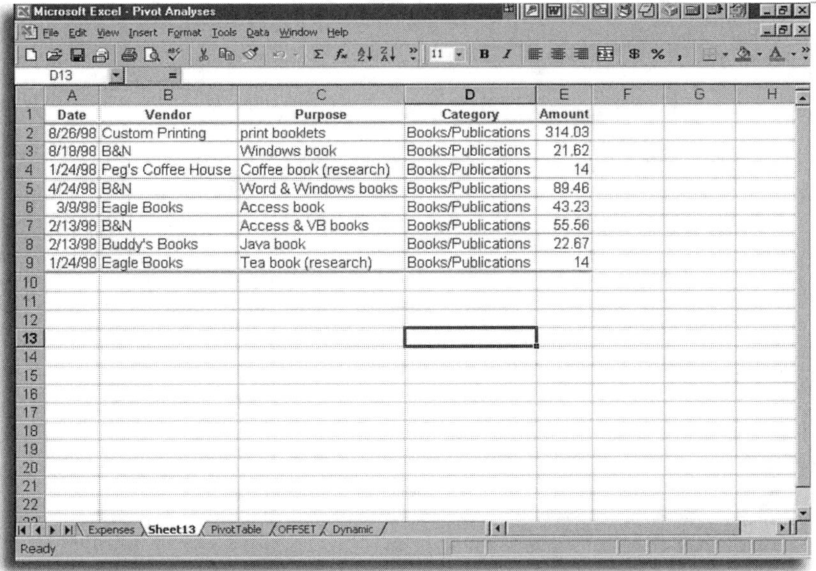

Date	Vendor	Purpose	Category	Amount
8/26/98	Custom Printing	print booklets	Books/Publications	314.03
8/18/98	B&N	Windows book	Books/Publications	21.62
1/24/98	Peg's Coffee House	Coffee book (research)	Books/Publications	14
4/24/98	B&N	Word & Windows books	Books/Publications	89.46
3/9/98	Eagle Books	Access book	Books/Publications	43.23
2/13/98	B&N	Access & VB books	Books/Publications	55.56
2/13/98	Buddy's Books	Java book	Books/Publications	22.67
1/24/98	Eagle Books	Tea book (research)	Books/Publications	14

FIGURE 19.22
The new worksheet table displays source data for the PivotTable cell I drilled down.

Formatting a PivotTable

PivotTables are candidates for formatting just like other worksheet tables. You can format

- Number display
- Cell and font color
- Field labels to display different text

Wasn't Formatting Previously More Work?

In versions of Excel earlier than Excel 97, number formatting was a longer procedure, but now, it's as easy as formatting worksheet tables. If you find that formatting disappears when you refresh a PivotTable, you need to activate the Preserve Formatting option: Right-click the PivotTable, click **Table Options**, click the **Preserve formatting** check box, and then click **OK**.

Formatting Numbers

The easiest way to format numbers in a PivotTable is the same way you format them in a worksheet table.

Format numbers in a PivotTable

1. Select the data cells you want to format.
2. On the **Format** menu, click **Cells**.
3. In the Format Cells dialog box, click the **Number** tab.
4. Set the Number formatting you want, and click **OK**.

   The PivotTable in Figure 19.23 looks a lot better now that it's formatted in a currency number format.

FIGURE 19.23
The Currency format is appropriate for my amount field.

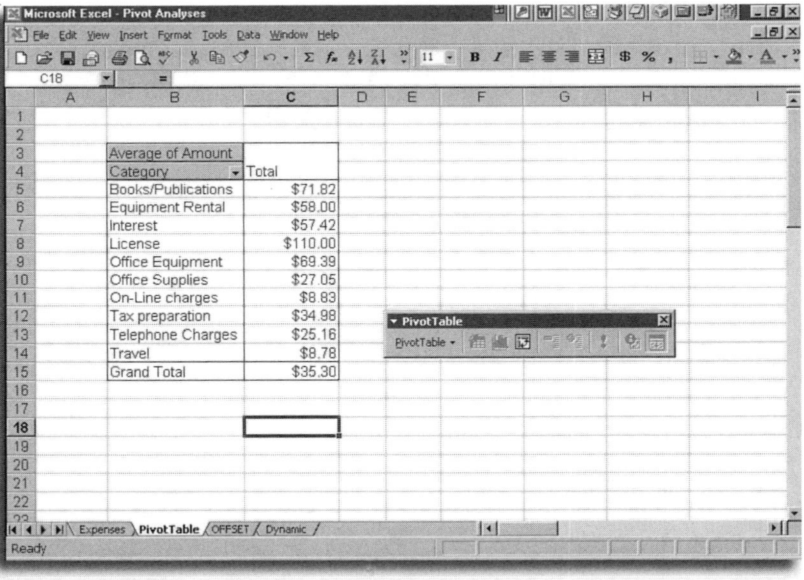
Microsoft Excel - Pivot Analyses
File Edit View Insert Format Tools Data Window Help
C18
Average of Amount
Category
Total
Books/Publications $71.82
Equipment Rental $58.00
Interest $57.42
License $110.00
Office Equipment $69.39
Office Supplies $27.05
On-Line charges $8.83
Tax preparation $34.98
Telephone Charges $25.16
Travel $8.78
Grand Total $35.30
PivotTable
Expenses PivotTable OFFSET Dynamic
Ready

There's a Currency Button on the Formatting Toolbar

The Currency button on the Formatting toolbar is faster, but it applies a different format. (It actually applies Accounting format, not Currency.) Currency places the dollar signs right next to each number, but Accounting places the dollar signs on the left side of the cell. Try both formats and see which you prefer.

SEE ALSO

➤ *To learn more about formatting numbers, see page 243.*

Formatting Tables

You can format PivotTables using the same techniques as for worksheet tables, but AutoFormat works especially well for PivotTables.

AutoFormat a PivotTable

1. Click any cell in the PivotTable.
2. On the **Format** menu, select **AutoFormat**.
3. Click a format in the Format preview area.
4. Click **OK**.

   The PivotTable in Figure 19.24 is formatted with the Report 9 format. The AutoFormat remains when you change, pivot, or refresh the PivotTable.

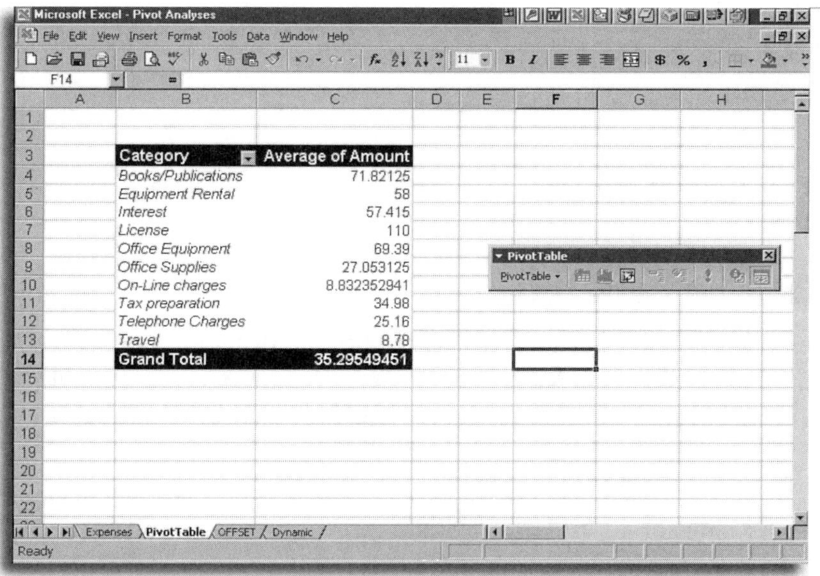

FIGURE 19.24
AutoFormat is a quick, easy way to apply a complete format to a PivotTable.

If the AutoFormat overrides your other formatting (the way it overrode my Currency formatting in Figure 19.24), you must reapply the formatting that the AutoFormat removed.

In Figure 19.25, I reformatted my number cells to Currency.

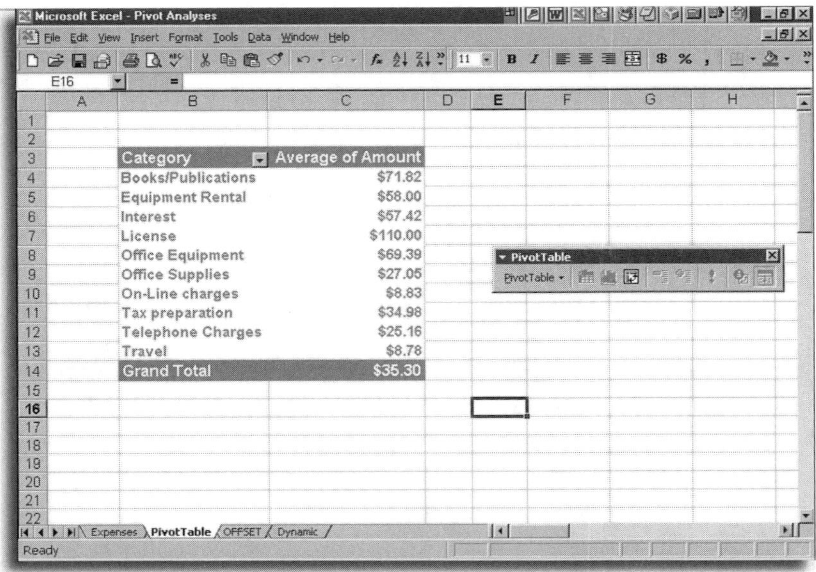

FIGURE 19.25
Reapply any formatting that the AutoFormat removed.

Changing Label Text

Sometimes, a data source has field names that are abbreviated, obscure, or unintelligible to anyone who didn't create the table. Those field names become the field labels in your PivotTable, but you can change the field labels in the PivotTable to display any text you want.

Change field label text

1. Click the field label you want to change.
2. Type the label text you want and press Enter.

The label text changes to your entry (as shown in Figure 19.26).

The Button Isn't Really a Button

The field label looks like a button, but it's really just a cell.

Working with PivotCharts

PivotCharts are a graphical representation of PivotTable data, linked to a PivotTable, and they work just like PivotTables. When you create a PivotChart, Excel creates both a PivotTable and a PivotChart that are linked to each other. The two objects are created on separate pages (the PivotChart is created on a new chart sheet, regardless of where you locate its PivotTable),

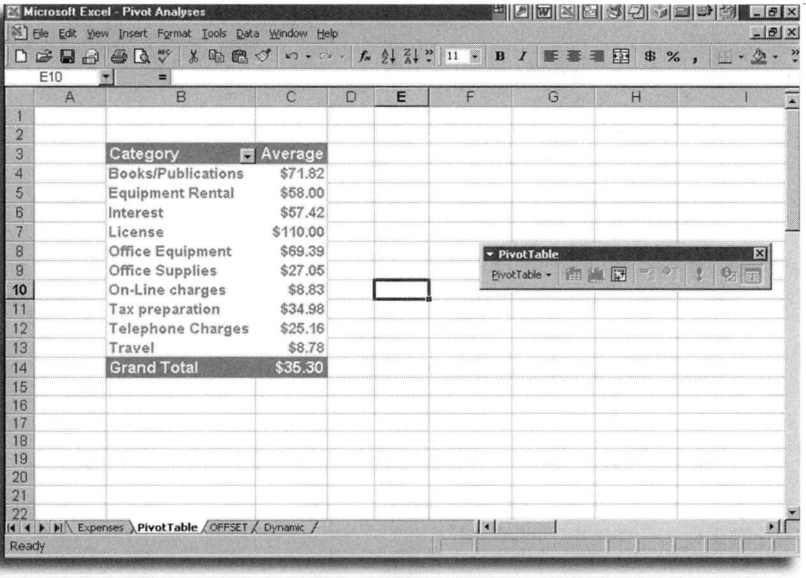

FIGURE 19.26
I changed the label Average of Amount (see Figure 19.25) to Average.

and they mirror one another. Any rearrangement (pivoting) you do in one is copied in the other.

In a PivotChart, you can

- Pivot the chart by dragging field buttons to new locations.
- Change data calculation by double-clicking the data field button and choosing a new function.
- Show or hide categories of data by clicking field buttons in the page, column, and row areas.
- Pivot the PivotChart by pivoting its linked PivotTable.

PivotCharts Versus Normal Charts

PivotCharts and normal charts are similar in many ways but different in little ways that can be annoying if you don't expect them. For example, some things you can do in normal charts that you can't do in PivotCharts are

- Move or resize chart titles.
- Move or resize the plot area by dragging.

- Change values by resizing a data marker.
- Reposition the legend by dragging.
- Move the PivotChart to a different workbook from the workbook of the linked PivotTable. (It becomes a static chart, unlinked to the data.)
- Create the PivotChart as an embedded chart object on an existing worksheet. (You can move it to an existing worksheet after it's created, but it's always created as a new chart sheet.)

PivotCharts use the same terminology that you find in PivotTables: field buttons; row, column, and page fields; and data area. They also use standard chart terminology: value and category axes, data markers, legends, and so forth. PivotCharts are a combination of PivotTable and normal chart, and are quite useful if you don't have your heart set on resizing or repositioning chart elements.

SEE ALSO

➤ *To learn more about creating normal (non-pivoting) charts, see page 385.*
➤ *To learn more about formatting charts, see page 403.*

Creating PivotCharts

Creating a PivotChart is just like creating a PivotTable. You use the same wizard and layout techniques (unless you create the PivotChart from an existing PivotTable—then you get an instant chart without wizard steps).

Creating a PivotChart from Raw Data

To create a PivotChart from raw detail data, follow the same steps as for creating a PivotTable.

Create a PivotChart from a worksheet table

1. Click in the worksheet source table from which you want to create a PivotTable.
2. On the **Data** menu, click **PivotTable and PivotChart Report**.

   The PivotTable and PivotChart Wizard starts (shown in Figure 19.27).

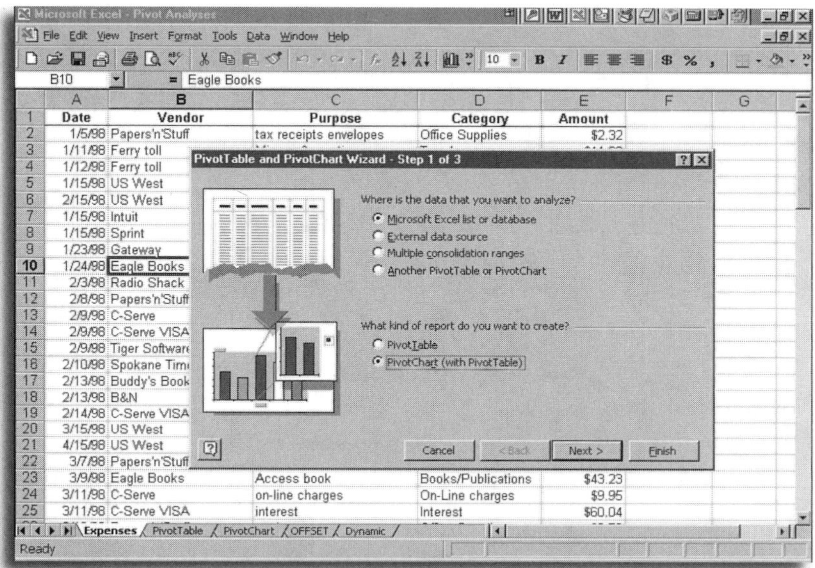

FIGURE 19.27
In the PivotTable and PivotChart Wizard Step 1, click the type of source data you're using, and click the PivotChart option.

3. In Step 1 of the wizard, click an option for the type of source data (in this case, a **Microsoft Excel list or database**).
4. Click **Next**.

   The Step 2 dialog box appears, and the worksheet table you clicked is defined as the source range. (The worksheet range is outlined with a moving border, as shown in Figure 19.28).
5. If the range is correct, click **Next**.

   If you want to use a named range instead of a range reference, type the name in the **Range** box and click **Next**.

   The wizard Step 3 appears, asking where you want to put the PivotChart's linked PivotTable. The PivotChart will be created on a new chart sheet, but you can locate its linked PivotTable wherever you want it.
6. If you have a worksheet set up to hold the linked PivotTable (as I do in this workbook, named PivotChart), click the **Existing** worksheet option; then, click the sheet tab, and click a cell in the worksheet where you want the upper-left corner of the PivotTable to be located (shown in Figure 19.29).

   If you want Excel to insert a new worksheet for the PivotTable, leave the **New worksheet** option selected.

It's More Efficient to Use the Same Data

If you've already created a PivotTable from the range in the Range box, you're asked whether you want to base the new PivotTable on the existing PivotTable. The best answer usually is **Yes** because your workbook will be smaller and all the PivotTables will be refreshed whenever you refresh one of them. In a second Step 2, you're asked which existing PivotTable you want to use. Click the one you want and then click **Next**.

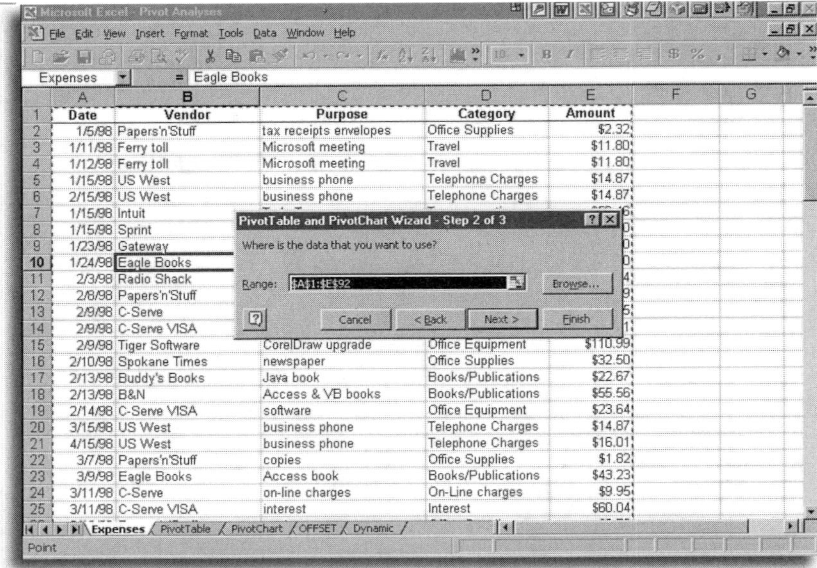

FIGURE 19.28
The range reference in the Range box is outlined with a moving border on the worksheet.

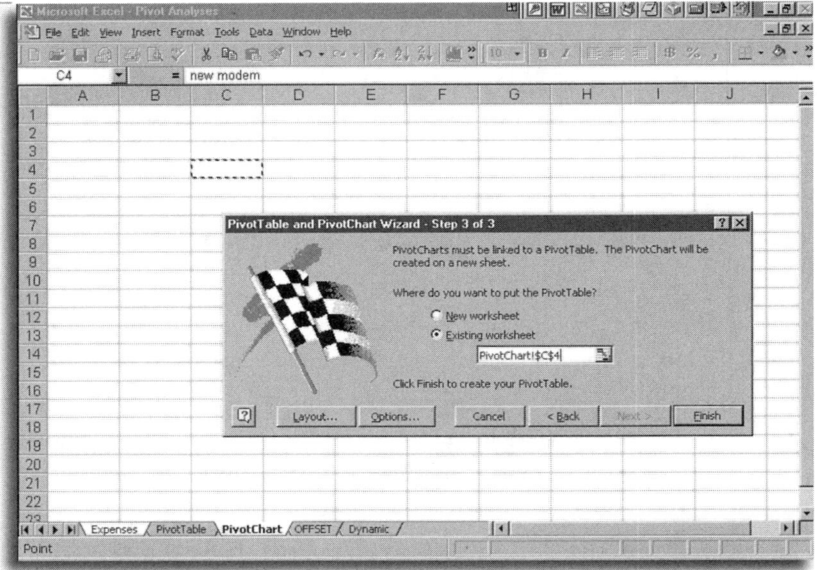

FIGURE 19.29
Tell Excel where to put the PivotChart's linked PivotTable. The PivotChart gets its own new chart sheet.

7. Click **Finish**.

   A new chart sheet appears with the PivotChart structure, as shown in Figure 19.30, and your source data headings appear in the PivotTable toolbar.

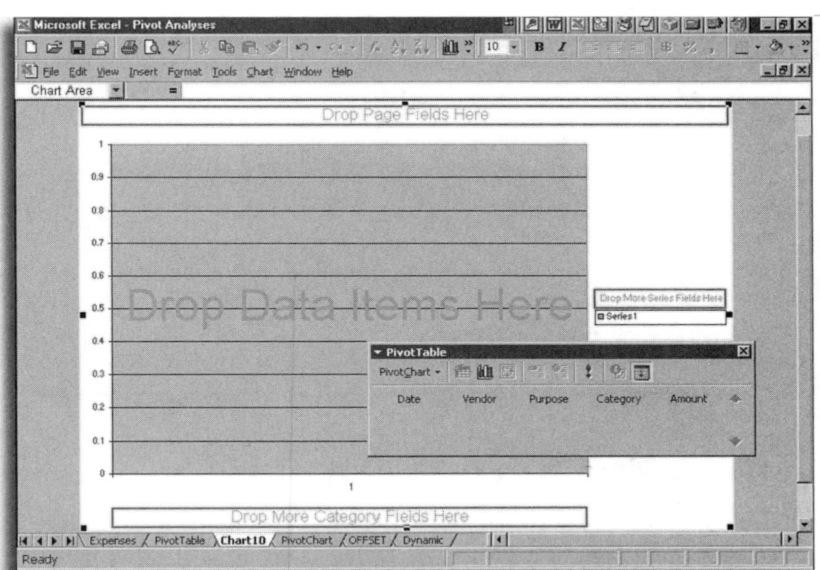

FIGURE 19.30
The new PivotChart structure works just like a new PivotTable structure.

8. Drag the field labels onto the PivotChart areas to lay out the structure of the PivotChart. (Everything you do in the PivotChart will be mimicked in the linked PivotTable.) ScreenTips appear wherever you point the mouse (just like in a normal chart).

   In Figure 19.31, I dragged the Category field button to the bottom of the chart (the category axis) and the Amount field button to the middle of the chart (the column axis).

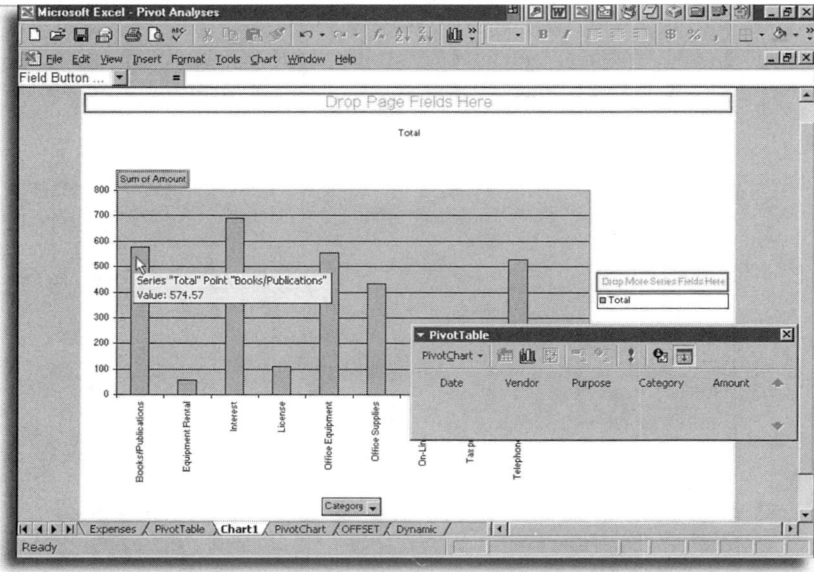

FIGURE 19.31
The default PivotChart is a column chart on a new chart sheet.

Creating a PivotChart from a PivotTable

When you create a chart from a PivotTable, you automatically get a PivotChart.

Create a PivotChart from a PivotTable

1. Click in the PivotTable from which you want to create a PivotChart.
2. On the PivotTable toolbar, click the **Chart Wizard** button (shown in Figure 19.32).

   A new PivotChart appears on a new chart sheet.

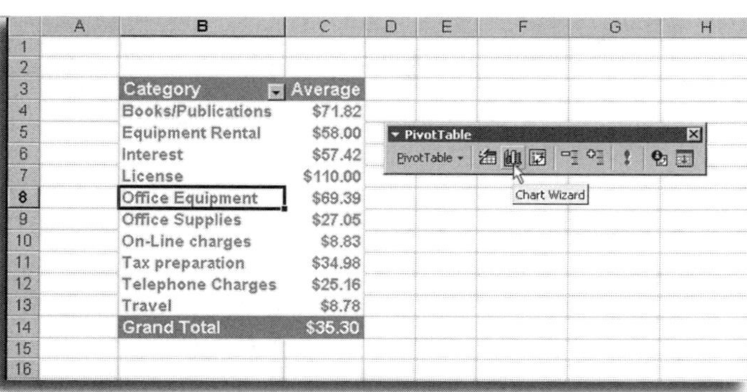

Category	Average
Books/Publications	$71.82
Equipment Rental	$58.00
Interest	$57.42
License	$110.00
Office Equipment	$69.39
Office Supplies	$27.05
On-Line charges	$8.83
Tax preparation	$34.98
Telephone Charges	$25.16
Travel	$8.78
Grand Total	$35.30

FIGURE 19.32
The Chart Wizard creates an instant PivotChart, no questions asked, when you create a chart from a PivotTable.

Creating a Normal Chart from a PivotTable

Because a long list of details makes a messy, incomprehensible chart, you must summarize the details before charting. A PivotTable is an efficient way to summarize them, but in Excel 2000, you can only create a PivotChart from a PivotTable, and you might prefer to create a normal chart instead.

The only way to create a normal chart from data in a PivotTable in Excel 2000 is to copy the data in the PivotTable and paste it as values, unlinked to its underlying details.

Create a normal chart from PivotTable data

1. Select the cells in the PivotTable that you want to chart.

   Select only the data labels and items you want to chart, as shown in Figure 19.33. (Don't select the grand totals or the extra PivotTable field buttons.)

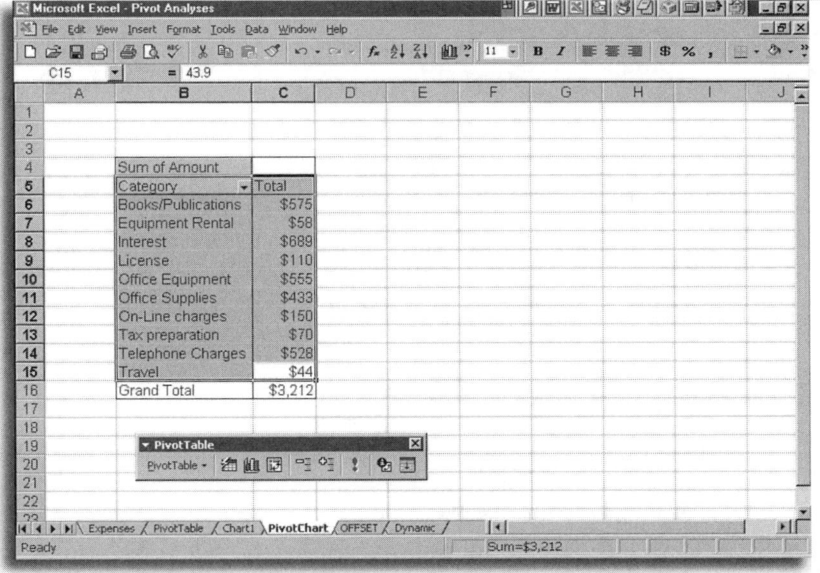

FIGURE 19.33
Don't select grand totals because their values are so large they'll make the chart unreadable.

2. On the toolbar, click **Copy**.
3. Right-click a different cell on the worksheet, and click **Paste Special**.

4. In the Paste Special dialog box, click the **Values** option, then click **OK**.

   The PivotTable values are pasted as an unlinked table (shown in Figure 19.34). You can create a normal chart from this table.

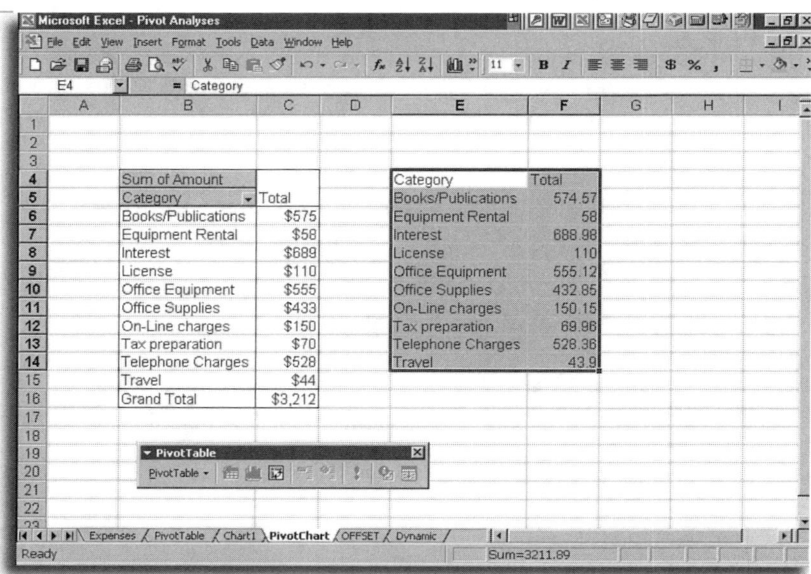

FIGURE 19.34
The PivotTable summarized your data efficiently, and you can create a normal chart from the pasted values.

SEE ALSO

➤ *To learn more about creating normal (non-pivoting) charts, see page 385.*

Rearranging PivotCharts

Because a PivotChart is a graphical version of a PivotTable, you can rearrange the layout of a PivotChart the same way you rearrange the layout of a PivotTable.

Rearrange a PivotChart

- To rearrange the layout, drag the field buttons to different areas on the chart.
- To remove a field, drag the field button off the chart.
- To add a field, drag the field button from the PivotTable toolbar onto the chart.

- To change the calculation function, double-click the data field button (in Figure 19.35, the Sum of Amount button), and select a different function in the PivotTable Field dialog box.
- To hide or show items on the category axis, click the down arrow on the category axis field button (in Figure 19.35, it happens to be named Category), and mark or clear check boxes for the items.

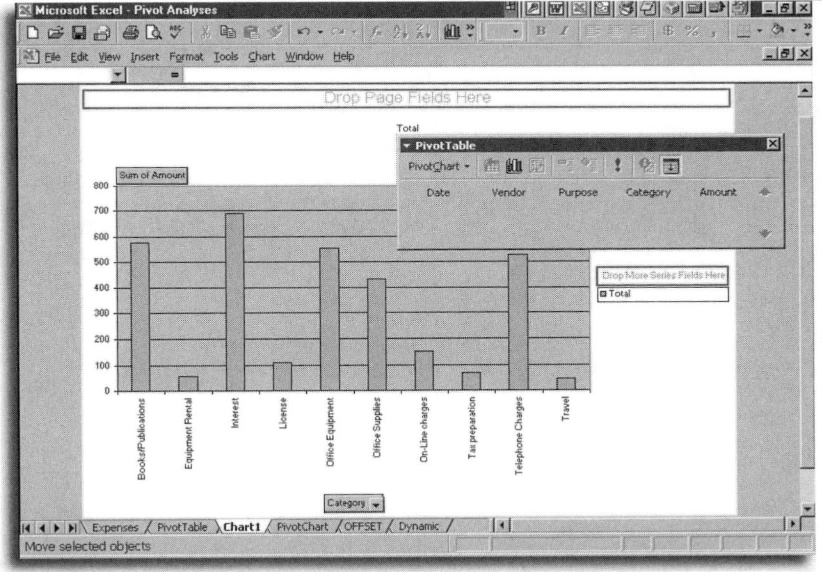

FIGURE 19.35
Rearrange a PivotChart using the same techniques as for a PivotTable.

Formatting PivotCharts

The first thing you might want to do is make the PivotChart look like a normal chart by hiding the layout guides and field buttons.

Hide the layout guides and field buttons

1. Right-click any field button, then click **Hide PivotChart Field Buttons** on the shortcut menu. (You can also find this command on the **PivotChart** menu on the PivotTable toolbar.)

The field buttons and layout guides are hidden, and the chart looks like a normal chart (as shown in Figure 19.36).

2. Close the PivotTable toolbar to get it out of view.

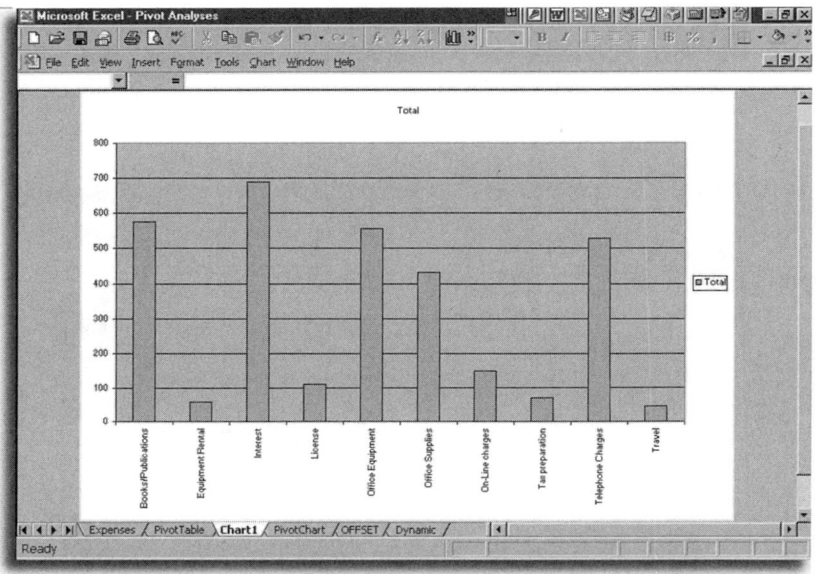

FIGURE 19.36
It looks like a normal chart (but you can't drag the titles around or resize the plot area).

You can rearrange the PivotChart by rearranging its linked PivotTable, or you can rearrange the PivotChart directly by showing its layout guides and field buttons.

Show the layout guides and field buttons

1. Right-click any toolbar and then click **PivotTable** to display the PivotTable toolbar.
2. Click the **PivotChart** menu and then click **Hide PivotChart Field Buttons**.

   The field buttons and layout guides are displayed, and the chart looks like a PivotChart.

SEE ALSO

➤ *To learn more about formatting charts, see page 403.*

Embedding a PivotChart on a Worksheet

If you prefer charts embedded as objects on worksheets, you can move the PivotChart to a worksheet after you create it.

Move a PivotChart to a worksheet

1. Right-click in the chart area or plot area, then click **Location** on the shortcut menu.
2. In the Chart Location dialog box, click the **As object in** option.
3. Select the worksheet name from the drop-down list, as shown in Figure 19.37; then, click **OK**.

How Do I Move It Back to a Chart Sheet?

Repeat the procedure for moving the PivotChart to a worksheet, but click the **As new sheet** option in the Chart Location dialog box.

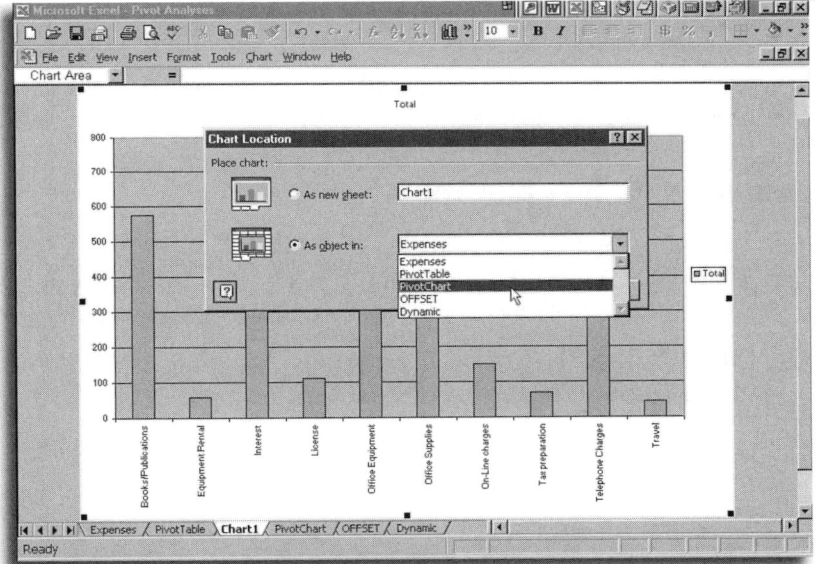

FIGURE 19.37
Choose any worksheet in the workbook.

The PivotChart is moved (not copied) to the worksheet, where it's an embedded chart object (as shown in Figure 19.38).

FIGURE 19.38

It's still a PivotChart, but now, it's a worksheet object.

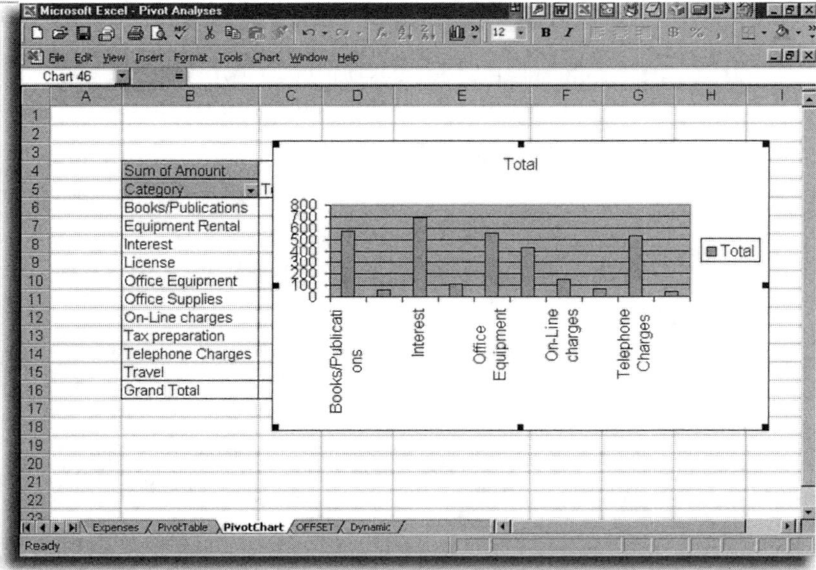

Formatting Colors and Fonts

Changing colors, fonts, chart types, and chart options in a PivotChart is identical to formatting in a normal chart. (Chapter 21, "Formatting a Chart," covers chart formatting in detail.)

SEE ALSO

➤ *To learn more about formatting charts, see page 403.*

PART

V

Charts

20 Creating a Chart 00

21 Formatting a Chart 00

22 Putting Data on a Map 00

CHAPTER

20

Creating a Chart

- Deciding what kind of chart you need
- Creating a chart
- Changing the chart type
- Changing the data displayed in a chart
- Changing a chart's orientation
- Moving and resizing a chart
- Changing a chart's location—on a worksheet or on its own chart sheet

Is a Chart the Same Thing as a Graph?

Yes, it's the same thing. The term *graph* is commonly used for graphically displayed data because charts used to be hand-drawn on graph paper, but in Excel, you only see the term *chart*.

Too Many Steps in the Wizard?

Want to create a chart really fast? Select your data, click the **Chart Wizard** button on the toolbar, and click **Finish** in Step 1 of the Chart Wizard.

What Are Custom Chart Types?

Excel's Custom chart types consist mostly of interesting formatting (except for user-defined types, where you save your own custom chart formats). Play with the custom formats, and see whether they display your data in a way that makes sense.

Creating a Chart with the Chart Wizard

A lot of folks are visually oriented and grasp data and comparisons more easily when it's presented graphically rather than as a bunch of numbers.

Excel's Chart Wizard guides you through the process of creating charts. If you change your mind about the chart after you finish it, you can change and reformat any part of it.

Creating a chart in Excel is a quick procedure: You select the data you want to chart, and then let the Chart Wizard help you build the chart. You have a multitude of choices available in the Chart Wizard, but any choice you make is easy to change after the chart is finished.

Chart your data

1. Select the data you want to include in your chart.
   - Drag to select a rectangular range of data, including any row and column labels that you want to appear in the chart.
   - Press the Ctrl key to select nonadjacent rows or columns.
   - Don't include grand totals in your data selection; they make the chart hard to read.
2. On the Standard toolbar, click **Chart Wizard.**

   The Chart Wizard starts (shown in Figure 20.1). Click the chart type and chart subtype you want. Click the **Custom Types** tab to use built-in or user-defined Custom chart types. (You can learn more about the different chart types in the next section, "Types of Charts.")

   To decide which chart type you want, you can preview your data in different types. Select a type (and subtype) and then click the **Press and Hold to View Sample** button. Your selection isn't permanent; if you later decide to change the chart type, it's easy. (See the section "Changing the Chart Type" later in this chapter.)
3. Click **Next**.

   Step 2 of the Chart Wizard appears (shown in Figure 20.2).

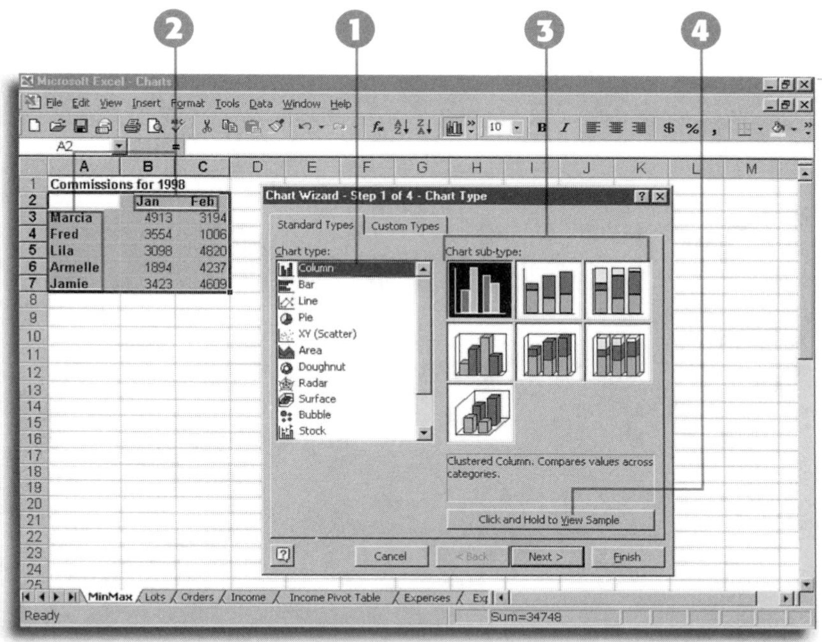

FIGURE 20.1

In Step 1 of the Chart Wizard, pick a chart type (and a different subtype if you want one).

1. Chart types
2. Include labels in data selection.
3. Chart subtypes
4. Click to preview your data.

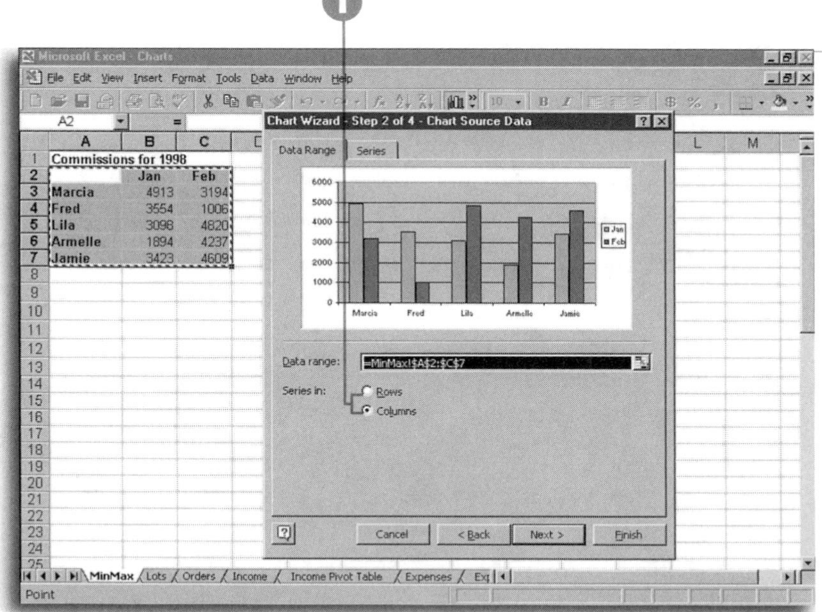

FIGURE 20.2

Click each Series in option button, look at the preview, and then use the option that shows your data in the orientation you want.

1. Pick an orientation.

4. Click the data orientation you want—**Rows** or **Columns**—and click **Next**.

   Step 3 of the Chart Wizard appears (shown in Figure 20.3).

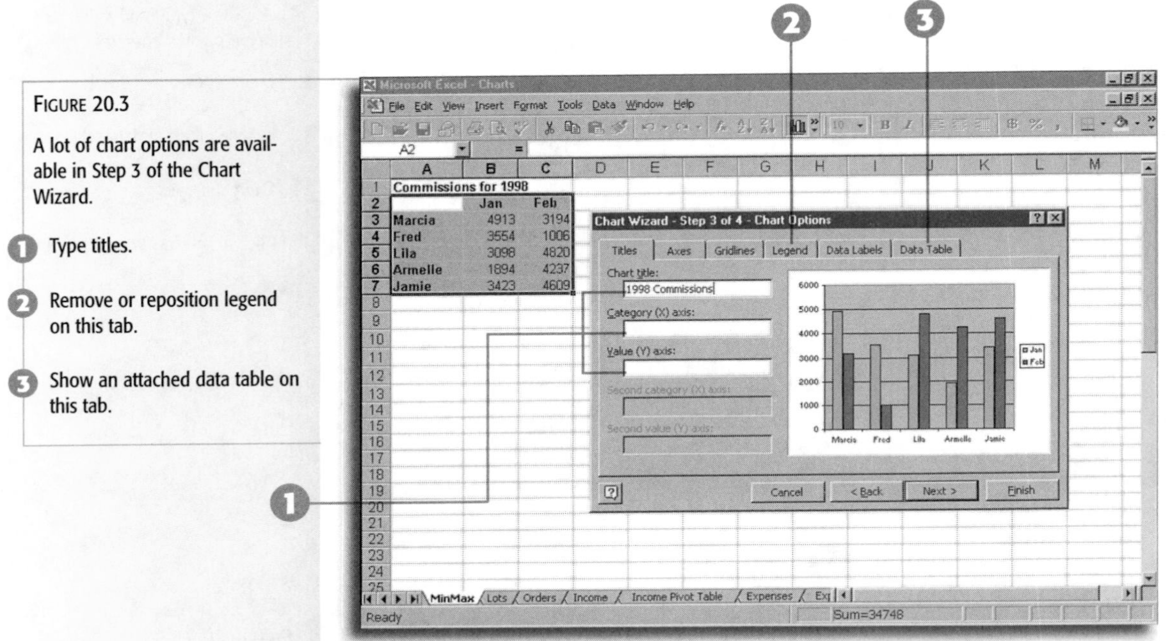

FIGURE 20.3

A lot of chart options are available in Step 3 of the Chart Wizard.

1. Type titles.
2. Remove or reposition legend on this tab.
3. Show an attached data table on this tab.

5. Set the chart options you want (such as chart titles, gridlines, and a legend) and click **Next**.

   Step 4 of the Chart Wizard appears (shown in Figure 20.4).

6. Click an option to create the chart as an object in the worksheet (as shown in Figure 20.5) or on a separate chart sheet, and click **Finish**.

   If you change the data in the worksheet, the chart updates automatically to reflect the changed data.

That's all there is to creating a chart. The real fun and magic happen when you format the chart, which is covered in Chapter 21, "Formatting a Chart." Some of the formatting changes I would make in the chart in Figure 20.5 follow: Change the number format on the y axis to currency, make the chart object larger, and change the colors in the chart.

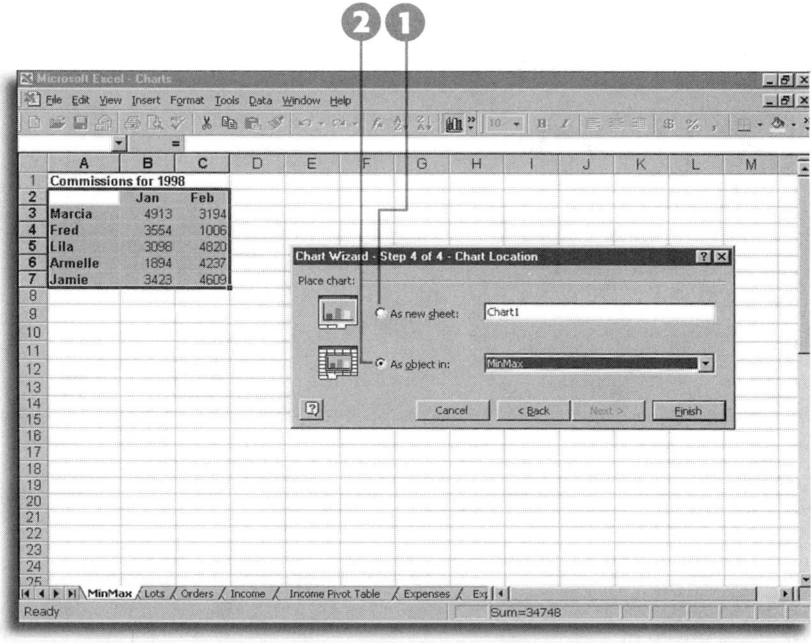

FIGURE 20.4
A chart sheet is a separate sheet in the workbook, like a worksheet that contains only a full-size chart.

1. Create chart sheet.
2. Create chart object on worksheet.

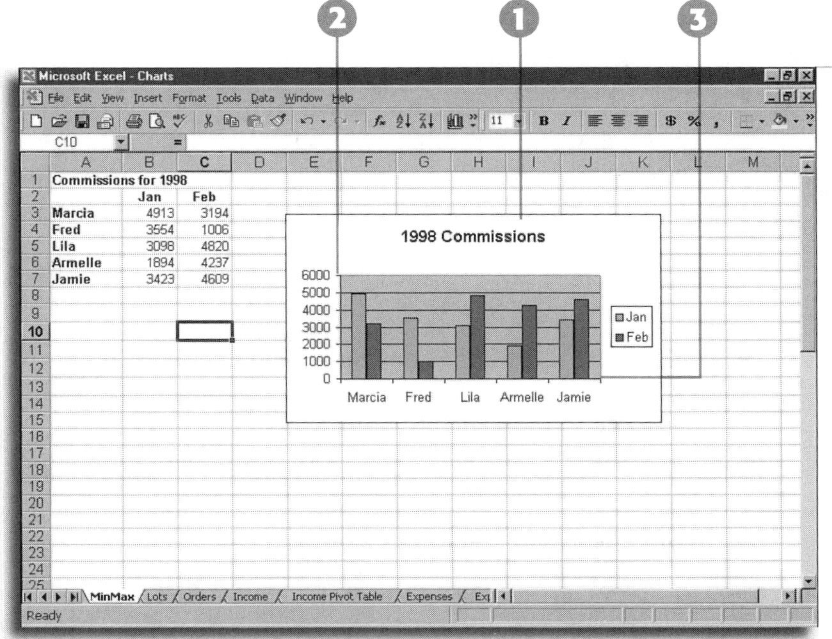

FIGURE 20.5
This chart is a chart object on the worksheet.

1. Chart object
2. Y axis
3. X axis

SEE ALSO

➤ *To learn more about formatting charts, see page 403.*

Types of Charts

When you create a chart, the first step is to choose a chart type. Many different types of charts are available, and some may seem unusual because you're not accustomed to seeing them or interpreting the data they present. The key ideas to keep in mind when you choose a chart type follow:

- What kind of data are you charting? Are you showing discrete comparisons between categories of data? Changes over time? Percentages of a whole? Correlations between two numeric values? Three sets of values, which are most easily displayed in a three-dimensional format?
- What kinds of charts is your audience accustomed to seeing and interpreting? If you choose a chart type your audience isn't familiar with, the audience is less likely to understand the data you're presenting.

The following figures show and explain the different kinds of charts you can create in Excel.

Using Different Series Markers in One Chart

To change the chart type of a single series (as I did in the Cylinder-Cone-Pyramid chart in Figure 20.6), right-click the series, click **Chart Type**, click the type you want for the series, and click **OK**.

The charts shown in Figure 20.6 are familiar to most audiences. The Line and Area charts display the same data. They are a good choice for showing changes in values over time because their lines suggest continuity between the data points. The Cylinder, Cone, and Pyramid markers are a 3D twist on the standard rectangular column chart marker.

The Column, Bar, Cylinder, Cone, and Pyramid charts all display the same data and are all good for comparing discrete categories of data at a specific point in time (such as total sales in each department for the month of January).

When you want to show how data breaks down into percentages of a total amount (for example, how your expenses budget was spent), the chart types shown in Figure 20.7 work best. The Pie chart is effective but can only display a single series of data. The Doughnut chart is less familiar to most audiences. It does the

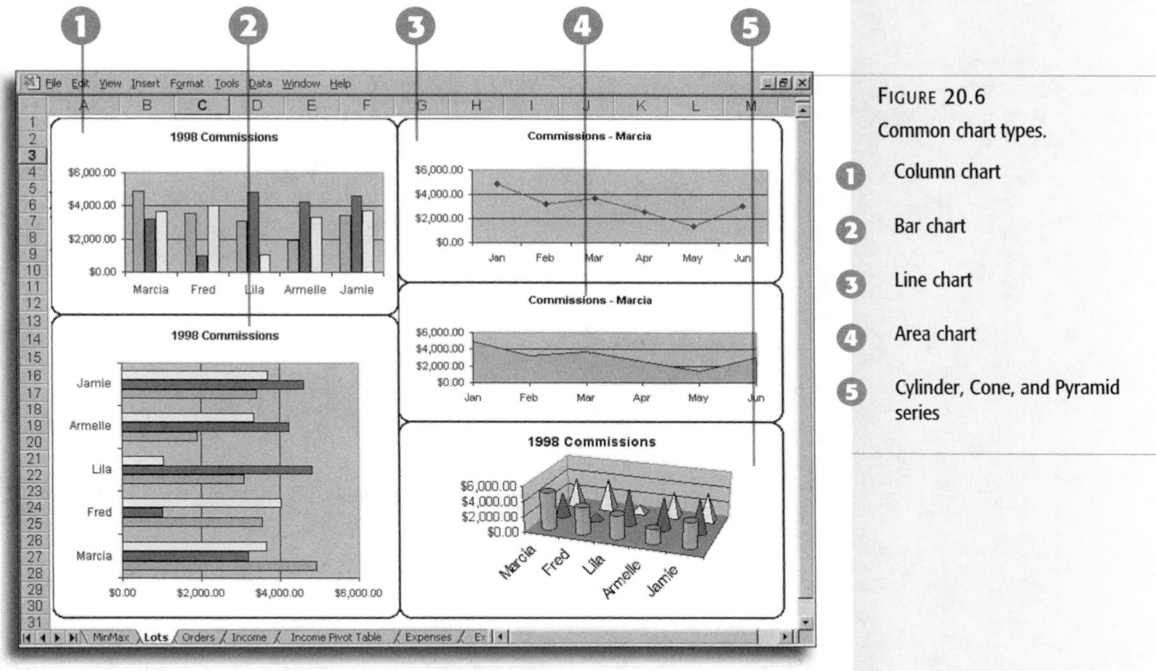

FIGURE 20.6
Common chart types.

1. Column chart
2. Bar chart
3. Line chart
4. Area chart
5. Cylinder, Cone, and Pyramid series

same job as the Pie chart, but for two or three series. If you want to compare percentages of a whole for more than two or three series, your best bet is the 100% Stacked Column chart. In any of these charts, however, your chart has more impact if you limit each series to a half-dozen data points.

For keeping track of investment performance, Excel has several versions of the Stock chart that you see in financial reports. (Two of them are shown in Figure 20.8.) The important thing to remember about creating a Stock chart is that the data source you want to chart must be laid out in the same order as the name of the chart. For example, the data for the Volume-Open-High-Low-Close chart is organized in the source table in this order: Date, Volume, Open, High, Low, Close.

The charts shown in Figure 20.9 have fairly specific applications, and they are all best used when your audience is familiar with the chart type. For example, Radar charts are not seen much in North America, and those audiences are usually baffled by the presentation.

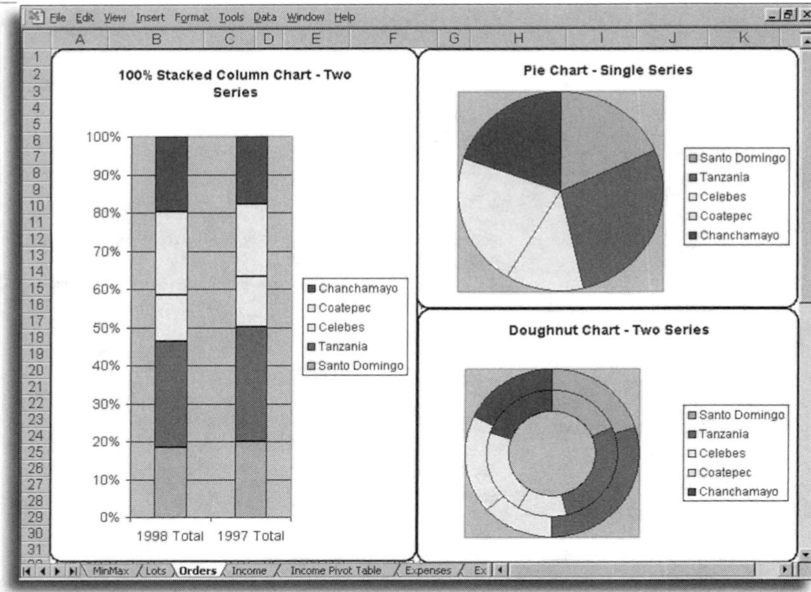

FIGURE 20.7

Pie charts, Doughnut charts, and the 100% Stacked subtype of the Column chart are all good for displaying percentages.

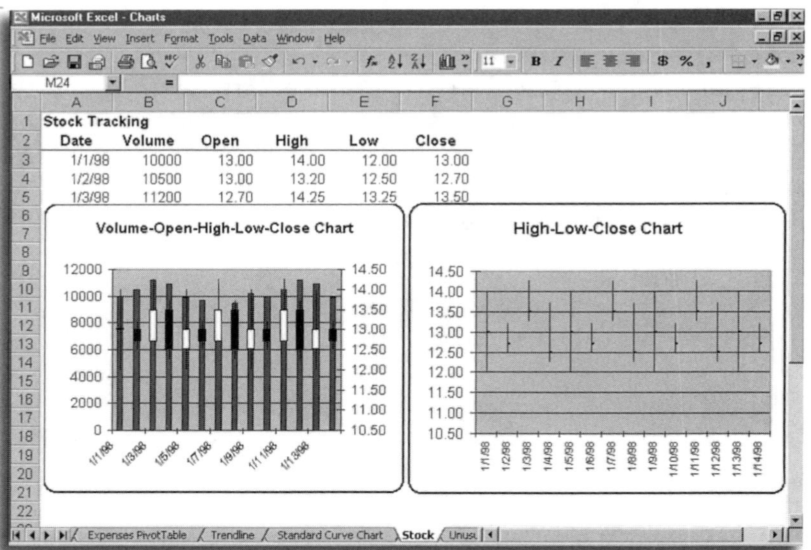

FIGURE 20.8

Stock charts are ideal for tracking the performance of stocks and futures prices.

XY scatter charts are common in scientific applications where two values are correlated, such as the height and weight of individuals in a test population. Bubble and Surface charts both give three-dimensional representations of three sets of data: The Surface chart shows an x axis, a y axis, and a z axis and can give an audience a feel for the data after they become familiar with the Surface chart type. In the Bubble chart, the size of each bubble point represents the z axis value for the point.

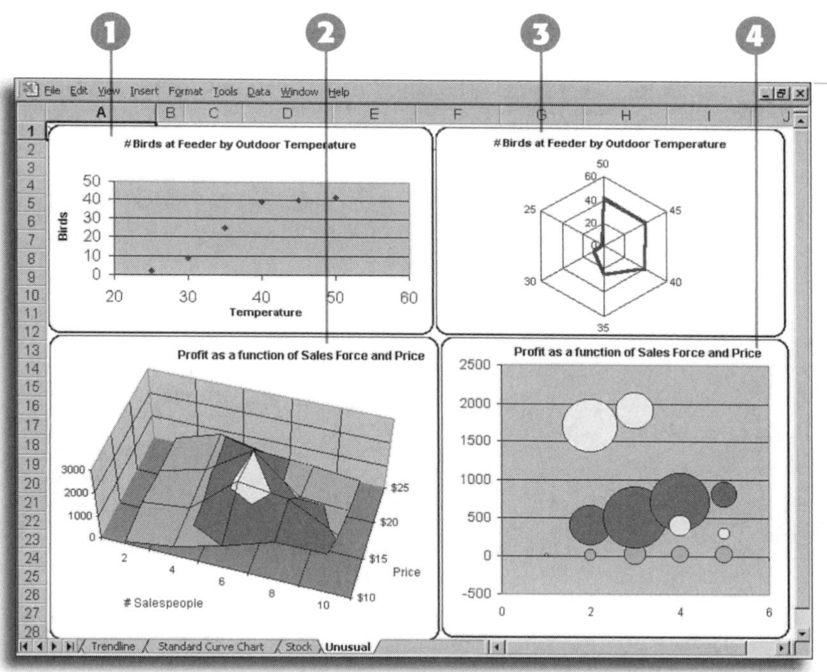

FIGURE 20.9

XY charts are common in scientific applications; Bubble, Radar, and Surface charts are unusual.

1. XY (scatter) chart
2. Surface chart
3. Radar chart
4. Bubble chart

SEE ALSO

➤ *To learn more about formatting chart lines, colors, and fonts, see page 404.*

Which Chart Element Is Which?

If you hold your mouse pointer over any chart element, a ChartTip appears with the name of the element and other information, depending on what's selected in the chart.

My Chart Toolbar Isn't Automatic

To open the Chart toolbar and return it to automatic behavior, click a chart object (to activate it), right-click any toolbar, and click **Chart**. The Chart toolbar appears when you click a chart object and disappears when you click the worksheet.

The Chart Toolbar

The Chart toolbar appears automatically whenever a chart object is active (that is, when you click a chart object), unless you close the toolbar to get it out of your way. After you've closed the Chart toolbar, you need to open it again to return its automatic behavior. (The Chart toolbar is shown in Figure 20.10, and Table 20.1 explains each button on the toolbar.)

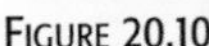

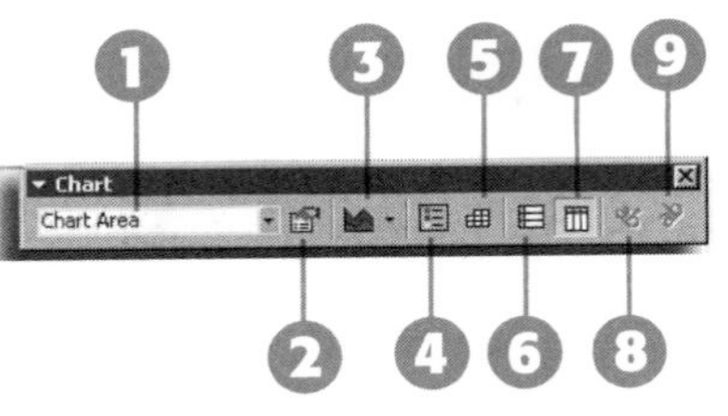

FIGURE 20.10

The buttons on the Chart toolbar help you make some common changes to your chart quickly.

1. Chart Objects
2. Format Object
3. Chart Type
4. Legend
5. Data Table
6. By Row
7. By Column
8. Angle Text Downward
9. Angle Text Upward

TABLE 20.1 Buttons on the Chart toolbar

Icon	Name	Purpose
Chart Area	Chart Objects	A list of all chart elements. To select a specific element, drop the list and click the element name.
	Format Selected Object	Opens a Formatting dialog box for the selected chart element.
	Chart Type	Opens a palette of chart types. To float the palette, drag its title bar away from the toolbar.
	Legend	Click to remove or replace the chart legend. When you remove the legend, the plot area resizes to fill the chart.
	Data Table	Click to add or remove a data table at the bottom of the chart.
	By Row	Changes orientation to put rows along the x axis.
	By Column	Changes orientation to put columns along the x axis.
	Angle Text Downward	Angles labels along selected axis to read from the upper left to the lower right.
	Angle Text Upward	Angles labels along selected axis to read from the lower left to the upper right.

Changing the Chart Type

After you've created a chart, you may decide that a different chart type would display your data better.

Change the chart type

1. Click the chart to select it.

2. On the **Chart** menu, click **Chart Type**.

   The Chart Type dialog box appears. (It's identical to the Step 1 dialog box shown in Figure 20.1.)

3. Select a chart type (and a different subtype if you want one).

4. Click **OK**.

   The chart type changes.

Changing Chart Data

Charts update automatically when the values in source ranges change, but if you add rows and columns of data to a source range, charts don't always automatically include the new rows and columns.

You have two easy ways to change the source range, depending on what kind of change you want to make:

- To add more rows or columns to the existing source range, drag the data border.
- To switch to a different source range, use the Chart Wizard.

Both techniques are shown in the following sections.

Adding More Data to a Source Range

In Figure 20.11, I've got a chart for three months of data. I added another month of data to the source range and need to add the new data to the chart.

SEE ALSO

➤ *To learn about using the OFFSET and COUNTA functions, see page 352.*

Add more data to an existing source range

1. Click near the chart perimeter to select the chart area.

   When the chart area is selected, the Name box reads `Chart Area` and handles appear around the chart border.

   When you select the chart area, colored borders appear around the source data range (shown in Figure 20.12).

Change Chart Type Quickly

For a quick but limited selection of chart types, click the down arrow on the **Chart Type** button on the Chart toolbar, and then click a chart type button. To switch between chart types rapidly, you can drag the chart type palette away from the toolbar and use it as a floating palette.

How Can I Change Just One Series?

To change the chart type of a single series (for example, to create a line series in a column chart), click a marker in the series that you want to change and select a chart type for the series.

Source Ranges That Adjust Automatically

You can use a named formula to define a *dynamic* source range that always includes any rows or columns you add to the data table. Create a named formula to define the source range, and type the formula name in the **Data** range box in Step 2 of the Chart Wizard.

FIGURE 20.11

I need to add the April data to the chart.

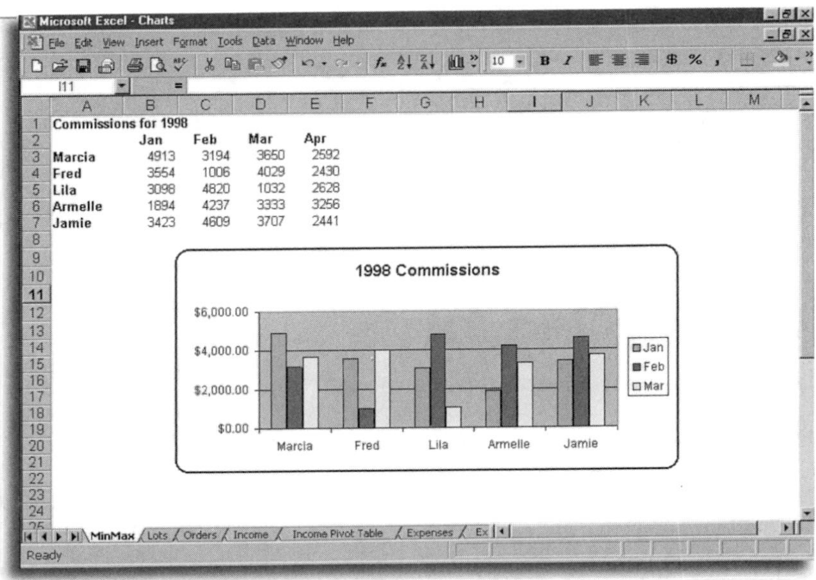

FIGURE 20.12

The source data in the chart is surrounded by colored borders.

1. Source data range borders
2. Drag fill handle

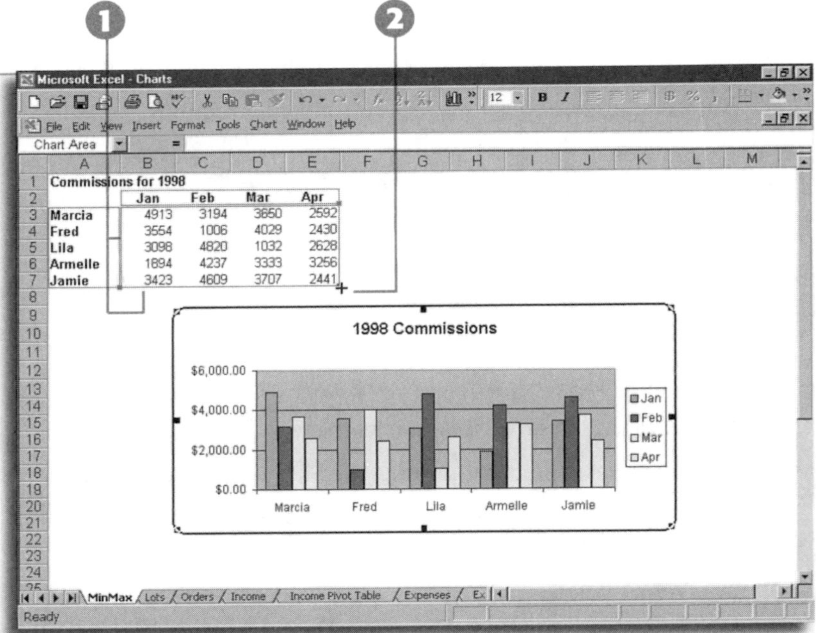

2. Drag the Fill handle on the colored source range borders to increase or decrease the source data range.

   When you release the Fill handle, all the data within the colored borders is included in the chart.

Changing the Data Source Range

If you've created a great chart, using the Chart Wizard is the easiest way to switch the data it displays to a different source range, either on the same worksheet or on another worksheet.

Change the data source range

1. Click the chart to select it.
2. Click the **Chart Wizard** button on the Standard toolbar.

   Step 1 of the Chart Wizard appears.
3. Click the **Next** button.
4. In Step 2 of the Chart Wizard, delete the reference in the **Data** range box, and enter a new source range by dragging to select the worksheet range you want.

   If you've named the worksheet range you want, type the range name in the **Data** range box.
5. Click **Finish**.

   The chart's data source is changed.

How Did You Turn Off the Gridlines?

To turn worksheet gridlines on or off, click **Tools** and then click **Options**. On the View tab, mark or clear the **Gridlines** check box.

Changing Chart Orientation

You can select the orientation you want in Step 2 of the Chart Wizard. You can put row labels along the horizontal axis or use column labels on the horizontal axis. When you create a chart, it's a good idea to take advantage of the opportunity to preview each orientation before you move on to the next step in the Chart Wizard.

After you finish the chart, however, you might change your mind about the orientation you chose. Fortunately, it's easy to change.

Change the orientation of an existing chart

1. Click the chart to select it and to display the Chart toolbar.

   If you closed the Chart toolbar earlier, right-click any toolbar and click **Chart** to display it.

2. On the Chart toolbar, click the **By Row or By Column** button.

   - Click the **By Row** button to put row data as data series along the chart's x axis.
   - Click the **By Column** button to put column data as data series along the chart's x axis.

   The chart orientation is switched each time you click the buttons.

Moving and Resizing a Chart

A newly created chart object is unlikely to be the right size or in the right position, but moving and resizing a chart is simple.

Move a chart

1. Click the chart near its perimeter so that the chart area is selected.

   You can tell the chart area is selected because the name **Chart Area** appears in the worksheet Name box and in the Chart Objects box. Handles appear around the chart border (as shown in Figure 20.13).

2. Drag the chart area to move the chart.

   You can grip the chart anywhere inside the chart area. If you accidentally drag the plot area or another element by mistake, click the **Undo** button on the toolbar and start again.

Use Gridlines for Perfect Alignment

To align the chart with worksheet gridlines, press the Alt key while you drag the chart. Release the Alt key after you release the mouse button to drop the chart.

Resize a chart

1. Click the chart near its perimeter so that the chart area is selected.

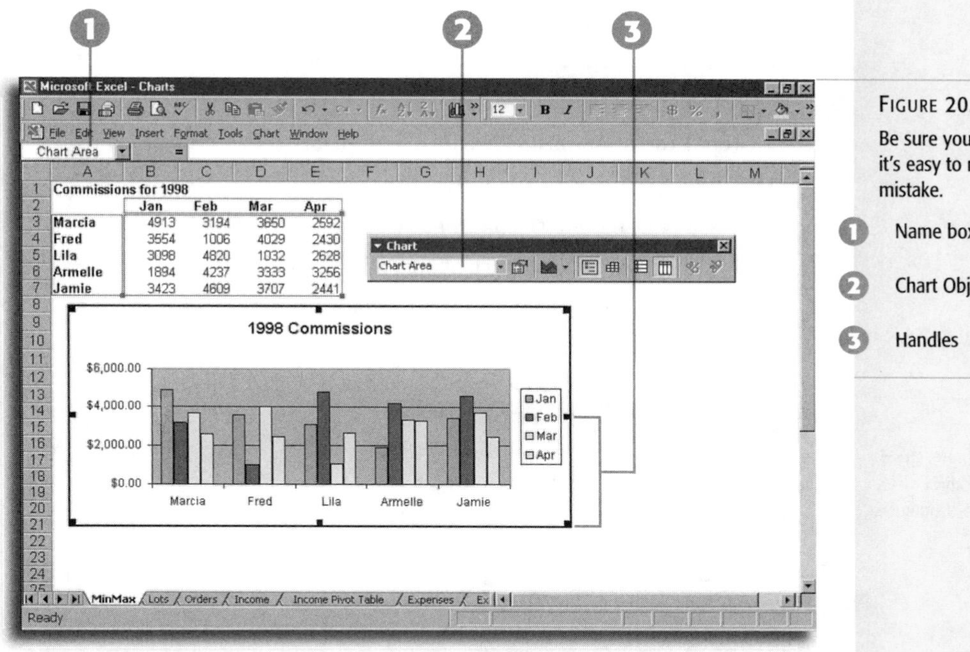

FIGURE 20.13

Be sure you move the chart area; it's easy to move the plot area by mistake.

1. Name box
2. Chart Objects box
3. Handles

2. Drag a chart handle (refer to Figure 20.13) to resize the chart.

   - Hold down the Shift key while you drag a corner handle to resize the chart proportionally. (The chart retains its original height-to-width ratio.)
   - Hold down the Ctrl key while you drag any handle to resize a chart symmetrically. (Both sides or top and bottom move in or out the same distance.)
   - Hold down the Alt key while you drag any handle to align the border with the worksheet gridlines.

Changing the Chart Location

You can easily move a chart from a worksheet to its own sheet in a workbook or from its own sheet onto a worksheet.

If you want to print a worksheet with a chart object next to the chart data, you need the chart on the worksheet as a chart object.

If you want to display the chart as a full-size sheet so that you can see a lot of details, it's easier to make the chart into a chart sheet.

You can decide where to place the chart when you create it in Step 4 of the Chart Wizard. If you need to change the chart location after you've created it, use the following procedures.

Change a chart object on a worksheet to a chart sheet

1. Right-click the chart object and then click **Location**.
2. In the Chart Location dialog box (shown in Figure 20.14), click the **As new sheet** option.

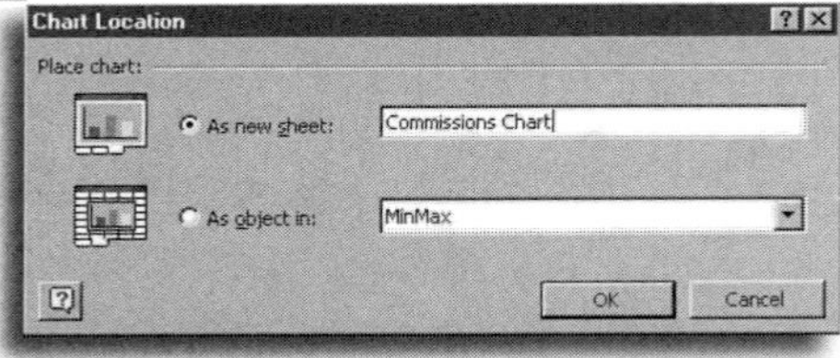

FIGURE 20.14
You can change the chart's sheet name in the Chart Location dialog box or later by double-clicking the sheet tab.

3. Type an appropriate name for the chart sheet (something more meaningful than Chart1).
4. Click **OK**.

   The chart becomes a separate chart sheet in the workbook. This chart in Figure 20.15 was stretched to fill the window by opening **View** and selecting **Sized with Window**. To return it to its original dimensions, click **View** and select **Sized with Window** again.

   If you want to show the data with the chart, click the **Data Table** button on the Chart toolbar. A table of the chart's source data is attached to the bottom of the chart. The data table will probably be as big as the chart itself, but you can click the data table to select it and then use the buttons on the Formatting toolbar to make the font smaller or bold or a different color. Figure 20.16 shows a chart on a chart sheet with a reformatted data table attached.

   To remove the data table, click the **Data Table** button again.

Print Chart and Worksheet Separately

If you want to print either the worksheet or the chart separately, you don't need to move the chart; just set printing options differently.

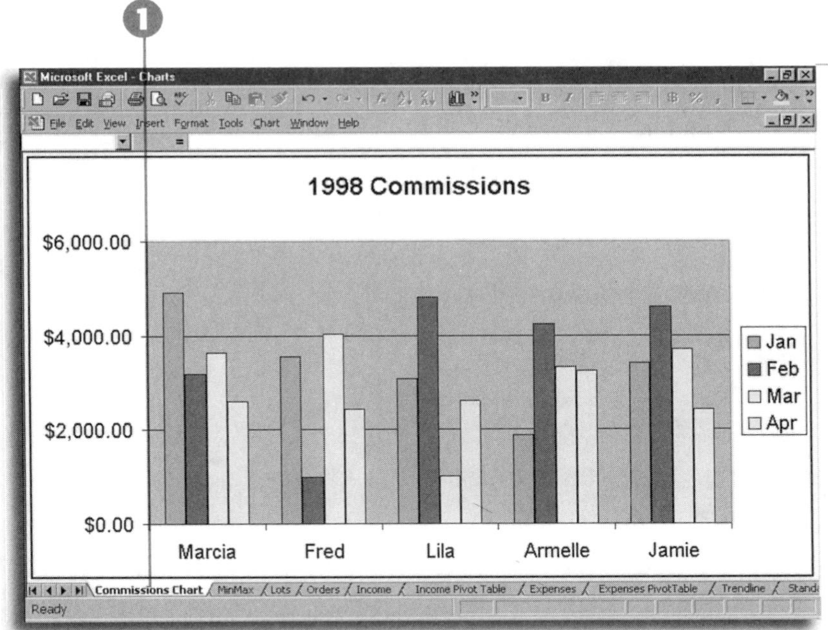

FIGURE 20.15
The chart is a separate chart sheet in the workbook.

1 Renamed sheet tab

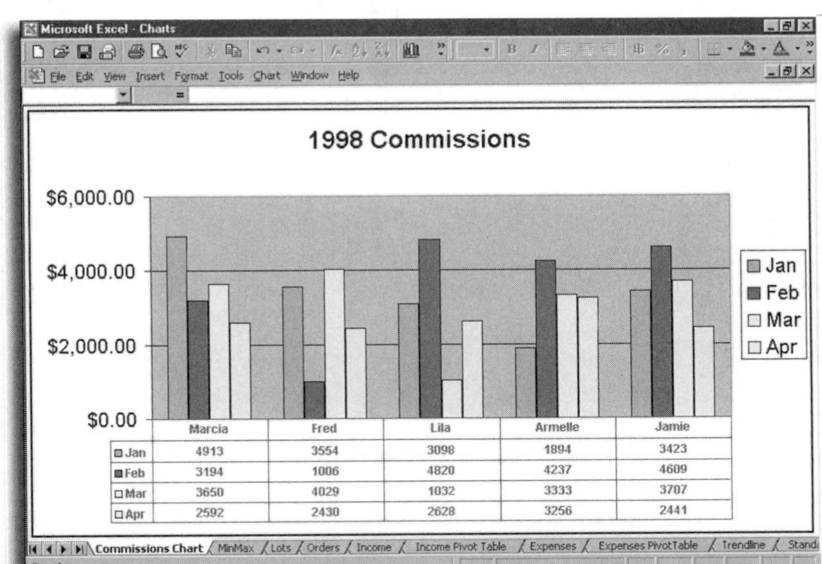

FIGURE 20.16
This chart has a data table attached; the data table was reformatted to make it look neater.

Change a chart sheet to a chart object on a worksheet

1. Right-click the chart area or plot area and click **Location**.
2. In the Chart Location dialog box, click the **As object in** option.
3. In the **As object in** drop-down list box, select the worksheet in which you want to place the chart object (as shown in Figure 20.17).

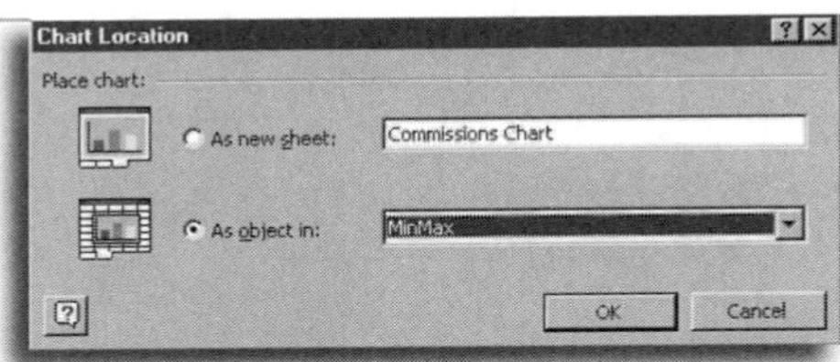

FIGURE 20.17
Pick a worksheet in the active workbook in which you want to place the chart object.

4. Click **OK**.

   The chart becomes an object on the worksheet. It may need reformatting when the size changes; the fastest way to make the font fit the smaller chart size is to select a new Font Size while the chart object is selected (as shown in Figure 20.18).

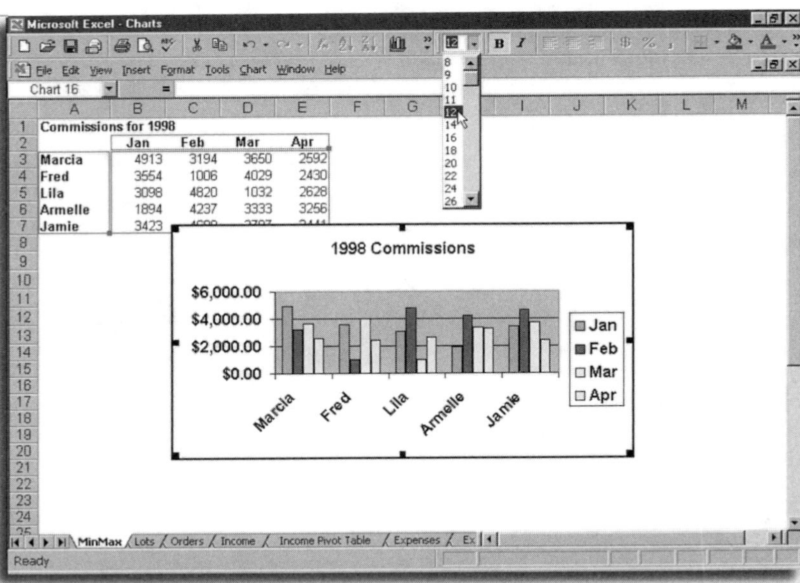

FIGURE 20.18
After you place the chart object in the worksheet, you can move and resize it.

SEE ALSO

➤ *To learn more about printing worksheets and charts, see page 449.*

CHAPTER

21

Formatting a Chart

- Changing colors, lines, and fonts
- Changing the axis scale
- Rearranging the series order
- Rotating, exploding, and resizing a pie chart
- Rotating the perspective in a 3D chart
- Adding a trendline
- Plotting data on a secondary axis
- Adding data markers to show values or labels

Formatting Chart Colors, Lines, and Fonts

Like worksheets, charts can present data in a utilitarian manner, or you can format them to make them look professional, graphically striking, or silly, depending on your audience.

When you first create a chart, you get Excel's default colors, fonts, and so on, and your chart looks like every other chart ever created in Excel 2000. But after you've created a chart, your options for changing the look of the chart are countless.

After you've spent a lot of time formatting a chart, you can save and reuse the entire formatting package for a chart as a custom chart format.

To keep your audience's attention during a presentation, make your charts visually attractive with color, line, and font formatting (as shown in Figure 21.1); to make a presentation involving several charts coherent and professional, give all the charts a uniform look by using the same formatting for all of them.

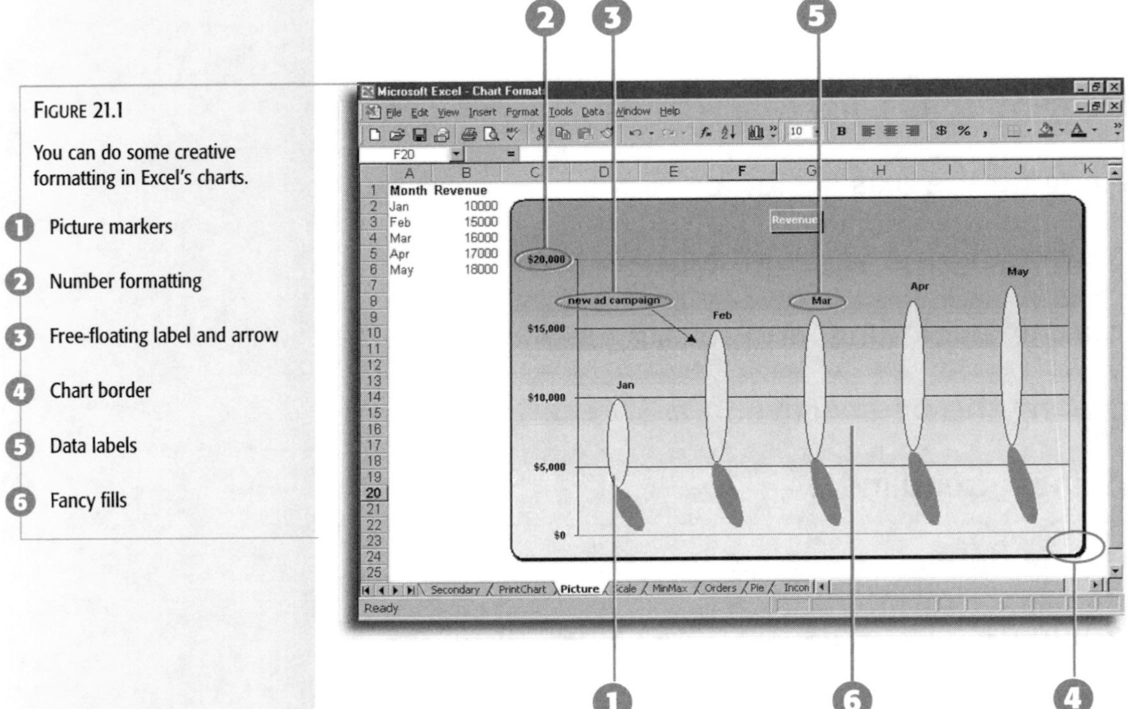

FIGURE 21.1

You can do some creative formatting in Excel's charts.

1. Picture markers
2. Number formatting
3. Free-floating label and arrow
4. Chart border
5. Data labels
6. Fancy fills

To format any element's color, line weight, font, or other characteristics, you select the element and then open the Format dialog box for that element. Sometimes, selecting an element is difficult because the element is small or overlapped by another element, but you can use a few different ways to select the chart element you want to format.

Quick Change Artist

For quick color changes, select the element; then, use the **Fill Color** or **Font Color** button on the Formatting toolbar. The selection is limited compared with what the dialog box offers, but it's much faster.

Change the formatting of chart colors, lines, or fonts

1. Do one of the following to select a chart element for formatting:
   - Click the element.
   - On the Chart toolbar, in the Chart Objects box, click the down arrow; then, click the name on the list.
   - Click any element; then, press the right or left arrow key to cycle through all elements in the chart.
2. Do one of the following to open the Format dialog box for the selected element:
   - Double-click the selected element.
   - On the Chart toolbar, click the **Format** button. (The button name is **Format *element***, depending on which element is selected.)
   - Right-click the selected element; then, click the **Format** command. (The command name is **Format *element***, depending on which element is selected.)
3. In the Format dialog box, select the formatting options you want.
4. Click **OK**.

Deleting a Chart Element

You can delete any element from a chart: individual series, elements you've added (such as a trendline), legend, data table, axes, and gridlines; anything in the chart can be deleted in the interest of showing only what you want to show and nothing else.

Delete a chart element

1. Select the element.
2. Press Delete.

   If you change your mind about a deleted element, click the **Undo** button (on the Standard toolbar) to replace the element.

Changing Axis Scale

Changing the scale of a chart axis can persuade an audience to accept your point of view. For example, suppose OkeyDokey forest has a chemical factory built along one side of it, and there's an argument about whether the factory is making life difficult for the trees in the forest. You've counted the number of trees per acre in four quadrants of the forest, and the counts are all between 100 and 200.

If you want to persuade an audience that there's no important difference between quadrants, you can show the data on a scale that runs 0 to 200 (as shown in Figure 21.2). To persuade the audience there's a big problem in Quad2 (next to the chemical factory), show the data on a narrow scale that runs from just below the minimum data point to just above the maximum data point (as shown in Figure 21.3). The data is valid, and it's perfectly fair to present the data either way, but you can control your audience's perception of the data by changing the scale you use to present it.

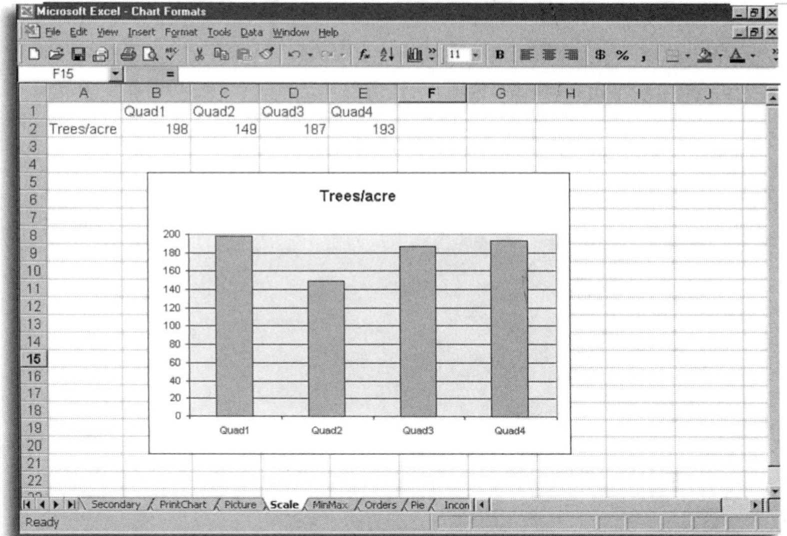

FIGURE 21.2
To persuade an audience that there's little difference in the data, use a large axis scale.

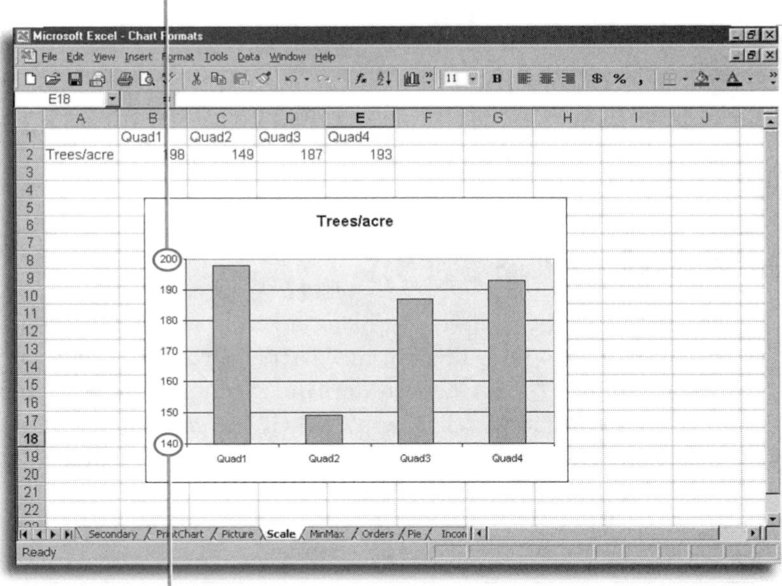

FIGURE 21.3
Use a narrow axis scale to show clear differences between data point values.

1. Minimum
2. Maximum

Change the axis scale in a chart

1. Select the axis.
2. On the Chart toolbar, click the **Format Axis** button.

   The Format Axis dialog box is displayed, as shown in Figure 21.4.

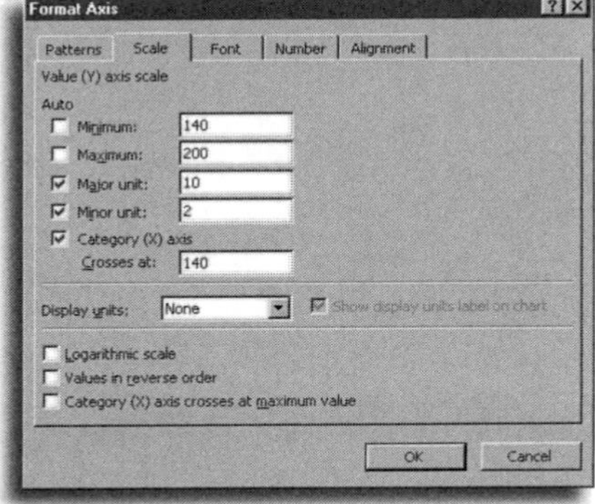

FIGURE 21.4

I've set the axis scale to run from 140 to 200.

3. On the Scale tab, type the maximum number for your custom scale in the **Maximum** box.
4. Type the minimum number you want in the **Minimum** box.
5. Click **OK**.

   The scale on the selected axis is changed.

Reordering the Series

When you create a chart, your data series are plotted in the order that Excel finds them in the chart's source range, but you are not limited to that series order. You might want to rearrange the series order in the chart, especially if you've created a 3D chart, in which a tall series in front can hide shorter markers behind it (as in the chart in Figure 21.5).

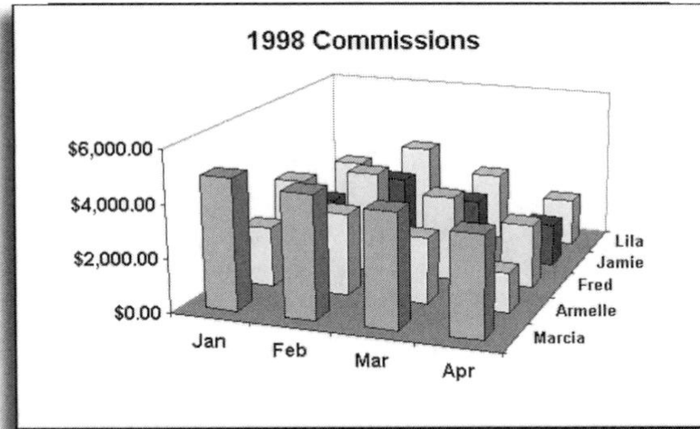

FIGURE 21.5
In this 3D column chart, the series in front hides the series behind it.

Reorder the series in a chart

1. Double-click any series in the chart.

   The Format Data Series dialog box is displayed, as shown in Figure 21.6.

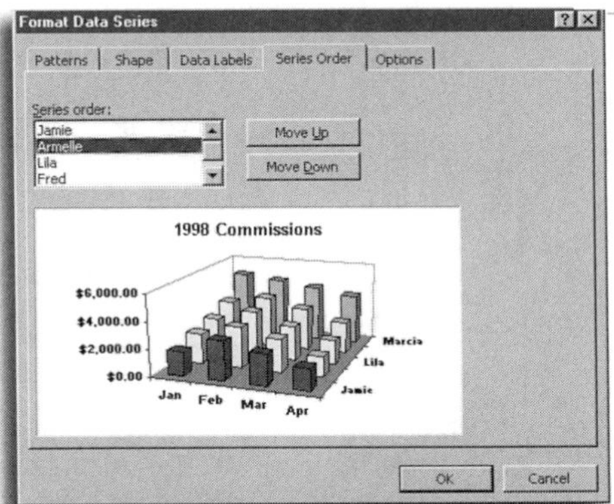

FIGURE 21.6
On the Series Order tab, you can rearrange the series in any order you want.

2. Click the **Series Order** tab.
3. Rearrange the series order: Click a series name, then click the **Move Up** and **Move Down** buttons to reposition it.
4. When you're finished, click **OK**.

   The resulting series order shown in Figure 21.7 is more readable. (You can also rearrange the series in 2D charts.)

If Your 3D Chart Is Too Tall

3D charts are usually created as tall as they are wide, which is seldom what you want. See the section "Changing 3D Perspective" later in this chapter to learn how to change the shape of a 3D block to make it flatter (or taller).

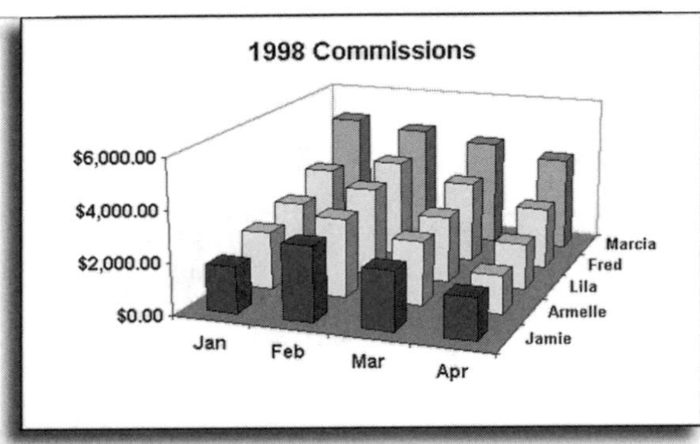

FIGURE 21.7

With the series rearranged, all markers are easier to see.

Doughnuts Work Like Pies

You can also resize a doughnut chart and explode its outer ring.

Resizing and Exploding a Pie Chart

Pie charts are great for showing how much of the total "pie" belongs to each data point, and if you make the pie larger and *explode* it by separating the slices (or pulling out a single slice), you can call attention to individual items in your data.

I demonstrate resizing and exploding a pie chart using the chart shown in Figure 21.8. In this default pie chart, the pie is a bit small, the legend is too large, and I want to call attention to the Tanzania value.

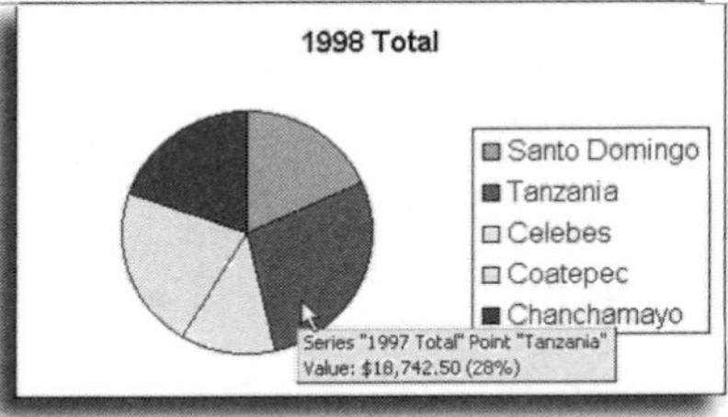

FIGURE 21.8

I want to rearrange this pie chart to highlight a particular value.

Making the Pie Bigger

I want to make the pie bigger; to do this, I'll make the legend smaller to make more room in the chart and then drag the plot area to make it larger.

Make the legend smaller

1. Click the legend border to select it.
2. On the Formatting toolbar, select a smaller font size in the **Font Size** box.

The entire legend is resized to accommodate the changed font size.

Make the plot area larger

1. Select the plot area.

   If it's difficult to locate the plot area with the mouse pointer, click the arrow on the **Chart Objects** box (on the Chart toolbar); then, click **Plot Area** on the list.

2. Make the plot area larger by dragging a corner; move the resized plot area by dragging inside a corner (as shown in Figure 21.9).

Have You Noticed the ScreenTip Values?

New Excel users who have been using a different spreadsheet software program are often pleasantly surprised to find that pointing to a data marker displays a ScreenTip with the data point's value.

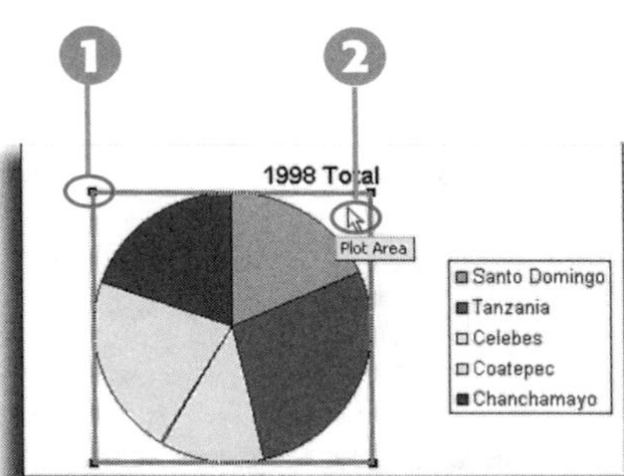

FIGURE 21.9
I made the legend smaller and the plot area larger.

1. Drag a handle to resize.
2. Drag just inside a corner to move.

Exploding the Pie

To call attention to a specific data point in a pie chart, you can drag that slice out of the pie; you can also explode the entire pie by dragging all slices away from the center of the pie.

Drag a single slice out of the pie

1. Click anywhere inside the pie.

   The series (the whole set of slices) is selected.

2. Click the slice you want to drag out.

   The single slice is selected, as shown in Figure 21.10.

Can I Have Two Slices?

You can drag two or more slices out of the pie; just drag each slice individually.

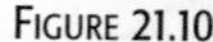

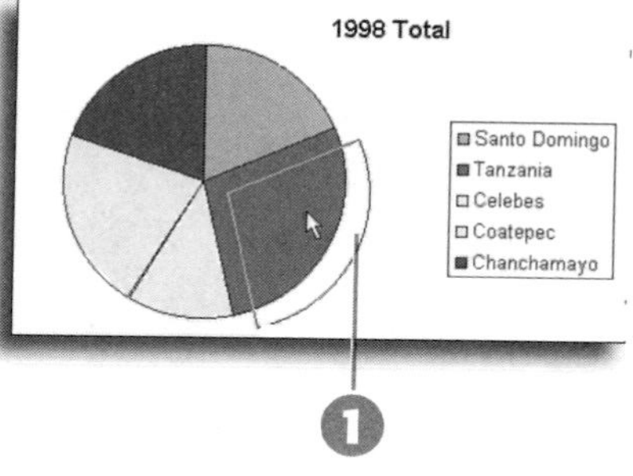

FIGURE 21.10

Click a slice twice (not a double-click) to select it.

1 Drag away from the center.

3. Drag the slice away from the center of the pie.

   Figure 21.11 shows the results of dragging a single slice out.

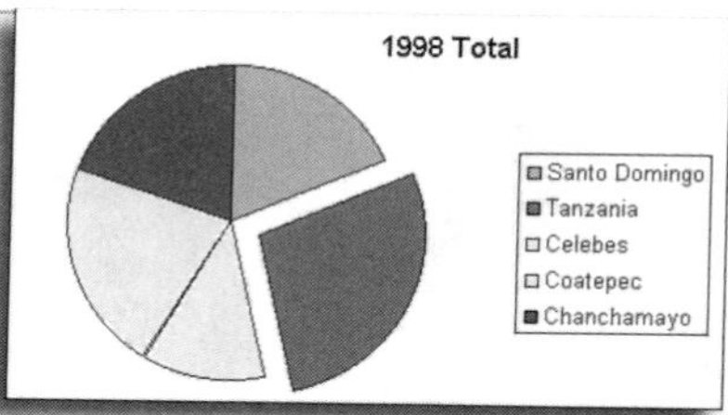

FIGURE 21.11

The Tanzania slice draws attention because it's separated from the pie.

To rejoin the slice to the pie, select the single slice and drag it back to the center of the pie.

Explode the entire pie

1. Click the pie to select the entire series (all the slices).
2. Drag any of the slices away from the center of the pie.

   All the slices separate from the pie, as shown in Figure 21.12.

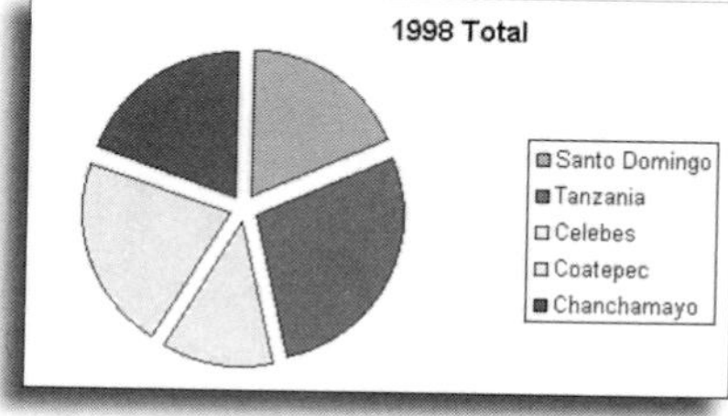

FIGURE 21.12

Explode the whole pie by dragging a slice in the selected series, rather than a single selected slice.

To rejoin the slices, select the series and drag a slice back to the center of the pie.

Changing 3D Perspective

A 3D chart can be an effective way to get your point across, but sometimes it's difficult to see all the markers in a 3D chart because they hide behind one another.

To bring hidden markers into view, you can rotate a 3D chart on all three axes. You can rotate it quickly by dragging a corner of the plot area, or more carefully by opening a dialog box that gives you precise control of the rotation.

A 3D chart has a few elements that 2D charts don't have: *walls* and a *floor*. Think of the chart as a box of markers with two of the sides cut away; the walls are the remaining sides of the box, and the floor is under the markers. If you click the walls or the floor, that element will display handles on each corner, and you can rotate, or spin, the chart in any direction by dragging a handle.

Changing Perspective by Dragging

Change the perspective of a 3D chart by dragging

1. Select the chart walls or floor.

   The element you select (walls or floor) will display a handle at each corner.

2. Drag a corner handle to rotate the chart, as shown in Figure 21.13.

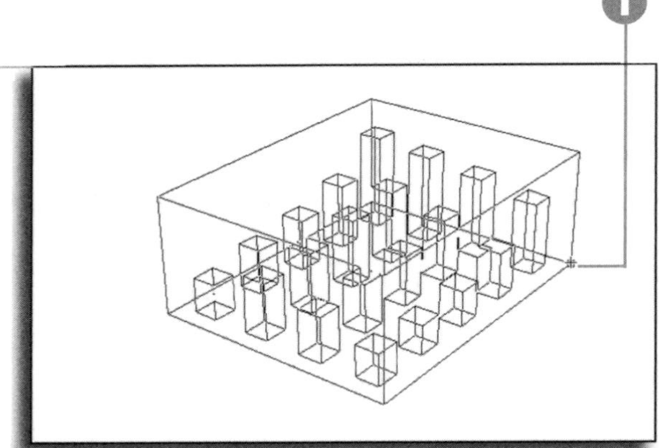

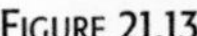
FIGURE 21.13

By holding down Ctrl, I can see what's happening to the chart markers while I rotate the chart.

1 Drag the corner to rotate a plot.

Here are a couple of hints for more precise dragging:

- Drag a front floor corner for greater precision and control.
- Hold down Ctrl while you drag to display a wire frame of the chart markers.

Changing Perspective Using a Dialog Box

Changing perspective by dragging a chart corner takes some practice (your chart can easily end up upside down and inside out), so here's a rotation technique that gives you more precise control over your chart's perspective.

Change perspective using a dialog box

1. Right-click anywhere in the chart or plot area.
2. Click **3-D View**.

   The 3-D View dialog box is displayed, as shown in Figure 21.14.
3. Rotate the chart around any of three axes (elevation, rotation, or perspective) by clicking the buttons.
4. When you're finished, click **OK**.

If your chart seems too small, you can often make it larger by changing the height-to-width ratio in the 3-D View dialog box: Changing the **Height** setting to 50 percent of base makes the chart wider and larger.

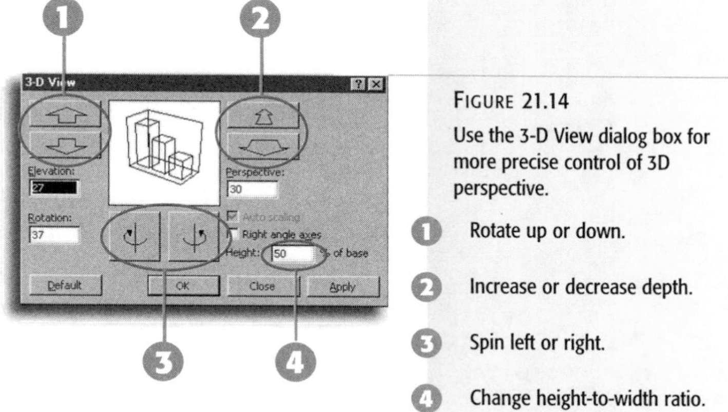

FIGURE 21.14

Use the 3-D View dialog box for more precise control of 3D perspective.

1. Rotate up or down.
2. Increase or decrease depth.
3. Spin left or right.
4. Change height-to-width ratio.

Adding a Trendline

Trendlines are of real value and are commonly used in the scientific arena. To create a trendline, Excel uses specific equations that calculate the data points in a chart and then draws the trendline that the equation calculates. Excel also calculates how well the points in the chart correlate to the trendline. (The *R-squared value* is the measure of how well the points and trendline correlate.)

The best chart type for a trendline is an XY (scatter) chart because the data normally charted in a scatter chart—two sets of numeric values—is the sort a trendline was designed to analyze; also, any other lines or solid markers tend to obscure the trendline. A trendline is a visual representation of a *regression analysis* of the data points; a regression analysis is a mathematical measurement of how closely data points fit a perfect line or curve.

Using Trendlines in Business Data

The one trendline that's useful in business (non-scientific) data is the *moving average*, which smoothes out fluctuations over time to give you a better overall picture of performance. See the section "Adding a Moving Average to Business Data" to learn more about moving averages.

Adding a Trendline to Scientific Data

Here's an example of a linear trendline in action. At a biotech company I once worked for, I performed chemical analyses of water samples, testing for trace amounts of a biochemical called endotoxin. Endotoxin reacts with a test chemical that turns it yellow; the concentration of endotoxin in a sample is determined by how long it takes the sample to turn yellow. The faster it turns yellow, the higher the concentration of endotoxin. (Endotoxin is measured in EU/ml, which means endotoxin units per milliliter.)

To make this test work, I produced a standard curve (a trendline) using endotoxin samples of known concentration; then, I tested the water samples and compared the results with the standard curve (the trendline) to determine endotoxin concentration in the water samples.

In the following example, I tested known concentrations and dilutions of endotoxin and show the results in Figure 21.15.

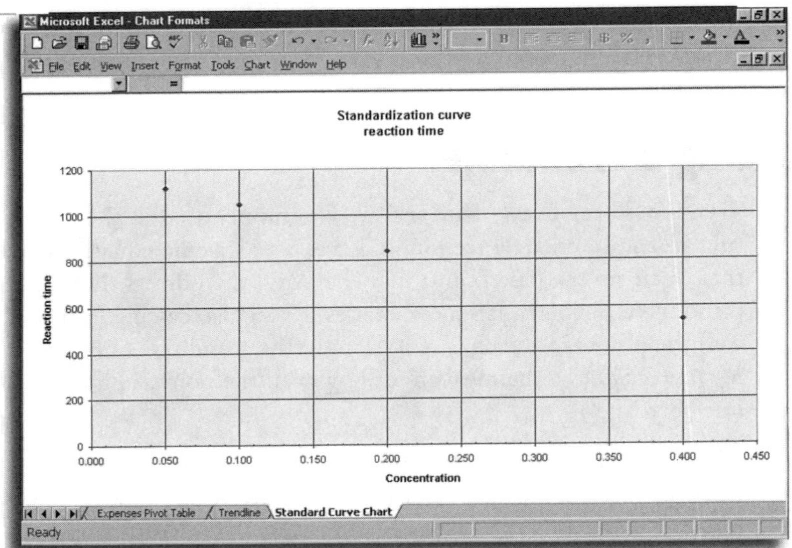

FIGURE 21.15

This XY scatter chart plots concentration against reaction time.

Add a trendline to a chart

1. Select the chart.
2. On the **Chart** menu, click **Add Trendline**.

   The Add Trendline dialog box is displayed, as shown in Figure 21.16.
3. On the Type tab, click the type of trendline you want to apply to your data.

   For more information on the mathematics of various trendline types, use Help to look up *trendline equations*. (In the Office Assistant balloon, type trendline equations, then click the **Equations of calculating trendlines** option.)

What Are the Trendline Equations?

To see the equation for each trendline: In the Add Trendline dialog box, on the Type tab, click the Help button in the upper-right corner; then, click a trendline type. A ScreenTip is displayed with the equation.

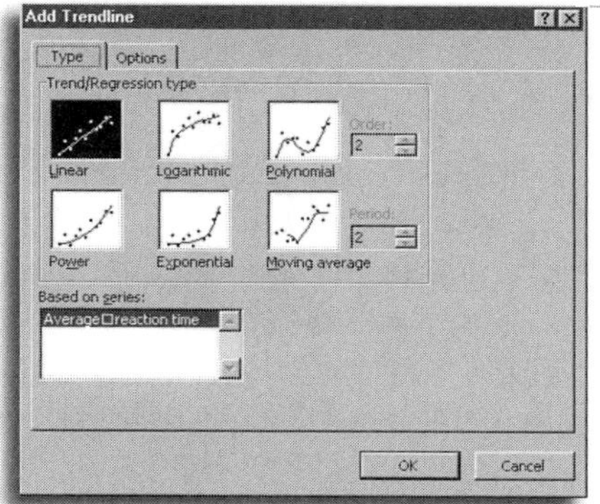

FIGURE 21.16

The type of trendline you choose depends on the data you've charted.

4. On the Options tab, click the **Display equation on chart** and **Display R-squared value on chart** check boxes (if you want to include the supporting mathematical results).
5. Click **OK**.

   The linear trendline for my chart is shown in Figure 21.17. To use this trendline, I draw a line from the y axis value (reaction time) to the trendline and then down to the x axis to find the concentration.

What's an R-squared Value?

The R-squared value tells me whether the trendline is a valid measuring stick for endotoxin concentration. An R-squared value of 1.0000 (or –1.0000) is a perfect correlation; to be valid, the trendline R-squared value must be at least 0.98. In Figure 21.17, the R-squared value of 0.9949 tells me the trendline is valid for measuring endotoxin concentration.

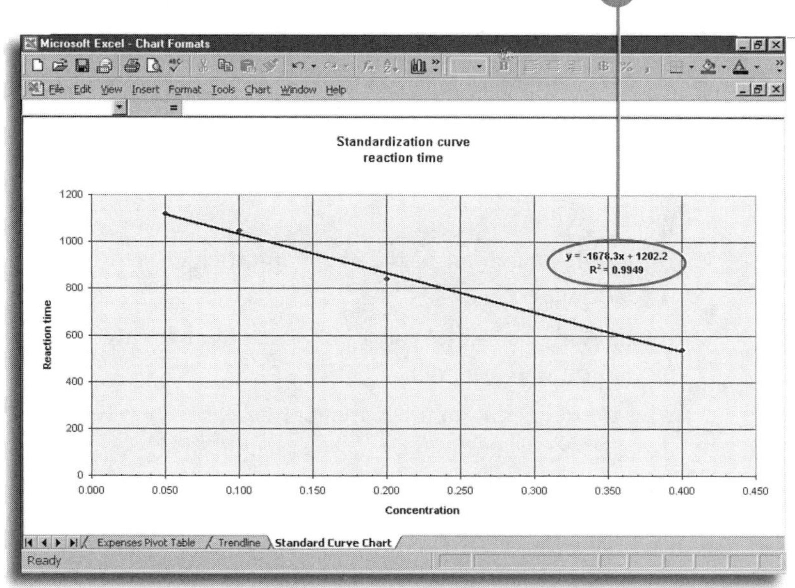

FIGURE 21.17

The R-squared value tells me this line is valid for determining sample concentrations.

1 Supporting math results

I used a linear trendline (which is appropriate for this data), and the trendline equation and resulting R-squared value are shown on the chart.

To use this trendline to determine the concentration of endotoxin in water samples, I mix the samples with the test chemical and then use the machine to time the color reaction. Next, I plot the reaction time against the trendline on the chart, and I find the corresponding endotoxin concentration. For example, in Figure 21.17, a reaction time of 800 seconds is equivalent to a concentration of approximately 0.24 EU/ml.

Adding a Moving Average to Business Data

Moving averages are useful in business data to smooth out fluctuations over time. They're particularly useful in tracking trends in data such as stocks and futures prices, factory output, workplace-accident rates, and seasonal sales of specific items.

A moving average can highlight regular, periodic increases or decreases in values so you can plan for the next increase or decrease. The following example shows a moving average applied to stock prices.

Add a moving average to a chart

1. Select the chart, and select the data series you want to apply the moving average to.

   Figure 21.18 shows a high-low-close chart of stock prices; I'll add a moving average to the high series. Also, I've changed the chart scale so the fluctuations in prices are more pronounced.

2. Right-click a marker in the series and then click **Add Trendline**.

3. In the Add Trendline dialog box, click the **Moving Average** picture on the Type tab.

   The Period is the number of data points that are averaged for each point on the moving-average line. There are no mathematical calculations to display.

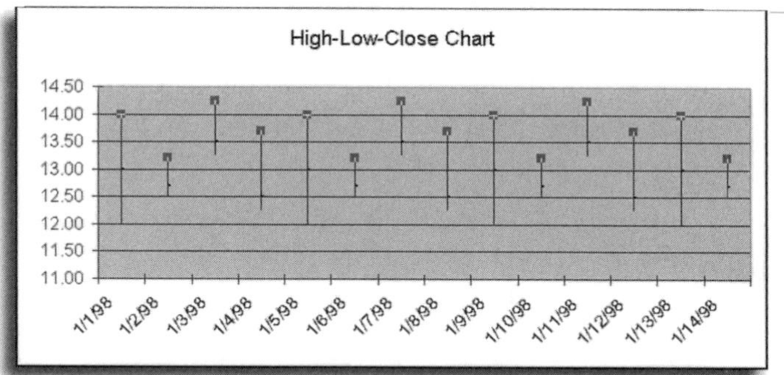

FIGURE 21.18
A trendline or moving average can only be added to a specific data series in a chart.

4. Click **OK**.

   The moving average in Figure 21.19 smoothes out the peaks and valleys in the daily "high" stock prices so that a regular trend is apparent. The moving average starts when there are a specified number of periods, or data points, to average (in this case, the first two "high" values). Each point in the moving average line is the average of the "high" values for that data marker and the previous data marker.

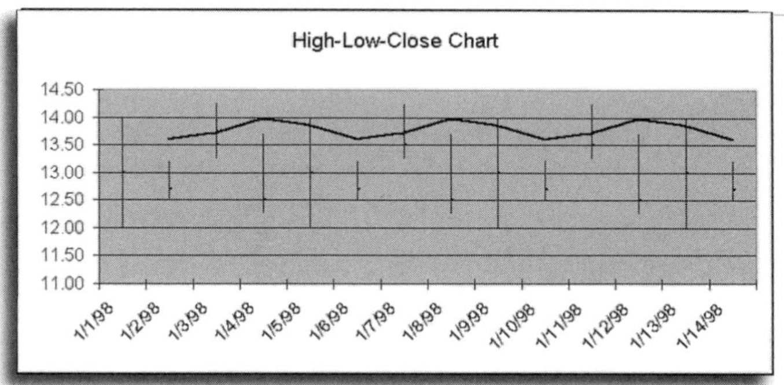

FIGURE 21.19
A moving average shows regular upswings and downswings more clearly than the raw data.

Adding a Secondary Axis

A *secondary axis* is ideal for comparing data that's related but is on two different scales. For example, suppose you are in charge of a department store sales staff, and your burning questions are: How are total sales related to the number of salespeople on the staff? Does adding salespeople result in more total sales revenue? At what point does a larger sales staff result in marginally larger sales revenues?

You might find an answer by charting total revenue versus number of salespeople for several months. But if total revenue is in excess of $10,000 and salespeople number between 10 and 20, how can you put both sets of numbers on the same chart? You can use a secondary axis.

In Figure 21.20, the Sales Force values are so much smaller than the Revenue values that they're "off the scale" and don't show up on the chart. This is my clue that I need a secondary axis.

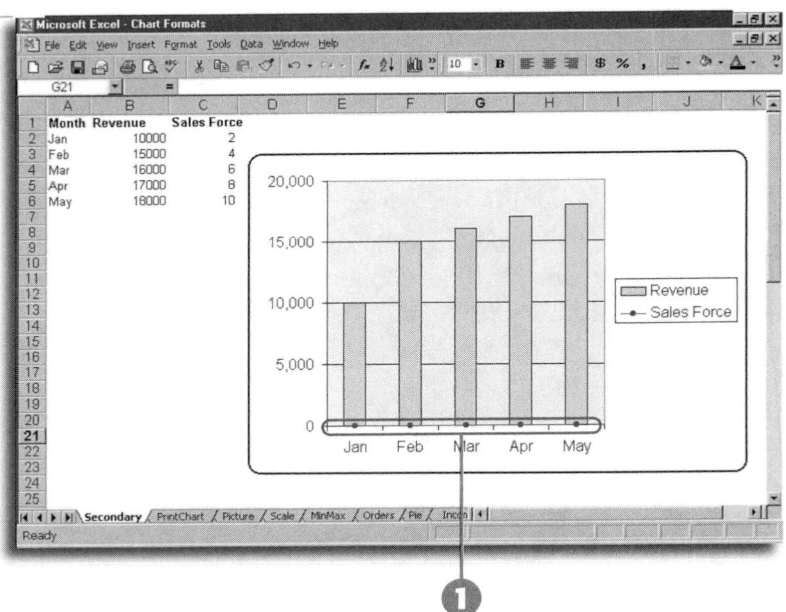

FIGURE 21.20

With a single axis, the Sales Force series is completely hidden.

1 The Sales Force data is hidden.

Add a secondary axis to a chart

1. Select the chart.
2. On the Chart toolbar, in the **Chart Objects** box, select the hidden series.
3. On the Chart toolbar, click the **Format Data Series** button.
4. In the Format Data Series dialog box (shown in Figure 21.21), on the Axis tab, click the **Secondary axis** option.

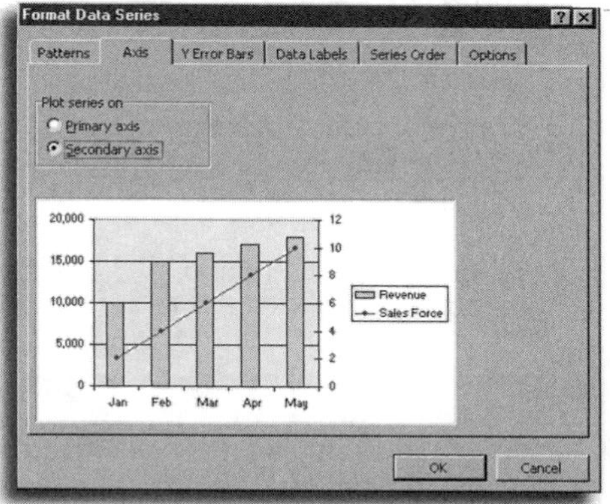

FIGURE 21.21
When you click the **Secondary axis** option, it is displayed in preview in the dialog box.

5. Click **OK**.

The selected series is plotted on a secondary axis, as shown in Figure 21.22.

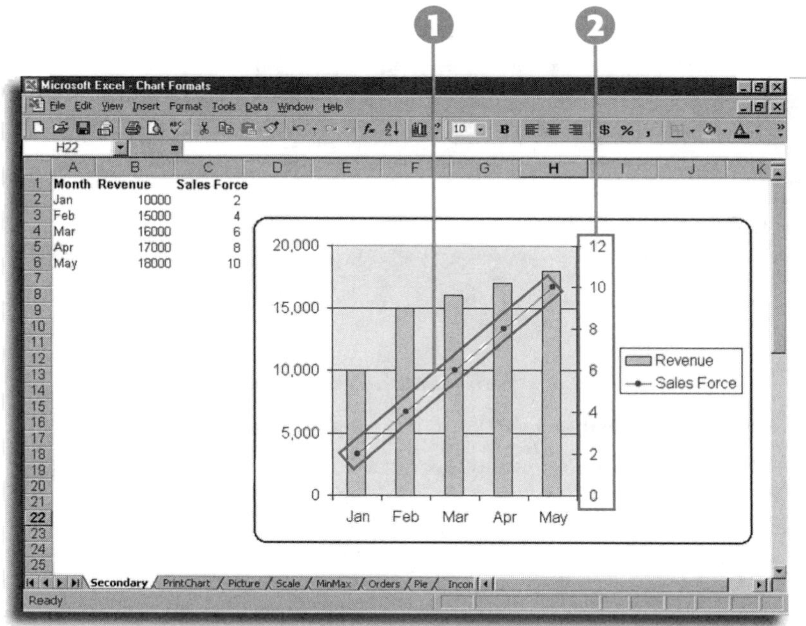

FIGURE 21.22
In addition to adding the secondary axis, I changed the series chart type to line for greater clarity.

1. Line chart type
2. Secondary axis

Adding Data Labels

Data labels add value to a chart by positioning data labels or values right next to their markers in the chart, as shown in Figure 21.23. The labels show text or values from the source range, so if you change text or values in the source range, the data labels on the chart are automatically updated. Data labels can be moved, formatted, and deleted as a group or individually.

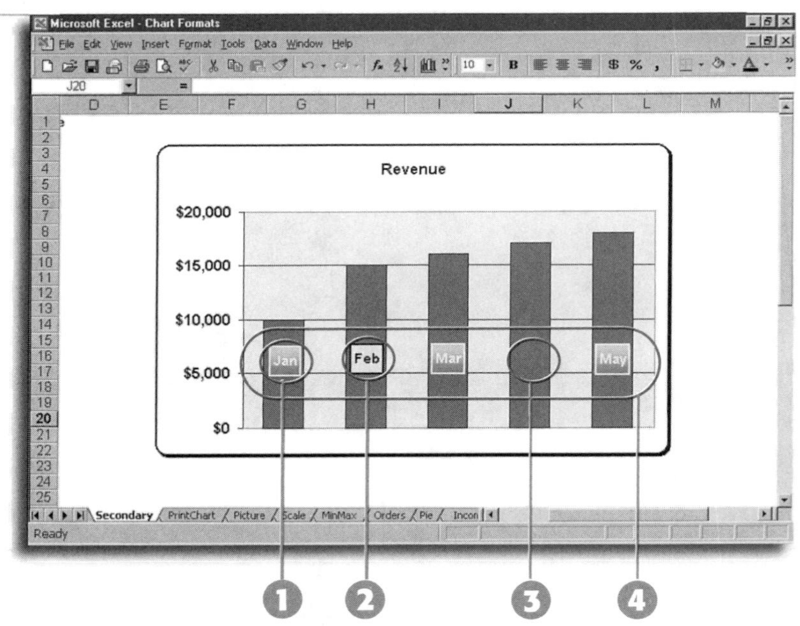

FIGURE 21.23

These data labels were added and then formatted as a group and repositioned individually.

1. Fill effects and border from Patterns tab
2. Single label formatted separately
3. Single label deleted
4. Data labels

Add Your Own Labels

To add a free-floating label anywhere on the chart: Select the chart area; then, type your label text (your text is displayed in the Formula bar), and press Enter. The label will display somewhere on the chart; you can format it and move it wherever you want. (To call attention to a specific item, use the Drawing toolbar to draw an arrow from the label to the item.)

Remove Those Data Labels

To remove data labels, select the set of labels; then, press Delete. To remove a single data label, select the single label by clicking it twice (not a double-click); then, press Delete.

➤ *For more information on drawing objects, see "Basic Drawing," page 564.*

Add data labels to a chart

1. Select the series you want to add data labels to.
2. On the Chart toolbar, click the **Format Data Series** button.

   The Format Data Series dialog box is displayed, as shown in Figure 21.24.

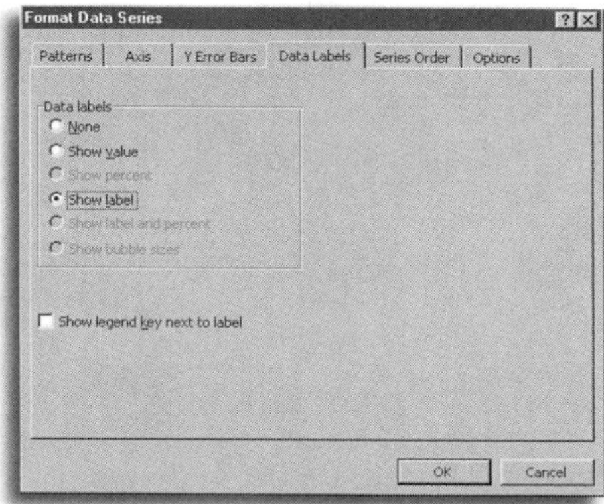

FIGURE 21.24
The types of data labels available depend on the type of chart you're adding them to.

3. On the Data Labels tab, click an option for the type of data label you want.

   For this example, I selected **Show label** so that my category labels display with the chart markers.

4. Click **OK**.

Format One Unique Label

To select a single label, click the label twice (not a double-click). Only the selected label is formatted.

Add a Data Table

To add (or remove) a *data table* at the bottom of a chart, click the **Data Table** button on the Chart toolbar. A data table is a picture of the chart's source data, attached to the bottom of the chart; you can use it to show all source values without showing the worksheet.

Format data labels

1. Click one of the labels.

   The set of labels for the series is selected.

2. Use the buttons on the Formatting toolbar to make quick changes to color, font, and font size.
3. Double-click one of the labels to open the Format Data Labels dialog box, where you can make a wider variety of formatting changes. (Be sure to double-click the data label, not the data point.)
4. Click **OK** to close the Format Data Labels dialog box when you're finished.

Creating Picture Markers

Picture markers can wake up a drowsy audience by adding a touch of whimsy to a chart. You can use any picture you want as data markers: clip art, objects you've created in Windows Paint, or even a company logo graphic (see Figure 21.25).

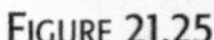

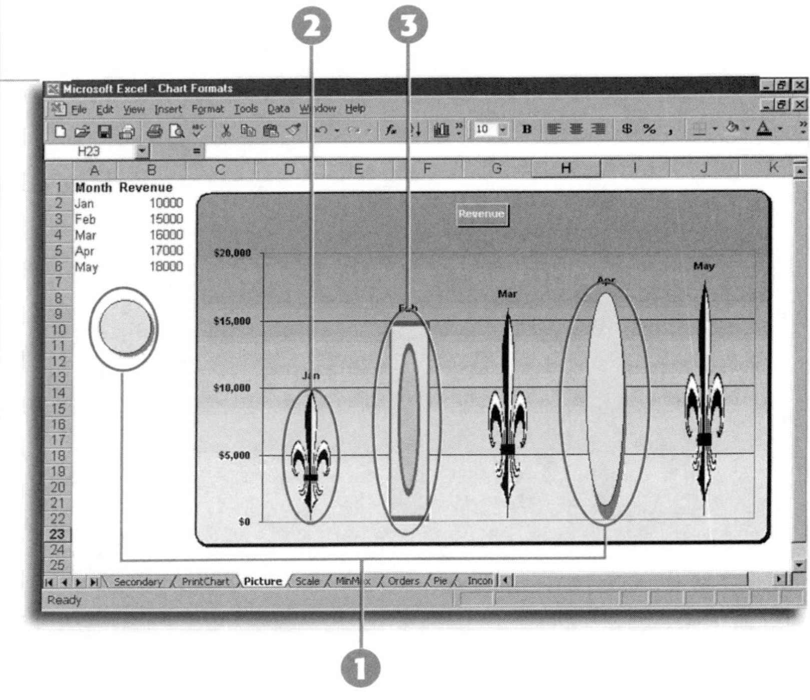

FIGURE 21.25

These picture markers are stretched; you can also stack them on top of one another.

1. Drawn on worksheet; then copied and pasted to marker
2. Clip art on Office 2000 CD
3. Created in Windows Paint

Create One Unique Marker

To create a picture marker for a single data marker, click the marker twice to select it (not a double-click); then, double-click the single marker and use the Patterns tab in the Format Data Point dialog box to create the new marker.

Create picture markers

1. Double-click the data series.

   The Format Data Series dialog box is displayed, as shown in Figure 21.26.

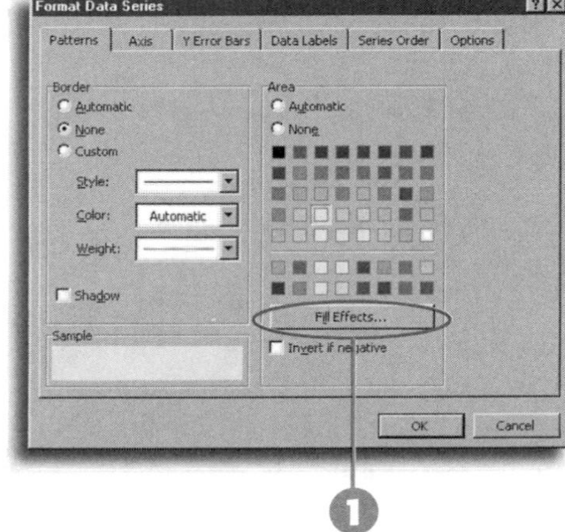

FIGURE 21.26

Use the Patterns tab to format data markers in myriad creative ways (even make them invisible!).

1. Fill Effects

2. On the Patterns tab, click the **Fill Effects** button.

   The Fill Effects dialog box is displayed, as shown in Figure 21.27.

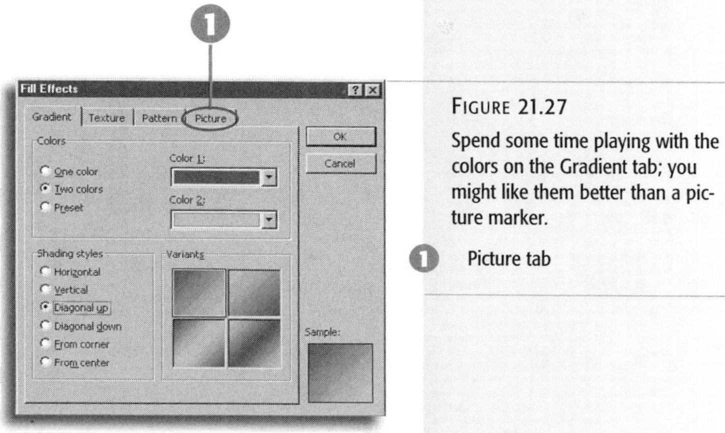

FIGURE 21.27
Spend some time playing with the colors on the Gradient tab; you might like them better than a picture marker.

1 Picture tab

3. In the Fill Effects dialog box, click the **Picture** tab.
4. On the Picture tab, shown in Figure 21.28, click the **Select Picture** button.

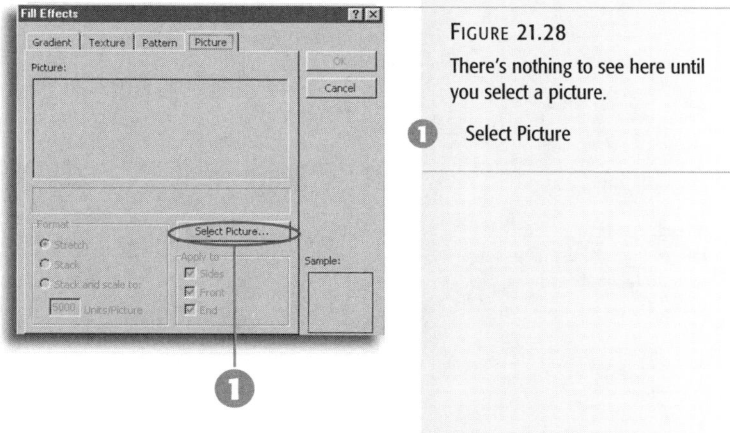

FIGURE 21.28
There's nothing to see here until you select a picture.

1 Select Picture

Draw Your Own Markers

Here's a quick way to create a simple picture marker: Use the Drawing toolbar to draw an object on the worksheet. Select and copy the object; then, select a data series (or single marker) and paste the object to replace the markers.

The Select Picture dialog box is displayed, as shown in Figure 21.29.

5. Navigate to a folder that contains the picture you want to use.

   Click the **Preview** button to look at the pictures before you choose one.

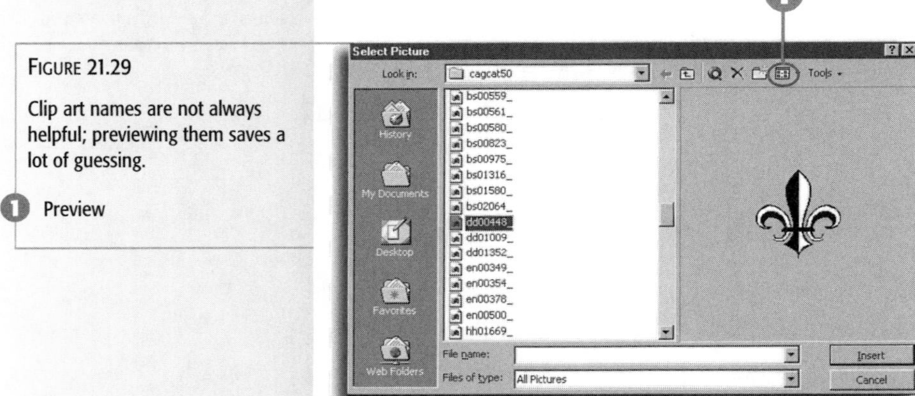

FIGURE 21.29

Clip art names are not always helpful; previewing them saves a lot of guessing.

1 Preview

6. Double-click the name of the picture you want.

   The picture is displayed on the Picture tab in the Fill Effects dialog box (shown in Figure 21.30).

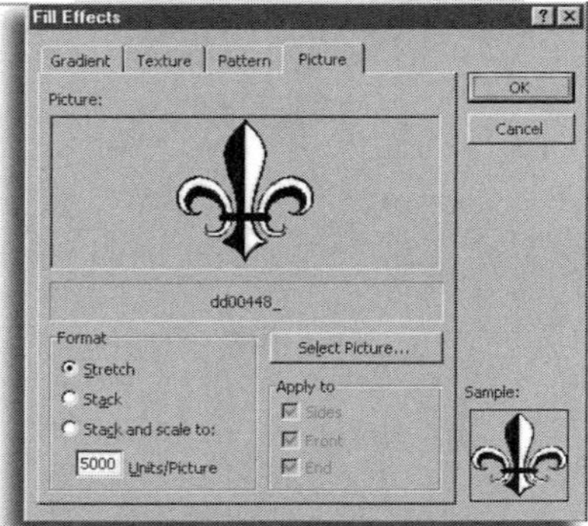

FIGURE 21.30

Stretch is usually the most interesting option, unless you want to retain the original picture proportions.

7. Decide whether you want to stretch, stack, or stack and scale the picture marker in the chart:
   - **Stretch** fills the picture marker to its value by stretching a single picture out of proportion.
   - **Stack** fills the picture marker to its value by stacking several pictures on top of one another; the picture retains its original size and proportions and might be cut off at the value level.
   - **Stack and scale** also stacks pictures on top of one another, retaining their original proportions, but it resizes the picture smaller so that each picture equals a specific number of data units in the chart (which you specify in the **Units/Picture** box).
8. Click **OK** to close the Fill Effects dialog box.
9. Click **OK** to close the Format Data Series dialog box.

   Your data markers are replaced by picture markers.

SEE ALSO

➤ *For more information on drawing objects, see "Basic Drawing," page 564.*

Beware of Stack and Scale

A smaller number of units per picture means more pictures per marker, which uses more computer memory and takes the chart longer to redraw.

Saving and Reusing Your Custom Chart Format

When you've put a lot of time into formatting all the elements of a chart (or if someone sends you a workbook containing a beautifully formatted chart that you want to use), you can save all that formatting work as a custom chart format. Then, you can apply all that painstaking formatting to new charts with just a couple of clicks.

To demonstrate, I'm going to save and then apply the formatting shown in Figure 21.31.

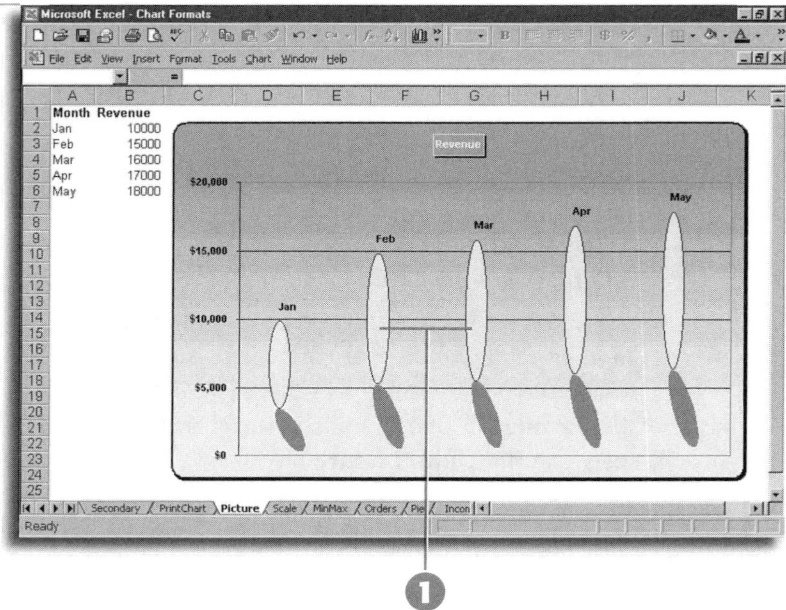

FIGURE 21.31

I spent a lot of time on this format. (I wish you could see it in color.)

1 Markers drawn on worksheet and then pasted to series

Save chart formatting as a custom chart format

1. Right-click the formatted chart.
2. Click **Chart Type**.

   In the Chart Type dialog box, click the **Custom Types** tab (shown in Figure 21.32). Click the **User-defined** option.

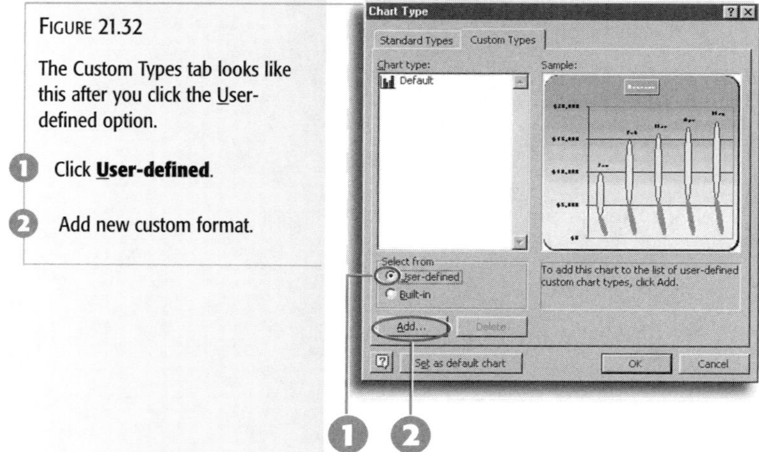

FIGURE 21.32

The Custom Types tab looks like this after you click the User-defined option.

1 Click **User-defined**.

2 Add new custom format.

3. Click the **Add** button.
4. In the Add Custom Chart Type dialog box that is displayed, type a name and memorable description for your custom format; then, click **OK**.

   The name is added to the Chart Type list, and when the name is selected, your description and a preview of the format are displayed in the dialog box.
5. Click **OK** to close the Chart Type dialog box and save the custom format.

Apply a custom chart format

1. Select your data and click the **Chart Wizard** button on the Standard toolbar to begin creating the chart.
2. In Step 1 of the Chart Wizard, click the **Custom Types** tab.
3. In the Custom Types tab, click the **User-defined** option.
4. In the **Chart Type** list, click the name of your custom format.
5. Continue creating the chart using the Chart Wizard.

If you've already created a chart, you can switch the chart type to your custom format. Right-click the chart area; then, click **Chart Type**. On the Custom Types tab, click **User-defined**; then, double-click the name of your custom format.

CHAPTER

22

Putting Data on a Map

- Creating a geographical data map
- Adding features to a data map
- Labeling items in a map
- Changing the position or size of a map
- Using the Map Control to fine-tune maps
- Creating custom pin maps

Are There More Maps?

Microsoft Map is a separate program included with Excel that generates predrawn maps on which you can display your data. A limited number of maps comes with Excel; you can buy more maps from the company that originally created the map program, MapInfo Corporation. To find them, click a map, and on the **Help** menu, click **How to Get More Data**.

Where Is Microsoft Map?

To use Microsoft Map, you must install it from your Office 2000 CD-ROM. You'll find it in the Excel category.

Introducing Microsoft Map

If you have data that's geographically oriented, such as sales by state, you might want to display the data on a geographical map instead of a chart.

In this chapter, I show you how to get started using maps to display your data and how to create a map with no data (called a *pin* map) to which you can add your own labels and information.

The Microsoft Map program has its own toolbar with buttons that you don't see elsewhere in Excel. This toolbar is displayed only when a map is active. Table 22.1 explains what each button does.

TABLE 22.1 Map toolbar buttons

Icon	Name	Purpose
	Select Objects	Allows mouse pointer to select objects for moving, sizing, and deleting.
	Grabber	Allows mouse pointer to drag image within map object.
	Center Map	Turns mouse pointer into an "X-marks-the-spot" symbol for designating a new map center. (Click it where you want to create a map center point.)
	Map Labels	Turns mouse pointer into a labeler to add labels to clicked map elements.
A	Add Text	Creates free-floating labels.
	Custom Pin Map	Turns mouse pointer into a pushpin to add pushpins to a pin map.
	Display Entire	Zooms out so entire original map is displayed.
	Redraw Map	Redraws flat map proportions after you move the image with the grabber.
	Map Refresh	Updates map with changed worksheet data (becomes available if worksheet data changes).
	Show/Hide Microsoft Map Control	Turns Microsoft Map Control dialog box on and off.
100%	Zoom Percentage of Map	Changes (zooms) map magnification.
	What's This? Help	Turns mouse pointer into a What's This? pointer for quick identification of map elements and toolbar buttons.

Creating a Geographical Data Map

If you want to show your data on a map, the data layout is important: The first column must contain geographical entries, such as cities, states, or countries. An appropriate data layout is shown in Figure 22.1. (Excel recognizes standard two-letter state abbreviations as well as full state names.)

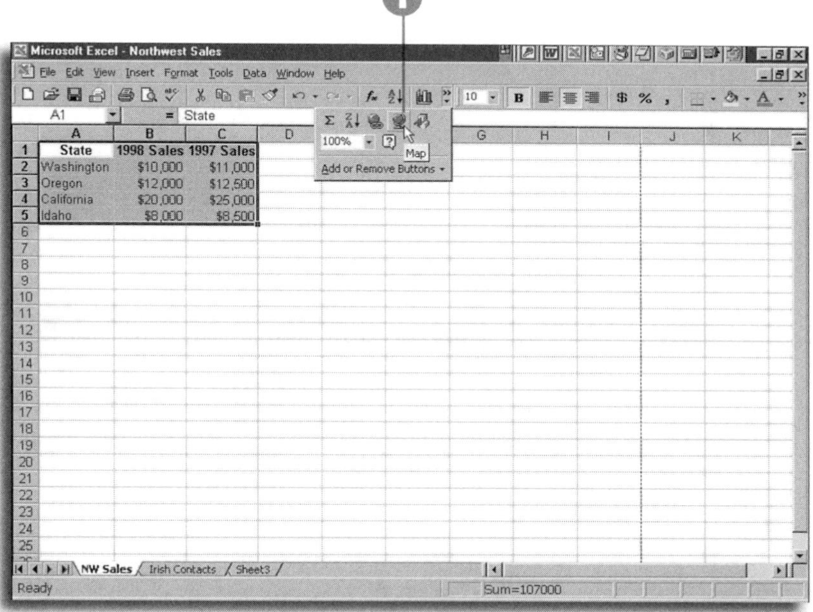

FIGURE 22.1
For a data map, build your source table so that geographical entries are in the leftmost column.

1 Map button

Create a data map

1. On the worksheet, select the data you want to map. (If you want the legend to include category names, include the column and row labels in your selection.)
2. On the Standard toolbar, click the **Map** button.

   Your mouse pointer becomes a crosshair, as shown in Figure 22.2.
3. Drag the crosshair diagonally across the worksheet to draw a rectangle.

   The rectangle will be your data map; don't worry about the dimensions because you can change size and shape later.

FIGURE 22.2

Drag the crosshair mouse pointer to draw a rectangle.

1 Rectangle

2 Crosshair pointer

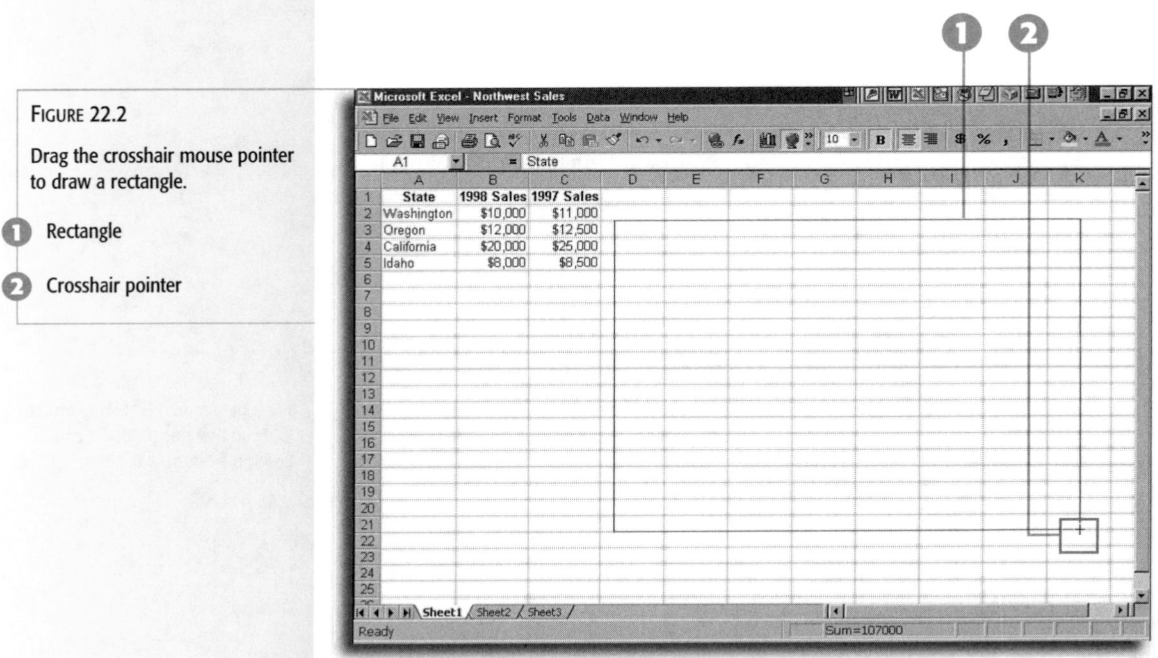

If Microsoft Map can guess which map you want from your data, that map is displayed. If not, you'll see one of two dialog boxes after you draw the map rectangle. (Both are shown in Figure 22.3.)

FIGURE 22.3

Which dialog box you see at this point depends on what Microsoft Map can guess from your data.

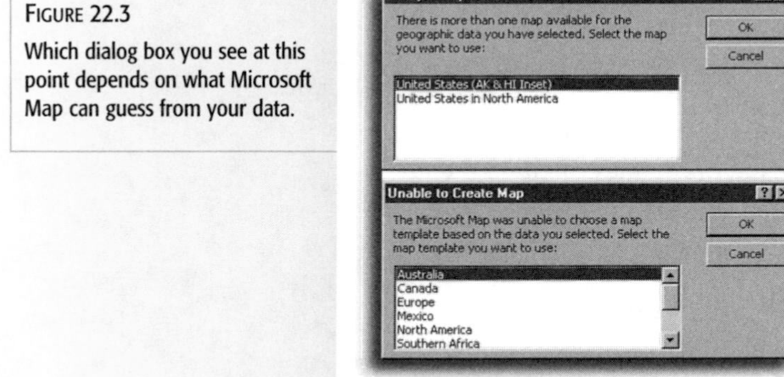

4. Whichever dialog box you see, double-click the map you want.

The map is displayed along with the Microsoft Map Control dialog box and the Map toolbar, as shown in Figure 22.4. Initially, only the data from the first category (in this case, 1998 Sales) is displayed. You add the remaining data and choose the format you want by using the Microsoft Map Control dialog box. To learn more about adding and formatting data series in a map, see the section "Using the Map Control," later in this chapter.

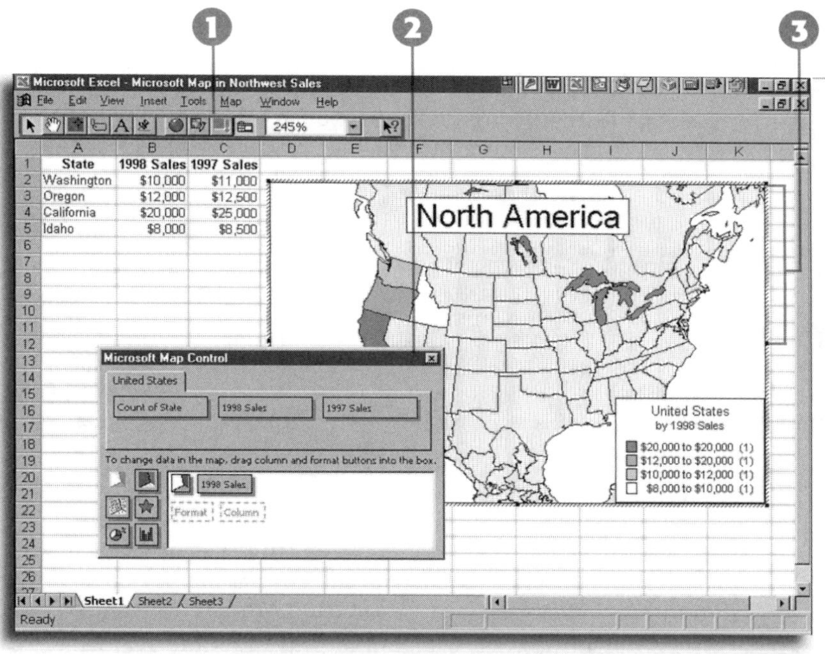

FIGURE 22.4
Once your map is created, use the Map Control to determine which data is shown on your map and how it's displayed.

1. Map toolbar
2. Map Control
3. Handles

To resize or reshape the map, click the map to select it; then, drag the handles on the map border.

To return to the worksheet, click a cell. The map becomes a worksheet object, and the Map toolbar is replaced by worksheet toolbars. To activate the map again, double-click the map object.

Adding Features to Your Map

You can add geographical features—such as cities, highways, and airports—to your map and then label the specific features to which you want to call attention.

Add geographical features to your map

1. Right-click the map; then, click **Features**.
2. In the Map Features dialog box (shown in Figure 22.5), click **check boxes** for the features you want displayed on the map.

   There are a lot of different features available for each map; to add more features (such as airports or postal codes) to the list in the Map Features dialog box, click the **Add** button, select a feature from the list, and click **OK**.

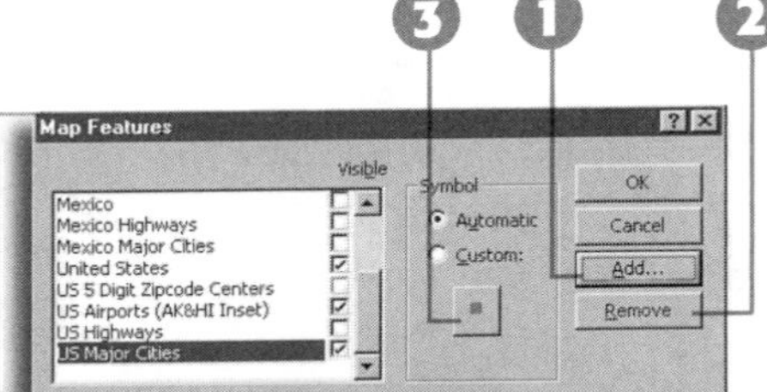

FIGURE 22.5

Several features are already attached to each map; you can choose to make them visible.

1. Add more features to the list.
2. Remove features from the list.
3. Click to pick your own symbol.

3. Click **OK**.

   Airports and major cities are shown on the map in Figure 22.6. In the Map Features dialog box, I added U.S. airports to the list and deselected Canada and Mexico features so that I could show airports on the map and limit the map to the continental United States.

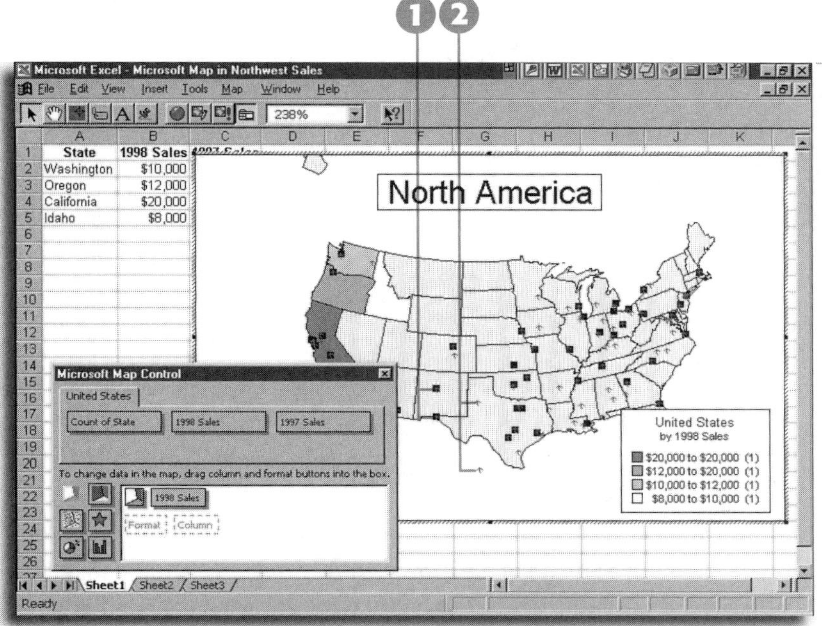

FIGURE 22.6

You can show airports, cities, and highways and then label just those you want to point out.

1. Major cities
2. Airports

Labeling Map Items

When you show map features, a lot of them are displayed. You'll want to label only those specific features on your map that you want to point out to your audience.

Label map items

1. On the **Tools** menu, click **Labeler**.

   The Map Labels dialog box is displayed, as shown in Figure 22.7.

2. In the Map Labels dialog box, click the down arrow in the Map **feature to label** box, and click the feature category you want to create labels for. (In Figure 22.8, I'm going to label a few airports.)

Refreshing the Map

When you're making changes to features as you set up the map, you'll sometimes see a message that says the data has changed and you must refresh the map before you can continue with whatever you're doing. Click **OK** in the message box to continue.

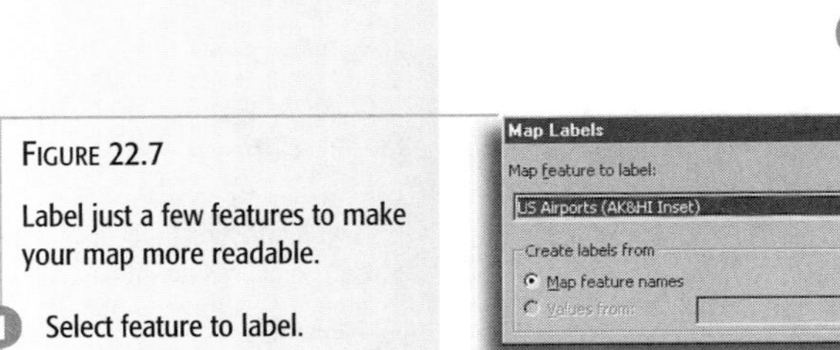

FIGURE 22.7

Label just a few features to make your map more readable.

1 Select feature to label.

3. Click **OK**.

   The mouse pointer becomes a crosshair again.

4. Hold the mouse crosshair over features on your map; feature names are displayed in ScreenTips.

5. When you see a ScreenTip that you want to use as a label, click it.

   Figure 22.8 shows labels for some airports in the Western United States. I repositioned and zoomed this map image to focus on my four states. (See the following section to learn how.)

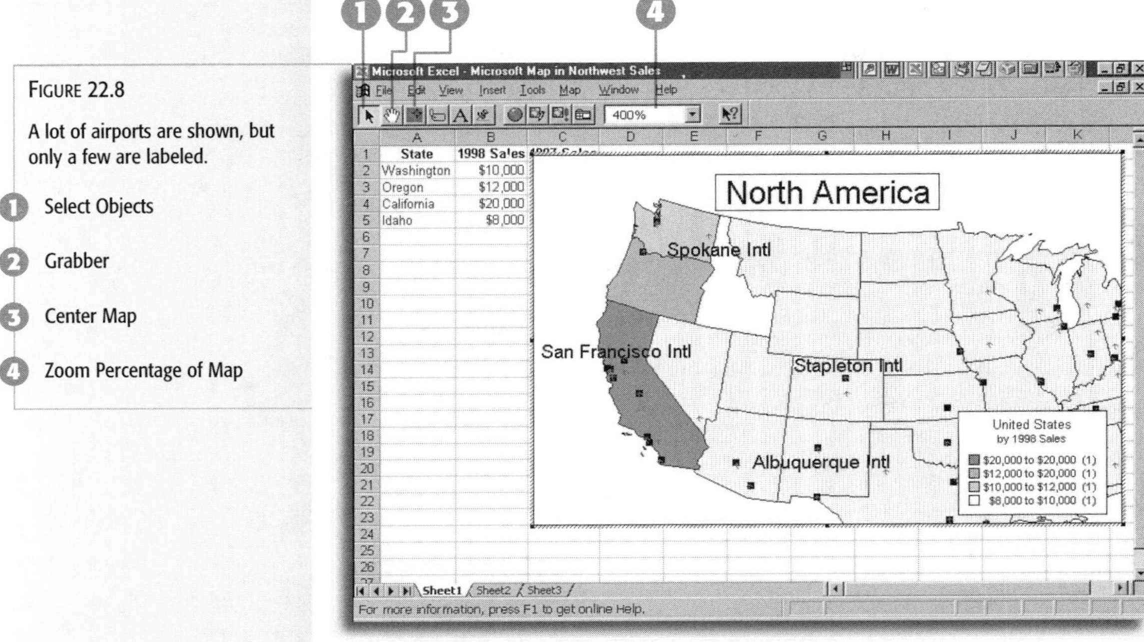

FIGURE 22.8

A lot of airports are shown, but only a few are labeled.

1 Select Objects

2 Grabber

3 Center Map

4 Zoom Percentage of Map

6. On the toolbar, click **Select Objects** to turn off the labeler.

   After you create labels, you can reposition them on the map by dragging their borders.

Repositioning and Enlarging a Map

You can resize and reposition a map object on your worksheet the same way you resize and reposition any graphical object; but with a map object, you can also do two more things:

- Reposition the map image within the object frame to help your audience focus on a specific portion of the map.
- Zoom into a specific portion of a large map, again to help your audience focus on a specific portion of the map.

Move a map within its object frame

1. On the Map toolbar, click the **Grabber** button.
2. Click the map image and drag it to a new position within its frame.
3. To recenter the map image in its frame, click **Center Map** on the toolbar; then, click the map spot that you want to put in the center of the map frame.

Zoom, or enlarge, the map

1. On the Map toolbar, click the down arrow on the **Zoom Percentage of Map** button. 100%
2. Click a higher zoom percentage to zoom in on the map.

   If the default percentages aren't quite right, you can type your own zoom percentage in the Zoom Percentage of Map button; then, press Enter.
3. On the Map toolbar, click the **Grabber** button; then, drag the zoomed image in its frame to position it precisely.

Using the Map Control

Your data can be shown on the map in several ways, including

- Regions colored by value
- Regions colored by category
- Small column charts overlaid on regions
- Small pie charts overlaid on regions
- Colored dots or symbols

To change the way data is displayed in your map, use the Microsoft Map Control dialog box, shown in Figure 22.9. You can show or hide the Map Control with the **Show/Hide Microsoft Map Control** button on the toolbar.

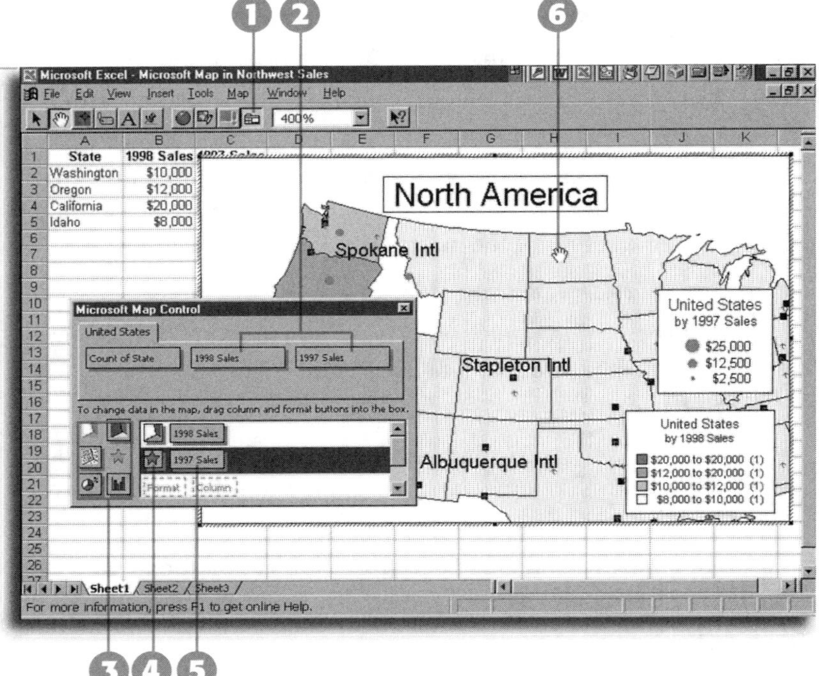

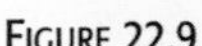
FIGURE 22.9

The Microsoft Map Control dialog box is where you control how data is displayed.

1. Show/Hide Microsoft Map Control
2. Worksheet data columns
3. Data format buttons
4. Drag format button into box…
5. …and then drag column button into box.
6. Grabber mouse pointer to move objects

Table 22.2 identifies the buttons in the Map Control.

TABLE 22.2 Map control buttons

Icon	Name	Purpose
	Value Shading	Shows each value level in a different color (can display only a single category of data values, as shown in Figure 22.10).
	Category Shading	Shows each category in a different color, instead of each value level.
	Dot Density	Shows values as lots of small dots; more dots (higher density) represent higher values.
	Graduated Symbol	Shows values as symbols of different sizes; larger symbols represent higher values (as shown in Figure 22.10).
	Pie Chart	Shows multiple categories of data as small pie charts overlaid on each region.
	Column Chart	Shows multiple categories of data as small column charts overlaid on each region.

Control your data display with the Map Control

1. On the toolbar, click the **Show/Hide Microsoft Map Control** button.

   If the Microsoft Map Control dialog box is already displayed, clicking the button will hide it; to follow these steps, make sure the Microsoft Map Control is displayed.

2. Drag a data format button from the lower-left portion of the dialog box into the big white box in the Map Control.

   In this example, I dragged the Graduated Symbol format button into the box.

3. Drag a data column button into the big white box in the Map Control.

   In this example, I dragged the 1997 Sales data button into the box.

   The format button lines up with the data button; that column of data is displayed on your map in the format you paired with it (as shown in Figure 22.10).

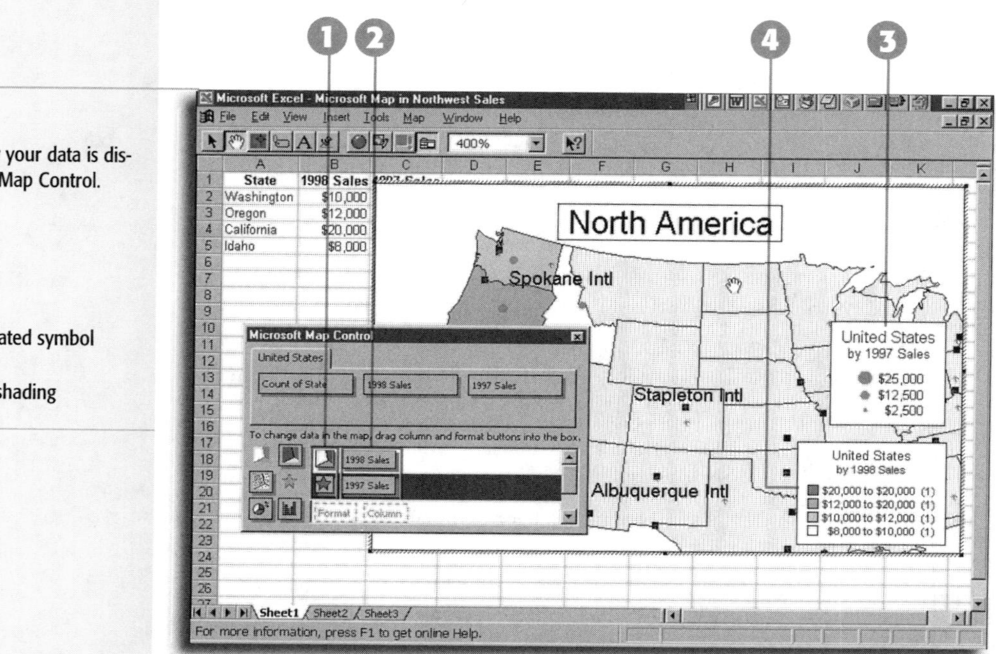

FIGURE 22.10

You control how your data is displayed with the Map Control.

1. Format
2. Data
3. 1997 by graduated symbol
4. 1998 in value shading

To remove data, or redo the data display, drag the format and data buttons away from the big white box in the Map Control. (A wastebasket symbol indicates removal.)

Creating Custom Pin Maps

A *pin map* is a map with pushpin markers in it; you can use pushpin markers in maps with data, but they are also a great way to customize a map with no data. You can use a pin map to show information such as where events are held or where you traveled on your vacation. In this example, I show you how to create a no-data map and then add your own pushpins and labels.

Create a pin map

1. On the Standard toolbar, click the **Map** button. (Don't select any data.)
2. Drag the crosshair to draw a rectangle for your map object.

3. In the Unable To Create Map dialog box, double-click a map.

   Your map object is created on the worksheet.

4. On the Map toolbar, click the **Custom Pin Map** button.

5. In the Custom Pin Map dialog box (shown in Figure 22.11), type a name for the pin map (something like `Summer Events` or `Contacts in Ireland`). After you name a set of custom map pins, they are available in the Custom Pin Map dialog box for other maps.

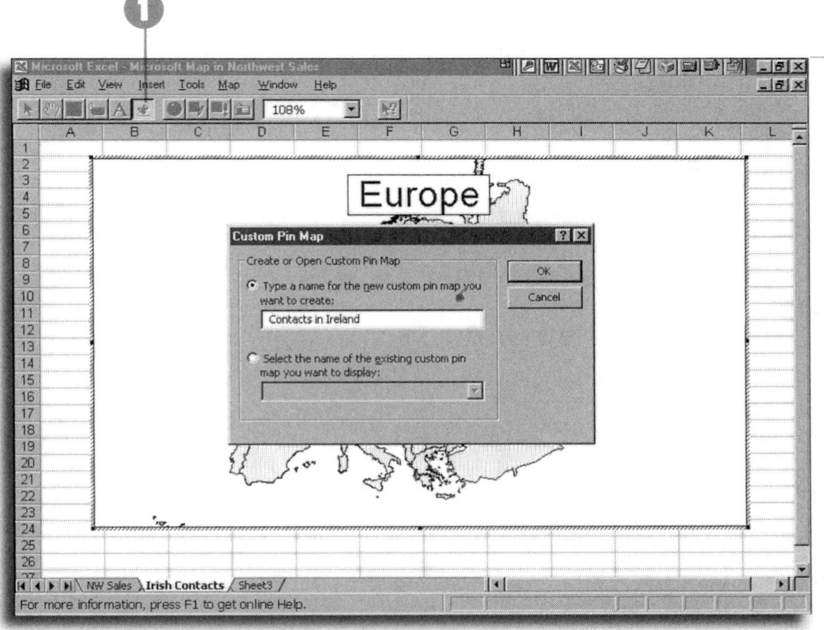

FIGURE 22.11

Name your pin map before you place and label the pins.

1 Custom Pin Map

6. Click **OK**.

   Your mouse pointer becomes a pushpin symbol.

7. Click the map to place each pushpin you want.

   Each time you place a pushpin, the Edit Text Object dialog box appears so you can enter label text for the pushpin. If you don't want to enter label text, click **Cancel** in the Edit Text Object dialog box.

8. When you finish placing pins on the map, click the **Select Objects** button on the Map toolbar.

9. If you didn't label your pushpins when you placed them, you can label them later by double-clicking the pushpin. You can also create free-floating labels without pushpins.

   To create free-floating labels, click the **Add Text** button; **A** then, click in the map where you want your label. Type the label and click **OK**.

Figure 22.12 shows a pin map with free-floating labels and an active pushpin mouse. I enlarged this map object and then zoomed and repositioned the map image. Any label on the map can be moved around after you click the Select Objects button.

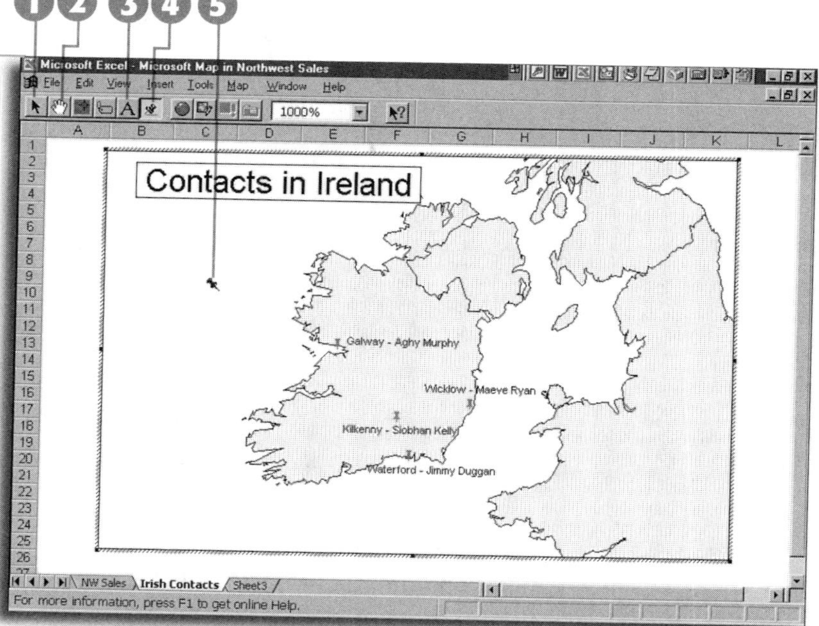

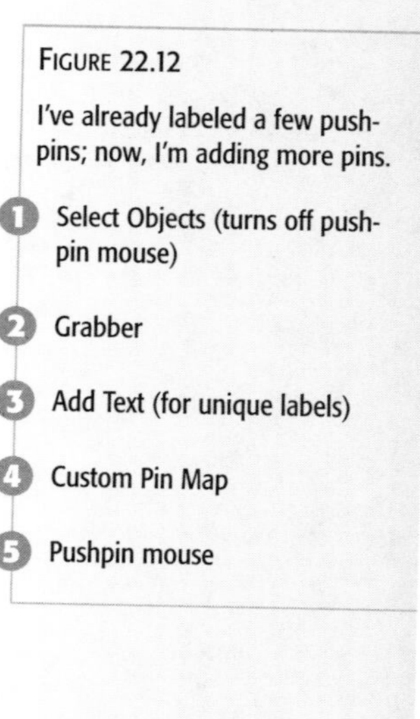
FIGURE 22.12

I've already labeled a few push-pins; now, I'm adding more pins.

1. Select Objects (turns off push-pin mouse)
2. Grabber
3. Add Text (for unique labels)
4. Custom Pin Map
5. Pushpin mouse

To either change the symbol of a pushpin or make it larger, right-click the pushpin you want to change, then click **Format** on the shortcut menu. The Symbol dialog box appears with lots of ways to change the symbol.

If the pushpin has no label, the Edit Text Object dialog box might appear instead of the shortcut menu; either enter text and click **OK**, or click **Cancel**, then click **Format** on the shortcut menu.

In the Symbol dialog box (shown in Figure 22.13), you can click a different symbol. To change the size of the pushpin, click the **Font** button, and in the Font dialog box, make your changes; click **OK** twice to close both dialog boxes. To select a symbol from a different font set, click the **Font** button, and in the Font dialog box, select a different font.

To change a label's font, right-click the label, then click **Format Font**, and change the font in the Font dialog box.

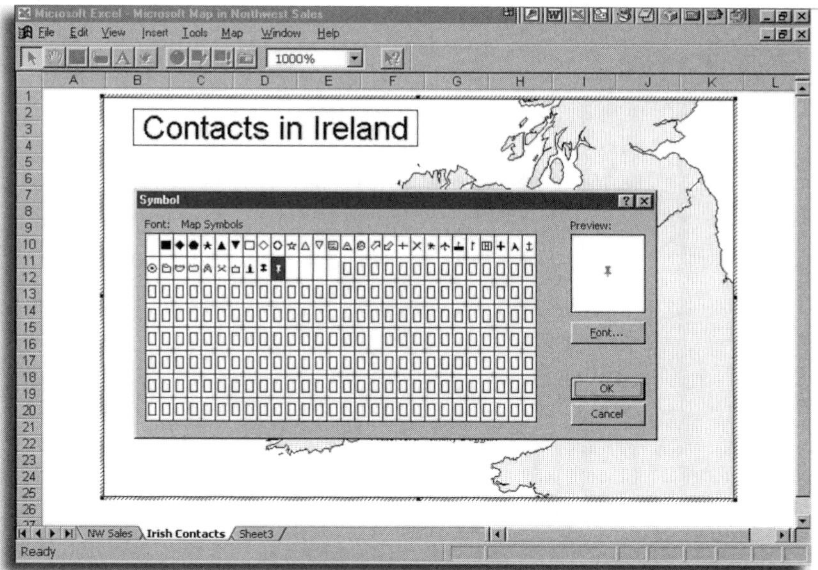

FIGURE 22.13
Pushpins are easier to see if you enlarge them; you can use different symbols for different types of places.

PART VI

Printing

23 Deciding What to Print 449

24 Formatting the Printed Page 461

CHAPTER

23

Deciding What to Print

- Previewing your worksheet before you print
- Printing a quick copy of an entire worksheet
- Printing a portion of a worksheet
- Printing a chart, with or without its worksheet data
- Printing an entire workbook

Previewing Printed Pages

Although Bill Gates envisions a utopian "paperless office," you and I know that it's a long, long way off. We still need to print information: to mail out, to pass around at company meetings, to give to the CEO who's still a bit computer-phobic, and to file as a backup to fragile electronic information storage.

You can print a worksheet with one click of a toolbar button, but you might not get the easy-to-read printed pages you want. You can save yourself time and paper if you develop the habit of *always* looking at your pages in Print Preview before you print.

Preview the worksheet before you print

1. Display the worksheet on your screen, as shown in Figure 23.1.

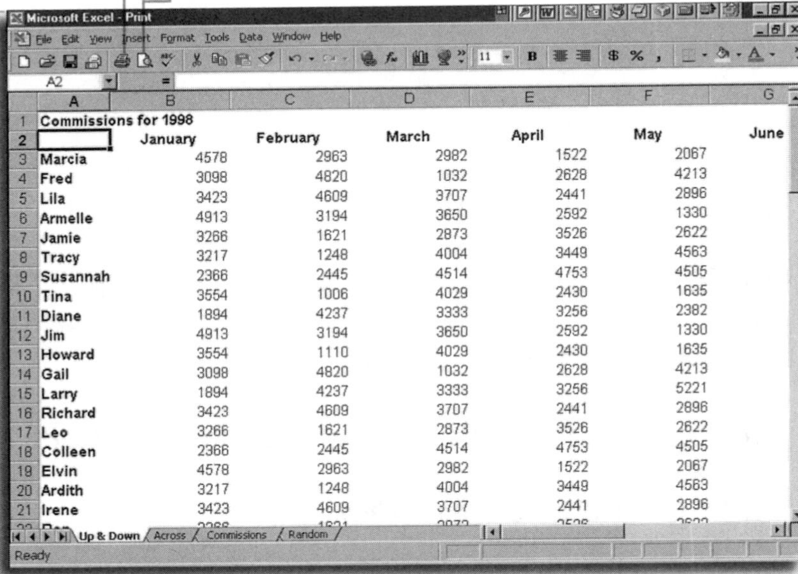

	A	B	C	D	E	F	G
1	Commissions for 1998						
2		January	February	March	April	May	June
3	Marcia	4578	2963	2982	1522	2067	
4	Fred	3098	4820	1032	2628	4213	
5	Lila	3423	4609	3707	2441	2896	
6	Armelle	4913	3194	3650	2592	1330	
7	Jamie	3266	1621	2873	3526	2622	
8	Tracy	3217	1248	4004	3449	4563	
9	Susannah	2366	2445	4514	4753	4505	
10	Tina	3554	1006	4029	2430	1635	
11	Diane	1894	4237	3333	3256	2382	
12	Jim	4913	3194	3650	2592	1330	
13	Howard	3554	1110	4029	2430	1635	
14	Gail	3098	4820	1032	2628	4213	
15	Larry	1894	4237	3333	3256	5221	
16	Richard	3423	4609	3707	2441	2896	
17	Leo	3266	1621	2873	3526	2622	
18	Colleen	2366	2445	4514	4753	4505	
19	Elvin	4578	2963	2982	1522	2067	
20	Ardith	3217	1248	4004	3449	4563	
21	Irene	3423	4609	3707	2441	2896	

FIGURE 23.1

I'll preview this worksheet before I print it.

1. Print
2. Print Preview

2. On the Standard toolbar, click the **Print Preview** button. 

   Your worksheet is displayed as printed pages, as shown in Figure 23.2. To zoom in on part of the page, click there with the zoom pointer; click again to see the whole page.

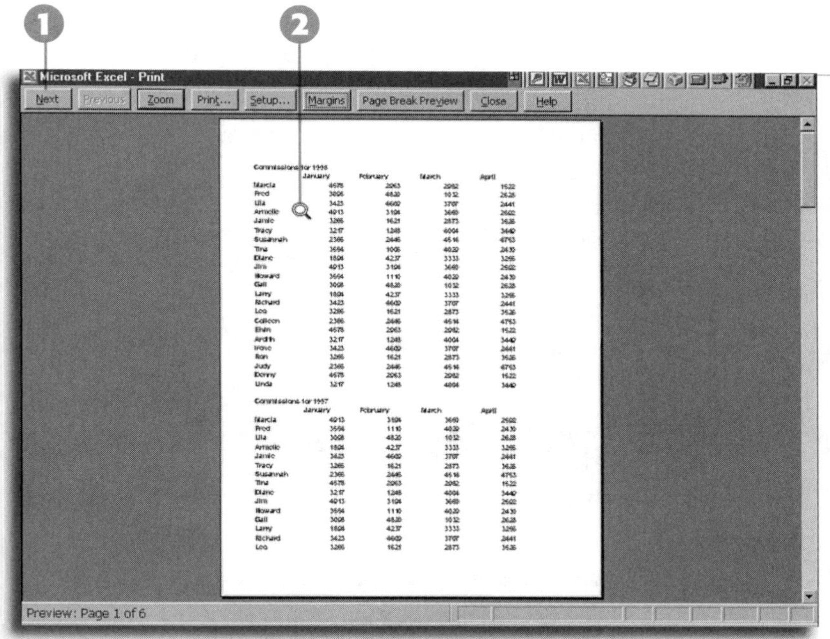

FIGURE 23.2
My worksheet is in Print Preview.

1. Button bar
2. Zoom pointer

There are nine buttons on the Print Preview button bar; Table 23.1 tells you what they do.

TABLE 23.1 Print Preview button bar

This Button	Does This
Next	Shows the next page.
Previous	Shows the previous page.
Zoom	Zooms in and out on the printed page, the same as the Zoom pointer; you can zoom with greater accuracy by clicking on the page instead of the button.

...continued

TABLE 23.1 Continued

This Button	Does This
Print	Opens the Print dialog box.
Setup	Opens the Page Setup dialog box.
Margins	Shows and hides page margins; you can change margins by dragging them with the mouse.
Page Break Preview	Switches to Page Break Preview, where you can see the page breaks and page order for the whole worksheet; to return to Print Preview from Page Break Preview, click the **Print Preview** button on the Standard toolbar; to return to the worksheet from Page Break Preview, open the **View** menu and click **Normal**.
Close	Returns to the worksheet.
Help	Opens a Print Preview help file.

SEE ALSO

➤ *To learn more about working in Page Break Preview, see page 464.*

Printing a Quick Copy of a Worksheet

You can quickly print a single copy of everything on a worksheet.

Use the Print button to quickly print a worksheet

1. Display the worksheet on your screen.
2. On the Standard toolbar, click the **Print** button.

   A copy of the entire worksheet is printed, using the default print settings.

Printing Part of a Worksheet

Hiding Columns or Rows Before You Print

To print nonadjacent columns or rows in a table, rather than the entire table, hide the columns or rows you don't want to print. (Select the rows or columns; then, right-click the selection and click **Hide**.)

You won't always want to print your entire worksheet. You can set a specific range as a print area, which will always be printed without the rest of the worksheet. You can also select a specific range of cells for a single printing. (The selection overrides a print area for the specific printing.)

Setting a Print Area

If you print the same worksheet table every week, you can set a print area that allows you to print the table quickly without selecting it first.

Set a print area in the worksheet

1. Select the range of cells you want to include in your print area, as I've done in Figure 23.3.

	A	B	C	D	E	F	G	H	I
1	Commissions for 1998								
2		January	February	March	April	May	June	July	August
3	Marcia	4578	2963	2982	1522	2067	3944	2605	4621
4	Fred	3098	4820	1032	2628	4213	1951	2099	4451
5	Lila	3423	4609	3707	2441	2896	1327	1429	3714
6	Armelle	4913	3194	3650	2592	1330	3002	4166	4324
7	Jamie	3266	1621	2873	3526	2622	2148	2094	3449
8	Tracy	3217	1248	4004	3449	4563	4542	4668	3612
9	Susannah	2366	2445	4514	4753	4505	4934	3523	4179
10	Tina	3554	1006	4029	2430	1635	4508	4472	1616
11	Diane	1894	4237	3333	3256	2382	2486	1818	1064
12	Jim	4913	3194	3650	2592	1330	3002	4166	4324
13	Howard	3554	1110	4029	2430	1635	4508	4472	1616
14	Gail	3098	4820	1032	2628	4213	1951	2099	4451
15	Larry	1894	4237	3333	3256	5221	2486	1818	1064
16	Richard	3423	4609	3707	2441	2896	1327	1429	3714
17	Leo	3266	1621	2873	3526	2622	2148	2094	3449
18	Colleen	2366	2445	4514	4753	4505	4934	3523	4179
19	Elvin	4578	2963	2982	1522	2067	3944	2605	4621
20	Ardith	3217	1248	4004	3449	4563	4542	4668	3612
21	Irene	3423	4609	3707	2441	2896	1327	1429	3714

FIGURE 23.3
You can set any range in a worksheet as a print area; the remainder of the worksheet isn't printed.

2. On the **File** menu, point to **Print Area**; then, click **Set Print Area**.

   The print area is set, and a dashed line is displayed around it in the worksheet. You can check it by clicking the **Print Preview** button; only the print area is displayed, as shown in Figure 23.4.

More About the Print Area

The print area is really a range named "Print_Area." (You can see it in the Define Name dialog box.) To create a self-adjusting, dynamic print area, define the name Print_Area with the OFFSET/COUNTA formula discussed in Chapter 19, "Summarizing Details with PivotTables and PivotCharts," in the section titled "Creating a Source Range That Changes Dynamically."

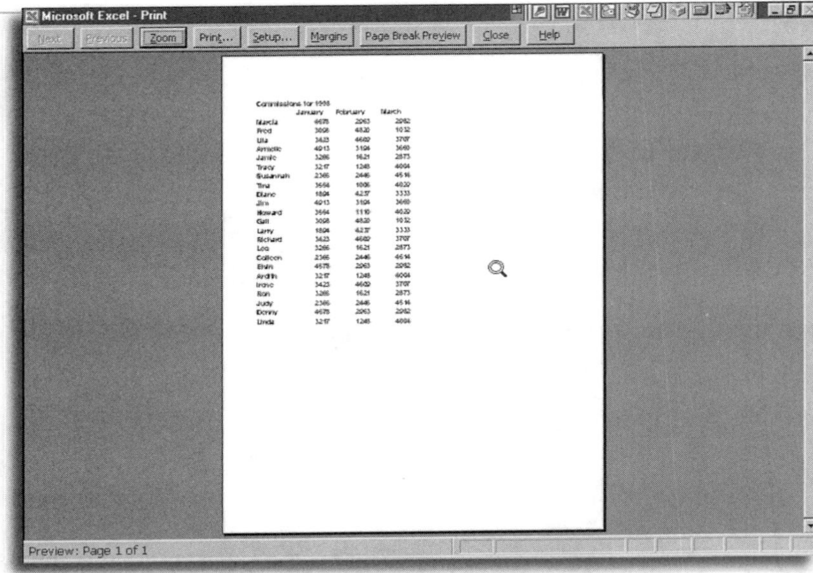

FIGURE 23.4
Only the print area is displayed in the preview.

Changing the Print Area

You don't need to remove a print area to set a new one; just set the new print area, and it will replace the previous print area.

Print Several Ranges with One Click

To set several different, nonadjacent print areas on the same worksheet, select one range; then, press Ctrl while you select the remaining ranges. On the **File** menu, point to **Print Area**; then, click **Set Print Area**. Each print area is printed on a separate page, and you can print them all with a single print command. To print them all on the same page, hide the rows and columns between the nonadjacent ranges, and then set a single print area that encompasses all of them.

Removing a Print Area

When a print area is no longer useful, you can remove it. To remove a print area, open the **File** menu, point to **Print Area**, and then click **Clear Print Area**.

SEE ALSO

➤ *To learn more about formatting printed pages, see page 461.*

Printing a Selected Range

To print a worksheet range "on-the-fly" or "just one time, right now," you can print a worksheet selection without setting a print area.

Print a selected range

1. Select the range you want to print.
2. On the **File** menu, click **Print**.

   The Print dialog box is displayed, as shown in Figure 23.5.

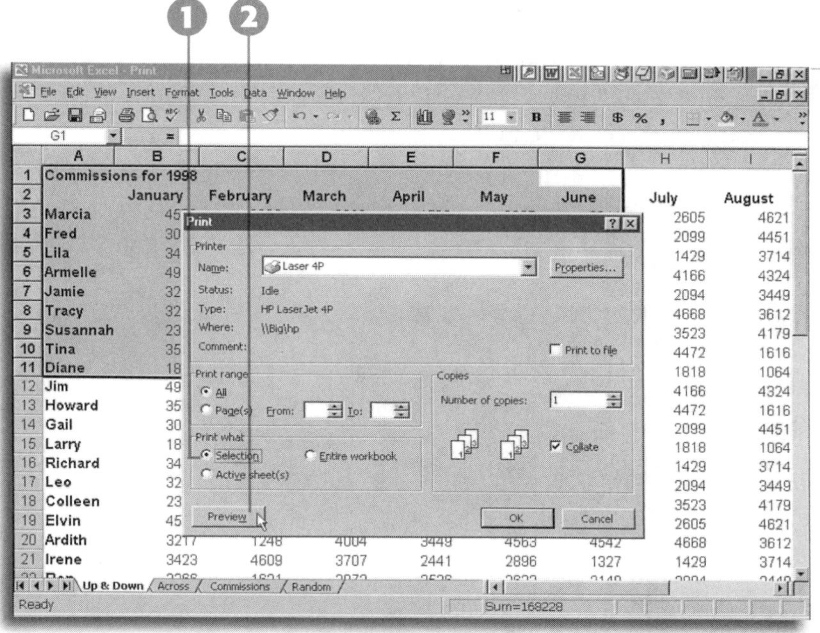

FIGURE 23.5

The Print dialog box is where you change default print settings.

1 Selection

2 Preview

3. Under **Print what**, click **Selection**.

   If you want to check your selection in Print Preview, click the **Preview** button before you click OK; from the Print Preview window, you can click the **Print** button (on the button bar) to print or the **Close** button to return to the worksheet and make further changes before printing.

4. Click **OK**.

Your selected range is printed.

Printing Specific Pages

Sometimes I catch an error after I've printed a worksheet that's several pages long. I have to change and reprint the pages with the corrections, but it's a waste of time and paper to reprint the entire worksheet.

Print specific pages from a worksheet

1. Display the worksheet in Print Preview (or look at your printed copy), and determine which pages you want to print.
2. On the **File** menu, click **Print**.

   The Print dialog box is displayed, as shown in Figure 23.6.

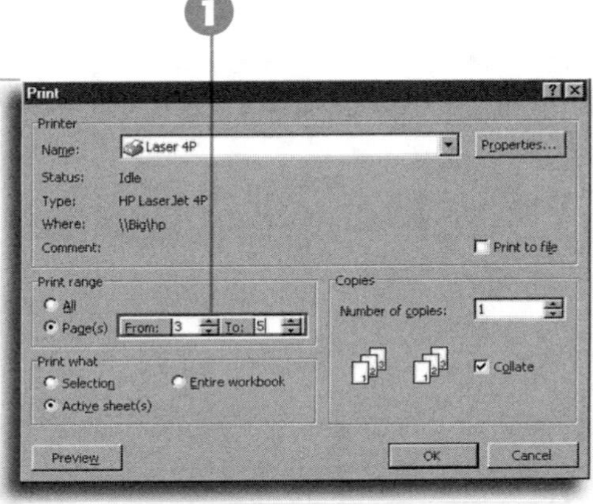

FIGURE 23.6

The Print dialog box lets you print only certain pages.

1 Print these pages.

3. Under **Print range**, click the **Page(s)** option.
4. Type the beginning and ending page numbers you want to print in the **From:** and **To:** boxes. To print just page 2, set **From:** and **To:** to 2. To print pages 3 through 5, set **From:** to 3, and **To:** to 5.
5. Click **OK**.

The pages you specified are printed.

SEE ALSO

➤ *To learn how to fit printed data onto a specific number of pages, see page 470.*

Printing a Chart

A chart can exist as a chart object on a worksheet, or it can stand alone as a separate chart sheet. If the chart is an object on a worksheet, you have three print choices:

- Print the chart alone.

- Print the worksheet alone.
- Print the worksheet with the chart on it.

SEE ALSO

➤ *To learn more about creating charts, see page 385.*
➤ *To learn more about formatting printed charts, see page 475.*

Printing a Chart Sheet

If a chart exists as a chart sheet, it is printed alone.

Print a chart sheet

1. Display the chart sheet.

   Check the chart page in Print Preview before you print so you won't be surprised. (Beautiful color charts often require color changes to be readable when printed on a black-and-white printer.)

2. On the Standard toolbar, click the **Print** button. 

The chart is printed. See Chapter 24, "Formatting the Printed Page," to learn about changes you can make to a printed chart.

SEE ALSO

➤ *To learn more about formatting printed pages, see page xx [Chapter 24].*

Printing a Chart Object

When a chart is an object on a worksheet, you can print it with the worksheet data, print the chart alone, or print the worksheet alone without removing the chart.

Printing the Chart Alone

You can print a chart object without its underlying worksheet by selecting the chart before you print.

Print a chart object without the worksheet data

1. Click in the chart. It doesn't matter which chart element is selected, so you can click anywhere in the chart.

   It's a good idea to check Print Preview at this point, in case you need to make color changes for printing.

2. On the Standard toolbar, click the **Print** button.

   The chart is printed as a full page, just as if it were a chart sheet.

Printing the Worksheet Alone

If you want to print the underlying worksheet without any charts, you need to make a minor change to the chart's properties to prevent it from printing.

Print the worksheet without the chart object

1. Right-click the chart area.
2. Click **Format Chart Area**.

   The Format Chart Area dialog box is displayed, as shown in Figure 23.7.

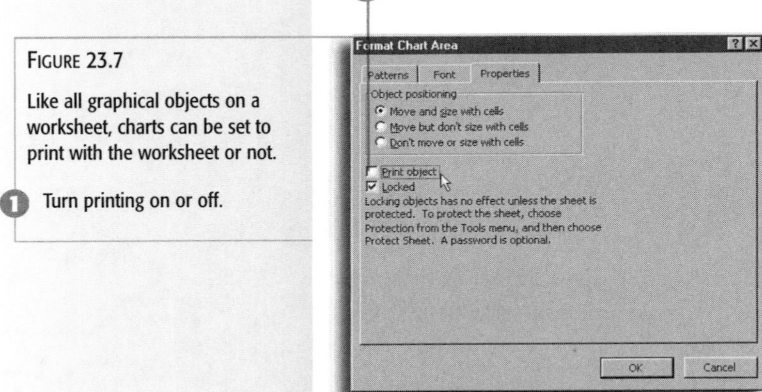

FIGURE 23.7

Like all graphical objects on a worksheet, charts can be set to print with the worksheet or not.

1 Turn printing on or off.

3. Click the **Properties** tab; then, click the **Print object** check box to clear it.
4. Click **OK**.

   If you check your worksheet in Print Preview at this point, the chart won't display.

To set the chart to print with the worksheet again, repeat the procedure to mark the **Print object** check box in step 3.

Printing the Worksheet with the Chart

Unless you make changes to the chart object's Print properties (as in the procedure described previously), the chart object is printed with the worksheet when you print the worksheet.

If you set a print area and the chart object is positioned outside the print area, the chart won't be printed unless you include it in the print area.

Printing an Entire Workbook

If you have several worksheets in a workbook and you need to print all of them, you can save yourself time by printing the entire workbook instead of printing each worksheet separately.

Print More Efficiently

To print a workbook efficiently, set up the print area and page orientation on each worksheet so that extraneous pages aren't printed.

Print an entire workbook

1. On the **File** menu, click **Print**.
2. Under **Print what**, click the **Entire workbook** option (shown in Figure 23.8).

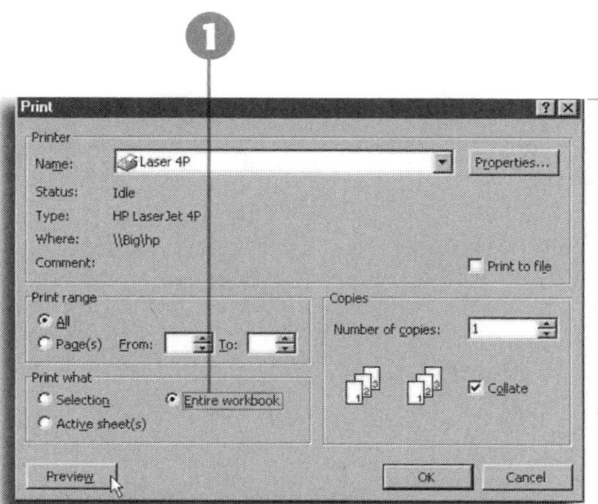

FIGURE 23.8
Printing the whole workbook can be a real time-saver.

1 Print whole workbook.

If you want to preview the pages that will be printed, click the **Preview** button. All the pages in the workbook will be displayed in Print Preview; to page through them one-by-one, click the **Next** button on the Print Preview button bar.

3. Click **OK**.

CHAPTER

24

Formatting the Printed Page

Changing page breaks, orientation, and paging order

Changing alignment of the data on the page

Changing page margins

Fitting data to a specific number of pages

Changing how data is labeled on each page

Creating page headers and footers

Printing worksheet gridlines (or not)

Changing worksheet colors to shades of gray or black and white

Printing charts with different sizes, alignments, and proportions

Changing Page Breaks

Excel automatically sets page breaks at the page margins, but the automatic page breaks often break information at inappropriate places in a table. You can change page breaks so that large tables are broken into pieces where you choose. There are two ways to set your own page breaks: in the worksheet and in Page Break Preview.

Changing Page Breaks in the Worksheet

Set page breaks

1. Display the worksheet in Print Preview (as shown in Figure 24.1), and determine where you need to reset page breaks.

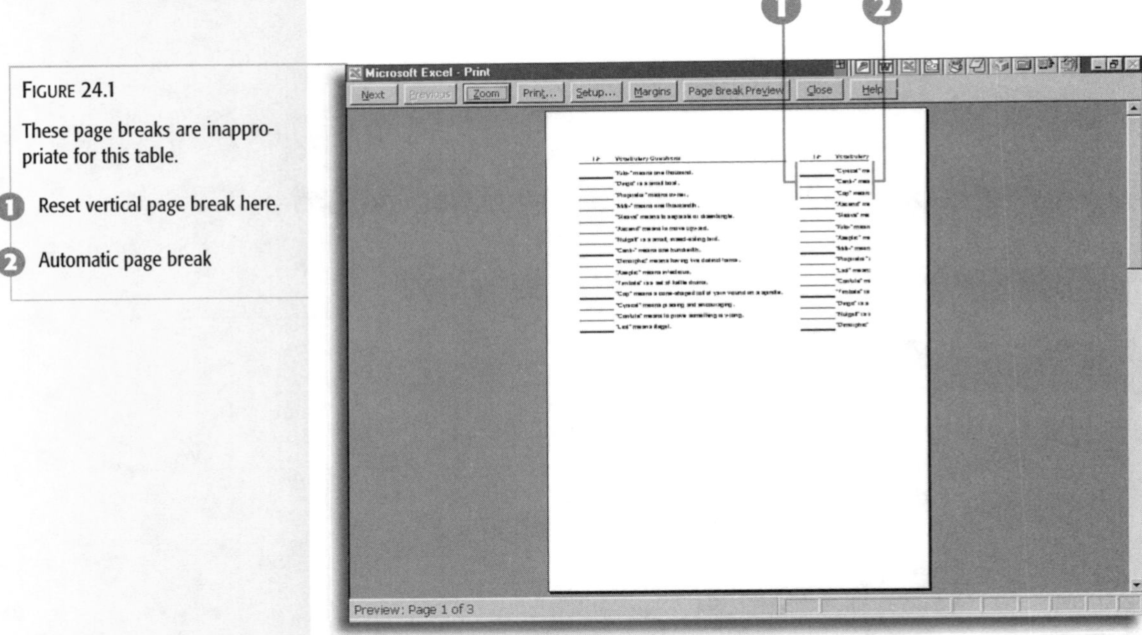

FIGURE 24.1

These page breaks are inappropriate for this table.

1 Reset vertical page break here.

2 Automatic page break

2. Click **Close** to close Print Preview and switch to Normal view.

   After you've opened a worksheet in Print Preview, the worksheet shows dashed lines where Excel has set automatic page breaks.

3. To set a new vertical page break, select the column on the right side of where you want the new page break (as shown in Figure 24.2).

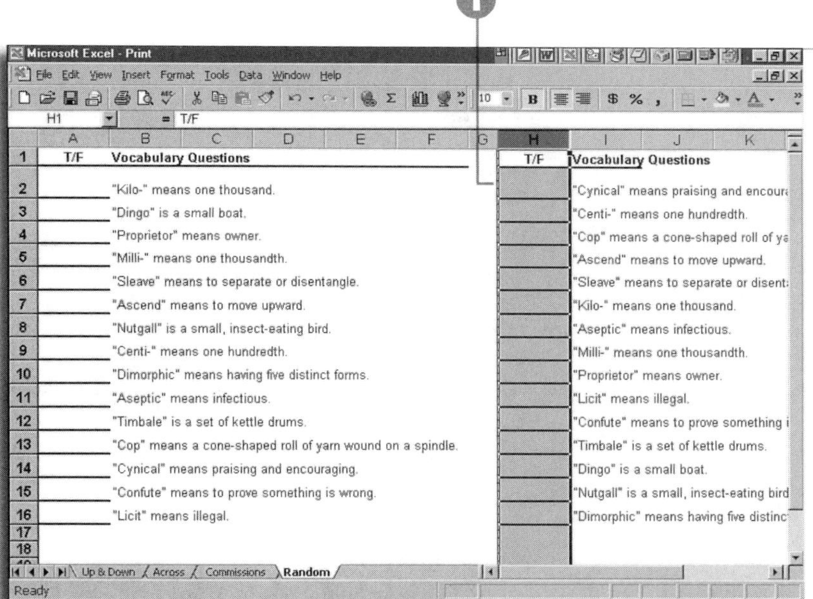

FIGURE 24.2
The new page break is created on the left side of the selected column.

1 Manual page break

4. On the **Insert** menu, click **Page Break**.

   A manual page break is created; it's a dashed line with longer dashes than the automatic page break.

5. To create a horizontal page break, select the row below the new page break.

6. On the **Insert** menu, click **Page Break**.

   A new horizontal page break is inserted.

Remove a Page Break

To remove a manual page break, click a cell below or on the right of the break line; then, open the **Insert** menu and click **Remove Page Break**.

Using Page Break Preview

Page Break Preview is a feature that shows you page breaks and page ordering from an "aerial view" and allows you to reset page break lines and print areas by dragging the lines.

You can also format cells, resize rows and columns, write formulas, and do just about anything you can do in Normal view.

Switch to Page Break Preview and change page breaks

1. On the **View** menu, click **Page Break Preview**.

   If you see a message welcoming you to Page Break Preview, click **OK**.

   The worksheet from Figure 24.1 is shown in Page Break Preview in Figure 24.3.

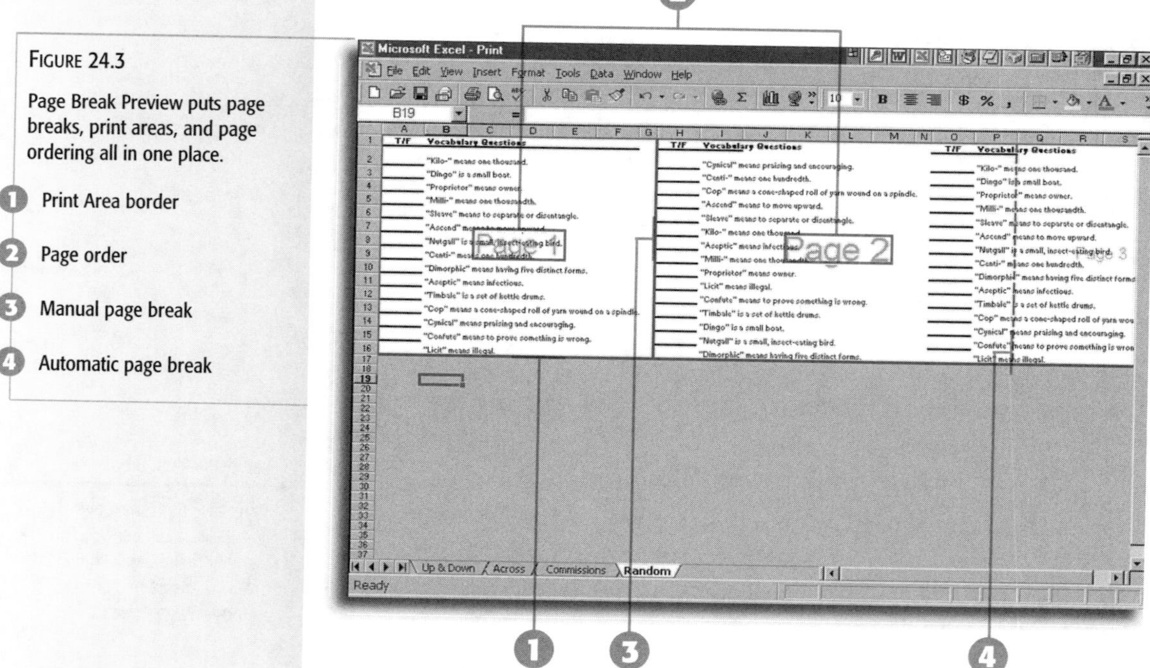

FIGURE 24.3

Page Break Preview puts page breaks, print areas, and page ordering all in one place.

1. Print Area border
2. Page order
3. Manual page break
4. Automatic page break

2. Point to the page break you want to move.
3. When the mouse pointer becomes a two-headed arrow, drag the break line to a new position.
4. To switch back to normal worksheet view, open the **View** menu and click **Normal**.

SEE ALSO

➤ *To learn more about setting print areas, see "Setting a Print Area," page 453.*

Set or Reset a Print Area Quickly

To reset a print area in Page Break Preview, drag the Print Area border lines to new positions.

Changing the Page Layout

Several aspects of the page layout usually need your attention:

- Orientation, either landscape or portrait
- Paging order, either over, then down or down, then over
- Centering the information on the page
- Changing page margins

All these items, and others, are set in the Page Setup dialog box.

Changing the Page Orientation

Some worksheets and charts need to be printed in a *landscape*, or wide, orientation, whereas others are better presented in a *portrait*, or tall, orientation.

Change page orientation

1. On the **File** menu, click **Page Setup**.

   The Page Setup dialog box is displayed, as shown in Figure 24.4.
2. On the **Page** tab, under **Orientation**, click the **Portrait** or **Landscape** option.
3. Click **OK** to close the dialog box or **Print Preview** to see the result of your change.

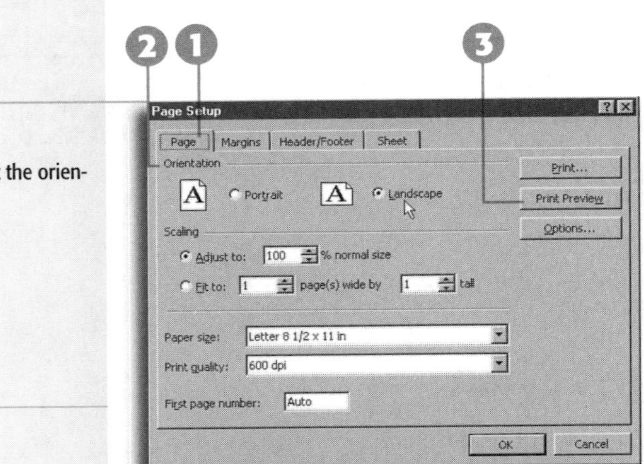

FIGURE 24.4

Use the **Page** tab to set the orientation.

1. Page tab
2. Orientation
3. Print Preview

Changing the Paging Order

Paging order is the order in which the pages in the worksheet are printed; if you have a worksheet that's several pages wide and several pages long, you can choose whether to have pages numbered across the width of the worksheet (as shown in Figure 24.5) or down the length (as shown in Figure 24.6).

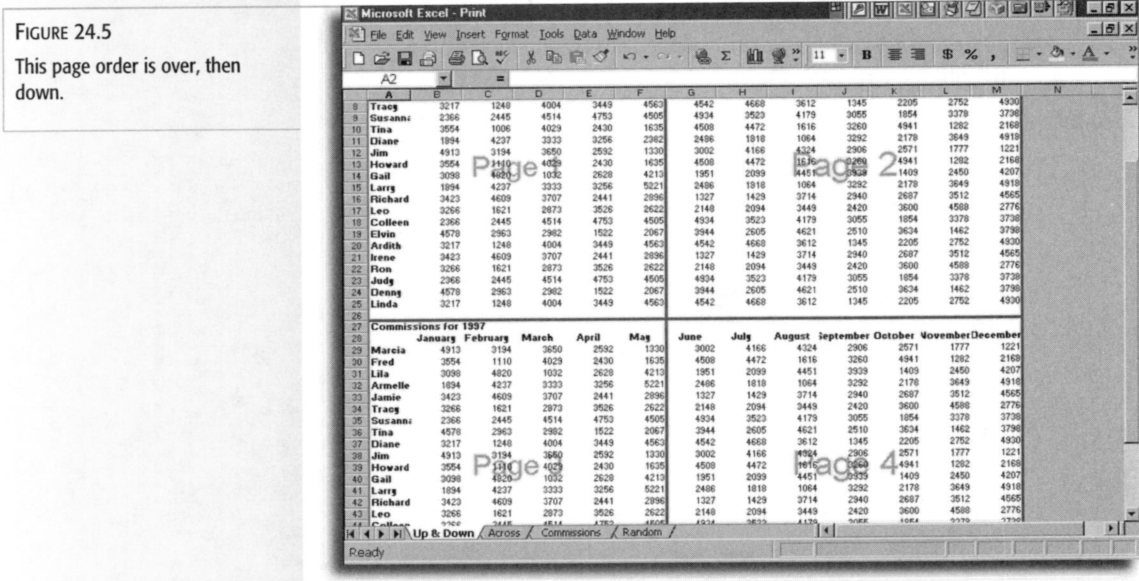

FIGURE 24.5

This page order is over, then down.

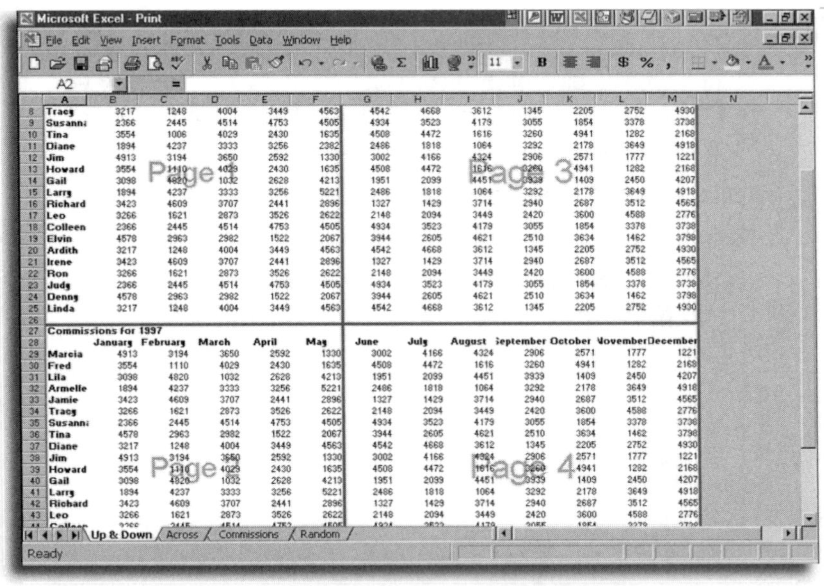

FIGURE 24.6
This page order is down, then over.

Change paging order

1. On the **File** menu, click **Page Setup**.
2. On the **Sheet** tab, shown in Figure 24.7, click an option under **Page order**.

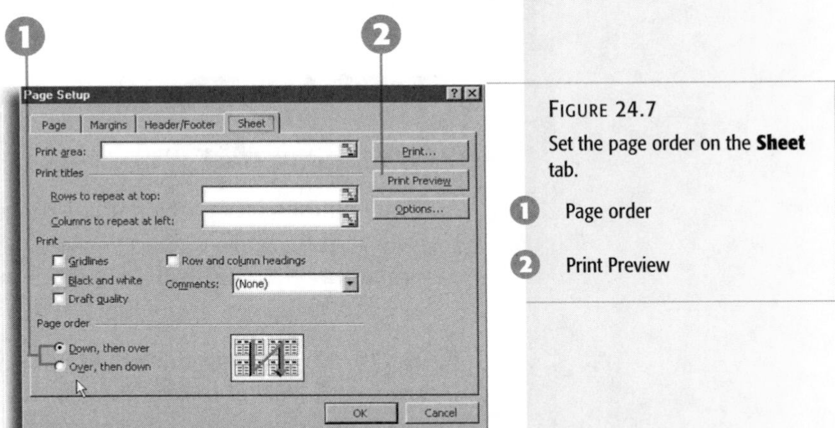

FIGURE 24.7
Set the page order on the **Sheet** tab.

1. Page order
2. Print Preview

3. Click **OK** to close the dialog box or **Print Preview** to see the new layout.

Changing the Centering

By default, the data on printed pages is aligned against the top and left margins. Often, your data looks better if it's centered horizontally (and sometimes vertically).

Center data on the printed page

1. On the **File** menu, click **Page Setup**.
2. On the **Margins** tab, shown in Figure 24.8, under **Center on page**, click check boxes for the centering you want.

   The Preview diagram shows you the results of your choices.
3. Click **OK**.

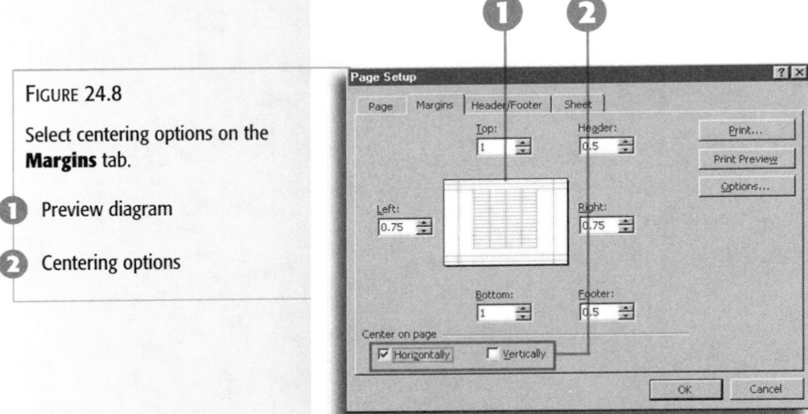

FIGURE 24.8

Select centering options on the **Margins** tab.

1. Preview diagram
2. Centering options

Changing Page Margins

Two common situations might prompt you to change the margins on your printed pages—to reduce the number of pages by fitting more rows or columns on each page and to change the size of a printed chart.

You can change margins precisely and identically by setting numerical margin measurements in a dialog box, or you can change them quickly by dragging the margin lines in Print Preview.

Changing Margins Precisely by Using the Dialog Box

To set margins with precision (for example, to make each margin exactly 1.5 inches), set them in the Page Setup dialog box.

Change margins using the Page Setup dialog box

1. On the **File** menu, click **Page Setup**.
2. On the **Margins** tab, shown in Figure 24.9, type margin measurements in the **Top**, **Bottom**, **Left**, and **Right** boxes.

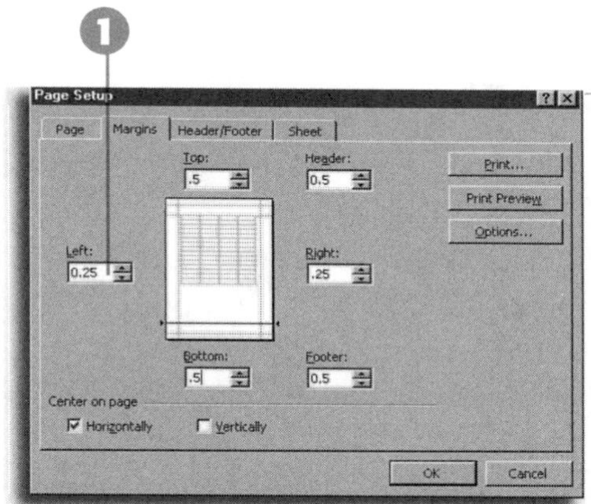

FIGURE 24.9
Set precise margins on the **Margins** tab.

1. Type precise measurements.

3. Click **OK** to close the dialog box or **Print Preview** to see the changed pages.

Changing Margins Quickly by Dragging Them

Often, you don't need precise margin measurements but want to change margins quickly.

Change margins quickly

1. Switch to Print Preview.
2. On the Print Preview button bar, click the **Margins** button (shown in Figure 24.10) to display margin lines on the page.

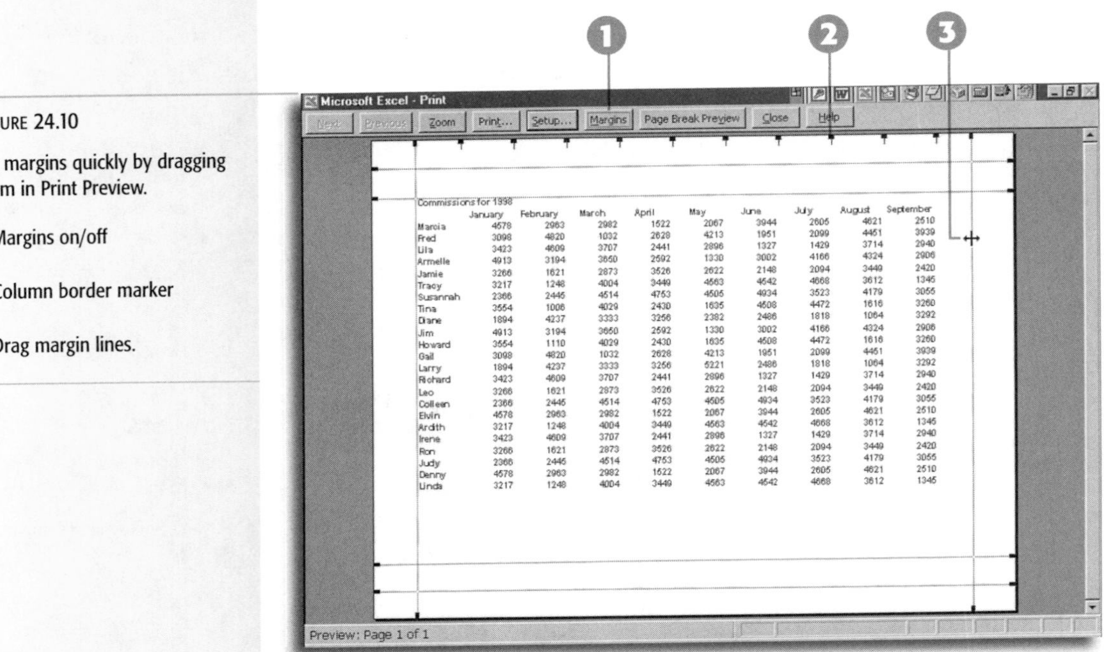

FIGURE 24.10

Set margins quickly by dragging them in Print Preview.

1 Margins on/off

2 Column border marker

3 Drag margin lines.

3. Point to a margin line; when the mouse pointer becomes a two-headed arrow, drag the line to a new position.
4. If you notice that a column is too narrow or too wide in Print Preview, drag its column border marker to resize it.

Printing a Worksheet on a Specific Number of Pages

Suppose you have a table of data that's just a few rows too long for three pages, but you don't want to print a fourth page. You can spend time messing with the margins and page layout to make the data fit on three pages, or you can have Excel shrink the data to fit precisely on three pages.

Fit data on a specific number of pages

1. On the **File** menu, click **Page Setup**.
2. On the **Page** tab (shown in Figure 24.11), under **Scaling**, click the **Fit to** option; then, type numbers in the **page(s) wide by** and **tall** boxes.

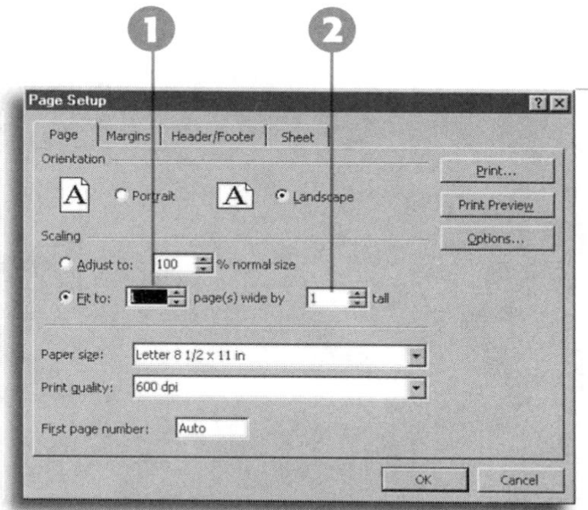

FIGURE 24.11

Fit data to a specific number of pages on the **Page** tab.

1. Fit on this many pages wide.
2. Fit on this many pages tall.

3. Click **OK** to close the dialog box or **Print Preview** to see the changed pages.

Give Your Pages Room to Grow

If you know your table will grow in length, but the number of columns won't change (perhaps a list of annual business expenses), set the **page(s) wide** box to 1 and the **tall** box to 50. Excel prints as many pages as there is data in the list, and the huge number of pages **tall** gives your list plenty of room to grow without changing the page setup.

Printing Row and Column Labels on Every Page

When you're printing a table that's several pages long or wide, only the first page has both column labels and row labels. On the remaining pages, where rows or columns don't have identifying labels, the data becomes rather meaningless. The solution to this problem is to set the rows and columns that contain labels as *print titles*, rows and columns that are printed on every page as labels to identify the data.

Don't Print Titles Twice

If you set print titles, don't include those rows and columns in the print area, or they'll be printed twice.

Create print titles

1. Display the worksheet in Normal view.
2. On the **File** menu, click **Page Setup**.
3. Click the **Sheet** tab (shown in Figure 24.12).
4. Under **Print titles**, click in the **Rows to repeat at top** box.
5. In the worksheet, click or drag the row selectors for the rows that contain column labels.

   The row references are entered in the box; these rows are repeated at the top of the data table on each printed page.

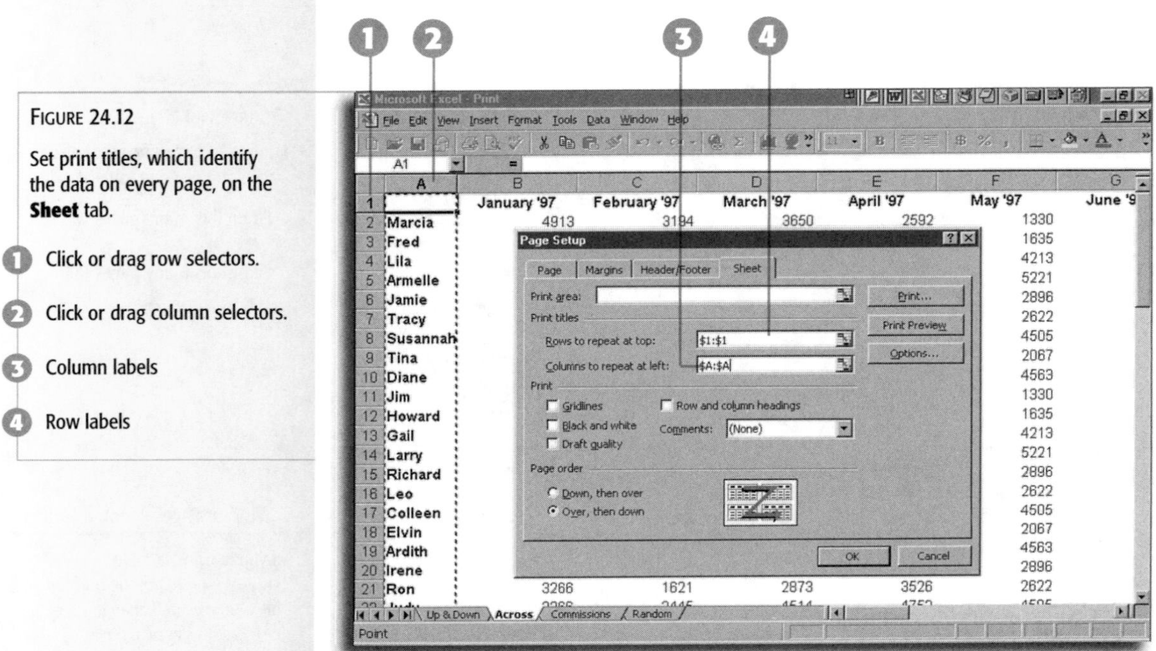

FIGURE 24.12

Set print titles, which identify the data on every page, on the **Sheet** tab.

1. Click or drag row selectors.
2. Click or drag column selectors.
3. Column labels
4. Row labels

6. Click in the **Columns to repeat at left** box.
7. In the worksheet, click or drag the column selectors for the columns that contain row labels.

   The column references are entered in the box; these columns are repeated on the left side of the data table on each printed page.
8. Click **OK** to close the dialog box or **Print Preview** to see the changed pages.

Creating a Custom Header or Footer

Headers and footers are an important part of the printed page; they can be displayed on every page and show information that's not part of the worksheet. Information that is often put in headers and footers includes a report title, page numbers, and the date and time the report was printed.

Headers and footers are created the same way; the only difference is that a header displays at the top of each page, and a footer displays at the bottom of each page.

Create a header (or footer)

1. On the **File** menu, click **Page Setup**.
2. Click the **Header/Footer** tab (shown in Figure 24.13).

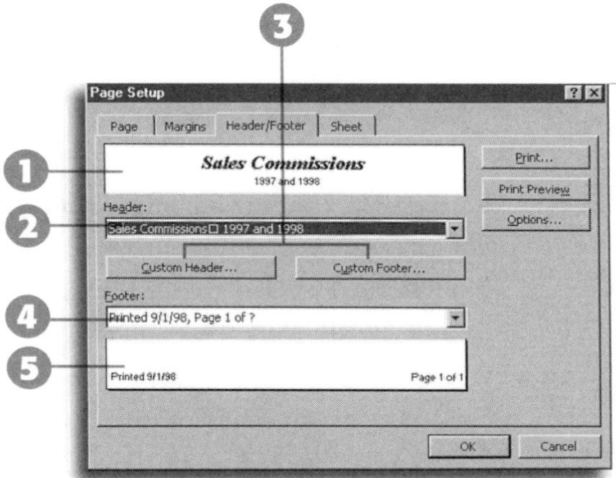

FIGURE 24.13
You create headers and footers the same way; the preview shows you what your header and footer look like on the printed page.

1. Header preview
2. Built-in headers
3. Create custom header or footer.
4. Built-in footers
5. Footer preview

3. To use a built-in header or footer, click the down arrow in the **Header** or **Footer** box; then, click the header or footer you want.

   Your selection is displayed in the preview window.

4. To create a custom header or footer, click the **Custom Header** or **Custom Footer** button.

   The Header (or Footer) dialog box is displayed with default entries. The dialog box (shown in Figure 24.14) has three windows: Entries in the left window are left-aligned in the header/footer, entries in the center window are centered in the header/footer, and entries in the right window are right-aligned in the header/footer.

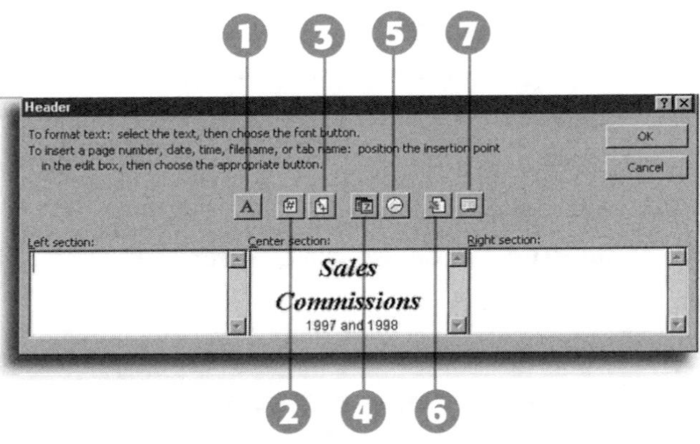

FIGURE 24.14

Custom headers and footers can be formatted and can show automatically updated information such as page numbers and dates.

1. Font
2. Page number
3. Total pages in document
4. Current date
5. Current time
6. Workbook name
7. Worksheet name

5. Click in the window for the alignment you want; then, type your custom header/footer text or click buttons to enter automatically updated information.

   Press Enter to start a new line in the header/footer.

6. Select text you want to format; then click the **Font** button (shown in Figure 24.14) and apply font formatting. Click **OK** to close the Format Font dialog box.
7. Click **OK** to close the Header (or Footer) dialog box.

   Check the header/footer in the preview window to be sure it's what you want.

8. Click **OK** to close the Page Setup dialog box, or click **Print Preview** to see the changed pages.

Customize Your Page Numbers (or Other Fields)

To create a footer that reads Page 1 of 4, type **Page** and then a space; click the **Page number** button; type a space, **of**, and a space; then click the **Total Pages** button. You can use this technique to customize any automatic fields in a header or footer.

Can't Remember What the Buttons Do?

For a quick explanation of what a button in the Header (or Footer) dialog box does, right-click a button and click the **What's This?** button that appears.

Printing Worksheet Gridlines

In Excel 2000 (and Excel 97), worksheet gridlines don't print by default, which is usually what you want. Sometimes, however, you might want to print the gridlines.

Print worksheet gridlines

1. On the **File** menu, click **Page Setup**.
2. On the **Sheet** tab, click the **Gridlines** check box.
3. Click **OK** to close the Page Setup dialog box, or click **Print Preview** to see the changed pages.

Printing in Black and White

I like to use cell colors in my worksheets to highlight important cells, but I don't want the cell colors (or shades of gray) printed. Instead of removing the cell colors, printing, and replacing the cell colors, I can tell Excel to print the worksheet in black and white, which hides any cell colors.

Print in black and white

1. On the **File** menu, click **Page Setup**.
2. On the **Sheet** tab, click the **Black and white** check box.
3. Click **OK** to close the Page Setup dialog box, or click **Print Preview** to see the changed pages.

SEE ALSO

➤ *To learn more about formatting worksheet cells with colors, see the section titled "Formatting Colors," page 235.*

Formatting Printed Charts

You might want to make two changes to your charts before printing:

- Change the size or proportions of the printed chart.
- Switch the colors of the data markers to black-and-white patterns for clear differentiation on a black-and-white printer.

SEE ALSO

➤ *To learn more about creating charts, see the section titled "Creating a Chart with the Chart Wizard," page 386.*

Resizing a Printed Chart

When you're about to print a chart without a worksheet (whether it's a chart sheet or a chart object), take a look at the chart page in Print Preview before you click the Print button. What you see might need some tweaking.

A printed chart is automatically stretched to fit within the margins of the printed page, which can stretch a tall or wide chart

Chart Options in the Page Setup Dialog Box

The chart options in the Page Setup dialog box only display when a chart object or chart sheet is selected before you open the **File** menu and click **Page Setup**.

completely out of proportion. You can change the size or proportions of your printed chart in the following ways:

- Change the page margins to resize and reposition the chart on its page.
- Select from three options in the Page Setup dialog box on the **Chart** tab. Table 24.1 explains the three options.

TABLE 24.1 **Printed chart size/scale options**

This Option	Does This
Use full page	Changes the size and shape of the chart to fill all the space within the margin lines.
Scale to fit page	Resizes the chart to fit within the margins without altering the chart's original height/width proportions.
Custom	Makes the printed chart the same size and shape as the chart object on the worksheet (which has little effect on a chart sheet).

Resize and reposition the chart on the page by changing the page margins

1. Display the chart in Print Preview.
2. On the button bar, click the **Margins** button to turn on margin lines.
3. Drag the margin lines (as shown in Figure 24.15); the chart will remain within them in accordance with the size/scale options set in the Page Setup dialog box.

Control the size and proportions of a chart within the printed-page margins

1. On the **File** menu, click **Page Setup** (or click the **Setup** button on the Print Preview button bar).
2. On the **Chart** tab (shown in Figure 24.16), click one of the three options under **Printed chart size**.

   Table 24.1 explains what each option does.
3. Click **OK** to close the Page Setup dialog box, or click **Print Preview** to see the changed page.

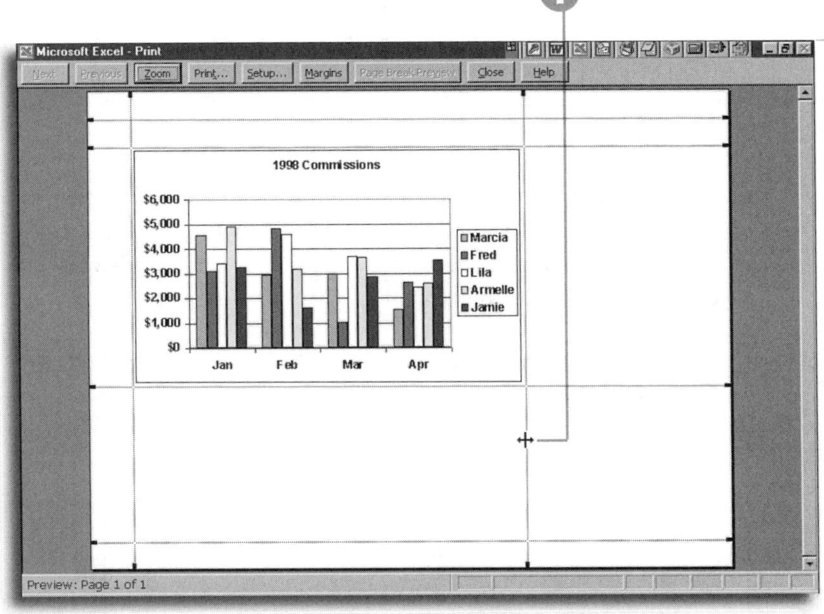

FIGURE 24.15

Resize and move the chart on its printed page by dragging its surrounding margin lines.

1. Drag.

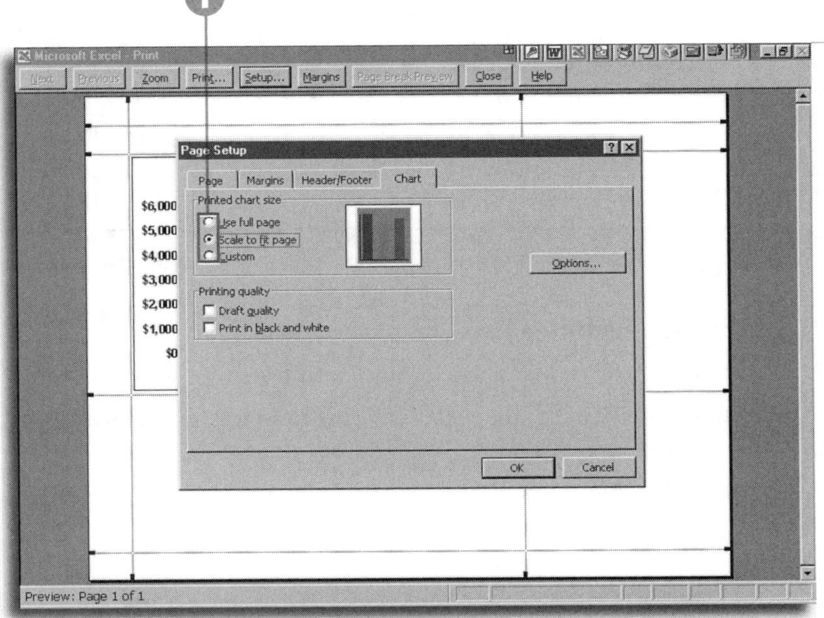

FIGURE 24.16

Set printed-chart size and scale options on the **Chart** tab.

1. These options control size and proportion.

Printing Data Markers in Black and White

If you're printing on a black-and-white printer, you'll be disappointed at what happens to your beautifully colored chart; sometimes the markers are difficult to differentiate and identify because they're all in shades of gray.

To solve this problem, you can print your chart with gray-shaded background fills and borders but have Excel switch the marker colors and their corresponding legend keys to black-and-white patterns, as shown in Figure 24.17.

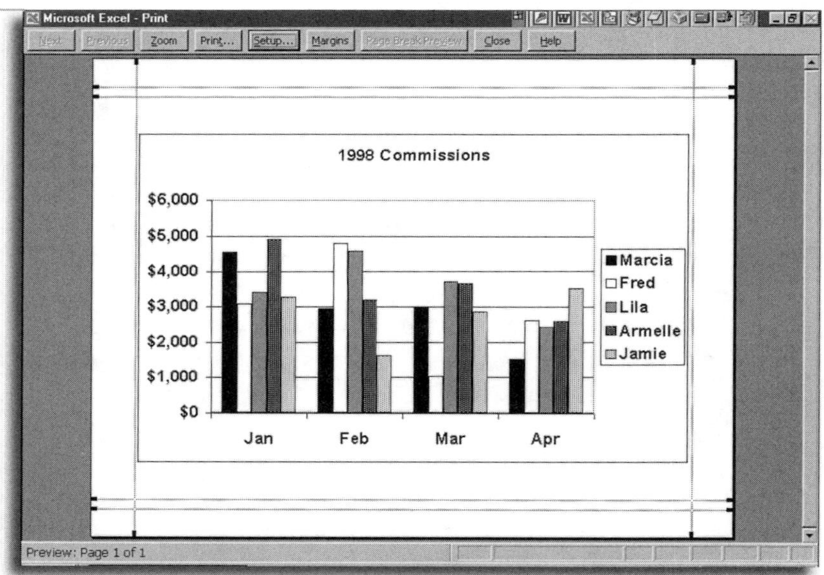

FIGURE 24.17
There's no question which marker is which in this chart now that the data markers are in black-and-white patterns.

Print data markers in black-and-white patterns

1. On the **File** menu, click **Page Setup**.
2. On the **Chart** tab, click the **Print in black and white** check box.
3. Click **OK** to close the Page Setup dialog box, or click **Print Preview** to see the changed pages.

PART

VII

Sharing Data with Other Users and Other Applications

25 Sharing a Workbook with Other Users 481

26 Sharing Data Between Applications 499

CHAPTER

25

Sharing a Workbook with Other Users

Finding out who's using a shared workbook

Saving a shared workbook

Reviewing changes and resolving conflicts in a shared workbook

Tracking changes in a shared workbook

Accepting and rejecting tracked changes

Merging shared workbooks

Printing a history of changes

Unsharing a workbook

Saving a workbook as read-only

Sharing a Workbook

If you share a workbook with others on a network, two or more people can use the workbook simultaneously. This arrangement comes in handy if a team is working feverishly on a project deadline or if several people need access to a list of common data such as expenses, orders, or purchases. When a workbook is shared, no one has to wait his or her turn to open and make changes in the workbook.

If a workbook isn't shared and someone else has it open when you try to open it, you'll get a message box that allows you to choose between opening the workbook as read-only (so you can read it but not make changes) or being notified by an onscreen message when the workbook is closed and available to you.

You can also work on two separate but identical copies of a shared workbook and then merge the two workbooks into one for the same results as simultaneously sharing the same workbook. This feature is handy if someone needs to take a copy of a workbook on the road, work on it away from the network, and then return to the office and combine his or her changes quickly into the original workbook.

Does This Really Work?

To test and practice sharing workbooks, you'll need to enlist the help of someone else on your network who can open a shared workbook simultaneously with you.

Before you can use a workbook simultaneously with another user (or use copies of a workbook you want to merge later), you must open the workbook and set its "shared" setting.

Share a workbook

1. On the **Tools** menu, click **Share Workbook**.

   The Share Workbook dialog box is displayed, as shown in Figure 25.1.

2. On the **Editing** tab, click the **Allow changes by more than one user at the same time** check box.

3. Click **OK**.

   A message tells you the workbook will be saved and asks if you want to continue. If your workbook is brand-new and hasn't been saved yet, you'll be asked to save it and give it a name at this point.

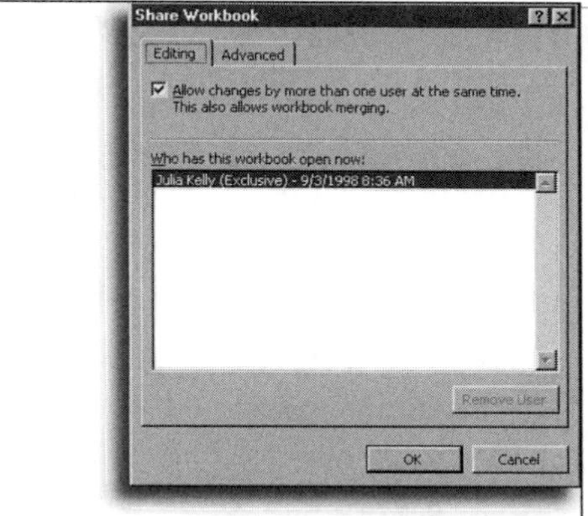

FIGURE 25.1
One quick click and the workbook is available to all.

4. Click **OK**.

The workbook is now shared, and the word [Shared] is displayed in the title bar as a reminder.

When you work in a shared workbook, you might find yourself unable to perform a task. To save you the frustration of wondering why it won't work, here are some things you can't do in a shared workbook:

- Delete worksheets.
- Insert or delete ranges. (However, you can insert or delete entire rows and columns.)
- Merge multiple cells into a single cell.
- Create conditional formats.
- Create or change data validation settings.
- Create or change charts, pictures, objects, or hyperlinks.
- Draw graphical objects with the Drawing toolbar.
- Create, change, or view scenarios.
- Create automatic subtotals.
- Group or outline data.
- Create or change PivotTables.
- Do anything involving macros.

Who Can Open My Workbook?

Your shared workbook can be opened by users with Excel 97 or Excel 2000, but not by users with any earlier version of Excel. To open the workbook in Excel 95, you need to unshare it and save it as a file type of 5.0/95 Workbook or 97-2000 & 5.0/95 Workbook.

SEE ALSO

➤ *To learn more about saving workbooks, see the section titled "Saving a File," page 46.*

Who's Using a Shared Workbook?

When you open a shared workbook, the word [Shared] in the title bar tells you it's available to others, but you can't tell from the title bar whether someone else is currently using the workbook (or who the current users are).

Removing a User

Any user can remove any other user from a shared workbook by selecting the name and clicking the **Remove user** button; this step might be necessary if someone is finished using the shared workbook but left it open. For more details about removing a user, right-click the **Remove user** button; then click the **What's This?** button that is displayed.

See who's currently using a shared workbook

1. On the **Tools** menu, click **Share Workbook**.
2. On the **Editing** tab, look at the **Who has this workbook open now** list (shown in Figure 25.2). The names come from Excel's **Tools**, **Options** dialog box, **General** tab, in the **User Name** box.

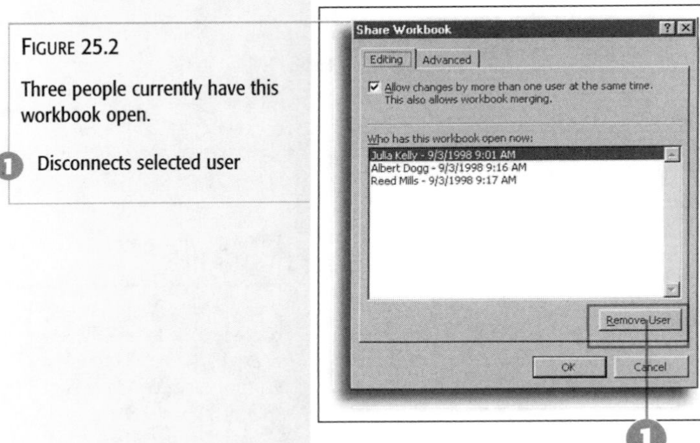

FIGURE 25.2

Three people currently have this workbook open.

1 Disconnects selected user

3. Click **OK** or **Cancel** to close the dialog box.

Saving a Shared Workbook

If more than one user has made entries in a shared workbook, you see the other entries when you save the workbook. Whoever saves the workbook gets to decide which changes to keep.

Save a shared workbook

1. On the toolbar, click **Save**.

   You might see a message that other users have made changes; if so, read it and click **OK** to close it.

   Changed cells have colored borders and a colored triangle in the upper-left corner; the color identifies who made the change. The colored borders and triangles disappear after changes are accepted or rejected (which you'll learn about in the following sections).

2. Point to a changed cell.

   A comment like the one in Figure 25.3 is displayed, with information about the changes.

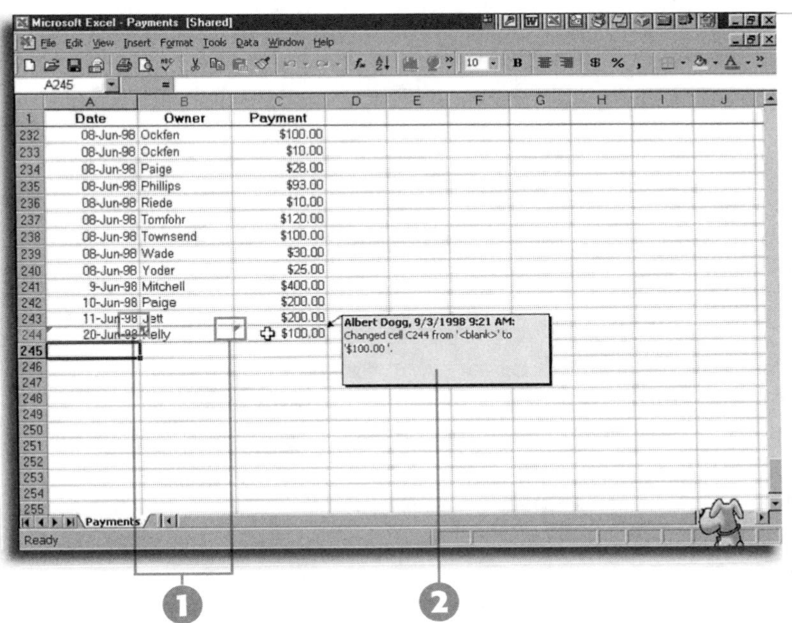

FIGURE 25.3

Every time the workbook is saved, each worksheet shows you where changes were made since you last saved.

1. Change indicator
2. Change comment

Reviewing Changes in a Shared Workbook

If two or more people have made changes to the same cell, a conflict arises when the workbook is saved: Which changes should Excel keep?

Excel keeps track of all the changes made in a shared workbook; you can review all the changes and decide individually which changes to keep, either when you save the workbook or later when you want to see what's been happening in the workbook while you were away.

Resolving Conflicts in a Shared Workbook

When you save a workbook that contains conflicting changes, you can resolve the conflicts in the Resolve Conflicts dialog box (shown in Figure 25.4) and accept or reject any changes.

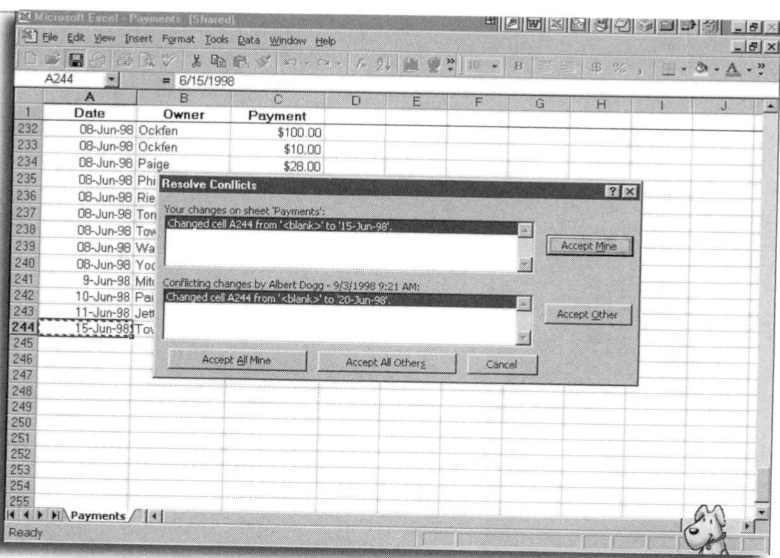

FIGURE 25.4

The Resolve Conflicts dialog box is displayed only when there are two or more saved changes to a cell.

I'm Not Conflict Oriented

To set up the shared workbook so that whoever saves the workbook gets his or her changes saved, open the **Tools** menu and click **Share Workbook**; on the **Advanced** tab of the Share Workbook dialog box, click the option for **The changes being saved win**. There won't be any conflicts to resolve.

If the Resolve Conflicts dialog box is displayed when you save the workbook, choose an option:

- To keep your change (displayed in the dialog box), click **Accept Mine**.
- To keep the other change displayed in the dialog box, click **Accept Other**.
- To keep only your changes throughout the worksheet without reviewing them, click **Accept All Mine**.
- To keep all the other changes in the worksheet without reviewing them, click **Accept All Others**.
- To postpone the conflict resolution until later, click **Cancel**. (You'll see a message that the worksheet hasn't been saved; click **OK** to continue.)

The Resolve Conflicts dialog box closes itself when you finish.

Tracking Changes in a Shared Workbook

If you've just opened a shared workbook and you want to see what changes have been made in your absence, you can highlight every changed cell on a worksheet and accept or reject any changes that were made.

Highlighting Changed Cells

You can see which cells have been changed by highlighting them.

Highlight changed cells

1. On the **Tools** menu, point to **Track Changes**; then, click **Highlight Changes**.

   The Highlight Changes dialog box is displayed, as shown in Figure 25.5.

2. Select the changes you want to see by clicking the **When**, **Who**, or **Where** check boxes and selecting alternatives from the drop-down lists.

   If your time is limited and you're only interested in changes in a specific part of a worksheet, click in the **Where** box, then drag to select the worksheet cells you want to check; only the selected cells will be checked for changes. To check the entire worksheet, leave the **Where** box and check box empty.

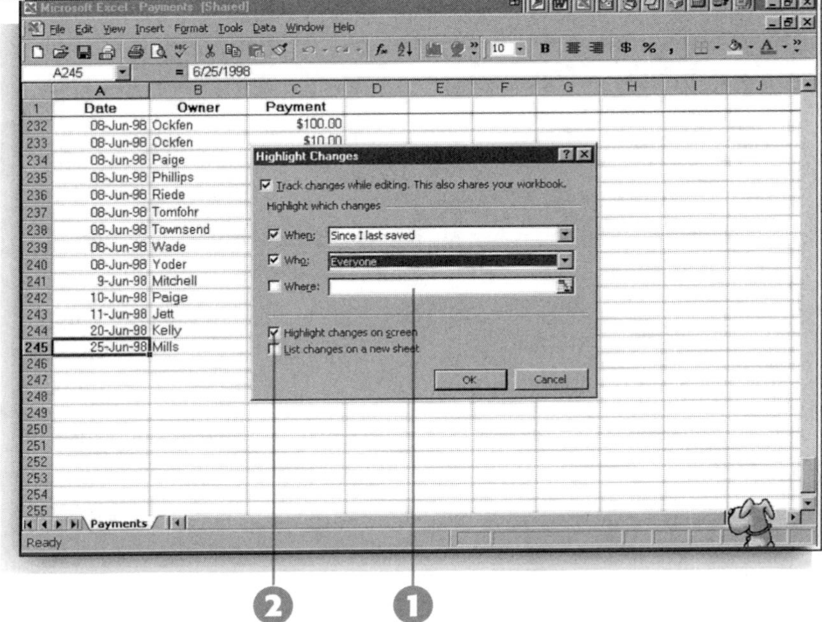

FIGURE 25.5

To save time, you can be quite specific about which changes you want to see.

1. Drag to enter a specific worksheet range.

2. Show the changed cells.

3. Click **OK**.

   All the changes you elected to see are highlighted with colored borders and change indicators, like the changed cells in Figure 25.6. The person's Excel user name is displayed in a comment when you point at a changed cell.

Accepting and Rejecting Tracked Changes

After you highlight changed cells, you can accept or reject the changes; you can review the changes individually to accept some and reject others, or you can accept or reject the whole set of highlighted changes.

Accept or reject changes

1. On the **Tools** menu, point to **Track Changes**; then, click **Accept or Reject Changes**.

   At this point, you might see a message that the workbook will be saved; click **OK** to continue. Then you might see the Resolve Conflicts dialog box; you'll have to accept or reject conflicting changes to satisfy the dialog box. (You might or might not see this message and dialog box before you see the Select Changes to Accept or Reject dialog box, depending on what has transpired among users of the shared workbook.)

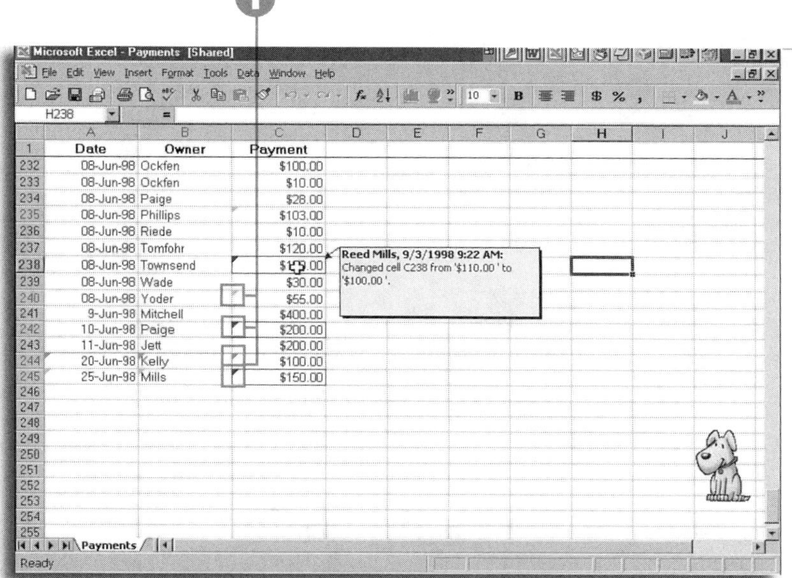

FIGURE 25.6
The cell borders and change indicators are different colors depending on who made the change.

1 Change indicators

The Select Changes to Accept or Reject dialog box is displayed, as shown in Figure 25.7.

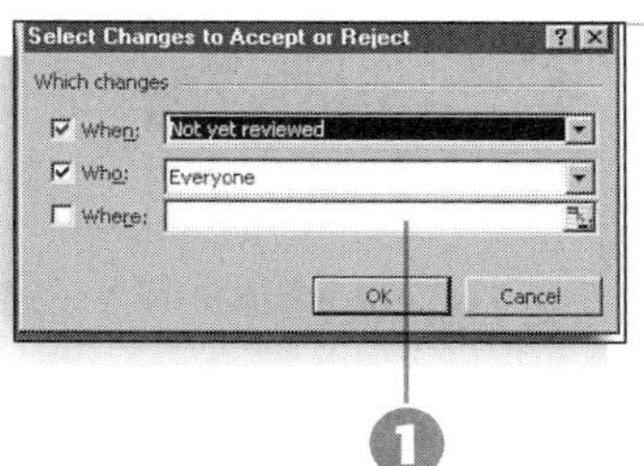

FIGURE 25.7
You can save time by narrowing the range of changes to accept or reject.

1 Click here; then, drag to limit worksheet range.

2. In the Select Changes to Accept or Reject dialog box, click the **When**, **Who**, or **Where** check boxes and select alternatives from the drop-down lists to limit the changes you want to see.

3. Click **OK**.

   If there are changes within the limits you set, the Accept or Reject Changes dialog box is displayed, as shown in Figure 25.8. (If there are no changes, you'll see a message to that effect; click **OK** to continue.)

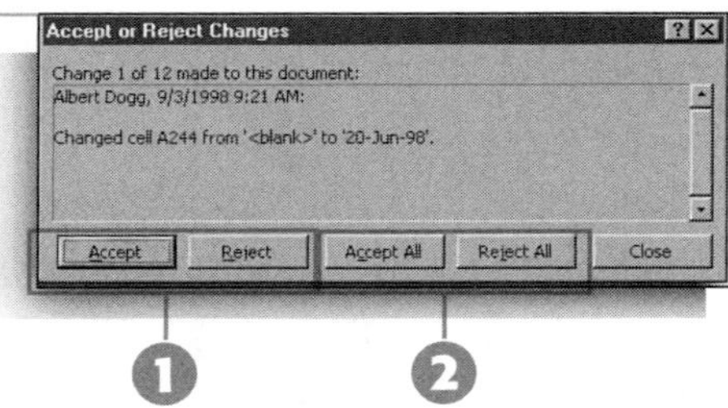

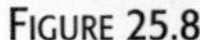
FIGURE 25.8

Sort through the changes individually, or accept or reject the whole lot.

1. Accept/reject the displayed change.
2. Accept/reject all the changes you specified.

4. To accept or reject changes, either individually or en masse, click the appropriate buttons in the dialog box.

   When all changes have been reviewed, the dialog box closes itself.

Merging Shared Workbooks

You can send identical copies of a workbook to others, let each make his or her own changes and additions to the workbook, and then merge all the copies back into a single workbook.

Workbooks must meet specific requirements so they can be merged:

- The original workbook must be "shared" before you make copies of it.
- In the original workbook, you must set a number of days to track the change history (on the Share Workbook dialog box's **Advanced** tab). By default, Excel keeps a change history for 30 days.
- The workbook copies must be merged before the change history days run out. (If you don't change any default settings, you've got a month.)

- You can only merge copies of the original workbook with each other. (Workbooks that are similar but are not copies won't merge.)
- Each copy of the workbook must have a different filename.

When you've made copies of a shared workbook and made changes to one or all of the copies, you can merge them all back together into a single workbook. In the merged workbook, you can highlight, accept, and reject changes and conflicting information just as if the changes had been made to a single shared workbook.

Merge copies of a shared workbook

1. Open the copy of the shared workbook that will become the main shared workbook.
2. On the **Tools** menu, click **Merge Workbooks**.

   If the merge workbook has any unsaved changes in it, you'll see a message asking you to save the workbook. Click **OK**.

   The Select Files to Merge Into Current Workbook dialog box is displayed; it looks and works like the Open and Save dialog boxes you're familiar with.
3. In the Select Files to Merge Into Current Workbook dialog box, click the name of a shared copy you want to merge.
4. Click **OK**.
5. Repeat steps 2 through 4 for each copy you want to merge into the main shared workbook.

The main shared workbook shows changes and conflicts with changed-cell colored borders and indicators.

Merge Several Copies at Once

If you're merging multiple shared copies that are all in the same folder, you can select all their names in step 3 and merge them all at once.

Printing a History of Changes

By default, Excel keeps track of the changes that have been made to a shared workbook for the past 30 days. For example, if a specific cell has been changed back and forth several times, each change in the tussle is tracked. You can print a change history—a separate worksheet that lists all the changes made to cells in your worksheet—as long as the workbook is shared.

How Much History Can I Keep?

You can change the number of days, or not keep track of the history at all, by changing the option under **Track changes** on the **Advanced** tab of the Share Workbook dialog box.

Print a history of all the changes Excel has tracked

1. On the **Tools** menu, point to **Track Changes**; then click **Highlight Changes**.
2. Clear the **When**, **Who**, and **Where** check boxes.
3. Click the **List changes on a new sheet** check box.
4. Click **OK**.

   A new worksheet is created, like the one shown in Figure 25.9. The worksheet has AutoFilter buttons so you can filter to hide changes you're not concerned with and then print the history (to show others who's been wrangling over which data).

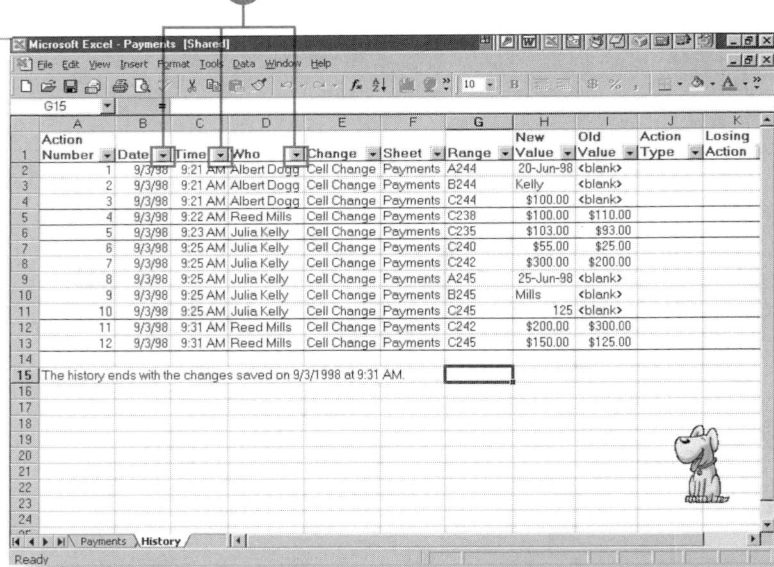

FIGURE 25.9

You can limit the change history with choices in the Highlight Changes dialog box and then further limit the display by filtering the changes with the AutoFilter buttons.

 AutoFilter buttons

SEE ALSO

➤ *For more information on using AutoFilter, see the section titled "Filtering a List on a Single Criterion," page 284.*

Unsharing a Workbook

The time might come when you need to be proprietary about a workbook—for example, if you want to create PivotTables or charts for a presentation. Because you can't do these things (or other important stuff) in a shared workbook, you'll need to unshare the workbook.

Unshare a workbook

1. On the **Tools** menu, click **Share Workbook**.
2. On the **Editing** tab, clear the **Allow changes by more than one user at the same time** check box; then click **OK**.

   A confirmation message is displayed.
3. If you're sure you want to unshare the workbook, click **Yes**. Otherwise, click **No**.

   The workbook is now available to only one user at a time. If you had a change history worksheet in the workbook, it's removed permanently.

Saving a Workbook as Read-Only (the Opposite of Sharing)

The opposite of sharing a workbook is to save it as read-only, so that others are reminded not to use it. (In its read-only state, others can read it but cannot save changes to it unless they save it with a different filename.)

If you have an unshared workbook open, anyone else who tries to open it can *only* open it as read-only. You can make the read-only setting permanent to remind others not to change it, even when you're not using it, but if the workbook isn't in use when they open it, the read-only message is only a reminder.

I Don't Want Anyone to See My Workbook at All

You can protect the workbook so nobody can open it without a password. In the Save Options dialog box, type a password in the **Password to Open** box. (This is a great idea for teachers who want to protect grade sheets from their bright, young hacker students.) Be careful: Passwords are case sensitive (jk is different from JK), and if you forget the password, you're out of luck.

Save a workbook as read-only

1. On the **File** menu, click **Save As**.
2. In the Save As dialog box, click the **Tools** button.
3. On the Tools menu, click **General Options**.
4. In the Save Options dialog box, click the **Read-only recommended** check box; then, click **OK**.

Read-Only Is Only a Reminder

If someone clicks **No** in the **Open as read-only?** message box, the workbook opens normally and he or she can save changes to it. The read-only status of the file is only a reminder, not true file security.

5. In the Save As dialog box, click **Save**.

   A message is displayed asking if you want to replace the existing file of the same name with the "new" file. (It's the same file, but this is how Excel makes the change.)

6. Click **Yes**.

   Other people are able to open the file and read its contents. (They'll see a message like the one in Figure 25.10, and they should, you hope, heed your request to open the file read-only by clicking **Yes**.)

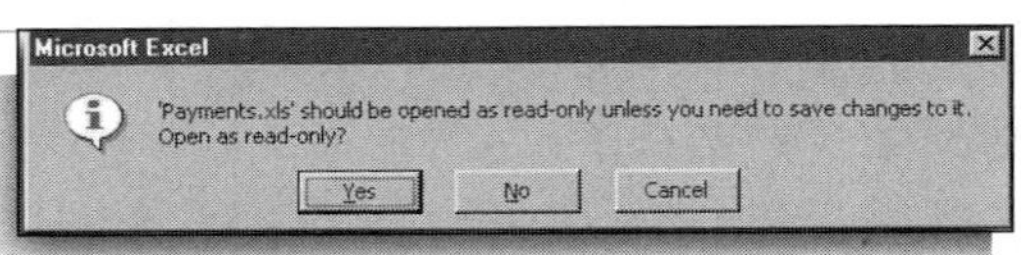

FIGURE 25.10

This message is a reminder to anyone who opens the workbook.

If they want to make changes, they'll have to either click **No** (and the file opens normally) or click **Yes** and then save the file with a different name.

To undo the read-only setting, repeat the steps to save a workbook as read-only, but clear the **Read-only recommended** check box in step 3.

SEE ALSO

➤ *To learn more about saving workbooks, see the section titled "Saving Files as Workbooks," page 46.*

Protecting Workbooks and Worksheets

When you've gone to great effort to create a complex worksheet or workbook full of intricately constructed formulas (as in the Theatre Seating workbook in Chapter 31, "Creative Worksheets"), you don't want other folks to inadvertently change or delete any of those formulas. Or you might have a worksheet with intricate graphical objects or an important chart, and you want to prevent others who open the workbook from changing those worksheet objects.

A few locks and keys are built into Excel to help you protect your work: You can protect an entire workbook, or individual worksheets in a workbook. Which you choose depends on what you want to protect or prevent.

You can protect the workbook if you want to prevent

- Deleting or inserting worksheets
- Renaming worksheets
- Copying or moving worksheets
- Hiding or unhiding worksheets
- Changing the size or shape of workbook windows
- Splitting or unsplitting panes
- Freezing or unfreezing panes

You can protect the worksheet if you want to prevent changes to

- Cell contents
- Charts
- Graphical objects
- Scenario definitions

You can protect and share a workbook at the same time if you want to share a workbook and make sure all the changes by others are tracked. (No one can remove change tracking.)

Protect a workbook

1. On the **Tools** menu, point to **Protection**, and click **Protect Workbook**.
2. In the Protect Workbook dialog box (shown in Figure 25.11), mark check boxes to protect **Structure** or **Windows** or both.

   Unless you really, seriously, desperately need to protect your work from changes by malicious evil-doers, my advice is don't use a password. Leave the **Password** box blank. (You'll be able to unprotect the workbook to make changes a lot more quickly.)
3. Click **OK**.

To unprotect the workbook so you can make changes to the window or worksheet arrangement, on the **Tools** menu, point to **Protection**, and click **Unprotect Workbook**. If you protected the workbook with a password, you'll have to enter the password and click **OK**.

I Am Paranoid About Changes

Anyone who knows Excel can unprotect your workbook and mess up your work, so to *really* protect the workbook, you can type a password in the **Password** box. Be careful, however; passwords are case sensitive, so if you type **JK**, the initials jk won't work. Also, if you forget your password, you're out of luck.

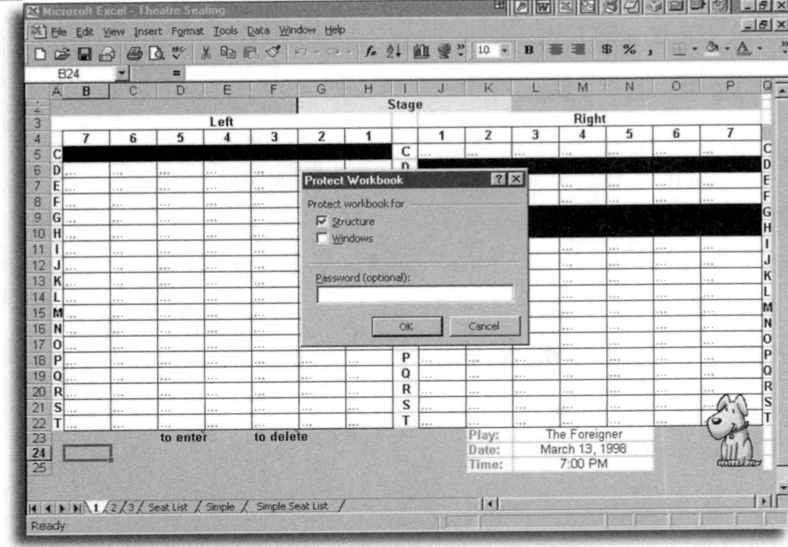

FIGURE 25.11

To prevent changes to the worksheet or window arrangement, you can protect the whole workbook.

Protect a worksheet

1. On the **Tools** menu, point to **Protection**, and click **Protect Sheet**.
2. In the Protect Sheet dialog box (shown in Figure 25.12), mark check boxes to protect **Contents**, **Objects**, or **Scenarios**.

   Clicking **Objects** protects graphic objects, including charts.

   Clicking **Scenarios** protects scenario definitions; different scenarios can be shown and viewed, but they can't be changed.

   Clicking **Contents** protects the contents of locked cells so they can't be changed. By default, all cells on worksheets are locked, so all the cells are protected when you protect your worksheet. If you want to protect formulas but allow users to enter values for those formulas to calculate, you need to unlock the cells where values can be entered, and then protect the worksheet. (See the next step by step exercise to learn how to unlock cells.)

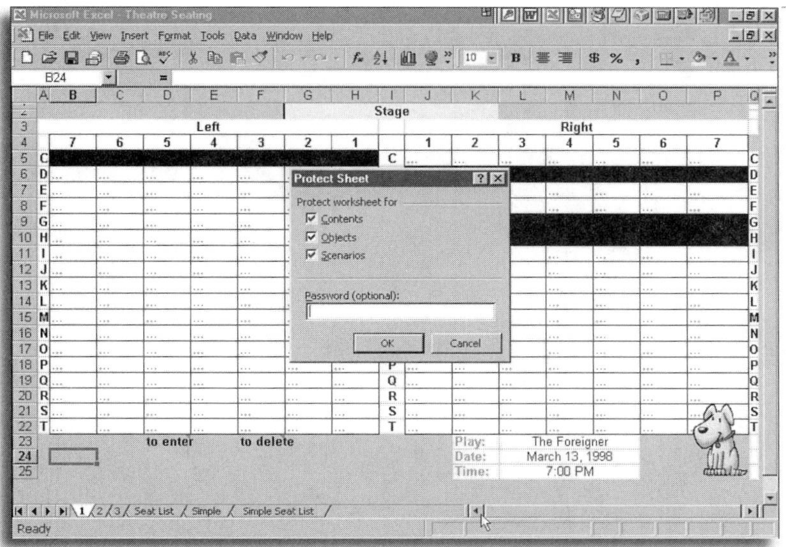

FIGURE 25.12
To prevent changes to your formulas or graphic objects, protect the worksheet.

As with workbook protection, unless you need to protect your work from others with bad intentions, my advice is don't use a password. Leave the **Password** box blank. (You'll be able to unprotect the worksheet to make changes more quickly without a password to enter.)

3. Click **OK**.

To unprotect the worksheet so you can make changes to your formulas, on the **Tools** menu, point to **Protection**, and click **Unprotect Sheet**. If you protected the worksheet with a password, you'll have to enter the password and click **OK**.

Unlock cells on a worksheet before protecting it

1. Select the specific cells you want to unlock (so their values can be changed).

   By default, all cells in a worksheet are locked.
2. Click **Format**, then click **Cells**.
3. In the Format Cells dialog box (shown in Figure 25.13), on the **Protection** tab, clear the **Locked** check box.

FIGURE 25.13

You need to unlock the cells you want to give users access to before you protect the worksheet.

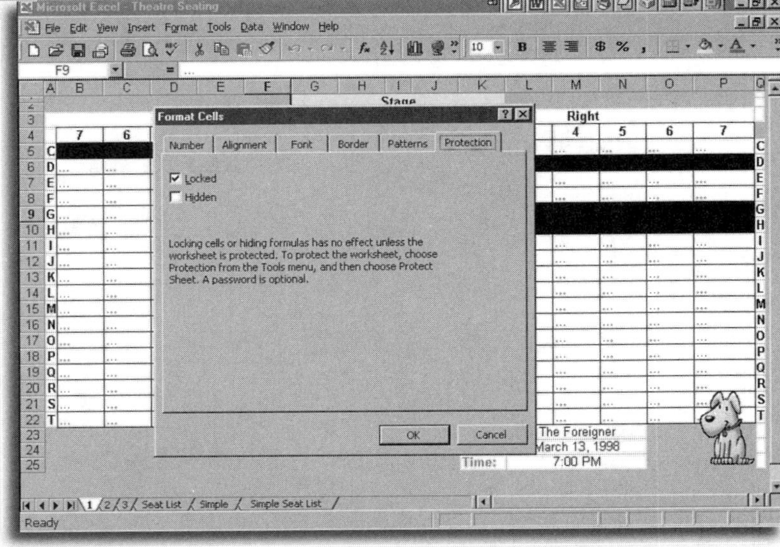

4. Click **OK**.

   Now you can protect the worksheet to prevent changes in locked cells, but allow others to enter data in the unlocked cells.

SEE ALSO

➤ *To learn more about selecting adjacent and nonadjacent cells, see the section titled "Selecting Cells in a Worksheet" in Chapter 5, page 85.*

Protect the change tracking in a shared workbook

1. On the **Tools** menu, point to **Protection**.
2. Click **Protect and Share Workbook**.
3. In the Protect Shared Workbook dialog box, mark the **Sharing with track changes** check box, then click **OK**.

Removing protection and sharing from the workbook are two separate steps. First, click **Tools**, point to **Protection**, and click **Unprotect Shared Workbook**; then, click **Tools**, click **Share Workbook**, and clear the **Allow changes** check box (and then click **OK**).

Can I Really Hide Worksheet Cells?

On the **Protection** tab in the Format Cells dialog box, a check box lets you "hide" cells. "Hidden" cells aren't really hidden—they're in plain view—but their formulas are hidden. If you hide a cell that contains a formula and then select the cell, nothing appears in the Formula bar. If you create an intricate formula that you don't want to share, you can hide and lock the cell and then protect the worksheet, and no one will be able to "borrow" your proprietary formula.

CHAPTER

26

Sharing Data Between Applications

Pasting, embedding, and linking objects

Sending data from Excel to Word

Sending data from Word to Excel

Changing the source of a link

Using Excel data in a PowerPoint slide

Sharing Data: Pasting, Embedding, and Linking Objects

The biggest advantage in having the Microsoft Office suite of programs on your computer is that they cooperate and share data with one another so well. By sharing data between programs, you can create reports that combine data from Word documents and Excel worksheets on the same page.

A table of data or chart in Excel can be copied to a Word document as simple data or a picture, as an embedded object that can be changed with Excel tools (without opening Excel), or as a linked object that's always current. Information in a Word document can be copied to an Excel worksheet using the same procedures.

There are several different ways to share data between programs, depending on what results you need:

- Pasting copied data from one program into another
- Embedding an object of copied data and formatting from one program into another
- Linking an object of information from one program into another

This chapter uses several new terms—*object*, *embed*, and *link*—that I'll explain before I show you how to use them to share data between programs. Refer to Table 26.1 for definitions and other useful information.

TABLE 26.1 Shared data definitions

Term	Definition	Double-Click Results	Editing Results
Object	A "container" of information that's inserted in another file.	Depends on whether the object is linked or embedded.	
Paste	Pasted data is inserted as text; it becomes part of the file into which it's pasted.	No special results; pasted data is not connected to its source.	

Term	Definition	Double-Click Results	Editing Results
Embed	An embedded object is connected to the program in which it was created, but not to its source file.	The source program opens so you can change the object with its own editing and formatting tools.	Editing changes only the embedded object, not the source file. A file containing an embedded object is larger because it contains all the object's data and formatting.
Link	A linked object is connected directly to its source file.	The source file and program both open so you can change the source file.	Editing changes a linked object's source file; all linked copies reflect changes. A file containing a linked object is smaller because it contains only the link.

Isn't Drag and Drop Faster?

If you drag cells from a worksheet and drop them in the document, you'll get an embedded object instead of a pasted table. (It's faster, if an embedded object is what you want.) Hint: To prevent window scrolling when you drag and drop, press Alt while you drag. (If you want to copy, not move, press Ctrl when you drop the cells in the Word document.) To drag and drop with a choice of paste options, use the right mouse button.

Sending Data from Excel to Word

If you're creating a report that's primarily a Word document, but you need to include an Excel chart or table, you can paste, embed, or link the Excel data into the Word document. The figures in the following sections show you what happens when you paste, embed, and link data from Excel to Word.

Copying and Pasting Data

When you copy and paste data from Excel into Word, the data becomes a table in the Word document. (If you copy and paste a chart, the chart is pasted as an embedded object.)

Paste data from Excel into Word

1. Open both the Excel worksheet and the Word document.
2. In the worksheet, select the data you want to copy and paste.
3. Right-click the selection; then click **Copy.**
4. Switch to Word.

5. Right-click in the document where you want to insert the table.

6. Click **Paste Cells**.

   The data is pasted as a table in the document, as shown in Figure 26.1. The worksheet cells become cells in a Word table and carry their formatting with them. To turn the gridlines on (or off), open Word's **Table** menu and click **Show Gridlines**.

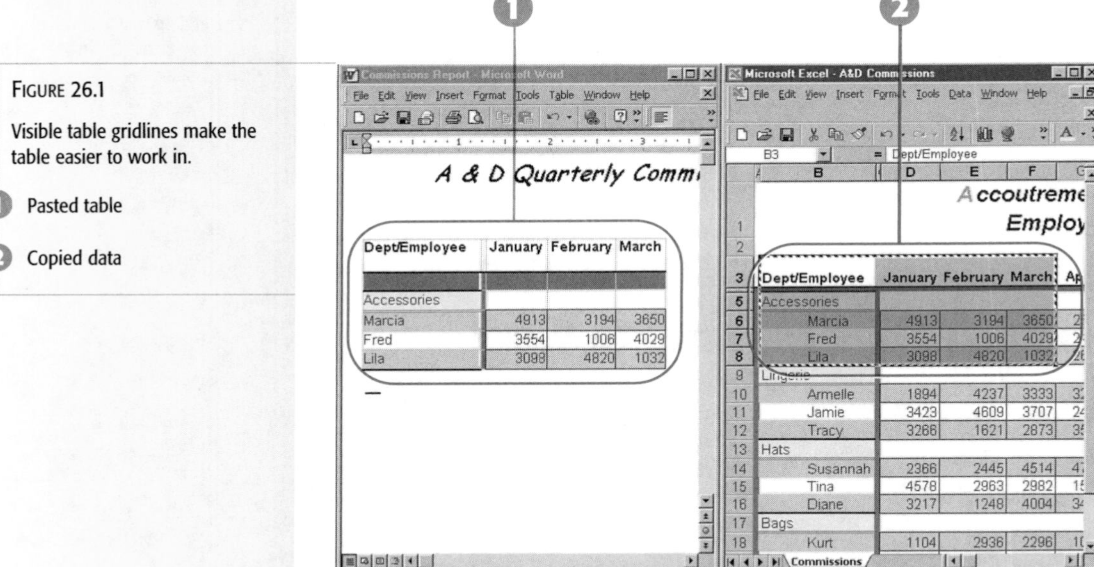

FIGURE 26.1

Visible table gridlines make the table easier to work in.

1 Pasted table

2 Copied data

You can work with the pasted data as you would any other Word table.

Embedding an Object

An embedded object is a picture of the data (table or chart) that's connected to its *source* program (the program in which it was created). The embedded object can be changed from within Word, using Excel's menu and toolbars.

In this example, I'll paste an embedded worksheet table. (You can use the same procedure to paste an embedded chart.)

Embed Excel data in a Word document

1. Open both the Excel worksheet and the Word document.
2. In the worksheet, select the data you want to embed.
3. Right-click the selection; then click **Copy.**
4. Switch to Word.
5. Click in the document where you want to embed the object.
6. On the **Edit** menu, click **Paste Special**.
7. In the Paste Special dialog box, be sure the **Paste** option is selected, and double-click **Microsoft Excel Worksheet Object**.

   The data is pasted as an embedded object in the document, as shown in Figure 26.2. The object "floats" on top of the document and can be moved anywhere. (Word text moves around to make room for it.)

The Right-Mouse Way

If you drag data with the right mouse button, you can choose **Move Here** or **Copy Here** from the shortcut menu when you drop the data in Word. Either command places an embedded object in the Word document.

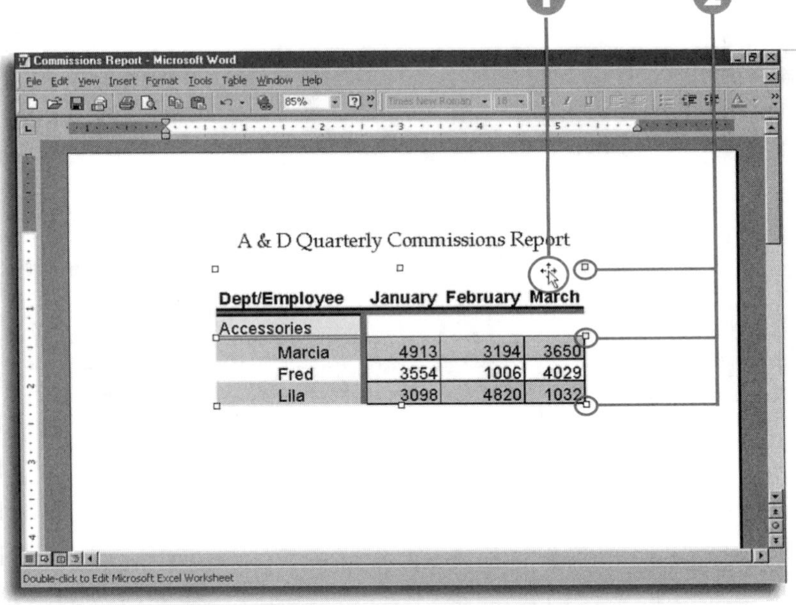

FIGURE 26.2

If you drag the object handles, the object stretches out of proportion.

1 Four-arrow "move" pointer

2 Object handles

To select the object, click it. To move it, drag from anywhere within the object with the four-arrow "move" pointer. To resize the object to fit your page, drag one of the handles around the border. If you stretch the object out of proportion by dragging the object handles, you can resize the object proportionally by holding down Shift or Ctrl while you drag a corner handle.

Change the embedded object

1. Double-click the embedded object.

   Excel opens within Word. (The title bar still says Word, but the menu and toolbars are Excel's, as shown in Figure 26.3.) Drag border handles to make the object window larger, or scroll in the window with the scrollbars.

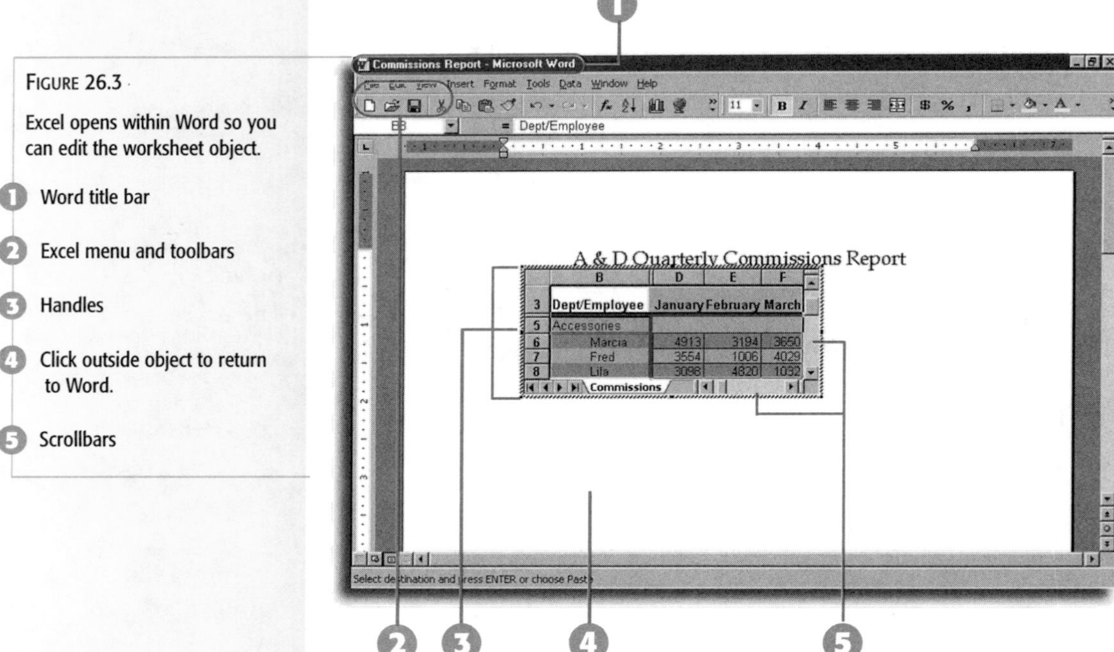

FIGURE 26.3

Excel opens within Word so you can edit the worksheet object.

1. Word title bar
2. Excel menu and toolbars
3. Handles
4. Click outside object to return to Word.
5. Scrollbars

2. Make changes using Excel's tools. (Because the object is embedded, changes you make don't affect the source file.)

   Be careful about dragging handles and scrolling: Whatever is displayed in the Excel window when you return to Word is what your object will display. (It could be a completely different part of the worksheet than you originally copied.)

3. To close Excel and return to Word, click in the Word document.

How Do I Delete an Embedded Object?

To delete an embedded object, click it; then press Delete. (Don't try to delete it while it's open for editing; click in the file that contains the object, then click the object once to select it.)

Linking to the Source File

Pasting a linked object is similar to pasting an embedded object, but the result is quite different. A *link* is just a short set of directions to the location of the source file (and if the source file is moved, the link might be broken). Linked data is especially useful if you need to make several copies of the same data, because if you need to make a change in the source data (such as correcting a misspelling), you only need to make the change once, in the source file; linked copies are all updated with the change automatically.

The Right-Mouse Method

If you drag data with the right mouse button, you can choose **Link Excel Object Here** from the shortcut menu to insert a linked object when you drop the data in Word.

For this example, I'll paste a linked chart from Excel to Word. (You can use the same quite procedure to paste a linked worksheet table.)

Paste linked Excel data into a Word document

1. Open both the Excel workbook and the Word document.
2. In the workbook, right-click the chart you want to link; then, click **Copy**.
3. Switch to Word.
4. Click in the document where you want to paste the linked chart.
5. On the **Edit** menu, click **Paste Special**.
6. In the Paste Special dialog box, be sure the **Paste link** option is selected, and double-click **Microsoft Excel Chart Object**.

   The chart is pasted as a linked object in the document, as shown in Figure 26.4. Like an embedded object, it can be moved anywhere in the document with the four-arrow "move" pointer. To resize the linked chart object proportionally, hold down Shift or Ctrl while you drag a corner handle.

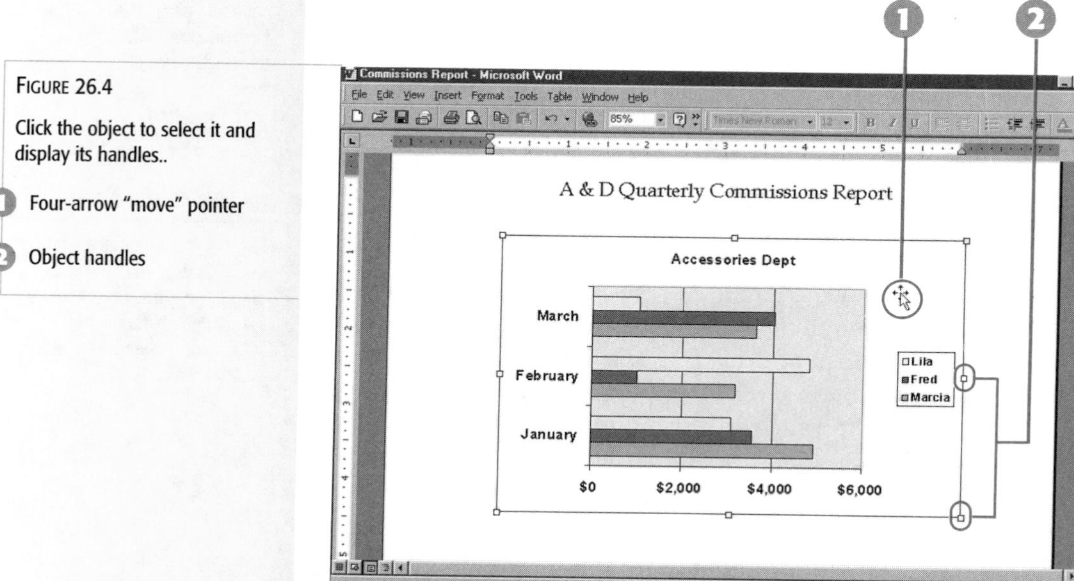

FIGURE 26.4

Click the object to select it and display its handles..

1. Four-arrow "move" pointer
2. Object handles

Because the object is linked, you change it by changing the source file.

Change the linked object

1. Double-click the linked object.

   Excel opens, and the source file opens in Excel (as shown in Figure 26.5).

2. Make changes in the source file.

   Changes in the source file are automatically reflected in the linked object.

3. To close Excel and return to Word, save the source file; then close the file and close Excel.

   If you don't save the source file, the linked object won't show your changes (because it only shows what's in the source file).

How Do I Delete a Linked Object?

To delete a linked object, click it; then press Delete.

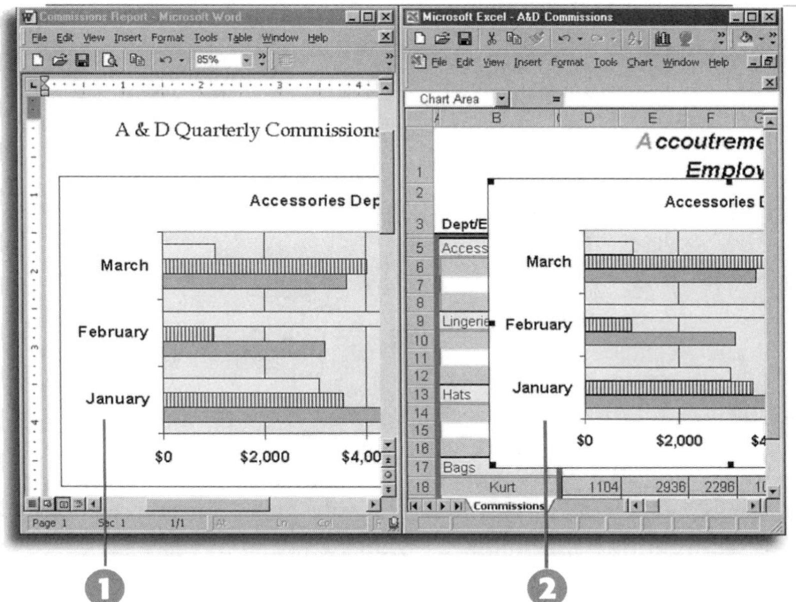

FIGURE 26.5

When you double-click a linked object, the source file opens in its original program.

1. Linked object in Word
2. Source file in Excel

When you open a document or workbook that contains linked objects, a message might ask you if you want to update the linked information; click **Yes** to update the file immediately or **No** to preserve the previous values.

To Ask or Not To Ask

If you want Excel to prompt you before updating linked information, open the **Tools** menu and click **Options**; on the **Edit** tab, click the **Ask to update automatic links** check box. To update automatically without being asked, clear the check box.

Do You Have a Bitmap Logo?

You can use these procedures to paste or embed a bitmap (.bmp) graphic; when you double-click an embedded graphic to edit it, Windows Paint opens (unless you have another paint program, such as CorelPaint, that opens instead).

Bringing Data from Word into Excel

Bringing data from Word into an Excel worksheet works very much like pasting, embedding, and linking Excel data into a Word document. The biggest difference is that if you copy Word text and paste it in a worksheet, each paragraph is pasted into a single cell; however, if you copy a Word table into Excel, each cell in the Word table is pasted into a cell in the worksheet.

Copying and Pasting Word Text to Excel

When you copy and paste data from Word into Excel, the Word text becomes data in worksheet cells.

The Classic Way

You can also use the standard Copy and Paste commands to paste Word text into Excel, but the drag-and-drop method is faster.

The Right-Mouse Way

If you drag data with the right mouse button, you can choose **Move Here** or **Copy Here** from the shortcut menu when you drop the text in Excel.

Drag Right

You can drag and drop an embedded Word object into a worksheet by dragging the text with the right mouse button; when you drop it, click **Copy Here as Document** on the shortcut menu.

Paste text from Word into Excel

1. Open both the Excel worksheet and the Word document, and arrange them side-by-side in two windows on your screen. (Right-click the taskbar and click **Tile Windows Vertically.**)
2. Select the Word text, drag it into the Excel window, and drop it in the cells where you want it.

   To move the text into Excel, drop it; to copy the text, hold down Ctrl while you drop it. (When you press Ctrl, the plus symbol on the mouse pointer indicates "copy".)

Embedding a Word Object in Excel

An embedded Word object is a picture of the text, connected to its *source* program (Word). The embedded object can be changed from within Excel, using Word's menu and toolbars.

Embed Word text in an Excel worksheet

1. Open both the Excel worksheet and the Word document.
2. In the Word document, select the text you want to embed.
3. Right-click the selection; then, click **Copy.**
4. Switch to Excel, and click in the worksheet where you want to embed the object.
5. On the **Edit** menu, click **Paste Special**.
6. In the Paste Special dialog box, be sure the **Paste** option is selected, and double-click **Microsoft Word Document Object**.

   The text is pasted as an embedded object in the worksheet. The object "floats" on top of the document and can be moved anywhere. It hides any cells it covers, unless you format the object's fill color to be No Fill. (Select the object, then click **No Fill** in the **Fill Color** button on the Formatting toolbar.)

   To change the embedded object's text, see the step by step exercise "Change the embedded object" earlier in this chapter. Changing an embedded object is the same regardless of which program the object is copied from or pasted into.

Linking a Word Object into Excel

The process of pasting a quite quite linked object is similar to pasting an embedded object, but a *link* is just a short set of directions to the location of the source file (and if the source file is moved, the link might be broken). Linked data is especially useful if you need to make several copies of the same data, because if you need to make a change in the source data (such as correcting a misspelling), you need to make the change only once, in the source file; linked copies are all automatically updated with the change.

It's a Right Drag

If you like using the right mouse button, here's another opportunity. Drag the text you want to link with the right mouse button, and when you drop it, click **Link Document Here** on the shortcut menu.

Paste linked Word text into an Excel worksheet

1. Open both the Excel workbook and the Word document.
2. In the Word document, select and right-click the text you want to link; then, click **Copy**.
3. Switch to Excel.
4. Click in the worksheet where you want to paste the linked text.
5. On the **Edit** menu, click **Paste Special**.
6. In the Paste Special dialog box, be sure the **Paste link** option is selected, and double-click **Microsoft Word Document Object**.

   The text is pasted as a linked object in the worksheet. Like an embedded object, it can be moved anywhere in the document with the four-arrow "move" pointer.

   To change the linked object's text, see the step by step exercise "Change the linked object" earlier in this chapter. Changing a linked object is the same regardless of which program the object is copied from or pasted into.

Changing a Link's Source

Excel automatically keeps track of the path to the link source, so if a linked object's source is renamed, Excel can find the source and keep the link updated. But if you want to change the object to reflect text in a different document, you can change the link's source.

Update a link

1. Open the Excel workbook that contains the linked object.
2. On the **Edit** menu, click **Links**.

   The Links dialog box is displayed, as shown in Figure 26.6. It lists all the links in the open workbook or document.

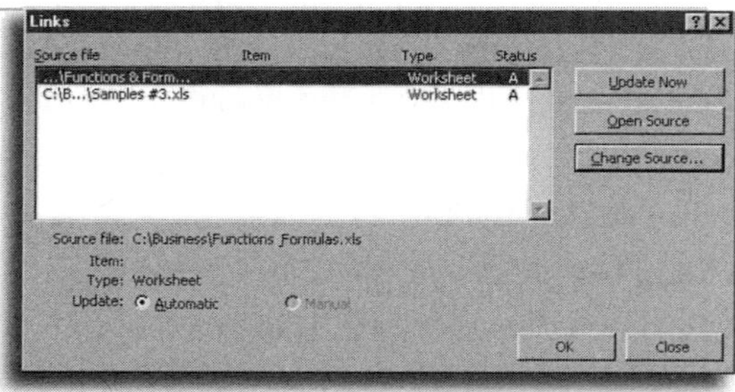

FIGURE 26.6

Click **Update Now** to show any changes in the source since you opened the file that contains the link.

3. Select the link you want to change; then click **Change Source**.

   The Change Links dialog box is displayed.
4. In the Change Links dialog box, change the filename. (Type the new path if the file is in a different folder.)
5. Click **OK**.

   The link in the Links dialog box is updated to the new file-name.
6. In the Links dialog box, click **OK**.

Now, your linked object displays current data from the new source.

Dragging a Hyperlink or Shortcut Icon into Excel

Another way to make Word data instantly accessible to someone reading your Excel worksheet is to create a hyperlink or a shortcut icon in the worksheet. Both are small and take up little worksheet space, but make the corollary data easily available to anyone who wants to see it.

For the link to work, the source document must be available on the computer or network, in folders that users have access to. (If you send the Excel file to someone off your network, the link won't work.)

Drag a link from Word into Excel

1. Arrange the Word and Excel windows side-by-side on your screen.

   The fastest way is to open both programs, right-click the taskbar, and click **Tile Windows Vertically**. (See Chapter 6, "Changing Your View of the Worksheet," to learn more about arranging multiple windows.)

2. Select the Word data you want to link.
3. Using the right mouse button, drag the data from the Word window to the Excel window, point to the cell where you want the link, and release the mouse button.
4. On the shortcut menu (shown in Figure 26.7), click **Create Shortcut Here** to drop the link as a shortcut icon; click **Create Hyperlink Here** to drop a hyperlink in the cell.

   When you click the link, Word and the linked document open.

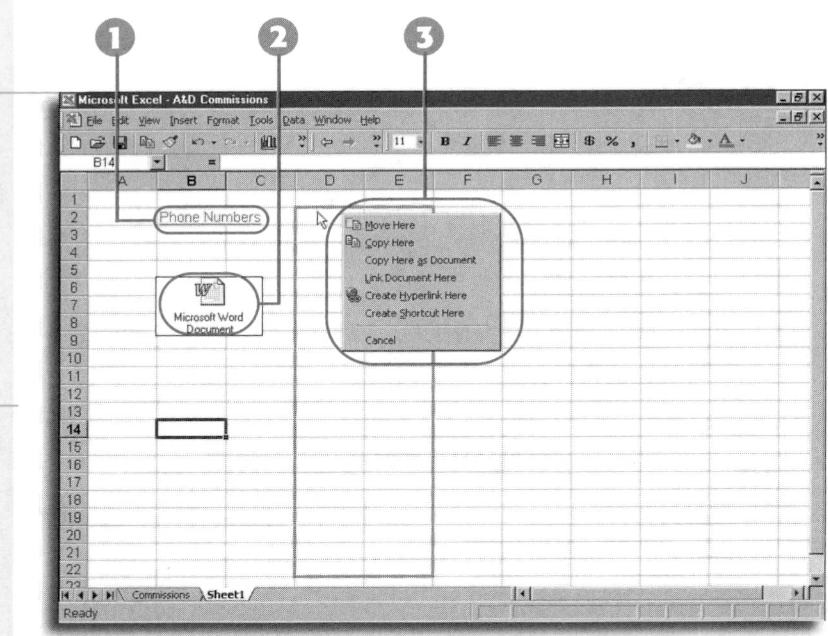

FIGURE 26.7

Use a shortcut link or a hyperlink to give a worksheet user access to corollary information.

1. Hyperlink
2. Shortcut link
3. Shortcut menu

SEE ALSO

➤ *To learn more about using hyperlinks in a worksheet, see the section titled "Using Hyperlinks," page 40.*

Pasting Excel Data to a PowerPoint Slide

Slide presentations that include Excel charts are colorful and powerful. Pasting a chart in a PowerPoint slide is usually a better idea than linking or embedding, because it's more easily transportable: You don't need either Excel or the source workbook on your laptop computer to support the object in the slide. Also, the charting feature in PowerPoint is the same lame charting feature that's in Word and Access; it's not as powerful, flexible, or easy to use as Excel's charting feature, so if you want to show a great chart in a PowerPoint slide, you'll get better results if you create the chart in Excel and paste it into the PowerPoint slide.

Paste a chart into a PowerPoint slide

1. Start PowerPoint, and open the slide you want to paste the chart into. (See *Using PowerPoint 2000* (Que, 1998) to learn about using PowerPoint.)

2. Switch to Excel.
3. Select the chart object or chart sheet you want to copy and paste.
4. On the toolbar, click the **Copy** button.
5. Switch to PowerPoint.
6. Click in the slide where you want to paste the chart.
7. On the **Edit** menu, click **Paste**.

   Your chart is pasted into the slide (as shown in Figure 26.8); you can resize the chart by dragging its handles, and then close Excel and finish creating your PowerPoint presentation.

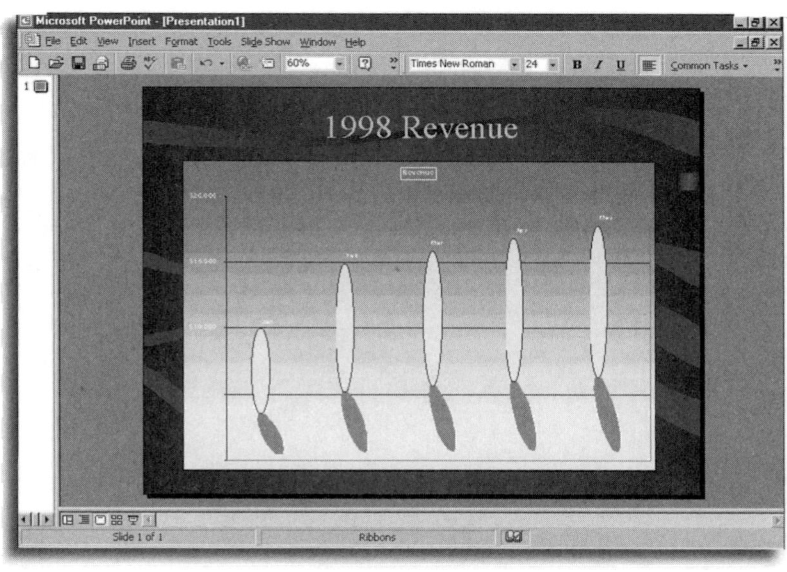

FIGURE 26.8
Fancy chart formatting can really spice up a PowerPoint presentation.

SEE ALSO

➤ *To learn more about creating Excel charts, see page 385.*

➤ *To learn more about exporting Excel data to an Access database, see the section titled "Sending Excel Data to Access," page 128.*

PART

VIII

Customizing and Automating

27 Customizing Your Excel Screen 517

28 Automating Repetitive Work with Macros 535

29 Using Excel's Built-In Templates 549

CHAPTER

27

Customizing Your Excel Screen

Using the Full Screen and Zoom features

Moving, hiding, and showing toolbars

Changing buttons in built-in toolbars

Creating your own personal toolbar

Adding and removing commands from the menu bar

Creating a new menu

Esoteric Display Changes

Other screen display changes aren't universally useful, but for unusual situations you'll want to know about them. On the **Tools** menu, click **Options**, and on the **View** tab, you'll find several check boxes under **Window options**. Those check boxes change settings for the active worksheet.

Customizing Screen Elements

The default screen display for your workbooks is functional and useful just the way it is, but on occasion, certain changes come in handy (especially if your monitor is only 15 inches or less, like mine).

Some customizing changes that come in handy are

- Switching to full screen to remove all extraneous clutter and see the maximum amount of worksheet possible
- Changing the magnification of your worksheet, or *zooming*, to see specific details close up and enlarged or lots of the worksheet, all reduced
- Personalizing your toolbars so that all the buttons, and only the buttons, you use are displayed
- Personalizing your menus to add and remove commands

I'll show you how to do all these things; you might find some of the changes quite useful.

Changing Your Screen Display

Two useful methods of changing how much Excel "real estate" you see on your screen are full screen and zooming. Both allow you to see much more of your worksheet; full screen does so by hiding everything except the menu bar and sheet tabs, and zooming does so by reducing the size of the cells. Which method you choose depends on what you want to do.

If you're formatting or setting page breaks, you don't need to see cell contents, but you do need to see as much of the worksheet as possible. In this case, you'd want to zoom out and see lots of small worksheet cells.

If you're working with the contents of cells but need to see more of the worksheet to maintain your train of thought, you might want to give full screen a try. Also, sometimes folks accidentally switch to full screen and can't find their way back to normal view, so I'll tell you how to recover from full screen.

Using the Full Screen

To get a big view of your worksheet, without extra screen elements taking up scarce screen space, you can switch to full screen.

To switch to full screen view, open the **View** menu and click **Full Screen**.

Full screen view hides the toolbars, the title bar, status bar, and the taskbar and leaves only your sheet, the scrollbars, and the menu bar in view (as shown in Figure 27.1).

Accoutrement & Deshabille, Inc.
Employee Commissions
1998

Dept/Employee	January	February	March	April	May	June	July	August	September	October	November
Accessories											
Marcia	4913	3194	3650	2592	1330	3002	4166	4324	2906	2571	1777
Fred	3554	1006	4029	2430	1635	4508	4472	1616	3260	4941	1282
Lila	3098	4820	1032	2628	4213	1951	2099	4451	3939	1409	2450
Lingerie											
Armelle	1894	4237	3333	3256	2382	2486	1818	1064	3292	2178	3649
Jamie	3423	4609	3707	2441	2896	1327	1429	3714	2940	2687	3512
Tracy	3266	1621	2873	3526	2622	2148	2094	3449	2420	3600	4588
Hats											
Susannah	2366	2445	4514	4753	4505	4934	3523	4179	3055	1854	3378
Tina	4578	2963	2982	1522	2067	3944	2605	4621	2510	3634	1462
Diane	3217	1248	4004	3449	4563	4542	4668	3612	1345	2205	2752
Bags											
Kurt	1104	2936	2296	1051	2310	3746	2918	3473	3675	1023	3778
Jill	1373	1246	2861	3949	1111	3683	1756	1954	1574	3440	1268
Elaine	3622	3486	1654	3092	1313	4869	3819	1757	1913	1058	3836
Jewelry											
Albert	3105	1886	2433	2325	3842	4861	2460	3008	4268	2538	2477

FIGURE 27.1
Full screen view can be a bit scary at first, because all your familiar landmarks are gone.

You won't want to work in full screen all the time. Because the menu is still in view, you can return to normal view easily.

To return your screen to Normal view, do one of the following:

- On the **View** menu, click **Full Screen**.
- On the keyboard, press Alt, then V, then U.

The Full Screen toolbar has only the one necessary button: **Close Full Screen**; it's an ideal toolbar candidate for adding one or two other buttons you find essential. To learn how to add other buttons to any toolbar, see the section "Personalizing Your Toolbars" later in this chapter.

It's Like Page Break Preview

Page Break Preview (see Chapter 24, "Formatting the Printed Page") is a zoomed-out view with more information displayed than in normal view.

SEE ALSO

› *To learn more about other ways to change your onscreen view, see the section titled "Using Multiple Windows," page xx (Ch. 6, "Changing Your View of the Worksheet").*

Zooming In and Out

Zooming in or out changes your screen display by magnifying or reducing the cells in the worksheet. It's very helpful when you want to format a larger area than you can normally see on your screen. You can zoom in or out to any magnification you choose; you can also select a range of cells and have Excel zoom in or out to frame just that range in your screen.

Zoom in or out by a specific percentage

1. On the Standard toolbar, click the down arrow next to the Zoom box. (If your toolbars are sharing one row, click the double arrow at the right end of the Standard toolbar to find the Zoom box.)

   The Zoom list drops down to show built-in Zoom percentages, as shown in Figure 27.2.

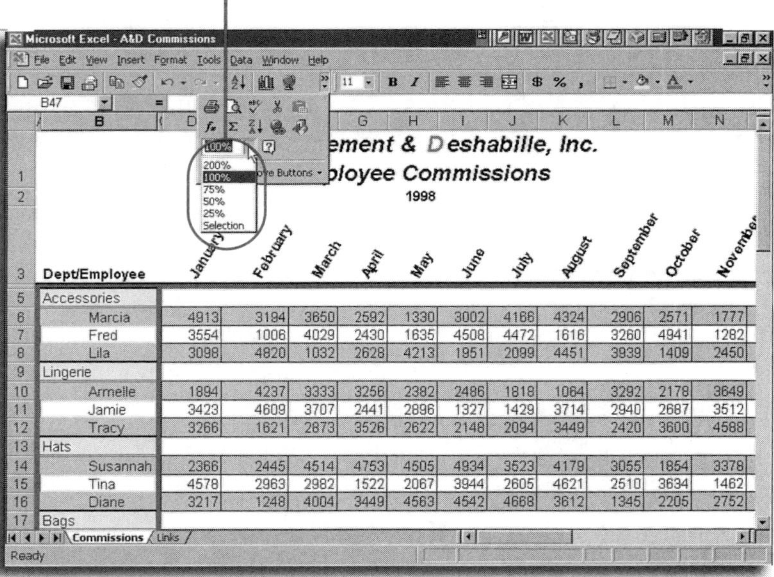

FIGURE 27.2

Pick a built-in zoom setting from the list, or type your own setting in the box.

1 Zoom

2. Click a percentage.

   Figure 27.3 shows two windows zoomed to different percentages.

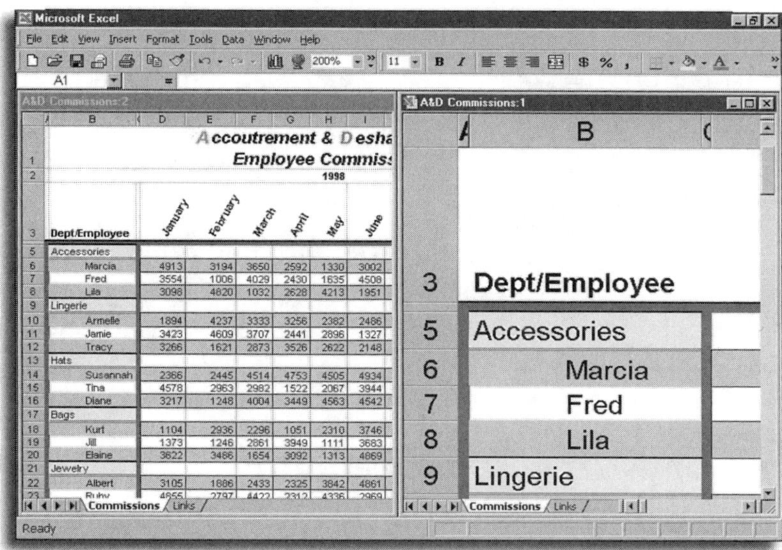

FIGURE 27.3
The left window is zoomed to 75%; the right window is zoomed to 200%.

To return the worksheet to a standard magnification, repeat steps 1 and 2, and click the 100% zoom setting.

Sometimes a setting of 85% or 120% is preferable to any built-in settings; you can zoom the view to any percentage you want.

Zoom to a custom percentage that's not on the list

1. On the Standard toolbar, click in the **Zoom** box.
2. Type your own percentage.
3. Press Enter.

If you want your selected range to fill the screen, without fiddling with finding the right zoom setting, you can tell Excel to zoom to fit your selection.

Zoom to fit your selection

1. Select the worksheet range.
2. On the Zoom button list, click **Selection**.

   Figure 27.4 shows a worksheet zoomed to fit a selected table.

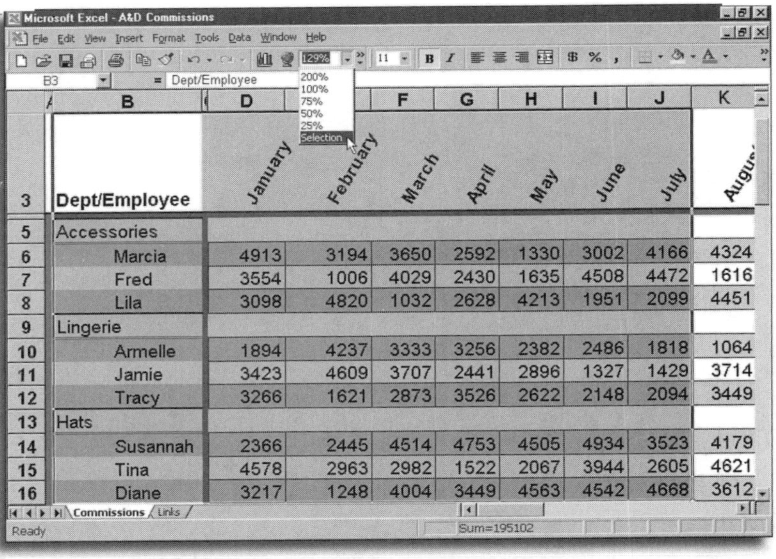

FIGURE 27.4

To view only your selection, zoom to it.

Which Buttons Are Multifunctional?

To figure out if a button is multifunctional, hold down the Shift key and click the button; if the button face changes, it's multifunctional. But don't release the mouse button while you're pointing at the button, or the button action will take effect; instead, slide the mouse pointer away from the toolbar before you release the mouse button.

Personalizing Your Toolbars

Excel has several built-in toolbars that you can personalize by deleting seldom-used buttons and adding new buttons. The Standard and the Formatting toolbars start with Excel by default, and you've probably already used these toolbars. Other useful toolbars are the Chart toolbar that displays when you create a chart (see Chapter 20, "Creating a Chart"), the PivotTable toolbar that displays when you create a PivotTable (see Chapter 19, "Summarizing Details with PivotTables and PivotCharts"), the Drawing toolbar (see Chapter 30, "Drawing Objects"), and others that you can show and explore when you're curious. All of them can be personalized.

Some of the things you'll want to know how to do with toolbars are

- Moving them around your screen, including "floating" and "docking"
- Showing them and hiding them
- Changing the buttons they display
- Creating a new toolbar

Many toolbar buttons are multifunctional with the Shift key (so you can reduce the number of buttons on a toolbar and make room for other buttons). For example, you can click the Sort Ascending button to sort a list in ascending order, or you can hold down Shift while clicking the same button to sort a list in descending order. Other multifunctional buttons include Save/Open, Print/Print Preview, Align Left/Align Right, and Center/Merge and Center.

Moving Toolbars

The usual position for a toolbar is "docked," or attached to, the top of your Excel window (right below the menu bar); but you can also dock toolbars against the bottom and sides of your Excel window or "float" them in the middle of the screen, as shown in Figure 27.5.

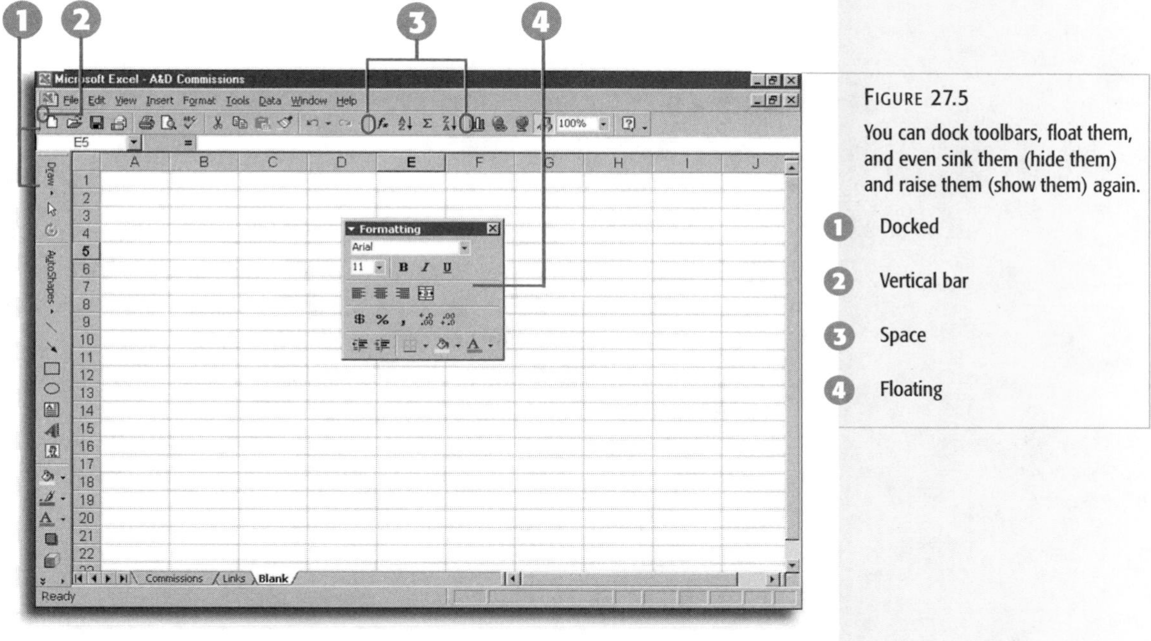

FIGURE 27.5

You can dock toolbars, float them, and even sink them (hide them) and raise them (show them) again.

1. Docked
2. Vertical bar
3. Space
4. Floating

The Best Display Is Your Own

The most efficient way to save screen space is to create your own custom toolbar, which contains only the buttons you use, and display it instead of the Standard and Formatting toolbars. (See the previous section, "Personalizing Your Toolbars," to learn how.)

Move a toolbar to a different location

1. Click the vertical bar at the left end of the toolbar, or click a space between buttons.
2. Drag the toolbar to a new position in the Excel window, and drop it.
   - If you drop the toolbar in the middle of the Excel window, it will float there; you can reposition a floating toolbar by dragging its title bar.
   - To change the shape of a floating toolbar (like the Formatting toolbar in Figure 27.5), drag one of its borders.
   - If you drag the toolbar to the bottom or side of the Excel window, it will dock against the edge of the window.

The toolbars stay where you left them, even after you close and reopen Excel.

Hiding and Showing Toolbars

Hiding and showing toolbars is important when you learn to create your own personalized toolbars; you'll want to hide the built-in toolbars and show your own instead.

Along with hiding and showing toolbars, you can choose to keep your Standard and Formatting toolbars in the same row (which means some of the buttons will always be hidden), or display them the traditional way, in two toolbar rows. If you're working on a 17-inch monitor, keeping both toolbars in the same row probably won't save you much screen space, but if you're working on a 15-inch or 14-inch monitor (or a laptop), you might find that extra half inch of worksheet invaluable.

Hide or show toolbars

1. Right-click any toolbar or the menu bar.

   The toolbar shortcut menu is displayed, as shown in Figure 27.6. If you don't see the name you want here, you'll find it in the Customize dialog box.

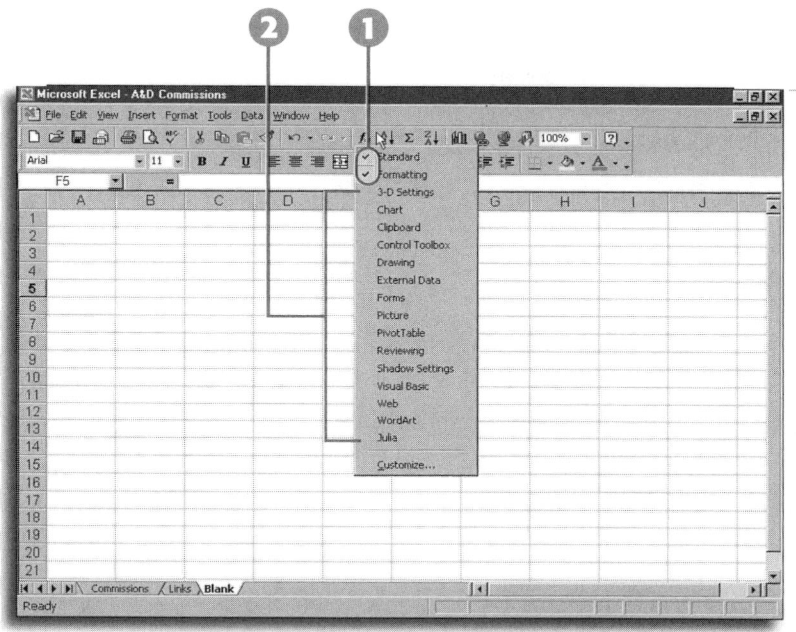

FIGURE 27.6
The toolbar shortcut menu is the quickest way to show and hide toolbars.

1 Shown

2 Hidden

2. Click the name of the toolbar you want to hide or show.

   The commands are all toggle commands: Click to show, and click again to hide. A toolbar name with a check mark is shown; no check mark means the toolbar is hidden.

3. If you don't see the name of the toolbar you want to hide or show, click **Customize**.

   The Customize dialog box is displayed, as shown in Figure 27.7.

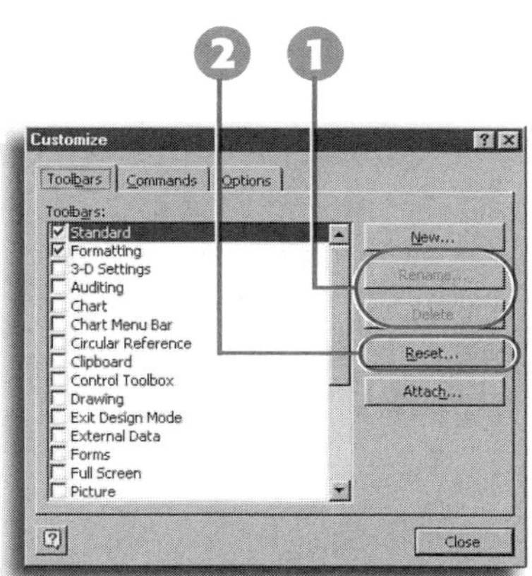

FIGURE 27.7
All the toolbars in your copy of Excel, both built-in and personal, are listed on the **Toolbars** tab.

1 Delete and rename personal toolbars.

2 Reset built-in toolbars.

Or Just Drag Them

You can also change your Standard/Formatting toolbars display by dragging them to share one row or occupy two rows.

Add and Remove Built-In Toolbar Buttons

To add or remove buttons quickly from built-in, docked toolbars, click the small down arrow at the right end, then click **Add or Remove Buttons**. A list of all the buttons assigned to that built-in toolbar appears; displayed buttons are check-marked. Click each button you want to show or hide, then click a worksheet cell to close the list. To add buttons that aren't on the built-in list, follow the step by step exercise "Add buttons to a toolbar" later in this chapter.

4. Click check boxes for toolbars you want to show; clear check boxes for toolbars you want to hide.
5. Click **Close** to finish.

Display toolbars in one row or two rows

1. Right-click any toolbar or the menu bar, and click **Customize**.
2. On the **Options** tab, click the **Standard and Formatting toolbars share one row** check box.

   Mark the check box to share one row and save screen space; clear the check box to show both toolbars, each in its own row. (The check box won't be available unless both the Standard and Formatting toolbars are displayed and docked.)
3. Click **Close** to finish.

Changing Buttons in Built-In Toolbars

The tremendous variety of buttons on the Standard and Formatting toolbars might not fit your needs precisely, but you can change any built-in toolbar to be exactly what you want. You can easily make these changes to any toolbar:

- Move buttons around for convenience.
- Delete buttons you never use.
- Add buttons you want.

Move toolbar buttons around and rearrange them

1. Press and hold down the Alt key.
2. Drag buttons to new positions on the toolbar, as shown in Figure 27.8.

   Drop a button between two other buttons to rearrange them; add a space between buttons by dragging a button just a bit to one side.

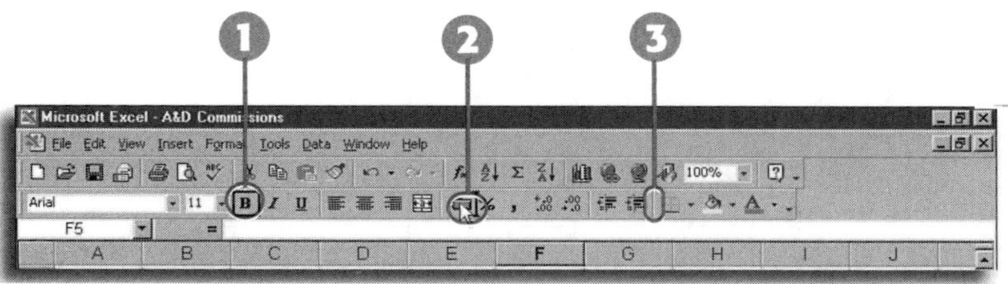

FIGURE 27.8

When you move a button, an insertion marker shows you where it will be inserted.

1 Moving this button

2 Insertion marker

3 Space

Delete buttons from a toolbar

1. Press and hold down the Alt key.
2. Drag the button away from the toolbar and drop it anywhere on the worksheet.

   The button is removed from the toolbar.

   If the toolbar is one of Excel's built-in toolbars and you make it unrecognizable, you can reset it to its original configuration.

Reset a built-in toolbar's original configuration

1. Right-click any toolbar; then click **Customize**.
2. On the **Toolbars** tab, click the name of the toolbar you want to reset.
3. Click the **Reset** button.

   If a message asks if you're sure, click **OK**.
4. Click **Close** when you're finished.

Add buttons to a toolbar

1. Show the toolbar you want to add buttons to.
2. Right-click any toolbar; then, click **Customize**.
3. On the **Commands** tab, click the category of commands where you'll most likely find the button you want.

   Toolbar buttons are all quick ways to use a menu command, so the buttons are sorted into categories that correspond to Excel's menus.
4. Scroll through the **Commands** list until you find the toolbar button you want.

Resetting Toolbars

You can reset built-in toolbars, but you cannot delete them; you can delete personal, custom toolbars, but you cannot reset them.

5. Drag the button away from the dialog box and drop it on the toolbar, as shown in Figure 27.9.

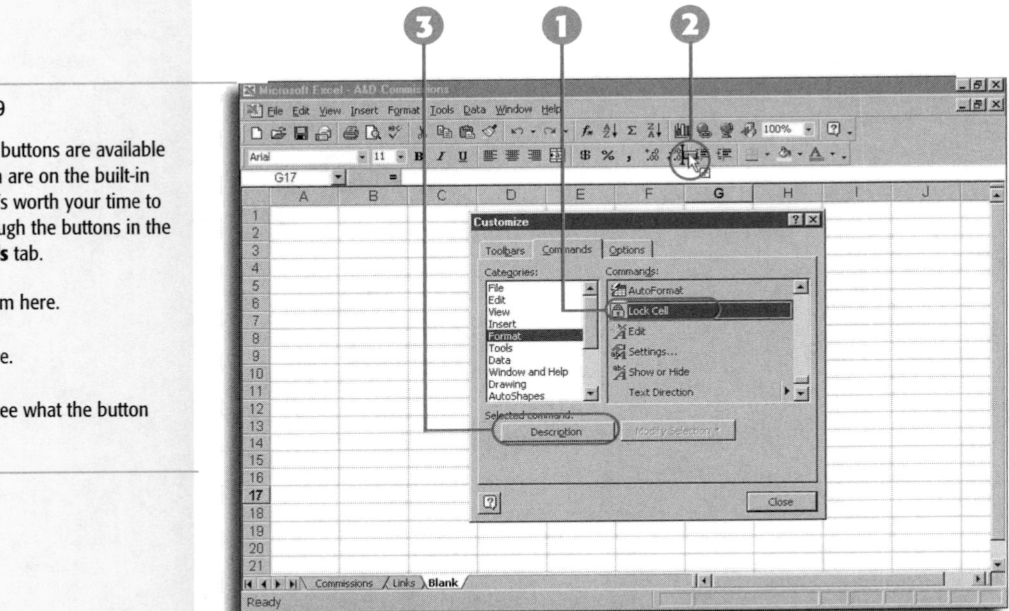

FIGURE 27.9

A lot more buttons are available to you than are on the built-in toolbars; it's worth your time to cruise through the buttons in the **Commands** tab.

1. Drag from here.
2. Drop here.
3. Click to see what the button does.

6. In the Customize dialog box, click **Close** when you finish.

SEE ALSO

➤ *To learn how to create a button or command to run a macro, see the section titled "Attaching a Macro to a Toolbar Button or Menu Command," page 543.*

Creating Personal Toolbars

Personal toolbars are about as customized as you can get in Excel; they're a great boon to efficiency and productivity because you have exactly the buttons you want at hand. If you share a computer with someone else, you can cause great strife if you mess with shared built-in toolbars; instead, you can use personal toolbars, which allow you to customize your workspace without messing up your co-worker's workspace.

Create a personal toolbar

1. Right-click any toolbar; then click **Customize**.
2. On the **Toolbars** tab, click **New**.

   The New Toolbar dialog box is displayed, as shown in Figure 27.10.

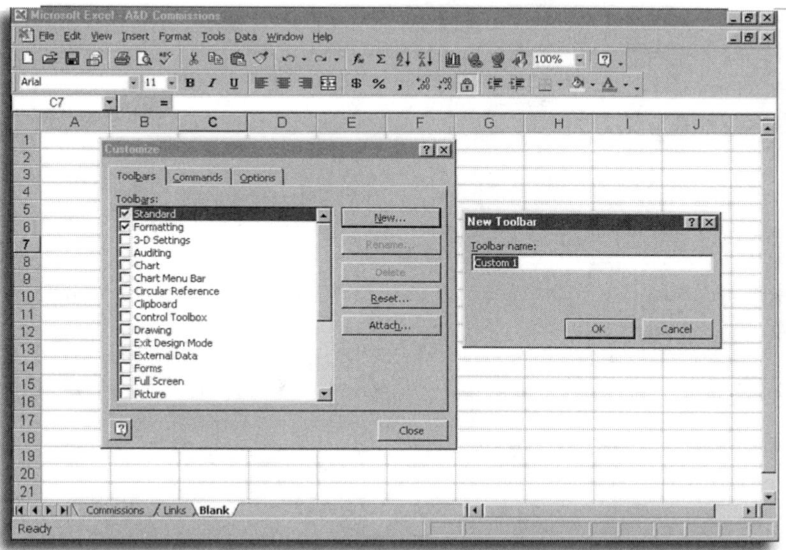

FIGURE 27.10
Your own name makes the toolbar very personal; you also can identify the toolbar by its purpose.

3. Type a name for your toolbar; then click **OK**.

   The new, empty, very small toolbar is displayed on your worksheet (shown in Figure 27.11).
4. On the **Commands** tab, click a category of commands that lists the buttons you want.
5. Scroll through the **Commands** list until you find the toolbar button you want.
6. Drag each button away from the dialog box and drop it on your new toolbar.
7. Repeat steps 4 through 6 until you've added all the buttons you want.
8. In the Customize dialog box, click **Close** when you finish.

   Figure 27.12 shows a personal toolbar I use a lot.

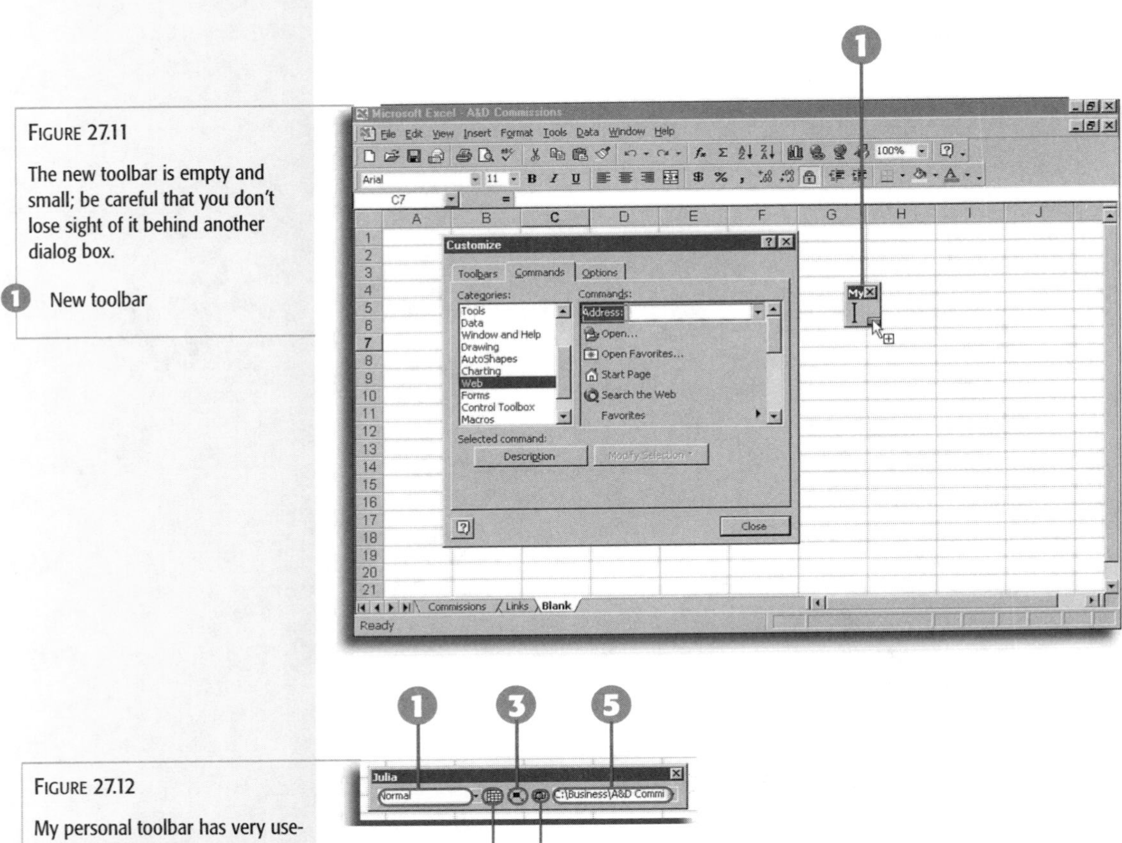

FIGURE 27.11

The new toolbar is empty and small; be careful that you don't lose sight of it behind another dialog box.

1 New toolbar

FIGURE 27.12

My personal toolbar has very useful buttons that aren't displayed on any built-in toolbars.

1 Style

2 Unmerge Cells

3 Select Current Region

4 Camera

5 Address

Customizing Your Menu Bar

You can customize your menu bar to remove commands you never use, add commands you want, and even add commands to run macros (which you learn more about in Chapter 28).

To alter your menu bar, you can remove an entire menu by holding down the Alt key while you drag the menu name away and drop it on the worksheet.

To restore the menu bar to its original configuration, with all its original menus and commands: In the Customize dialog box, on the **Toolbars** tab, click the name **Worksheet Menu Bar**; then click the **Reset** button.

A new feature in Office 2000 is a menu display that hides commands you seldom use. If you look for a command on a specific menu and don't see it, click the double-down arrow at the bottom of the menu to display all the commands. If you find this behavior annoying, you can switch back to classical menus, in which all commands are displayed. When you set or change command-display behavior in Excel 2000, the setting applies to all Office 2000 programs (so don't be surprised when Word, PowerPoint, and Access menus all have the same display you set in Excel).

Don't Mess with Someone Else's Workspace

If you share a computer with someone else, I strongly advise you not to mess with the menus, because a co-worker who doesn't know what you did to his menu bar can become irate when he can't find a command.

Change the command display mode

1. Right-click the menu bar; then, click **Customize**.
2. On the **Options** tab, click the **Menus show recently used commands first** check box.

   Mark the check box for the new Office 2000 hide-the-commands display; clear the check box for classical, show-all-the-commands display.

   If you mark the check box in step 2, you can also mark or clear the **Show full menus after a short delay** check box. If you mark this check box, each menu will automatically display all its commands if you click the menu name and point to it for a couple of seconds.
3. When you're finished, click **Close**.

Add a command to a menu

1. Right-click the menu bar; then, click **Customize**.
2. On the **Commands** tab, click the category and then locate the command you want to add to a menu.
3. Drag the command from the dialog box to the menu bar, and hold the mouse pointer over the specific menu item you want to add the command to.

   The menu drops down so you can place the command where you want it, as shown in Figure 27.13.

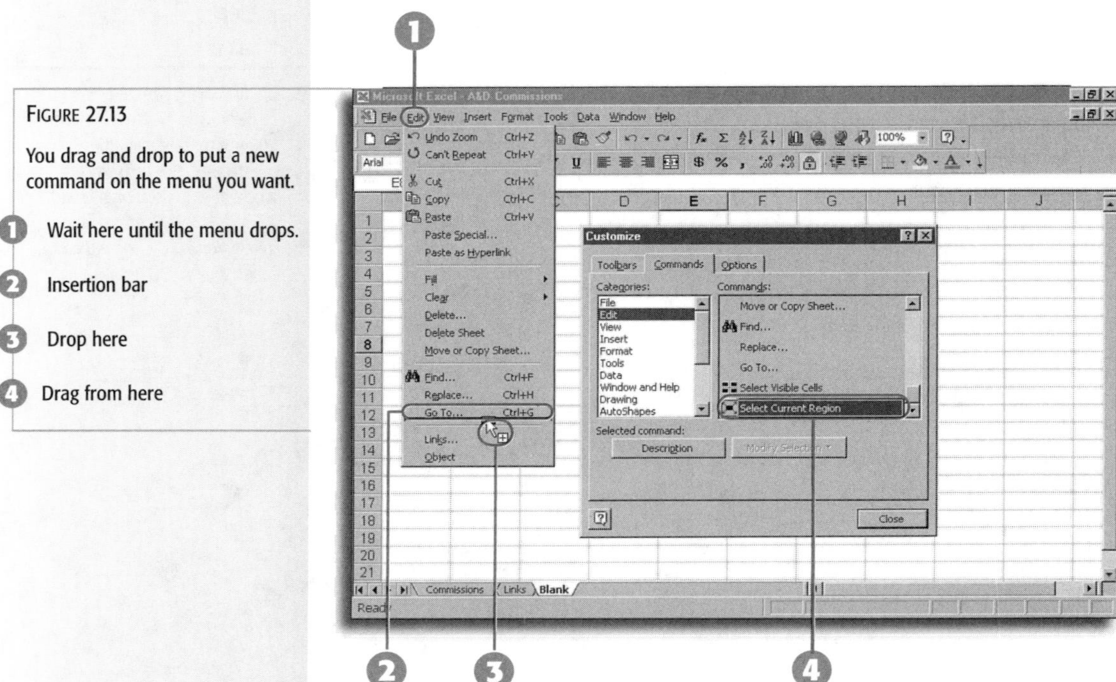

FIGURE 27.13

You drag and drop to put a new command on the menu you want.

1 Wait here until the menu drops.

2 Insertion bar

3 Drop here

4 Drag from here

4. Drop the command in position on the menu.
5. When you're finished, click the **Close** button to close the Customize dialog box.

Remove a command from a menu

1. Right-click the menu bar; then, click **Customize**.

   You won't actually use the Customize dialog box, but it must be displayed to render the menus customizable.
2. Click a menu to display it; then drag the command away and drop it on the worksheet.
3. When you're finished, click **Close** to close the Customize dialog box.

Create a new menu for your menu bar

1. Right-click the menu bar; then click **Customize**.
2. On the **Commands** tab, scroll to the bottom of the category list, and click **New Menu**.

3. From the **Commands** list, drag the **New Menu** command from the dialog box and drop it on the menu bar (as shown in Figure 27.14).

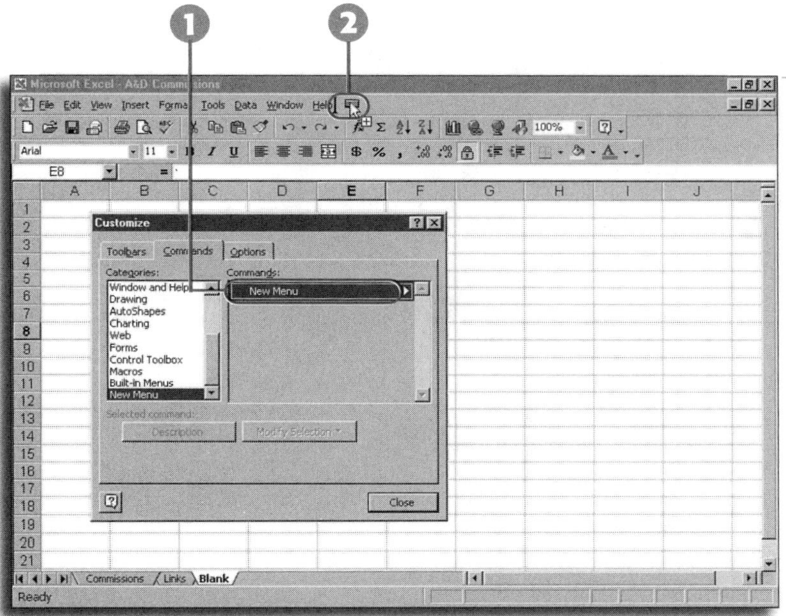

FIGURE 27.14

When you move a button, an insertion marker shows you where it will be inserted.

1 Drag from here.

2 Drop here.

A new, empty menu is added to the menu bar.

4. Right-click the new menu.

   A shortcut menu is displayed, as shown in Figure 27.15.

5. In the **Name** box, delete the default name New Menu and type the menu name you want; then, press Enter.

6. Use the step by step exercise "Add a command to a menu" earlier in the chapter to add commands.

   Your new menu will be blank, and therefore very small, until you add commands to it; so be careful that you don't drop that first command on the menu bar by mistake.

7. When you're finished, click **Close** to close the Customize dialog box.

   To remove a custom menu, press the Alt key while you drag the menu name away from the menu bar; then, drop the dragged menu name anywhere on the worksheet.

Can I Make a Shortcut Key?

You can designate a shortcut key, or *hotkey*, for a menu or command name by adding an ampersand (&) to the left of the letter. For example, to make the *u* in the menu name "Stuff" a hotkey, type the name **St&uff** in the **Name** box. The new menu name will be **Stuff**.

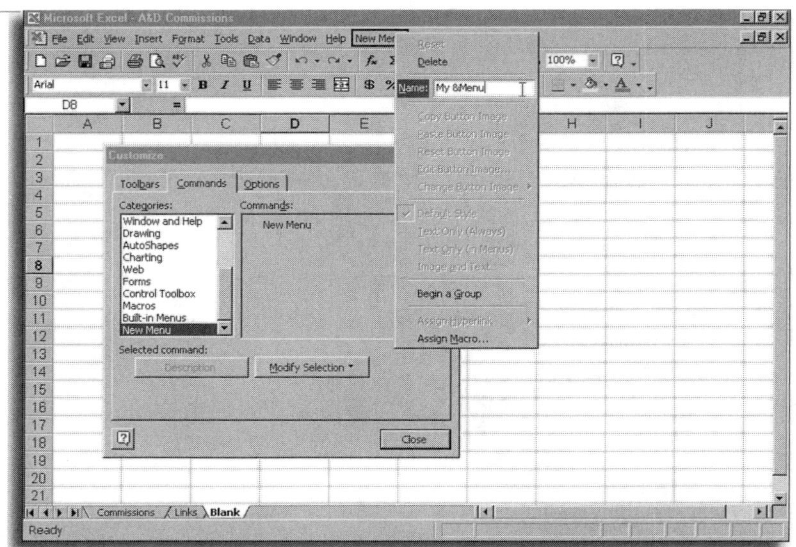

FIGURE 27.15

To insert a space line left of the menu name (to create visual groups on the menu bar), click **Begin a Group** on the shortcut menu.

CHAPTER

28

Automating Repetitive Work with Macros

Recording a macro

Running a macro

Editing a macro

Attaching a macro to a toolbar button or menu command

Creating a toggle macro

Introducing Macros

Some of your Excel tasks are bound to be repetitive. For example, you might import and consolidate sales information on a weekly basis and then format and subtotal the new table the same way every time. Rather than performing the same formatting and subtotaling tasks over and over again, you can create a macro that will perform the sequence of tasks for you.

A *macro* is a series of instructions, written in a programming language called Visual Basic for Applications (VBA), that Excel can follow. To create a macro, you don't need to understand the programming language; you only need to know what Excel commands you want the macro to perform for you. You record the commands by performing them (clicking and typing and so forth), and the *macro recorder* translates them into VBA, which Excel reads as if a professional programmer had written it. Recording a macro is similar to recording music on a tape recorder: You don't need to understand how the music is recorded onto the tape; you only need to know what music you want to record.

After your macro is recorded, you can run it from the Macro dialog box, or you can attach it to a menu command or toolbar button.

Recording a Macro

Plan and Test Your Macro

It's a good idea to rehearse your planned macro steps before you actually record the macro and then test the macro after you record it.

Before you record a macro, plan out exactly what you want the macro to do and in what order. After you start the macro recorder, every cell you click, everything you type, and every command you select are recorded in a manner similar to a tape recorder.

Name your macro to reflect the actions it performs so that it is easy to identify later. Macro names cannot include spaces or periods, so if you include more than one word, you must separate the words with an underscore, as in My_Cool_Macro, or use initial capitals to separate the words, as in MyCoolMacro.

Record a macro

1. On the **Tools** menu, point to **Macro**; then, click **Record New Macro**.

   The Record Macro dialog box is displayed, as shown in Figure 28.1.

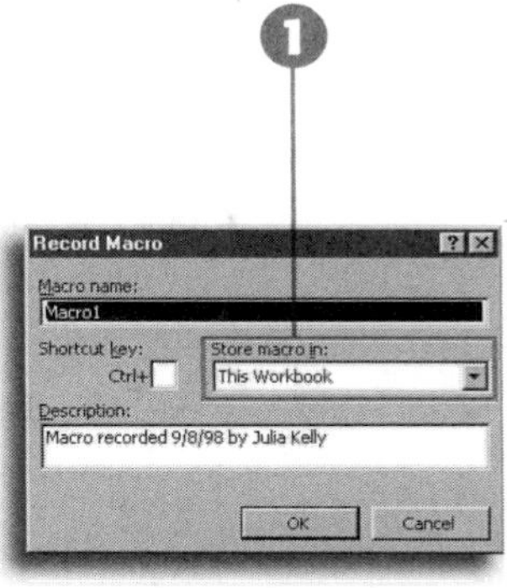

FIGURE 28.1
A macro stored in This Workbook is available only in this workbook; to make a macro always available, store it in the Personal Macro Workbook.

1 Where the macro is available

2. In the **Macro name** box, type an identifiable name for the macro.

   No spaces or periods are allowed in the name, and it must begin with a letter.

3. In the **Shortcut key** box, type a shortcut key, or hotkey, that you can click to run the macro. The Crtl key is automatically included in any macro keyboard shortcut.

   Be careful that you don't assign a keyboard shortcut that you use for other workbook activities, such as Ctrl+C to copy or Ctrl+V to paste, because the macro will override the existing keyboard shortcut.

4. In the **Store macro in** list, select a workbook to store the macro in.

   A macro stored in This Workbook is available only when this particular workbook is open. To make a macro available all the time, in any workbook, click the down arrow on the **Store macro in** box and select **Personal Macro Workbook**.

A Shifty Shortcut

You can include the Shift key in your keyboard shortcut if you click in the **Shortcut key** box and press Shift+*key*. For example, if you click in the **Shortcut key** box and press Shift+D, your shortcut key is Ctrl+Shift+D. (You press all three keys at the same time to run the macro.)

What's the Personal Macro Workbook?

The Personal Macro Workbook is a hidden file that Microsoft Excel creates when you select the Personal Macro Workbook option; it opens automatically whenever you start Microsoft Excel, but you won't see it because it's hidden.

5. Select the text in the **Description** box, and type your own memorable macro description.
6. Click **OK**.

   The macro recorder starts recording immediately, and the Stop Recording toolbar (shown in Figure 28.2) is displayed with two buttons on it: Stop Recording and Relative Reference. You can move this toolbar out of the way while you record the macro if you need to; moving the toolbar won't be recorded.

   - Click the **Stop Recording** button to stop the macro recorder when you finish performing the macro steps.
   - Click the **Relative Reference** button to switch between recording relative and absolute references.

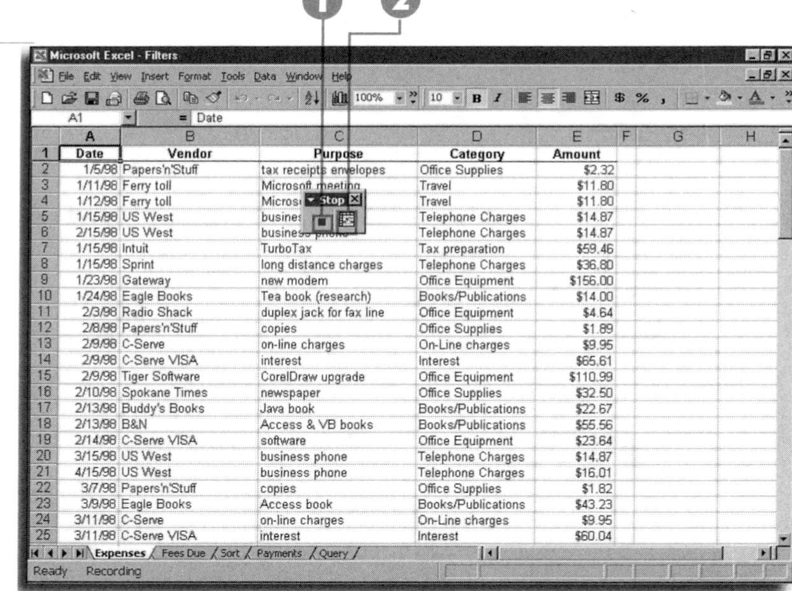

	A	B	C	D	E
1	Date	Vendor	Purpose	Category	Amount
2	1/5/98	Papers'n'Stuff	tax receipts envelopes	Office Supplies	$2.32
3	1/11/98	Ferry toll	Microsoft meeting	Travel	$11.80
4	1/12/98	Ferry toll	Micros	Travel	$11.80
5	1/15/98	US West	busines	Telephone Charges	$14.87
6	2/15/98	US West	busines	Telephone Charges	$14.87
7	1/15/98	Intuit	TurboTax	Tax preparation	$59.46
8	1/15/98	Sprint	long distance charges	Telephone Charges	$36.80
9	1/23/98	Gateway	new modem	Office Equipment	$156.00
10	1/24/98	Eagle Books	Tea book (research)	Books/Publications	$14.00
11	2/3/98	Radio Shack	duplex jack for fax line	Office Equipment	$4.64
12	2/8/98	Papers'n'Stuff	copies	Office Supplies	$1.89
13	2/9/98	C-Serve	on-line charges	On-Line charges	$9.95
14	2/9/98	C-Serve VISA	interest	Interest	$65.61
15	2/9/98	Tiger Software	CorelDraw upgrade	Office Equipment	$110.99
16	2/10/98	Spokane Times	newspaper	Office Supplies	$32.50
17	2/13/98	Buddy's Books	Java book	Books/Publications	$22.67
18	2/13/98	B&N	Access & VB books	Books/Publications	$55.56
19	2/14/98	C-Serve VISA	software	Office Equipment	$23.64
20	3/15/98	US West	business phone	Telephone Charges	$14.87
21	4/15/98	US West	business phone	Telephone Charges	$16.01
22	3/7/98	Papers'n'Stuff	copies	Office Supplies	$1.82
23	3/9/98	Eagle Books	Access book	Books/Publications	$43.23
24	3/11/98	C-Serve	on-line charges	On-Line charges	$9.95
25	3/11/98	C-Serve VISA	interest	Interest	$60.04

FIGURE 28.2

You'll need two buttons when you're in the middle of recording a macro.

1 Stop Recording

2 Relative Reference

7. Perform all the steps you want the macro to perform for you when you run it.
8. When you finish, click the **Stop Recording** button on the Stop Recording toolbar.

   The macro recorder stops recording your actions, and the Stop Recording toolbar is no longer displayed.

Running a Macro

After you've recorded a macro, it's a good idea to test it and iron out any little glitches before you store it permanently or pass it along to someone else.

When you run a macro, it carries out all the actions that you performed while you were recording.

Run a macro

1. On the **Tools** menu, point to **Macro**; then click **Macros**.

   The Macro dialog box is displayed.
2. Click the macro name; then click **Run**.

   The macro runs, and the macro actions you recorded are executed.

If you started your recorded macro by selecting a cell and the recorder used absolute references, the cell you selected will be selected by the macro. But there are two other possibilities:

- If your macro begins by selecting a cell and the recorder used relative references, the macro selects a cell relative to the cell that's already selected when you run the macro. If you have problems with your macro beginning in an unexpected cell, the relative versus absolute setting could be the source of your trouble. Either re-record the macro with the Relative Reference button turned off (not highlighted or depressed), or edit the macro to replace the relative reference with an absolute reference.
- If you didn't intend for the macro to begin by selecting a cell, but instead you want the macro to begin carrying out

If the Stop Recording Toolbar Doesn't Appear

You can also stop recording by clicking **Tools**, **Macro**, **Stop Recording**. If the Stop Recording toolbar doesn't appear when you begin recording, it's because it was closed (by clicking its X box) while recording a previous macro. To return it to normal behavior so it appears while you record, start recording a macro; then right-click any toolbar and click **Stop Recording**.

Or Type It

If you recorded your macro with a keyboard shortcut, just type the keyboard shortcut to run the macro.

Am I Recording Relative or Absolute?

If the Relative Reference button is depressed or highlighted, you're recording relative references; if the button isn't depressed or highlighted, you're recording absolute references.

procedures in whatever cell you select before running the macro, either re-record your macro and don't select a starting cell after you turn on the recorder, or edit the macro to remove the cell selection at the start of the macro.

Editing a Macro

Just as comments in your worksheets can document how they are set up, you can add comments to your macro to document it so that you and other users can understand what it's doing later. You can also edit a macro by changing recorded actions to correct a problem or to refine the macro. Because macros are written in VBA, you need to understand VBA and programming to make serious changes to a recorded macro, but you can make smaller changes that don't require a course in programming. (For example, if you misspell a word while recording a text entry, you can edit the spelling in the module rather than re-recording the entire macro.)

Macros are stored in a Visual Basic module hidden in the workbook. To read and edit your macros, you open the module using the Visual Basic Editor. With the Visual Basic Editor, you can add comments to the macro to explain individual steps, and you can edit the steps themselves to change or correct them without recording the macro again.

Edit a macro

1. On the **Tools** menu, point to **Macro**; then click **Macros**.

   The Macro dialog box is displayed.

2. Select the macro name you want to edit; then click **Edit**.

   The Visual Basic Editor opens (shown in Figure 28.3) with the selected macro displayed in the window on the right. You can switch between a workbook and your macro by clicking the button on either the taskbar or toolbar.

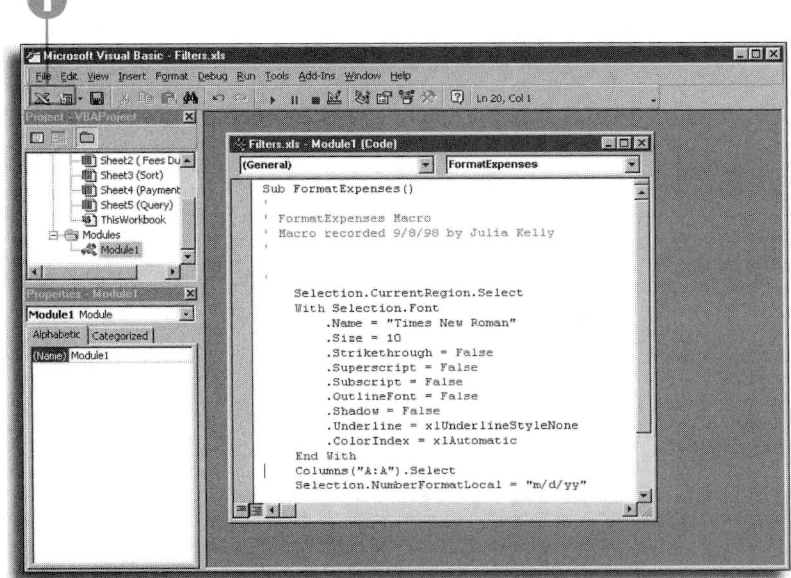

FIGURE 28.3

The Visual Basic Editor is a separate program within Excel that gives you access to your macros.

1 Return to Excel.

In the macro, some text is displayed in green, some in blue, and some in black. Green text indicates a comment and is ignored by Microsoft Excel when the macro is run. Blue text indicates *keywords* that Microsoft Excel recognizes (in this case, `Sub`, `With`, `False`, `End With`, and `True`). Black text indicates macro steps. Comments are always preceded by an apostrophe, which tells Microsoft Excel that they are comments.

The macro begins with the word `Sub` in blue text, followed by the macro name and a pair of parentheses (in this example, `FormatExpenses()`). Everything else after this line is a step in the macro, until you reach the line that reads `End Sub` (in blue).

To document a macro, add comments to individual sections, either immediately above the section, on the same line as the section, or immediately following the section. It doesn't matter which you choose, as long as you are consistent.

Add a comment to a macro

1. Type an apostrophe and then the comment.
2. Click away from the comment line, or press Enter.

   The comment automatically turns green after you click away from the line (as shown in Figure 28.4). The apostrophe tells Microsoft Excel that the text is a comment rather than a step. Adding comments will not affect the macro when you run it, as long as you remember to add the apostrophe at the beginning of the line. (If you forget, you'll see an error message when you run the macro again.)

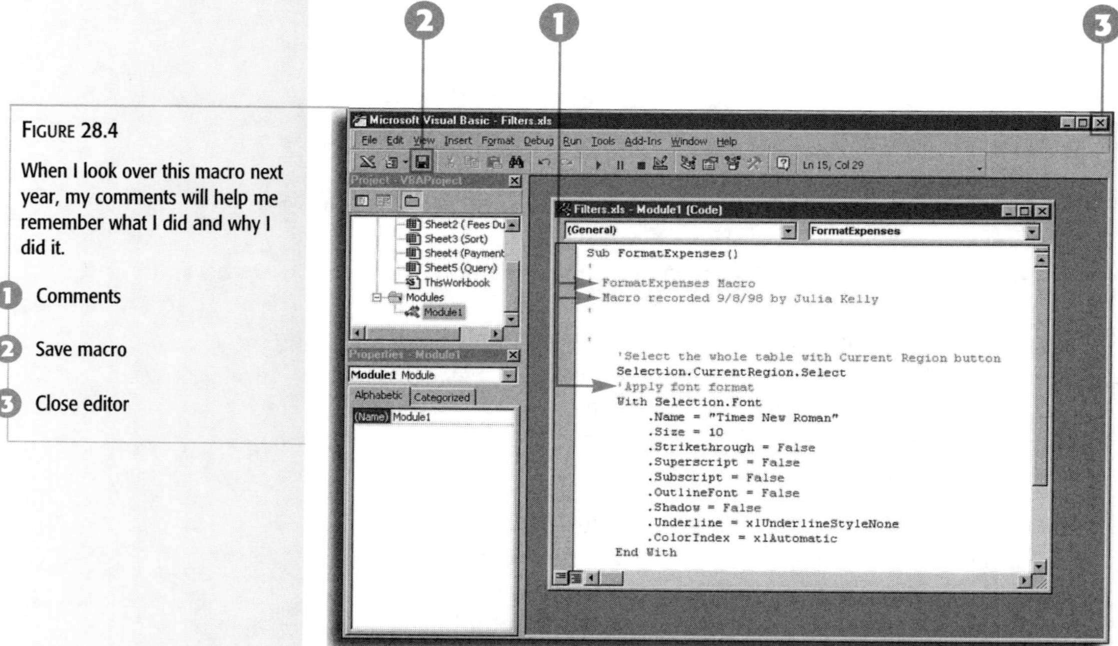

FIGURE 28.4

When I look over this macro next year, my comments will help me remember what I did and why I did it.

1. Comments
2. Save macro
3. Close editor

3. When you finish editing the macro, click the **Save** button on the toolbar.
4. To close the Visual Basic Editor and return to Excel, click its **Close** button.

Attaching a Macro to a Toolbar Button or Menu Command

After you record a macro, you can run it more quickly by attaching it to a button or menu command.

Create a menu command or toolbar button to run the macro

1. Right-click a toolbar; then, click **Customize**.
2. On the **Commands** tab, scroll down the list of categories, and click **Macros**.
3. In the **Commands** list (shown in Figure 28.5), do one of the following:
   - To create a menu command, drag **Custom Menu Item** up to the menu bar, hold it over the menu you want, and then drop it into position on the menu.
   - To create a toolbar button, drag **Custom Button** onto a toolbar.

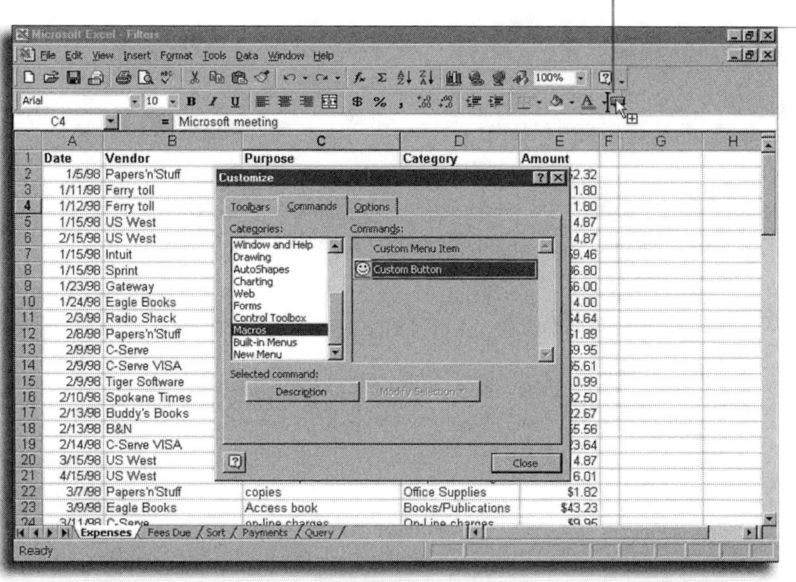

FIGURE 28.5

First, create the custom menu command or toolbar button; then, assign the macro to it.

1. Drag Custom Button to toolbar.

How About a Command Shortcut Key?

To create a shortcut key for your new menu command, type an ampersand (&) to the left of the shortcut key letter in the command name. For example, to create the command name MyMacro, type the name **M&yMacro** in the **Name** box.

4. Right-click the new button or menu command.
5. In the shortcut menu that is displayed (shown in Figure 28.6), give the button or command a name in the **Name** box.

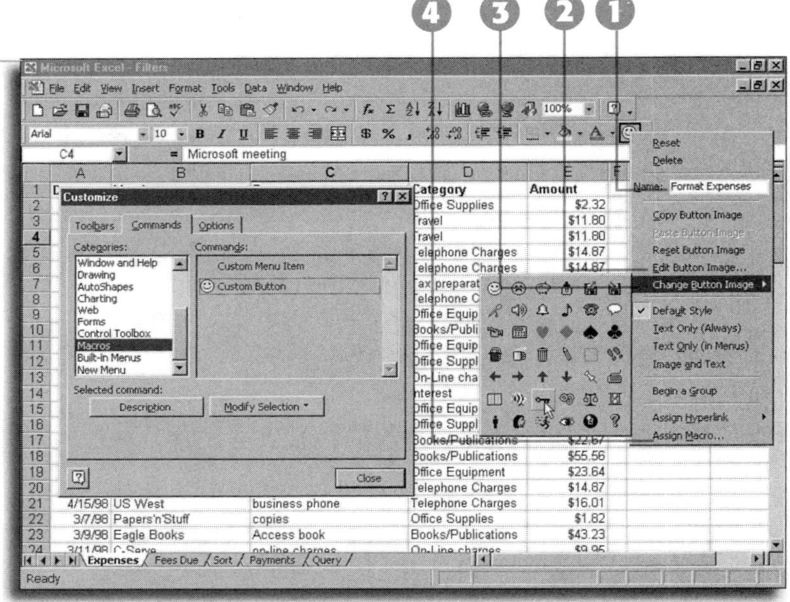

FIGURE 28.6

You can also change or edit the button face.

1. Name button/command
2. Draw your own button face.
3. Pick new button face.
4. Assign macro.

6. In the shortcut menu, click **Assign Macro**.

   The Assign Macro dialog box is displayed.
7. Click the macro name you want to assign to the button or command; then, click **OK**.
8. In the Customize dialog box, click **Close**.

To test the macro, click the button or menu command.

SEE ALSO

➤ *To learn more about creating custom menus and commands, see the section titled "Creating Personal Toolbars," page 528.*

➤ *To learn more about creating custom toolbar buttons, see the section titled "Customizing Your Menu Bar," page 530.*

Creating a Toggle Macro

A toggle is something you click to turn on and click again to turn off (such as the Bold formatting button or the AutoFilter command). You can reduce some commands to a single click by creating a macro and then editing the macro to turn it into a toggle macro. To explain more clearly, I'll show you how to create one of my favorite toggle macros: turning fixed-decimal entry on and off.

This macro is simple to record and then requires a minor edit in the Visual Basic Editor to make it a toggle.

Fixed-decimal entry is something I use whenever I have lots of currency figures to enter in an expenses list; it allows me to type only the dollars and cents, and it inserts the decimal point for me at the two-decimal-place position (which is a lot faster). I don't want it on when I'm not entering currency figures, however, so I want to be able to turn it on and off easily. For clarity in this demonstration (and to make your macro match the one shown in the figures), be sure the fixed-decimal setting is turned off (check box cleared) before you begin recording.

Where's This Fixed-Decimal Feature?

To find the actual on/off check box, open the **Tools** menu, click **Options**, and then click the **Edit** tab. To turn the fixed-decimal setting on or off, click the **Fixed decimal** check box (leave **Places** set at **2**). To make this macro simple, leave the **Fixed decimal** check box cleared (off) before you begin recording the macro.

Record the initial macro

1. On the **Tools** menu, point to **Macro**; then click **Record New Macro**.

   The Record Macro dialog box is displayed.

2. In the **Macro name** box, type the name `ToggleDecimal`.
3. Leave the **Shortcut key** box empty, unless you're sure you want (and can remember) a shortcut key.
4. Store the macro in the Personal Macro Workbook.

   The Personal Macro Workbook is a hidden workbook that makes the macro available to any workbook you're working in.

5. Select the text in the **Description** box, and type `Toggles two fixed decimal places on and off`.

More About the Personal Macro Workbook

The Personal Macro Workbook doesn't exist until you store a macro in it. Excel creates it to hold the macro, keeps it hidden (unless you unhide it), and opens it every time you start Excel—which is how your macro is made *global*, or available to every workbook you open. To keep it out of your way, keep it hidden unless you're editing a macro that's stored in it.

6. Click **OK**.

   The macro recorder starts, and the Stop Recording toolbar is displayed.

7. On the **Tools** menu, click **Options**; then click the **Edit** tab.
8. Click the **Fixed decimal** check box, and leave **Places** set at 2.
9. Click **OK** to close the dialog box.
10. On the Stop Recording toolbar, click the **Stop Recording** button.

    The macro recorder stops recording your actions.

Next, you'll edit the macro to make it a toggle, but because the macro is stored in a hidden workbook (the Personal Macro Workbook), you'll have to unhide the workbook before you can edit the macro. (A macro stored in This Workbook or New Workbook is not hidden; only the Personal Macro Workbook is hidden.)

Edit the macro to make it toggle on and off

1. On the **Window** menu, click **Unhide**.
2. In the Unhide dialog box, be sure **Personal** is selected; then click **OK**.

   The Personal Macro Workbook looks like an empty workbook; don't type anything in it. You're only going to edit the macro stored there.

3. On the **Tools** menu, point to **Macro**; then click **Macros**.
4. Select the name **ToggleDecimal**; then click **Edit**.

   The Visual Basic Editor opens, and your macro should look similar to the one in Figure 28.7. The macro tells Excel to turn on the fixed-decimal setting. I'm going to change the macro action to read as follows:

   ```
   Application.FixedDecimal = Not Application.FixedDecimal
   ```

   This tells Excel that whatever the setting is, it should make it the opposite.

Mine Says False, Not True

If you had **Fixed Decimal** turned on before you started this macro and cleared the check box instead of marking it in the previous procedure, your macro will read False instead of True and have an extra line. To make your macro match the figures in this demonstration, be sure you start recording the macro with **Fixed Decimal** turned off.

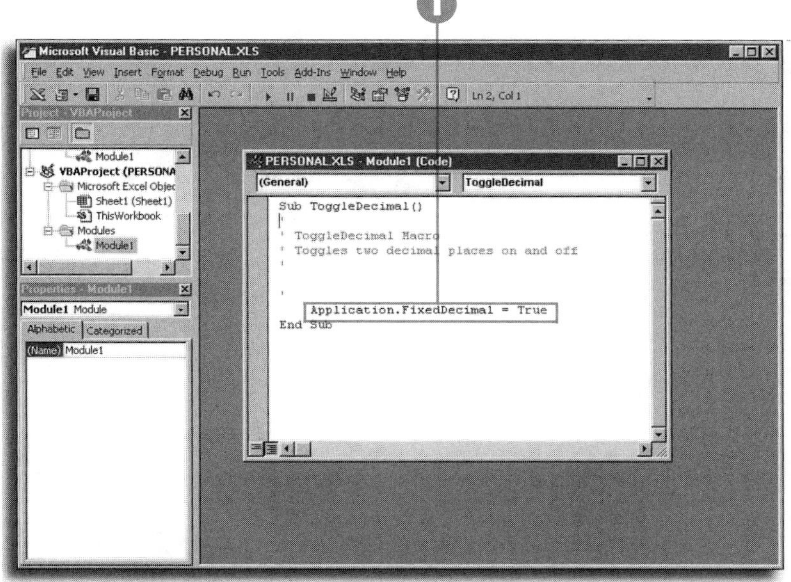

FIGURE 28.7
I'm going to edit this simple macro into a toggle macro.

1 Macro action

5. In the module, select the words `Application.FixedDecimal`; then, press Ctrl+C to copy it.
6. Double-click the keyword **True** to select it; then, click Ctrl+V to paste the copied words in its place.
7. Enter the word **`Not`** after the equal sign; then click away from the line. (Leave a space between the word Not and the pasted words.)

   Your module should look like the one in Figure 28.8. The word Not is changed into a blue keyword.
8. On the **File** menu, click **Close and Return to Microsoft Excel**.

   The VB Editor closes, and the Personal workbook is open. (The title bar should read Microsoft Excel - Personal.) You'll hide the Personal workbook before you exit Excel, but first, you'll finish working with your macro. You won't save Personal until after it's hidden and you exit Excel; when you exit Excel, you'll be asked if you want to save Personal.

Do Macro Stuff Before You Hide the Workbook

When you hide the Personal workbook, you'll discover that you can't assign, edit, delete, or mess with its macros in any way without unhiding it; so save yourself a step by making toolbar buttons and menu commands now, before you hide it.

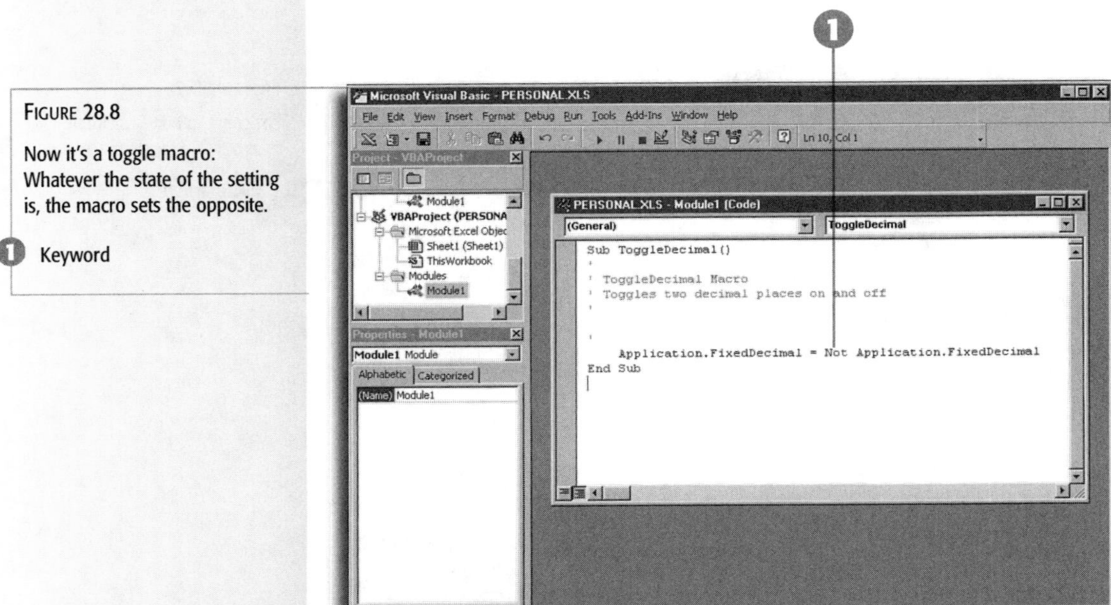

FIGURE 28.8

Now it's a toggle macro: Whatever the state of the setting is, the macro sets the opposite.

1 Keyword

Hiding the Personal Workbook Is Important

If you don't hide the Personal workbook, it will open every time you start Excel; to get it out of your way, you must remember to hide it.

Please Don't Forget You Did This!

Please don't forget you created this macro and then call Microsoft Product Support for help in fixing Excel's entry behavior, because they'll probably get mad at *me* for having taught you this. To help you remember, make the button or command name very obvious and easy to find again later.

9. Assign the macro to a button or menu command before you hide the Personal Macro Workbook. (See the section "Attaching a Macro to a Toolbar Button or a Menu Command" earlier in this chapter.)

10. On the **Window** menu, click **Hide** to hide the Personal Macro Workbook. (Don't close it, just hide it.)

    When you exit Excel, you'll be asked if you want to save changes to Personal.xls; at that point, you'll click **Yes**. Excel will save the hidden workbook and then exit.

Now you can give it a try.

Open a new workbook. In any cell, type **123** and press Enter. Then click your toggle button or command, type **123**, and press Enter again. When the toggle is "on", your entry will read `1.23`; when the toggle is "off", the entry reads `123`.

When you close Excel after working in the Personal Macro Workbook, you'll be asked if you want to save the changes you made in the Personal Macro Workbook. Click **Yes**.

CHAPTER

29

Using Excel's Built-In Templates

- Working with templates
- Installing the Template Wizard add-in
- Entering automated information in the template
- Setting up a database for a new template
- Setting up a database for an existing template
- Saving copies of a template to collect summary data

Working with Templates

SEE ALSO

➤ *To learn more about templates, see page 45.*

Excel comes with three built-in Spreadsheet Solutions templates, including Invoice and Expense Statement templates, that can save you considerable time by automating data collection. The Template Wizard sets up the automatic data collection for you, links each saved copy of the template to its appropriate database, and collects the summary data from every saved copy of the template. The resulting workbook database is a list of data from which you can subtotal or create PivotTables, like any other list in Excel.

You can use the built-in templates, as described in Chapter 3, "Saving Files and Using Templates," without installing the Template Wizard. The difference is that without the Template Wizard, you won't be able to compile and track data from copies of the template.

To collect summary data from every saved copy of a Spreadsheet Solutions template, you need the Template Wizard add-in installed and loaded. *Installing* copies the add-in from the CD-ROM into your computer. Loading the add-in makes it available for Excel to use.

What's a Template?

A template is like a preprinted pad of paper. You can tear off new, ready-to-use copies that only need new data entered. All the labeling, formatting, and formulas you need are already in place.

Why Isn't Every Add-In Loaded?

Each loaded add-in uses more of your system resources and memory and slows Excel down just a bit. For maximum performance, you should have installed only the add-ins that you use. Load an add-in when you need to use it, and unload it when you don't need it.

Installing the Template Wizard Add-In

To find out if you've already installed the Template Wizard add-in, open the **Tools** menu, select **Add-Ins**, and look for the **Template Wizard with Data Tracking** check box in the list of add-ins (shown in Figure 29.1). Click the **Template Wizard with Data Tracking** check box to load the Template Wizard (and clear the check box to unload it when you're finished using it).

Are There More Spreadsheet Solutions Templates?

You can download more Spreadsheet Solutions templates from Microsoft for free. Open the **Help** menu, select **Office on the Web**, and click **Free Stuff** to launch your Internet browser and go directly to the electronic warehouse.

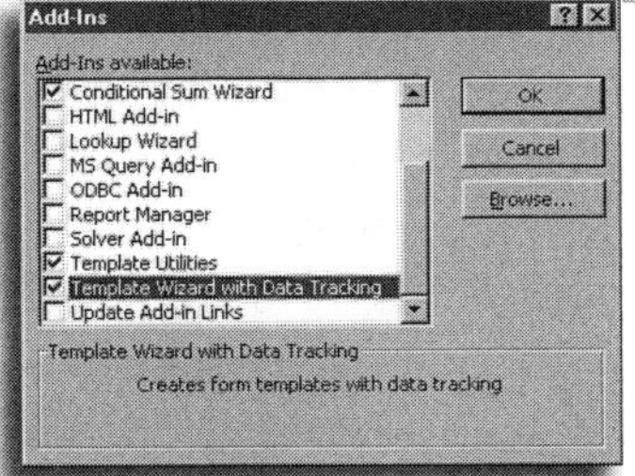

FIGURE 29.1
Load add-ins only when you need to use them.

If the Template Wizard isn't installed, you see a message asking if you'd like to install it now. Be sure your Office 2000 CD-ROM is in the CD drive, and click **Yes**. The add-in will install itself with no further input from you.

SEE ALSO

➤ *For more information on personalizing Excel's Spreadsheet Solutions templates, see page 53.*

Entering Automated Information in the Template

Some of the Spreadsheet Solutions templates, like the Expense Statement template, require employee information that gets collected in the summary database along with the totals.

The macros in the Spreadsheet Solutions templates enable you to automatically enter customized information, such as names, addresses, and employee numbers. These macros save time and prevent errors for everyone who uses a copy of the template.

Customize a Spreadsheet Solutions template with automated information

1. Open the **File** menu and select **Open**.
2. Navigate to your Library folder. (The default path is C:\Program Files\Microsoft Office\Office\Library.) The path in your computer may be different if you changed the folder during installation.

3. Double-click the workbook named **Common**.

   The Common workbook opens (shown in Figure 29.2). It's a workbook of information shared by all the Spreadsheet Solutions templates. It contains sample employee data to guide you in filling in your own company data.

   You can also enter company data on the Product and Service Catalog worksheet.

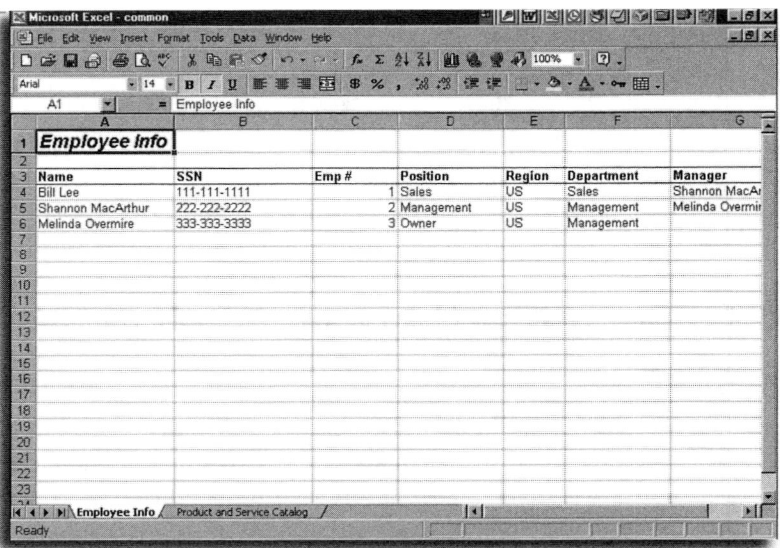

FIGURE 29.2

The Common workbook is a file where you can keep employee data that some of your Spreadsheet Solutions templates require.

4. In the Common workbook, delete the sample data and enter your own data.
5. Save and close the Common workbook.

Now you can open a copy of any Spreadsheet Solutions template that requires employee data, and enter employee information from a list rather than typing it. For example, if you have the Expense Statement template installed, you notice a **Select Employee** button in the Employee Information area. Click the button, select a name, click **OK**, and all the correct employee information is automatically entered.

I Forgot How to Open My Spreadsheet Solutions Template

Open the **File** menu, click **New**, and double-click a template on the **General** tab, where your customized templates are stored.

SEE ALSO

➤ *For more information on opening copies of templates, see page 51.*

Setting Up the Collection Database

You can set up the link between a Spreadsheet Solutions template and its collection database when you first customize the template, or after you've customized and saved the template.

Setting Up a Database While You Set Up a New Template

If you are customizing a Spreadsheet Solutions template and database for the first time, the Template Wizard guides you through the entire process.

Set up a new Spreadsheet Solutions template and collection database

1. Open the **File** menu and select **New**.
2. In the New dialog box, click the **Spreadsheet Solutions** tab.
3. Double-click the icon for the Spreadsheet Solutions template that you want to set up.

   A message warning you about macro viruses may appear; click **Enable Macros**.

   A new copy of the template appears. (A copy of the Invoice template is shown in Figure 29.3.)

Templates for Everyone

If you want to give others access to copies of a customized template, be sure the Templates folder where you save the customized template is a public-access folder on your network.

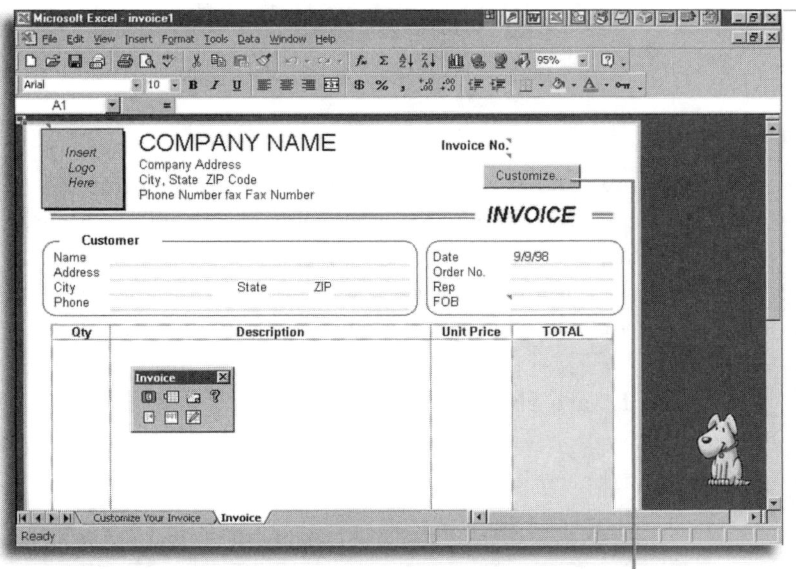

FIGURE 29.3

A new invoice template that I want to customize.

1 Customize

4. Click the **Customize** button.
5. Fill in all the customization information you want on the Customize Your Invoice worksheet.

SEE ALSO

➤ *For more about customizing the template, see page 52.*

6. Find the **Template Wizard Database** box in the Default Information area (shown in Figure 29.4). The path and workbook name you see there lead to the linked database for this template.

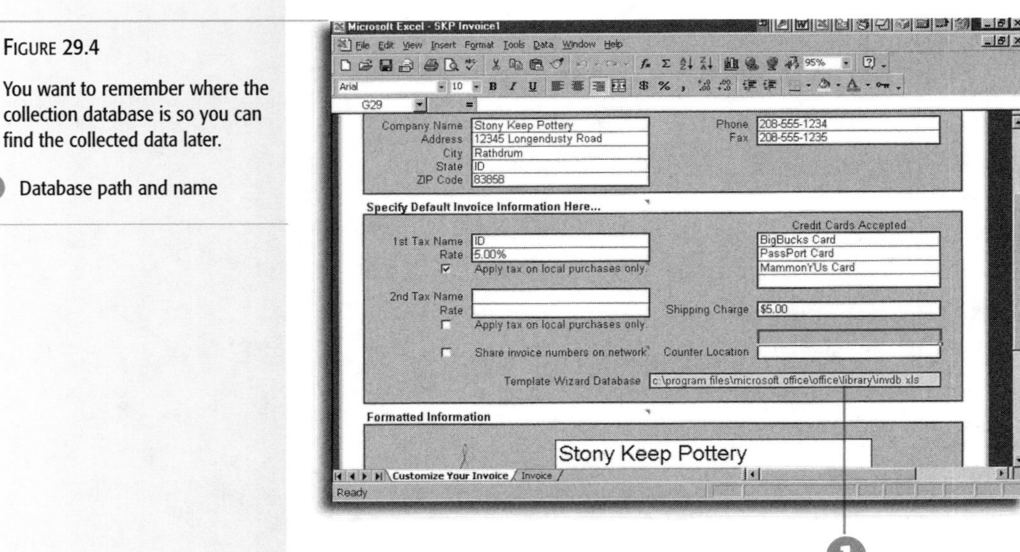

FIGURE 29.4

You want to remember where the collection database is so you can find the collected data later.

1 Database path and name

Because you're creating the template with the Template Wizard installed and loaded, its link to its database is automatically set up for you. If you want to, you can change the database using the procedures in the next section, "Setting Up a Database for an Existing Template."

7. At the top of the customizing worksheet, click the **Lock/Save Sheet** button.

The Lock/Save Sheet button saves your changes and protects the worksheet from further, inadvertent changes.

8. In the Lock/Save Sheet dialog box, click **OK**.
9. In the Save Template dialog box, give the template a name and click **Save**.

   You see a message with information about your new template. Read it and click **OK** to continue.
10. Close the template.

Now you can open copies of your template, enter data, save and close the copies, and the data is collected in the linked database.

Setting Up a Database for an Existing Template

In the previous procedure, you set up a new Spreadsheet Solutions template and linked it to an automatic-tracking database; however, you can also set up a Spreadsheet Solutions template without linking it to a database, and later change your mind about tracking the data. This procedure begins with an existing Spreadsheet Solutions template that's not linked to a database and creates a linked database for it.

Create a linked database for an existing Spreadsheet Solutions template

1. Open the **File** menu and select **New**.
2. In the New dialog box, double-click the icon for the customized template that you want to link to a database.

   Because you're linking a template you've already created (such as my SKP Invoice, shown in Figure 29.5), you find it on the General tab.

   Be sure you click the **Enable Macros** button in the macro warning message that appears.
3. In the new template copy, click the **Customize** button.

   The hidden customizing worksheet appears (shown in Figure 29.6).

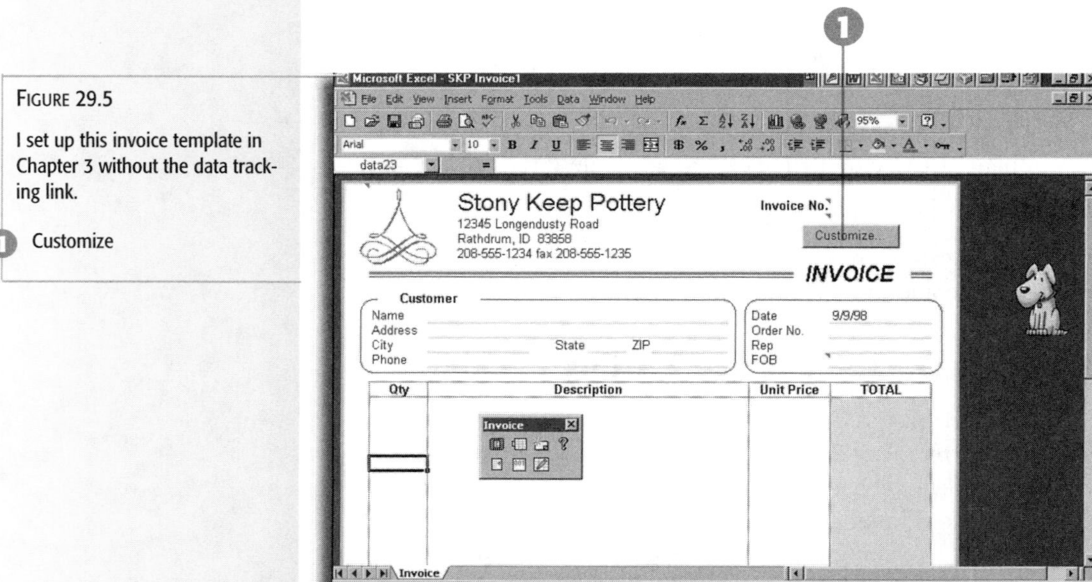

FIGURE 29.5

I set up this invoice template in Chapter 3 without the data tracking link.

1 Customize

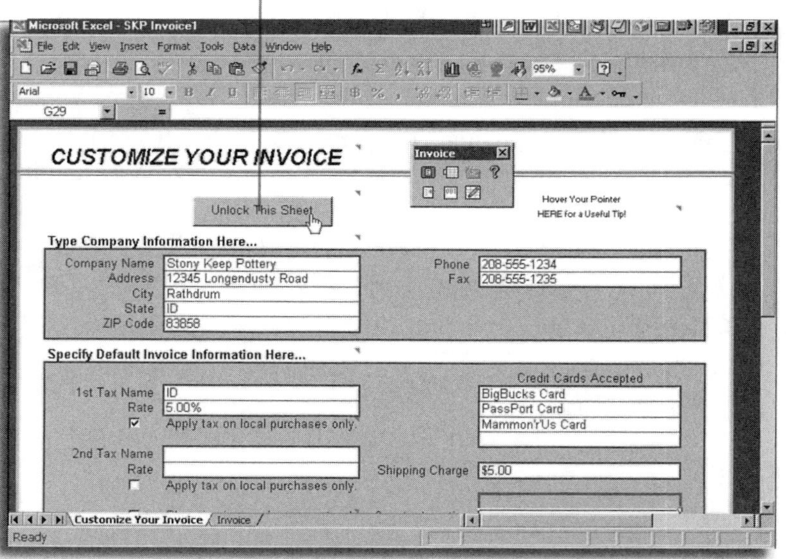

FIGURE 29.6

The hidden worksheet in the template does the automation work.

1 Unlock the worksheet.

4. Click the **Unlock This Sheet** button so that you can make changes to the template, and click **OK** in the warning message that appears.
5. Scroll to the Default Information area and look for the **Template Wizard Database** box (shown in Figure 29.7). (Each template is a little different.)

This Worksheet Is a Bit Confusing

To learn about any particular data cell on the customize worksheet, click the cell or point to a comment indicator. A comment or text box appears with explanatory information.

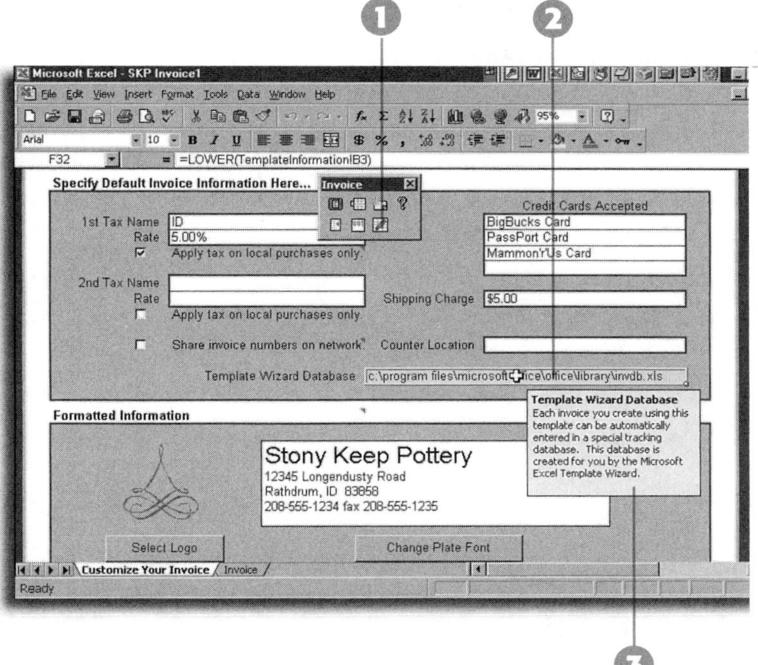

FIGURE 29.7

Each template serves a different purpose and requires different automation information.

1. Capture data in a database
2. Path to database
3. Message appears when I click the cell.

Take a look at the path in the Template Wizard Database box so you know where to find the data collection database later.

6. To create a different database for the template, or change the data that's collected, click the **Capture Data in a Database** button on the Invoice template toolbar.
7. In the Create and Interact with Database dialog box, click the **Create a new Template Database** option and click **OK**.

   The Template Wizard starts.

Create a New Database for Your Template

To change the database, you must first save a workbook to be the database in the Library folder. The contents must be recognizable to the Template Wizard, so the easiest way is to create a copy of the default database (the name in the **Template Wizard Database** box) and give it a new name.

8. Follow the steps in the Template Wizard to set up a new database for your template.

If anything in the Template Wizard is confusing, click the **Help** button in the wizard step. The Template Wizard help files are remarkably direct and helpful.

Saving Copies of the Template to Collect Summary Data

When a template is linked to its collection database and you open a copy of the template to create an invoice (or whatever) for a customer, saving the template-copy workbook involves an extra step. Excel asks whether you want to create a new record in the collection database.

Only One Record Is Saved

By default, the collection database collects only a single line of summary data from each copy of the template. To collect more or different data from a template, click the **Capture Data in a Database** button on the Invoice template toolbar, follow the Template Wizard steps, and click the wizard's **Help** button when you need more information.

In this procedure, you are no longer customizing a template; you've opened a copy of the template, which is a normal workbook.

Collect summary data from template copies in the collection database

1. Open and fill out the template-copy workbook, and click the **Save** button on the Standard toolbar.
   The Template File - Save to Database dialog box appears (shown in Figure 29.8).

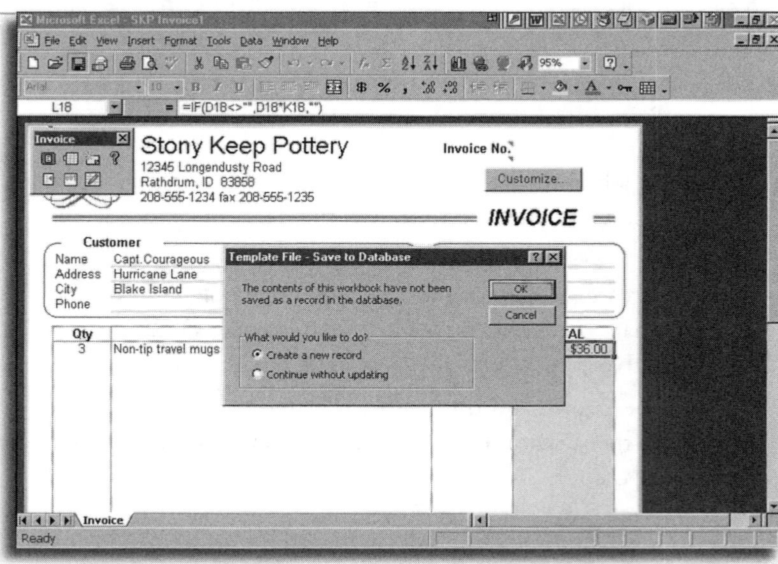

FIGURE 29.8
You can choose whether to save the data in the collection database or not.

2. To save the data in the database, be sure the **Create a new record** option is selected and then click **OK**.

   If instead you want to save the workbook without saving the data to a database, click the **Continue without updating** option and click **OK**.

   The Save As dialog box appears.

3. Continue saving the workbook normally. Be sure to navigate to the folder in which you save your business workbooks, and give the workbook an identifiable name.

   At this point, the template copy is a normal workbook, and you can save it with file properties (such as keywords) to make it easier to locate later.

4. Close the workbook.

SEE ALSO

- *For more information on saving workbooks as templates, see page 50.*
- *For more information on opening copies of templates, see page 51.*
- *For more information on personalizing Excel's Spreadsheet Solutions templates, see page 53.*

Using the Collection Database

After you've saved a couple of template workbooks that are linked to a collection database, you can open the database to work with the collected data.

Open a collection database

1. On the Standard toolbar, click **Open**.
2. In the Open dialog box, navigate to your Library folder. (The default path is C:\Program Files\Microsoft Office\Office\Library; it may be different in your computer.)
3. Double-click the name of the collection database linked to your template.

Can't Remember the Database Name?

In the Open dialog box, you can right-click a likely filename and click **Quick View** to glimpse what's in the mysterious file.

The name of the default database for the Spreadsheet Solutions Invoice template is INVDB. The default name for the Expense Statement's database is EXPDB. The default name for the Purchase Order template database is PODB. For other templates, be sure you remember the database name.

Your collection database opens (a sample invoice collection database is shown in Figure 29.9). You can consolidate, subtotal, chart, and add PivotTables to the collected data to evaluate it.

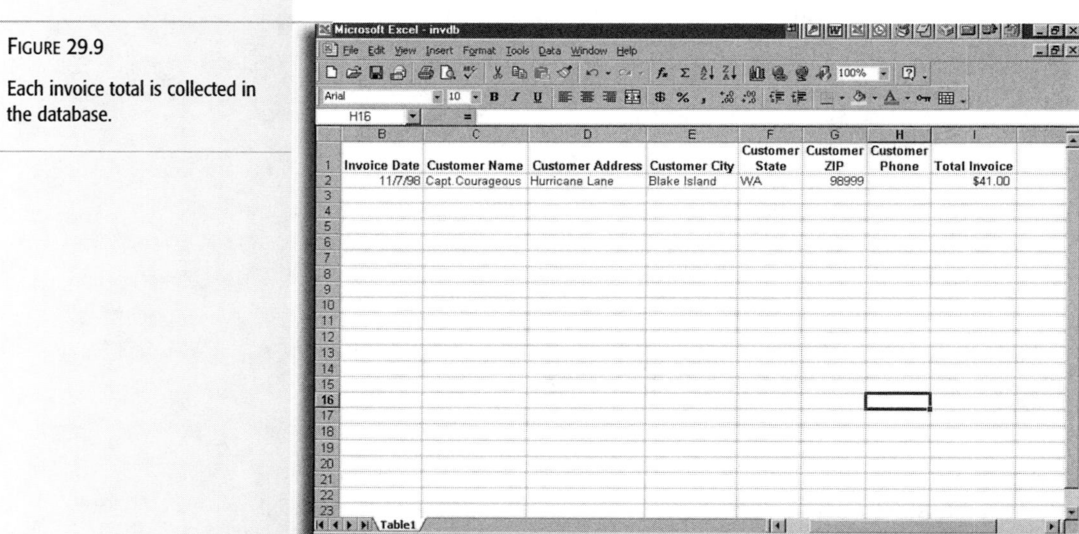

FIGURE 29.9

Each invoice total is collected in the database.

SEE ALSO

➤ *To learn more about consolidating and subtotaling lists, see page 328.*

➤ *To learn more about charting data, see page 386.*

➤ *To learn more about creating PivotTables, see page 346.*

PART

IX

Creative Excel

30 Drawing Objects 563

31 Creative Worksheets 575

32 Creative Charts 593

CHAPTER

30

Drawing Objects

Drawing basic shapes

Creating AutoShapes

Drawing text boxes

Changing your graphical objects

Converting objects to 3D

Creating WordArt objects

Basic Drawing

Excel isn't about art; nevertheless, like other Office 2000 programs, it has extensive tools for drawing graphical objects. What's more, your graphical objects can be functional. You can assign a macro to a drawn object and run the macro by clicking the object.

I'll give you a basic overview of drawing objects. If you're artistic by nature, you can further investigate and practice drawing objects after I get you started in the right direction.

You Can More Quickly Access the Drawing Toolbar

You can show and hide the Drawing toolbar even more quickly by clicking the Drawing button on the Standard toolbar.

To draw anything in Excel, start by displaying the Drawing toolbar: Right-click any toolbar and click Drawing. The Drawing toolbar most likely appears docked at the bottom of your Excel screen (shown in Figure 30.1). Table 30.1 explains the buttons on the Drawing toolbar.

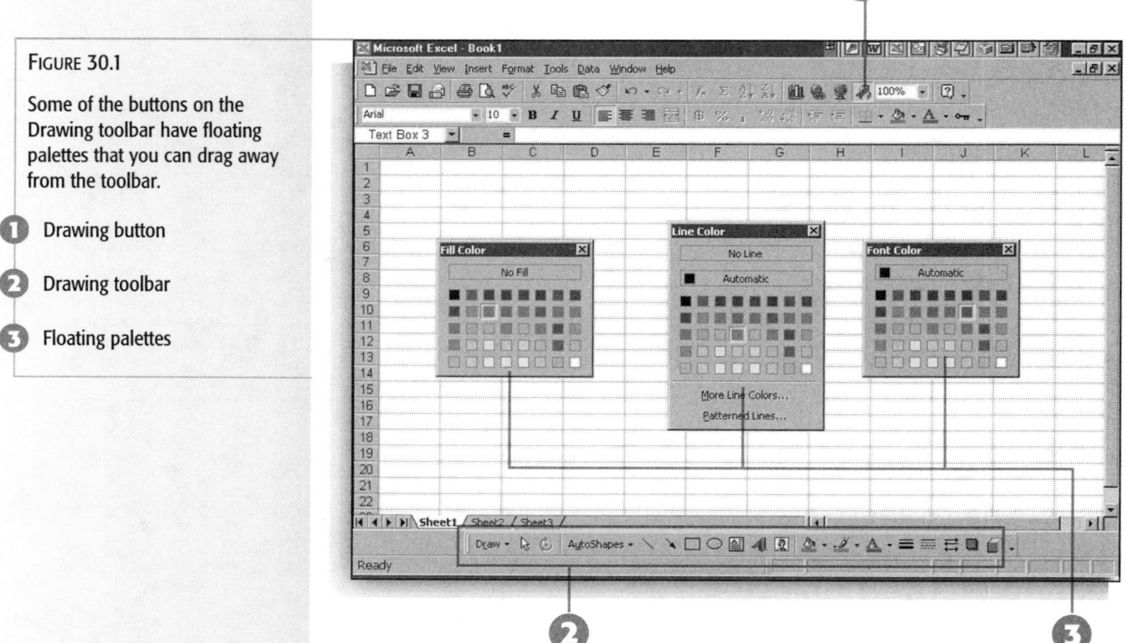

FIGURE 30.1

Some of the buttons on the Drawing toolbar have floating palettes that you can drag away from the toolbar.

1. Drawing button
2. Drawing toolbar
3. Floating palettes

TABLE 30.1 **Buttons on the Drawing toolbar**

Icon	Name	Purpose
Draw	Draw	Shows a menu with more drawing commands.
	Select Objects	Enables the mouse pointer to select objects; click to deactivate it when you want to select a worksheet cell.
	Free Rotate	Enables you to rotate an object with the mouse.
AutoShapes	AutoShapes	Shows a menu of AutoShape categories.
	Line	Draws a straight line.
	Arrow	Draws an arrow.
	Rectangle	Draws a rectangle or square.
	Oval	Draws an oval or circle.
	Text Box	Draws a box that holds text.
	Insert WordArt	Starts the WordArt applet.
	Fill Color	Shows a palette of colors to fill a selected object.
	Line Color	Shows a palette of colors for selected lines, arrows, or object borders.
	Font Color	Shows a palette of colors for selected text.
	Line Style	Shows a palette of line weights (thickness) for selected lines, arrows, or object borders.
	Dash Style	Shows a palette of line dash styles for selected lines, arrows, or object borders.
	Arrow Style	Shows a palette of arrow styles for selected lines or arrows.
	Shadow	Shows a palette of shadows for selected objects.
	3D	Shows a palette of 3D styles for converting selected objects.

Basic shapes include lines and arrows, rectangles, and ovals.

Draw a basic graphic object

1. Click the button for the shape you want to draw (line, arrow, rectangle, or oval).

   The mouse pointer becomes a crosshair for drawing.

2. Click and drag the crosshair across the screen, diagonally to create an oval or rectangle, or in the direction you want to create a line or arrow (shown in Figure 30.2). If your object isn't quite the shape or location you want, you can move it and reshape it later.

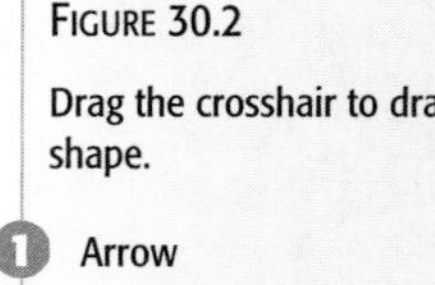

FIGURE 30.2

Drag the crosshair to draw the shape.

1. Arrow
2. Rectangle
3. Handles
4. Oval
5. Four-arrow move pointer

I Want Them All to Be the Same

To format several objects at once, select them as a group: Either press and hold down Shift while you click to select individual objects, or click the **Select Objects** button and then draw a rectangle around the group of objects that you want to select.

The following are some tips for drawing and formatting basic shapes:

- To draw a perfectly vertical or horizontal line, hold down Shift while you draw the line. (Shift forces the line into 15-degree angles.)
- To draw any object from the center out, hold down Ctrl while you draw.

- To draw a perfect square or circle, hold down Shift while you draw a rectangle or oval.
- To convert an arrow to a line or a line to an arrow, or to change the direction of an arrow, select the line or arrow object and choose a different style from the **Arrow Style** button.
- To change line or border weight (thickness), select the object, and then select a line weight from the **Line Style** button.
- To move an object, click it and drag it with the four-arrow move pointer.
- To resize or reshape an object, click it and drag a handle.
- To align an object with worksheet gridlines, press Alt while you move the object or drag a handle. The object border snaps to the nearest gridline.
- To draw several lines, arrows, rectangles, or ovals, double-click the button for the shape you want and draw a lot of objects. Click the button to deactivate it when you're finished.
- To copy a shape, press Ctrl while you drag and drop the object.
- To assign a macro to an object, right-click the object, click **Assign Macro**, click the macro name, and then click **OK**.

SEE ALSO

➤ *For more information on creating macros to automate a worksheet, see page 535.*

Creating AutoShapes

AutoShapes are built-in complex shapes, such as banners, flowchart symbols, and block arrows, that you can select from a menu. After you create an AutoShape, you can move, resize, reshape, and color it just like any other object.

Create an AutoShape graphic

1. On the Drawing toolbar, click the **AutoShapes** menu.
2. On the **AutoShapes** menu, point to a category and click a shape (shown in Figure 30.3).

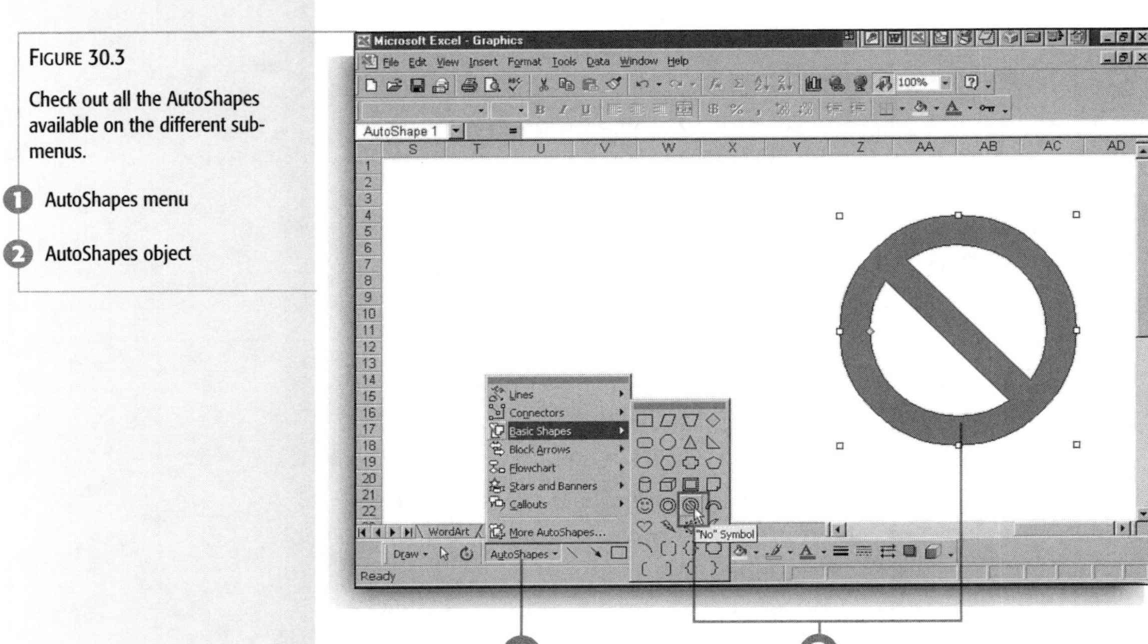

FIGURE 30.3

Check out all the AutoShapes available on the different sub-menus.

1. AutoShapes menu
2. AutoShapes object

3. Either click the worksheet to create an instant AutoShape, or drag the crosshair across the worksheet to draw the AutoShape.

   The AutoShape is created; all the moving, shaping, and formatting tips mentioned previously apply to AutoShapes.

   Many AutoShapes have an adjustment handle—a small yellow diamond that appears when the AutoShape is selected. You can drag the adjustment handle to alter a prominent feature of the shape, such as the shape or size of an arrow's point. You have to drag the handle on your specific shape to see what changes it makes.

Drawing Text Boxes

Charts, Too

Although I'm only discussing worksheets in these procedures, all these objects can also be drawn in charts.

Text boxes are free-floating text labels that you can use to add information to a worksheet or chart. You can format them as colored, bordered rectangular objects and change their fonts. You can also leave them as transparent and place them on top of other graphics to make it look as though the graphic object contains text (shown in Figure 30.4).

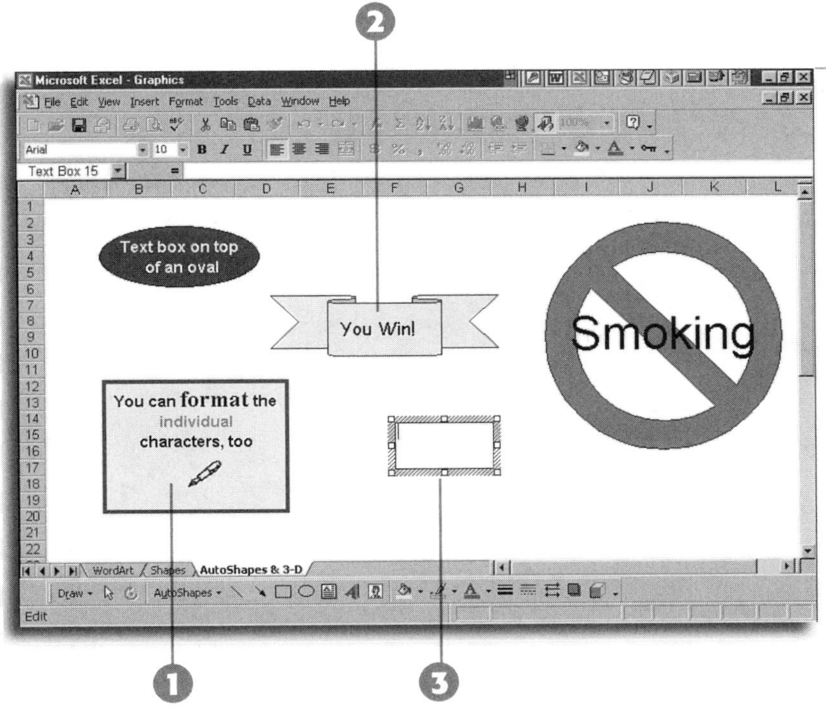

FIGURE 30.4
You can add a lot of information to a worksheet or chart with text boxes.

1. Text box with border, fill color, and formatted text
2. Text box on AutoShapes banner
3. New text box with insertion pointer

Create a text box

1. On the Drawing toolbar, click the **Text Box** button.

   The mouse becomes a sword shape, which changes to a crosshair when you begin to draw the box.

2. In the worksheet, drag the mouse pointer diagonally to draw the text box.

   When you release the mouse button, a text box is created and an insertion point flashes in the box.

3. Type the text you want.

   You can edit and format the text the same way you would text in a cell.

4. Click away from the text box to finish.

The Sword-Shaped Mouse Pointer

If you click the sword-shaped pointer, rather than drag across the worksheet, a small text box is created that precisely fits the text you type in it.

To edit text in a finished text box, click the text box. The text box is selected, and the insertion point appears in the text.

To delete a text box, click it, click its border, and then press Delete.

Converting Objects to 3D

Most objects can be converted to a **3D** shape. You know a selected object is not convertible if the shapes on the 3D menu are grayed out.

Convert a drawn object to a 3D shape

1. Select the object.
2. On the Drawing toolbar, click the **3D** button.
3. On the 3D palette, click a 3D shape.

   The object is converted to 3D.

For more interesting 3D effects, click the **3D Settings** button on the 3D palette. (Table 30.2 explains what the buttons on the 3D Settings toolbar do for you.) A few effects are shown in Figure 30.5, but the best way to learn what these settings can do for you is to create an object and test the different effects yourself.

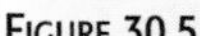

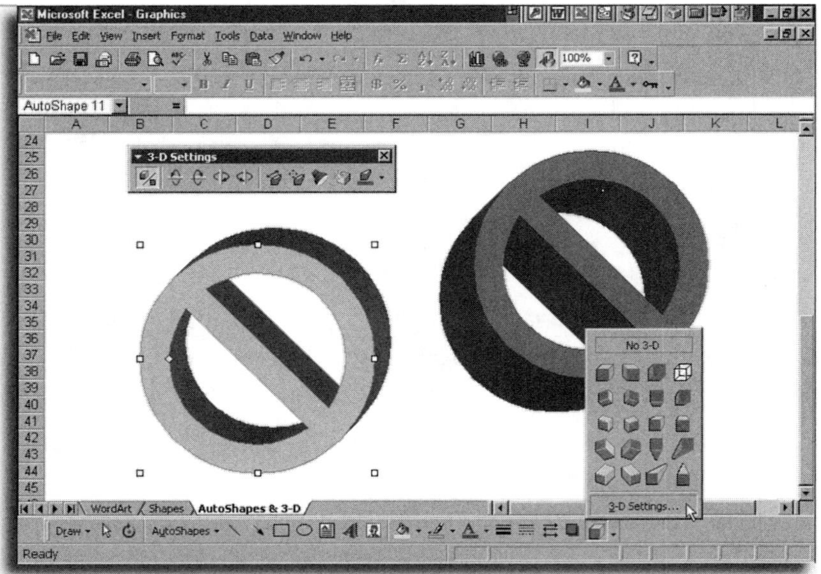

FIGURE 30.5

Be careful with three-dimensional effects; you could get hooked!

TABLE 30.2 **3D Settings toolbar**

Icon	Name	Purpose
	3D On/Off	Toggles the 3D effect on and off.
	Tilt Down	Tilts perspective down.
	Tilt Up	Tilts perspective up.
	Tilt Left	Tilts perspective left.
	Tilt Right	Tilts perspective right.
	Depth	Enables you to choose the depth of the third dimension.
	Direction	Enables you to change the three-dimensional direction.
	Lighting	Enables you to change the directional source of light and shadow on the object.
	Surface	Enables you to choose a material-surface effect.
	3D Color	Enables you to change the color of the third dimension.

Creating WordArt Objects

WordArt in Office 2000 is a more powerful, more memory-intensive version of the mini-program that creates curved and shaped pictures from your text. WordArt creates arresting graphics, but a word of caution is in order: Don't plan on printing it unless your printer has a lot of memory. My printer is a Hewlett-Packard LaserJet 4P with the standard 2MB of memory that it came with. It's a little workhorse of a printer, but 2MB of memory isn't enough to print a page with even the smallest WordArt graphic in it.

Create a WordArt graphic

1. On the Drawing toolbar, click the **Insert WordArt** button.

   The WordArt palette of text shapes appears (shown in Figure 30.6).

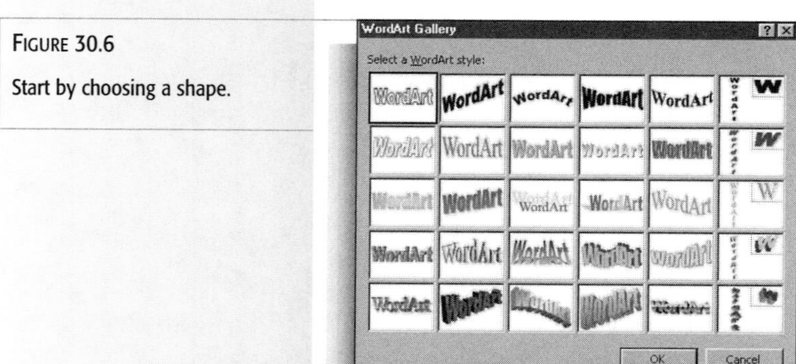

FIGURE 30.6

Start by choosing a shape.

2. Double-click a shape.

   The Edit WordArt Text dialog box appears (shown in Figure 30.7).

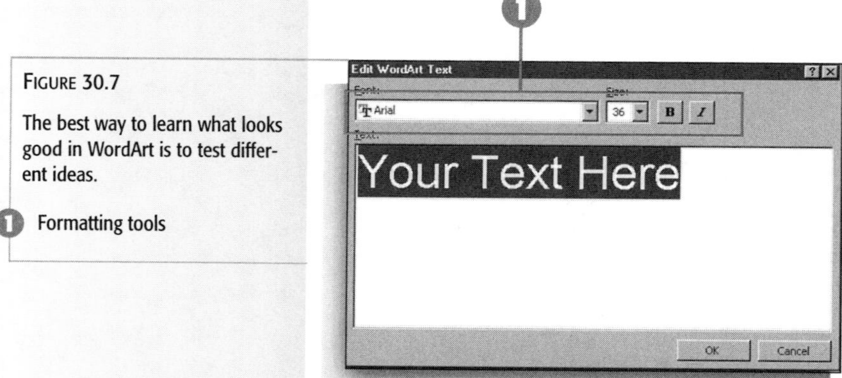

FIGURE 30.7

The best way to learn what looks good in WordArt is to test different ideas.

1 Formatting tools

3. Type your text in the **Text** box.
4. Use the formatting tools in the Edit WordArt Text dialog box to format your text.
5. Click **OK**.

   Your WordArt object is created (shown in Figure 30.8). The WordArt toolbar appears when the graphic object is selected. Table 30.3 explains what the WordArt toolbar buttons do.

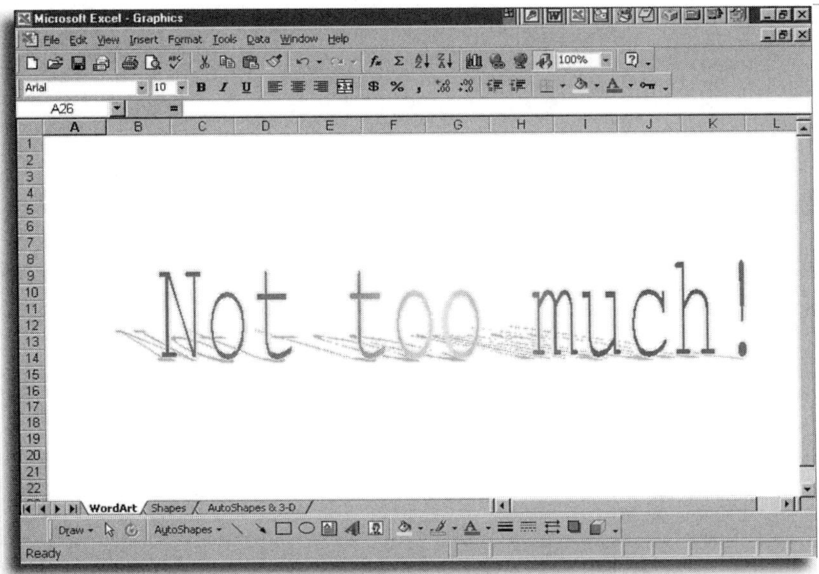

FIGURE 30.8
Don't get too carried away, or your data is overshadowed by the graphics.

TABLE 30.3 WordArt Toolbar buttons

Icon	Name	Purpose
	Insert WordArt	Adds a new WordArt object.
Edit Text...	Edit Text	Enables you to change text in a selected WordArt object.
	WordArt Gallery	Enables you to change the shape of a selected WordArt object.
	Format WordArt	Opens the Formatting dialog box for a selected WordArt object.
	WordArt Shape	Gives you more WordArt shapes from which to choose.
	Free Rotate	Enables you to rotate the object. (Drag a corner dot to rotate.)
	WordArt Same Letter Heights	Makes all letters in WordArt object the same height.
	WordArt Vertical Text	Changes WordArt text alignment to vertical.
	WordArt Alignment	Lets you change how words are stretched and aligned.
	WordArt Character Spacing	Enables you to tighten or loosen letter spacing in a WordArt object.

CHAPTER

31

Creative Worksheets

Combining AutoFilter, macros, and printing in a creative business solution

Creating an Excel approach that makes business in a theatre reservations office more efficient

Creative Approaches to Worksheet Applications

This chapter is about creative ways to combine different techniques covered in this book. It's by no means exhaustive, and if you really get interested in creative worksheet techniques, you can find a lot more to learn. I hope these two examples inspire you to look for ways to be creative with your own Excel work.

I'll show you two real-life Excel projects that I created as solutions for clients' questions. First, I'll show you the finished project and explain how it works, and then I'll guide you through the creation of a simple example of each. The procedures for creating these projects are loose and general because I want you to inject your own creativity into the process.

Kurt's Invoice—a Creative Invoice Solution

My friend Kurt wanted to figure out how to make an invoice out of a long parts-and-prices list. His original idea was to write a VBA program; however, I'm not a programmer by nature, so I always look for an easier route. In this case, I thought AutoFilter might be the perfect answer.

To demonstrate the solution, I've created an invoice for the fictitious Stony Keep Soap and Pottery company, which sells handmade vegetable soaps and handmade pottery pieces.

How Kurt's Invoice Works

Figure 31.1 shows the finished worksheet. To create the invoice for an order, you type a quantity for each item ordered. The worksheet has formulas that automatically calculate item totals and an invoice total.

The two text boxes on the worksheet run macros. One macro filters and prints the invoice, and the other macro returns the worksheet to its original condition, ready to take another order.

This invoice is designed to be filled out and printed, but not saved as individual Excel files. It could be saved as a template if you want to keep a copy of each separate invoice.

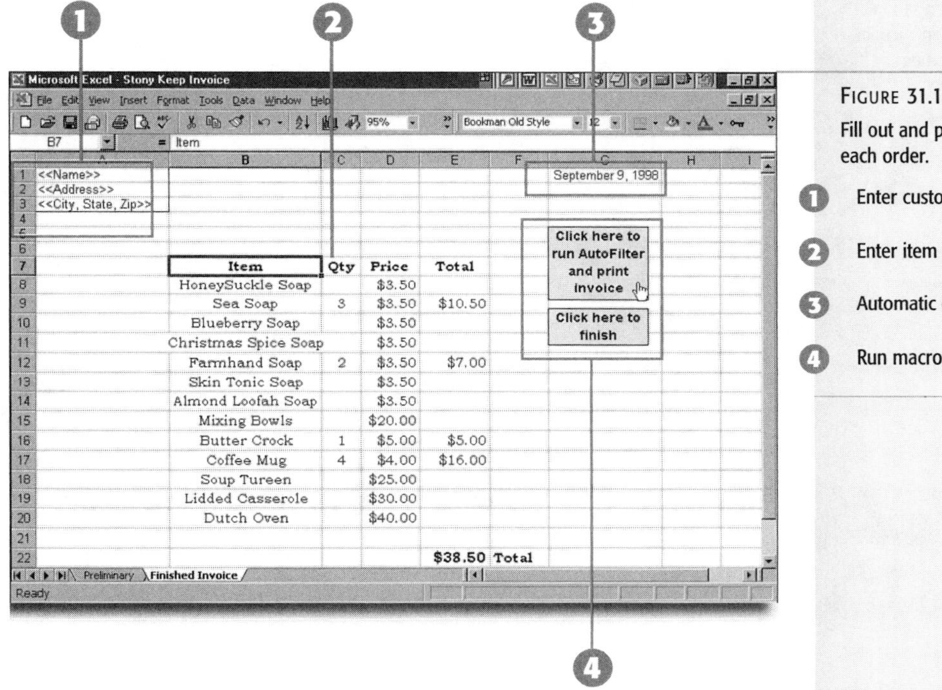

FIGURE 31.1
Fill out and print the invoice for each order.

1. Enter customer info.
2. Enter item quantities.
3. Automatic current date
4. Run macros by clicking.

After you type quantities for each item ordered, click the upper text box. Its assigned macro activates AutoFilter, filters the table for nonblanks in the Qty column, and then sends the page to the printer. (Figure 31.2 shows a sample invoice in print preview.) The macro is edited to print two copies, one for the customer and one for the business.

After the invoice is sent to the printer, click the lower text box. Its assigned macro removes the AutoFilter and deletes the data in the Qty column so the invoice worksheet is ready for another order.

The invoice is not designed so that each individual invoice is saved electronically because, for many small businesses with small hard drives, that's impractical; instead, they keep paper invoices in file cabinets.

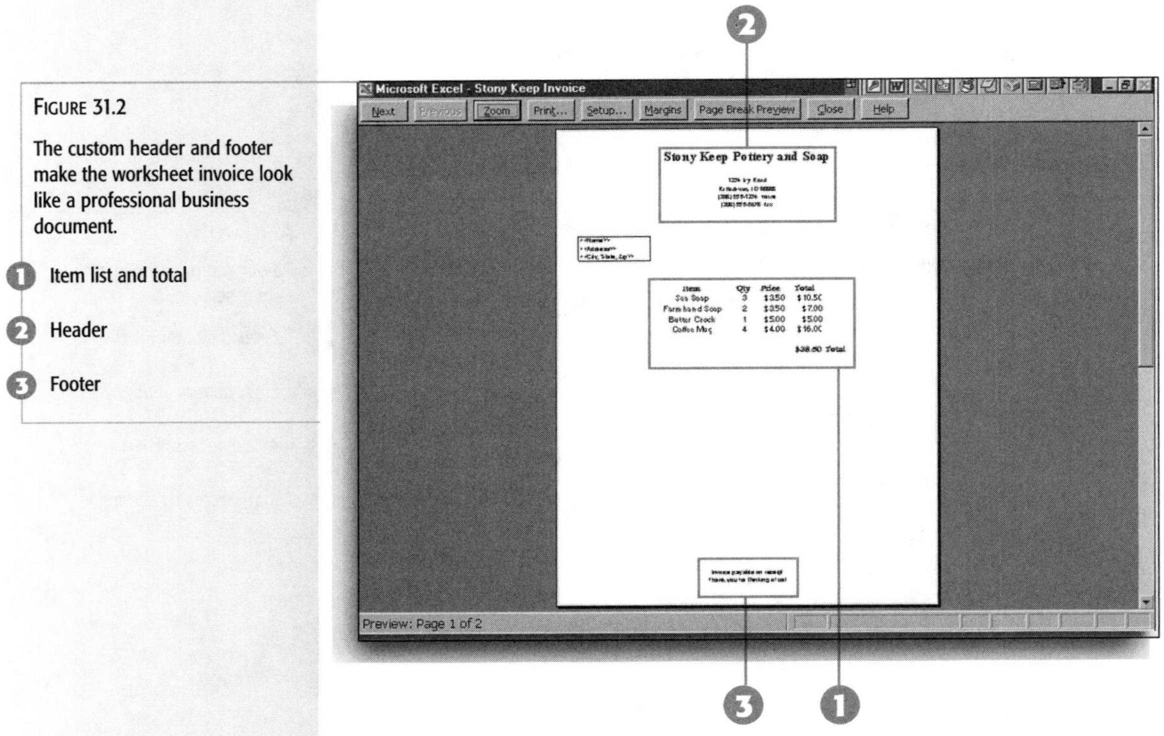

FIGURE 31.2

The custom header and footer make the worksheet invoice look like a professional business document.

1 Item list and total

2 Header

3 Footer

Setting Up the Invoice Worksheet

First, set up your invoice with all the product entries, formulas, and formatting that's needed to make the printed invoice look professional.

Create the invoice worksheet

1. Open a new workbook, and save it with an appropriate name.
2. Create a custom header and footer for the invoice:
   - Enter your business name, address, and phone number in the header.
   - Format the header text with eye-catching font and font sizes.
   - Type the appropriate business text in the footer, such as `Invoice due and payable on receipt` and `Thank you for your order!`.

3. Make worksheet entries as shown in Figure 31.3.
   - The entries in the upper-left corner of the worksheet are placeholders to remind you to enter the customer's name and address. I placed a border around this group of cells so that the customer information is visually set apart in the printed page. (The worksheet gridlines won't be printed.)
   - In cell G1, type `=today()` so that the current date is always shown when you fill out and print the invoice.
   - Enter an items list in the middle range, and include columns for Item, Qty, Price, and Total.

   A short list of mock data is enough to get the invoice set up; you can add lots of items and prices after the invoice is finished and functional.

   You can move this list around later to make it look good on the printed page, but cell B7 is a good starting point for the upper-left corner of your list.

Be Creative

Remember, I'm showing you how I created my invoice solution; feel free to alter these steps to make your project unique and personal.

	A	B	C	D	E	F	G
1	<<Name>>						September 9, 1998
2	<<Address>>						
3	<<City, State, Zip>>						
7		Item	Qty	Price	Total		
8		HoneySuckle Soap		$3.50			
9		Sea Soap		$3.50			
10		Blueberry Soap		$3.50			
11		Christmas Spice Soap		$3.50			
12		Farmhand Soap		$3.50			
13		Skin Tonic Soap		$3.50			
14		Almond Loofah Soap		$3.50			
15		Mixing Bowls		$20.00			
16		Butter Crock		$5.00			
17		Coffee Mug		$4.00			
18		Soup Tureen		$25.00			
19		Lidded Casserole		$30.00			
20		Dutch Oven		$40.00			
22					$0.00	Total	

Preliminary | Finished Invoice

FIGURE 31.3

Choose the fonts you want to set off each section of the worksheet.

SEE ALSO

➤ *To learn about using labels in formulas, and using the IF function in a nested formula, see pages 194 and 207.*

4. Enter the formulas for the item totals. I entered the formula `=IF(ISBLANK(Qty),"",Qty*Price)` in cell E8 and used AutoFill to copy it down the list.
   - The item totals are calculated by multiplying the Price column label by the Qty column label in the Qty*Price portion of the formula.
   - The item total is nested in an IF formula that reads "If the Qty value is blank, then show nothing; otherwise, multiply the Qty value by the Price value." This prevents the invoice from displaying extra zeroes. It isn't necessary, but it's a nice touch.
5. Enter a total sum for the ordered items with the SUM function. Use AutoSum on the Standard toolbar to enter it quickly. Be sure the summed range includes all the cells in the Total column. (Figure 31.4 shows a sample item total formula and the list total formula.)
6. Add any other formulas you want, such as tax and shipping, below the list total.

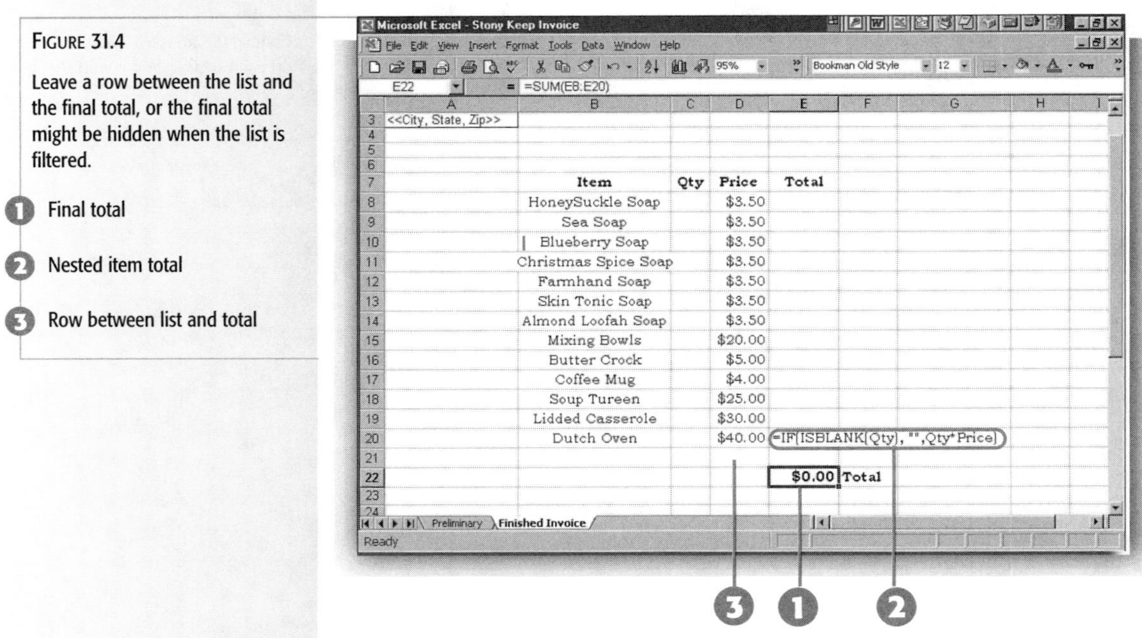

FIGURE 31.4

Leave a row between the list and the final total, or the final total might be hidden when the list is filtered.

1 Final total

2 Nested item total

3 Row between list and total

7. Take a look at the invoice in print preview; it should look similar to the one shown in Figure 31.5. If yours looks unbalanced, show the margins, rearrange column widths and margin lines to fix it, and then return to normal view.

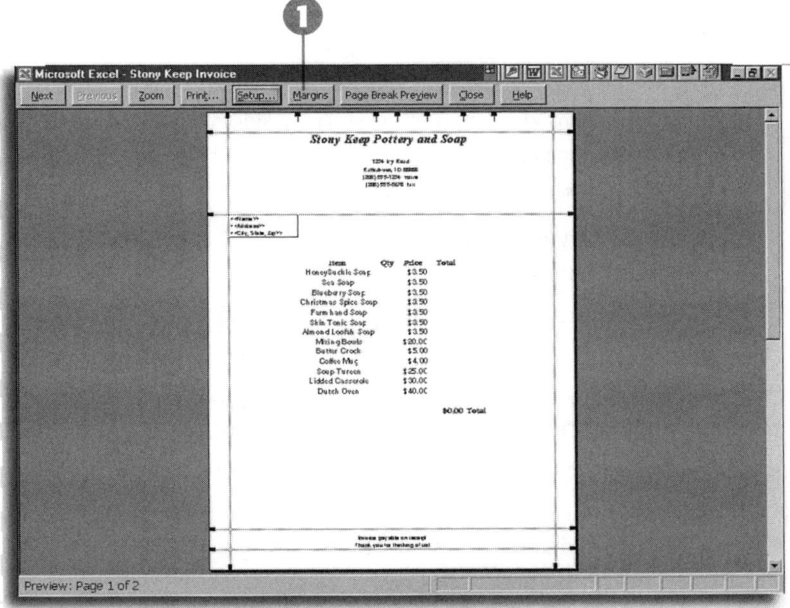

FIGURE 31.5
Your invoice ought to look similar to this one.

1 Margins

SEE ALSO

➤ *To learn more about the TODAY() function, see page 196.*
➤ *To learn more about nested IF functions, see page 194.*
➤ *To learn more about writing formulas with labels, see page 207.*

Automating the Invoice with Macros

Now you can add the macros that turn this invoice into an efficient business solution, and if you have lots of orders waiting to be filled, these macros can save you considerable time.

Macro Warning

When you open a workbook that contains macros, even your own, you're warned that macros can contain viruses—and it's quite possible, if your workbook has been in someone else's computer. These macros, however, are your own, and they're safe.

Oops, It's Printing

After you click the Print button, Excel attempts to print the invoice page, but you don't need it printed. If your printer is on, it's printed. If you get a message complaining that your printer isn't on, click **Cancel** to stop the print process and get rid of the message. It doesn't matter whether you click Cancel before or after you stop recording, because the macro records the Print command but not the Cancel command.

Create the macros that automate the invoice

1. Start the macro recorder. (On the **Tools** menu, select **Macro**, and click **Record New Macro**.)
2. Give the macro a name such as `FilterAndPrint`.
3. Store the macro in **This Workbook**.
4. Click **OK** and record the following steps.
5. Click the Item column label (cell B7 in my example).

   This step makes the macro start by selecting that cell so that AutoFilter can locate the list.
6. On the **Data** menu, select **Filter**, and click **AutoFilter**.
7. In the Qty column, click the filter arrow and click **(NonBlanks)**.
8. On the Standard toolbar, click **Print**.
9. On the Stop Recording toolbar, click **Stop Recording**.

   The macro recorder stops recording, and your worksheet is filtered. (The list is hidden by the filter because there aren't any entries in the Qty column.)
10. Start the macro recorder again (see step 1) to record the clean-up macro. Name it `Finish`, store it in **This Workbook**, and click **OK**.
11. Click the Item column label.

    You want the macro to start there, even if you've clicked elsewhere in the worksheet between macros.
12. Turn off the AutoFilter. (On the **Data** menu, select **Filter**, and then click **AutoFilter**.)
13. Select the cells in the Qty column, and press Delete.

    You can select as many cells below the column label as you want, but *don't* select the column label. If your list of items grows longer later, you can edit the macro to change the selected range.

    It doesn't matter that there's no data to be deleted right now because you're only recording steps for the macro.
14. Stop recording. (On the Stop Recording toolbar, click **Stop Recording**.)

Editing the Macro

The macro recorder recorded a default print setting of one copy, but I want to print two copies (one for the customer and one for my files). I can edit the macro to change the number of copies it prints.

You Always Have Another Way

Another way to control the number of copies is to record the macro by opening **File**, selecting **Print**, and setting the **Number of copies** to 2.

Inspect and edit your macros

1. On the **Tools** menu, select **Macro**, and click **Macros**.

   The Macro dialog box appears (shown in Figure 31.6).

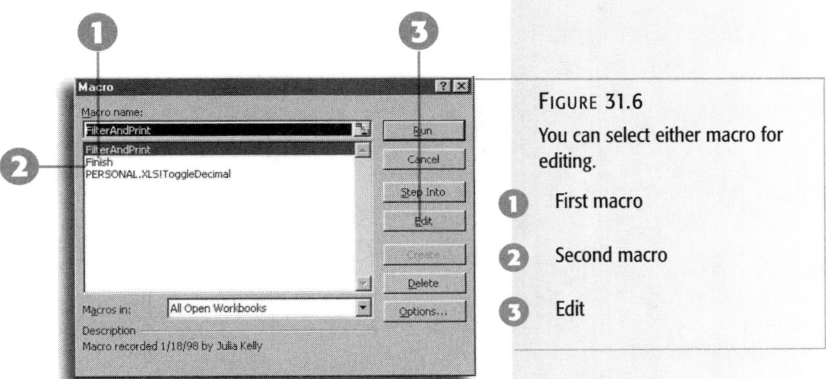

FIGURE 31.6
You can select either macro for editing.

1. First macro
2. Second macro
3. Edit

2. Click either macro name and click **Edit**.

   The Visual Basic Editor opens to your two macros (as shown in Figure 31.7).

3. In the last line of the FilterAndPrint macro (see Figure 31.7), where it reads `Copies:=1`, change the number `1` to **`2`**.

   (It should read `Copies:=2.`)

   This change makes the macro print two copies instead of the default single copy.

4. Close the Visual Basic Editor. (Click its **Close** button.)

5. Save your workbook.

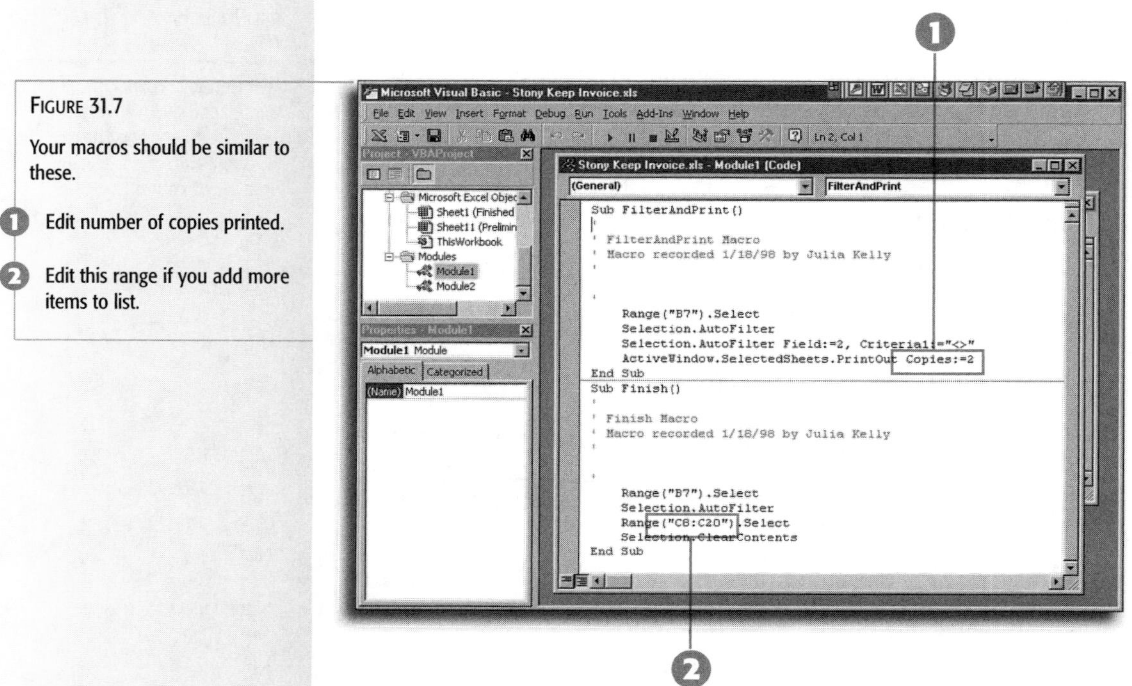

FIGURE 31.7

Your macros should be similar to these.

1 Edit number of copies printed.

2 Edit this range if you add more items to list.

Making the Macros Handy

Macros in a worksheet are timesavers only if they are easy for anyone who uses the worksheet to find and run them. Of course, you can add them to menus and toolbar buttons, but these macros are intended to be limited to this workbook, so it's not useful to have them taking up space on a menu or toolbar. Fortunately, you can run macros from graphical objects in a worksheet, which makes them constantly available but only in the workbook where they're stored. If you assign your macros to text boxes, you can run and explain each macro with its own graphical object.

Add text boxes to run the macros

1. Display the Drawing toolbar.
2. On the invoice sheet, create two text boxes similar to the ones in Figure 31.8.

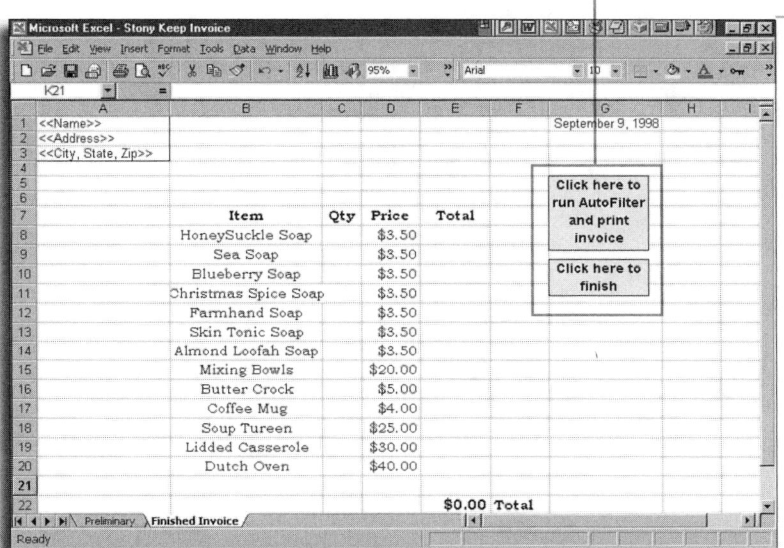

FIGURE 31.8

Text boxes are convenient because they can contain instructions, but you can use other graphic objects instead.

1 Formatted text boxes

3. Arrange the text boxes the way you want them on the worksheet.
4. Select both text boxes (press Shift and click both), and then double-click the border on one of them.

   Double-clicking the border selects the object. Double-clicking inside the text box selects the text for editing.

   The Format Object dialog box appears (shown in Figure 31.9).
5. On the **Properties** tab, click the **Don't move or size with cells** option, clear the **Print object** check box, and click **OK**.

   Setting these properties prevents the text boxes from appearing on the printed invoice pages and from moving or stretching when the list is filtered.

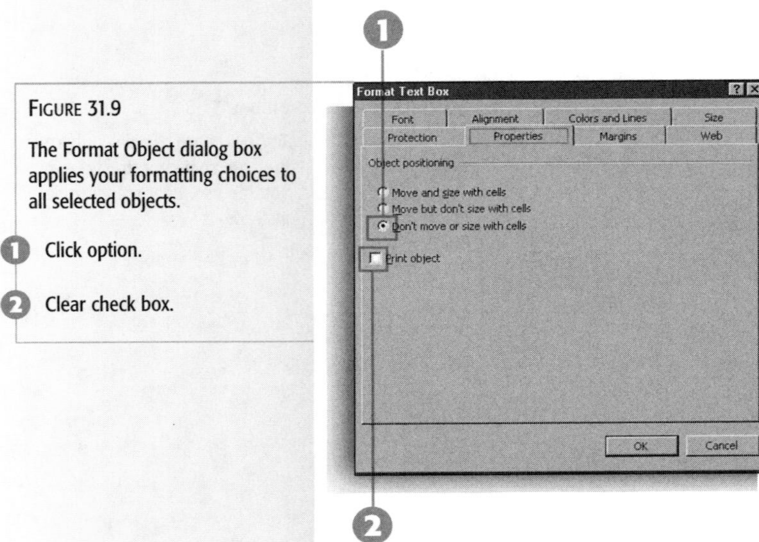

FIGURE 31.9

The Format Object dialog box applies your formatting choices to all selected objects.

1 Click option.

2 Clear check box.

I Can't Select Any Cells!

If you've been playing with graphic objects and you suddenly can't select any cells, click the **Select Objects** button on the Drawing toolbar to turn it off.

Okay, Now How Do I Select It?

From here on out, if you need to select the text box to move it or edit it, either right-click it or press Ctrl while you click it.

6. Click the worksheet to deselect the text boxes.
7. Right-click the border on the top text box, and click **Assign Macro**.
8. In the Assign Macro dialog box, click the **FilterAndPrint** macro name and click **OK**.

   The macro is assigned to the text box. When you point to the text box, the mouse pointer becomes a small pointing hand, and if you click the text box, the macro runs.
9. Repeat steps 7 and 8 to assign the Finish macro to the lower text box.

That's it! To test your invoice and macros, type a few entries in the Qty column, click the first text box, and click the second text box to finish the invoice process. (If your printer is turned on, two pages are printed.)

SEE ALSO

➤ *For more information on recording macros, see page 536.*
➤ *For more information on editing a macro after you've recorded it, see page 540.*
➤ *For more information on creating text boxes on a worksheet, see page 569.*

Theatre Seating

This project was a solution for a local community theatre that wanted to trade in its old plastic-and-grease-pencil reservations board for an electronic system. Not only are the entries more legible, but the reservations data can be tracked for other purposes by sending the Excel data to an Access database. The project consists of two different worksheets: a seating chart, with one copy for each show, and a single seat list that compiles all the names, phone numbers, and reserved seat numbers from all the seating charts in a neat list. (Figure 31.10 shows one of the seating charts.)

Oh, Yeah, Like I Really Need This

I sincerely doubt that many of you will ever need this particular project, but I want to fire your imaginations about what kinds of unusual and creative approaches you can take with Excel in your own work. I'm sure many of you will get much more creative than this.

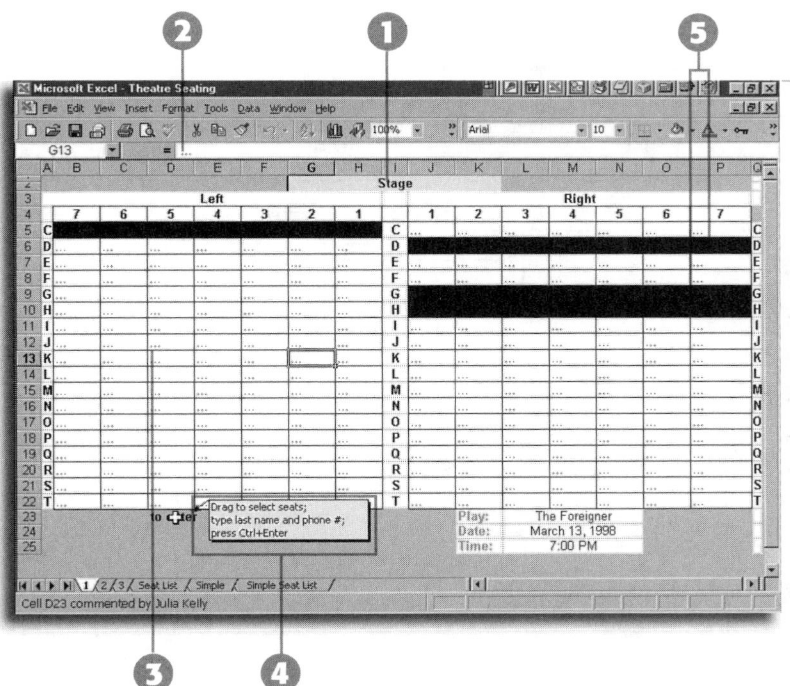

FIGURE 31.10

This seating chart is complex because of the way the theatre is laid out.

1. Worksheet is formatted to resemble the specific theatre.
2. Read full entry here.
3. "..." keeps seat visually open.
4. Comments with instructions
5. These seats are nonexistent in this theatre.

How the Seating Chart Works

To use the seating chart, drag to select a group of seats for a patron, depending on the number and location of seats. Then type the patron's last name and phone number, and press

Ctrl+Enter to enter the identical data in all the selected cells (which fills the seats). That's it; the seat list worksheet automatically records your entries.

The entries in the seating chart aren't entirely legible unless you click a cell and read its entry in the Formula bar, because each cell's entry is truncated by the entry in the cell to its right. You want to keep the entries truncated so that you can see at a glance which seats are still open. To keep a seat open, fill it with the entry .... To cancel seat reservations, replace the patron data with the ... entry in each seat. (Figure 31.11 shows the seat list worksheet, where seats and patron information are automatically recorded in a more familiar format.)

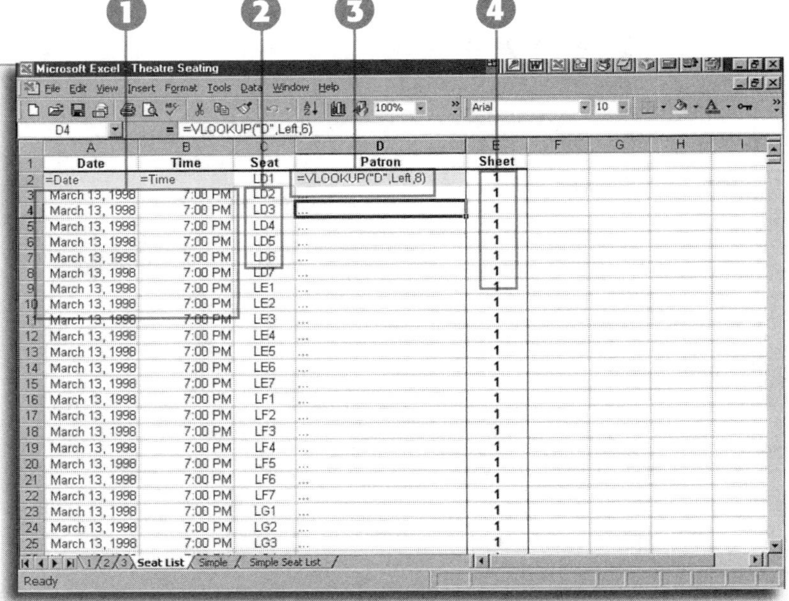

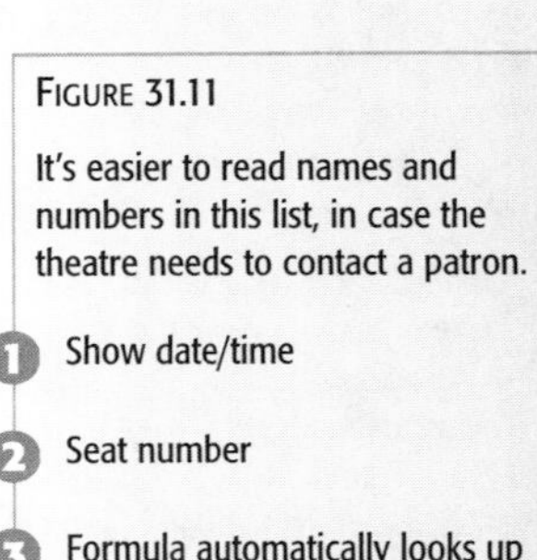

FIGURE 31.11

It's easier to read names and numbers in this list, in case the theatre needs to contact a patron.

1. Show date/time
2. Seat number
3. Formula automatically looks up seat data in a named range.
4. Quick reminder of the data source

Creating the Seating Chart Workbook

The fully functional seating chart I created for my local theatre is a bit complex because most real-life projects are complex. I'll show you a simplified version, however, of how I combined Excel's features to make the project work. (The point of this demonstration is to show you how you can use Excel to do more than filter and subtotal lists of numbers.)

Create a simple version of this project

1. Create a worksheet that looks like the one in Figure 31.12.

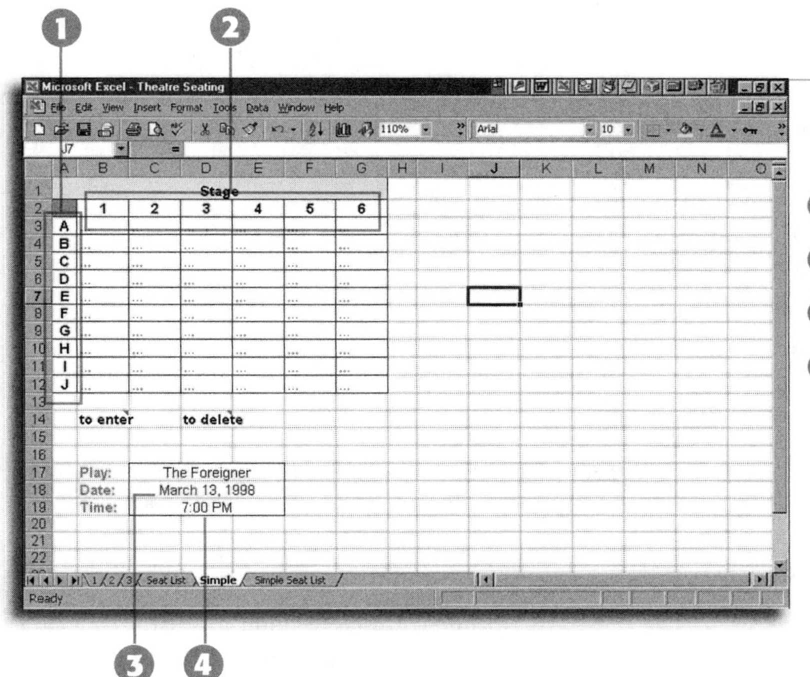

FIGURE 31.12
This is a simplified version of my theatre seating chart.

1. Theatre row letters
2. Seat numbers within each row
3. Cell named Date
4. Cell named Time

2. Select the range of seat cells and name them **Seats**, and then name the **Date** cell and the **Time** cell.

   In this example, I've named the range A3:G12 "Seats." My LOOKUP formula needs the row labels in Column A but doesn't need the column labels in Row 2.
3. Add any helpful comments you might need (especially if someone else uses the workbook).
4. Save the workbook.
5. On a different worksheet, create the table shown in Figure 31.13.

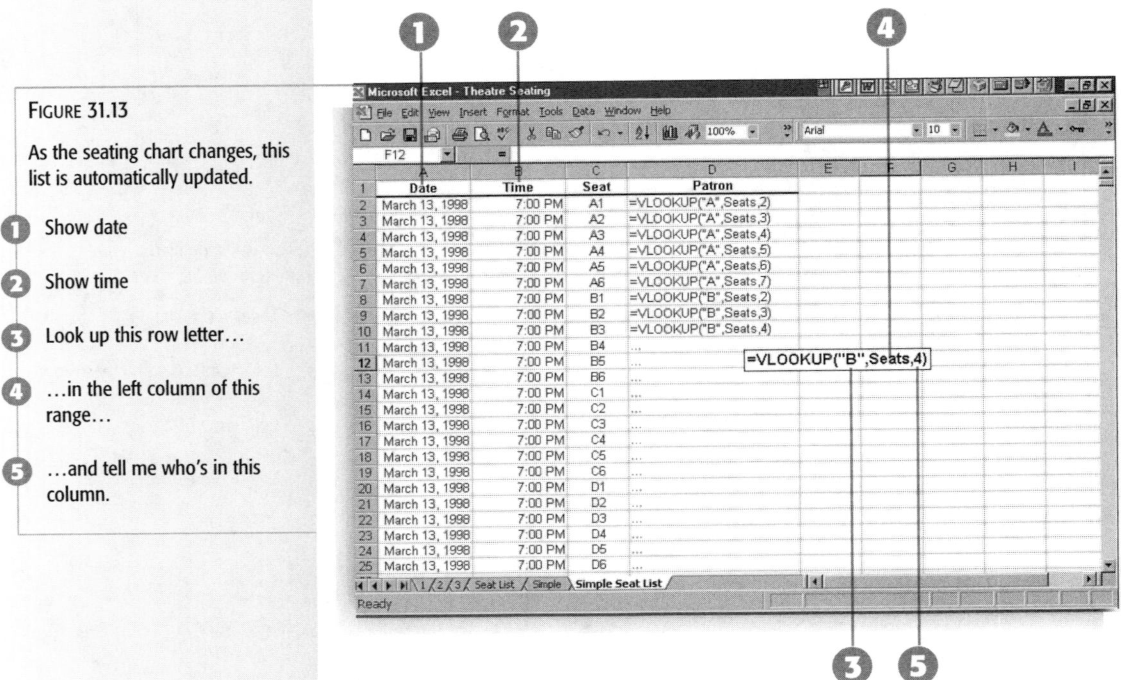

FIGURE 31.13

As the seating chart changes, this list is automatically updated.

1. Show date
2. Show time
3. Look up this row letter…
4. …in the left column of this range…
5. …and tell me who's in this column.

I've shown the formulas I used to build this list. They all use named cells and ranges on the seating chart worksheet.

6. Enter the formulas that look up data in the seating chart.

   My VLOOKUP formula looks up a value (the row letter) in the leftmost column of a named range (Seats) and returns the value from the column I specify (the seat number).

7. Enter some names in the seating chart to test your seat list. Your VLOOKUP formulas may need some tweaking to be sure they all look up what you intend.

   Figure 31.14 shows the completed seating chart and seat list side-by-side in two windows so that I can test them easily.

To use the seating chart for several performances, create a copy of the finished worksheet for each performance. Change only the data that's different for each performance. (You need to check, and possibly change, the range names on each seating chart.) Add more VLOOKUP formulas to the seat list to look up data from each seating chart.

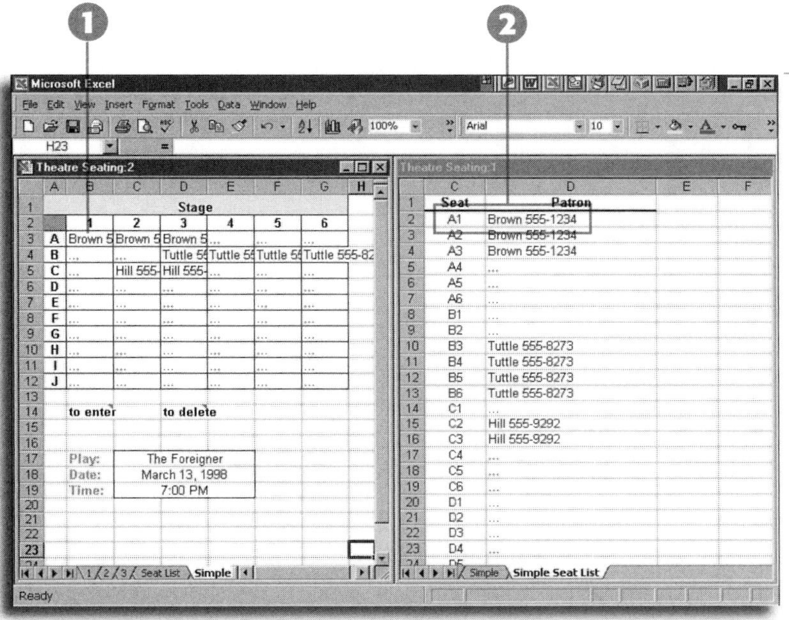

FIGURE 31.14

I can test the seat list easily by using two windows to view my formulas and source data side-by-side.

1 Seat and patron

2 Seat and patron

SEE ALSO

➤ *For more information on writing a VLOOKUP formula, see page 190.*

➤ *For more information on naming cells and ranges, see page 202.*

➤ *For more information on using named cells and ranges in formulas, see page 206.*

➤ *For more information on copying worksheets, see page 90.*

CHAPTER

32

Creative Charts

Creating a bar chart that shows data with long labels

Creating a stacked column chart that combines specific sets of data in each column

Creating a dynamic chart display

Creative Approaches to Charting

The Chart Wizard is a highly capable charting engine, but occasionally, you may need to display data that requires a little more creativity than you find in the Chart Wizard alone. This chapter contains a couple of creative approaches to charting that might come in handy for you, but more than that, I want to get you thinking about how you can use the Chart Wizard in combination with other Excel features to get exactly what you need.

I'm going to show you two real-life solutions to clients' data display questions: a chart display that combines a transparent chart and the worksheet underneath it, and a stacked column chart that relies on a special data layout to compare information.

I'm also going to show you a clever way to allow worksheet readers to choose the chart they want to see, by creating a variety of charts and using worksheet controls such as option buttons to choose which chart to display.

Giff's Chart

A client of mine (his name is Giff, and I named this chart after him) conducted a survey of company employees, averaged the responses, and wanted to chart them on a bar chart that showed the questions alongside the bars. The problem was that the Chart Wizard had difficulty showing all the data just the way he wanted it displayed, so I combined an embedded chart with the worksheet beneath it. (The result is shown in Figure 32.1. These aren't real survey questions.)

I probably could've used several ways to achieve the result my client wanted; however, the way I show you is meant to remove any perceived limitations on what you're able to do with a chart. Be warned: When you get creative like this, it takes more time and tweaking to get what you want.

Figure 32.2 shows the data with which I started. Next, I'll show you how I created the finished chart. (My explanation isn't detailed because I want you to experiment to find out what you can do.)

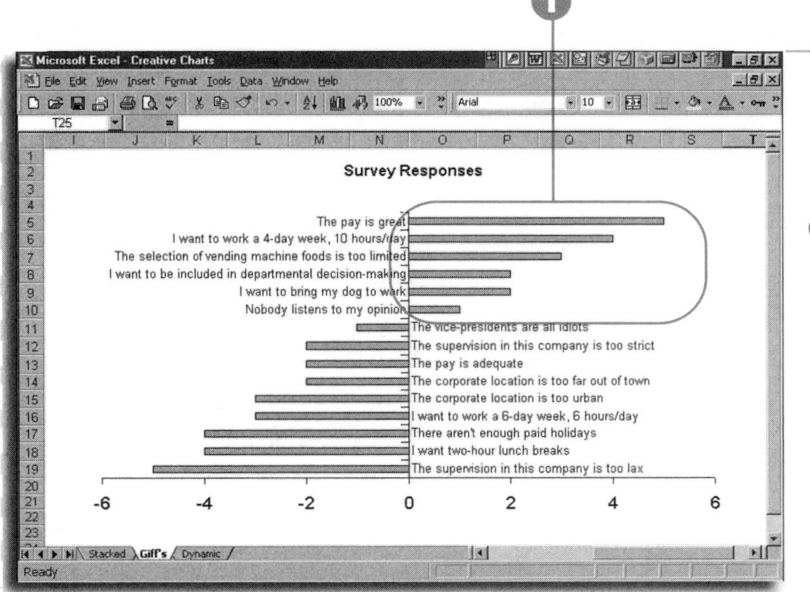

FIGURE 32.1
The data labels are actually entries in the worksheet beneath the chart, and the chart background is transparent.

❶ Source data sorted to show bar lengths from high to low

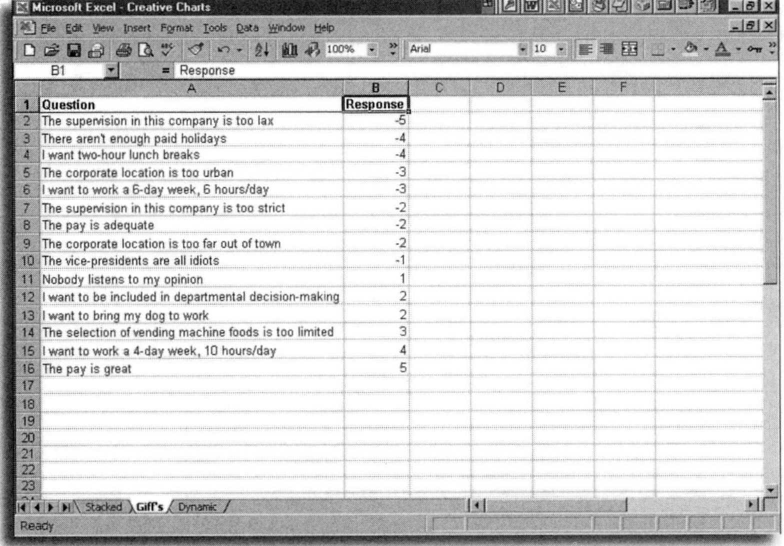

Question	Response
The supervision in this company is too lax	-5
There aren't enough paid holidays	-4
I want two-hour lunch breaks	-4
The corporate location is too urban	-3
I want to work a 6-day week, 6 hours/day	-3
The supervision in this company is too strict	-2
The pay is adequate	-2
The corporate location is too far out of town	-2
The vice-presidents are all idiots	-1
Nobody listens to my opinion	1
I want to be included in departmental decision-making	2
I want to bring my dog to work	2
The selection of vending machine foods is too limited	3
I want to work a 4-day week, 10 hours/day	4
The pay is great	5

FIGURE 32.2
The data is simple, but I need to show the entire survey question, legibly, next to each marker in the chart.

Create Giff's chart

1. Sort the data so that the bar chart markers make a symmetrical picture, with marker values sorted from high to low.
2. Copy the data and paste it to another location in the worksheet, where you want to build the chart. (Copy the values, too, so you can re-sort them.)

   The chart is not connected to the values in the worksheet that become the data labels. This is a drawback, but it is worth it to get the finished chart I want.
3. Sort the pasted data in the opposite order and delete the values (as shown in Figure 32.3).

   You have to re-sort the data because a bar chart presents data in the opposite order from which it's laid out in the source table. (This is one of those facts that isn't written down anywhere, but you figure it out when you start to play with charts.)

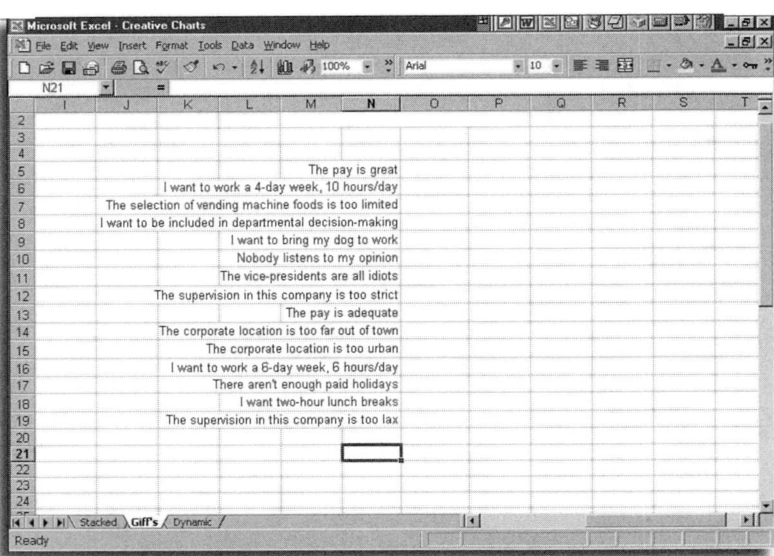

FIGURE 32.3

To use this technique, you need to sort the label data so that it matches the bar values in the chart.

4. Put the labels with positive values in one worksheet column and right-align the cells.
5. Move the labels with negative values one column to the right and left-align those cells (as shown in Figure 32.4).

6. Select all the label cells, and format them with a **Vertical** alignment of **Center** (on the Format Cells dialog box, **Alignment** tab).

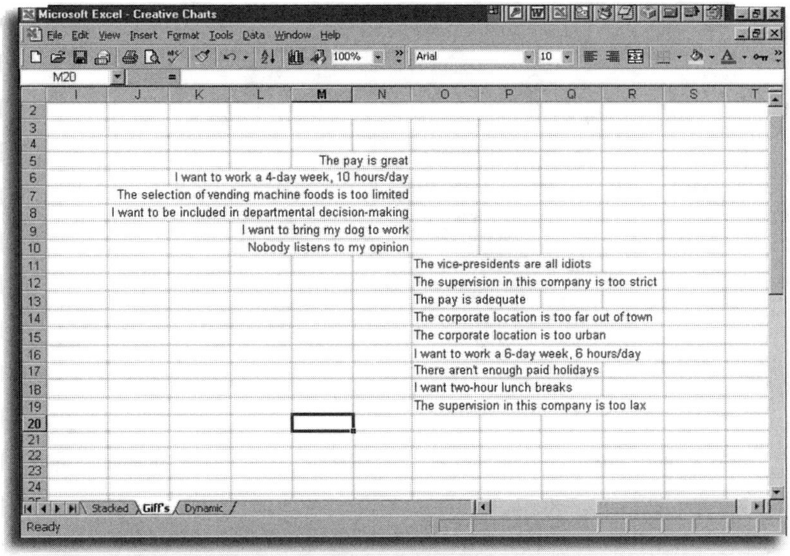

FIGURE 32.4
This label layout makes more sense after the chart is laid over it.

7. Create a bar chart from the source data.
   - In Step 2 of the Chart Wizard, put the series in **Columns**.
   - In Step 3 of the Chart Wizard, remove the legend and gridlines.

   The finished chart looks like the one shown in Figure 32.5. Next, I'll format it to make it work with the worksheet labels.
8. Double-click the central axis, and in the Format Axis dialog box, click the **Patterns** tab.
9. In the **Patterns** tab, under **Tick mark labels**, click **None**, and then click **OK**.

   The axis labels are removed, but the tick marks remain.
10. Double-click the chart area. On the **Patterns** tab, under **Border**, select **None**; under **Area**, select **None**, and then click **OK**.

Draw Attention to Specific Bars

You can make an individual bar stand out from the rest by changing its color or adding a striped pattern. Click the bar twice (not a double-click) to select it, double-click the selected bar, and change its color and pattern on the **Patterns** tab in the Format Data Point dialog box.

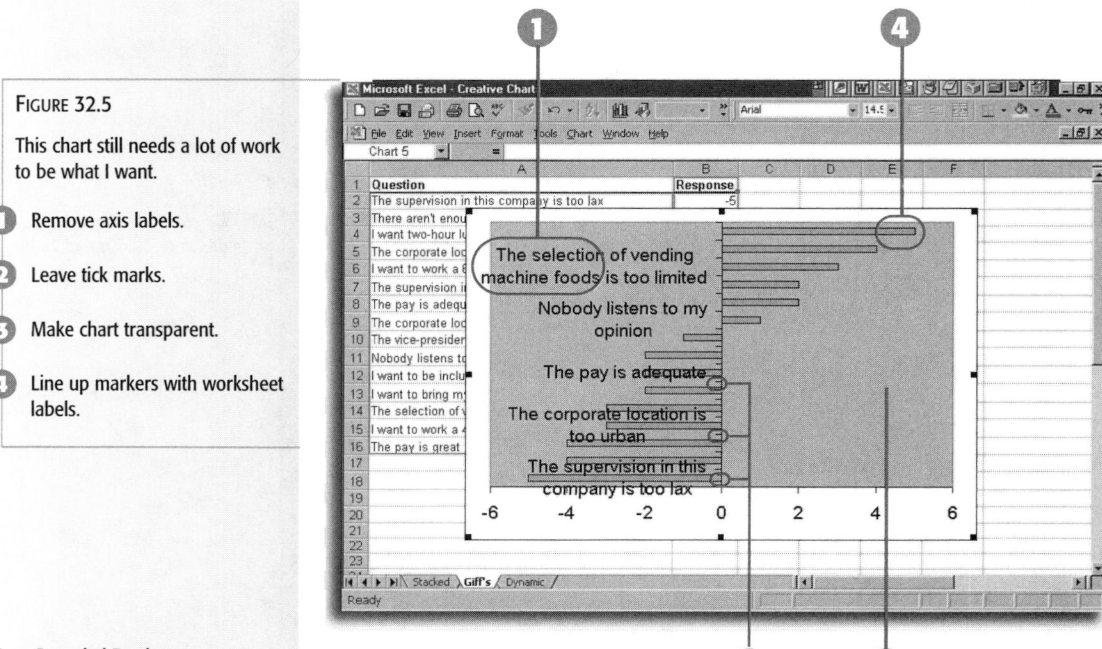

FIGURE 32.5

This chart still needs a lot of work to be what I want.

1. Remove axis labels.
2. Leave tick marks.
3. Make chart transparent.
4. Line up markers with worksheet labels.

Try a Rounded Border

Another nice touch is a round-cornered border for an invisible chart. Instead of removing the chart area border, click the **Round corners** check box and change the border color and line weight to add more visual interest.

11. Double-click the plot area. On the **Patterns** tab, under **Border**, select **None;** under **Area**, select **None** and then click **OK**.

    This makes the chart area and plot area transparent and borderless so the markers and axes float on the worksheet. You can't see through the chart yet because the chart object is still selected (see Figure 32.6). When you click the worksheet, however, you see the transparent chart overlaid.

12. Right-click the chart area and click **Format Chart Area**.
13. On the **Properties** tab, click the **Don't move or size with cells** option and then click **OK**.

    This keeps the chart from resizing when you resize the worksheet rows beneath it.

14. Resize the chart to be large on the worksheet and then click in a worksheet cell.

Because you can't see the worksheet cells beneath the chart when the chart is selected, you leave the chart in one place and move the column and row borders beneath it to line up the labels and markers.

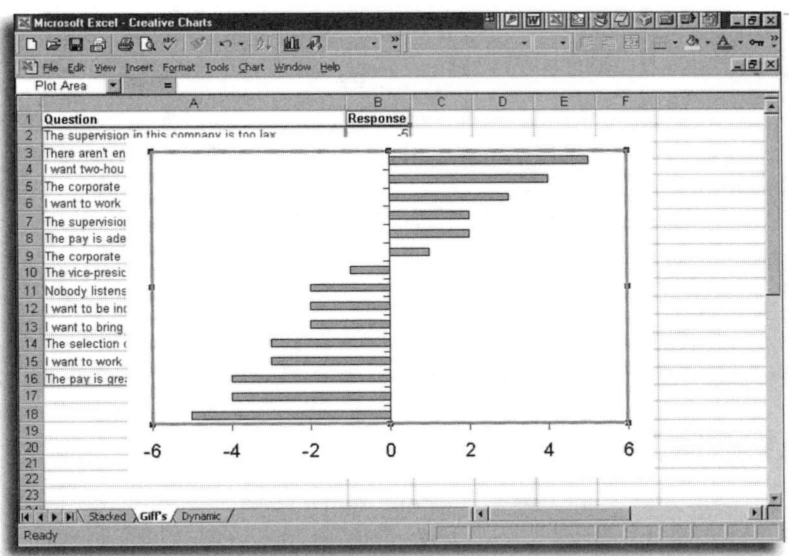

FIGURE 32.6
What remains is to line up the worksheet labels with the chart markers.

15. Drag the column border nearest the central axis to line it up precisely under the center axis.
16. Select and drag each row border to line it up with a tick mark. This makes each vertically centered label line up with its marker.
17. When all the dragging is done, turn off the worksheet gridlines. (On the **Tools** menu, click **Options**, and on the **View** tab, clear the **Gridlines** check box.)

    If your chart doesn't look like the one in Figure 32.7, keep tweaking it until you get what you want.

This chart is an example of the creative things you can do if you don't limit yourself to the built-in features in Excel.

SEE ALSO

➤ *To learn more about creating a chart, see page 385.*
➤ *To learn more about sorting data, see page 269.*

FIGURE 32.7

Voilá! Now, play with this and see what else you can do.

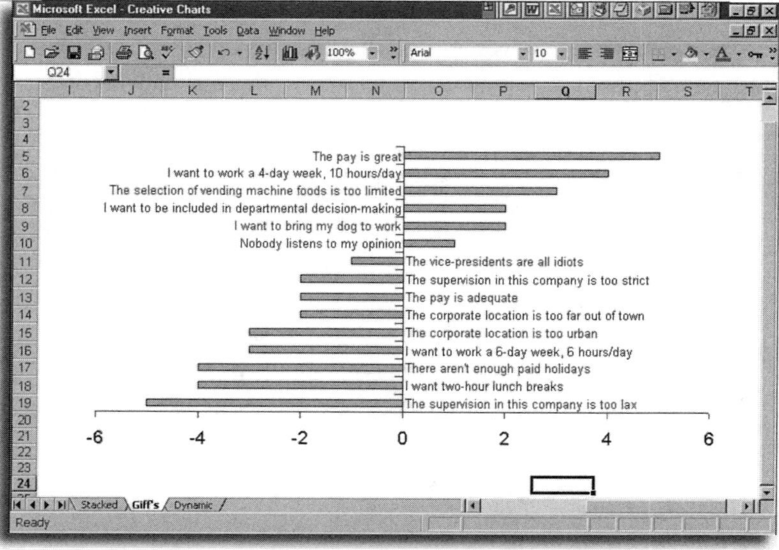

Stacked Columns

Another client had a quick question: How can I show income versus expenses in the same chart and in a stacked column format so that one column shows all the income and the other column shows all the expenses? The answer is shown in Figure 32.8.

FIGURE 32.8

This is a neat, efficient way to compare income and expenses graphically.

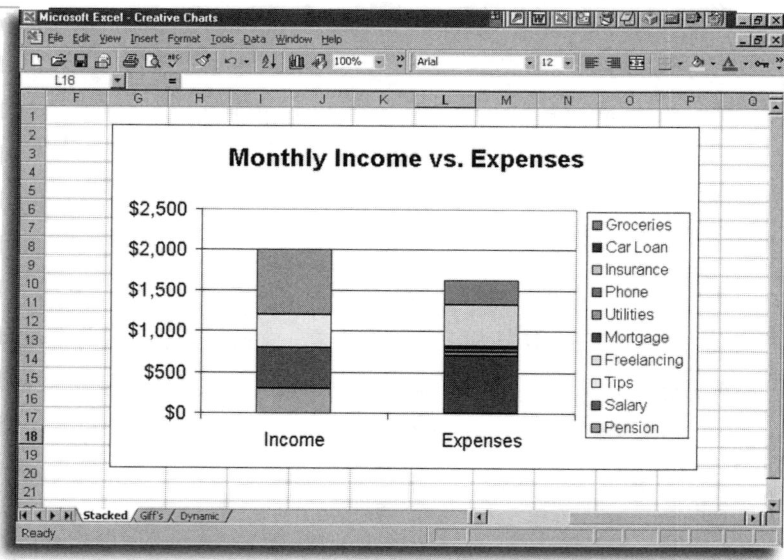

This is a pretty simple solution that relies on the layout of the chart's source data.

Figure 32.9 shows the data layout. The data for each stacked column is in its own category. I charted the series in rows in Step 2 of the Chart Wizard. It's not a complex solution; rather, it's one of those simple ideas that can be frustratingly elusive until someone points it out.

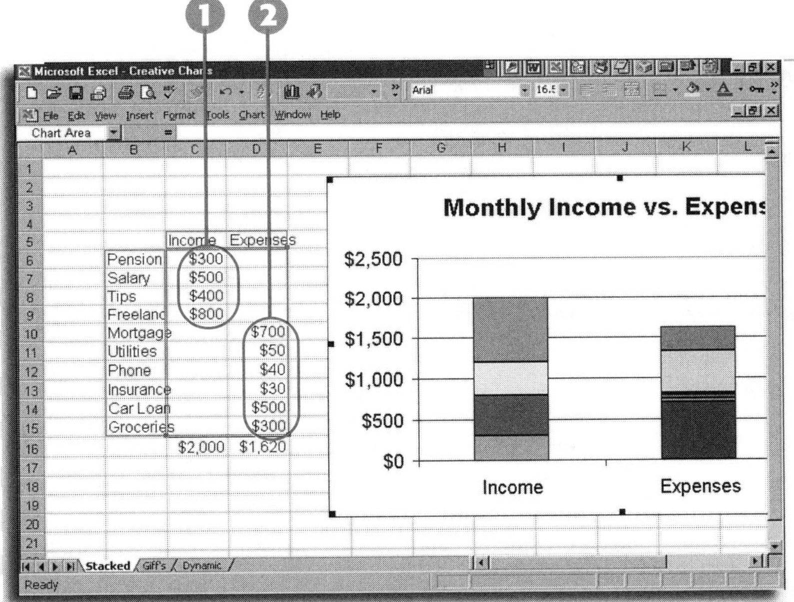

FIGURE 32.9
Changing the source data layout can change your chart radically.

1. Income stacked column
2. Expenses stacked column

SEE ALSO

➤ *To learn more about creating a chart, see page 385.*

Dynamic Chart Display

Here's your dilemma: You need to send charted data to your company's CEO, who can barely use a computer, let alone Excel. You want to give the CEO a bright, colorful, electronic file because it's dazzling and impressive, but you need to make the file as simple as possible to use. One solution is shown in Figure 32.10.

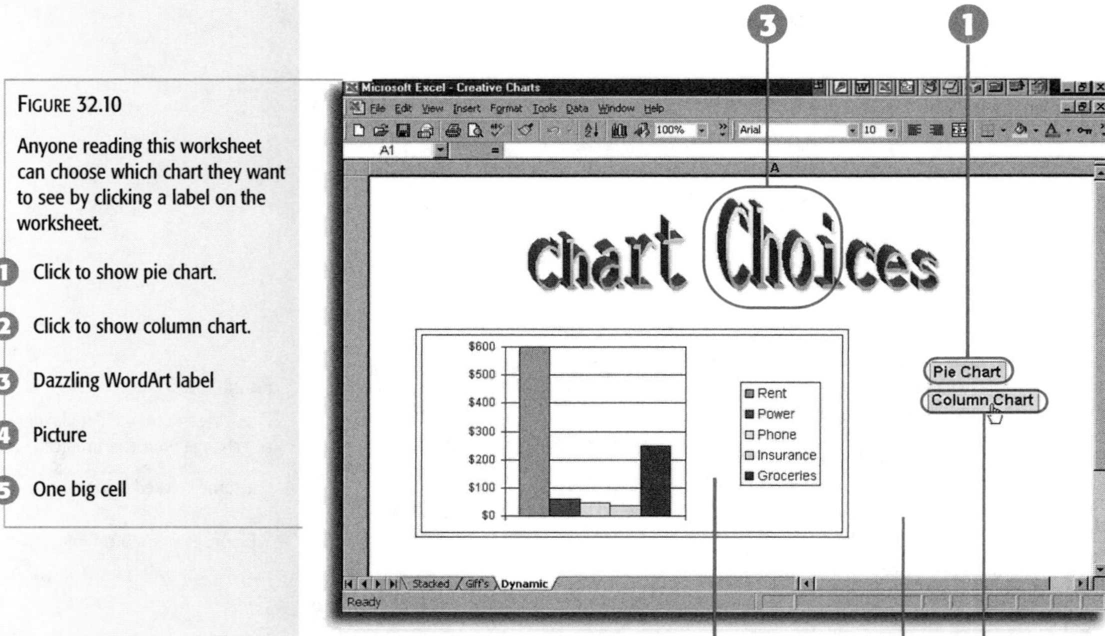

FIGURE 32.10

Anyone reading this worksheet can choose which chart they want to see by clicking a label on the worksheet.

1. Click to show pie chart.
2. Click to show column chart.
3. Dazzling WordArt label
4. Picture
5. One big cell

The worksheet in Figure 32.10 has a big WordArt label, two text boxes with macros attached, and a picture of a chart. The actual charts that appear in the picture are located elsewhere on the worksheet, out of view. The worksheet area behind the objects is one big cell (larger than the screen area), so the display isn't cluttered by selected cells.

If readers want to see the data in a pie chart, they click the Pie Chart label, and a macro attached to the text box shows the pie chart in the picture. If they want to see the data displayed in a column chart instead, they click the Column Chart label.

The two charts and their data are elsewhere on the worksheet, shown in Figure 32.11.

The chart picture in Figure 32.10 is actually a picture of the cells behind each chart, taken with the Camera button. A picture of cells displays all objects that overlay the cells, and because each chart fits the pictured cells perfectly, all the picture shows is the chart.

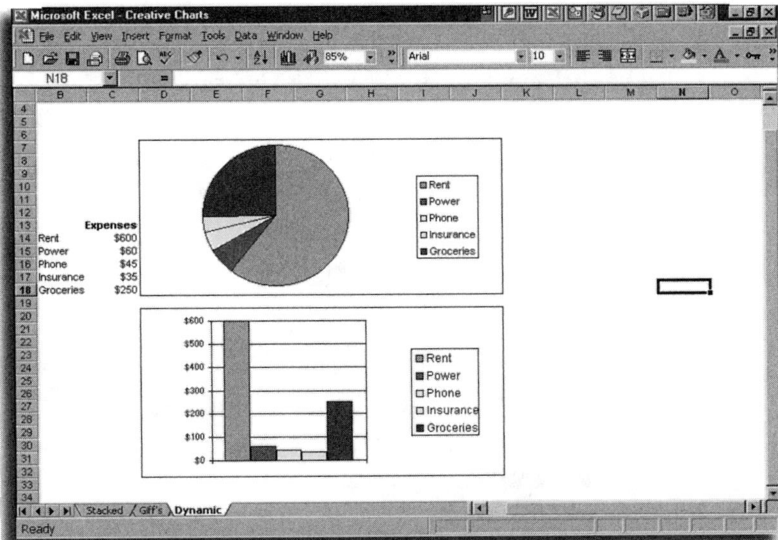

FIGURE 32.11

Both charts use the same data and fit precisely over their background cell ranges.

Using the Camera button to take a picture is the only new procedure involved in creating this worksheet; all other procedures used to create this dynamic chart display (such as creating charts, resizing rows and columns, recording macros, creating text boxes and attaching macros, and creating WordArt) are covered elsewhere in this book.

To create a dynamic chart display, follow this general outline of procedures:

- Start by putting the Camera button on a toolbar.
- Create the charts on a different area of the worksheet (away from cell A1).
- Fit each chart precisely to the cells behind it.
- Name each range of cells that's overlaid by a chart.
- Resize cell A1 to be larger than the screen area.
- Take a picture of one chart range and paste it in place.
- Record a macro that changes the picture.
- Draw text boxes (or other graphic objects) to be click labels.
- Attach the macros to the click labels.
- Create a WordArt worksheet title.

First, put the Camera button on the toolbar of your choice.

Put the Camera button on a toolbar

1. Right-click any toolbar, then click **Customize**.
2. On the **Commands** tab (shown in Figure 32.12), click the **Tools** category, then scroll down to find the **Camera** button.

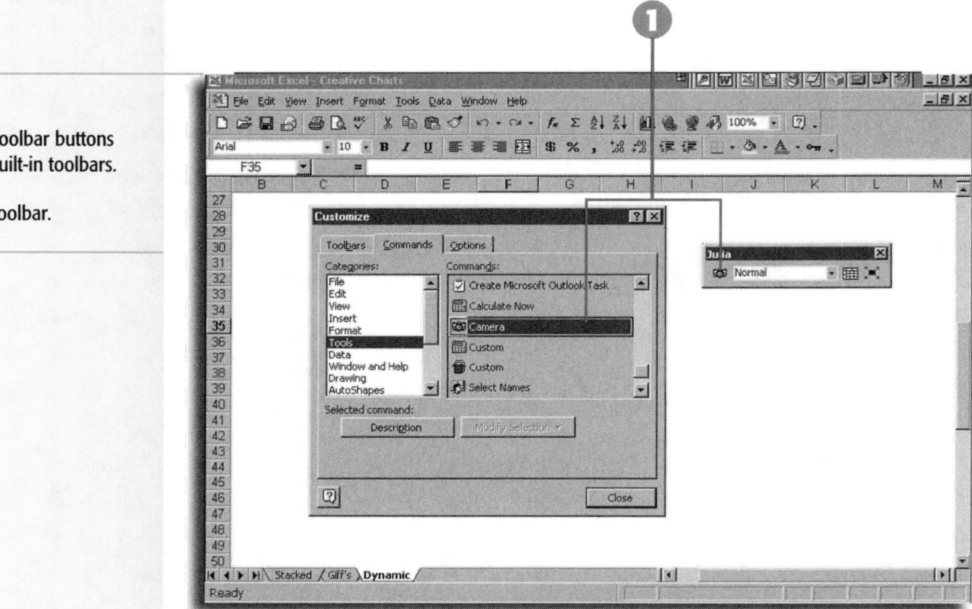

FIGURE 32.12

A lot of useful toolbar buttons aren't on any built-in toolbars.

1 Drag to any toolbar.

3. Drag the Camera button onto any toolbar.
4. Click **Close** to close the Customize dialog box.

SEE ALSO

➤ *To learn more about putting new buttons on toolbars, see page 527.*

Next, you'll create all the charts you want the user to be able to display.

Create the charts on a different area of the worksheet

1. Copy the data you want to chart to an area of the worksheet that's below and right of cell A1.

Cell A1 will be resized to be larger than the screen area, and you want your data near the big cell (so you can work with it easily) but not right next to cell A1. In Figure 32.13, my data is in the range B13:C18.

2. Create the first chart from the data, and size it to fit precisely over the cells behind it. In Figure 32.13, my pie chart fits over the range D18:J18.

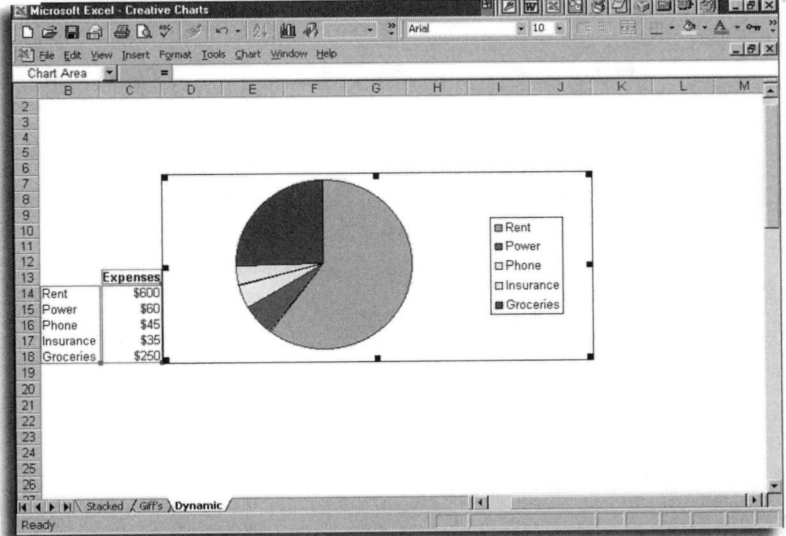

FIGURE 32.13
Press Alt to snap objects to worksheet gridlines.

Press Alt while you drag the chart area to align one corner precisely with cell borders (the corner will snap to the nearest gridlines); then, press Alt while you drag handles to snap the remaining chart borders into alignment with cell borders.

You want the chart to fit perfectly over the range of cells because you'll take a picture of the range, and if the chart doesn't fit perfectly, cell borders will show in the picture (or part of the chart will be hidden).

3. Create a copy of the first chart, and align it over a range of cells near the first chart. Because it's a copy, it already fits a range of cells and will snap into perfect position if you press Alt while you move it.

Experiment with the Picture

After you finish creating pictures of the charts, you can experiment with moving and resizing the charts to get a feel for what happens to the picture.

SEE ALSO

➤ *To learn more about creating charts, see page 385.*

Next, name the range of cells behind each chart so that your macros will be able to easily identify each range.

I'm Mouse-Oriented; How Do I Use the Keys?

Use an arrow key to move to a cell behind the upper-left corner of the chart. Hold down Shift while you press the down-arrow key to select all the cells down the left side of the chart; then, continue to hold Shift while you use the right-arrow key to select all the cells to the right side of the chart.

Name the ranges behind the charts

1. Select the range of cells covered by a chart.

   Either move the chart temporarily to select the range of cells behind it with the mouse, or leave the chart in position and use the arrow and Shift keys to select the hidden cells.

2. Click in the **Name** box, type a name for the range, and press Enter.

   To make the macro procedures easier, use a name that identifies the chart. In this example, I named my ranges "PieChart" and "ColChart."

3. Repeat the naming process for each chart.

   Now, you can move quickly to each range by selecting its name in the Name box list (shown in Figure 32.14), and you'll be able to identify each range by name in your macros.

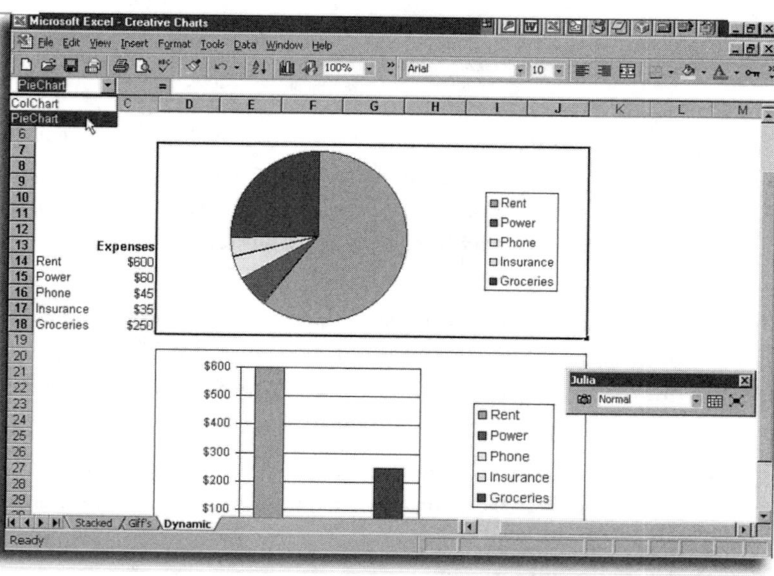

FIGURE 32.14

Remember, no spaces are allowed in range names.

SEE ALSO

➤ *To learn more about naming cells, see page 202.*

Now, you need to create the big cell so that all your objects lie on top of the one big cell and a user can't mess up the great display by clicking cells.

Resize cell A1 to be larger than the screen area

1. Select cell A1.
2. Drag the bottom border of Row 1 down below the bottom of the screen.
3. Drag the right border of Column A beyond the right edge of the screen.

   Reduce your worksheet magnification to 75% to drag farther if you need to. Figure 32.15 shows my finished worksheet zoomed to 75% magnification with cell A1 selected.

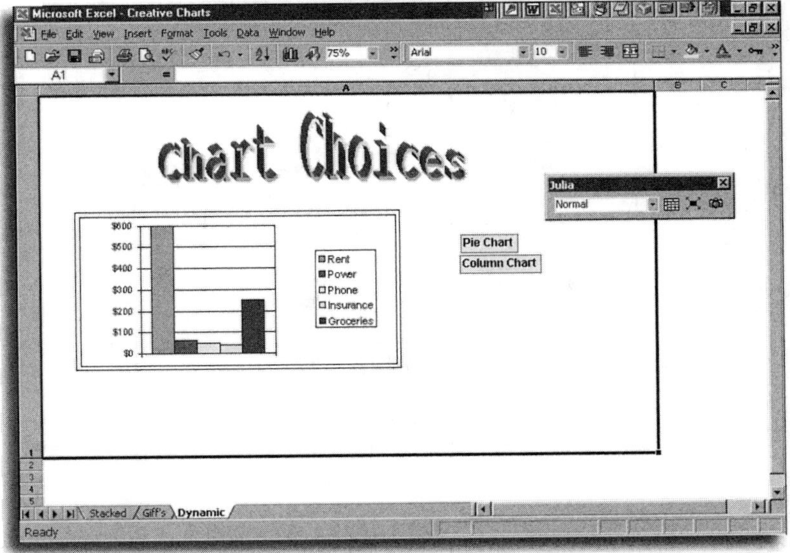

FIGURE 32.15
At 75% magnification, it's easier to see how big cell A1 is.

SEE ALSO

➤ *To learn more about resizing rows and columns, see page 224.*

Next, take a picture of one chart range and place it in your big cell.

Take a picture of one chart range

1. In the Name box, click one of your chart-range names.

   The range is selected, and the neatly fitted chart is in view on your screen.

2. On the toolbar, click the **Camera** button.

   The mouse button becomes a crosshair (shown in Figure 32.16); wherever you click, the picture will be pasted.

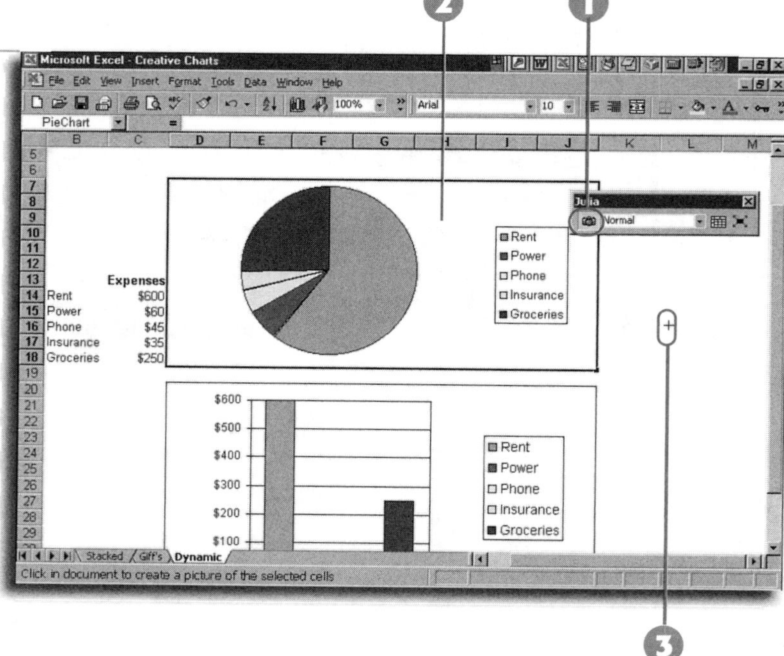

FIGURE 32.16

Click the crosshair mouse pointer to paste the picture.

1. Camera button
2. Selected range
3. Crosshair

3. Press Ctrl+Home to move quickly to cell A1, your big cell.
4. Click the crosshair in the big cell to paste the picture, then move the picture to an appropriate onscreen location (as shown in Figure 32.17).

   You've pasted a picture of worksheet cells, including any data and objects they contain. Because your chart is fitted to the cell range, you get a perfect picture of your chart.

My Picture Has Two Borders

If your chart picture has two borders, one is the chart border, and one is the picture border. To remove the picture border, right-click the picture, then click **Format Picture**. On the **Colors and Lines** tab, under **Line**, drop the **Color** list, click **No Line**, and then click **OK**. To remove the chart border, select the chart and format the chart area to have no border.

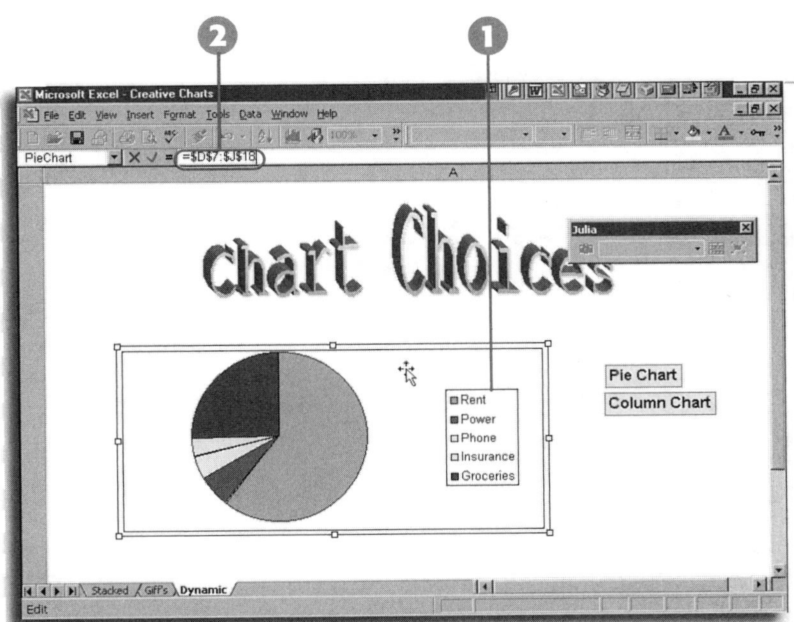

FIGURE 32.17

You'll change the picture's range reference to a range name in your macros.

1. Picture
2. Picture's range reference

When you click the picture to select it, the equation in the Formula bar shows which cells are displayed in the picture. When you create the macros, you'll change the formula to point to named ranges.

Record a macro that changes the picture

1. On the **Tools** menu, point to **Macro**, then click **Record New Macro**.

   If the Macro command is unavailable, you probably have the picture selected; click in the worksheet to select a cell, then click the commands.

2. In the Record Macro dialog box (shown in Figure 32.18), give the new macro an easily identifiable name. (The two macros in this example are named "Pie" and "Column".)

3. In the **Store macro in** list, select **This Workbook**.

   You don't need this macro available anywhere but in this workbook to change this chart display.

4. Click **OK**.

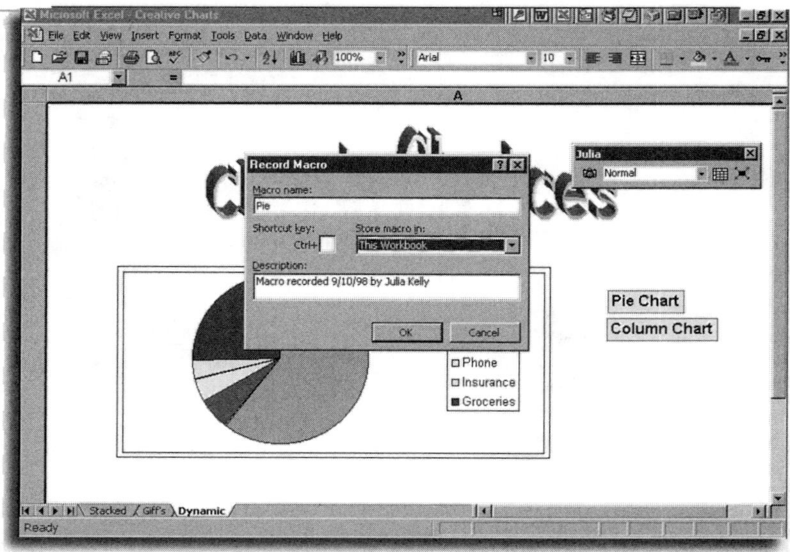

FIGURE 32.18

Give the macro an intuitive name, and store it in this workbook.

The macro recorder starts, and the Stop Recording toolbar is visible on your worksheet. The next few steps are the steps your macro will perform.

5. Click the picture to select it.
6. In the Formula bar, select the range reference, and in its place, type one of your chart range names (as shown in Figure 32.19).

   Use the range name that corresponds to the macro name so when you run the macro, you display the correct chart. (For example, I named this macro "Column" and typed the range name "ColChart" to display my column chart.)
7. Press Enter to complete the formula.
8. Click anywhere in the big cell (cell A1).
9. On the Stop Recording toolbar, click the **Stop** button.
10. Repeat steps 1 through 9 for each chart range you want to display in the picture.

    In this example, I have two charts to display (a pie chart and a column chart), so I created two macros.

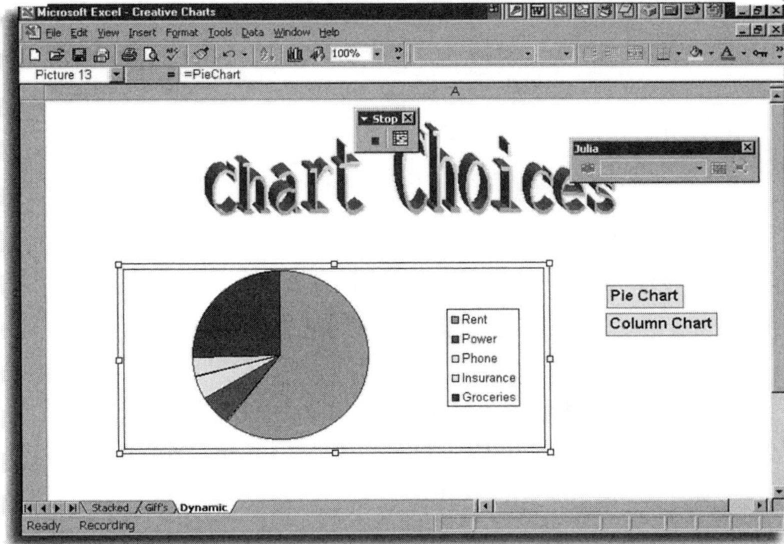

FIGURE 32.19
It's a good idea to coordinate the macro name and range name.

SEE ALSO

➤ *To learn more about recording macros, see page 535.*

Next, it's a good idea to test the macros.

Test the macros

1. Click **Tools**, point to **Macro**, and click **Macros**.
2. In the Macro dialog box, click the name of chart macro.
3. Click **Run**.

   The picture should display the chart recorded in the macro.
4. Repeat steps 1 through 3 for each macro you recorded.

When all the macros pass muster, you can create text box labels and attach the macros to them.

Draw text boxes and assign macros to them

1. Display the Drawing toolbar.
2. In the big cell, draw a text box (or any graphic object you like) for each macro.
3. Right-click a text box and click **Assign Macro**.
4. In the Assign Macro dialog box, click the name of the macro you want to assign to the selected object, then click **OK**.

5. Repeat steps 3 and 4 to assign a macro to each text box.

   You can format the text boxes or graphic objects at any time; after you assign macros to the objects, right-click them and click the object's **Format** command to change formatting.

SEE ALSO

➤ *To learn more about drawing graphic objects on worksheets, see page 563.*

Now, you can test your macros again, this time by clicking each of the objects.

The final step is to add a splashy WordArt title to make the worksheet sparkle.

Create a WordArt worksheet title

1. On the Drawing toolbar, click the **Insert WordArt** button.
2. Create a great WordArt title in the big cell.

SEE ALSO

➤ *To learn more about drawing graphic objects on worksheets, see page 563.*

You're done! Now, get creative and see what else you can do to make this dynamic chart presentation even better.

This example displays different chart types for the same data, but you can show charts of different data, perhaps data for each quarter or each division. You can also show tables of data by taking pictures of the worksheet cells that contain the data because anything in or on the named range can be shown in the picture.

To make the screen presentation look even more customized, click **Tools**, then click **Options**, and on the **View** tab, turn off the row and column headers, both scrollbars, and the sheet tabs. While you're there, you can also hide the Formula bar and status bar. Figure 32.20 shows a worksheet with all these elements hidden. Users can't scroll around or open other worksheets.

Here's one thing you should *not* do: *Don't* protect the sheet to prevent users from moving the picture, because then your macros won't work.

This short chapter is not meant to be a comprehensive treatise on creative charting, just enough to inspire you to try new approaches with your own data.

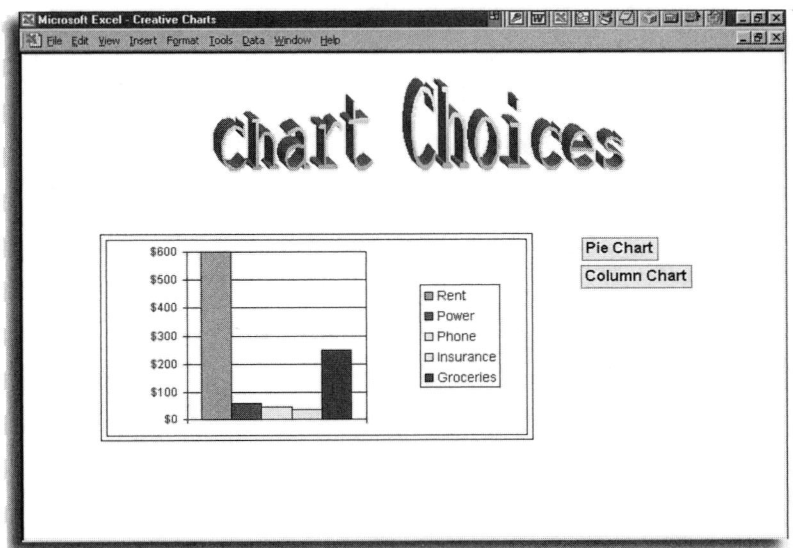

FIGURE 32.20
With all the normal worksheet elements hidden, it doesn't look like a worksheet any more.

Glossary

absolute reference A cell reference that specifies the exact address of a cell. An absolute reference takes the form A1, B3, and so on.

activate (chart) Select a chart for editing or formatting. To activate a chart sheet, click the sheet tab. To activate a chart object on a worksheet, click the chart.

active cell The selected cell. You can enter or edit data in the active cell.

active sheet The sheet that you are currently working on. When a sheet is active, the name on the sheet tab is bold.

active window The window that you are currently using or that is currently selected. Only one window can be active at a time, and keystrokes and commands affect the active window.

add-in Files that can be installed to add commands and functions to Excel.

address, cell The location of a cell on a sheet. The cell address consists of a column address and a row address, such as F12, in which F is the sixth column on the sheet and 12 is the twelfth row on the sheet.

address, Internet The address of a Web site on the Internet. It usually takes the form `http://www.something.com`. *See also* URL.

alignment The horizontal (or vertical) position of text within a cell.

argument Information you supply to a function for calculation. An argument can be a value, reference, name, formula, or another function.

arrow keys The up-arrow, down-arrow, left-arrow, and right-arrow keys (and diagonal keys on some keyboards) that are used to move the insertion point one cell at a time or to select from a menu or a list of options.

ascending A method of ordering a group of items from lowest to highest, such as from A to Z or 1 to 10.

AutoFill A feature that allows you to create a series of incremental or fixed values on a worksheet by dragging the fill handle with the mouse.

AutoFormat (for charts) A combination of chart type, chart subtype, and other formatting characteristics, such as patterns and font, that you can quickly apply to a chart to change its appearance. In addition to Excel's built-in AutoFormats, you can create your own custom (user-defined) AutoFormats.

AutoFormat (for PivotTables) Built-in sets of formatting characteristics specifically for PivotTables.

AutoFormat (for worksheet tables) Built-in sets of formatting characteristics specifically for worksheet tables.

axes Borders on the plot area that provide a frame of reference for measurement or comparison. On most charts, data values are plotted along the y axis and categories are plotted along the x axis. On a typical column chart, the x axis is the horizontal axis and the y axis is the vertical axis. Pie and doughnut charts have no axes, radar charts have a single central axis, and scatter charts have two value axes. Some 3D charts have three axes (x, y, and z) for values, categories, and series.

border A line that goes around text, cells, or tables. You can assign a variety of line styles and colors to a border.

cell The intersection of a column and a row.

cell reference The set of column and row coordinates that identifies a cell location on a worksheet. Also known as the cell address.

chart A graphical representation of worksheet data. A chart can be a chart object (located on a worksheet) or a chart sheet (located on a separate sheet). Charts are linked to the data they were created from and are automatically updated when worksheet changes are made.

chart area The entire background in the chart, just outside the plot area. When the chart area is selected, uniform font characteristics can be applied to all text in the chart.

chart object A chart located on a worksheet. A chart object behaves like other worksheet objects.

chart sheet A sheet in a workbook containing a chart. When a chart sheet is active, the chart on the chart sheet is automatically activated.

chart type A chart type is a specific kind of chart, such as area, bar, column, line, pie, doughnut, radar, XY (scatter), 3D area, 3D bar, 3D column, 3D line, 3D pie, or 3D surface. Each chart type has at least one subtype that's a variation of the original chart type.

Chart Wizard A series of dialog boxes that guides you through the steps required to create a new chart (or modify settings for an existing chart).

check box A box that indicates with a check mark that a feature is turned on or off.

circular references A formula that refers to its own cell, either directly or indirectly.

Clipboard A temporary holding area for data that is cut or copied. Up to 12 items remain on the Clipboard until you clear it. You can paste cut or copied data from the Clipboard to another location, worksheet, workbook, or application.

Clipboard toolbar A toolbar with icons for each cut or copied data item on the Clipboard; it appears automatically when there are two or more items on the Clipboard. Click an icon to paste its data.

collapse To click the small minus symbol next to a group heading to hide the items in that group.

column A vertical range of cells. Each column is identified by a unique letter or letter combination (such as A, Z, or CF).

column heading The label at the top of a column.

comment A note that explains, identifies, or comments on the information in a specific cell or range of cells.

comparison criteria A set of search conditions used to filter data. Comparison criteria can be a series of characters you want matched, such as apple, or an expression, such as >300.

comparison operator A mathematical symbol used to compare two values (such as =, >, <, =>, =<, or <>).

constant A cell value that does not start with an equal sign. For example, the date, the value 345, and text are all constants.

copy To duplicate information from one location to another, either within a workbook, to another workbook, or to a file in another program.

cursor The flashing vertical line that shows where text is entered (for example, in a cell during in-cell editing). Also known as the insertion point.

custom sort order A non-alpha, non-numeric sort order, such as Low, Medium, High or Monday, Tuesday, Wednesday. You can use one of the built-in custom sort orders, or create your own using the Tools, Options, Custom Lists dialog tab.

cut To remove selected information from one location so you can paste it to another location within the workbook, to another workbook, or to a file in another program.

data form A dialog box that you can use to see, change, add, and delete records from a list or database or to find specific records based on criteria you specify. You can display the data form for a list or database by clicking Data, Form.

data label A label that provides additional information about a data marker in a chart. Data labels can be applied to a single marker, an entire data series, or all data markers in a chart. They may be formatted and moved but not sized.

data marker A column, bar, area, dot, slice, or other symbol in a chart that represents a single data point or value originating from a worksheet cell. Related data markers in a chart compose a data series.

data point An individual value plotted in a chart that originates from a single cell in a worksheet. Data points are represented by data markers.

data region A range of cells containing data and bounded by empty cells.

data series A group of related data points in a chart that originate from a single worksheet row or column. Each data series in a chart is distinguished by a unique color or pattern. You can plot one or more data series in a chart. (A pie chart is limited to one series.)

database A range of cells containing data that is related to a particular subject or purpose. The first row in the database contains field names. Each additional row in the database is one record; each column in the database is one field. In Excel, a database is also known as a list.

default A predefined setting that is built into a program and used when you do not specify an alternative setting. For example, a worksheet might have a default font setting of Arial, 10-point text.

delimiter A character, such as a tab, space, or comma, that separates fields of data in a text file.

dependents Cells containing formulas that refer to the active cell.

descending order Highest to lowest, such as Z to A or 10 to 1.

destination area The range of cells you select to hold the summarized data when using the Consolidate command. The destination area can be on the same worksheet as the source data, or it can be on a different worksheet.

dialog box A box that appears when you choose a command that requires additional information. It may include areas in which you type text or numbers and view or change settings for options related to the command. If you don't understand an option, right-click it, and then click the What's This button that appears.

drag and drop A mouse technique for directly moving or copying a set of information from one location to another. To drag an object, position the pointer over the object, hold down the mouse button while you move the mouse, and then release the mouse button when the object is positioned where you want it.

drop-down list box A single box with uneditable text and an arrow, paired with a drop-down list that appears when the user selects the arrow.

edit To add, delete, or change information, such as text or graphics.

embed To insert an object from a source program into a destination document. An embedded object maintains a connection to its original application so that you can open the original application and edit the embedded object by double-clicking the object. *See also* link.

embedded object Data (such as text or graphics) that you can edit using the full resources of its source program while it is in a destination document. *See also* embed.

expand To click the plus symbol next to a group heading to display the items in the group.

export The process of converting and saving a file to be used in a another program. *See also* import.

external reference In a formula, a reference to a cell, range, or named area on a different worksheet.

field In a list or database, a column of data that contains a particular type of information, such as Last Name, Phone Number, or Quantity.

file A document that you create or save with a unique filename. In Excel, a file is a workbook.

file format The format, such as text, Word, dBASE, FoxPro, and so on, of the file in which data is stored.

fill handle The small black square in the lower-right corner of the selected cell or range (only visible if **Allow cell drag and drop** is turned on). When you position the mouse pointer over the fill handle, the pointer changes to a black cross. Drag the fill handle to copy contents to adjacent cells or to create a series. Dragging the fill handle with the right mouse button displays a shortcut menu.

filter A set of criteria you can apply to records to show specific records. The records that match your criteria are listed, and all others are hidden.

floating palette A palette that can be dragged away from its toolbar. *See also* palette.

floating toolbar A toolbar that appears in a window with a title bar, stays on top of the other windows, and is not fixed in position.

folder A container in which workbooks, other program files, and other folders are stored on your computer disks. Folders can help you organize your documents by grouping them into categories, as you would organize paper documents into file folders.

font A collection of letters, numbers, and special characters that share a consistent and identifiable typeface, such as Courier or Times New Roman.

footer Text that appears at the bottom of every printed page. *See also* header.

format The way text and cells appear on a page. Types of formats include character, number, cell border, color, and more. Styles can contain any combination of these formats.

formula An equation that produces a new value from existing values. A formula always begins with a equal sign (=).

Formula bar A bar near the top of the Excel window that you can use to enter or edit values and formulas in cells or charts. Displays the formula or constant value from the active cell or object.

free-floating label A label that's not linked to a chart object and can be moved anywhere on the chart.

function A built-in formula that uses a series of values (arguments) to perform an operation and returns the result of the operation. You can use the Function Wizard to select a function and enter it into a cell.

Goal Seek A tool for finding the input value a formula needs in order to return a specific result. You can enter your goal value, select the variable that you want to change, and then let Excel find the value that will return your goal.

graphic object A line or shape (such as a button, text box, ellipse, rectangle, arc, or picture) you draw using the tools on the toolbar or a picture you paste into Excel.

gridlines Lines that Excel displays on a worksheet to visually separate columns and rows into cells. By default, Excel doesn't print the worksheet gridlines, but you can choose to print them.

gridlines (chart) Lines in a chart that extend from the tick marks on an axis across the plot area. Gridlines come in various forms: horizontal, vertical, major, minor, and various combinations. They make it easier to view and evaluate data in a chart.

group In an outline or PivotTable, detail rows or columns that are subordinate to a summary row or column.

handles Small black squares located around the perimeter of selected graphic objects, chart items, or chart text. By dragging the handles, you can move, copy, or size the selected object, chart item, or chart text.

header Text that appears at the top of every printed page. *See also* footer.

icon A small graphic that represents an object, such as a program, a disk drive, or a document. When you double-click an icon, the item the icon represents opens.

import The process of converting and opening a file that was created in a another program. *See also* export.

insert To enter text, data, or a graphic into a document, cell, or dialog box. You can also insert cells, rows, and columns into a worksheet. You insert information at the insertion point. *See also* insertion point.

insertion point A flashing vertical line that shows the text entry point (also known as the cursor). It appears in a cell or text box when you click the mouse pointer there.

installing an add-in Copying the add-in program from the CD-ROM onto your hard drive so it becomes available to a main program such as Excel. *See also* loading an add-in.

Internet The worldwide network of networks. It encompasses the World Wide Web, FTP (file transfer protocol for transferring files between computers), and e-mail services, among other things.

intranet A local network, usually within a company or organization, that the public doesn't have access to.

label Text you provide to identify data.

landscape The horizontal orientation of a page; opposite of *portrait*, or vertical, orientation.

legend A box containing entries and keys that help to identify the data series or categories in a chart. The keys, to the left of each entry, show the colors assigned to the data markers in the chart.

link A data connection between a dependent worksheet (the worksheet that will use the data) and a source worksheet (the worksheet in which the original data resides). The dependent worksheet is updated whenever the data changes in the source worksheet. You can link graphics, text, and other types of information between a source file and a dependent file. *See also* embed.

list A range of cells containing data that is related to a particular subject or purpose. In Excel, the terms list and database are used interchangeably.

loading an add-in Activating an installed add-in so that a main program, such as Excel, can use the features provided by the add-in. *See also* installing an add-in.

macro A sequence of VBA commands you can record and then run to automate your work. A macro can be assigned to a shortcut key, button, or object for easy use.

marquee *See* moving border.

mixed reference In a formula, a combination of a relative reference and an absolute reference. A mixed reference takes the form $A1 or A$1, where A is the column cell address and 1 is the row cell address. For example, the mixed reference $A1 always refers to column A, regardless of the position of the cell containing the formula. The row address 1 refers to the row in relation to the cell containing the formula. If the cell containing the formula is copied down one row, the mixed reference $A1 changes to $A2.

move To transfer information from one location to another, either within a workbook, to another workbook, or to a file in another program.

moving average A type of trendline applicable to business data; it smoothes out data fluctuations by averaging sets of data values to give a better picture of changes over time.

moving border A moving dotted line that surrounds a cell or range of cells. For example, a moving border appears around a cell or range that has been cut or copied or around a cell or range you are inserting into a formula.

name A unique identifier you create to refer to a cell, a range, or a formula. When you use names in a formula, the formula is easier to read and maintain than a formula containing cell references.

nonadjacent selection A selection of two or more cells or ranges that do not touch each other.

normal style The style applied to all cells on sheets until another style is applied.

Office Assistant The gatekeeper for Microsoft help. You can change its interface to any of several different characters. (If you don't like it, you can hide it or uninstall it.)

OLE (Object Linking and Embedding) A technology for exchanging data between different programs. Drag and drop and linking and embedding are examples of OLE features. *See also* link *and* embed.

open database connectivity (ODBC) A driver manager and a set of ODBC drivers that enable applications to use Structured Query Language (SQL) as a standard language to access data created and stored in another format, such as FoxPro or Access.

option button A button for selecting one of a group of mutually exclusive options.

options The choices in a dialog box.

outline A summary report of worksheet data that contains several nested levels of detail data and summary data for each level of detail. The user can change the view of the outline to show or hide as much detail as they want.

palette A dialog box containing choices for color and other special effects. A palette appears when you click a toolbar button, such as Border or Fill Color. *See also* floating palette.

pane Panes allow you to view different areas of a large worksheet simultaneously. You can horizontally or vertically split a window into two panes, or you can split a window both vertically and horizontally to display four panes.

paste To insert cut or copied text into a new location.

paste area The destination for data that has been cut or copied.

path The location of a file within a computer file system. The path indicates the filename preceded by the disk drive, folder, and subfolders in which the file is stored. If the file is on another computer on a network, the path also includes the computer name.

personal macro workbook A hidden workbook that contains macros that are available every time you start Excel. When you record a macro, you can choose to record it into your personal macro workbook.

PivotChart A flexible chart presentation that uses a PivotTable as a data source; it can be pivoted like a PivotTable.

PivotTable An interactive worksheet table that enables you to summarize and analyze data from existing databases, lists, and tables. Use the PivotTable Wizard to specify the database, list, or table you want to use and to define how you want to arrange the data in the PivotTable. Once you create a PivotTable, you can reorganize the data by dragging fields and items.

PivotTable column field A field that is assigned a column orientation in a PivotTable. Items associated with a column field are displayed as column labels.

PivotTable data In a PivotTable, the summarized data calculated from the data fields of a source list or table.

PivotTable data area The part of a PivotTable that contains summary data. Values in each cell of the data area represent a summary of data from the source records or rows.

PivotTable detail item An item associated with an inner row or column field in a PivotTable.

PivotTable field A category of data that is derived from a field in a source list or table. For example, the Year field in a source list or database becomes the Year field in a PivotTable. Items from the source list or table, such as 1994, 1995, and so on, become subcategories in the PivotTable.

PivotTable item A subcategory of a PivotTable field. Items in a PivotTable are derived from unique items in a database field or from unique cells in a list column. In a PivotTable, items appear as row, column, or page labels.

PivotTable page field A field that is assigned to a page orientation in a PivotTable. Items in a page field are displayed one at a time in a PivotTable.

PivotTable row field A field that is assigned a row orientation in a PivotTable. Items associated with a row field are displayed as row labels.

plot area The area of a chart in which data is plotted. In 2D charts, it is bounded by the axes and encompasses the data markers and gridlines. In 3D charts, the plot area includes the chart's walls, axes, and tick-mark labels.

portrait A term used to refer to vertical page orientation; opposite of *landscape*, or horizontal, orientation.

precedents Cells that are referred to by the formula in the active cell.

precision The number of digits Excel uses when calculating values. By default, Excel calculates with a maximum of 15 digits of a value (full precision). If **Precision as displayed** is selected (on the Tools, Options, Calculation tab), Excel rounds values to the number of digits displayed on the worksheet before calculating; the **Precision as displayed** setting cannot be undone and applies to all worksheets in the workbook.

preview A view that displays your document as it will appear when you print it. Items such as text and graphics appear in their actual positions.

print area An area of a worksheet that is specified to be printed.

print titles Rows or columns that you set to print at the top or left of every page. For example, if you select Row 1 for a print title, Row 1 is printed at the top of the data on every page. If you select Column A for a print title, Column A is printed at the left of the data on every page.

program A computer software package, such as a word processor, spreadsheet, presentation designer, or relational database.

protection, workbook A method of preventing changes to the structure or windows in a workbook.

protection, worksheet A method of preventing changes to the cell contents, objects, or scenarios on a worksheet.

public files Network files that are available to everyone on the network.

publish Save an Excel file as an interactive Web page for posting to an Internet or intranet site.

query A means of finding exactly the data you want from a data source.

query definition Information that the Query Wizard uses to connect to and determine which data to retrieve from a data source. A query definition can include table names, field names, and criteria. A query definition is sent to a data source for execution in the form of a Structured Query Language (SQL) statement.

range Two or more cells on a worksheet.

record A single row in a list or database. The first row of a database usually contains field names, and each additional row in the database is a record. Each record in the database contains the same categories (fields) of data as every other record in the database.

reference The location of a cell or range of cells on a worksheet, indicated by column letter and row number. For example, B2 and C3:D4 are references. *See also* address, cell.

reference type The type of reference: absolute, relative, or mixed. A relative reference (such as A1) in a formula indicates the location of the referenced cell relative to the cell containing the formula. An absolute reference (such as A1) always refers to the exact location of the referenced cell. A mixed reference (such as $A1 or A$1) is half relative and half absolute.

refresh data To update a PivotTable or a query.

relative reference Specifies the location of a referenced cell in relation to the cell containing the reference. A relative reference takes the form A4, C12, and so on.

result cell A cell on the worksheet that is recalculated when a new scenario is applied.

row A horizontal set of cells. Each row is identified by a unique number.

R-squared value A calculated value that indicates how valid the correlation in a trendline is.

scale In a chart, the scale determines what values are displayed on an axis, at what intervals the values occur, and where one axis crosses another.

scenario A named set of input values that you can substitute in a worksheet model to perform what-if analysis.

Scenario Manager An add-in that allows you to create, view, and summarize scenarios.

scrollbars The shaded bars along the right side and bottom of the Excel window. With scrollbars, you can scroll from top to bottom in a long sheet or from side to side in a wide sheet.

secondary axis In a chart with more than one series, a secondary axis allows you to plot a series along a different value axis so that you can create two different value scales in the same chart.

select To highlight a cell or a range of cells on a worksheet or choose an object or a chart item. The selected cells, objects, or chart items will be affected by the next command or action.

shortcut An object that acts as a pointer to a document, folder, or program. If you double-click the shortcut, the object opens.

shortcut menu A context-sensitive menu that shows a list of commands relative to a selected item; it appears when you right-click the item.

sort key The field name or criteria by which you want to sort data.

sort order A way to arrange data based on value or data type. An ascending sort order sorts text from A to Z, numbers from the smallest negative number to the largest positive number, and dates and times from the earliest to the latest. A descending sort order is the opposite of an ascending sort order, except for blanks, which are always sorted last. If you choose a custom sort order, an ascending sort order is the order in which the items appear in the Sort Options dialog box.

source The document or program in which the data was originally created.

source data for PivotTables The list, database, or table used to create a PivotTable. Source data can be an Excel list or database, an external data source such as a dBASE or Microsoft Access file, Excel worksheet ranges with labeled rows and columns, or another PivotTable.

source worksheet The worksheet referred to by an external reference formula. The source worksheet contains the value used by the external reference formula.

split bar The horizontal or vertical line dividing a split worksheet. You can change the position of the split bar by dragging it or remove the split bar by double-clicking it.

status bar The bar at the bottom of the screen that displays information about the selected command or tool or an operation in progress.

Structured Query Language (SQL) A language used for retrieving, updating, and managing data.

style A named combination of formats that can be applied to a cell or range. If you redefine the style to be a different combination of formats, all cells to which the style was applied will automatically change to reflect the new formats. A style can include (or exclude) formats for number, font, alignment, borders, patterns, and protection.

subtotal row A row that displays one or more subtotals for columns in an Excel list. A list can contain multiple, nested subtotal rows.

summary data For automatic subtotals and worksheet outlines, the Total rows or columns that summarize detail data. Summary data is usually adjacent to and below the detail data.

summary function The calculation you direct Excel to use when combining source data in a PivotTable or a consolidation table or when inserting automatic subtotals in a list or database. Examples of summary functions include sum, count, and average.

table One or more rows of cells commonly used to display numbers and other items for quick reference and analysis. Items in a table are organized into rows (records) and columns (fields).

template A workbook that you create and then use as the basis for other, similar workbooks. You can create templates for workbooks, worksheets, and chart sheets.

text box A rectangular graphic object in which you can type text.

text file A file that contains only unformatted text information, often as tab-delimited or comma-delimited lists.

tick marks In a chart, small lines that intersect an axis like divisions on a ruler. Tick marks are part of and can be formatted with an axis.

title bar The horizontal bar at the top of a window that displays the name of the document and program that appears in that window.

toolbar A bar on which buttons for commands reside. You can change any toolbar or create new toolbars by adding, deleting, or rearranging buttons. Toolbars can be moved, or docked, at any edge of a program window. *See also* floating toolbar.

trendline A graphical representation of a trend in a data series. Trendlines are used to study problems of prediction, also called regression analysis. Trendlines can be added to data series in 2D area, bar, column, line, and XY (scatter) chart type groups and can be formatted.

trendline label Optional text for a trendline, including either the regression equation or the R-squared value or both. A trendline label may be formatted and moved; it cannot be sized.

UNC The address of a file on a local network.

URL Universal Resource Locator; the address of a Web site on the Internet. *See also* address, Internet.

VBA (Visual Basic for Applications) A programming language used in Excel and other application programs.

Visual Basic Editor A small program included in Office 2000 where all Visual Basic editing operations take place; it replaces the old Excel Visual Basic module and is pretty much identical to the programming environment for Visual Basic 5.0.

Web page A document posted on the World Wide Web.

Web site A set of Web pages and a home page; the home page is the Web page through which the other Web pages at the site can be accessed.

wildcard character A character (? or *) that stands for one or more other characters in search criteria. Used to find or filter data on a worksheet. An asterisk (*) represents any number of characters. A question mark (?) represents any single character in the same position as the question mark. To search for a literal question mark or asterisk, precede it with a tilde (~). For example, to search for asterisk, search for ~*.

workbook An Excel file that contains at least one sheet.

worksheet The primary document you use in Excel to store and manipulate data. A worksheet consists of cells organized into columns and rows and is always part of a workbook. Several worksheets can appear in one workbook, and you can switch among them easily by clicking their tabs with the mouse.

World Wide Web The part of the Internet where Web sites and Web pages are posted.

x axis On most charts, categories are plotted along the x axis. On a typical column chart, the x axis is the horizontal axis.

XY (scatter) chart A 2D chart that has numeric values plotted along both axes, rather than values along one axis and categories along the other axis. This type of chart is typically used to analyze scientific data to see whether one set of values is related to another set of values.

y axis On most charts, data values are plotted along the y axis. On a typical column chart, the y axis is the vertical axis. When a secondary axis is added, it is a secondary y axis.

Y intercept In a chart, the point at which a trendline meets the y axis. Setting the y intercept enables you to change the way data appears in a chart without actually changing the scale of the axis.

Index

Symbols

error, 207
#DIV/0! error, 207
#N/A error, 207
#NAME? error, 207
#NULL! error, 208
#NUM! error, 208
#REF! error, 207
#VALUE! error, 207
& (ampersand). *See* **CONCATENATE function**
*** (asterisk), 164**
^ (caret), 164
(=) equal sign, 165
/ (forward slash), 164
– (minus sign), 164
+ (plus sign), 164
100% stacked column charts, 390
3-D charts
perspectives, 413-414
reordering series, 408
3D options for graphics, 569
3D source areas, 331-332

A

absolute cell references, 162
absolute references, copying formulas, 166
accepting changes to shared workbooks, 487-488
Access, data
importing from Excel, 126-127
sending to Excel, 123-125
actual values, 244
Add Custom Chart Type dialog box, 427
Add Trendline dialog box, 416
Add-Ins dialog box, 176
adding. *See also* **inserting**
buttons to toolbars, 527
cells together, 160-161
commands to menus, 531
comments
to macros, 540-541
to worksheets, 150-152
data to chart source ranges, 395
fields to PivotTables, 357, 361
graphics, 237-239
hyperlinks, 39-40
worksheets, 86-87
adjustment handles, AutoShapes, 567
airports, adding to maps, 436
aligning
charts on worksheets, 398
data on pages, 466-467
graphics, 567
alignment, changing page layout, 466-467
alternative scenarios, 318
alternative solutions, comparing, 316
Analysis Toolpak add-in, 176
Answer Wizard, help window, 21
applying built-in styles, 258
area charts, 390
arguments, 175
SUBTOTAL, 294
arithmetic operators, 164
arranging
multiple windows, 101, 104
PivotCharts, 375-376
arrows, drawing, 565-566
art. *See* **graphics**
ascending order, sorting, 270
Assign Macro dialog box, 611
assigning macros, 542-543, 610
auditing, 171
AutoCalculate, 160, 295
AutoComplete, repeating entries, 114
AutoCorrect, 153-155
AutoFill, 111-112
formulas, copying, 165-166
growth series, 113
relative references, copying, 165-166
AutoFilter
filtering tables, 284
Kurt's invoice example, 577
AutoFilter button, 71-72
AutoFormat
PivotTables, 366-367
tables, formatting, 236-237
automated information, entering into templates, 551-552
automated invoices, 576
AutoFilter option, 577
formulas, 579
headers/footers, 578
macros, 581-583
name/address placeholders, 578
automating Excel actions. *See* **macros**
AutoShapes, adjustment handles, 567
AutoSum, 160-161
AutoSum button, 76, 160
AVERAGE function, 178, 182-183
axes
chart orientation, 397
charts
scale changes, 406
secondary, 419-420

B

backwards calculation, 312
Bar charts, 390
bar colors, charts, 597
behavior of Office Assistant, 23-24

best-fitting columns and rows, 224

blending. *See* merging

borders
- charts, 598, 608
- formatting, 230-232

Borders toolbar, 231

Bubble charts, 391

built-in
- database templates, opening, 558-559
- graphics, 567
- styles, applying, 258
- templates. *See* Spreadsheet Solutions templates

buttons
- adding to toolbars, 527
- AutoFilter, 71-72
- AutoSum, 76, 160
- Chart toolbar, 391
- Circle Invalid Data, 206
- Clear Clipboard, 144
- deleting from toolbars, 526
- Desktop, 32
- Drawing toolbar, 564-565
- Enable Macros, 54, 555
- External Data toolbar, 302-303
- Favorites, 32
- Formatting toolbar, 17-18
- History, 31
- Last Folder, 32
- Map Control, 440
- Map toolbar, 432
- Margins, 469
- moving, 526
- multifunctional, 522
- My Documents, 31
- Paste All, 144
- Picture toolbar, 239-241
- PivotTable toolbar, 354-355
- Print, 452
- Print Preview, 450-452
- Property Toolbox, 73
- Redo, 139
- Refresh, 74
- Spelling, 155
- Spreadsheet Solutions toolbar, 56
- Standard toolbar, 15-17
- toolbars, 217
- Undo, 139
- Unlock This Sheet, 555
- Up One Level, 32
- Web Folders, 32
- WordArt toolbar, 571

C

calculating
- cells without formulas, 160
- filtered lists, 293-296
- filtered records with AutoCalculate, 295

calculations
- interactive Web pages, changing, 73-74
- PivotTables, changing, 361-362

Camera button, 603

Cancel Refresh button, 303

cartoon thing. *See* Office Assistant

cell addresses. *See* cell references

cell color (fill color), formatting colors, 233-234

cell location. *See* cell references

cell names, 198-200

cell references, 82, 161, 176. *See also* cell names
- types of, 162-163
- updating, 147

cells, 82
- adding together, 160-161
- changed highlighting, 487
- copying, 141, 144
- data, entering, 110
- deleting, 147-148
- dependent, finding, 171
- entries,
  - *editing, 134*
  - *shrinking to fit, 226-227*
- formulas
  - *calculating without, 160*
  - *writing, 202-203*
- inserting, 147-148
- merging, 229
- moving, 140-142
- naming, 200-202
- number formatting, 243-245
- precedent, finding, 171
- selecting in worksheets, 85
- unlocking before protecting, 495
- unmerging, 229

center-out drawing, 566

centering data on pages, 466-467

Change Links dialog box, 509

changeable layout tables. *See* PivotTables

changes
- finding in shared workbooks, 486-489
- shared workbooks
  - *accepting, 487-488*
  - *finding, 485*
  - *history of printing, 491*
  - *protecting, 496*
  - *rejecting, 487-488*

changing. *See also* editing
- calculations
  - *interactive Web pages, 73-74*
  - *PivotTables, 361-362*
- cell reference types, 163
- column width, 222
- command display mode, 530-531
- data source ranges, 349-353
- defaults, worksheets, 88
- field labels, PivotTables, 367-368
- formatting dates and time, 247
- formulas, 170- 171
- Office Assistant's behavior, 23-24
- page breaks, 462-463
- page layout, 465-469
- PivotCharts, 379
- PivotTables
  - *arrangements, 355-361, 365*

column fields to row fields, 357
layout, 356
row fields to column fields, 356
print area, 454
row height, 222
styles, 259-261

chart sheets
naming, 399
workbooks, 389
worksheets, 398-400

Chart toolbar, 391-393

Chart Type dialog box, 394, 427

Chart Wizard, 385
PivotTable toolbar, 354

charts, 385-386. *See also* PivotCharts
100% stacked column, 390
aligning on worksheets, 398
Area charts, 390
axes
orientation, 397
scale changes, 406
secondary, 419-420
Bar charts, 390
bar colors, 597
bar patterns, 597
Bubble charts, 391
Column charts, 390
column labels, 386
comparative column, 599
Cone charts, 390
creating from PivotTables, 372-373
creative techniques, 594
custom chart formats, 427-429
Custom types, 386
Cylinder charts, 390
Cylinder-Cone-Pyramid charts, 390
data labels, 420-423
data orientation, 386
data series, reordering, 408
data tables, 423
deleting elements, 405
Doughnut charts, 390
dynamic displays, 600-612
formatting, 404-405, 474-476
graphics, 568
gridlines, 386
income versus expenses, 599
legends, 386
Line charts, 390
moving, 397-398
objects, printing, 457
orientation, 397
percentage display, 390
picture markers, 423-426
Pie charts, 390
exploding, 411-412
versus PivotCharts, 369-370
PivotTables, 344
printing, 398, 456-458
Pyramid charts, 390
Radar charts, 390
resizing, 475-476
rounded borders, 598
row labels, 386
series markers, 390
changing series, 395
sheets, printing, 456-457
sizing, 398
source ranges, 394-395
stacked columns, 599
Stock charts, 390
styles, 388
Surface charts, 391
text boxes, 568
titles, 386
transparent, 594, 596-598
trendlines, 415
types, 388
changing, 394
worksheet combinations, 594
XY scatter, 390

ChartTips, 393

choices, user dynamic chart displays, 600-612

Circle Invalid Data button, 206

circles, drawing, 566

Circular error, 208

cities, adding to maps, 436

Clear Clipboard button, 144

closing
Excel, 14-15
files, 41-42
windows, 104
workbooks, 41

collection databases, opening, 558-559

colors
cell color (fill color), formatting, 233-234
chart formatting, 405
formatting, 232-234
hiding for printing, 474
PivotCharts, changing, 379
text color (font color), formatting, 233

column breaks, 462

column charts, 390
stacked, 599

column fields
changing to row fields (PivotTables), 357
PivotTable terms, 344

column labels, charts, 386

columns
best-fitting, 224
deleting, 145-147
hiding, 226
while printing, 452
inserting, 146
outlining, 339
parsing, 149-150
precise measurements, setting, 224
separating, 149-150
unhiding, 226
widths, changing, 222

combining. *See* merging

command display mode, changing, 530-531

commands
adding to menus, 531
removing from menus, 531
What's This? (Help menu), 26

comments
adding
to macros, 540-541
to worksheets, 150-152

deleting, 153
editing, 152-153

comparative column charts, 599

comparing solutions and scenarios, 316

CONCATENATE function, 178, 197-198

conditional number formats, 251-252

Conditional Sum Wizard, SUMIF function, 184-185

Cone charts, 390

configurations, resetting toolbars, 526

configuring Spreadsheet Solutions database, 552-555

conflicts, shared workbooks, 486

Consolidate dialog box, 329, 332

consolidating, 328
lists, 328-329, 331
destination areas, 328
source areas, 331-332
tables, 328
updating, 331

constants, 205

contents, protecting, 495

Contents tab, help window, 20

Context and Index help files, 20

Convert Text to Columns Wizard, 150

Convert to Microsoft Access dialog box, 126

converting
formulas to values, 205
numbers, actual values to displayed values, 253-255

copies, shared workbooks, 491

copying. *See also* pasting
cells, 141, 144
data. *See* data, copying
entries, 165-166
formatting with Format Painter, 234-236
formulas, 165-166
relative references with AutoFill, 165-166
styles from other workbooks, 262-264
values, 165-166
workbooks, 49
worksheets, 89-92

correlations, displaying via trendlines, 414

COUNTIF function, 178, 185-187

Create Names dialog box, naming cells, 201-202

Create New Data Source dialog box, 298

Create Shortcut dialog box, 12

creating. *See also* customizing
charts from PivotTables, 372-373
conditional number formats, 251-252
custom lists with AutoFill, 111-112
dynamic ranges with named formulas, 352
footers, 471-473
headers, 471-473
invoice numbering system, 196
new menus for menu bar, 531-532
personal toolbars, 527-529
PivotCharts, 371-372
PivotTables, 346, 348-349
print titles, 470-471
queries, 298-299
scenarios, 318-319, 321
shortcuts, 13, 33
styles by example, 261-262
toggle macros, 544-547
Web folders, 32

creative chart techniques, 594

creative worksheet techniques, 576

crosstab tables. *See* PivotTables

Custom AutoFilter dialog box, 293

custom chart formats, 427-429

Custom chart types, 386

custom format codes, 249-250

custom lists, 275-277
Creating with AutoFill, 111-112

Custom Pin Map dialog box, 442

custom sort order, sorting lists, 275-277

custom templates, 51-52

Customize dialog box, 524, 603

customizing
menu bars, 529-532
screen elements, 518
Spreadsheet Solutions templates, 52-54
templates, 551-552
toolbars, 521-522

Cylinder charts, 390

Cylinder-Cone-Pyramid charts, 390

D

data. *See also* entries
aligning on pages, 466-467
centering on pages, 466-467
charts, changing, 394
copying
from other programs, 121-122, 124
from Word, 122-123
from Word to Excel, 506
to Word from Excel, 501
deleting, 138-139
dragging and dropping from Access, 125

editing, 134-136
entering
with AutoFill, 111-112
with data entry forms, 115-117
duplicate data in multiple cells, 114
into a single cell, 110
validating, 117-118
into worksheets, 110
extracting, 283
with Query Wizard, 296-298
finding, 136-137
importing
from Access to Excel, 123-124
from Excel to Access, 126-128
pasting
from Excel to PowerPoint, 511-512
from Excel to Word, 501
from Word to Excel, 507
PivotTables, summarizing, 343-344
replacing, 137-138
sending
from Excel to Word, 501
from Word to Excel, 506
sharing, 500-501
shrinking to fit, 469-470

data area, PivotTable terms, 344

data display options for maps, 441

data entry forms, entering data, 115-117

data labels, charts, 420-423

data maps, 433-435

data markers, printing in black and white, 476

data orientation, charts, 386

Data Range Properties button, 303

data series, reordering charts, 408

data source ranges
changing, 349-353
charts, 395

data sources
creating PivotTables from same data source, 349
defining, 298

data tables, charts, 423

data validation, 110
removing, 119

Data Validation dialog box, 117

databases
collection, opening, 558-559
Spreadsheet Solutions, 552-555

dates
footers/headers, 474
formatting, 246-247

decimal places macros, 544

defaults
custom templates, opening, 52
worksheets, changing, 88

Define Name dialog box, naming cells, 202

defining data sources, 298

deleting
buttons from toolbars, 526
cells, 147-148
chart data labels, 422
columns, 145-147
comments, 153
data, 138-139
embedded objects, 505
items from charts, 405
linked objects, 506
map data, 441
rows, 145-147
scenarios, 323
styles, 264-265
text boxes, 569
worksheets, 86

delimiters, 130

dependent cells, finding, 171

descending order, sorting, 270

deselecting worksheets, 82

Desktop button, 32

destination areas, 328

details, showing PivotTables, 362-364

dialog boxes
Add Custom Chart Type, 427
Add Trendline, 416
Add-Ins, 176
Arrange Windows, 101
Assign Macros, 611
AutoCorrect, 154
Change Links, 509
Chart Type, 394, 427
Consolidate, 329, 332
Convert to Microsoft Access, 126
Create Names, 201-202
Create New Data Source, 298
Create Shortcut, 12
Custom AutoFilter, 293
Custom Pin Map, 442
Customize, 524, 603
Data Validation, 117
Define Name, 202
Edit Text Object, 442
File Properties, 47
Fill Effects, 423
Find, 136
Format Axis, 406
Format Cells, 218, 231-233, 235
Format Data Series, 420
Goal Seek, 314
Insert Hyperlink, 40
Lock/Save Sheet, 54, 554
Macro, 610
Map Features, 436
Map Labels, 436
Merge Styles, 264
Microsoft Map Control, 441
New Web Query, 307
ODBC Microsoft Excel Setup, 298
Page Setup, 465, 468
Paste Function, 176, 184-185

Print, 455
Record Macro, 536, 608
Resolve Conflicts, 485-486
Run Query, 307
Save As Type, 48
Save Template, 554
Scenario Manager, 318
Scenario Values, 319
Select Picture, 424
Select Workbook, 298
Share Workbook, 482
Show Pages, 360
Sort, 273
Style, 260
SUBTOTAL, 297, 333
SUMIF, 185
Template File - Save to Database, 557
Top 10 AutoFilter, 292
Unable to Create Map, 442

disagreements, 485-486

displayed values, 244

displaying
dynamic charts. *See* dynamic chart displays
Formatting toolbar, 216
percentages in charts, 390
toolbars, 18, 524-525

Doughnut charts, 390
exploding, 410-412

drag-and-drop
cell editing, 141
data from Access, 125

dragging worksheets to another workbook, 92

drawing, 566-568

Drawing button, Standard toolbar, 564

drawing objects, 564

Drawing toolbar, 564
3D button, 569
AutoShapes option, 567
buttons, 564-565
Insert WordArt button, 571
Text Box button, 568

dynamic chart displays, 600-607, 609-610, 612
assigning macros, 610
borders, 608
Camera button, 603
creating the charts, 604
naming ranges behind chart, 606
recording macros, 608
resizing cell A1, 606
taking pictures of one chart range, 607
testing macros, 610
Wordart worksheet titles, 611

dynamic data tables. *See* PivotTables

dynamic ranges, 351-353

dynamic source ranges, charts, 395

E

Edit Query button, 303

Edit Text Object dialog box, 442

editing. *See also* changing
cells, 134
chart type, 394
comments, 152-153
custom templates, 51-52
data, 134-136
embedded objects, 503-504
interactive Web pages, 69, 76
linked objects, 505-506
macros, 539
scenarios, 322
static Web pages, 63-64
text boxes, 569
toggle macros, 545-546

effects for 3D graphics, 570

elements of charts, 405

embedded objects, 503-505

embedding
data, 500
Excel objects in Word, 502-503
PivotCharts in worksheets, 378
Word objects in Excel, 507-508

Enable Macros button, 54, 555

enlarging
maps, 439
Pie chart plot area, 410

entering
data
with AutoFill, 111-112
with data entry forms, 115-117
into a single cell, 110
validation, 117-118
into worksheets, 110
duplicate data in multiple cells, 114

entries. *See also* data
cells, editing, 134
copying, 165-166
repeating, 113-114
shrinking to fit in a cell, 226-227
worksheet presentation, 219-221
wrapping to multiple lines, 227-228

equations for trendlines, 416

errors. *See also* mistakes
#####, 207
#DIV/0!, 207
#N/A, 207
#NAME?, 207
#NULL!, 208
#NUM!, 208
#REF!, 207
#VALUE!, 207
Circular, 208
locating, 205, 208-209

examples of creative worksheets, Kurt's invoice, 576-579, 581-583

Excel
closing, 14-15
embedding Word objects, 507-508
exiting, 14-15
Formatting toolbar, buttons, 17-18
new features
menu display, 529
Office 2000 Clipboard, 123
Rocky the dog, 18
Standard toolbar, buttons, 15-17

Start menu, 12
starting, 11-14
exiting Excel, 14-15
exploding charts, 409-412
External Data toolbar buttons, 602-303
extracting data, 283. *See also* filtering
with Query Wizard, 296-298

F

Favorites button, 32
Field Dialog, PivotTable toolbar, 355
field labels, PivotTables
changing, 367-368
terms, 344
fields
filtering, 357, 361
file extensions, 53
file properties
files, finding, 36-38
keywords, 36
saving, 47-48
text, 36
File Properties dialog box, 47
filenames, spaces in, 63
files. See also workbooks
closing, 41-42
file properties, finding, 36-38
multiples, opening, 35
opening, 30-33
with hyperlinks, 41
non-Excel files, 33-34
read-only, 35
safely, 35
Quick View, finding, 38-40
saving, 46-49
Fill Color button, Formatting toolbar, 405
fill color, 233-234
fill effects, chart picture markers, 423
Fill Effects dialog box, 423
filtered lists, calculating, 293-295
with SUBTOTAL function, 295-296
filtered records, calculating, 295
filtering. *See also* extracting data
AutoFilter, 284
lists
with multiple criteria, 286, 288-290, 292-293
with one criterion, 284
on a criteria range, 289, 292
on the highest and lowest numbers in a number field, 292-293
tables with AutoFilter, 284
on two criteria in the same field, 288-290
on two different fields, 288-289
filters, queries, 296
Find dialog box, 136
finding
changes in shared workbooks, 485-487, 489
data, 136-137
dependent cells, 171
files, 36-40
hidden buttons on toolbars, 216
invalid data, 209-210
mistakes, 171-172
precedent cells, 171
values, 251-252
floating palettes, 233
font color, 233
Font Color button, Formatting toolbar, 405
fonts
chart formatting, 405
formatting, 217-218
PivotCharts, changing, 379
footers
creating, 471-473
parts-list invoices, 578
printing, 474
Format Axis dialog box, 406
Format Cells dialog box, 218, 231-233, 235
Format Data Series dialog box, 420
Format Painter, copying formatting, 234-236
Format Painter toolbar, number formatting, 246
Format Report, PivotTable toolbar, 354
formats, saving files, 48
formatting
best-fitting columns and rows, 224
borders, 230-232
cells
merging, 229
precise measurements, 224
charts, 404, 474-476
colors, 405
custom chart formats, 427-429
data labels, 423
fonts, 405
lines, 405
colors, 232-234
dates, 246-247
entries
aligning, 219-221
indenting, 221
rotating, 221
shrinking to fit in a cell, 226
wrapping to multiple lines, 227-228
fonts, 217-218
Format Painter, copying, 234-236
graphics, 566
adding, 237-239
hiding rows and columns, 226
number formatting, 243-245
numbers
conditional number formats, 251-252
PivotTables, 365, 368
special format codes, 250
as text, 247-249, 251

pages, 461-464
part numbers, 247-249, 251
Picture toolbar, 239, 241
PivotCharts, 376, 378-379
PivotTables, 364-365, 367
resizing columns and rows, 222
styles. *See* styles
tables with AutoFormat, 236-237
time, 246-247
transposing tables and lists, 228-229
unhiding rows and columns, 226
WordArt, 571
ZIP codes, 247-249, 251

Formatting toolbar, 215
buttons, 17-18
displaying, 216
Fill Color button, 405
Font Color button, 405
restoring to default, 216

Formula bar, editing data, 134-135

Formula Palette, 177
SUMIF function, 184

formulas. ***See also*** **functions**
buttons
AutoSum, 76
Refresh, 74
calculating cells without formulas, 160
changing, 170- 171
converting to values, 205
copying, 165-166
dynamic ranges, 352
errors, locating, 208-209
links, updating, 169
OFFSET function, 352
PMT, 313
protecting, 498
testing, 179
tracing, 171-172
writing, 178, 164-165
AVERAGE function, 182
CONCATENATE function, 198
COUNTIF function, 187
functions, 176-178
labels, 203-204, 208
LEFT function, 195-196
linking workbooks, 166-167, 169
MAX function, 180-181
MIN function, 180
named cells, 202
SUM formula, 178
SUMIF function, 184-185
VLOOKUP function, 188, 190-191

free-floating chart labels, 422

free-floating labels, pin maps, 443

freezing panes, 96

Full Screen view, screen displays, 518-519

functions, 159, 175-176. ***See also*** **formulas**
Analysis Toolpak add-in, 176
AVERAGE, 178, 182-183
CONCATENATE, 178, 197-198
COUNTIF, 178, 185-187
Formula Palette, 177
formulas, writing, 176-178
HLOOKUP, 178, 188-191
IF, 178, 191-192
LEFT, 178, 195-197
MAX, 178, 180-182
MIN, 178, 180
NOW, 178, 194
OFFSET, 352
PMT, 178, 192-193
RAND, 277
RIGHT, 178, 195-197
SUBTOTAL, 294-295
SUM, 178-179
SUMIF, 178, 184-185
TODAY, 178, 194
VLOOKUP, 178, 188-191

G

geographical maps, 433, 436
source tables, 433

Giff's chart-worksheet example, 594-596

Goal Seek
answering problems, 312-316
backwards calculation, 312
loan amounts, 312-314

Goal Seek dialog box, 314

Goal Seeking tool, backwards calculations, 312

graphics, 564
3D options, 569
adding, 237-239
aligning, 567
assigning macros, 567
AutoShapes, 567
built-in, 567
drawing, formatting, 565-566
moving, 567
pasting into worksheets, 237-238
resizing/reshaping, 567
shaping text via WordArt, 571
text boxes, 568

graphs. ***See*** **charts**

gridlines
charts, 386
hiding, 234
printing, 233, 473

grouping items in a field, PivotTables, 355-356

growth series, AutoFill, 113

guides, PivotCharts, 377

H

headers
creating, 471-473
parts-list invoices, 578
printing, 474

help, 18
Office Assistant, 18-20
What's This?, 25

help files, Contents and Index, 20

Help menu commands, What's This?, 26

help window, 20-23

Helper. ***See*** **Office Assistant**

hidden buttons, 216-217

Hide Detail, PivotTable toolbar, 355

Hide/Display Fields, PivotTable toolbar, 355
hiding
colors, 474
columns, 226
for printing, 452
gridlines, 234
guides, PivotCharts, 377
help window, 23
inner field details, PivotTables, 358
Office Assistant, 24
rows, 226, 338
for printing, 452
subtotal levels, 334, 337
toolbars, 524
zero values, 255
highlighting changed cells, 487
highways, adding to maps, 436
History button, 31
HLOOKUP function, 178, 188-191
horizontal lines, 566
hyperlinks, 39-41. *See also* links

I

IF function, 178, 191-192
importing
data
from Access, 123-124
from Excel to Access, 126-128
text files, 128-130
in-cell editing feature, 134
income versus expenses charts, 599
Index tab, help window, 20
inner field, PivotTable terms, 346
inner field details, PivotTables, 358
Insert Hyperlink dialog box, 40
Insert WordArt button, Drawing toolbar, 571
inserting
cells, 147-148
columns, 146
rows, 146
installing
Microsoft Map, 432
Template Wizard, 550
interactive Web pages, 60, 71-73
AutoFilter, 71-72
calculations, changing, 73-74
editing, 69, 76
Property Toolbox, 73
saving, 66-67, 69
updating, 76-77
invalid data, finding in worksheets, 209-210
investment tracking, charts, 390
invisible charts, 596-598
invoices
numbering system, 196
parts-lists, 576
attaching macro to graphic, 583
AutoFilter option, 577
formulas, 579
headers/footers, 578
macro editing, 583
macros, 581-582
name/address placeholders, 578
item, PivotTable terms, 344

J-L

keywords, searches, 36, 48

labels, 198. *See also* cell names; print titles
chart columns and rows, 386
chart data, 420-423
formulas, writing, 203-204, 208
map items, 436-437
pin maps, 443
Last Folder button, 32
leaving. *See* exiting Excel
LEFT function, 178, 195-197
legends
charts, 386
Pie charts, shrinking, 410
limitations of shared workbooks, 482-483
Line charts, 390
linear regression, 415-417
linear series, 113
linear trendlines, 415
lines, drawing, 565-566
linked data, pasting in Word, 505
linked objects, 505-506
linked Word text, pasting into Excel worksheets, 508-509
linking
data, 500
objects to Word, 504-505, 508
Spreadsheet Solutions database to existing templates, 555
links
dragging from Word to Excel, 510-511
formulas, updating, 169
sources, changing, 509
updating, 509
lists. *See also* tables
consolidating, 328-329, 331
destination areas, consolidating, 328
filtering
with multiple criteria, 286, 288-290, 292-293
with one criterion, 284
sorting. *See also* sorting, lists
transposing, 228-229
loans, Goal Seek, 312-314
locating. *See also* finding
errors, 205, 208-209

Lock/Save Sheet dialog box, 54, 554

M

Macro dialog box, 610

macros, 535-536
assigning, 610
to graphics, 567
to menu commands, 542-543
to toolbars, 542-543
automating invoices, 576
comments, adding, 540-541
decimal places macros, 544
editing, 539
naming, 536
recording, 536-538, 608
running, 539-540
with text boxes, 584
shortcut keys, 537
testing, 539-540, 610
toggle macros. *See* toggle macros
viruses, Spreadsheet Solutions templates, 53-54

Map Control, 439-441

Map Features dialog box, 436

Map Labels dialog box, 436

Map toolbar, buttons, 432

maps, 432
adding geographic features, 436
data display control via Map Control, 439-441
data maps, 433-435
deleting data, 441
enlarging, 439
geographical, 433, 436
labeling items, 436-437
pin maps, 441-442
resizing, 435, 438

Margins button, 469

margins, changing, 467-469

marker labels for charts. *See* data labels

MAX function, 178, 180-182
formulas, writing, 180-181

menu bars
customizing, 529-532
new menus, creating, 531-532

menu commands, 531
assigning macros, 542-543
shortcut keys, 544

menu display, new feature, 529

menus, 531-532

Merge Styles dialog box, 264

merging
cells, 229
shared workbooks, 488-490
styles from other workbooks, 264

Microsoft Map, installing, 432

Microsoft Map Control dialog box, 441

Microsoft Office Manager (MOM). *See* Office Shortcut bar

MIN function, 178-180

mistakes
finding, 171-172
undoing, 139

mixed cell references, 162

mixed references, copying formulas, 166

mixed-up sort, 277

MOM (Microsoft Office Manager). *See* Office Shortcut bar

moving
buttons, 526
cells, 140-142
charts, 397-398
PivotCharts, to worksheets, 378
toolbars, 522-524
worksheets, 90-92

moving around in. *See* navigating worksheets

moving maps on worksheets, 439

multifunctional toolbar buttons, 522

multiple windows, 96-98
arranging manually, 101, 104

multiple workbook users. *See* shared workbooks

My Documents button, 31

N

Name box, naming cells, 201

named cells, writing formulas, 202-203

naming
cells, 200-202
chart sheets, 399
macros, 536
worksheets, 79-80

naming ranges behind charts, 606

navigating worksheets, 82, 85

new features
menu display, 529
Office 2000 Clipboard, 123
Rocky the dog, 18

New Web Query dialog box, 307

normal style, 258

Normal view, screen displays, 519

NOW function, 178, 194

number formatting, 243, 245
Format Painter toolbar, 246

number series, AutoFill, 112

Numbered Pages view, 463-464

numbers
converting actual values to displayed values, 253-255
fields, filtering highest and lowest numbers, 292-293

formatting
conditional number formats, 251-252
dates, 246-247
PivotTables, 365, 368
special format codes, 250
as text, 247-249, 251
time, 246-247

O

objects
embedding
Excel objects in Word, 502-503
Word objects in Excel, 507-508
linking to Word documents, 504-505, 508
protecting, 495
ODBC Microsoft Excel Setup dialog box, 298
Office 2000 Clipboard, 123, 142
Office Assistant
behavior, changing, 23-24
help, 18-20
hiding, 24
reinstalling, 25
removing from your computer, 24-25
Office Clipboard toolbar, pasting, 144-145
Office Shortcut bar, 15
Excel, starting, 13-14
OFFSET function, 352
on/off macros. *See* **toggle macros**
opening
Chart toolbar, 393
collection database, 558-559
custom templates, 50-52
files, 30-33
with hyperlinks, 41
non-Excel, 33-34
as read-only, 35
safely, 35
and starting Excel at the same time, 33
multiple files, 35
new workbooks, 30
Spreadsheet Solutions templates, 552
static Web pages, 61
templates, 31
workbooks, existing, 31-33
orientation
chart data, 386
charts, 397
outer field, PivotTable terms, 344
outlining, 338-339
ovals, drawing, 565

P

Page Break Preview, 463-464
page breaks, 462-463
page field item, PivotTable terms, 344
page fields, PivotTables, 344, 358-359
page layout, changing, 465-469
Page Number view, 463-464
page numbers, printing, 474
page ordering, 465
page orientation, 465
Page Setup dialog box, 465
changing margins, 468
pages
formatting, 461-464
margins, 468
panes, 96-98
parsing columns, 149-150
part numbers, formatting, 247-249
parts-list invoices, 576
AutoFilter option, 577
formulas, 579
headers/footers, 578
macros, 581-583
name/address placeholders, 578
passwords, workbooks, 493. *See also* **protecting**
Paste All button, 144
Paste Function dialog box, 176
SUMIF function, 184-185
pasting
data, 500
from Excel to PowerPoint, 511-512
from Excel to Word, 501
from Word to Excel, 507
graphics into worksheets, 237-238
linked data in Word, 505
linked Word text into Excel worksheets, 508-509
with Office Clipboard toolbar, 144-145
patterns, charts, 597
percentage display in charts, 390
personal lists, sorting, 275-277
Personal Macro Workbook, 537
personal toolbars, 527-529
personalizing. *See* **customizing**
perspectives, 3D charts, 413-414
picture markers, charts, 423-426
Picture toolbar, buttons, 239-241
pictures. *See* **graphics**
Pie charts, 390
exploding, 409, 411-412
legends, shrinking, 410
plot area, enlarging, 410
rejoining slices, 411
resizing, 409
pin maps, 432, 441-443
PivotChart Wizard, 346
PivotCharts, 368-369
versus charts, 369-370
creating, 371-372

embedding in worksheets, 378
formatting, 376, 378-379
guides, 377
moving to worksheets, 378
rearranging, 375-376

PivotTable and PivotChart Wizard, PivotTable toolbar, 355

PivotTable charts. *See* PivotCharts

PivotTable Menu, PivotTable toolbar, 354

PivotTable toolbar, 354-355

PivotTables, 324-325, 343
AutoFormat, 366-367
changing
arrangement of, 355-361, 365
calculations, 361-362
column fields to row fields, 357
row fields to column fields, 356
charts, 344
creating, 372-373
creating, 346-349
data, summarizing, 343-344
details, showing, 362-364
field labels, changing, 367-368
fields, 357, 361
formatting, 364-365, 367
grouping items in a field, 355-356
inner field details, 358
page fields, 358-359
refreshing, 353-355
rotating, 356
separate pages, 359-360, 364
terms, 344-346
troubleshooting, 349

plot area of charts
Pie charts, enlarging, 410
transparent, 597-598

PMT formula, 313

PMT function, 178, 192-193

postal codes, adding to maps, 436

PowerPoint, pasting data from Excel, 511-512

precedent cells, finding, 171

precise measurements, columns and rows, 224

presentation, worksheets, 219-221

preventing changes. *See* protecting

previewing printed pages, 450-452

print area, 452-454

Print button, 452

Print dialog box, 455

Print Preview, 450

Print Preview button bar, 451-452
Margins button, 469

print titles, 470-471. *See also* labels

printed charts, resizing, 475-476

printing
across, then down, 465
in black and white, 474
charts, 398, 456-458
data markers, 476
down, then across, 465
gridlines, 233, 473
hiding columns and rows, 452
print area, 452-453
with Print button, 452
with Print Preview, 450-452
print titles, 470-471
ranges, 453-454
shared workbooks, change history, 491
shrinking data to fit, 469-470
specific pages, 455-456
tables, 453-454
WordArt problems, 571
workbooks, 458-459
worksheets
with charts, 398
without charts, 457-458

Property Toolbox button, 73

protecting
cells, unlocking, 495
changes in shared workbooks, 496
contents, 495
formulas, 498
objects, 495
scenarios, 495
shared workbooks, 494
workbooks, 493-494
worksheets, 493-495

pushpin maps, 441-442
resizing pins, 443

Pyramid charts, 390

Q

queries
creating, 298-299
filters, 296
refreshing, 305
reusing, 305-307
saving, 305

Query Parameters button, 303

Query Wizard, 296
extracting data, 296-298
running, 299-300, 302

querying Web pages, 307

Quick View, finding files, 38-40

quitting. *See* exiting

R

R-squared values, trendlines, 415-417

Radar charts, 390

RAND function, 277

random order, sorting lists, 277-280

ranges, printing, 453-454. *See also* dynamic ranges

read-only files, opening, 35

read-only workbook status, 492-493